American Government

Readings on Continuity and Change

Second Edition

American Government

Readings on Continuity and Change

Second Edition

ROBERT HARMEL
Texas A&M University

St. Martin's Press   New York

Senior editor: Don Reisman
Manager, publishing services: Emily Berleth
Project management: Beckwith-Clark, Inc.
Cover design: Sheree Goodman
Cover photo: Image Bank © Kay Chernush

Library of Congress Catalog Card Number: 92-50016
Copyright © 1993 by St. Martin's Press, Inc.

For information, write:
St. Martin's Press, Inc.
175 Fifth Avenue
New York, NY 10010

ISBN: 0-312-03716-3

ACKNOWLEDGMENTS

"The Constitution as an Elitist Document," by Michael Parenti. From *How Democratic Is the
Constitution?* edited by Robert A. Goldwin and William A. Schambra, © 1980, The
American Enterprise Institute for Public Policy Research. Reprinted with the permission
of The American Enterprise Institute for Public Policy Research, Washington, D.C.

"The Framers' Intentions," by David G. Smith. *From the Convention and the Constitution:
The Political Ideas of the Founding Fathers* by David G. Smith, St. Martin's Press, 1965,
New York. Reprinted by permission of the author.

"The Political Structure of Constitution Making," by Calvin C. Jillson and Cecil L. Eubanks.
Reprinted from "The Political Structure of Constitution Making: The Federal Convention
of 1787," by Calvin C. Jillson and Cecil L. Eubanks, in *American Journal of Political Science*,
Volume 28, Number 3, August 1984, by permission of the University of Texas Press.

"Amending the Constitution." Reprinted from *Framers of the Constitution*. Washington, D.C.:
National Archives and Records Administration, 1986.

"The Other Amendment: Why Is the 14th Amendment Important to the Bill of Rights?" by
John Neary. John Neary, *Life* Magazine © 1991, The Time Inc. Magazine Company.
Reprinted with permission.

"Doesn't Congress Have Ideas of Its Own?" by Abraham Ribicoff. Reprinted from *The Satur-
day Evening Post,* © 1964.

"The Imperial Presidency," by Arthur M. Schlesinger, Jr. From *The Imperial Presidency* by Arthur M. Schlesinger, Jr. Copyright © 1973 by Arthur M. Schlesinger, Jr. Reprinted by permission of Houghton Mifflin Company. All rights reserved.

To these future participants in American politics:

Chris Dale
Vickie and Kristine Petersen
Rachel, Kayme, Naomi, and Paul Fritz
Jenna and Bruce Holman
and Charles and Christine Wu

Preface

As Madison Avenue would say, *American Government: Readings on Continuity and Change* is an American government reader "with a difference." In many respects, it resembles a number of fine readers already in print: its contents cover the broad range of topics normally covered in American government classes; it is organized according to the standard outline for such classes; and it includes classics and important historical documents along with a majority of contemporary pieces. The "difference" is the book's emphasis on continuity and change, which runs throughout the various sections of the book, and which highlights the dynamic quality of American politics. Collectively, the seventy-five readings provide a picture of a political system that has undergone tremendous change, but within a basic framework that has endured for over two centuries. More than half of the readings deal directly with change. Others provide important historical background, and some others deal primarily with significant continuities in American politics. Change within continuity has been one of the most important features of the American political system, and this book has been specifically designed to reflect that quality.

New to the Second Edition
Though the second edition of this book differs from the first in some important respects, it continues the same central focus: continuity and change in American government and politics, with nearly all readings being either of historical importance (such as Federalist papers and Supreme Court cases) or documenting and analyzing change. And again, several pieces predict future trends; others offer suggestions for reform.

The new edition goes beyond the first in

- giving consideration to the lasting impact of the **"conservative Reagan era"** and the policies formulated in those years (Readings #15, #34, #75)
- giving more attention to the impact of the **media** in American politics (#31, #32, #49, #50)
- giving more attention to the **nominating phase** of the electoral process (Chapter Nine)
- covering some new trends and controversies, including the **recentralization of power within the House of Representatives** (#54), the **lessening impact of individual interest groups** as the number of them rises (#47), the issue of **strict vs. loose constructionism** in the Supreme Court (#62, #63), the **increasing involvement of the House and of state/local governments in the foreign policy area** (#16, #68), and what could prove to be fundamentally important changes in **political values** (Chapter Six)

- giving attention to some foci not covered (or only barely so) in the first edition, such as the **"other" federal courts** (#66), **direct marketing** (#42), the **cabinet** (#60), the **amendment process** (#5, #28), and the importance of the **"black vote"** in presidential elections (#35).

Structurally, there are four new chapters in the second edition, covering **constitutional change** (Chapter Two), **political values and issues** (Chapter Six), the **presidential nominating process** (Chapter Nine), and **policy-making** (Chapter Eighteen). In addition, a number of the readings are cross-listed (set within brackets in the Table of Contents) for additional chapters where they are of special relevance.

Though some of the readings are "historical" and as such are not subject to change, every effort has been made to make the book as current as possible. Fully thirty-three of the seventy-five readings are new for this edition, and an additional six are based on updates of material included in the first edition. Sixteen of the readings are from sources published since 1991, and another fourteen were published in 1989 or 1990.

Using the Book in the Classroom

American Government has been specifically designed to be *useful* in American government classes. Although students will learn a great deal simply by reading the selections, the class as a whole will benefit even more from actively discussing them. And as readings on change are inherently well suited to generating discussion, so the emphasis of this book should contribute to its usefulness. Some of the readings will raise questions concerning the likely consequences of certain changes that have already been implemented; others will stimulate thinking about the possible impact of proposed reforms. In addition, a number of readings with potentially controversial content are offset by others with alternative points of view (for instance, Michael Parenti and David G. Smith, Theodore Roosevelt and William Howard Taft, Edward S. Greenberg and Susan Love Brown et al.); such readings can support "debate" on important topics. In selecting the readings, I placed a good deal of emphasis on their "discussibility." If a reading could not easily be used to stimulate class discussion (or discussion outside the class, for that matter), I chose not to include it.

The book is also organized to maximize usefulness in a variety of class structures. The organization uses the standard, systems-analysis approach of setting-inputs-institutions-outputs. However, instructors whose courses are structured differently will have no difficulty rearranging the various chapters. To facilitate this, I have written *separate chapter introductions*, rather than broader introductions to the four main parts. In addition, brief introductions to the selections themselves add even greater flexibility by equipping each reading to "stand alone."

Besides the chapter and selection introductions, I have also provided a brief introduction to Part Four, "The Outputs." While there is a general understanding of what constitutes the setting, the inputs, and the institutions of American government and politics, the concept of *outputs* is treated in a variety of ways in some texts and classes, and often it is not treated at all. The six readings in Part Four do not cover a range of specific policy areas, but instead deal with two of the broadest questions concerning the policy process and its outputs: who rules and who wins? The readings provide alternative answers that should serve to stimulate discussion and debate.

The book's emphasis on continuity and change clearly involves looking at the past as well as the present of the American system. An underlying assumption of this anthology is that we cannot fully understand current institutions and events without taking history—whether recent or distant—into account. For instance, many references are made in these pages to the experiences and intentions of the framers. And because their concerns influenced the shaping of the Constitution, including the document it replaced, both the Articles of Confederation and the Constitution of the United States of America are provided in full in the *Documents* section at the end of the book.

Acknowledgments

An anthology is, by definition, a collective effort. The authors of the readings in this book deserve the bulk of the credit for whatever success it has. I, of course, bear full responsibility for the choice of material and for any internal deletions, as well as for changes in many of the titles and removal of many footnotes that appeared in the selections when they were first published. I am grateful to the publishers of the original works for granting permission to reprint them.

As in the first edition, I need to acknowledge debts to friends and associates who have helped in very important ways. At Texas A&M, I am especially indebted to my colleagues John Robertson, Roberto Vichot, Charles Wiggins, Jon Bond, and Samuel Wu; and to my graduate assistants, Kevin O'Neill and Rachel Gibson. And at St. Martin's, Don Reisman has been an exceptionally encouraging, thoughtful, and helpful editor.

I'd like to thank the following reviewers for St. Martin's Press: Marvin Alisky, Arizona State University; Arthur English, University of Arkansas at Little Rock; Mary E. Guy, University of Alabama–Birmingham; Terry L. Heyns, Kansas State University; Alan N. Katz, Fairfield University; Jeffrey Kraw, Wagner College; Robert W. Langran, Villanova University; Michael D. Martinez, University of Florida; Brigitte Nacos, Columbia University; Robert M. Peace, Southwest Missouri State University; Ronald R. Pope, Illinois State University; Diane E. Schmidt, Southern Illinois University–Carbondale; and Stella Z. Theodoulou, California State University–Northridge.

Finally, I want to express my thanks to the students of Political Science 206 at Texas A&M, who have been the inspiration for this book.

Robert Harmel

Note to Instructors

We would like to note the availability of an instructor's manual that contains approximately 600 test questions, including multiple choice and essay/discussion items. For more information, please write St. Martin's Press, College Desk, 175 Fifth Avenue, New York, NY 10010; or contact your local St. Martin's sales representative.

Contents

PART TWO
Sources of Inputs 223

American Government

Readings on Continuity and Change

Second Edition

Introduction

For approximately two centuries, Americans have lived under the same governmental system that was outlined by fifty-five men in Philadelphia in 1787. During the same time span, Denmark has had three different political systems, Russia six, Austria seven, France nine, and Greece twelve.* Of the political systems existing today, only the United Kingdom's is older. There is no denying the fact that America's basic political system has had remarkable "staying power." But that, in turn, is not to deny the equally important fact that *within* the basic arrangement, there has been much change.

The story of change in American government and politics must begin with the writing of the Constitution itself, which was, first and foremost, a document *of change*. The framers were sent to Philadelphia to *change* the Articles of Confederation, which had served for six years as the structure for a loose collection of sovereign states, much as the United Nations structures a collection of sovereign nations today. National government under the Articles consisted only of a one-house Congress; it was intended to be "small" government. Passage of any law required agreement of nine of the thirteen states; it was intended to be a weak and nearly powerless national government. The framework provided by the Articles of Confederation had served an important function for the first few years of independence, allowing time to mold a national identity from thirteen separate, colonial states. But it had not served well the needs for security and efficient commerce. So the framers met to *amend* the Articles, but soon arrived at the conclusion that the necessary changes were so many and so fundamental that it would be preferable to *replace* the Articles with a completely new document.

Some things were carried over, including preservation of important policy areas in which the states could exercise independent action, continuation of an important role for Congress within the national government, and most importantly, continued rejection of monarchy in favor of republican government. But now, states would no longer be the only powerful governmental actor. Congress would be joined by a separate executive and an independent judiciary, and "government by the people" would be extended (through popular election of the House of Representatives) to the national level.

The Constitution that was written in Philadelphia has proven to be abnormally durable. But the primary reason for the persistence of this document *of* change is that it allowed so much room *for* change. In other words, the key to its longevity has been its *adaptability*.

---

*Based on the editor's analysis of data collected by Ted Robert Gurr for his study of Polity Persistence and Change (data available from the Inter-university Consortium for Political Research, study #5010).—*Editor's Note.*

Not only was an amendment process provided for changing the document itself, but even more importantly, room was provided for changing *within* the system. The Constitution is not a rigid document, as compared to other constitutions. The "gaps" and "holes" that were left to be filled in later, and the "vague language" that was open to interpretation and re-interpretation, have resulted in a system that could be adapted to changing needs and circumstances. Such time honored "institutions" of American politics as political parties and the Supreme Court's power of judicial review were not even mentioned in the Constitution, but both were developed anyway, as they were needed. The president's cabinet is only indirectly referenced and the very important committee system of Congress is not mentioned at all, and so it has been possible to alter both of them over time without changing the Constitution. It is commonplace today to acknowledge growth in the powers of the presidency and of the national level of government, presumably in response to the changing nature of demands being placed upon government. To the extent that these observations are correct (and the weight of the evidence suggests they are), the changes have taken place gradually *within* the system provided by the Constitution.

Indeed, a case can be made for the argument that what the framers wrote into their Constitution has been no more important, in providing durability, than what they left out. The gaps, the holes, the vague language—all have been important in providing room for adapting government and politics to changing needs and circumstances. Allowances for change under the Constitution, along with the ability to amend it when necessary, have reduced any need to replace it.

This book is about continuity and change in American politics. Many of the readings mention continuities; almost all deal with change. The imbalance in favor of change undoubtedly reflects, in part, the editor's impression that it is more interesting to read and to write about change than about continuity. Nonetheless, it is also true that by studying change we are also, in a way, studying continuity. Any thorough review of the continuities and changes in the American political system must ultimately arrive at this conclusion: the single greatest *continuity* in American politics is *change!*

PART ONE

The Setting

CHAPTER ONE

The Framers
and the Constitution

That the framers were meeting in Philadelphia to structure change in the political system is not debatable. They had, after all, been chosen by their states to attend a convention called by Congress "for the sole and express purpose of revising the Articles of Confederation." *Why* they made the particular changes they did, on the other hand, is and has been the subject of much debate. At least since Charles Beard wrote his now classic and much maligned (and defended) *An Economic Interpretation of the Constitution* in 1913, debate has raged over the motives and intentions of the framers. Were they altruistic men, driven by a philosophy of what would be the good and wise thing to do for society as a whole, or were they, as Beard argued, a group of monied businessmen, bankers, and landowners, whose primary interests were those of the class they represented? Three of the four readings in this chapter offer different answers to that question. Michael Parenti concludes, as did Beard, that the Constitution is basically an elitist document, while David Smith argues that the framers were motivated more by national than self interests. Calvin Jillson and Cecil Eubanks find merit in both arguments, but as applied to different parts of the Constitution.

As the framers went about the business of deciding whether or not to change certain elements of the American system, one of the topics for heated discussion was the implementation of democracy itself. Though it is taken for granted today, not all of the delegates in Philadelphia assumed that "the people" could or should be trusted to make important political decisions. The first reading in this chapter is a small portion of James Madison's personal notes on the debates in the Constitutional Convention, and recounts some of the debate over "democracy."

1 / A Debate on Trusting the People
James Madison

Recognizing that he was participating in an historically important event, James Madison requested and received permission to take thorough notes on the proceedings at the Constitutional Convention.* Madison's notes are today considered to be the most important single source of information on the debates, even though they are undoubtedly colored to some extent by Madison's own views and biases.

The following excerpt from Madison's notes recounts the debate over the method for selection of the House of Representatives. The members of the unicameral Congress under the Articles of Confederation had been selected by state legislatures, and that same method would now be used for selection of members to the "second branch" of Congress, the Senate. The question discussed below is whether the members of the House of Representatives should also be chosen by state legislatures or instead by "the people," using direct election. Some delegates felt that extending national governance to "the people," implying the "lowest" as well as the "superior" classes of society, would be too risky. Others, including Madison, argued that popular election of at least one house would be "essential" to durable, stable, democratic government.

Resol: 4. first clause "that the new members of the first branch of the National Legislature ought to be elected by the people of the several States" being taken up,

Mr. Sherman opposed the election by the people, insisting that it ought to be by the State Legislatures. The people he said, immediately should have as little to do as may be about the Government. They want information and are constantly liable to be misled.

Mr. Gerry. The evils we experience flow from the excess of democracy. The people do not want virtue, but are the dupes of pretended patriots. In Massachusetts it had been fully confirmed by experience that they are daily misled into the most baneful measures and opinions by the false reports circulated by designing men, and which no one on the spot can refute. One principal evil arises from the want of due provision for those employed in the administration of Government. It would seem to be a maxim of democracy to starve the public servants. He mentioned the popular clamour in Massachusetts for the reduction of salaries and the attack made on that of the Governor though secured by the spirit of the Constitution itself. He had

*Smith, Edward Corwin, ed., *The Constitution of the United States,* 11th edition (New York: Barnes and Noble Books, 1979, p. 8). To get the most complete picture of how the debates ultimately resulted in the arrangements that we find in the Constitution, see Wilbourne E. Benton, *1787: Drafting the U.S. Constitution* (2 volumes) (College Station, Texas: Texas A&M University Press, 1986). Benton annotates each section of the Constitution on the basis of seven delegates' convention notes, including those of James Madison.—*Editor's Note.*

he said been too republican heretofore: he was still however republican, but had been taught by experience the danger of the levilling spirit.

Mr. Mason, argued strongly for an election of the larger branch by the people. It was to be the grand depository of the democratic principle of the Government. It was, so to speak, to be our House of Commons—It ought to know & sympathise with every part of the community; and ought therefore to be taken not only from different parts of the whole republic, but also from different districts of the larger members of it, which had in several instances particularly in Virginia, different interests and views arising from difference of produce, of habits &c &c. He admitted that we had been too democratic but was afraid we should incautiously run into the opposite extreme. We ought to attend to the rights of every class of the people. He had often wondered at the indifference of the superior classes of society to this dictate of humanity & policy; considering that however affluent their circumstances, or elevated their situations, might be, the course of a few years, not only might but certainly would, distribute their posterity throughout the lowest classes of Society. Every selfish motive therefore, every family attachment, ought to recommend such a system of policy as would provide no less carefully for the rights and happiness of the lowest than of the highest orders of Citizens.

Mr. Wilson contended strenuously for drawing the most numerous branch of the Legislature immediately from the people. He was for raising the federal pyramid to a considerable altitude, and for that reason wished to give it as broad a basis as possible. No government could long subsist without the confidence of the people. In a republican Government this confidence was peculiarly essential. He also thought it wrong to increase the weight of the State Legislatures by making them the electors of the national Legislature. All interference between the general and local Government should be obviated as much as possible. On examination it would be found that the opposition of States to federal measures had proceded much more from the officers of the States, than from the people at large.

Mr. Madison considered the popular election of one branch of the National Legislature as essential to every plan of free Government. He observed that in some of the States one branch of the Legislature was composed of men already removed from the people by an intervening body of electors. That if the first branch of the general legislature should be elected by the State Legislatures, the second branch elected by the first—the Executive by the second together with the first; and other appointments again made for subordinate purposes by the Executive, the people would be lost sight of altogether; and the necessary sympathy between them and their rulers and officers, too little felt. He was an advocate for the policy of refining the popular appointments by successive filtrations, but thought it might be pushed too far. He wished the expedient to be resorted to only in the appointment of the second branch of the Legislature, and in the Executive & judiciary branches of the Government. He thought too that the great fabric to be raised would be more stable and durable, if it should rest on the solid foundation of the people themselves, than if it should stand merely on the pillars of the Legislatures.

Mr. Gerry did not like the election by the people. The maxims taken from the British constitution were often fallacious when applied to our situation which was extremely different. Experience he said had shewn that the State legislatures drawn immediately from the people did not always possess their confidence. He had no objection however to an election by the people if it were so qualified that men of honor & character might not be unwilling to be joined in the appointments. He seemed to think the people might nominate a certain number out of which the State legislatures should be bound to choose.

Mr. Butler thought an election by the people an impracticable mode.

On the question for an election of the first branch of the national Legislature by the people.

Mass. ay. Connect. divided. N. York ay. N. Jersey no. Penn. ay. Delaware divided. Virginia ay. N. Carolina ay. S. Carolina no. Georgia ay.

2 / The Constitution as an Elitist Document
Michael Parenti

In a book published in 1913, economic historian Charles Beard presented evidence that most of the fifty-five men who "wrote" the Constitution were themselves part of the United States' early upper-class, falling into occupational categories whose economic interests had suffered under the Articles of Confederation. Though several of Beard's data were later shown to be faulty, his general thesis still rings true for some who subscribe to the elitist view of the Constitution.

In the Beardian tradition, Michael Parenti argues in the following article that the Constitution was written as an essentially nondemocratic, elitist document. Furthermore, the Constitution still continues today to serve the conservative interests of the "propertied class" at the expense of other citizens.

Class and Power in Early America
It is commonly taught that in the eighteenth and nineteenth centuries men of property preferred a laissez-faire government, one that kept its activities to a minimum. In actuality, they were not against a strong state but against state restrictions on business enterprise. They never desired to remove civil authority from economic affairs but to ensure that it worked *for*, rather than against, the interests of property. This meant they often had to move toward new and stronger state formations.

Adam Smith, who is above suspicion in his dedication to classical capitalism, argued that, as wealth increased in scope, government would have to perform still greater services on behalf of the propertied class. "The necessity of civil government," he wrote, "grows up with the acquisition of valuable property."[1] More importantly, Smith argued seventy years before Marx, "Civil authority, so far as it is instituted for the security of property, is in reality instituted for the defense of the rich against the poor, or of those who have some property against those who have none at all."[2]

Smith's views of the purposes of government were shared by the rich and the wellborn who lived in America during the period between the Revolution and the framing of the Constitution. Rather than keeping their distance from government, they set the dominant political tone.

> Their power was born of place, position, and fortune. They were located at or near the seats of government and they were in direct contact with legislatures and government officers. They influenced and often dominated the local newspapers which voiced the ideas and interests of commerce and identified them with the good of the whole people, the state, and the nation. The published writings of the leaders of the period are almost without exception those of merchants, of their lawyers, or of politicians sympathetic with them.[3]

The United States of 1787 has been described as an "egalitarian" society free from the extremes of want and wealth which characterized the Old World, but there were landed estates and colonial mansions that bespoke an impressive munificence. From the earliest English settlements, men of influence had received vast land grants from the crown. By 1700, three-fourths of the acreage in New York belonged to fewer than a dozen persons. In the interior of Virginia, seven persons owned a total of 1,732,000 acres. By 1760, fewer than 500 men in five colonial cities controlled most of the commerce, banking, mining, and manufacturing on the eastern seaboard and owned much of the land.

Here and there could be found farmers, shop owners, and tradesmen who, by the standards of the day, might be judged as comfortably situated. The bulk of the agrarian population were poor freeholders, tenants, squatters, and indentured and hired hands. The cities also had their poor—cobblers, weavers, bakers, blacksmiths, peddlers, laborers, clerks, and domestics, who worked long hours for meager sums.

As of 1787, property qualifications left perhaps more than a third of the white male population disfranchised. Property qualifications for holding office were so steep as to prevent most voters from qualifying as candidates. Thus, a member of the New Jersey legislature had to be worth at least 1,000 pounds, while state senators in South Carolina were required to possess estates worth at least 7,000 pounds, clear of debt. In addition, the practice of oral voting, the lack of a secret ballot, and an "absence of a real choice among candidates and programs" led to "widespread apathy."[4] As a result, men of substance monpolized the important offices. "Who do they represent?" Josiah Quincy asked of the South Carolina legislature. "The laborer, the mechanic, the tradesman, the farmer, the husbandman or yeoman? No, the representatives are almost if not wholly rich planters."[5]

Dealing with Insurgency

The Constitution was framed by financially successful planters, merchants, lawyers, and creditors, many linked by kinship and marriage and by years of service in Congress, the military, or diplomatic service. They congregated in Philadelphia in 1787 for the professed purpose of revising the Articles of Confederation and strengthening the powers of the central government. They were impelled by a desire to do something about the increasingly insurgent spirit evidenced among poorer people. Fearful of losing control of their state governments, the framers looked to a national government as a means of protecting their interests. Even in a state like South Carolina, where the propertied class was distinguished by the intensity of its desire to avoid any strong federation, the rich and the well-born, once faced with the possibility of rule by the common people "and realizing that a political alliance with conservatives from other states would be a safeguard if the radicals should capture the state government. . . gave up 'state rights' for 'nationalism' without hesitation."[6] It swiftly became their view that a central government would be less accessible to the populace and would be better able to provide the protections and services that their class so needed.

The landed, manufacturing, and merchant interests needed a central government that would provide a stable currency; impose uniform standards for trade; tax directly; regulate commerce; improve roads, canals, and harbors; provide protection against foreign imports and against the discrimination suffered by American shipping; and provide a national force to subjugate the Indians and secure the value of western lands. They needed a government that would honor at face value the huge sums of public securities they held and would protect them from paper-money schemes and from the large debtor class, the land-hungry agrarians, and the growing numbers of urban poor.

The nationalist conviction that arose so swiftly among men of property during the 1780s was not the product of a strange transcendent inspiration; it was not a "dream of nation-building" that suddenly possessed them as might a collective religious experience. (If so, they were remarkably successful in keeping it a secret in their public and private communications.) Rather, their newly acquired nationalism was a practical and urgent response to material conditions affecting them in a most immediate way. Gorham of Massachusetts, Hamilton of New York, Morris of Pennsylvania, Washington of Virginia, and Pinckney of South Carolina had a greater identity of interest with each other than with debt-burdened neighbors in their home counties. Their like-minded commitment to a central government was born of a common class interest stronger than state boundaries.

The rebellious populace of that day has been portrayed as irresponsible and parochial spendthrifts who never paid their debts and who believed in nothing more than timid state governments and inflated paper money. Little is said by most scholars of the period. . .about the actual plight of the common people, the great bulk of whom lived at a subsistence level. Farm tenants were burdened by heavy rents and hard labor. Small farmers were hurt by the low prices merchants offered for their crops and by the high costs for merchandised goods. They often bought land at inflated prices, only to see its value collapse and to find themselves unable to meet their mortgage obligations. Their labor and their crops usually were theirs in name only. To survive, they frequently had to borrow money at high interest rates. To meet their debts, they mortgaged their future crops and went still deeper into debt. Large numbers were caught in that cycle of rural indebtedness which is the common fate of agrarian peoples in many countries to this day. The artisans, small tradesmen, and workers (or "mechanics," as they were called) in the towns were not much better off, being "dependent on the wealthy merchants who ruled them economically and socially."[7]

During the 1780s, the jails were crowded with debtors. Among the people, there grew the feeling that the revolution against England had been fought for naught. Angry, armed crowds in several states began blocking foreclosures and sales of seized property, and opening up jails. They gathered at county towns to prevent the courts from presiding over debtor cases. In the winter of 1787, farmers in western Massachusetts led by Daniel Shays took up arms. But their rebellion was forcibly put down by the state militia after some ragged skirmishes.

Containing the Spread of Democracy
The specter of Shays' Rebellion hovered over the delegates who gathered in Philadelphia three months later, confirming their worst fears about the populace. They were determined that persons of birth and fortune should control the affairs of the nation and check the "leveling impulses" of that propertyless multitude which composed "the majority faction." "To secure the public good and private rights against the danger of such a faction," wrote James Madison in *Federalist* No. 10, "and at the same time preserve the spirit and form of popular government is then the great object to which our inquiries are directed." Here Madison touched the heart of the matter: how to keep the *spirit* and *form* of popular government with only a minimum of the *substance*, how to provide the appearance of republicanism without suffering its leveling effects, how to construct a government that would win mass acquiescence but would not tamper with the existing class structure, a government strong enough both to service the growing needs of an entrepreneurial class while withstanding the egalitarian demands of the poor and propertyless. . . .

The delegates spent many weeks debating their interests, but these were the differences of merchants, slave owners, and manufacturers, a debate of haves versus haves in which each group sought safeguards within the new Constitution for its particular concerns. Added to this were the inevitable disagreements that arise over the best means of achieving agreed-upon ends. Questions of structure and authority occupied a good deal of the delegates' time: How much representation should the large and small states have? How might the legislature be organized? How should the executive be selected? What length of tenure should exist for the different officeholders? *Yet, questions of enormous significance, relating to the new government's ability to protect the interests of property, were agreed upon with surprisingly little*

debate. For on these issues, there were no dirt farmers or poor artisans attending the convention to proffer an opposing viewpoint. The debate between
haves and have-nots never occurred.

The portions of the Constitution giving the federal government the power
to support commerce and protect property were decided upon after amiable
deliberation and with remarkable dispatch considering their importance.
Thus all of Article I, Section 8 was adopted within a few days. This section
gave to Congress the powers needed by the propertied class for the expansion
of its commerce, trade, and industry. . . .

Some of the delegates were land speculators who expressed a concern
about western holdings; accordingly, Congress was given the "Power to dispose
of and make all needful Rules and Regulations respecting the Territory or
other Property belonging to the United States. . . ." Some delegates speculated
in highly inflated and nearly worthless Confederation securities. Under Article VI, all debts incurred by the confederation were valid against the new
government, a provision that allowed speculators to make generous profits
when their securities were honored at face value.[8]

In the interest of merchants and creditors, the states were prohibited
from issuing paper money or imposing duties on imports and exports or interfering with the payment of debts by passing any "Law impairing the
Obligation of Contracts." The Constitution guaranteed "Full Faith and
Credit" in each state "to the Acts, Records, and judicial Proceedings" of other
states, thus allowing creditors to pursue their debtors more effectively.

The property interests of slave owners were looked after. To give the slave-
owning states a greater influence, three-fifths of the slave population were to
be counted when calculating the representation deserved by each state in the
lower house. The importation of slaves was allowed until 1808. Under Article
IV, slaves who escaped from one state to another had to be delivered to the
original owner upon claim, a provision unanimously adopted at the convention.

The framers believed the states acted with insufficient force against popular uprisings, so Congress was given the task of "organizing, arming, and disciplining the Militia" and calling it forth, among other reasons, to "suppress
Insurrections." The federal government was empowered to protect the states
"against domestic Violence." Provision was made for "the Erection of Forts,
Magazines, Arsenals, dock-Yards and other needful Buildings" and for the
maintenance of an army and navy for both national defense and to establish
an armed federal presence within the potentially insurrectionary states—a
provision that was to prove a godsend a century later when the army was used
repeatedly to break strikes by miners, railroad employees, and factory workers.

In keeping with their desire to contain the majority, the founders in-
serted "auxiliary precautions" *designed to fragment power without democratizing it.* By separating the executive, legislative, and judiciary functions and
then providing a system of checks and balances among the various branches,
including staggered elections, executive veto, Senate confirmation of appointments and ratification of treaties, and a bicameral legislature, they hoped
to dilute the impact of popular sentiments. They also contrived an elaborate

and difficult process for amending the Constitution. *To the extent that it existed at all, the majoritarian principle was tightly locked into a system of minority vetoes, making sweeping popular actions nearly impossible.*

The propertyless majority, as Madison pointed out in *Federalist* No. 10, must not be allowed to concert in common cause against the established economic order. First, it was necessary to prevent unity of public sentiment by enlarging the polity and then compartmentalizing it into geographically insulated political communities. The larger the nation, the greater the "variety of parties and interests" and the more difficult it would be for a majority to find itself and act in unison. As Madison argued, "A rage for paper money, for an abolition of debts, for an equal division of property, or for any other wicked project will be less apt to pervade the whole body of the Union than a particular member of it.... " An uprising of impoverished farmers could threaten Massachusetts at one time and Rhode Island at another, but a national government would be large and varied enough to contain each of these and insulate the rest of the nation from the contamination of rebellion....

Plotters or Patriots?

The question of whether the founders were motivated by financial or national interest has been debated since Charles Beard published *An Economic Interpretation of the Constitution* in 1913. It was Beard's view that the delegates were guided by their class interests. Arguing against Beard's thesis are those who believe that the framers were concerned with higher things than lining their purses and protecting their property. True, they were moneyed men who profited directly from policies initiated under the new Constitution, but they were motivated by a concern for nation building that went beyond their particular class interests, the argument goes. To paraphrase Justice Holmes, these men invested their belief to make a nation; they did not make a nation because they had invested. "High-mindedness is not impossible to man," Holmes reminded us.

That is exactly the point: High-mindedness is one of man's most common attributes even when, or especially when, he is pursuing his personal and class interest. The fallacy is to presume that there is a dichotomy between the desire to build a strong nation and the desire to protect property and that the delegates could not have been motivated by both. In fact, like most other people, they believed that what was good for themselves was ultimately good for the entire society. Their universal values and their class interests went hand in hand; to discover the existence of the "higher" sentiment does not eliminate the self-interested one....

...The point is not that they were devoid of the grander sentiments of nation building but that *there was nothing in the concept of nation which worked against their class interest and a great deal that worked for it....*

...Even if we deny that the framers were motivated by the desire for personal gain that moves others, we cannot dismiss the existence of their class interest. They may not have been solely concerned with getting their own hands in the till, although enough of them did, but they were admittedly preoccupied with defending the propertied few from the propertyless many—for the ultimate benefit of all, as they understood it. . . .

The small farmers, tradesmen, and debtors who opposed a central government have been described as motivated by self-serving parochial interests—as opposed to the supposedly higher-minded statesmen who journeyed to Philadelphia and others of their class who supported ratification. How or why the propertied rich became visionary nation builders is never explained. In truth, it was not their minds that were so much broader but their economic interests. Their motives were neither higher nor lower than those of any other social group struggling for place and power in the United States of 1787–1789. They pursued their material interests as single-mindedly as any small freeholder—if not more so. Possessing more time, money, information, and organization, they enjoyed superior results. How could they have acted otherwise? For them to have ignored the conditions of governance necessary for the maintenance of their enterprises would have amounted to committing class suicide—and they were not about to do that. They were a rising bourgeoisie rallying around a central power in order to advance their class interests. Some of us are quite willing to accept the existence of such a material-based nationalism in the history of other countries, but not in our own.

Finally, those who argue that the founders were motivated primarily by high-minded objectives consistently overlook the fact that the delegates repeatedly stated their intention to erect a government strong enough to protect the haves from the have-nots. They gave voice to the crassest class prejudices and never found it necessary to disguise the fact—as have latter-day apologists—that their uppermost concern was to diminish popular control and resist all tendencies toward class equalization (or "leveling," as it was called). Their opposition to democracy and their dedication to the propertied and moneyed interests were unabashedly and openly avowed. Their preoccupation was so pronounced that one delegate did finally complain of hearing too much about how the purpose of government was to protect property. He wanted it noted that the ultimate objective of government was the ennoblement of mankind—a fine sentiment that evoked no oppositon from his colleagues as they continued about their business.

An Elitist Document

More important than conjecturing about the framers' motives is to look at the Constitution they fashioned, for it tells a good deal about their objectives. It was, and still is, largely an elitist document, more concerned with securing property interests than personal liberties. Bills of attainder and ex post facto laws are expressly prohibited, and Article I, Section 9, assures us that "the Privilege of the Writ of Habeas Corpus shall not be suspended, unless when in Cases of Rebellion or Invasion the public Safety may require it," a restriction that leaves authorities with a wide measure of discretion. Other than these few provisions, the Constitution that emerged from the Philadelphia Convention gave no attention to civil liberties.

When Colonel Mason suggested to the Convention that a committee be formed to draft "a Bill of Rights"—a task that could be accomplished "in a few hours"—the representatives of the various states offered little discussion on the motion and voted almost unanimously against it. The Bill of Rights, of course, was ratified only after the first Congress and president had been elected.

For the founders, liberty meant something different from democracy; it meant liberty to invest and trade and carry out the matters of business and enjoy the security of property without encroachment by king or populace. The civil liberties designed to give all individuals the right to engage actively in public affairs were of no central concern to the delegates and, as noted, were summarily voted down. . . .

The twentieth-century concept of social justice, involving something more than procedural liberties, is afforded no place in the eighteenth-century Constitution. The Constitution says nothing about those conditions of life that have come to be treated by many people as essential human rights—for instance, freedom from hunger; the right to decent housing, medical care, and education regardless of ability to pay; the right to gainful employment, safe working conditions, and a clean, nontoxic environment. Under the Constitution, equality is treated as a *procedural* right without a *substantive* content. Thus, "equality of opportunity" means equality of opportunity to move ahead competitively and become unequal to others; it means a chance to get in the game and best others rather than to enjoy an equal distribution and use of the resources needed for the maintenance of community life. . . .

If the Constitution is so blatantly elitist, how did it manage to win enough popular support for ratification? First, it should be noted that it did not have a wide measure of support, initially being opposed in most of the states. But the same superiority of wealth, leadership, organization, control of the press, and control of political office that allowed the rich to monopolize the Philadelphia Convention worked with similar effect in the ratification campaign. Superior wealth also enabled the Federalists to bribe, intimidate, and, in other ways, pressure and discourage opponents of the Constitution. At the same time, there were some elements in the laboring class, especially those who hoped to profit from employment in shipping and export trades, who supported ratification.

Above all, it should be pointed out that the Constitution never was submitted to popular ratification. There was no national referendum and none in the states. Ratification was by state convention composed of elected delegates, the majority of whom were drawn from the more affluent strata. . . .

In sum, the framers laid the foundation for a national government, but it was one that fit the specifications of the propertied class. They wanted protection from popular uprisings, from fiscal uncertainty and irregularities in trade and currency, from trade barriers between states, from economic competition by more powerful foreign governments, and from attacks by the poor on property and on creditors. The Constitution was consciously designed as a conservative document, elaborately equipped with a system of minority checks and vetoes, making it hard to enact sweeping popular reforms or profound structural changes, and easy for entrenched interests to endure. It provided ample power to build the services and protections of state needed by a growing capitalist class but not the power for a transition of rule to a different class or to the public as a whole....

Notes

1. Adam Smith, *An Inquiry into the Nature and Causes of the Wealth of Nations* (Chicago: Encyclopaedia Britannica, Inc., 1952), p. 309.
2. Ibid., p. 311.
3. Merrill Jensen, *The New Nation* (New York: Random House, 1950), p. 178.
4. Sidney H. Aronson, *Status and Kinship in the Higher Civil Service* (Cambridge, Mass.: Harvard University Press, 1964), p. 49.
5. Ibid, p. 49.
6. Merrill Jensen, *The Articles of Confederation* (Madison: University of Wisconsin Press, 1948), p. 30.
7. Ibid., pp. 9–10. "In addition to being frequently in debt for their lands," Beard noted, "the small farmers were dependent upon the towns for most of the capital to develop their resources. They were, in other words, a large debtor class, to which must be added, of course, the urban dwellers who were in a like unfortunate condition." Charles A. Beard, *An Economic Interpretation of the Constitution of the United States* (New York: Macmillan, 1936), p. 28.
8. See Beard, *An Economic Interpretation*, passim. The profits accrued to holders of public securities were in the millions. On the question of speculation in western lands, Hugh Williamson, a North Carolina delegate, wrote to Madison a year after the convention: "For myself, I conceive that my opinions are not biassed by private Interests, but having claims to a considerable Quantity of Land in the Western Country, I am fully persuaded that the Value of those Lands must be increased by an efficient federal Government." Ibid., p. 50. Critiques of Beard have been made by Robert E. Brown, *Charles Beard and the American Constitution* (Princeton, N.J.: Princeton University Press, 1956) and Forrest McDonald, *We the People—The Economic Origins of the Constitution* (Chicago: Chicago University Press, 1958).

3 / The Framers' Intentions
David G. Smith

In contrast to the arguments offered by Beard and others who have attributed anti-democratic motives to the framers, Smith contends that the writers of the Constitution were driven by a desire to develop a republican government that could withstand the "disharmony" of their day. Rather than being chiefly motivated by economic self-interests, they were motivated by more "national" and political concerns.

According to the interpretation suggested in this [reading], the delegates were attempting *in the main* to create a political system and not to protect property. They were also attempting *principally* not to defeat democracy but to devise strong constitutional and political supports for a federal republic. They had a large and generous vision of the future. They also understood the limitations of their constitutional and political resources. They sought to connect their ambitious vision of the future with their present political world.

The Founding Fathers: Accused and Defended

The indictment by Beard, Smith, and Parrington includes three counts.* One is that making and adopting the Constitution was an act of usurpation. Another is that the Constitution was designed largely to protect property interests, especially personalty or property other than land. The last count is that the Constitution was antidemocratic both in design and in substance. . . .

Defense: An Alternate Interpretation

The bill of particulars given above is, so far as it goes, true. The main issue with Beard, Smith, Parrington and other idol-smashers, however, is the interpretation of the acts of the delegates. Interpretation depends upon context; and an alternate interpretation depends upon enlarging the context within which the delegates acted. That enlarged context is the "disharmonious society" for which the Constitution was made. That context does not destroy the anti-Convention indictment. It simply demonstrates that the indictment can be subsumed as incidental to a bigger purpose: to erect a large political edifice upon weak constitutional foundations.

We return briefly to the eighteenth-century society. . . . The society was disharmonious because it tended toward group and sectional particularism, and because the political attitudes needed to support common republican government were not firmly set nor strongly entrenched. There were few of the moderating influences that we associate with democracy in modern, urban, and industrialized societies: intersectional ties, a national economy, and a wide sharing and communication of political attitudes. Eighteenth century society, furthermore, lacked many of the institutional resources with which to create a "reasonable" or "moderate" politics, to borrow the language of that time. Parties were loose factional assemblages; and political communication was poorly organized. Under all these circumstances, and despite all that worked in favor of republican government, the danger of expanding or "cumulative" political conflict was a very real, if not always present, threat.

The language of the delegates in Convention supports a view that they were primarily concerned with creating a constitution for a "disharmonious society" lacking adequate supports for a moderate federal republic. Their speeches and their language do not support an interpretation that they wanted

---

*J. Allen Smith, *The Spirit of American Government* (New York: Macmillan, 1907); Vernon Parrington, *Main Currents in American Thought* (New York: Harcourt, Brace, and Co., 1927).—*Editor's Note.*

primarily to defeat democracy or erect an antipopular oligarchy. In the florid oratory of the opening days of the Convention the delegates denounced the democratic provisions of the Articles and of the state constitutions, the rage for paper money, and the unreasonableness of the people. But for the most part, they spoke of different fears: of cabal and faction; of dissolution or consolidation; of monarchy or popular upheaval. They were fearful mainly not of democracy or attacks upon property, but of continuing, unchecked tendencies to an extreme, and of political expressions that would undermine republican government itself.

The constitution the delegates constructed indicates also that, whatever may have been their other concerns, they were fundamentally engaged in an attempt to strengthen the American polity so that the future republican government could function effectively. Their strategy—logical under the circumstances—included three principal methods or aims. One was to withdraw especially fruitful sources of contention from the most quarrelsome and heated centers of political dispute and thereby limit a tendency toward cumulative political conflict. Another technique of the delegates was to strengthen both the political and nonpolitical bonds of unity. And lastly, also in keeping with rational strategy under prevalent political conditions, they sought to create an artificial frame of government to limit and to sublimate the natural tendencies of politics in their "disharmonious society."

The delegates withdrew power from the states; especially they withdrew some principal objects of political contention from the reach of local democracy. The Constitution prohibited interference with contracts or with commerce among the states. It also enjoined each state to grant "full faith and credit" to the public acts, records, and judicial proceedings of other states and to recognize for the citizens of each state the "privileges and immunities" of citizens in the several states.

By one account, in these provisions the delegates acted to limit democracy and to protect property. By another, they attempted to remove sources of contention from the power of the states, to provide for a national citizenship and for a new government with power to act as representative and trustee of citizens possessed of a dual citizenship.

Actually, the delegates in Convention seemed to be relatively indifferent to the *internal* politics of the states. They did not consistently take the side of debtors or creditors, democrats or oligarchs. Nor did they appear to fear local democracy as such. They did not care, either, how many heads were broken on the local level. But they were intensely and continuously concerned with political conflict that weakened the union, undermined a growing nationhood, or threatened the stability of a republican government.

Aside from the provisions cited and those designed to secure national control of foreign relations, the states were left substantially in charge of their own affairs. They retained their traditional police power almost in its entirety, along with control over property, crime, civil injuries, and social arrangements. The delegates removed from the states very little. Indeed, to have done so would have, in their view, both threatened to create a monarchy, centralized discontent, and made the common government itself too much subject to contention. Instead, they sought to create an additional tier of government and a new constituency principally to defend and represent what citizens enjoyed in common as Americans.

Those objects of political controversy that the delegates sought to protect from the states were critical in amending the major defects of their disharmonious society. A national commerce and protection of common rights would contribute both to a national citizenship and to removing causes of dissension among the states. Their protection would encourage both political and economic growth. And by putting them out of the reach of the states and local governments, some of the heat would be removed from a politics that tended dangerously toward cumulative and uncontrollable conflict.

Aside from an attempt to withdraw certain subjects of contention from state action, the delegates were also especially concerned to strengthen the bonds of union. The contract and commerce clauses, indeed all of those clauses of the Constitution that deal with property, need to be read in this context. The delegates set up protections for property, for commerce, and for sound money. They particularly sought to protect the foundations upon which personalty and economic endeavor rested. To follow the delegates in Convention is revealing. They discuss property, the commerce clause, and conflicts of debtors and creditors. But they talked directly about these matters very little. They are discussed almost wholly in conjunction with *other* objects: navigation acts, the slave trade, the burden of taxation, etc.

Property found its place among many other interests, and especially as an adjunct to *political* objectives such as military strength and corporate unity, or *social* objectives such as access to unappropriated resources and equality of status. Usually, the delegates seemed primarily interested in settling upon one or another social or political objective. The battles in the Convention about these interests or ends were often fierce. When agreement was reached, economic arrangements appeared to follow pretty much as a matter of course and even of indifference. Often they were simply taken over from some clause in the Articles, or from a practice made familiar by their colonial experience. One may say, then, that economic and property arrangements were subordinate to the interests of federal union, political stability, and the future economic and social development within the United States. The delegates adopted those property arrangements they felt would conduce the long-term interests of the nation they saw growing from their efforts.

Property was protected; and a measure of control over property and especially personalty was withdrawn from the states. The delegates may have incidentally benefited the interests of creditors or merchants or speculators. In fact, they did not seem specifically to want to protect them. In any case, they had other ends. One was withdrawing a source of controversy from direct political action by the states. The delegates were also filling out and giving specific character to a conception of national citizenship and of future national development. And they were, finally, artificially strengthening the polity by associating union and common republican government with economic advantage and development.

The delegates' treatment of democracy, or popular government, probably appears by contemporary standards the most suspect of all their deeds. Notice again, however, that an interpretation of their actions depends upon the context in which they are read. Their actions could have been aimed at weakening democracy. They could also have been intended to strengthen artificially a republican government under circumstances requiring precisely that approach to secure a popular government on a national scale. The delegates sought to erect a national government. They sought to establish a dual citizenship under which people would be at once members of a locale and of a state, but would share in a joint venture of federal and republican government. They created scope for an additional layer or level of government, an independent government with its own machinery of courts, its own taxing powers, and a capacity to develop loyalties. They knew the tendencies of the politics of their time. Consequently, they sought equally to guard against the most dangerous tendencies of the government they were creating.

The Founding Fathers called themselves supporters of republican government, by which they meant representative government, derived from the great bulk of the people, but so arranged as to secure stability and government of the wise and virtuous. They meant by "wise and virtuous" primarily wise in the ways of politics and filled with republican virtue. The delegates understood from their own experience that the government, to work at all, required political leaders at the national level with considerable disinterested devotion to the republic. Remember their experience: their enormous efforts and great difficulty in getting the project started and their many frustrations. They had seen how readily jealousies could set individuals and sections against each other. From their experience—under colonial governments, during the Revolution, under the Articles—they knew that a stratum of patriots was not only a necessary support to government, but a needed security against factionalism, cabal, or disruptive parochialism.

A prime objective of the Convention was, therefore, to provide for moderate and independent leadership for the nation in spite of the masses or popular majorities, especially those within the states. The delegates feared also a plebiscitary chief on the national scene or a widespread populistic democracy. Against these dangers, they devised a set of "republican remedies" to apply to the federal government itself. Their "republican remedies" had another purpose: to complete and perfect the representative republic itself.

The representative devices in the Constitution serve both to temper political will and to supplement and complete it by providing representation for interests that might otherwise remain unheard. Representation in the Constitution was the subject of sectional and factional compromise. These compromises had also (and were understood to have) a broad tendency to supplement and expand political representation. In sum, the representative arrangements in the Constitution, whatever other purposes they had, were also designed to offset the defects of political representation that arose from an inadequately organized politics.

Today, we are apt to think of checks and balances, separation of powers, and indirect representation as devices to restrain the "tyranny of the majority," and to thwart popular government. In part they have that effect. But in the eighteenth century, they were good republican and democratic devices and, in fact, applied consistently and rigorously by radical republicans in the states. When commending such devices in the Convention, the delegates sometimes spoke of the danger of majorities or omnipotent legislatures. A more central concern was cabal and faction: the threats of silent and sinister accumulations of power and of the disruption of the polity by minority interests. The delegates were trying to generate a national will, not defeat it. A central danger, as they saw it, was that such a will would not be representative, that it would be a will proclaiming itself the representative of the whole but masking designs for power, pelf, and preferment. Separation of powers, checks and balances, and representative formulae would work to counteract the natural tendencies of politics built on a primitive economic and social base. Such devices were also vital for nourishing the government itself: to secure confidence in it; to win the support of disinterested patriots; and to afford a security against fecund evils.

A democrat might say that the delegates took too low a view of politics. Perhaps they did. But that judgment misses one of the unique and original contributions of the Founding Fathers. They contrived an alternate and supplementary system of institutions to remedy the deficiencies of their own political society. The delegates' constitutional methods of fragmentation, of withdrawal and delegation, and of nourishing a patriot elite are directed to this object. They wished to stimulate loyalty to the principles of republican government. They wanted also to generate power in the whole system. They sought to achieve both these ends by limiting politics—that is, politics in the ordinary sense of the word. But in constraining and narrowing the method of politics, they supplemented the Constitution, providing for alternate methods, other modes for the resolution of conflict, and for stimulating patriotic energies.

Eighteenth-century philosophers often spoke of a social contract and of a political contract or contract of government. These terms are useful in the present context. The task for the delegates was to build a nationwide political contract upon an untried and possibly inadequate foundation. For this purpose, they required more than a simple principal-agent model of government. Neither the existing society nor contemporary political institutions could sustain a republican government based upon a direct connection between political will and government response. Supporting the political contract required artful measures. Consequently, the delegates contrived methods to strengthen particular political institutions by formal constitutional provisions and to sublimate intense political passions by utilizing the forces of social and economic evolution. American politics was "judicialized." Many issues that involved property, citizenship, and the development of the nation were reserved from the direct or speedy expression of popular will. Even ordinary political decision was closely associated with the politics of federalism and an intricate constitutional system of representation and separation of powers. According to one view of democracy, the delegates dethroned the people and set up an antidemocratic scheme of government. But "politics" in the narrow usage of that term is a small part of the whole of the life of man, and even a small part of what most understand democracy to be. Whether the delegates' conception of the right relation between citizens, the society, and the state, between the social contract and the contract of government, was an ungenerous one or even an antipopular one, remains to be discussed. . . . Certainly we can say, however, that their conception was statesmanlike.

Conclusion

The intention of the delegates probably cannot be finally known. But if we establish a purpose that included a wider intention and motive than that imputed by Beard or Smith, we lay a foundation for the ensuing discussion. Without alleging proof, it would be useful to state what seems the most plausible interpretation of the delegates' intentions.

In the context of their society and their experience with the colonial and revolutionary governments, the delegates' activities in behalf of the new government seem to have been directed primarily at a simple, coherent set of *political* objectives. They seem to have been aiming at (1) withdrawing particular objects of contention from local majorities; (2) attempting to secure a common interest; (3) securing the support for the "representative republic" of a stratum of "wise and virtuous" leaders who would put republican principles above personal and factional interest; and (4) devising a scheme of representation and checks and balances that would complete that government and prevent it in turn from developing cumulative tendencies toward an extreme.

The delegates, in Convention and out of it, appear to have been doing what people have generally thought they were. They protected property, but especially in order to remove sources of discord, foster economic growth, and develop interest in the government. They destroyed the dependence of the government upon the states, but more in the interests of a national citizenship than fear of democracy. Similarly, they added to central government the "salutary checks" of republican government as much to complete a representative will as to restrain it. In Convention and out of it they did not act as if they were trying to execute a *coup* for their faction, defend property, or silence democrats in the states. They were men engaged in a task intellectually and practically of enormous difficulty: to conceive a successful constitution and launch a nation. That task required great initiative and sound principles of strategy and philosophy. . . .

Beard and Smith remind us that the Founding Fathers lived long ago and that they made a Constitution to serve, initially, a society of a few million farmers. There is no security that their philosophy will continue to serve us, especially at times when new popular creeds are struggling for recognition.

To their credit, however, the Founding Fathers did not finally settle the issue between republican government and responsiveness to popular creeds or democratic majorities. Instead, they initiated a dialogue between the people as ultimate sovereign and the people as *populus*, as trustee for the nation.

4 / The Political Structure of Constitution Making

Calvin C. Jillson and Cecil L. Eubanks

As demonstrated in the previous readings by Parenti and Smith, attempts to explain the actions of the framers in writing the Constitution have produced two "competing theories," one stressing material self-interests and the other stressing what Calvin Jillson and Cecil Eubanks call "rational" philosophical thinking. In this reading the authors review the debates and decisions that were made in Philadelphia, in light of this controversy. They conclude that both explanations are correct, but that they apply to different types of decisions.

. . .One line of interpretation has consistently argued for the centrality of ideas and political principles to the outcome of the Convention's debates, while the other has stressed the importance of practical politics and economic interests. . . .

Conflicting Interpretations: Principle versus Interest
Americans entered the twentieth century convinced that British Prime Minister William Gladstone had captured the special character of the American Constitution in describing it as "the most wonderful work ever struck off at a given time by the brain and purpose of man" (Smith, 1980, p. 94). Yet, less than a decade into the new century, J. Allen Smith (1907) set the tone for an explicitly materialist interpretation of the Convention's work by arguing that "the American scheme of government was planned and set up to perpetuate the ascendancy of the property-holding class" (p. 298). Charles A. Beard (1913) elaborated this "economic interpretation" of the motives of the Framers and the outcome of their deliberations. He concluded that "the members of the Philadelphia Convention which drafted the Constitution were, with a few exceptions, immediately, directly, and personally interested in, and derived economic advantages from, the establishment of the new system" (1913, p. 324).

By mid-century, the charges against the Founders had become less personal, but no less materialist in character. John P. Roche (1961). . . concluded that the Constitution was no more than a particularly impressive example of "political improvisation" (p. 810). It was "a patchwork sewn together under the pressure of both time and events by a group of extremely talented democratic politicians" (p. 815). Though Roche did not intend his reading to "suggest that the Constitution rested on a foundation of impure or base motives" (p. 801) many analysts feared that the cumulative impact of his and other materialist interpretations of the Founding had diminished the nation's sense of direction and purpose. Walter Lippmann (1955) concluded that "the public philosophy [that guided the nation's early development] is in large measure intellectually discredited among contemporary men.... The signs and seals of legitimacy, or rightness and of truth, have been taken over by men who reject...the doctrine of constitutional democracy" (pp. 136–37).

The recovery of a sound and effective "public philosophy" did not come quickly. Fully twenty years after Lippmann wrote, Martin Diamond (1976) was forced to conclude that "the old root American ideas have been challenged on nearly every front and cast into doubt by the most powerful contemporary intellectual currents" (p. 3). In defense of the Founders and the political system that they created, Diamond adopted and promoted a view that clearly, even combatively, emphasized the impact of ideas and political principles over material interests in the Convention. He argued that "the Convention supplies a remarkable example of...how theoretical matters govern the disposition of practical matters" (Diamond, 1981, p. 30). In Diamond's view, "the debate over the Constitution was a climactic encounter between two rival political theories of how the ends of democratic consent, liberty and competent government can best be obtained" (1981, p. 54). Despite the profound impact of Diamond's work on many students of American political ideas and institutions, others have continued to embrace the predominately materialist view that we have identified with Smith, Beard, and Roche.

Despite the persistence of this long-standing dispute within the tradition of constitutional studies,....we seek to demonstrate that debate moved between two levels of constitutional construction and that these levels represented significant shifts in the relative importance of political principles and material interests in the Convention....

At the "higher" level, the constitution-maker wrestles with general questions concerning the scope, scale, and form appropriate to government. Will the regime be an aristocratic, democratic, or mixed republic? Will the government have a legislative or an executive focus? Will its legislature be bicameral or unicameral? Will its executive be one man or several? These questions are less likely to be decided with reference to the economic status, social role, or material characteristics of the constitution-maker than with reference to his philosophical assumptions concerning the interplay among human nature, political institutions, and the good society.

As the general institutional design and the relationships that will pertain among its component parts become clear, the individual constitution-maker moves closer to the realm of practical politics. The questions that dominate this "lower" level of constitutional design concern the regulation of political behavior through rules governing such specific matters as citizenship, suffrage and voting, eligibility to office, and representation. The choices made concerning these matters determine the context of day-to-day politics at the operational or practical level. Therefore, questions at this level are much more likely to be decided with direct reference to the political, economic, and social characteristics of the chooser, his state, or his region than with reference to his philosophical principles.. . .

The Extended Republic versus Traditional Republicanism: Power and Principle

The Convention's first two weeks of substantive debate, 29 May to 9 June, saw a fundamentally important clash of ideas at the "higher" level of constitutional choice (Jensen, 1964, p. 43; Smith, 1965, pp. 36–41).. . . Madison's theory of the "extended republic" sought to offer a positive new approach to providing "a republican remedy for the diseases most incident to republican government" (Earle, 1937, p. 62).

. . .As Martin Diamond (1972) correctly noted: "The main thrust of the opposition resulted from the more general argument that only the state governments (small republics), not some huge central government, could be made effectively free and republican" (p. 635).. . .

James Madison and those members of the Convention who sought to enhance dramatically the authority and independence of the national government moved decisively and successfully to capture the Convention's agenda and therewith to set the tone of its deliberations. The adoption, on 29 May, of Madison's Virginia Plan gave the "extended republic" men an initial edge because their general principles obviously underlay its specific provisions. On 30 May, they sought to solidify this potential advantage by putting the Convention on record in favor of radical change. Therefore, Edmund Randolph moved "that a *national* Government [ought to be established] consisting of a *supreme* Legislative, Executive and Judiciary" (Farrand, 1911, vol. 1, p. 33).

Many delegates sympathized with this root and branch approach, but others were wary, preferring the incremental approach to the Convention's business enunciated by John Dickinson of Delaware. Dickinson simply thought that wholesale change was unnecessary. "We may resolve therefore,. . . that the confederation is defective; and then proceed to the definition of such powers as may be thought adequate to the objects for which it was instituted.. . . The enquiry should be—

1.   What are the legislative powers which we should vest in Congress.
2.   What judiciary powers.
3.   What executive powers" (Farrand, 1911, vol. 1, p. 42).

. . .[A] dramatic division [existed] within the Convention over how to proceed and over the purposes and intentions that underlay the alternative approaches. The extended republic men sought to undertake immediately the radical changes necessary to institute a truly national government, while the small republic men favored incremental changes in the existing Confederation.. . .

The extended republic men from the Middle Atlantic region, led by Virginia's Madison and by Pennsylvania's James Wilson and Robert Morris, held the early initiative. This largely reflected the fact that the small republic men had yet to formulate an acceptable balance between national and state authority that could be offered as a coherent alternative to Madison's Virginia Plan. As a consequence, their opposition lacked the conviction and cohesion that characterized the support for Madison's extended republic. This uncertainty was evident in the fact that two of the small republic delegations, Massachusetts and North Carolina, gave substantial support to the extended republic cause....

Madison's vision of a great commercial republic, ruled by a powerful national government that would regulate with competence and justice the activities of the several states, was directly challenged by John Dickinson on 2 June. In Dickinson's view, the critical problem posed by government in a free society was the danger that authority might concentrate and become tyrannical (Bailyn, 1969, pp. 55-93). To minimize this constant danger, Dickinson argued, the national government should remain weak and "the Legislative, Executive, & Judiciary departments ought to be made as independent [separate] as possible" (Farrand, 1911, vol. 1, p. 86).

On 4 June,...Madison carefully presented and explained the theoretical underpinnings of his "extended republic." William Pierce of Georgia recorded that "Mr. Madison in a very able and ingenious Speech...proved that the only way to make a Government answer all the end of its institution was to collect the wisdom of its several parts in aid of each other [by blurring a pure separation of powers] whenever it was necessary" (Farrand, 1911, vol. 1, p. 110). By stressing the principle of "checks and balances" as a supplement and buttress to a strict "separation of powers," the extended republic men sought to create a governmental structure in which each department was fully capable of and motivated to self-defense. If the integrity of the structure and its ability to forestall tyranny by maintaining separate centers of power could be depended upon, then great power could be given to the national government in the knowledge that one branch would check potential abuses of the other.

As the full implications of Madison's program became clearer to the small republic men, they struggled with increasing determination against the idea that substantial authority at the national level could be either necessary or safe....

Madison's opponents knew that additional powers would have to be granted to a central government, but the idea of a truly national government clashed directly with the philosophical assumptions with which they (and most Americans with them) had been operating since before the revolution. Yet, bereft of viable alternatives, these "men of shaken faith" could oppose only half-heartedly when Madison contended that "it was incumbent on [them] to try this [extended republic] remedy, and...to frame a republican system on such a scale & in such a form as will control all the evils which have been experienced" (Farrand, 1911, vol. 1, p. 136). While the conflict remained at this "higher" level of constitutional choice, the small republic men cast about for alternatives to Madison's frighteningly radical approach. None came readily to hand (Diamond, 1981, p. 27).

Large States versus Small States: Power and Interest
On 7 June the tenor of the questions before the Convention began to drift from the high plane of theory to the rough and tumble of practical, interest-driven power politics. Dickinson opened the discussion on 7 June by restating the modest commitment of the small republic men to "the preservation of the States in a certain degree of agency" (Farrand, 1911, vol. 1, p. 153). James Wilson, on behalf of the supporters of the Virginia Plan, observed that the "doubts and difficulties" surrounding the place of the state governments in the proposed system derived from the threat that they seemed to pose to the independence and effectiveness of the national government; "he wished to keep them from devouring the national Government" (ibid.).

Those delegates who followed the logic of Madison's extended republic expected any initiative left with the state governments to be misused. Their theoretical principles told them that small republics had always been violent and short-lived because interested local majorities, possessed of the means, invariably acted unjustly. Therefore, Charles Pinckney proposed "that the National Legislature should have authority to negative all [State] Laws which they should judge to be improper" (Farrand, 1911, vol. 1, p. 164). Madison seconded the Pinckney motion, saying that he "could not but regard an indefinite power [Pinckney had called it a "universality of power"] to negative legislative acts of the States as absolutely necessary to a perfect system" (ibid.).

Elbridge Gerry, Gunning Bedford, and William Paterson sprang to the defense of the states. Gerry scornfully rejected the idea of "an indefinite power to negative legislative acts of the States" as the work of "speculative projector(s)" whose theory had overwhelmed their experience and their judgment (Farrand, 1911, vol. 1, pp. 164–65). Bedford reminded his small state colleagues of the dangers inherent in such a plan. Paterson reinforced Bedford's remarks by holding up "Virginia, Massachusetts, and Pennsylvania as the three large States, and the other ten as small ones" (p. 178). He concluded that "the small States will have everything to fear. . . . New Jersey will never confederate on the plan before the Committee. She would be swallowed up" (ibid., pp. 178–79). James Wilson responded in kind for the large states. He said that "if the small States [would] not confederate on this plan, Pennsylvania and [he presumed] some other States, would not confederate on any other" (ibid., p. 180). This exchange indicates how quickly and decisively the Convention's focus shifted from general theories about the nature of republican government to the impact of various modes of representation on particular states and regions. It also highlights the interest-laced character (who gets what, when, and how) of discussion at the "lower" level of constitutional choice.

. . . [T]he voting alignments changed [dramatically] when the Convention's attention shifted from "higher" to "lower" level questions of constitutional choice. During the Convention's first two weeks, the states of the Deep

South (the Carolinas and Georgia) had been wary of Madison's plan to place great power at the national level. Nonetheless, the extended republic men had successfully overcome the objections of the delegates from the Northeast and the Deep South to establish firmly the principle of a strong national government. Now the question was who would wield this great power? Under these new circumstances, the rapidly growing states of the Deep South joined Massachusetts, Pennsylvania, and Virginia to pursue proportional representation in both houses of the national legislature. The large states were opposed by five smaller states from the Middle Atlantic region demanding equal representation in at least one brach of the proposed legislature.. . .

The confrontation intensified on 11 June when Roger Sherman of Connecticut suggested that seats in the House of Representatives be allocated to the states in proportion to the number of free inhabitants, with each state to have one vote in the Senate. The large state men still demanded proportional representation in both houses. Rufus King of Massachusetts and Wilson of Pennsylvania countered with a motion proposing "that the right of suffrage in. . .[the House of Representatives] ought not to be according to the rule established in the Articles of Confederation [equality], but according to some equitable ratio of representation," which after some discussion passed seven to three with one abstention (Farrand, 1911, vol. 1, p. 196). The large state coalition unanimously voted yes and was joined by Connecticut in pursuance of Sherman's suggested compromise. New York, New Jersey, and Delaware opposed the measure, while the Maryland delegates were divided. Wilson then sought to reinforce the allegiance of the southerners to the large state coalition by awarding them a three-fifths representation for their slaaves. Only New Jersey and Delaware opposed (ibid., p. 201). Pressing the large state advantage, Wilson and Alexander Hamilton moved that "the right of suffrage in the 2nd branch [the Senate] ought to be according to the same rule as in the 1st branch" (ibid., p. 202). They were successful by. . .[a] six-to-five alignment.. . . Thus, proportional representation in both houses, for a time, had been achieved by the triumph of the large states.

The opposing coalitions held firm through 29 June, when Connecticut's Oliver Ellsworth again declared the need for a compromise settlement. Wilson, arguing against any compromise by the large states on this crucial issue, adamantly rejected the idea, saying, "If a separation must take place, it could never happen on better grounds" (Farrand, 1911, vol. 1, p. 482). Gunning Bedford of Delaware answered for the small states, "I do not, gentlemen, trust you. If you possess the power, the abuse of it could not be checked; and what then would prevent you from exercising it to our destruction?" (ibid., p. 500).

With the proceedings obviously at a dangerous impasse, a compromise committee was chosen on 2 July.. . . On 5 July, Gerry delivered the report of his committee to the Convention. It proposed: "That in the first branch of the Legislature each of the States now in the Union be allowed one Member for every forty thousand inhabitants.. . . That in the second Branch of the Legislature each State shall have an equal Vote" (Farrand, 1911, vol. 1, p. 524).

Between 5 July and 16 July when the Connecticut Compromise was finally adopted, the North and the South battled over the apportionment of seats in the House of Representatives through two additional compromise committees and interminable floor debates to insure that the regions of the new nation would be institutionally positioned to defend their paramount interests (Jillson, 1981, pp. 36–41).

Executive Power and Citizen Participation: Principle and Interest

The coalitions that had aligned behind conflicting views of republican government during the Convention's first two weeks resurfaced immediately following the Connecticut Compromise as the Convention's focus turned again to questions at the "higher" level of constitutional choice. These familiar coalitions, still divided by philosophical differences concerning the nature of republican government, controlled the Convention's business for the next five weeks, well into late August. The small republic men sought to control the potential for abuse of governmental power by means of a strict separation of departments, a modest empowerment, and the use of explicit constitutional prohibitions and restraints where danger still seemed to lurk. Madison repeatedly enunciated the counterargument in favor of "checks and balances" as a supplement to a pure "separation of powers" that the extended republic men considered definitive and to which they frequently referred during debate over questions at the "higher" level of constitutional choice.....

Slavery, Commerce, Executive Selection and the West: State and Regional Interest

As the Convention moved into late August, several critical issues at the "lower" level of constitutional choice, including some provision for the critical regional issues of slavery and commercial regulation, for executive selection, and for control of the western lands, stood unresolved.....

When debate on the slave trade opened on the morning of 22 August, General Charles Cotesworth Pinckney went directly to the regional economics of the conflict between the states of the Upper South (Maryland and Virginia of the middle state coalition) and the states of the Lower South (the Carolinas and Georgia of the peripheral coalition) on this volatile issue. General Pinckney said, "South Carolina & Georgia cannot do without slaves. As to Virginia she will gain by stopping the importations. Her slaves will rise in value, & she has more than she wants" (Farrand, 1911, vol. 2, p. 371). For the shipping interests so dear to the northern wing of the peripheral coalition Pinckney held out the prospect that "the more slaves, the more produce to employ the carrying trade; The more consumption also, and the more of this, the more revenue for the common treasury" (ibid.).

Though Dickinson and others from the middle Atlantic argued that further importations were "inadmissible on every principle of honor and safety," King spoke for the dominant peripheral coalition when he remarked that "the subject should be considered in a political light only" (Farrand, 1911, vol. 2, p. 372). Viewed from this practical perspective, King feared that "the exemption of slaves from duty whilst every other import was subjected to it, [was] an inequality that could not fail to strike the commercial sagacity of the Northn & middle States" (ibid., p. 373). General Pinckney agreed that allowance for a modest duty would "remove one difficulty," and G. Morris quickly moved to broaden the ground for compromise to include the sensitive regional concerns of slavery and commercial regulation, saying, "these things may form a bargain among the Northern & Southern States" (ibid., p. 374). A compromise committee of one member from each state was quickly appointed.

Luther Martin, Maryland's representative on the committee, later reported that the substance of the committee's report involved an interregional quid pro quo between the northern and southern wings of the peripheral coalition. "The eastern States, notwithstanding their aversion to slavery, were very willing to indulge the southern States, at least with a temporary liberty to prosecute the slave-trade, provided the southern States would, in their turn, gratify them, by laying no restrictions on navigation acts" (Farrand, 1911, vol. 3, pp. 210-11). The Deep South would be allowed to continue importing slaves until at least 1800, while the northern states would be allowed to set commercial policy by simple majority vote of the national legislature.

The Commerce and Slave Trade Compromise was reported to the floor on 24 August but was not debated until 25 August. In the interim, the Convention returned to the complex issue of executive selection. Again, the Middle Atlantic states were powerless against a united coalition of peripheral states. The precise question before the Convention was whether the Periphery's preference for legislative selection would be exercised by separate ballots in the House and Senate, or, as Rutledge now suggested, in the hope of driving a wedge between Pennsylvania and Virginia and their small state allies, by "joint ballot" of both houses voting together. Sherman immediately objected that the "joint ballot" would deprive the smaller states "represented in the Senate of the negative intended them in that house." When the vote was taken, New Hampshire, Massachusetts, and the Carolinas were supported by the largest of the Middle Atlantic states, Pennsylvania, Maryland, and Virginia, in approving the measure seven to four. Delegates from the smaller states quickly sought to reestablish their influence in the presidential selection process by proposing that each state delegation should have one vote even if the polling was done by "joint ballot." The motion was lost by a single vote, five to six, when Pennsylvania and Virginia again joined the peripheral states to turn back their former allies. The remnants of the Middle Atlantic state coalition successfully avoided final defeat by postponing the issue.

When debate on the provisions of the Commerce and Slave Trade Compromise opened on the morning of 25 August, General Pinckney moved to extend the period during which free importation of slaves would be allowed from 1800 to 1808. On this amendment, and on the entire clause as amended, the commercial northeast, New Hampshire, Massachusetts, and Connecticut, anticipating northern control over commercial regulation in direct exchange for their support on this matter of the slave trade, joined the Deep

South to defeat the Middle Atlantic states of New Jersey, Pennsylvania, Delaware, and Virginia. With the southern half of the compromise thus easily confirmed, the northern sections dealing with commercial regulation were postponed and did not reappear until 29 August.

In the interim, the delegates from South Carolina maneuvered to gain additional security for their property in slaves....

Despite the assurances offered by General Pinckney, opinion in the southern delegations ran strongly to the view that commercial regulation by simple majority was an invitation to southern destruction. Mason argued strenuously that "the *Majority* will be governed by their interests. The Southern States are the *minority* in both Houses. Is it to be expected that they will deliver themselves bound hand & foot to the Eastern States?" (Farrand, 1911, vol. 2, p. 451).... Despite this deeply rooted southern opposition, a solid bloc of six northern states, ranging from New Hampshire to Delaware, joined only by South Carolina, defeated Maryland, Virginia, North Carolina, and Georgia on the question.

South Carolina's service to the northern states was quickly rewarded by an additional increment of security for her property in slaves. The Convention approved Butler's proposal that "any person bound to service...[escaping] into another State...shall be delivered up to the person justly claiming their service or labor" (Farrand, 1911, vol. 2, p. 454). But, the cost to larger southern interests, in which South Carolina obviously shared, was high. South Carolina's blind pursuit of security for her property in slaves broke the South as an effective force in the Convention.

...[T]he tone of the Convention's final days was unmistakably set by the debates that began on 30 August over control of the unsettled western lands. Daniel Carroll of Maryland opened this confrontation by moving to strike out a provision requiring "the consent of the State to [lands under its jurisdiction] being divided" (Farrand, 1911, vol. 2, p. 461). Carroll argued that this was an absolutely fundamental point with those states that did not hold claims to vast tracts of the western territory (Jensen, 1966, p. 150; Rakove, 1979, p. 352).

Pennsylvania's James Wilson opposed Carroll's motion, arguing that "he knew nothing that would give greater or juster alarm than the doctrine, that a political society is to be torne asunder without its own consent" (Farrand, 1911, vol. 2, p. 462). This argument struck the delegates from the smaller states as yet another brazen rejection of principle in favor of interest. Luther Martin said that "he wished Mr. Wilson had thought a little sooner of the value of *political* bodies. In the beginning, when the rights of the small States were in question, they were phantoms, ideal beings. Now when the Great States were to be affected, political Societies were of a sacred nature" (ibid., p. 464). When the votes were counted, New Jersey, Delaware, and Maryland stood alone.

It was eminently clear to the delegates from the smaller states that the Convention was once again slipping out of control and that dangerous consequences could result. If the larger states effectively dominated the executive selection process and the vast resources represented by the unsettled lands in the West, their stature in the new system could only be enhanced, while that of the smaller states would just as certainly decline. With these concerns foremost in the minds of the delegates from the smaller states, a committee of one member from each state was appointed on 31 August to resolve matters that still remained undecided.... [I]t was not until 4 and 5 September that it delivered the main components of its complex and controversial compromise report to the full Convention.

   ...The small states...emerged from the Brearley Committee determined to defend a report that was designed to enhance dramatically their potential for influence in the new government (Warren, 1928, p. 664).

   Most of the members of the new majority of small and northern states had long preferred executive selection by specially chosen electors to legislative selection. The Brearley Committee report envisioned a return to electoral selection, but perhaps more importantly, the failure of any candidate to receive a majority of the electoral votes would result in the reference of the five leading candidates to the Senate (where the small states had an equal vote with the large states) for final selection. Madison, Morris, and Mason feared that the Senate would ultimately decide "nineteen times in twenty" (Farrand, 1911, vol. 2, p. 500). Further, treaties, as well as ambassadorial, Supreme Court, and other major administrative appointments were to be made by the President only "with the Advice and Consent of the Senate" (ibid., pp. 498–99). And finally, although the House would charge the President in impeachable offenses, the final disposition of these charges would occur in the Senate. These provisions gave the smaller states what many of the delegates thought would be fearfully direct control over the appointment, conduct in office, and removal of the President. Both the larger states and the Deep South opposed these dramatic enhancements of senatorial authority. Yet, as the Convention entered its final days, neither the large states nor the southern states were in a position to oppose effectively the Brearley Committee report and the determined phalanx of small Middle Atlantic and northeastern states that stood behind it.

   The great fear of many delegates was that the powers added to the Senate to enhance the role of the small states in the new government had set the stage for aristocracy. Much of 5 September was taken up by the expression of such fears and by the search for ways to alleviate them without reducing the influence of the smaller states over the process of executive selection....

   ...[The] response was immediate and overwhelmingly positive when Connecticut's Roger Sherman, speaking for the dominant majority of small northern states, proposed that recourse in the event that no candidate had a majority of the electoral votes for president should not be to the Senate, but to "the House of Representatives...each State having one vote" (Farrand, 1911, vol. 2, p. 527).... This solution allowed the small states to retain their dominant position in the executive selection process, while simultaneously alleviating the fear that the Senate had come to be a dangerously powerful body. With this last and most difficult question finally resolved, the Convention hurried toward adjournment.

Conclusion

. . .Throughout this essay, we have sought to show that the debates and decisions of the Federal Convention bear the distinctive marks of that grudging accommodation between principles and interests that is characteristic of democratic politics.

General principles, such as republicanism, federalism, separation of powers, checks and balances, and bicameralism, define the structure of government only in vague outlines. Therefore, discussion of general principles serves merely to identify the broad paths along which the general interests and the common good of the community can be pursued. Other considerations, primarily deriving from diverse political, economic, and geographic interests, suggest and often virtually determine the modifications, adjustments, and allowances that principled consistency must make to political expediency. James Madison made precisely this point in a letter that accompanied a copy of the new Constitution sent to Jefferson in Paris in late October 1787. Madison explained that "the nature of the subject, the diversity of human opinion, . . . the collision of local interests, and the pretensions of the large & small States will . . . account . . . for the irregularities which will be discovered in [the new government's] structure and form" (Farrand, 1911, vol. 3, p. 136). . . .

We conclude that the Federal Convention of 1787, from its opening day on 25 May until its final adjournment on 17 September, confronted two distinct, but intimately related, aspects of constitutional design. The first was general. What kind of republican government should be constructed? As the delegates considered and discussed alternative visions of the relationship between human nature, the institutions of government, and the quality of the resulting social order, the temper and tone of their deliberations was quiet and philosophical. Some measure of detachment was possible at the "higher" level of constitutional choice because the debates over general principles provided little indication of precisely how the choice of one set of principles over another would affect the specific interests of particular individuals, states, or regions.

While the delegates considered questions of basic constitutional design, they seemed almost oblivious to the conflicts of interest that inevitably arose as they moved to the "lower" level of constitutional choice, where their theories and principles would be shaped and molded into practical arrangements for governing. When distributional questions came to the fore, debate intensified, tempers flared, and conflict predominated. Questions touching upon the allocation of representatives and presidential electors, the status of slavery, and regulation of the nation's commerce and its western lands directly affected the political, economic, and social interests of distinct classes, states, and regions. Indeed, it was only at this "lower" level of constitutional construction, where interests clashed so loudly, that the Convention was threatened with dissolution.

References

Bailyn, Bernard, 1969. *The ideological origins of the American Revolution.* Cambridge: Harvard University Press.

Beard, Charles A. 1913. *An economic interpretation of the Constitution of the United States.* New York: Macmillan.

Diamond, Martin. 1972. The Federalist. In Leo Strauss and Joseph Cropsey, eds., *History of political philosophy,* 2d ed. Chicago: Rand McNally: pp. 631–51.

_____. 1976. The American idea of man: The view from the founding. In Irving Kristol and Paul Weaver, eds., *The Americans: 1976.* Lexington, Mass.: Lexington Books, pp. 1–23.

_____. 1981. *The founding of the democratic republic.* Itasca, Ill.: Peacock.

Earle, Edward Mead, ed. 1937. *Federalist papers.* New York: Modern Library.

Farrand, Max. 1911. *The records of the Federal Convention of 1787.* 4 vols. New Haven: Yale University Press.

Jensen, Merrill. 1964. *The Articles of Confederation: An interpretation of the social-constitutional history of the American Revolution 1774–1781.* Madison: University of Wisconsin Press.

Jillson, Calvin. 1979. The executive in republican government. The case of the American founding. *Presidential Studies Quarterly,* 9 (Fall):386–402.

_____. 1981. The representation question in the Federal Convention of 1787: Madison's Virginia plan and its opponents. *Congressional Studies,* 8 (1):21–41.

Lippmann, Walter. 1955. *The public philosophy.* New York: Mentor.

Roche, John P. 1961. The founding fathers: A reform caucus in action. *American Political Science Review,* 55 (December):799–816.

Smith, David G. 1965. *The Convention and the Constitution.* New York: St. Martin's.

Smith, J. Allen. 1907. *The spirit of American government.* Reprint ed. Cambridge: Belknap Press, 1965.

Smith, Page. 1980. *The shaping of America: A people's history of the young republic.* Vol. 3. New York: McGraw-Hill.

Warren, Charles. 1928. *The making of the Constitution.* Reprint ed. New York: Barnes & Noble, 1967.

CHAPTER TWO

Constitutional Change: The Amendments

Though the framers of the Constitution left substantial room in their document for changes to be made without altering the basic arrangements, they also provided means for changing the document itself in those extreme situations that might call for it. The amendment process, as laid out in Article V, requires involvement of both the state and national levels. Congress is involved at the stage of proposing amendments, either doing so itself when two-thirds of both houses agree, or by calling a convention to do so when two-thirds of the state legislatures request it. The states must then ratify a proposed amendment in order for it to take effect, by agreement of either three-fourths of the legislatures or three-fourths of specially called state conventions.

Over the more than two hundred years since the Constitution itself was ratified, it has been amended only twenty-seven times, and the main effect of one of those (the Twenty-first) was to repeal another (the Eighteenth). This must be considered a remarkably small number, especially given that ten of the amendments (the first ten, also called the Bill of Rights) were ratified in the first few years under the Constitution.

The entire history of effecting change by amendment is discussed in the first reading of this chapter. The second reading focuses upon what is often called "the other amendment," the Fourteenth.

5 / Amending the Constitution

National Archives

The framers, in devising an amendment process that requires substantial support at both the national and state levels, clearly did not intend for amendments to be adopted easily or quickly. In reviewing the history of using the process, the authors conclude that while it has resulted in some important changes, the process may have proven too slow and cumbersome at times.

Since 1787 the Constitution has been considerably modified to perfect, amplify, and keep it abreast of changing times. The main mechanisms have been amendments and judicial interpretation. The amending process is outlined in Article V of the Constitution. Amendments may be proposed to the states either by Congress, based on a two-thirds vote in both houses, or by a convention called by Congress at the request of the legislatures of two-thirds of the states. Ratification requires the approval of three-fourths of the states, either by their legislatures or special conventions as Congress may direct. No national constitutional convention has ever been called, and the only amendment ratified by special state convention was the 21st.

The number of amendments to date totals [27]* the first 10 of which (Bill of Rights) were enacted shortly after ratification of the original document. Those that have been accepted have survived a grueling process. Thousands of proposals for amendments of all sorts—praiseworthy and frivolous, realistic and impractical, even including suggestions for a virtually new Constitution—have been recommended over the years by congressmen, political scientists, and others. But these have either failed to win the favor of Congress or the states.

Of the successful amendments, some, reflecting changing national aspirations and mores as well as fundamental social transformations, have produced governmental reforms and social changes. Others have refined the constitutional structure for such purposes as democratizing the political system, improving its functioning, or relieving associated abuses. The first 10 amendments came into being because of fear of national governmental tyranny.

Except for the Bill of Rights, before World War I amendments were relatively rare. For 122 years after 1791, when the Bill of Rights was adopted, only five (two in the early years of the republic and three in the aftermath of the Civil War) were enacted—or an average of one about every 25 years. Since 1913, on the other hand, the nation has approved 12*, or 1 every 6½*

---

*There were twenty-six amendments when this selection was written in 1986. An amendment proposed in 1789 and finally ratified in 1992 [as the Twenty-seventh) makes it unconstitutional for a congressional pay raise to take effect in the same term in which it was adopted.—*Editor's Note.*

years or so. The increased frequency in recent times is doubtless to a considerable extent attributable to the rapidity of social and economic change.

The Bill of Rights

From the beginning regarded as virtually a part of the original Constitution, the Bill of Rights was mainly designed to prevent the federal government from infringing on the basic rights of citizens and the states. Essentially a reassertion of the traditional rights of Englishmen as modified and strengthened by the American experience, these measures had already been delineated in various forms—in the Northwest Ordinance of 1787; the declarations, or bills, of rights that had been adopted by most states, either separately or as part of their constitutions; the Declaration of Independence (1776); the Declaration of Rights that the First Continental Congress had issued in 1774; and early colonial manifestoes.

During the Constitutional Convention and the ratification struggle in the states, many objections had been made to the exclusion from the Constitution of similar guarantees. When ratifying, many states expressed reservations and suggested numerous amendments, especially a bill of rights. North Carolina, decrying the absence of a declaration of rights in the Constitution, even refused to ratify in 1788 and did not do so until the following year, after the new government had been established and by which time such provisions had been proposed for addition to the instrument.

Washington called attention to the lack of a bill of rights in his inaugural address, and the First Congress moved quickly to correct this fault. Madison, in a prodigious effort, synthesized most of the amendments the states had recommended into nine propositions. The House committee, on which he sat, expanded these to 17. The Senate, with House concurrence, later reduced the number to 12. Meantime, the decision had been made to append all amendments to the Constitution rather than to insert them in the text at appropriate spots, as Madison had originally desired.

By December 1791 the States had ratified the last 10 of the 12 amendments Congress had submitted to them in September 1789. The first of the two that were not sanctioned proposed a future change in the numerical constituency of representatives and in their number; the second would have deferred any changes in congressional salaries that might be made until the term of the succeeding Congress.

The first amendment, covering the free expression of opinion, prohibits congressional interference with the freedom of religion, speech, press, assembly, and petition. Amendments two through four guarantee the rights of citizens to bear arms for lawful purposes, disallow the quartering of troops in private homes without the consent of the owner, and bar unreasonable searches and seizures by the government.

Amendments five, six, and eight essentially provide protection against arbitrary arrest, trial, and punishment, principally in federal criminal cases though over the course of time the judiciary has held that many of the provisions also apply in state cases. Mainly to prevent harassment of the citizenry by governmental officials, these measures established the right of civilian defendants to grand jury indictments for major crimes; prohibit "double jeopardy," or duplicate trial, for the same offense, as well as self-incrimination; deny deprivation of "life, liberty, or property without due process of law"; ensure the right of the accused to have legal counsel, be informed of the nature and cause of the accusation, subpoena witnesses on his own behalf, confront the witnesses against him, and receive an expeditious and public jury trial; and ban excessive bails and fines, as well as "cruel and unusual punishments." The fifth amendment also prohibits the government seizure of private property under the doctrine of eminent domain without proper compensation.

The seventh amendment guarantees the right of a jury trial in virtually all civil cases.

Amendment nine states that the rights enumerated in the Constitution are not to be "construed to deny or disparage others retained by the people." The 10th amendment, somewhat different from the other nine because of its allusion to the states, reserves to them and the people all "powers not delegated to the United States by the Constitution, nor prohibited by it to the States."

Contrary to a popular misconception, the main body of the Constitution also contains various safeguards similar to those in the Bill of Rights that protect citizens and the states against unreasonable actions. Article I prohibits the government from suspending the writ of *habeas corpus*, which would otherwise allow arbitrary arrest, and both the national government and the states from enacting bills of attainder (legislative punishment of crimes) and *ex post facto* laws (retroactively making acts criminal). Article III requires a jury trial for federal crimes and limits the definition of treason and penalties for the offense.

Article IV guarantees that the acts, records, and judicial proceedings of one state are valid in all the others; grants to citizens of every state the privileges and immunities of the others as defined by law; warrants the representative government and territorial integrity of the states; and promises them the protection of the national government against foreign invasion and domestic insurrection. Article VI excludes religious tests for officeholding.

Nevertheless, it is the Bill of Rights that has become the main bulwark of the civil liberties of the American people. These measures, which make the Constitution a defender of liberty as well as an instrument of governmental power, represented another swing of the pendulum. The Articles of Confederation had created a weak league of semi-independent states. As a result, citizens looked primarily to the states for protection of their basic rights, which were defined in constitutions or separate declarations. Then the Constitution provided a strong central government. This was counterbalanced by the Bill of Rights, which allowed continuance of such a government with full regard for the rights of the people.

In recent decades, the Bill of Rights has acquired increased significance to all citizens because the Supreme Court has ruled that many parts of it are applicable to the states as well as to the federal government.

Subsequent Amendments

The 11th amendment, which was passed by Congress in 1794 and ratified the next year, was engendered by state objections to the power of the federal judiciary and represents the only occasion to date whereby an amendment has limited its authority. Curtailing federal power in actions brought against individual states, the measure denies the federal courts jurisdiction over private suits brought against one state by citizens of another or of a foreign country.

The 12th amendment, which won the approbation of Congress in 1803 and state approval the following year, is a constitutional accommodation to the formation of political parties. Many of the Founding Fathers, who had themselves not been immune to divisiveness, had feared their growth, which they believed would stimulate factional strife. But parties soon proved to be necessary vehicles for the nation's political life.

As they grew, the method of electing the President and Vice President as originally set forth at Philadelphia became cumbersome and controversial, if not practically unworkable. The election of 1796 produced a President and Vice President of different parties. In 1800 a tied electoral vote occurred between members of the same party, and the House of Representatives was forced to choose a President. These two experiences created the necessary sentiment to modify the electoral process. The principal provision of the 12th amendment required future electors to cast separate ballots for the two executives.

For more than six decades after the ratification of the 12th, no further amendments were enacted. Then the Civil War crisis created three, the so-called "national supremacy" amendments, which congressional Radical Reconstructionists proposed. The 13th, sent out to the states in 1864 and ratified in 1865, was the first attempt to use the amending process to institute national social reform. It followed upon Lincoln's limited and preliminary action in the Emancipation Proclamation (1863) to free the slaves. Although the amendment declared slavery and involuntary servitude (except as punishment for crimes) to be unconstitutional, it did not provide blacks with civil rights guarantees equal to those of whites.

During the Reconstruction period, therefore, two more additions to the Constitution became the law of the land. Their main objectives were to insure the rights of black men to full citizenship. Ultimately, however, because of their broad phraseology, the two amendments have come to have significant repercussions for all citizens. The 14th, proposed in 1866 and ratified 2 years later, decrees that all persons born or naturalized in the United States are citizens of the nation and of the state in which they live. The legislation also forbids the states from making any laws that abridge the "privileges or immunities of citizens of the United States," deprive them of "life, liberty, or property, without due process of law," or deny them the "equal protection of the laws."

The amendment also expanded representation in the House of Representatives from that contained in the original Constitution (the free, essentially white, population plus three-fifths of all slaves) to include all persons except untaxed Indians. Another provision stated that the representation of states arbitrarily denying the vote to adult men would be reduced. The measure also barred from federal officeholding those Confederates who had held federal or state offices before the Civil War, except when Congress chose to waive this disqualification, and ruled invalid all debts contracted to aid the Confederacy as well as claims for compensation covering the loss or emancipation of slaves.

The most important goal for which the amendment was added to the Constitution, the legal equality of blacks, was not fully realized until the 24th outlawed the poll tax in 1964. The attempt to limit the political participation of ex-Confederate leaders failed. In recent years, however, the Supreme Court has often used the amendment to achieve fuller state conformance with the Bill of Rights. Furthermore, judicial interpretations have broadened the meaning of such key phrases as "privileges or immunities" "due process," and "equal protection of the laws." Congress has also passed new enforcement legislation.

Despite the legislative efforts of the Radical Republicans, black men continued to be denied equal voting rights. In 1869, therefore, Congress passed and the next year the states ratified the 15th amendment. Attempting to protect the rights of ex-slaves it explicitly stated: "The right of citizens of the United States to vote shall not be denied or abridged by the United States or by any State on account of race, color, or previous condition of servitude."

Not until 1913 was the Constitution again changed. Before that time, Congress had only enjoyed the power to levy direct taxes in proportion to the populations of the states. During the late 19th century, the need for a federal income tax began to become apparent to many people in the country, but the Supreme Court on various occasions declared such a tax to be unconstitutional. By 1909 support for it was strong enough to warrant passage of the 16th amendment. Many Congressmen who voted affirmatively felt the states would never approve the action. Yet, 4 years later, they ratified it. The income tax quickly became a principal source of federal revenue and facilitated governmental expansion.

Later in 1913 the states approved another amendment, which Congress had sanctioned the previous year. The 17th authorized the direct election of senators by the voters rather than by state legislatures, as specified in the Constitution. The original method had long been a target of reformers. Numerous times between 1893 and 1911 the House of Representatives proposed amendments calling for popular selection of senators. The Senate, however, apparently concerned among other things about the tenure of its members and resenting the invasion of their prerogatives by the lower House, refused to give its stamp of approval to the legislation. But, by the latter year, pressure for change had become intense, particularly because the popular image of the Senate had become that of a millionaires' club divorced from the interests of the people. That same year, an Illinois election scandal helped turn the tide. Also, many states had by that time adopted senatorial preference primaries as an expression of popular sentiment to the legislators.

The highly controversial "prohibition" amendment, the 18th, cleared Congress in 1917 and was ratified 2 years later. It prohibited the manufacture, sale, or transportation of intoxicating liquors for beverage purposes and their importation into or exportation from the United States. This legislation was the result of nearly a century of temperance efforts to eliminate or limit use of alcoholic beverages. But unsuccessful enforcement and opposition by large elements of the public, particularly in urban areas, soon doomed the "noble experiment." In the only instance when an amendment has been repealed by another, the 21st, which was both proposed and ratified in 1933, voided the 18th. It returned control of alcohol to states and local jurisdictions, which could choose to remain "dry" if they so preferred.

The persistence of reformers likewise produced the 19th amendment, passed in 1919 and ratified the next year. Equal voting rights in federal and state elections were granted to women. Especially after the Civil War, they had begun to improve their legal status, and some states in the West had granted them the right to vote. During the early years of the 20th century, more states extended the privilege. These and other factors, coupled with the efforts of suffragists, facilitated adoption of the amendment. It marked a major step toward fuller political equality for women.

Congress gave its imprimatur to the so-called "lame duck" amendment, the 20th, in 1932 and it became effective the next year. Designed mainly to hasten and smooth the post-election succession of the President and Congress, it specified that the terms of the President and Vice President would begin on January 20 following the fall elections instead of on March 4 and required Congress to convene on January 3, when the terms of all newly elected Congressmen were also to begin. Correcting another defect in the Constitution was the stipulation that the Vice President-elect would succeed to the highest office in the land in the event the President-elect died before his inauguration or no President-elect had qualified.

Proposed to the states by Congress in 1947, the 22d amendment was ratified in 1951. Aimed in large part at preventing the repetition of the unprecedented four terms to which Franklin D. Roosevelt had been elected as President, it limited the service of chief executives to a maximum of the traditional two full terms. Vice Presidents succeeding to the office were to be restricted to one term if the unexpired portion of that to which they succeeded was longer than 2 years. The incumbent, Harry S. Truman, who was serving when this amendment was added to the Constitution, was exempted from it, though he did not choose to run for a second full term.

District of Columbia residents won the right to vote for presidential electors in the 23d amendment, which gained congressional approval in 1960 and was ratified the following year. It was part of the endeavor to obtain for D.C. residents political rights equal to those of citizens of the states. Although this step fell short of the "home rule" sought for the District, it was a major step toward more extensive political participation by its citizens.

The civil rights struggle of black people in the 1950s and early 1960s resulted in the 24th amendment, which was proposed in 1962 and ratified 2 years later. It outlawed poll taxes as a prerequisite for voting in federal elections. This device had long been used in some places to limit political participation, especially by blacks.

The long illnesses of Presidents Woodrow Wilson and Dwight D. Eisenhower and the assassination of President John F. Kennedy, coupled with the enormous contemporary importance of the presidency, gave rise to the 25th amendment. It was passed by Congress in 1965 and ratified in 1967. Steps to be followed in the event of presidential disability were outlined, and a method was established for expeditiously filling vacancies in the office of Vice President. When there is no Vice President, the President will nominate a replacement, who needs only approval by a congressional majority. In the event of presidential disability, the Vice President will temporarily hold the office of Acting President.

The 26th amendment, proposed and ratified in 1971, provided another extension of the franchise. In recognition of the increasing contributions of youth to American society, the minimum voting age in all elections was lowered to 18 years. Although a few states, in accordance with their discretionary rights at the time, had earlier reduced the voting age from 21, this constitutional addition made the national franchise uniform in terms of minimum age.

Despite its numerous advantages, the amendment process has proven to be less than perfect as a vehicle of change. Although the rigorous procedure required to enact amendments has prevented hasty and ill-advised action, it has on occasion delayed the inauguration of badly needed reforms. The brief and sometimes imprecise wording of the amendments, as well as of the Constitution itself, has necessitated prolonged and complex interpretation by the Supreme Court. The public and various governmental organs have on occasion failed to heed or fully execute our highest national law.

Whatever the flaws in our constitutional system, it enunciates our democratic principles and provides a superlative formula and instrument of government, which has established its primacy among the efforts of men to govern themselves. Yet the true guardian of our sacred charter of liberties is the vigilance of the people.

6 / The Other Amendment: Why Is the 14th Important to the Bill of Rights?

Life Magazine Staff

The first ten amendments, the "Bill of Rights," were written to guarantee that certain rights would not be infringed upon by the government. In this case, though, "the government" meant specifically the national level of government; the Bill of Rights was not originally intended to limit actions of states. Adoption of the Fourteenth Amendment in 1868 marked the beginning of a process by which that amendment's words would eventually be construed as applying nearly all of the limits to the states as well. The experience of the Fourteenth Amendment demonstrates not only the impact of the amendment process itself but also the central role that one amendment may play in a longer and broader process of constitutional change. In this case, decades of Supreme Court decisions have significantly broadened the Fourteenth Amendment's impact.

Section I. All persons born or naturalized in the United States, and subject to the jurisdiction thereof, are citizens of the United States and of the State wherein they reside. No State shall make or enforce any law which shall abridge the privileges or immunities of citizens of the United States; nor shall any State deprive any person of life, liberty, or property, without due process of law; nor deny to any person within its jurisdiction the equal protection of the laws.

The first and fundamental tenet of the 14th Amendment makes sure that the most basic rights of American citizens won't be trampled on by state governments. And since first enacted by Congress in 1868 to ensure that the rights of newly freed slaves would be respected by the states, the 14th Amendment has become a powerful, multipurpose legal tool—still hotly debated— that is often the most vital link Americans have to the Bill of Rights. As remarkable as it may seem today, the guarantees of the first 10 amendments were written only to protect against actions by the federal government, despite James Madison's warnings that "it was equally necessary that [essential rights] be secured against the State Governments." Many of the states already had their own bills of rights, and the founders were more fearful of central authority than that of the states.

Even after the Civil War played to its bloody end, and the 14th Amendment was adopted, strongly held and prickly traditions of states' rights kept the amendment—and the Bill of Rights—at bay. In the late 19th century. . . Justice John Marshall Harlan, called an "eccentric" by a later Supreme Court justice, was a lonely advocate of total incorporation, more than once arguing, as he did in an 1884 dissent, that the due process clause of the 14th

Amendment dictates that all of the personal liberties and protections of the federal Bill of Rights apply to the states.

Not until 1925 did the tide begin to turn. In *Gitlow v. New York*, the Court opened the floodgates of incorporation: "Freedom of speech and of the press," wrote Justice Edward T. Sanford for the majority, "which are protected by the First Amendment from abridgment by Congress—are among the fundamental personal rights and 'liberties' protected by the due process clause of the Fourteenth Amendment from impairment by the States."

The *Gitlow* ruling...was soon followed by a series of Supreme Court decisions incorporating the rights to counsel in capital crimes, to religious freedom and to freedom of assembly—a piecemeal nationalization of rights eventually articulated in a 1937 decision introducing the notion of an honor roll of superior rights.

Writing for the majority in *Palko v. Connecticut*, Justice Benjamin N. Cardozo declared the need to distinguish between those rights that were "of the very essence of a scheme of ordered liberty" and those without which "justice would not perish." The right to free speech qualifies, explained Cardozo; a grand jury indictment would not. (Justice Oliver Wendell Holmes Jr. had suggested his own test of whether a state violated due process: Does the state action "make you vomit"?)

Over the next 30 years, in a series of landmark decisions, the Court continued to extend the reach of the "citizens' rights" amendment to include Fourth Amendment protection against unreasonable search and seizure, Fifth Amendment protections against double jeopardy and self-incrimination, Sixth Amendment rights to counsel, a public trial and impartial jury, and Eighth Amendment prohibitions on cruel and unusual punishment, among others.

Still not incorporated under its wide umbrella are the Second and Third Amendments, the Fifth's right to a grand jury, the Seventh's right to jury trials in civil cases and the Eighth's prohibition on excessive bail. But these are considered minor omissions in the country's seemingly inexorable passage to judicial support of personal liberties. It is now accepted that states may grant greater rights than the federal Bill of Rights, but never less—a testament to the long and difficult road traveled by the 14th Amendment.

In fact, this freight train of an amendment goes beyond the Bill of Rights. Its equal protection clause was the lever with which the Court outlawed segregation in *Brown v. Board of Education* in 1954. And in 1973 its due process guarantee of personal liberty was invoked in the landmark abortion rights case of *Roe v. Wade....*

Whether its authors intended it or whether they didn't, the 14th Amendment now incorporates some of those rights listed by James Madison—whose own amendment proposal to protect citizens from the states was killed by the Senate in 1789—and enables the Bill of Rights to guarantee all of us, at last, protection under one law of the land.

CHAPTER THREE

Separation of Powers

By the time the framers met to change the Articles of Confederation (and actually wrote the new Constitution), it had become obvious to most of them that the existing Confederation's compact national government, consisting of a Congress but no separate executive or judiciary, was simply insufficient for effectively meeting even the limited objectives of the confederal government. In fact, after the Constitution had been written, George Washington noted that establishment of the three separate branches had been "unnecessary to be insisted upon, because it is well known, that the impotence of Congress under the former confederation, and the inexpediency of trusting more ample prerogatives to a single body, gave birth to the different branches which constitute the present general government."*

In addition to the immediate, practical advantages, separation of powers also offered a means of protection against tyrannical rule in the future. Separation of powers, in principle, is an arrangement for spreading power among different units of the same level of government, so as to make it more difficult for any set of officials to rule without regard for the will of others. In practice, the framers established a structure involving three branches—legislative, executive, and judicial, with "separate" powers that overlapped sufficiently to provide for a system of checks and balances. In *The Federalist* no. 47 and no. 48, included as readings in this chapter, James Madison defended the design by recalling experiences of state governments whose more exacting separation of powers had failed to prevent legislatures from usurping executive powers.

While the constitutional structure involves all three branches, separation of powers as a political issue at the national level has tended to focus on the *actual* distribution of power that exists between president and Congress, a distribution that has at times shifted in favor of one branch or the other. The framers designed an executive branch to replace the administration-by-congressional committee that had been the case under the Articles of Confederation. Though it was agreed that the executive should be powerful enough to serve as an effective check on Congress, the Constitution itself was left relatively vague with regard to specific presidential responsibilities. While many presidents have left their mark on the institution by expanding presidential responsibilities, the development of presidential power has not been a process of steady growth relative to Congress.

At times in our history, such as the presidencies of Andrew Jackson and Richard Nixon, it has been argued that presidential powers have grown too great, with the result of an ineffective Congress. At other times, though, it has seemed that Congress was in a position to overpower the executive. Readings in this chapter deal with two different eras of perceived "imbalance" between congressional and presidential powers. Woodrow Wilson, writing as a student of political science in the 1880s, described a situation in which Congress seemed capable of dominating

---

*Quoted in Louis Fisher, *President and Congress*, (New York: The Free Press, 1972, pp. 5-6).— *Editor's Note.*

both the executive and the judiciary. To the extent that Wilson's assessment was correct, the situation began to change shortly thereafter, and by the 1940s and 1950s the presidency had met if not passed the Congress. The story of the ascendency of the presidency, to the point of becoming "imperial" in the Nixon era, is ably told by Arthur Schlesinger, Jr., in another reading in this chapter. Looking at the other side of the same coin, then-Senator Abraham Ribicoff wrote in 1964 that Congress had willingly handed to the presidency the responsibility for legislative initiation, which in Ribicoff's view was Congress's business. Ribicoff's article is included here as well.

Congress may have willingly given presidents more responsibilities over the years, but has it also given presidents the capacity to fulfill the heightened expectations of the office? Theodore Lowi, in the final reading in this chapter, says the answer is "no," and therein lies a major problem for the entire system. Lowi suggests that a solution to the problem may lie in "building down" the presidency, building up the parties, and finding new ways of forcing Congress to share in responsibilities that it seems so willing to delegate.

7 / Federalist Papers no. 47 and no. 48

James Madison

In submitting their new Constitution to the states for ratification, the framers were aware that they were recommending some major departures from the governmental status quo. The changes involved in strengthening the position of the national government, for example, were certain to raise eyebrows. In fact, well-considered arguments against the new Constitution had already emanated from some "anti-federalists." The Federalist Papers, a set of eighty-five newspaper articles authored by "Publius" (actually James Madison and Alexander Hamilton, with some help from John Jay), were put forth as arguments for ratification, and especially to counter the arguments of the anti-federalists. In providing thoughtful explanations for a large federal republic, separation of powers with checks and balances, and representative government, the authors produced what has recently been described as "an American contribution to the classics of political thought."*

In Federalist no. 47 and Federalist no. 48, James Madison (as Publius) responds to arguments of opponents of ratification that the three branches were not made separate enough. In fact, the Constitution does provide for some overlapping of responsibilities within the separation-of-powers system; for example, the president's power to veto legislation and the Senate's power to approve presidential appointments. Specifically, Madison is responding to the charges that such overlapping

*Levy, Michael B., Political Thought in America, (Homewood, IL: The Dorsey Press, 1982, p. 77).—Editor's Note.

of powers destroys "all symmetry and beauty of form" among the separate branches, and exposes "some of the essential parts of the edifice to the danger of being crushed by the disproportionate weight of the other parts."

In drawing upon the state governments' experiences with separation of powers, Madison argues that while none of the state constitutions had achieved total separation of powers, some that had come closest to exacting separation on "parchment," had seen their legislatures, in practice, usurp executive and judicial powers. Effective protection against one branch becoming tyrannical, Madison argued, was to be found in the checks and balances provided in some overlapping of responsibilities.

Number 47
The Particular Structure of the New Government and the Distribution of Power Among its Different Parts

To the People of the State of New York: Having reviewed the general form of the proposed government and the general mass of power allotted to it, I proceed to examine the particular structure of this government, and the distribution of this mass of power among its constituent parts.

One of the principal objections inculcated by the more respectable adversaries to the Constitution, is its supposed violation of the political maxim, that the legislative, executive, and judiciary departments ought to be separate and distinct. In the structure of the federal government, no regard, it is said, seems to have been paid to this essential precaution in favor of liberty. The several departments of power are distributed and blended in such a manner as at once to destroy all symmetry and beauty of form, and to expose some of the essential parts of the edifice to the danger of being crushed by the disproportionate weight of other parts.

No political truth is certainly of greater intrinsic value, or is stamped with the authority of more enlightened patrons of liberty, than that on which the objection is founded. The accumulation of all powers, legislative, executive, and judiciary, in the same hands, whether of one, a few, or many, and whether hereditary, self-appointed, or elective, may justly be pronounced the very definition of tyranny. Were the federal Constitution, therefore, really chargeable with the accumulation of power, or with a mixture of powers, having a dangerous tendency to such an accumulation, no further arguments would be necessary to inspire a universal reprobation of the system. I persuade myself, however, that it will be made apparent to every one, that the charge cannot be supported, and that the maxim on which it relies has been totally misconceived and misapplied. In order to form correct ideas on this important subject, it will be proper to investigate the sense in which the preservation of liberty requires that the three great departments of power should be separate and distinct.

The oracle who is always consulted and cited on this subject is the celebrated Montesquieu. If he be not the author of this invaluable precept in the science of politics, he has the merit at least of displaying and recommending it most effectually to the attention of mankind. Let us endeavor, in the first place, to ascertain his meaning on this point.

The British Constitution was to Montesquieu what Homer has been to the didactic writers on epic poetry. As the latter have considered the work of the immortal bard as the perfect model from which the principles and rules of the epic art were to be drawn, and by which all similar works were to be judged, so this great political critic appears to have viewed the Constitution of England as the standard, or to use his own expression, as the mirror of political liberty; and to have delivered, in the form of elementary truths, the several characteristic principles of that particular system. That we may be sure, then, not to mistake his meaning in this case, let us recur to the source from which the maxim was drawn.

On the slightest view of the British Constitution, we must perceive that the legislative, executive, and judiciary departments are by no means totally separate and distinct from each other. The executive magistrate forms an integral part of the legislative authority. He alone has the prerogative of making treaties with foreign sovereigns, which, when made, have, under certain limitations, the force of legislative acts. All the members of the judiciary department are appointed by him, can be removed by him on the address of the two Houses of Parliament, and form, when he pleases to consult them, one of his constitutional councils. One branch of the legislative department forms also a great constitutional council to the executive chief, as, on another hand, it is the sole depositary of judicial power in cases of impeachment, and is invested with the supreme appellate jurisdiction in all other cases. The judges, again, are so far connected with the legislative department as often to attend and participate in its deliberations, though not admitted to a legislative vote.

From these facts, by which Montesquieu was guided, it may clearly be inferred that, in saying "There can be no liberty where the legislative and executive powers are united in the same person, or body of magistrates," or, "if the power of judging be not separated from the legislative and executive powers," he did not mean that these departments ought to have no *partial agency* in, or no *control* over, the acts of each other. His meaning, as his own words import, and still more conclusively as illustrated by the example in his eye, can amount to no more than this, that where the *whole* power of one department is exercised by the same hands which possess the *whole* power of another department, the fundamental principles of a free constitution are subverted. This would have been the case in the constitution examined by him, if the king, who is the sole executive magistrate, had possessed also the complete legislative power, or the supreme administration of justice; or if the entire legislative body had possessed the supreme judiciary, or the supreme executive authority. This, however, is not among the vices of that constitution. The magistrate in whom the whole executive power resides cannot of himself make a law, though he can put a negative on every law; nor administer justice in person, though he has the appointment of those who do administer it. The judges can exercise no executive prerogative, though they are shoots from the executive stock; nor any legislative function, though they may be advised with by the legislative councils. The entire legislature can perform no judiciary act, though by the joint act of two of its branches the judges may be removed from their offices, and though one of its branches is possessed of the judicial power in the last resort. The entire legislature, again, can exercise no executive prerogative, though one of its branches constitutes the supreme executive magistracy, and another, on the impeachment of a third, can try and condemn all the subordinate officers in the executive department.

The reasons on which Montesquieu grounds his maxim are a further demonstration of his meaning. "When the legislative and executive powers are united in the same person or body," says he, "there can be no liberty, because apprehensions may arise lest *the same* monarch or senate should *enact* tyrannical laws to *execute* them in a tyrannical manner." Again: "Were the power of judging joined with the legislative, the life and liberty of the subject would be exposed to arbitrary control, for *the judge* would then be *the legislator.* Were it joined to the executive power, *the judge* might behave with all the violence of *an oppressor.*" Some of these reasons are more fully explained in other passages; but briefly stated as they are here, they sufficiently establish the meaning which we have put on this celebrated maxim of this celebrated author.

If we look into the constitutions of the several States, we find that, notwithstanding the emphatical and, in some instances, the unqualified terms in which this axiom has been laid down, there is not a single instance in which the several departments of power have been kept absolutely separate and distinct. New Hampshire, whose constitution was the last formed, seems to have been fully aware of the impossibility and inexpediency of avoiding any mixture whatever of these departments, and has qualified the doctrine by declaring "that the legislative, executive, and judiciary powers ought to be kept as separate from, and independent of, each other *as the nature of a free government will admit; or as is consistent with that chain of connection that binds the whole fabric of the constitution in one indissoluble bond of unity and amity.*" Her constitution accordingly mixes these departments in several respects. The Senate, which is a branch of the legislative department, is also a judicial tribunal for the trial of impeachments. The President, who is the head of the executive department, is the presiding member also of the Senate; and, besides an equal vote in all cases, has a casting vote in case of a tie. The executive head is himself eventually elective every year by the legislative department, and his council is every year chosen by and from the members of the same department. Several of the officers of state are also appointed by the legislature. And the members of the judiciary department are appointed by the executive department.

The constitution of Massachusetts has observed a sufficient though less pointed caution, in expressing this fundamental article of liberty. It declares "that the legislative departments shall never exercise the executive and judicial powers, or either of them; the executive shall never exercise the legislative and judicial powers, or either of them; the judicial shall never exercise the legislative and executive powers, or either of them." This declaration corresponds precisely with the doctrine of Montesquieu, as it has been explained, and is not in a single point violated by the plan of the convention. It goes no farther than to prohibit any one of the entire departments from exercising the powers of another department. In the very Constitution to which it is prefixed, a partial mixture of powers has been admitted. The executive magistrate has a qualified negative on the legislative body, and the Senate, which is a part of the legislature, is a court of impeachment for members both of the executive and judiciary departments. The members of the judiciary department, again, are appointable by the executive department, and removable by the same authority on the address of the two legislative branches. Lastly, a number of the officers of government are annually appointed by the legislative department. As the appointment to offices, particularly executive offices, is in its nature an executive function, the compilers of the Constitution have, in this last point at least, violated the rule established by themselves.

I pass over the constitutions of Rhode Island and Connecticut, because they were formed prior to the Revolution, and even before the principle under examination had become an object of political attention.

The constitution of New York contains no declaration on this subject; but appears very clearly to have been framed with an eye to the danger of improperly blending the different departments. It gives, nevertheless, to the executive magistrate, a partial control over the legislative department; and, what is more, gives a like control to the judiciary department; and even blends the executive and judiciary departments in the exercise of this control. In its council of appointment members of the legislative are associated with the executive authority, in the appointment of officers, both executive and judiciary. And its court for trial of impeachments and correction of errors is to consist of one branch of the legislature and the principal members of the judiciary department.

The constitution of New Jersey has blended the different powers of government more than any of the preceding. The governor, who is the executive magistrate, is appointed by the legislature; is chancellor and ordinary, or surrogate of the State; is a member of the Supreme Court of Appeals, and president, with a casting vote, of one of the legislative branches. The same legislative branch acts again as executive council of the governor, and with him constitutes the Court of Appeals. The members of the judiciary department are appointed by the legislative department, and removable by one branch of it, on the impeachment of the other.

According to the constitution of Pennsylvania, the president, who is the head of the executive department, is annually elected by a vote in which the legislative department predominates. In conjunction with an executive council, he appoints the members of the judiciary department, and forms a court of impeachment for trial of all officers, judiciary as well as executive. The judges of the Supreme Court and justices of the peace seem also to be removable by the legislature; and the executive power of pardoning in certain cases, to be referred to the same department. The members of the executive council are made EX-OFFICIO justices of peace throughout the State.

In Delaware, the chief executive magistrate is annually elected by the legislative department. The speakers of the two legislative branches are vice-presidents in the executive department. The executive chief, with six others, appointed, three by each of the legislative branches, constitutes the Supreme Court of Appeals; he is joined with the legislative department in the appointment of the other judges. Throughout the States, it appears that the members of the legislature may at the same time be justices of the peace; in this State, the members of one branch of it are EX-OFFICIO justices of the peace; as are also the members of the executive council. The principal officers of the executive department are appointed by the legislative; and one branch of the latter forms a court of impeachments. All officers may be removed on address of the legislature.

Maryland has adopted the maxim in the most unqualified terms; declaring that the legislative, executive, and judicial powers of government ought to be forever separate and distinct from each other. Her constitution, notwithstanding, makes the executive magistrate appointable by the legislative department; and the members of the judiciary by the executive department.

The language of Virginia is still more pointed on this subject. Her constitution declares, "that the legislative, executive, and judiciary departments shall be separate and distinct; so that neither exercise the powers properly belonging to the other; nor shall any person exercise the powers of more than one of them at the same time, except that the justices of county courts shall be eligible to either House of Assembly." Yet we find not only this express exception, with respect to the members of the inferior courts, but that the chief magistrate, with his executive council, are appointable by the legislature; that two members of the latter are triennially displaced at the pleasure of the legislature; and that all the principal offices, both executive and judiciary, are filled by the same department. The executive prerogative of pardon, also, is in one case vested in the legislative department.

The constitution of North Carolina, which declares "that the legislative, executive, and supreme judicial powers of government ought to be forever separate and distinct from each other," refers, at the same time, to the legislative department, the appointment not only of the executive chief, but all the principal officers within both that and the judiciary department.

In South Carolina, the constitution makes the executive magistracy eligible by the legislative department. It gives to the latter, also, the appointment of the members of the judiciary department, including even justices of the peace and sheriffs; and the appointment of officers in the executive department, down to captains in the army and navy of the State.

In the constitution of Georgia, where it is declared "that the legislative, executive, and judiciary departments shall be separate and distinct, so that neither exercise the powers properly belonging to the other," we find that the executive department is to be filled by appointments of the legislature; and the executive prerogative of pardon to be finally exercised by the same authority. Even justices of the peace are to be appointed by the legislature.

In citing these cases, in which the legislative, executive, and judiciary departments have not been kept totally separate and distinct, I wish not to be regarded as an advocate for the particular organizations of the several State governments. I am fully aware that among the many excellent principles which they exemplify, they carry strong marks of the haste, and still stronger of the inexperience, under which they were framed. It is but too obvious that in some instances the fundamental principle under consideration has been violated by too great a mixture, and even an actual consolidation, of the different powers; and that in no instance has a competent provision been made for maintaining in practice the separation delineated on paper. What I have wished to evince is, that the charge brought against the proposed Constitution, of violating the sacred maxim of free government, is warranted neither by the real meaning annexed to that maxim by its author, nor by the sense in which it has hitherto been understood in America. This interesting subject will be resumed in the ensuing paper.

Publius

Number 48
These Departments Should not be so far Separated as to Have no Constitutional Control Over each Other

To the People of the State of New York: It was shown in the last paper that the political apothegm there examined does not require that the legislative, executive, and judiciary departments should be wholly unconnected with each other. I shall undertake, in the next place, to show that unless these departments be so far connected and blended as to give to each a constitutional control over the others, the degree of separation which the maxim requires, as essential to a free government, can never in practice be duly maintained.

It is agreed on all sides, that the powers properly belonging to one of the departments ought not to be directly and completely administered by either of the other departments. It is equally evident, that none of them ought to possess, directly or indirectly, an overruling influence over the others, in the administration of their respective powers. It will not be denied, that power is of an encroaching nature, and that it ought to be effectually restrained from passing the limits assigned to it. After discriminating, therefore, in theory, the several classes of power, as they may in their nature be legislative, executive, or judiciary, the next and most difficult task is to provide some practical security for each, against the invasion of the others. What this security ought to be, is the great problem to be solved.

Will it be sufficient to mark, with precision, the boundaries of these departments, in the constitution of the government, and to trust to these parchment barriers against the encroaching spirit of power? This is the security which appears to have been principally relied on by the compilers of most of the American constitutions. But experience assures us, that the efficacy of the provision has been greatly overrated; and that some more adequate defence is indispensably necessary for the more feeble, against the more powerful, members of the government. The legislative department is everywhere extending the sphere of its activity, and drawing all power into its impetuous vortex.

The founders of our republics have so much merit for the wisdom which they have displayed, that no task can be less pleasing than that of pointing out the errors into which they have fallen. A respect for truth, however, obliges us to remark, that they seem never for a moment to have turned their eyes from the danger to liberty from the overgrown and all-grasping prerogative of an hereditary magistrate, supported and fortified by an hereditary branch of the legislative authority. They seem never to have recollected the danger from legislative usurpations, which, by assembling all power in the same hands, must lead to the same tyranny as is threatened by executive usurpations.

In a government where numerous and extensive prerogatives are placed in the hands of an hereditary monarch, the executive department is very justly regarded as the source of danger, and watched with all the jealousy which a zeal for liberty ought to inspire. In a democracy, where a multitude of people exercise in person the legislative functions, and are continually exposed, by their incapacity for regular deliberation and concerted measures, to the ambitious intrigues of their executive magistrates, tyranny may well be apprehended, on some favorable emergency, to start up in the same quarter. But in a representative republic, where the executive magistracy is carefully limited, both in the extent and the duration of its power; and where the legislative power is exercised by an assembly, which is inspired, by a supposed influence over the people, with an intrepid confidence in its own strength; which is sufficiently numerous to feel all the passions which actuate a multitude, yet not so numerous as to be incapable of pursuing the objects of its passions, by means which reason prescribes; it is against the enterprising ambition of this department that the people ought to indulge all their jealousy and exhaust all their precautions.

The legislative department derives a superiority in our governments from other circumstances. Its constitutional powers being at once more extensive, and less susceptible of precise limits, it can, with the greater facility, mask, under complicated and indirect measures, the encroachments which it makes on the coordinate departments. It is not unfrequently a question of real nicety in legislative bodies, whether the operation of a particular measure will, or will not, extend beyond the legislative sphere. On the other side, the executive power being restrained within a narrower compass, and being more simple in its nature, and the judiciary being described by landmarks still less uncertain, projects of usurpation by either of these departments would immediately betray and defeat themselves. Nor is this all: as the legislative department alone has access to the pockets of the people, and has in some constitutions full discretion, and in all a prevailing influence, over the pecuniary rewards of those who fill the other departments, a dependence is thus created in the latter, which gives still greater facility to encroachments of the former.

I have appealed to our own experience for the truth of what I advance on this subject. Were it necessary to verify this experience by particular proofs, they might be multiplied without end. I might find a witness in every citizen who has shared in, or been attentive to, the course of public administrations. I might collect vouchers in abundance from the records and archives of every State in the Union. But as a more concise, and at the same time equally satisfactory, evidence, I will refer to the example of two States, attested by two unexceptionable authorities.

The first example is that of Virginia, a State which, as we have seen, has expressly declared in its constitution, that the three great departments ought not to be intermixed. The authority in support of it is Mr. Jefferson, who, besides his other advantages for remarking the operation of the government, was himself the chief magistrate of it. In order to convey fully the ideas with which his experience had impressed him on this subject, it will be necessary to quote a passage of some length from his very interesting "Notes on the State of Virginia," p. 195. "All the powers of government, legislative, executive, and judiciary, result to the legislative body. The concentrating these in the same hands, is precisely the definition of despotic government. It will be no alleviation, that these powers will be exercised by a plurality of hands, and not by a single one. One hundred and seventy-three despots would surely be as oppressive as one. Let those who doubt it, turn their eyes on the republic of Venice. As little will it avail us, that they are chosen by ourselves. An *elective despotism* was not the government we fought for; but one which should not only be founded on free principles, but in which the powers of government should be so divided and balanced among several bodies of magistracy, as that no one could transcend their legal limits, without being effectually checked and restrained by the others. For this reason, that convention which passed the ordinance of government, laid its foundation on this basis, that the legislative, executive, and judiciary departments should be separate and distinct, so that no person should exercise the powers of more than one of them at the same time. *But no barrier was provided between these several powers.* The judiciary and the executive members were left dependent on the legislative for their subsistence in office, and some of them for their continuance in it. If, therefore, the legislature assumes executive and judiciary powers, no opposition is likely to be made; nor, if made, can be effectual; because in that case they may put their proceedings into the form of acts of Assembly, which will render them obligatory on the other branches. They have accordingly, *in many* instances, *decided rights* which should have been left to *judiciary controversy,* and *the direction of the executive, during the whole time of their session, is becoming habitual and familiar."*

The other State which I shall take for an example is Pennsylvania; and the other authority, the Council of Censors, which assembled in the years 1783 and 1784. A part of the duty of this body, as marked out by the constitution, was "to inquire whether the constitution had been preserved inviolate in every part; and whether the legislative and executive branches of government had performed their duty as guardians of the people, or assumed to themselves, or exercised, other or greater powers than they are entitled to by the constitution." In the execution of this trust, the council were necessarily led to a comparison of both the legislative and executive proceedings, with the constitutional powers of these departments; and from the facts enumerated, and to the truth of most of which both sides in the council subscribed, it appears that the constitution had been flagrantly violated by the legislature in a variety of important instances.

A great number of laws had been passed, violating, without any apparent necessity, the rule requiring that all bills of a public nature shall be previously printed for the consideration of the people; although this is one of the precautions chiefly relied on by the constitution against improper acts of the legislature.

The constitutional trial by jury had been violated, and powers assumed which had not been delegated by the constitution. Executive powers had been usurped. The salaries of the judges, which the constitution expressly requires to be fixed, had been occasionally varied; and cases belonging to the judiciary department frequently drawn within legislative cognizance and determination.

Those who wish to see the several particulars falling under each of these heads, may consult the journals of the council, which are in print. Some of them, it will be found, may be imputable to peculiar circumstances connected with the war; but the greater part of them may be considered as the spontaneous shoots of an ill-constituted government.

It appears, also, that the executive department had not been innocent of frequent breaches of the constitution. There are three observations, however, which ought to be made on this head: *first*, a great proportion of the instances were either immediately produced by the necessities of the war, or recommended by Congress or the commander-in-chief; *secondly*, in most of the other instances, they conformed either to the declared or the known sentiments of the legislative department; *thirdly*, the executive department of Pennsylvania is distinguished from that of the other States by the number of members composing it. In this respect, it has as much affinity to a legislative assembly as to an executive council. And being at once exempt from the restraint of an individual responsibility for the acts of the body, and deriving confidence from mutual example and joint influence, unauthorized measures would, of course, be more freely hazarded, than where the executive department is administered by a single hand, or by a few hands.

The conclusion which I am warranted in drawing from these observations is, that a mere demarcation on parchment of the constitutional limits of the several departments, is not a sufficient guard against those encroachments which lead to a tyrannical concentration of all the powers of government in the same hands.

Publius

8 / Congressional Government

Woodrow Wilson

Before becoming the twenty-eighth president (1913–1921), Woodrow Wilson had
studied the national government as a political scientist, and had concluded that
Congress had become the dominant branch, ruling both the executive and the
judiciary "with easy mastery and with a high hand." The following selection is from
Wilson's *Congressional Government*, written in 1883–84 and earning for Wilson
a doctoral degree in 1886.

. . .We are the first Americans to hear our own countrymen ask whether the
Constitution is still adapted to serve the purposes for which it was intended;
the first to entertain any serious doubts about the superiority of our own institutions as compared with the systems of Europe; the first to think of
remodeling the administrative machinery of the federal government, and of
forcing new forms of responsibility upon Congress. . . .

The leading inquiry in the examination of any system of government
must, of course, concern primarily the real depositaries and the essential
machinery of power. There is always a centre of power: where in this system
is that centre? In whose hands is self-sufficient authority lodged and through
what agencies does that authority speak and act? The answers one gets to
these and kindred questions from authoritative manuals of constitutional exposition are not satisfactory, chiefly because they are contradicted by self-
evident facts. It is said that there is no single or central force in our federal
scheme; and so there is not in the federal *scheme*, but only a balance of powers
and a nice adjustment of interactive checks, as all the books say. How is it,
however, in the practical conduct of the federal government? In that, unquestionably, the predominant and controlling force, the centre and source
of all motive and of all regulative power, is Congress. All niceties of constitutional restriction and even many broad principles of constitutional limitation have been overridden, and a thoroughly organized system of congressional control set up which gives a very rude negative to some theories of
balance and some schemes for distributed powers, but which suits well with
convenience, and does violence to none of the principles of self-government
contained in the Constitution. . . .

It is noteworthy that Mr. Adams, possibly because he had himself been
President, describes the executive as constituting only *"in some degree"* a check
upon Congress, though he puts no such limitation upon the other balances
of the system. Independently of experience, however, it might reasonably have
been expected that the prerogatives of the President would have been one
of the most effectual restraints upon the power of Congress. He was constituted
one of the three great coordinate branches of the government; his functions
were made of the highest dignity; his privileges many and substantial—so

great, indeed, that it has pleased the fancy of some writers to parade them as exceeding those of the British crown; and there can be little doubt that, had the presidential chair always been filled by men of commanding character, of acknowledged ability, and of thorough political training, it would have continued to be a seat of the highest authority and consideration, the true centre of the federal structure, the real throne of administration, and the frequent source of policies. Washington and his cabinet commanded the ear of Congress, and gave shape to its deliberations; Adams, though often crossed and thwarted, gave character to the government; and Jefferson, as President no less than as Secretary of State, was the real leader of his party. But the prestige of the presidential office has declined with the character of the Presidents. And the character of the Presidents has declined as the perfection of selfish party tactics has advanced.

It was inevitable that it should be so. After independence of choice on the part of the presidential electors had given place to the choice of presidential candidates by party conventions, it became absolutely necessary, in the eyes of politicians, and more and more necessary as time went on, to make expediency and availability the only rules of selection. As each party, when in convention assembled, spoke only those opinions which seemed to have received the sanction of the general voice, carefully suppressing in its "platform" all unpopular political tenets, and scrupulously omitting mention of every doctrine that might be looked upon as characteristic and as part of a peculiar and original programme, so, when the presidential candidate came to be chosen, it was recognized as imperatively necessary that he should have as short a political record as possible, and that he should wear a clean and irreproachable insignificance. "Gentlemen," said a distinguished American public man, "I would make an excellent President, but a very poor candidate." A decisive career which gives a man a well-understood place in public estimation constitutes a positive disability for the presidency; because candidacy must precede election, and the shoals of candidacy can be passed only by a light boat which carries little freight and can be turned readily about to suit the intricacies of the passage.

I am disposed to think, however, that the decline in the character of the Presidents is not the cause, but only the accompanying manifestation, of the declining prestige of the presidential office. That high office has fallen from its first estate of dignity because its power has waned; and its power has waned because the power of Congress has become predominant. The early Presidents were, as I have said, men of such a stamp that they would under any circumstances have made their influence felt; but their opportunities were exceptional. What with quarreling and fighting with England, buying Louisiana and Florida, building dykes to keep out the flood of the French Revolution, and extricating the country from ceaseless broils with the South American Republics, the government was, as has been pointed out, constantly busy, during the first quarter century of its existence, with the adjustment of foreign relations; and with foreign relations, of course, the Presidents had everything to do, since theirs was the office of negotiation.

Moreover, as regards home policy also those times were not like ours. Congress was somewhat awkward in exercising its untried powers, and its machinery was new, and without that fine adjustment which has since made it perfect of its kind. Not having as yet learned the art of governing itself to the best advantage, and being without that facility of legislation which it afterwards acquired, the Legislature was glad to get guidance and suggestions of policy from the Executive.

But this state of things did not last long. Congress was very quick and apt in learning what it could do and in getting into thoroughly good trim to do it. It very early divided itself into standing committees which it equipped with very comprehensive and thorough-going privileges of legislative initiative and control, and set itself through these to administer the government. Congress is (to adopt Mr. Bagehot's description of Parliament) "nothing less than a big meeting of more or less idle people. In proportion as you give it power it will inquire into everything, settle everything, meddle in everything. In an ordinary despotism the powers of the despot are limited by his bodily capacity, and by the calls of pleasure; he is but one man; there are but twelve hours in his day, and he is not disposed to employ more than a small part in dull business: he keeps the rest for the court, or the harem, or for society." But Congress "is a despot who has unlimited time,—who has unlimited vanity, —who has, or believes he has, unlimited comprehension,—whose pleasure is in action, whose life is work." Accordingly it has entered more and more into the details of administration, until it has virtually taken into its own hands all the substantial powers of government. It does not domineer over the President himself, but it makes the Secretaries its humble servants. Not that it would hesitate, upon occasion, to deal directly with the chief magistrate himself; but it has few calls to do so, because our latter-day Presidents live by proxy; they are the executive in theory, but the Secretaries are the executive in fact. At the very first session of Congress steps were taken towards parceling out executive work amongst several departments, according to a then sufficiently thorough division of labor; and if the President of that day was not able to direct administrative details, of course the President of today is infinitely less able to do so, and must content himself with such general supervision as he may find time to exercise. He is in all every-day concerns shielded by the responsibility of his subordinates.

It cannot be said that this change has raised the cabinet in dignity or power; it has only altered their relations to the scheme of government. The members of the President's cabinet have always been prominent in administration; and certainly the early cabinets were no less strong in political influence than are the cabinets of our own day; but they were then only the President's advisers, whereas they are now rather the President's colleagues. The President is now scarcely the executive; he is the head of the administration; he appoints the executive. Of course this is not a legal principle; it is only a fact. In legal theory the President can control every operation of every department of the executive branch of the government; but in fact it is not practicable for him to do so, and a limitation of fact is as potent as a prohibition of law.

But, though the heads of the executive departments are thus no longer simply the counselors of the President, having become in a very real sense members of the executive, their guiding power in the conduct of affairs, instead of advancing, has steadily diminished; because while they were being made integral parts of the machinery of administration, Congress was extending its own sphere of activity, was getting into the habit of investigating and managing everything. The executive was losing and Congress gaining weight; and the station to which cabinets finally attained was a station of diminished and diminishing power. There is no distincter tendency in congressional history than the tendency to subject even the details of administration to the constant supervision, and all policy to the watchful intervention, of the Standing Committees.

I am inclined to think, therefore, that the enlarged powers of Congress are the fruits rather of an immensely increased efficiency of organization, and of the redoubled activity consequent upon the facility of action secured by such organization, than of any definite and persistent scheme of conscious usurpation. It is safe to say that Congress always had the desire to have a hand in every affair of federal government; but it was only by degrees that it found means and opportunity to gratify that desire, and its activity, extending its bounds wherever perfected processes of congressional work offered favoring prospects, has been enlarged so naturally and so silently that it has almost always seemed of normal extent, and has never, except perhaps during one or two brief periods of extraordinary political disturbance, appeared to reach much beyond its acknowledged constitutional sphere.

It is only in the exercise of those functions of public and formal consultation and cooperation with the President which are the peculiar offices of the Senate, that the power of Congress has made itself offensive to popular conceptions of constitutional propriety, because it is only in the exercise of such functions that Congress is compelled to be overt and demonstrative in its claims of over-lordship. The House of Representatives has made very few noisy demonstrations of its usurped right of ascendency; not because it was diffident or unambitious, but because it could maintain and extend its prerogatives quite as satisfactorily without noise; whereas the aggressive policy of the Senate has, in the acts of its "executive sessions," necessarily been overt, in spite of the closing of the doors, because when acting as the President's council in the ratification of treaties and in appointments to office its competition for power has been more formally and directly a contest with the executive than were those really more significant legislative acts by which, in conjunction with the House, it has habitually forced the heads of the executive departments to observe the will of Congress at every important turn of policy. Hence it is that to the superficial view it appears that only the Senate has been outrageous in its encroachments upon executive privilege. It is not often easy to see the true constitutional bearing of strictly legislative action; but it is patent even to the least observant that in the matter of appointments to office, for instance, senators have often outrun their legal right to give or withhold their assent to appointments, by insisting upon being first consulted concerning nominations as well, and have thus made their constitutional assent to appointments dependent upon an unconstitutional control of nominations.

This particular usurpation has been put upon a very solid basis of law by that Tenure-of-Office Act, which took away from President Johnson, in an hour of party heat and passion, that independent power of removal from office with which the Constitution had invested him, but which he had used in a way that exasperated a Senate not of his own way of thinking. But though this teasing power of the Senate's in the matter of the federal patronage is repugnant enough to the original theory of the Constitution, it is likely to be quite nullified by that policy of civil-service reform which has gained so firm, and mayhap so lasting, a footing in our national legislation; and in no event would the control of the patronage by the Senate have unbalanced the federal system more seriously than it may some day be unbalanced by an irresponsible exertion of that body's semi-executive powers in regard to the foreign policy of the government. More than one passage in the history of our foreign relations illustrates the danger. During the simple congressional session of 1868–9, for example, the treaty-*marring* power of the Senate was exerted in a way that made the comparative weakness of the executive very conspicuous, and was ominous of very serious results. It showed the executive in the right, but feeble and irresolute; the Senate masterful, though in the wrong. Denmark had been asked to part with the island of St. Thomas to the United States, and had at first refused all terms, not only because she cared little for the price, but also and principally because such a sale as that proposed was opposed to the established policy of the powers of Western Europe, in whose favor Denmark wished to stand; but finally, by stress of persistent and importunate negotiation, she had been induced to yield; a treaty had been signed and sent to the Senate; the people of St. Thomas had signified their consent to the cession by a formal vote; and the island had been actually transferred to an authorized agent of our government, upon the faith, on the part of the Danish ministers, that our representatives would not have trifled with them by entering upon an important business transaction which they were not assured of their ability to conclude. But the Senate let the treaty lie neglected in its committee-room; the limit of time agreed upon for confirmation passed; the Danish government, at last bent upon escaping the ridiculous humiliation that would follow a failure of the business at that stage, extended the time and even sent over one of its most eminent ministers of state to urge the negotiation by all dignified means; but the Senate cared nothing for Danish feelings and could afford, it thought, to despise President Grant and Mr. Fish, and at the next session rejected the treaty, and left the Danes to repossess themselves of the island, which we had concluded not to buy after all.

. . . [F]rom whatever point we view the relations of the executive and the legislature, it is evident that the power of the latter has steadily increased at the expense of the prerogatives of the former, and that the degree in which the one of these great branches of government is balanced against the other is a very insignificant degree indeed. For in the exercise of his power of veto, which is of course, beyond all comparison, his most formidable prerogative, the President acts not as the executive but as a third branch of the legislature. As Oliver Ellsworth said, at the first session of the Senate, the President is, as regards the passage of bills, but a part of Congress; and he can be an efficient, imperative member of the legislative system only in quiet times, when parties are pretty evenly balanced, and there are no indomitable majorities to tread obnoxious vetoes under foot.

...The balances of the Constitution are for the most part only ideal. For all practical purposes the national government is supreme over the state governments, and Congress predominant over its so-called coordinate branches. Whereas Congress at first overshadowed neither President nor federal judiciary, it now on occasion rules both with easy mastery and with a high hand; and whereas each State once guarded its sovereign prerogatives with jealous pride, and able men not a few preferred political advancement under the governments of the great commonwealths to office under the new federal Constitution, seats in state legislatures are now no longer coveted except as possible approaches to seats in Congress; and even governors of States seek election to the national Senate as a promotion, a reward for the humbler services they have rendered their local governments....

Judge Cooley, in his admirable work on "The Principles of American Constitutional Law," after quoting Mr. Adams's enumeration of the checks and balances of the federal system, adds this comment upon Mr. Adams's concluding statement that that system is an invention of our own. "The invention, nevertheless, was suggested by the British Constitution, in which a system almost equally elaborate was then in force. In its outward forms that system still remains; but there has been for more than a century a gradual change in the direction of a concentration of legislative and executive power in the popular house of Parliament, so that the government now is sometimes said, with no great departure from the fact, to be a government by the House of Commons." But Judge Cooley does not seem to see, or, if he sees, does not emphasize the fact, that our own system has been hardly less subject to "a gradual change in the direction of a concentration" of all the substantial powers of government in the hands of Congress; so that it is now, though a wide departure from the form of things, "no great departure from the fact" to describe ours as a government by the Standing Committees of Congress. This fact is, however, deducible from very many passages of Judge Cooley's own writings; for he is by no means insensible of that expansion of the powers of the federal government and that crystallization of its methods which have practically made obsolete the early constitutional theories, and even the modified theory which he himself seems to hold.

He has tested the nice adjustment of the theoretical balances by the actual facts, and has carefully set forth the results; but he has nowhere brought those results together into a single comprehensive view which might serve as a clear and satisfactory delineation of the Constitution of to-day; nor has he, or any other writer of capacity, examined minutely and at length that internal organization of Congress which determines its methods of legislation, which shapes its means of governing the executive departments, which contains in it the whole mechanism whereby the policy of the country is in all points directed, and which is therefore an essential branch of constitutional study. As the House of Commons is the central object of examination in every study of the English Constitution, so should Congress be in every study of our own. Any one who is unfamiliar with what Congress actually does and how it does it, with all its duties and all its occupations, with all its devices of management and resources of power, is very far from a knowledge of the constitutional system under which we live; and to every one who knows these things that knowledge is very near.

Though some of Wilson's words probably exaggerated the ineffectiveness of the presidency, his view—shared by others in his day—does suggest that the relationship of president and Congress has changed markedly since the beginning of this century. In fact by the time of his next book, published as *Constitutional Government in the United States* in 1908, Wilson himself would argue that a significant change toward greater presidential power had already taken place.

9 / Doesn't Congress Have Ideas of Its Own?

Abraham Ribicoff

In 1964, then-Senator Abraham Ribicoff (from Connecticut) wrote the following article, lamenting what he saw as a Congress that was no longer doing its job. Congress was simply reacting to presidential proposals, Ribicoff argued, and hence was failing in its obligation to initiate legislation on its own. Eighty years after Woodrow Wilson had written *Congressional Government*, Senator Ribicoff was describing a far different congressional role than that portrayed in Wilson's book.

In all the recent uproar about Congress—the public dismay with its balkiness, the cries for its reform—the real trouble with Congress has been overlooked. It is simply that Congress has surrendered its rightful leadership in the lawmaking process to the White House.

No longer is Congress the source of major legislation. It now merely filters legislative proposals from the President, straining out some and reluctantly letting others pass through. These days no one expects Congress to devise the important bills. Instead, the legislative views of the President dominate the press, the public and the Congress itself.

This is all wrong. Making laws, not just scrutinizing them, is the job of Congress. That job requires initiation, not simply passive reaction to executive branch requests. Yet Congress has surrendered the job—so completely that the press and the nation now "score" a president's success by the number of his requests he gets through Congress. In the scoring, a presidential request approved by Congress counts as a victory, and a rejected request counts as a defeat. . . .

It is not the President who is at fault. His office is, under the Constitution, a position of extraordinary leadership—in the nation and the entire world. It is part of his job to give Congress his recommendations for needed legislation. . . .

I have no quarrel with the way the President discharges *his* responsibilities. My point is that Congress has failed to exercise its own.

I do not mean just a failure to pass bills. There have been failures in this respect. Some needed bills have not been passed and many that were approved were unduly delayed. For these failures Congress has received much criticism. Some of that criticism is deserved, though the accomplishments of Congress last year are far greater than is generally recognized. The test-ban treaty and major bills for college aid, vocational education, medical schools, air pollution control, mental health, mental retardation and job retraining were all approved in 1963. In fact, I predict the complete record of the 88th Congress, including the tax cut and, in all likelihood, a strong civil rights law, will mark it as one of the most productive in recent years.

The critics of Congress have really missed the point. Their sole concern is the failure of Congress to enact presidential bills. They don't even consider whether Congress is doing any lawmaking on its own. What these critics really prefer is a parliamentary form of government. They want executive and legislative power to be joined, as in the British parliament, so that a policy decision made by the Government's leadership can be automatically made the law of the land. But the genius of our constitutional system is that it separates executive and legislative power and provides for two coequal branches of government. This is a great strength of our nation and it should not be diminished. But if the system is to work effectively, both branches must fully exercise their constitutionally assigned functions.

My concern is the failure of Congress to realize the full extent of its own role in the legislative process. Congress need not and should not be content simply to react to presidential requests. Congress should make its own independent assessments of the nation's problems and come up with its own answers. If legislation is needed, Congress, too, has prime responsibility for developing a bill. Yet this is not what happens in practice.

Look how the process works. There was widespread agreement last year that there should be legislation to revise the income tax laws. What happened? Congress convened on January 9, 1963. Did it start to conduct hearings into the entire problem of taxation? It did not. It did absolutely nothing until the President had drafted *his* tax proposal and sent it to the Hill. Then the Ways and Means Committee of the House began hearings—not a general inquiry into the entire problem, but a hearing into the pros and cons of the President's program.

The first witness was the Secretary of the Treasury. He said the program was good. Other witnesses followed who said part of the program was good and part was bad. When the hearings were over, the committee met in executive session and began a line-by-line examination of each recommendation sent up by the President. Some of these proposals were adopted, some rejected and a few modified. The committee added scarcely any provisions on its own initiative.

The committee then drafted a bill to put its decisions—or, more accurately, the decisions of the executive branch as modified by the committee—into legislative language. (Congress deserves credit for doing this bill-drafting. Usually the executive branch sends its recommendations to Congress with draft bills already prepared.) After Rules Committee approval, the bill went to the House floor, where amendments were not permitted.

Then the whole process began again in the Senate. In February, the bill completed its round trip and ended up back where it started: on the President's desk.

The process is simply wrong: The President's proposal should be looked at with care, but it should not be the beginning, middle and end of the story. There is absolutely no reason for Congress to spend all its time deciding whether the President's proposal is good or bad. Let Congress provide its own answers to the problem. Let the hearings roam broadly over the entire field of taxation and the economy, and when they are concluded, let the people's elected representatives draw up a bill that they believe is right.

When I entered the President's Cabinet [H.E.W.] three years ago, I was frankly surprised at the deferential attitude some members of Congress exhibited toward the executive branch. Of course, I know they make critical speeches and cut budget requests, but beneath these headline-making events is an unreported story of silent acquiescence to administration views.

Representatives and senators often called me to find out what position the administration would take on a bill of theirs or what type of draft legislation would be submitted by the White House. I was sorry they put so much emphasis on what position I would take. I was more interested in knowing what position *they* would take.

It is the same story here in the Senate. I have heard ranking members privately admit that their pet bills were doomed because of opposition from the executive branch. "Why don't you ask for hearings on that bill?" I asked a colleague the other day. "It sounds to me like a really good idea."

"It's no use," he replied, "The administration is dead set against it. It wouldn't have a chance."

In the House Education and Labor Committee last year, the Kennedy aid-to-education bill was being considered. The President had packaged many separate proposals in one bill and urged Congress to pass the entire bill. What was the reaction in the committee? "This is terrible; the President has got to set priorities. He should tell us which proposals he really wants; otherwise how are we to proceed?"

When I served in the Cabinet, I had an obligation to present the administration's view of what was important. But now that I serve in the
legislative branch, I should not just mark time until the executive branch
makes up my mind for me. I was elected to make judgments for myself and
my constituents. That is the business of everyone in Congress.

A practice that started many years ago as an orderly procedure for consolidating views within the executive branch has now grown into an unofficial pre-veto power. This is the practice of referring nearly all proposed legislation to the Budget Bureau and the various agencies of government for a
report of the administration's position. Say you have a proposal to cut the
tariff on widgets. You draft a bill, and it is referred to the Finance Committee. Then the bill goes "downtown" for reports from the administration. It
may be looked at by the Commerce Department, Treasury Department, State
Department, Tariff Commission and the Budget Bureau.

Weeks later the replies come back, "No," says the executive branch, "we
have carefully considered this bill and we would be just as happy if it didn't
pass." Unless your bill has acquired the popularity of apple pie, that reply
from the administration means the end of the line. Chances are there won't
even be a hearing. Prospects for ultimate passage are virtually nil.

Let us have the views of the executive branch. Often extremely constructive suggestions are made in executive reports; they improve the proposed bill.
But if the Congress permits the administration's disapproval to bring the
legislative process to a complete stop, it makes a great mistake.

If the administration seriously believes that a proposed bill is contrary
to the public interest, the Constitution sets out the appropriate procedure
to be followed: the presidential veto. Yet many people have come to believe
that when a political party controls both the White House and the Congress,
the veto should be put on the shelf. If a Democratic Congress passes a bill
that so displeases a Democratic President that he must veto it, then—people
think—somewhere along the line somebody goofed. According to this popular
notion, Democrats in Congress should not embarrass the President by sending up a bill he doesn't like.

This is nonsense. The Congress has a job to do—making laws. The President has one too—reviewing those laws and either signing or vetoing them.
Yet when one party controls both branches, it is rare for Congress to send
the White House a major bill that will be vetoed. To some, this may show
harmony between the executive and legislative branches. To me it shows that
Congress is not doing the job the people elected it to do.

I think that, no matter which party controls the executive and legislative
branches, the legislative process would work far better if several bills incurred vetoes during each Congress, including bills dealing with matters of
high public interest. These vetoes would show that Congress has thrown off
its complete dependence on administration approval. It would also make the
issues more meaningful to the country.

In the election of 1948, the Taft-Hartley Act was a clear-cut issue before
the voters precisely because it had been vetoed by President Truman and

passed over his veto. Again, the need for housing legislation was brought clearly into focus in 1959 when President Eisenhower vetoed a housing bill. The broad scope of the bill that ultimately became law two years later under President Kennedy is due in large part to the sharpening of the issue after the Eisenhower veto. The same can be said of the Water Pollution Control Act Amendments of 1961. A broad, national antipollution program was enacted the year after President Eisenhower referred to the problem as "uniquely local."

Because lawmaking in Congress is now so heavily influenced by the views of the executive branch, a subtle distortion has occurred in the press and so in the minds of the public. Whenever the President sends one of his proposals to Congress, reporters immediately ask senators and representatives what they think of the President's bill. They don't ask Senator X what he thinks should be done—whether he thinks any bill is needed, and if so, what kind of a bill he thinks best. Their inquiry is always confined to the alternatives of being for or against the President's bill.

The result is that a large part of the public, especially people who do want something done about the particular problem, tends to think that the only answer is the President's answer. Being for the President's bill is a good position, and being opposed is bad. And as the bill goes through the legislative process, these people are led to believe that any change in the President's bill is a setback for him, and the elimination of some provision a total defeat....

I believe the best way to insure responsible action by Congress is to give Congress heavy responsibilities. The men and women here want to do a good job for their constituents and their country. They are capable of doing it.

But if all the emphasis is on whether they approve or disapprove of what the President has recommended, then they will continue to spend too much of their time reacting to the White House. Turn the spotlight on what *they* think should be done and what *they* are prepared to do, and there will be constructive results.

Congress has a big job to do—and an important one. But first *Congress* must decide to do it.

10 / The Imperial Presidency

Arthur M. Schlesinger, Jr.

In stark contrast to Woodrow Wilson's observations of a weak and relatively powerless presidency at the turn of the century, Arthur Schlesinger, Jr., wrote in 1973 of an "imperial presidency." Schlesinger was not alone in his appraisal of an executive whose powers had grown well beyond a balance with Congress; others referred to the same phenomenon with words such as "presidential autocracy" and "presidential arrogance." Writing after the first term of Richard Nixon and at the time of the Watergate revelations, Schlesinger argues that while the imperial presidency was essentially a creation of foreign policy, it grew to incorporate a massive role in domestic policy as well. The imperial presidency, though not limited to the Nixon era, may have reached its peak during that administration.

The Imperial Presidency was essentially the creation of foreign policy. A combination of doctrines and emotions—belief in permanent and universal crisis, fear of communism, faith in the duty and the right of the United States to intervene swiftly in every part of the world—had brought about the unprecedented centralization of decisions over war and peace in the Presidency. With this there came an unprecedented exclusion of the rest of the executive branch, of Congress, of the press and of public opinion in general from these decisions. Prolonged war in Vietnam strengthened the tendencies toward both centralization and exclusion. So the imperial Presidency grew at the expense of the constitutional order. Like the cowbird, it hatched its own eggs and pushed the others out of the nest. And, as it overwhelmed the traditional separation of powers in foreign affairs, it began to aspire toward an equivalent centralization of power in the domestic polity.

I

... [I]n the case of Franklin D. Roosevelt and the New Deal... [the] extraordinary power flowing into the Presidency to meet domestic problems by no means enlarged presidential authority in foreign affairs. But... the case of FDR and the Second World War and Harry S. Truman and the steel seizure [showed] that extraordinary power flowing into the Presidency to meet international problems could easily encourage Presidents to extend their unilateral claims at home. Now, twenty years later, the spillover effect from Vietnam coincided with indigenous developments that were quite separately carrying new power to the Presidency. For domestic as well as for international reasons, the imperial Presidency was sinking roots deep into the national society itself.

One such development was the decay of the traditional party system. For much of American history the party has been the ultimate vehicle of political expression. Voters inherited their politics as they did their religion. It was as painful to desert one's party as to desert one's church. But this had begun to change. The Eisenhower period, marked by a President who considered himself above party and by an electorate which decided to balance the Republican President with a Democratic Congress, ushered in a time of decline in the parties. By the 1970s ticket-splitting had become common. Independent voting was spreading everywhere, especially among the young. Never had party loyalties been so weak, party affiliations so fluid, party organizations so irrelevant....

As the parties wasted away, the Presidency stood out in solitary majesty as the central focus of political emotion, the ever more potent symbol of national community. When parties were strong and media weak, Presidents were objects of respect but not of veneration. There were no great personal cults of Rutherford B. Hayes and Benjamin Harrison. Now voters wanted not only to respect but to adore their Presidents, even when, as in the cases of Johnson and Nixon, they found the effort difficult and unrewarding. For their part, historians and political scientists discovered in the images of the two Roosevelts and Wilson, strong Presidents using power for enlightened ends, the model of the Presidency to teach their students and hold up before aspiring politicians. The electronic revolution, having helped dissolve the parties, also helped exalt the Presidency by giving the man in the White House powerful means, first through radio and then through television, to bring his presence and message into every home in the land. Almost alone, Justice Jackson had said in the steel case, the President filled the public eye and ear.

At the same time, the economic changes of the twentieth century had conferred vast new powers not just on the national government but more particularly on the Presidency. The depression of the 1930s had left little doubt that government must thereafter underwrite economic activity and regulate the excesses of business. But the New Deal had been limited by the fact that the levers of private economic power remained in the hands of the political opposition. Then the Second World War strengthened both the techniques and the habits of centralized control. The combination of the New Deal and the war, E. S. Corwin wrote in 1947, had begun to transform a Constitution of Rights into a Constitution of Powers: "the Constitution of peacetime and the Constitution of wartime have become, thanks to the New Deal, very much the same Constitution."[1] But if a Constitution of powers, it was still a Constitution of limited powers—limited during the Second World War by standards of equity written into legislation and sustained in administration; limited in Truman's case by his own instinct and, on the occasion his instinct failed, by the Supreme Court; limited in Eisenhower's case by his disbelief in government; limited in Kennedy's case by instinct and narrow political margins; limited in all these cases by the capacity of corporate managers to resist government control employed for purposes they disliked.

But the trend toward the managed economy had set in. As Keynes himself had once dealt with the economic consequences of Versailles, Americans were now required to deal, in Samuel Lubell's phrase, with the political consequences of Keynes.[2] For Keynesianism made the federal budget the center of economic control and thereby gave presidential government the means, tempered only by what slight modification Congress might force through its taxing and appropriation powers, of deciding the levels of spending and the allocation of government outlays, which meant deciding the social priorities and, to an unprecedented degree, the economic pattern of American society.

There was, alas, no alternative to centralized economic responsibility. History had demonstrated beyond any social interest in further experiment that a high-technology economy would not, left alone, necessarily, or even probably, balance out at levels of high employment. It had demonstrated further that unregulated private ownership generated excessive inequality in the distribution of income, wealth and power and could not restrain greed from exploiting human labor or from despoiling the natural environment. No one, not even those businessmen who eulogized free enterprise at every public banquet, really wanted to get back on the roller coaster of boom and bust, or return to the bucket shop and sweatshop. National control was the only way to civilize industrial society. But national control without firm mechanisms of equality could quickly degenerate into a system of favoritism, of injustice and of graft.

The Keynesian instrumentalities of government were an intelligent response to public necessity. But they were instrumentalities designed for executive use. Congress showed no capacity to organize across-the-board control of spending or to alter the aggregates of spending in response to the needs of the economy. But, if the President could control employment and investment through the manipulation of the budget, he could do this for the benefit of the industries and regions that gave him steadiest support. And his power to create new economic situations through executive action enabled him to foreclose both decisions by other bodies—Congress, for example—and movement in other directions. The managed economy, in short, offered new forms of unilateral power to the President who was bold enough to take action on his own. "The drive for presidential power," Lubell wrote in 1973, "has been a drive to commit the future.... Once the fishhook of commitment becomes lodged in a nation's throat, voter opinion will thrash about furiously, like a powerful but helpless sailfish."[3] The combination of exasperation and impotence increasingly characterized American politics in domestic as well as in foreign affairs.

II

The imperial Presidency, born in the 1940s and 1950s to save the outer world from perdition, thus began in the 1960s and 1970s to find nurture at home. Foreign policy had given the President the command of peace and war. Now the decay of the parties left him in command of the political scene, and the Keynesian revelation placed him in command of the economy. At this extraordinary historical moment, when foreign and domestic lines of force converged, much depended on whether the occupant of the White House was moved to ride the new tendencies of power or to resist them.

For the American Presidency was a peculiarly personal institution. It remained, of course, an agency of government, subject to unvarying demands and duties no matter who was President. But, more than most agencies of government, it changed shape, intensity and ethos according to the man in charge. Each President's distinctive temperament and character, his values, standards, style, his habits, expectations, idiosyncrasies, compulsions, phobias recast the White House and pervaded the entire government beyond. The executive branch, said Clark Clifford, was a chameleon, taking its color from the character and personality of the President.[4] The thrust of the office, its impact on the constitutional order, therefore altered from President to President. Above all, the way each President understood it as his personal obligation to inform and involve the Congress, to earn and hold the confidence of the electorate and to render an accounting to the nation and posterity determined whether he strengthened or weakened the constitutional order.

Historically most Presidents had felt it a duty to keep close to the people. They characteristically exposed themselves, for example, to a wide range of national opinion. They appointed political chieftains of substance and following to their cabinet. They stayed in constant touch with the leadership of their party in Congress and in the states. They engaged in far-flung correspondence. They read the newspapers; McKinley spent two hours every morning at it. For a good deal of the first century of the republic, they held weekly *levées* and were accessible even to casual visitors to Washington. They deemed it a basic requirement of the job, in a phrase Garfield once quoted from Lincoln, "to take a bath in public opinion."[5]

Even as the nation grew more populous and public business more complicated, Presidents like the two Roosevelts and Wilson found their own ways of taking baths in public opinion. All of them had their monarchical moments. It has latterly become fashionable to say that the imperial Presidency began with FDR. But FDR, though he delighted in power, did not in the later royal style frown on argument and dissent in the presidential presence. Quite the contrary: he valued obstinate and opinionated men (who else could have put up for a dozen years with Harold Ickes?) and made debate a fundamental method of government. Even during the Second World War, Roosevelt continued to believe, as he showed when he began to plan for peace, that a strong President had to be, when possible, strong *with* the Congress, not strong *against* the Congress.

It was in the years after the Second World War that the Presidency, first with Truman and then more vehemently with Johnson and Nixon, acquired pretensions to powers construed not only as inherent but as exclusive. Personality continued to modify the evolution of the office. In the case of Truman his exceptional directness, openness and lack of affectation considerably offset the impact his unilateral exercise of power might have had on the institution. He declined to remove the Presidency from the people and was far too spontaneous an American democrat to fit comfortably into the imperial Presidency. No doubt there were royal elements in Eisenhower's occupancy of the White House, but his Whiggishness confined them largely to the ceremonial side of the office. Kennedy's Presidency was too short to permit confident generalization; but his ironic and skeptical intelligence customarily kept the Presidency in healthy perspective. Johnson, however, poured an insatiable personality, a greed for consensus and an obsession with secrecy into the institution. The office now began to swell to imperial proportions.

The Johnson Presidency provoked George Reedy's brilliant and influential book *The Twilight of the Presidency*, the first sustained analysis of the office in its imperial phase. Seeing everything through the Johnsonian prism, Reedy may have failed to distinguish the psychological requirements of a particular President from the structural requirements of the Presidency. But his account was filled with insight and prophecy. The analysis was based on what might be called Reedy's Law: "Isolation from reality is inseparable from the exercise of power."[6] His portrait of the White House as a court was not unduly exaggerated. I am not sure, though, that even a court need aid and abet presidential isolation. And I am quite sure that the White House need not necessarily be, as Reedy at times suggested, a Byzantine court.[7] That was not one's experience in the Kennedy years nor particularly one's reading of the Roosevelt, or Jackson, years. Most of all, I think he may have understated the capacity Presidents have to overcome isolation if they wish to do so. Reedy's Law was penetrating but not absolute.

One of the great myths of American political folklore was that the Presidency, with its "awesome" responsibilities, was the loneliest job in the world. This was nonsense. "No one in the country," said John F. Kennedy, "is more assailed by divergent advice and clamorous counsel."[8] Any President who accepted the obligation of accountability and the discipline of consent knew he must incorporate within himself a nation of diverse values and discrepant objectives. The fact that the decision he made was technically his own did not mean that a sensitivity to what his associates and Congress and the country thought could possibly be excluded from the inscrutable processes of decision. These things played more intensively on conscientious Presidents than anyone outside could possibly imagine.

No one, if he wished it, could see a greater variety of people than the President or consult a wider range of opinion or tap more diversified sources of knowledge. Reedy well described how every White House assistant in New Deal days recalled the experience of bringing a report to FDR and "discovering, in the course of the conversation, that the president had gained from some mysterious, outside source knowledge of aspects of the project of which the assistant himself was not aware." When a President used all his manifold resources to gather information, it became both risky and futile for a member of his staff to hold out on him.[9] I was always astonished at how much more President Kennedy seemed to know about what was going on, including the adverse items, than members of his staff did. In Kennedy's case the Bay of Pigs had provided a salutary if costly lesson in the perils of presidential isolation. One reason for the difference between the Bay of Pigs and the missile crisis was that fiasco had instructed Kennedy in the importance of uninhibited debate in advance of major decision.

But, if the White House provided unparalleled facilities to enable a President to find out everything that was going on, it also, if a President wanted to be shielded from bad news and vexatious argument, gave him unparalleled facilities to fulfill that ambition too. Reedy's book was an illuminating generalization from Reedy's own President projected less persuasively on the Presidency in general. Ironically his thesis applied more precisely to Johnson's successor than to Johnson himself. For Johnson, after all, had his three television sets and three wire service tickers in the Oval Office. He made his angry morning dash through the newspapers and the *Congressional Record*. He could not abide being alone. Even the company of courtiers could tell an intelligent and curious man a good deal; and Johnson's court was brighter than most. In addition, Johnson talked to, even if he too seldom listened to, an endless stream of members of Congress and the press. He unquestionably denied himself reality for a long time, especially when it came to Vietnam. But in the end reality broke through, forcing him to accept unpleasant truths he did not wish to hear. Johnson's personality was far closer than Truman's to imperial specifications. But the fit was by no means perfect.

III

With Nixon there came, whether by weird historical accident or by unconscious national response to historical pressure and possibility, a singular confluence of the job with the man. The Presidency, as enlarged by international delusions and domestic propulsions, found a President whose inner mix of vulnerability and ambition impelled him to push the historical logic to its extremity.

A more traditional politician like Hubert Humphrey, if he had been elected in 1968, a more conscientious politician like George McGovern, if he had made it in 1972, would doubtless have tempered the tendency to gather everything into the White House. But Nixon, underneath a conventional exterior, was a man with revolutionary dreams. The structural forces tending to transfer power to the Presidency were now reinforced by compulsive internal drives—a sense of life as a battlefield, a belief that the nation was swarming with personal enemies, a flinching from face-to-face argument, an addiction to seclusion, a preoccupation with response to crisis, an insistence on a controlled environment for decision. For a man so constituted, the imperial Presidency was the perfect shield and refuge. But Nixon not only had an urgent psychological need for exemption from the democratic process. He also boldly sensed an historical opportunity to transform the Presidency—to consolidate within the White House all the powers, as against Congress, as against the electorate, as against the rest of the executive branch itself, that a generation of foreign and domestic turbulence had chaotically delivered to the Presidency.

Speculation about motivation is ordinarily unprofitable, and psychobiography is a notoriously underdeveloped science. Nonetheless, because the Presidency is so peculiarly personal an institution, and because the psychic drives of the man who sits in the Oval Office so fundamentally affect the impact of each particular Presidency, and because Nixon's destiny was to carry the logic of the imperial Presidency to the point of no return, one cannot avoid pondering why he did things it never occurred to Truman or Eisenhower or Kennedy or even Johnson to attempt.

In *Six Crises*, itself a revealing title, Nixon had written in a revealing phrase about the "warfare of politics."[10] Politics was indeed for him a succession of battles *à toute outrance*, to be fought against cunning and vicious foes with every weapon at hand. "He is the only major American politician in our history," an observer wrote in 1960, "who came to prominence by techniques which, if generally adopted, would destroy the whole fabric of mutual confidence on which our democracy rests."[11] As the observer in question, I took care to make the point subjunctively. People change in politics and life; and one could not hold forever against Nixon what he said about Jerry Voorhis in 1946 or Helen Gahagan Douglas in 1950 or Adlai Stevenson in 1952 ("Adlai the appeaser. . .who got a Ph. D. from Dean Acheson's College of Cowardly Communist Containment") or Dean Acheson thereafter, especially in contrast to Dulles ("Isn't it wonderful finally to have a Secretary of State who isn't taken in by the Communists, who stands up to them?"). There was always the possibility of the new Nixon. Indeed, after his trips to Peking and Moscow in 1972, he seemed an honors graduate of the College of Cowardly Communist Containment himself.

Yet it was easier to alter policies than sets of mind. "I believe in the battle," Nixon told an interviewer during his high after his victory in 1972, "whether it's the battle of a campaign or the battle of this office.... It's always there wherever you go. I, perhaps, carry it more than others because that's my way." It was indeed his way. His concern through life had been to master the panic stirred within him by crisis, to be, when the moment arrived, calm, balanced, objective. He told his post-election interviewer proudly, "I have a reputation for being the coolest person in the room."

To assure coolness in the clutch, he believed, it was essential above all to simplify the arena of decision. This meant withdrawal from the provocations of criticism and argument. The President, said Tom Charles Huston, who served for a year as domestic security planner in the White House, "abhors confrontations, most particularly those based on philosophical convictions."[12] Nixon himself observed, "The [presidential] office as presently furnished probably would drive President Johnson up the wall. He liked things going on. He kept three TV sets here.... I could go up the wall watching TV commentators. I don't. I get my news from the news summary the staff prepares every day." The White House itself evidently drove him up the wall too. He deserted the light and lovely Oval Office for a small working room in the Executive Office Building; Joseph Alsop, an admirer, called him an agoraphobe. Even more soothing was Camp David, the old Shangri-La of FDR, high on the Catoctin Mountain of Maryland. Nixon now transformed FDR's rural retreat into an armed fortress, where he sought shelter behind a triple fence and a forest overflowing with Marines. "I find that up there on top of a mountain," he said, "it is easier for me to get on top of the job."[13]

Every President reconstructs the Presidency to meet his own psychological needs. Nixon displayed more monarchical yearnings than any of his predecessors. He plainly reveled in the ritual of the office, only regretting that it could not be more elaborate. What previous President, for example, would have dreamed of ceremonial trumpets or of putting the White House security force in costumes to rival the Guards at Buckingham Palace? Public ridicule stopped this. But Nixon saw no problem about using federal money, under the pretext of national security, to adorn his California and Florida estates with redwood fences, golf carts, heaters and wind screens for the swimming pool, beach cabanas, roof tiling, carpets, furniture, trees and shrubbery.

IV

Comic opera dress for White House guards and heaters for the San Clemente swimming pool were unimportant except as the expression of a regal state of mind. What mattered much more was the extent to which the same state of mind led Nixon, far more even than Johnson, to banish challenge from the presidential environment.

Notes

1. e. S. Corwin, *Total War and the Constitution* (New York, 1947), 172.
2. In this analysis I have shamelessly appropriated insights from Samual Lubell's original and arresting book *The Future While It Happened* (New York, 1973). Mr. Lubell developed some of his points further in an important five-part series released by the *New York Times* Special Features (though, oddly, not printed in the *New York Times*), June 3–7, 1973.
3. Lubell, *Future While It Happened*, 13.
4. Clark Clifford, "The Presidency As I Have Seen It," in Emmet Hughes, *The Living Presidency* (New York, 1973), 315.
5. T. C. Smith, *Life and Letters of James A. Garfield* (New Haven, 1925), II, 1044.
6. I take this formulation from a mimeographed paper (1966), "Problems of Isolation in the Presidency," prepared by Mr. Reedy for a conference at the Center for the Study of Democratic Institutions.
7. George E. Reedy, *The Twilight of the Presidency* (New York, 1970), 90–93.
8. Kennedy's introduction to Theodore C. Sorensen, *Decision-Making in the White House* (New York, 1963), xiii.
9. Reedy, *Twilight*, 96.
10. Richard M. Nixon, *Six Crises* (New York, 1962), 317.
11. Arthur M. Schlesinger, Jr., *Kennedy or Nixon: Does It Make Any Difference?* (New York, 1960), 10.
12. Huston, writing in the conservative magazine *The Alternative*, as quoted in Lou Cannon, "The Siege Psychology and How It Grew," *Washington Post*, July 29, 1973.
13. The interview quotations are from Saul Pett, *Washington Post*, January 14, 1973.

11 / Presidential Power: Restoring the Balance

Theodore J. Lowi

The presidency has grown over time because our expectations of the government have grown—especially since the 1930s—and because we have come to rely on the executive even more than Congress to fulfill those expectations. Theodore Lowi deals in the following article with what he sees as presidential incapacity for meeting the growing expectations within the system of separation of powers. Lowi considers arguments concerning two proposals—a six-year presidential term and cabinet government—and concludes that neither is a viable solution to the problem. The author places greatest confidence in "building down" the presidency, and especially in reducing the expectations that Americans have of the presidency. That alone could restore greater balance to the system.

In a single office, the presidency, the great powers of the American people have been invested, making it the most powerful office in the world. Its power is great precisely because it is truly the people's power, in the form of consent regularly granted. But there is great uncertainty about the terms of the social contract. We can know that virtually all power, limited only by the Bill of Rights, has been granted. And we can know that when the presidents take the oath of office they accept the power and the conditions for its use: the promise of performance must be met. But we cannot know what is adequate performance. No entrepreneur would ever sign a contract that leaves the conditions of fulfillment to the subjective judgment of the other party. This is precisely what has happened in the new social contract underlying the modern government of the United States.

The system of large positive national government in the United States was a deliberate construction, arising out of the 1930s. The urgency of the times and the poverty of government experience meant that the building was done exuberantly but improvisationally, without much concern for constitutional values or history. The modern presidency is the centerpiece of that construction. Considered by many a triumph of democracy, the modern American presidency is also its victim.

The gains from presidential government were immediate. Presidential government energized the executive; it gave the national government direction; it enhanced the capacity of presidential leadership to build national consensus and to overcome the natural inertia of a highly heterogeneous society. The costs of presidential government were cumulative. Most of the costs result from the fact that the expectations of the masses have grown faster than the capacity of presidential government to meet them. . . .

The Imperial/Plebiscitary Presidency

Richard Nixon was brought up on the imperial presidency and had no serious misgivings about it. Imperial meant something established, neither extreme nor extraordinary. Schlesinger could conceive of an imperial presidency precisely because it was already a real thing and not a figment of his or of Richard Nixon's imagination. Schlesinger chose the characterization *imperial* because it connotes a strong state with sovereignty and power over foreigners, as well as rank, status, privilege, and authority, and it also connotes the president's power and responsibility to do whatever he judges necessary to maintain the sovereignty of the state and its ability to keep public order, both international and domestic. The imperial presidency turns out on inspection, therefore, to be nothing more nor less than the discretionary presidency grounded in national security rather than domestic government. Characterizing the presidency as plebiscitary is not at all inconsistent; it is an attempt to capture the same factors and at the same time to tie them to the greatest source of everyday pressure on the presidency—. . . the American people and their expectations. Nixon's understanding of this situation in all its aspects was probably more extensive and complete than that of any other modern president. He understood it to a fault. If so, he was operating logically and sanely under the following assumptions:

The first assumption is that the president and the state are the same thing, that president is state personified. The second is that powers should be commensurate with responsibilities. Since most of the responsibilities of state were intentionally delegated to the president, there is every reason to assume that Congress and the people intended that there be a capacity to carry them out.

The third assumption, intimately related to the second, is that the president should not and cannot be bound by normal legal restrictions. To put this indelicately, the president's actions must be considered above the law or subject to a different kind of law from those of ordinary citizens. While not free to commit any crime merely for the sake of convenience, the president nevertheless cannot be constantly beset by considerations of legality when the state itself is or seems to be at issue.

The first three assumptions lead inexorably toward a fourth, which is that any *deliberate* barriers to presidential action must be considered tantamount to disloyalty. Barriers to presidential action can be tolerated up to a point, and it is probable that most presidents, including Richard Nixon, have prided themselves on their uncommon patience with organized protests, well-meaning but embarrassing news leaks, journalistic criticism, and organized political opposition. But there is a point beyond which such barriers cannot be tolerated, and as that point is approached, confidential knowledge of the identities and contentions of the organizers of obstructions must be gathered. When the intentions of these organizers are determined, to the president's satisfaction, to be malicious, it would be foolish for the president to wait until they are fully set in train.

If these assumptions only barely approximate Nixon's understanding of the presidency, then his actions, including his crimes, are entirely consistent and rational, quite possibly motivated by the highest sense of public interest. To reach that conclusion, however, is not to exonerate Nixon but only to bring the system and all its presidents into question. The Gulf of Tonkin incident involved a much greater deceit than Watergate. And Nixon's connection between himself and the state was never so intimate as that made by President Lyndon B. Johnson, who was even able to define the Vietnam War in personal terms: "I won't be the first to lose a war."

"Lying in state" is common practice. Presidents operate on the brink of failure and in ignorance of when, where, and how failure will come. . . . They don't know what's going on—yet they are responsible for it.

. . .Their main obligation is to preserve the myth that they are reserving themselves for the big decisions. This permits them to remain ignorant of most of what is happening; it permits them to leave most of the decisions to staff and most governing to administrators. This is presidential government. *This is presidential government?* It has frequently been observed that one of the main functions of a presidential press conference is the opportunity it provides to brief the president in order to keep him abreast of what is going on. What is presidential government between press conferences?

The presidency has great powers. The president is their victim. And so, unless we act, are we.

. . .The decade of 1962–1972 was one of the most remarkable in the history of American government. It began in almost unprecedented optimism and ended on the eve of despair. It was a period of unprecedented prosperity and of deep decline in respect for all big institutions, including corporations. It was a decade of tremendous public policy expansion and also a decade in which one president was disgraced and another was about to be deposed. . . .

The connection between expansion of government and crises of authority did not go unnoticed. During the 1970s a number of important changes were made that were intended, in one way or another, to restore balance between president and Congress. They simply were not adequate to attain that end, however, because they failed to meet one or more of the following criteria. An appropriate reform would have to deal effectively with the excessive personification of American government in the presidency. At a minimum this would require deflation of public expectations about the capacity of presidents, as individuals, to govern without collective responsibility. A good reform would have to deal with the plebiscitary nature of the presidency. Personification would be less of a problem if the only constituency were Congress and the Washington community. Therefore, a good reform would cool if not break up altogether the love affair between the masses and the president. A good reform would contribute to constitutional balance. Such balance does not have to take the form of the original Separation of Powers, although much can be said for that. As long as the American system rejects a single moral code, however, it must respect Madison's admonition that "auxiliary precautions" are necessary. The approach does not have to be Madison's, but the reform must be judged according to whether it improves the prospect of balancing power against power, ambition against ambition. Two of the most ambitious attempts to increase congressional power vis-à-vis the president—the War Powers Resolution and the Congressional Budget and Impoundment Control Act—failed to bring about any such improvement.

. . .War Powers provisions and added congressional budget controls righted no fundamental wrongs. Balance did not replace imbalance. Congress continues to delegate and defer, preferring as always to fight little battles rather than confront constitutional causes. The president continues to be plebiscitary, and presidential behavior continues to show the stresses of that situation. Parties continue to live, and decline, at the periphery. Members of Congress continue to rely, and increasingly, on political action committees (PACs), pushing parties further to the periphery. And the people, *en masse*, continue to vacillate between excessive expectations and unwarranted indignation. No wonder some of us are tempted from time to time to revive old proposals, especially if they look like panaceas. The panacea that will not die but will not, as yet, be accepted, is the constitutional provision limiting presidential tenure to one six-year term.

This remedy for excesses of presidential power is as old as the presidency itself. A nonrepeatable term was considered at the Constitutional Convention and was proposed in Congress as early as 1821 or 1826, depending on which presidential historian you consult. Although there is no open and shut case either way regarding this proposal, something important ought to be learned from the fact that it has been so attractive to so many people yet always falls short of being adopted.

The points in favor of the single six-year presidential term can be outlined simply and briefly. It would enable the president to devote all of his time to the job. Many a staffer and president-watcher has observed that a president begins his reelection campaign shortly after his inauguration. Moreover, the argument goes, the president would be free of partisan considerations and could be the leader of all the people. The single six-year term proposal enjoyed a particularly strong revival in the mid-1970s because of the assumption that Watergate would not have occurred at all if the Nixon people had not been so obsessed with reelection.

Everything that can be said in favor of the single six-year term boils down to the single argument that politics should be taken out of the office. As James MacGregor Burns observed, this issue is indicative of the ambivalence of the American people, including American presidents, toward the presidency itself and all its power. Every president between Harry Truman and Jimmy Carter, with the possible exception of Dwight Eisenhower, seems to have at one time or another favored a severe constitutional limitation on presidential tenure.[1] They may later have switched their positions, but that in itself is indicative of ambivalence toward the power and the potential imbalance in the office.

The case against the single six-year term reform is more complex but at least equally compelling—considerably more compelling to some people. First, any constitutional limit on the number of terms that can be served is a violation of democratic principles, which favor accountability through election, of which reelection is an essential part. On this ground the Twentieth Amendment, limiting presidents to two four-year terms, was also an extremely dubious reform. Second, even if we can justify an exception to the principle of accountability through election, it is impossible to determine the ideal length of the single term. Woodrow Wilson made this point in his case against the single six-year term, "Four years is too long a term for a president who is not the true spokesman of the people [and] is too short a term for a president who is doing, or attempting, a great work of reform, and who has not had time to finish it."[2]

Another strong argument against the single six-year term is that it would remove the presidency still further from party politics and thrust it still further into mass politics. Adoption of important policies requires a long and involved process of mobilizing support. Presidential leadership is needed, but the role it plays here is not simple. Freedom from reelection cannot alter that but can change the process, reinforcing the plebiscitary character of the presidency by freeing the president from party but not from popularity.

It is also persuasively argued that a president elected to a single six-year term would still have a gigantic bureaucracy to confront. As unwieldly as that gigantic bureaucracy is, it is more responsive to a popularly supported president and an enthusiastic Congress than to anything else.

While all those points are worth making in an evaluation of the single six-year term, it is curious to me that one of the most telling points against the single, nonrepeatable term has not been advanced. . . . This kind of constitutional limitation on elections is generally a product of systems with weak or nonexistent political parties. Since there is no party continuity or corporate party integrity in such systems, there is no basis for putting trust in the desire for reelection as a safeguard against bad management. Better under those conditions to operate on the basis of negative assumptions against incumbents. . . . And though the association of the nonrepeatable election with weak political parties is not in itself an argument against the limitation, the fallout from this association does contribute significantly to the negative argument. To put the matter bluntly, single-term limitations are strongly associated with corruption. In any weak party system, including the national presidential system, the onus of making deals and compromises, both shady and honorable, rests heavily upon individual candidates. Without some semblance of corporate integrity in a party, individual candidates have few opportunities to amortize their obligations across the spectrum of elective and appointive jobs and policy proposals. The deals tend to be personalized and the payoffs come home to roost accordingly. If that situation is already endemic in conditions of weak or no parties, adding to it the limitation against reelection means that the candidates and officials, already prevented from amortizing their deals across space, are also unable to amortize their obligations across time. This makes for a highly pressurized situation, where all the deals have to be personal and immediate. And it is a highly corrupting situation, turned from bad in the absence of a party ticket to worse in the absence of the time perspective produced by the prospect of reelection. . . .

The single six-year term for presidents is a reform comparable to the party and campaign finance reforms of the 1970s. It is an effort to compensate for the absence of a viable party system, but it is a compensation ultimately paid for by further weakening of the party system itself. Observers, especially foreign observers, have often noted that one source of weakness in American political parties is the certainty of election every two or four years. This, they say, is already an unjustifiable limitation on the electoral process, not only because any artificial limitation on elections is a violation of democratic principles but also because when elections are set in a certain and unchangeable cycle, political parties do not have to remain alert but can disappear into inactivity until a known point prior to the next election. In contrast, parliamentary systems in which elections can be called essentially at any time, depending upon political advantage or the maturation of a certain issue, require relatively continuous alertness on the part of party leaders, party candidates, and party workers. To rigidify matters by going beyond the determinacy of the electoral cycle to add an absolute rule of one term would hang still another millstone around the neck of already doddering political parties.

I can only hope that the addition of this argument to the negative case will contribute to a definitive and final rout of the single six-year term as a reform. . . .

Clearly one of the most desirable reforms would be a real cabinet around the presidency. A cabinet combines the advantages of a single chief executive with those of a plural executive. A cabinet would cut down, without eliminating, the personification of government in the plebiscitary presidency. Any number of advantages flow from the introduction of collective responsibility.

Unfortunately, this proposal runs afoul of a law governing all reform proposals: *There is an inverse relationship between feasibility and effectiveness.* A small step toward the development of a cabinet might have been taken after 1976, when Ronald Reagan identified his vice presidential running mate before the balloting and proposed that such a step be made a rule of the Republican party. If this same principle were expanded slightly, a true cabinet might develop. The important part of the early naming of appointees would be to identify the group *as a group* and to associate the members with the president and with the electoral process. This practice would give voters a much better sense of the shape and direction of the eventual administration, and at the same time it would provide the president with a true basis for sharing his responsibilities.

Effective as a cabinet would be, it is not feasible as long as the political parties are as weak as they are. Preelection identification of top appointees might help restore some strength to the national political parties, but a number of other conditions favorable to strong parties would also have to prevail. The point is that a cabinet is an instrument of party government and is difficult to conceive or construct without a minimum of party continuity and organizational integrity. At the present time, both the major parties fall below this minimum. . . .

Presidential Power: If Building It Up Won't Work, Try Building It Down

America approaches the end of the twentieth century with an enormous bureaucratized government, a plebiscitary presidency, and apparent faith that the latter can impose on the former an accountability sufficient to meet the rigorous test of democratic theory. Anyone who really shares this faith is living under a happy state of delusion. Anyone who does not believe and argues it nevertheless is engaging in one of Plato's Noble Lies; that is to say, the leaders do not believe it but believe it is in the public interest that the rest of us believe it. Then there are others who don't believe it but would like to make it the truth by giving the president more and more help. Presidents have themselves tried nearly everything to build for themselves a true capacity to govern.

Congress, with few exceptions, has cooperated. The Supreme Court, with two minor exceptions, has cooperated. The public seems willing to cooperate in making truth out of the noble lie by investing more and more power in the presidency. The intellectuals, perhaps most of all, have cooperated. If that's not enough, then it's possible nothing is enough.

Since building up the presidency has not met the problem of presidential capacity to govern, the time has come to consider building it down. Building down goes against the mentality of American capitalism, whose primary measure of success is buildups. [Buildups] are so important to American corporate managers that they fake them if necessary, through anything from useless mergers to misrepresentation of profits. Very few leaders have tried to succeed by making a virtue of building down. There was Bismarck, who perceived greater strength in a "smaller Germany." There may be a case or two of weekly magazines whose publishers have sought to strengthen their position by abandoning the struggle for a maximum mass subscription in favor of a smaller and more select but stable readership. But most leaders, in commerce and government, are guilty of what Barry Goldwater popularized in the 1960s, "growthmanship." In many circumstances, building up is an illusory solution, or, at best, a short-term gain.

The most constructive approach to building down the presidency would be the strengthening of political parties. If party organizations returned to the center of presidential selection, they would build down the presidency by making collective responsibility a natural outcome of the selection process rather than an alien intruder. Real parties build down the presidency in constructive ways by making real cabinets possible. The present selection process and the present relationship between the president and public opinion produced the star symbol that renders a president's sharing power almost inconceivable. The selection process with parties involved makes the star system itself hard to conceive of.

A three-party system comes into the picture in at least two ways. First, if a two-party system is indeed an anachronism in modern programmatic governments, a three-party system could be the most reasonable way to make real parties possible. Second, a three-party system might build down the presidency by making it more of a parliamentary office. This development would constitute something of a return to the original intent of the Founders' design, a selection process culminating in the House of Representatives. The French improved upon their system by mixing theirs with ours to create the Fifth Republic. It is time we consider mixing ours with theirs. The Fifth Republic established a better balance than we have by successfully imposing an independently elected president upon a strong parliament, giving the parliament the leadership lacking in the Fourth Republic but keeping the popularly elected president tied closely to it.

The crying need to impose parliamentary responsibility in our independently elected president can be accomplished without formally amending the Constitution. Just as the two-party system transformed the presidential selection system and thereby the presidency, so would a three-party or multiparty system transform the presidency, by bringing Congress back into the selection process. This transformation could, in addition, give Congress incentive to confront the real problems of the presidency. Although I admit that is unlikely, the probability could be improved as more of its members came to realize that Congress's survival as an institution may depend upon depriving the presidency of its claim to represent the Great American Majority. The presidency must be turned into a more parliamentary office.

Presidents who are products of the present system are also unlikely to try to change it—unless they come to recognize its inherent pathologies. The first president to recognize these pathologies will want to build down the presidency, and his or her legacy will be profound and lasting. A president who recognizes the pathology of the plebiscitary presidency will demand changes that will ward off failure and encourage shared responsibility. At a minimum, a rational president would veto congressional enactments delegating powers so broad and so vague that expectations cannot be met. This step in itself would build down the presidency in a very special way: It would incorporate more of Congress into the presidency because the clearer the intentions and the criteria of performance written into a statute, the more responsibility for its outcomes would be shared by the majority in Congress responsible for its passage. Such a way of building down alone would not produce a third party, but it would make the presidency more parliamentary, and thus more accommodating to strong parties and to three parties or more. Put this way, the prospect does not seem so unrealistic. To accomplish it, the president must simply make an analysis of the situation. A president must simply change his point of view.

Institutional reform is desperately needed, but the struggle for reform must be sensitive to the probability that there are no specific and concrete solutions for the problems of the plebiscitary presidency. One of the mischievous consequences of mixing technology and democracy is *belief in solutions*. Solutions are for puzzles. Big government is not a puzzle. The plebiscitary presidency is not a puzzle. Each is a source of important problems because, like all institutions, each is built on some basic contradictions. These contradictions will not go away, because they are the result of mixing highly desirable goals that don't mix well. There is, for example, a contradiction between representation and efficiency. There is a contradiction between specialization and humanization. There is a contradiction between the goal of treating everyone equally and the goal of giving special attention to individual variation. There tend to be contradictions wherever demand is intense and supply is limited. Problems in any institution are likely to grow in importance and danger whenever people lose their appreciation for the contradictions inherent in an institution and proceed to maximize one side of a contradiction at the expense of the other. For such contradictions and the problems of balance among desirable but contradictory goals, *coping* is a more realistic goal than *solving*. Successful coping comes mainly from understanding, and the chief barrier to understanding is ideology—the steadfast defense of existing practices and existing distributions of power.

On one point at least there is strong agreement between my argument and Ronald Reagan: his observation that where once government was part of the solution it is now part of the problem. Since I have been arguing the same thing at least since 1969,[3] I celebrate Reagan's recognition of the truth and regret the fact he does not actually believe it. He embraced big government and embraced, nay, enlarged the plebiscitary presidency more than most of his predecessors. Why do all recent presidents and important presidential aspirants look back with such admiration to Harry Truman, a man of such ordinary character and talents? I think they do so because Truman was the last president who was made bigger by the office he occupied. This is not to say that recent presidents have made more mistakes than presidents of the past. It is to say that they have been diminished by having to achieve so much more than past presidents and by having to use so much more deception to compensate for their failures. Modern presidents blame their failures on everything but the presidency, when the fault is the presidency more than anything else. It is there that successful coping must begin, with a change of attitude toward the plebiscitary presidency that will enable presidents and presidential candidates to confront the contradictions in the modern presidency rather than by embracing the office as it is.

Notes

1. James MacGregor Burns, *The Power to Lead: The Crisis of the American Presidency* (New York: Simon & Schuster, 1984), 181–82.
2. Quoted in Thomas E. Cronin, *The State Of the Presidency*, 2d ed. (Boston: Little, Brown, 1980), 356. This is an excerpt from Cronin's own excellent assessment of the single six-year term.
3. "The crisis of the 1960s is at bottom a political crisis, a crisis of public authority. During the Depression, stability was regained after a spectacular but unrevolutionary turn to government.... But today government itself is the problem." Theodore J. Lowi, *The End of Liberalism*, 1st ed. (New York: Norton, 1969), xiii.

CHAPTER FOUR

Federalism and Intergovernmental Relations

By 1787, the framers had already experienced six years of a very weak national government under the Articles of Confederation. The word *confederation* itself implies weak national government serving the common purposes of stronger state governments, and it is difficult to imagine national government being much weaker than it was under the Articles. Though the national government was given some potentially important "external" powers, including the "power of determining on peace and war," it was given few "internal" powers. Missing, for instance, was the power to regulate interstate or foreign commerce and, most importantly for being able to carry out its other limited powers, the Congress was given no independent taxing authority. The states, on the other hand, retained their "sovereignty, freedom, and independence," along with all powers not expressly delegated to the Congress.

Six years of experience provided ample evidence that the states could not cooperate sufficiently to achieve what the framers saw as the national good.* Economic and political problems were dramatically joined in events such as Shays' Rebellion, and Congress was impotent to help solve either the causes or the violent effects.

When the framers met in Philadelphia, confederation would give way to federalism. The national government would be given commerce powers and, most importantly, an effective power to tax. Other powers would be granted or denied to the national or state governments, but not all of the aspects of the federal arrangement would be clearly spelled out in the Constitution. Sufficient issues would remain to fuel future debates in both the political and judicial arenas. There would be enough room for both levels to vie for expanded powers, to maneuver for the upper hand.

Just as imbalances of power among the branches of the national government continue to occur and to be a source of some concern, even within a structure of checks and balances, so has the distribution of power among levels of government changed within the structure of federalism. The framers intended the national government to be more powerful than it had been under the Articles of Confederation, but exactly how powerful, relative to the states, remains a debated issue more than 200 years after the Constitution was written.

The fact that the levels of government not only compete with one another but also depend upon one another for resources and services complicates matters in American federalism. Money that is spent by state or local governments may

---

*While this was the pervasive view of those in attendance at the Convention, there was much less agreement outside the Convention over the desirability of stronger national government. This would become quite evident during the ratification process, as ardent anti-federalists spoke strongly against the new Constitution.—*Editor's Note.*

actually have been collected by the national government, matched by state funds, and spent according to guidelines established by Congress. Intergovernmental relations are so complex today that it is very difficult to assess credit or blame for many programs that defy an easy answer to the question: where does the *power* lie?

The readings of this chapter demonstrate that American federalism is complex, changeable, and above all, debatable. James Madison's *Federalist* no. 39 and Chief Justice John Marshall's opinion in *McCulloch v. Maryland* both clarify some of the important issues that continue to sustain debate over states' rights versus national powers. Charles Rice argues that faulty application of the Fourteenth Amendment (also discussed in Chapter Two) in constraining state and local governments has contributed to an imbalance of power in favor of Washignton, and hence to the erosion of federalism. John Shannon describes a number of recent developments that have contributed to a relationship among the three layers of government that is increasingly competitive, both politically and financially. John Kincaid documents transition from a situation where international affairs was almost exclusively the domain of the national government to one where state and local governments are significantly involved in a number of ways. In the final reading in this chapter, David Kennedy suggests that one continuity of American federalism, the "law of appropriateness," can help the untrained observer to understand what is going on even in today's complex world of intergovernmental relations.

12 / *Federalist Paper* no. 39

James Madison

In *Federalist* no. 39, James Madison (as Publius) responds to allegations of anti-federalists that the new Constitution was designed not to produce federalism, but rather to effectively replace a loose confederation of state governments by national government. Madison argues that the proposed system is a mixture of the national and federal forms, within which the states remain powerful.

Number 39 The Conformity of the Plan to Republican Principles
To the People of the State of New York: The last paper having concluded the observations which were meant to introduce a candid survey of the plan of government reported by the convention, we now proceed to the execution of that part of our undertaking.

The first question that offers itself is, whether the general form and aspect of the government be strictly republican. It is evident that no other form would be reconcilable with the genius of the people of America; with the fundamental principles of the Revolution; or with that honorable determination which animates every votary of freedom, to rest all our political experiments on the capacity of mankind for self-government. If the plan of the convention, therefore, be found to depart from the republican character, its advocates must abandon it as no longer defensible.

What, then, are the distinctive characters of the republican form? Were an answer to the question to be sought, not by recurring to principles, but in the application of the term by political writers, to the constitutions of different States, no satisfactory one would ever be found. Holland, in which no particle of the supreme authority is derived from the people, has passed almost universally under the denomination of a republic. The same title has been bestowed on Venice, where absolute power over the great body of the people is exercised, in the most absolute manner, by a small body of hereditary nobles. Poland, which is a mixture of aristocracy and of monarchy in their worst forms, has been dignified with the same appellation. The government of England, which has one republican branch only, combined with an hereditary aristocracy and monarchy, has, with equal impropriety, been frequently placed on the list of republics. These examples, which are nearly as dissimilar to each other as to a genuine republic, show the extreme inaccuracy with which the term has been used in political disquisitions.

If we resort for a criterion to the different principles on which different forms of government are established, we may define a republic to be, or at least may bestow that name on, a government which derives all its powers directly or indirectly from the great body of the people, and is administered by persons holding their offices during pleasure, for a limited period, or during good behavior. It is *essential* to such a government that it be derived from the great body of the society, not from an inconsiderable proportion, or a favored class of it; otherwise a handful of tyrannical nobles, exercising their oppressions by a delegation of their powers, might aspire to the rank of republicans, and claim for their government the honorable title of republic. It is *sufficient* for such a government that the persons administering it be appointed, either directly or indirectly, by the people; and that they hold their appointments by either of the tenures just specified; otherwise every government in the United States, as well as every other popular government that has been or can be well organized or well executed, would be degraded from the republican character. According to the constitution of every State in the Union, some or other of the officers of government are appointed indirectly only by the people. According to most of them, the chief magistrate himself is so appointed. And according to one, this mode of appointment is extended to one of the coordinate branches of the legislature. According to all the constitutions, also, the tenure of the highest offices is extended to a definite period, and in many instances, both within the legislative and executive departments, to a period of years. According to the provisions of most of the constitutions, again, as well as according to the most respectable and received opinions on the subject, the members of the judiciary department are to retain their offices by the firm tenure of good behavior.

On comparing the Constitution planned by the convention with the standard here fixed, we perceive at once that it is, in the most rigid sense, conformable to it. The House of Representatives, like that of one branch at least of all the State legislatures, is elected immediately by the great body of the people. The Senate, like the present Congress, and the Senate of

Maryland, derives its appointment indirectly from the people. The President is indirectly derived from the choice of the people, according to the example in most of the States. Even the judges with all other officers of the Union, will, as in the several States, be the choice, though a remote choice, of the people themselves. The duration of the appointments is equally conformable to the republican standard, and to the model of State constitutions. The House of Representatives is periodically elective, as in all the States; and for the period of two years, as in the State of South Carolina. The Senate is elective, for a period of six years; which is but one year more than the period of the Senate of Maryland, and but two more than that of the Senates of New York and Virginia. The President is to continue in office for the period of four years; as in New York and Delaware the chief magistrate is elected for three years, and in South Carolina for two years. In the other States the election is annual. In several of the States, however, no constitutional provision is made for the impeachment of the chief magistrate. And in Delaware and Virginia he is not impeachable till out of office. The President of the United States is impeachable at any time during his continuance in office. The tenure by which the judges are to hold their places, is, as it unquestionably ought to be, that of good behavior. The tenure of the ministerial offices generally, will be a subject of legal regulation, conformably to the reason of the case and the example of the State constitutions.

Could any further proof be required of the republican complexion of this system, the most decisive one might be found in its absolute prohibition of titles of nobility, both under the federal and the State governments; and in its express guaranty of the republican form to each of the latter.

"But it was not sufficient," say the adversaries of the proposed Constitution, "for the convention to adhere to the republican form. They ought, with equal care, to have preserved the *federal* form, which regards the Union as a *Confederacy* of sovereign states; instead of which, they have framed a *national* government, which regards the Union as a *consolidation* of the States." And it is asked by what authority this bold and radical innovation was undertaken? The handle which has been made of this objection requires that it should be examined with some precision.

Without inquiring into the accuracy of the distinction on which the objection is founded, it will be necessary to a just estimate of its force, first, to ascertain the real character of the government in question; secondly, to inquire how far the convention were authorized to propose such a government; and thirdly, how far the duty they owed to their country could supply any defect of regular authority.

First.—In order to ascertain the real character of the government, it may be considered in relation to the foundation on which it is to be established; to the sources from which its ordinary powers are to be drawn; to the operation of those powers; to the extent of them; and to the authority by which future changes in the government are to be introduced.

On examining the first relation, it appears, on one hand, that the Constitution is to be founded on the assent and ratification of the people of

America, given by deputies elected for the special purpose, but, on the other, that this assent and ratification is to be given by the people, not as individuals composing one entire nation, but as composing the distinct and independent States to which they respectively belong. It is to be the assent and ratification of the several States, derived from the supreme authority in each State,— the authority of the people themselves. The act, therefore, establishing the Constitution, will not be a *national*, but a *federal* act.

That it will be a federal and not a national act, as these terms are understood by the objectors; the act of the people, as forming so many independent States, not as forming one aggregate nation, is obvious from this single consideration, that it is to result neither from the decision of a *majority* of the people of the Union, nor from that of a *majority* of the States. It must result from the *unanimous* assent of the several States that are parties to it, differing no otherwise from their ordinary assent than in its being expressed, not by the legislative authority, but by that of the people themselves. Were the people regarded in this transaction as forming one nation, the will of the majority of the whole people of the United States would bind the minority, in the same manner as the majority in each State must bind the minority; and the will of the majority must be determined either by a comparison of the individual votes, or by considering the will of the majority of the States as evidence of the will of a majority of the people of the United States. Neither of these rules has been adopted. Each State, in ratifying the Constitution, is considered as a sovereign body, independent of all others, and only to be bound by its own voluntary act. In this relation, then, the new Constitution will, if established, be a *federal*, and not a *national* constitution.

The next relation is, to the sources from which the ordinary powers of government are to be derived. The House of Representatives will derive its powers from the people of America; and the people will be represented in the same proportion, and on the same principle, as they are in the legislature of a particular State. So far the government is *national*, not *federal*. The Senate, on the other hand, will derive its powers from the States, as political and coequal societies; and these will be represented on the principle of equality in the Senate, as they now are in the existing Congress. So far the government is *federal*, not *national*. The executive power will be derived from a very compound source. The immediate election of the President is to be made by the States in their political characters. The votes allotted to them are in a compound ratio, which considers them partly as distinct and coequal societies, partly as unequal members of the same society. The eventual election, again, is to be made by that branch of the legislature which consists of the national representatives; but in this particular act they are to be thrown into the form of individual delegations, from so many distinct and coequal bodies politic. From this aspect of the government, it appears to be of a mixed character, presenting at least as many *federal* as *national* features.

The difference between a federal and national government, as it relates to the *operation of the government*, is supposed to consist in this, that in the former the powers operate on the political bodies composing the Confederacy, in their political capacities; in the latter, on the individual citizens composing the nation, in their individual capacities. On trying the Constitution by this criterion, it falls under the *national*, not the *federal* character; though perhaps not so completely as has been understood. In several cases, and particularly in the trial of controversies to which States may be parties, they must be viewed and proceeded against in their collective and political capacities only. So far the national countenance of the government on this side seems to be disfigured by a few federal features. But this blemish is perhaps unavoidable in any plan; and the operation of the government on the people, in their individual capacities, in its ordinary and most essential proceedings, may, on the whole, designate it, in this relation, a *national* government.

But if the government be national with regard to the *operation* of its powers, it changes its aspect again when we contemplate it in relation to the extent of its powers. The idea of a national government involves in it, not only an authority over the individual citizens, but an indefinite supremacy over all persons and things, so far as they are objects of lawful government. Among a people consolidated into one nation, this supremacy is completely vested in the national legislature. Among communities united for particular purposes, it is vested partly in the general and partly in the municipal legislatures. In the former case, all local authorities are subordinate to the supreme; and may be controlled, directed, or abolished by it at pleasure. In the latter, the local or municipal authorities form distinct and independent portions of the supremacy, no more subject, within their respective spheres, to the general authority, than the general authority is subject to them, within its own sphere. In this relation, then, the proposed government cannot be deemed a *national* one; since its jurisdiction extends to certain enumerated objects only, and leaves to the several States a residuary and inviolable sovereignty over all other objects. It is true that in controversies relating to the boundary between the two jurisdictions, the tribunal which is ultimately to decide, is to be established under the general government. But this does not change the principle of the case. The decision is to be impartially made, according to the rules of the Constitution; and all the usual and most effectual precautions are taken to secure this impartiality. Some such tribunal is clearly essential to prevent an appeal to the sword and a dissolution of the compact; and that it ought to be established under the general rather than under the local governments, or, to speak more properly, that it could be safely established under the first alone, is a position not likely to be combated.

If we try the Constitution by its last relation to the authority by which amendments are to be made, we find it neither wholly *national* nor wholly *federal*. Were it wholly national, the supreme and ultimate authority would reside in the *majority* of the people of the Union; and this authority would be competent at all times, like that of a majority of every national society, to alter or abolish its established government. Were it wholly federal, on the other hand, the concurrence of each state in the Union would be essential to every alteration that would be binding on all. The mode provided by the plan of the convention is not founded on either of these principles. In requiring more than a majority, and particularly in computing the proportion by *States*, not by *citizens*, it departs from the *national* and advances towards the *federal* character; in rendering the concurrence of less than the whole number of States sufficient, it loses again the *federal* and partakes of the *national* character.

The proposed Constitution, therefore, is, in strictness, neither a national nor a federal Constitution, but a composition of both. In its foundation it is federal, not national; in the sources from which the ordinary powers of the government are drawn, it is partly federal and partly national; in the operation of these powers, it is national, not federal; in the extent of them, again, it is federal, not national; and, finally, in the authoritative mode of introducing amendments, it is neither wholly federal nor wholly national.

Publius

13 / *McCulloch v. Maryland*
4 Wheaton 316 (1819)

Though it was clear from the time of the writing of the Constitution that the authors intended the national government to be more powerful than it had been under the Articles of Confederation, questions arose early on—and persist today—concerning the exact relationship of national to state powers within the federal system. Three decades after ratification of the Constitution, the Supreme Court was presented with an opportunity to address the most fundamental principles involved in the debate over state vs. national powers.

The case of *McCulloch v. Maryland* (1819) arose out of Congress's chartering of a national bank in Baltimore, and the state of Maryland's attempt to tax that bank. James McCulloch, a cashier for the national bank, refused to pay the tax, and Maryland subsequently won support in a state court for its efforts to obtain the money. Though McCulloch lost in his appeal to the state's highest court, he was ultimately vindicated in his appeal to the U.S. Supreme Court.

In writing the Court's opinion, Chief Justice John Marshall indicated that the Supreme Court had considered two related questions: (1) did Congress have the power to incorporate the bank, and (2) if so, did a state have the right to tax such a bank? Based primarily upon the "supremacy clause" of Article 6 and the "necessary and proper clause" of Article 1, the Court found in favor of Congress's "implied" power to create the bank and against Maryland's right to tax it. In short, the decision upheld an "expansion" of national power at the expense of the states. Many later decisions, based in part on the precedent of *McCulloch v. Maryland*, would do likewise.

Marshall, Ch. J., delivered the opinion of the court:

In the case now to be determined, the defendant, a sovereign state, denies the obligation of a law enacted by the legislature of the Union, and the plaintiff, on his part, contests the validity of an act which has been passed by the legislature of that state. The constitution of our country, in its most interesting and vital parts, is to be considered; the conflicting powers of the government of the Union and of its members, as marked in that constitution, are to be discussed; and an opinion given, which may essentially influence the great operations of the government. No tribunal can approach such a question without a deep sense of its importance, and of the awful responsibility involved in its decision. But it must be decided peacefully, or remain a source of hostile legislation, perhaps of hostility of a still more serious nature; and if it is to be so decided, by this tribunal alone can the decision be made. On the Supreme Court of the United States has the constitution of our country devolved this important duty.

The first question made in the cause is, has Congress power to incorporate a bank?

It has been truly said that this can scarcely be considered as an open question, entirely unprejudiced by the former proceedings of the nation respecting it. The principle now contested was introduced at a very early period of our history, has been recognized by many successive legislatures, and has been acted upon by the judicial department, in cases of peculiar delicacy, as a law of undoubted obligation. . . .

It will not be denied that a bold and daring usurpation might be resisted, after an acquiescence still longer and more complete than this. But it is conceived that a doubtful question, one on which human reason may pause, and the human judgment be suspended, in the decision of which the great principles of liberty are not concerned, but the respective powers of those who are equally the representatives of the people, are to be adjusted; if not put at rest by the practice of government, ought to receive a considerable impression from that practice. An exposition of the constitution, deliberately established by legislative acts, on the faith of which an immense property has been advanced, ought not to be lightly disregarded.

The power now contested was exercised by the first Congress elected under the present constitution. The bill for incorporating the bank of the United States did not steal upon an unsuspecting legislature, and pass unobserved. Its principle was completely understood, and was opposed with equal zeal and ability. After being resisted, first in the fair and open field of debate, and afterwards in the executive cabinet, with as much persevering talent as any measure has ever experienced, and being supported by arguments which convinced minds as pure and as intelligent as this country can boast, it became a law. The original act was permitted to expire; but a short experience of the embarrassments to which the refusal to revive it exposed the government, convinced those who were most prejudiced against the measure of its necessity and induced the passage of the present law. It would require no ordinary share of intrepidity to assert that a measure adopted under these circumstances was a bold and plain usurpation, to which the constitution gave no countenance.

These observations belong to the cause; but they are not made under the impression that, were the question entirely new, the law would be found irreconcilable with the constitution.

In discussing this question, the counsel for the state of Maryland have deemed it of some importance, in the construction of the constitution, to consider that instrument not as emanating from the people, but as the act of sovereign and independent states. The powers of the general government, it has been said, are delegated by the states, who alone are truly sovereign; and must be exercised in subordination to the states, who alone possess supreme dominion.

It would be difficult to sustain this proposition. The convention which framed the constitution was indeed elected by the state legislatures. But the instrument, when it came from their hands, was a mere proposal, without obligation, or pretensions to it. It was reported to the then existing Congress of the United States, with a request that it might "be submitted to a convention of delegates, chosen in each state by the people thereof, under the recommendation of its legislature, for their assent and ratification." This mode of proceeding was adopted; and by the convention, by Congress, and by the state legislatures, the instrument was submitted to the people. They acted upon it in the only manner in which they can act safely, effectively, and wisely, on such a subject, by assembling in convention. It is true, they assembled in their several states—and where else should they have assembled? No political dreamer was ever wild enough to think of breaking down the lines which separate the states, and of compounding the American people into one common mass. Of consequence, when they act, they act in their states. But the measures they adopt do not, on that account, cease to be the measures of the people themselves, or become the measures of the state governments.

From these conventions the constitution derives its whole authority. The government proceeds directly from the people; is "ordained and established" in the name of the people; and is declared to be ordained, "in order to form a more perfect union, establish justice, insure domestic tranquillity, and secure the blessings of liberty to themselves and to their posterity." The assent of the states, in their sovereign capacity, is implied in calling a convention, and thus submitting that instrument to the people. But the people were at perfect liberty to accept or reject it; and their act was final. . . .

It has been said that the people had already surrendered all their powers to the state sovereignties, and had nothing more to give. But, surely, the question whether they may resume and modify the powers granted to government does not remain to be settled in this country. Much more might the legitimacy of the general government be doubted, had it been created by the states. The powers delegated to the state sovereignties were to be exercised by themselves, not by a distinct and independent sovereignty, created by themselves. To the formation of a league, such as was the confederation, the state sovereignties were certainly competent. But when "in order to form a more perfect union," it was deemed necessary to change this alliance into an effective government, possessing great and sovereign powers, and acting directly on the people, the necessity of referring it to the people, and of deriving its powers directly from them, was felt and acknowledged by all.

The government of the Union, then (whatever may be the influence of this fact on the case), is, emphatically, and truly, a government of the people. In form and in substance it emanates from them. Its powers are granted by them, and are to be exercised directly on them, and for their benefit.

This government is acknowledged by all to be one of enumerated powers. The principle, that it can exercise only the powers granted to it, would seem too apparent to have required to be enforced by all those arguments which its enlightened friends, while it was depending before the people, found it necessary to urge, that principle is now universally admitted. But the question respecting the extent of the powers actually granted, is perpetually arising, and will probably continue to arise, as long as our system shall exist.

In discussing these questions, the conflicting powers of the general and state governments must be brought into view, and the supremacy of their respective laws, when they are in opposition, must be settled.

If any one proposition could command the universal assent of mankind, we might expect it would be this—that the government of the Union, though limited in its powers, is supreme within its sphere of action. This would seem to result necessarily from its nature. It is the government of all; its powers are delegated by all; it represents all, and acts for all. Though any one state may be willing to control its operations, no state is willing to allow others to control them. The nation, on those subjects on which it can act, must necessarily bind its component parts. But this question is not left to mere reason; the people have, in express terms, decided it by saying, "this constitution, and the laws of the United States, which shall be made in pursuance thereof," "shall be the supreme law of the land," and by requiring that the members of the state legislatures, and the officers of the executive and judicial departments of the states shall take the oath of fidelity to it.

The government of the United States, then, though limited in its powers, is supreme; and its laws, when made in pursuance of the constitution, form the supreme law of the land, "anything in the constitution or laws of any state to the contrary notwithstanding."

Among the enumerated powers, we do not find that of establishing a bank or creating a corporation. But there is no phrase in the instrument which, like the articles of confederation, excludes incidental or implied powers; and which requires that everything granted shall be expressly and minutely described. Even the 10th amendment, which was framed for the purpose of quieting the excessive jealousies which had been excited, omits the word "expressly," and declares only that the powers "not delegated to the United States, nor prohibited to the states, are reserved to the states or to the people;" thus leaving the question, whether the particular power which may become the subject of contest has been delegated to the one government, or prohibited to the other, to depend on a fair construction of the whole instrument. The men who drew and adopted this amendment had experienced the embarrassments resulting from the insertion of this word in the articles of confederation, and probably omitted it to avoid those embarrassments. A constitution, to contain an accurate detail of all the subdivisions of which its great powers will admit, and of all the means by which they may be carried into execution, would partake of a prolixity of a legal code, and could scarcely be embraced by the human mind. It would probably never be understood by the public. Its nature, therefore, requires, that only its great outlines should be marked, its important objects designated, and the minor ingredients which compose those objects be deduced from the nature of the objects themselves. That this idea was entertained by the framers of the American constitution, is not only to be inferred from the nature of the instrument, but from the language. Why else were some of the limitations, found in the ninth section of the 1st article, introduced? It is also, in some degree, warranted by their having omitted to use any restrictive term which might prevent its receiving a fair and just interpretation. In considering this question, then, we must never forget that it is a constitution we are expounding.

Although, among the enumerated powers of government, we do not find the word "bank" or "incorporation," we find the great powers to lay and collect taxes; to borrow money; to regulate commerce; to declare and conduct a war; and to raise and support armies and navies. The sword and the purse, all the external relations, and no inconsiderable portion of the industry of the nation, are entrusted to its government. It can never be pretended that these vast powers draw after them others of inferior importance, merely because they are inferior. Such an idea can never be advanced. But it may with great reason be contended, that a government, entrusted with such ample powers, on the due execution of which the happiness and prosperity of the nation so vitally depends, must also be entrusted with ample means for their execution. The power being given, it is the interest of the nation to facilitate its execution. It can never be their interest, and cannot be presumed to have been their intention, to clog and embarrass its execution by withholding the most appropriate means. Throughout this vast republic, from the St. Croix to the Gulf of Mexico, from the Atlantic to the Pacific, revenue is to be collected and expended, armies are to be marched and supported. The exigencies of the nation may require that the treasure raised in the north should be transported to the south, that raised in the east conveyed to the west, or that this order should be reversed. Is that construction of the constitution to be preferred which would render these operations difficult, hazardous, and expensive? Can we adopt that construction (unless the words imperiously require it) which would impute to the framers of that instrument, when granting these powers for the public good, the intention of impeding their exercise by withholding a choice of means? If, indeed, such be the mandate of the constitution, we have only to obey; but that instrument does not profess to enumerate the means by which the powers it confers may be executed; nor does it prohibit the creation of a corporation, if the existence of such a being be essential to the beneficial exercise of those powers. It is, then, the subject of fair inquiry, how far such means may be employed....

But [the] constitution of the United States has not left the right of Congress to employ the necessary means for the execution of the powers conferred on the government to general reasoning. To its enumeration of powers is added that of making "all laws which shall be necessary and proper, for carrying into execution the foregoing powers, and all other powers vested by this constitution, in the government of the United States, or in any department thereof.". . .

The result of the most careful and attentive consideration bestowed upon this clause is, that if it does not enlarge, it cannot be construed to restrain the powers of Congress, or to impair the right of the legislature to exercise its best judgment in the selection of measures to carry into execution the constitutional powers of the government. If no other motive for its insertion can be suggested, a sufficient one is found in the desire to remove all doubts respecting the right to legislate on that vast mass of incidental powers which must be involved in the constitution, if that instrument be not a splendid bauble.

We admit, as all must admit, that the powers of the government are limited, and that its limits are not to be transcended. But we think the sound construction of the constitution must allow to the national legislature that discretion, with respect to the means by which the powers it confers are to be carried into execution, which will enable that body to perform the high duties assigned to it, in the manner most beneficial to the people. Let the end be legitimate, let it be within the scope of the constitution, and all means which are appropriate, which are plainly adapted to that end, which are not prohibited, but consist with the letter and spirit of the constitution, are constitutional....

After the most deliberate consideration, it is the unanimous and decided opinion of this court that the act to incorporate the bank of the United States is a law made in pursuance of the constitution, and is a part of the supreme law of the land....

It being the opinion of the court that the act incorporating the bank is constitutional, and that the power of establishing a branch in the state of Maryland might be properly exercised by the bank itself, we proceed to inquire: Whether the state of Maryland may, without violating the constitution, tax that branch?

That the power of taxation is one of vital importance; that it is retained by the states; that it is not abridged by the grant of a similar power to the government of the Union; that it is to be concurrently exercised by the two governments: are truths which have never been denied. But, such is the paramount character of the constitution that its capacity to withdraw any subject from the action of even this power, is admitted. The states are expressly forbidden to lay any duties on imports or exports, except what may be absolutely necessary for executing their inspection laws. If the obligation of this prohibition must be conceded—if it may restrain a state from the exercise of its taxing power on imports and exports—the same paramount character would seem to restrain, as it certainly may restrain, a state from such other exercise of this power, as is in its nature incompatible with, and repugnant to, the constitutional laws of the Union. A law, absolutely repugnant to another, as entirely repeals that other as if express terms of repeal were used.

On this ground the counsel for the bank place its claim to be exempted from the power of a state to tax its operations. There is no express provision for the case, but the claim has been sustained on a principle which so entirely pervades the constitution, is so intermixed with the materials which compose it, so interwoven with its web, so blended with its texture, as to be incapable of being separated from it without rendering it into shreds.

This great principle is, that the constitution and the laws made in pursuance thereof are supreme; that they control the constitution and laws of the respective states, and cannot be controlled by them. From this, which may be almost termed an axiom, other propositions are deduced as corollaries, on the truth or error of which, and on their application to this case, the cause has been supposed to depend. These are, 1st. that a power to create implies a power to preserve. 2d. That a power to destroy, if wielded by a different hand, is hostile to, and incompatible with these powers to create and to preserve. 3d. That where this repugnancy exists, that authority which is supreme must control, not yield to that over which it is supreme.

These propositions as abstract truths, would, perhaps, never be controverted. Their application to this case, however, has been denied; and, both in maintaining the affirmative and the negative, a splendor of eloquence, and strength of argument seldom, if ever, surpassed, have been displayed.

The power of Congress to create, and of course to continue, the bank, was the subject of the preceding part of this opinion; and is no longer to be considered as questionable.

That the power of taxing it by the states may be exercised so as to destroy it, is too obvious to be denied....

If we apply the principle for which the state of Maryland contends, to the Constitution generally, we shall find it capable of changing totally the character of that instrument. We shall find it capable of arresting all the measures of the government, and of prostrating it at the foot of the states. The American people have declared their Constitution and the laws made in pursuance thereof, to be supreme; but this principle would transfer the supremacy, in fact, to the states....

...The people of all the states have created the general government, and have conferred upon it the general power of taxation. The people of all the states, and the states themselves, are represented in Congress, and, by their representatives, exercise this power. When they tax the chartered institutions of the states, they tax their constituents; and these taxes must be uniform. But when a state taxes the operations of the government of the United States, it acts upon institutions created, not by their own constituents, but by people over whom they claim no control. It acts upon the measures of a government created by others as well as themselves, for the benefit of others in common with themselves. The difference is that which always exists, and always must exist, between the action of the whole on a part, and the action of a part on the whole—between the laws of a government declared which, when in opposition to those laws, is not supreme.…

The court has bestowed on this subject its most deliberate consideration. The result is a conviction that the states have no power, by taxation or otherwise, to retard, impede, burden, or in any manner control the operations of the constitutional laws enacted by Congress to carry into execution the powers vested in the general government. This is, we think, the unavoidable consequence of that supremacy which the constitution has declared.

We are unanimously of opinion that the law passed by the legislature of Maryland, imposing a tax on the Bank of the United States, is unconstitutional and void.

Marshall was generally correct in observing that "the question respecting the extent of the powers actually granted [to the national government] is perpetually arising, and will probably continue to arise, as long as our system shall exist." However, the decision in *McCulloch v. Maryland* itself established lasting answers for some of the most fundamental constitutional questions, and in so doing, effectively limited the range for serious, subsequent debate about allowable national powers.

14 / The Bill of Rights, Incorporation, and the Erosion of Constitutional Federalism

Charles Rice

In Chapter Two, a reading titled "The Other Amendment" reviews the process by which the Supreme Court has construed the Fourteenth Amendment as applying most of the Bill of Rights' limits on government to the states. In this reading, Charles Rice argues that the Supreme Court has done so in error, with the unfortunate consequence of contributing to the erosion of federalism.

The Constitution of the United States is the first instance in all history of the creation of a government possessing only limited powers. The Magna Charta, the Petition of Right, the English Bill of Rights, and all the other previous efforts to restrain government had merely imposed restrictions on the otherwise unlimited power of government. The framers of the Constitution, however, created a new government which would possess only the powers delegated to it. To be sure, some implied powers were delegated, and some of the delegated powers, such as the power to regulate interstate commerce, were subject to elastic interpretation. Nevertheless, the federalism ordained by the Constitution rested upon the essential principle that the federal government was given only the powers delegated and that all other governmental power remained with the states. This principle was embodied in the Constitution even before the adoption of the Tenth Amendment. Thus, Article I, Section 1 provides: "All legislative powers herein granted. . . ." The Tenth Amendment merely reaffirmed the principle, as if to say, "And we really mean it."

Various factors have contributed to the erosion of federalism in constitutional theory and practice—the changed character of the economy, the conferral on the federal government by the Sixteenth Amendment of an unlimited power to tax income, the direct election of senators provided by the Seventeenth Amendment, the effect of four major wars in seven decades, and others. This [selection], however, will focus on a little-noticed but decisive reason for the shift in governmental power from the states to Washington in matters affecting basic aspects of local government and community life. Consider a few examples.

When a twelve-year-old girl was shot and killed not long ago in the crossfire of a gang fight in Chicago's Cabrini-Green housing project, why could the police not respond to the demands of residents and columnists that they search the project, seize all the illegal weapons, and arrest their possessors?

When a small midwestern city finds that the newest addition to its downtown business district is a bar featuring totally nude dancing, why are the authorities unable to close the place down?

When a public school teacher responds to the requests of all the parents of her kindergarten class by allowing the children to recite the Romper Room grace—"God is great, God is good, Let us thank Him for our food"—before their cookies and milk, why is that teacher subject to injunction as a violator of the First Amendment to the U. S. Constitution?

Why are public high schools and colleges required to recognize a homosexual club on the same basis as they recognize other student clubs such as a stamp club or a history club?

Why are unborn human beings killed each year in this country in numbers equivalent to the combined populations of Boston, Denver, and Seattle, with the states unable to do anything effective to prevent it?

Why is a public figure who is financially destroyed by a falsehood published by a newspaper unable to recover a dime unless he proves the falsehood was published with actual malice?

These are questions about which many Americans are concerned. The answer in each case is that the states and communities are prevented from doing anything because of the incorporation doctrine. This has nothing to do with corporations. It is, rather, an invention of the Supreme Court of the United States by which that Court, contrary to the intent of the Constitution, has succeeded in binding the states uniformly by every requirement of the first eight amendments of the Bill of Rights as those requirements are interpreted by the Supreme Court.

The first eight amendments to the Bill of Rights were intended by the First Congress and by the states that approved them to protect the specified rights against invasion by the federal government. The state governments were not bound by those provisions. For protection of their rights against invasion by state governments, the people relied primarily upon state constitutions.

The Fourteenth Amendment, adopted in 1868, provides that "No State shall...abridge the privileges or immunities of citizens of the United States; nor shall any State deprive any person of life, liberty, or property, without due process of law; nor deny to any person within its jurisdiction the equal protection of the laws." In a line of decisions beginning more than six decades ago, the Supreme Court has held that virtually all of the protections of the first eight amendments of the Bill of Rights are included in the "liberty" protected by the Fourteenth Amendment due process clause and that therefore the states are as fully obliged to comply with them as is the federal government. Therefore, in the view of the Court, "The Fourteenth Amendment has rendered the legislatures of the states as incompetent as Congress to enact" laws in violation of, for example, the clause of the First Amendment, which provides, "Congress shall make no law respecting an establishment of religion."[1]

The Court has interpreted the Bill of Rights so as to include also rights not specified therein, which rights, arising from its own interpretation, it has proceeded to apply against the states. For example, in 1965 the Supreme Court struck down as unconstitutional a Connecticut law prohibiting the use of contraceptives. To accomplish this, the Court had to find a right of reproductive privacy in the Bill of Rights so as to hold that the due process clause of the Fourteenth Amendment forbids Connecticut to violate it. Less resourceful jurists might have said, as Justice Black did in dissent, that the framers did not have reproductive privacy in mind when they proposed the Bill of Rights and that therefore the Connecticut law did not violate the Fourteenth Amendment. The majority of the Court, however, discovered such a right of privacy in the "penumbras formed by emanations from the Bill of Rights."[2] This ruling was the precursor of *Roe v. Wade*,[3] in which the Supreme Court held that the unborn child is not a person for purposes of the Fourteenth Amendment and that the right of privacy prevents the states from prohibiting abortion....

The legislative history of the Fourteenth Amendment demonstrates that the application by the Supreme Court of the Bill of Rights to the states fits Justice Holmes's description, in another context, of "an unconstitutional assumption of powers by courts of the United States which no lapse of time or respectable array of opinion should make us hesitate to correct."[4] In his definitive analysis of that legislative history, Charles Fairman exhaustively analyzes the "mountain of evidence" from the congressional debates, the state ratifying proceedings, and other original sources in support of his conclusion that the framers and ratifiers of the Fourteenth Amendment did not intend to make the Bill of Rights applicable against the states. He contrasts this "mountain of evidence" with "the few stones and pebbles that made up the theory that the Fourteenth Amendment incorporated Amendments I to VIII."[5]

Nor can it be soundly argued that the Fourteenth Amendment applied some but not all of the provisions of the first eight amendments against the states. This selective incorporation theory, as Louis Henkin wrote, "finds no support in the language of the amendment, or in the history of its adoption, and it is truly more difficult to justify than Justice Black's position that the Bill of Rights was wholly incorporated."[6]

In this matter, the Supreme Court prefers its own fictional version to the actual meaning of the Constitution. A central feature of the Constitution is the division of powers between the federal and state governments. The Supreme Court's erroneous application of the Bill of Rights against the states has imposed an artificial uniformity which obliterates that division of powers in important areas. It is also counterproductive in that it frustrates that capacity for innovation and local diversity which is itself a significant safeguard of liberty.

This erroneous application of the Bill of Rights against the states is a major contribution to the congestion on the docket of the Supreme Court itself. Various proposed remedies for that congestion, such as higher standards for counsel and a new intermediate court of appeals, miss the point that an essential cause of the Supreme Court's overload is the Court's own misinterpretation of the Fourteenth Amendment's guarantee of due process of law; the Court interprets that guarantee so as to make every state and local subdivision uniformly subject to the prohibitions contained in the Bill of Rights in matters of speech, religious expression, admissibility of illegally seized evidence against a criminal defendant, and the like. Since the Court mandates one uniform rule in these matters, there must be one interpreter, which is, of course, the Supreme Court itself. Hence the avalanche of appeals to the Court....

Respect for the intent of the Constitution requires that the Supreme Court abandon its erroneous doctrine that applies the Bill of Rights against the states. But a proper interpretation of the Fourteenth Amendment would not leave the states free from all federal restraint in the matter of individual rights. The Supreme Court has misconstrued the due process clause of the Fourteenth Amendment so as to bind the states strictly by the Supreme Court's interpretations of the Bill of Rights. But another clause of that amendment, the privileges and immunities clause, was intended to require the states to protect basic rights, including the rights to life, property, personal security, and mobility....

In the *Slaughter-House Cases*,[7] the Supreme Court drained the privileges or immunities clause of meaning by holding that it protected only a limited category of privileges of "a citizen of the United States." This error has been compounded by the Supreme Court's erroneous interpretation of the due process clause of the Fourteenth Amendement as a guarantee of virtually every right, substantive as well as procedural, protected by the first eight amendments to the Bill of Rights against infringement by the federal government.

The errors discussed here are fundamental. So are the consequences in terms of the erosion of federalism. And the remedy should likewise be fundamental. What is needed is a reversal of the incorporation doctrine and a reversal of the *Slaughter-House Cases* so as to restore the three clauses of the Fourteenth Amendment—privileges or immunities, equal protection, and due process—to their proper functions. The amendment was serviceable as conceived by its framers. And it can be made serviceable again, whether through corrective action by Congress in the exercise of its Section 5 power to enforce the amendment by "appropriate legislation" or through the recovery by the Supreme Court of a sense of its own responsibility to interpret the Constitution rather than to amend it.

Notes

1. *Abington School District v. Schempp,* 374 U.S. 203, 215 (1963).
2. *Griswold v. Conn.,* 381 U.S. 479, 484 (1965).
3. *Roe v. Wade,* 410 U.S. 113 (1973).
4. *Black & White Taxicab Co. v. Brown & Yellow Taxicab Co.,* 276 U.S. 518, 533 (1928) (Holmes, J., dissenting).
5. Fairman, *Does the Fourteenth Amendment Incorporate the Bill of Rights?,* 2 Stan. L. Rev. 5, 134 (1949).
6. Henkin, *"Selective Incorporation" in the Fourteenth Amendment,* 73 Yale L.J. 74, 77 (1963); *see also* R. Berger, *Death Penalties: The Supreme Court's Obstacle Course* (Cambridge: Harvard Univ. Press, 1982), pp. 15–16.
7. *Slaughter-House Cases,* 83 U.S. (16 Wall.) 36 (1872).

15 / Competitive Federalism— Three Driving Forces

John Shannon

Though American federalism has long been described as a cooperative arrangement, John Shannon argues that it must be seen as a competitive situation as well, with the levels of government competing against one another for limited resources. Three recent developments—federal tax reform, the ending of general revenue sharing, and a Supreme Court decision—have all contributed to what now might be called "fend-for-yourself" federalism.

If students of American federalism were asked to make a list of the most significant intergovernmental developments of the last three decades, three actions of the 1985–87 period probably would survive the final cut:

- The U.S. Supreme Court decision in *Garcia v. San Antonio Metropolitan Transit Authority* (1985)
- The reform of the federal income tax (1986)
- The demise of the federal revenue sharing program (1986)

The *Garcia* Decision

In a 5–4 vote, *Garcia* overturned *National League of Cities v. Usery* (1976) by holding that the commerce clause of the Constitution granted the Congress the authority to regulate the wages of local government transit workers. In this case, it required the local authority to adhere to national minimum wage standards. . . .

From an historical perspective, *Garcia* can be viewed as putting one of the finishing judicial touches on a congressional deregulation process that began in earnest during the Depression. That searing national crisis forced the Congress and a reluctant Supreme Court to accede to the Roosevelt Administration's call for a New Deal—the unprecedented use of national government power to overhaul and jump-start a badly stalled economy. By 1942, the nation had witnessed the collapse of most of the constitutional barriers to federal entry into areas once considered the exclusive preserves of the states.

Federal Tax Reform

The far-reaching overhaul of the federal income tax code in 1986 produced some pluses and minuses for the state-local sector. On the plus side, there emerged the revenue windfall opportunity. By broadening the federal individual income tax base, the Congress automatically created a revenue windfall opportunity for those income tax states that conform their tax base definitions to those in the federal tax code. Not wanting to be viewed as taking advantage of this situation, most of the income tax states returned the "windfall" to their taxpayers by lowering tax rates and raising personal exemptions and standard deductions. On the minus side, federal income taxpayers can no longer claim the payment of state and local sales taxes as itemized personal deductions on the federal 1040. . . .

The sharp reduction in the top federal corporate and individual income tax rates also puts a keener edge on state and local tax competition. Because the cut in federal tax rates reduced the amount of state and local taxes that can be "written off" on the federal tax returns, upper income taxpayers and business firms are now more sensitive to interjurisdictional tax differentials. To stay competitive, virtually all of the income tax states with high nominal rates (ranging from 10 percent up to 16 percent) pulled their rates down into the high single-digit range.

The Death of Revenue Sharing

The federal revenue sharing program passed away slowly. By freezing the outlays year after year, a fairly hostile Congress made sure that this aid program would twist slowly in the inflationary winds. Pushed by the Reagan Administration, the Congress finally put an end to its revenue sharing with local governments in 1986—six years after lopping off the state portion.

A brief epitaph for the federal revenue sharing program might read as follows:

- 1964—first proposed to reduce an expected federal budget surplus
- 1972—finally pushed through a reluctant Congress
- 1986—sacrificed on the Gramm-Rudman-Hollings altar of fiscal discipline

The rise and fall of federal revenue sharing serve as sharp reminders of the remarkable turnabout in the fiscal fortunes of Washington and the state-local sector over the last two decades. In the mid-60s, the massive fiscal advantage enjoyed by the national government triggered the demand for revenue sharing to redress this intergovernmental fiscal imbalance. By the mid-80s, towering federal budget deficits prompted the Congress to zero it out.

The fall-off in federal aid flows and the wipeout of revenue sharing have caused a sea change in the expectations of state and local officials—when forced to search for "new money," they look to their own resources.

A Summing Up—Competitive Federalism

Three disparate developments—the *Garcia* decision, federal tax reform, and the revenue sharing wipeout—all have one thing in common. In each instance, the action gave competitive (fend-for-yourself) federalism a vigorous push forward.

Several considerations suggest that the adjective "competitive" best describes the current state of American federalism. Unlike the situation that prevailed over the first 150 years, the national government is no longer constitutionally restricted to a narrow area of governance. Now, a "deregulated" federal government can move into virtually any domestic area and compete for policy leadership. Unlike the more recent past (the 1950s and 1960s), however, Washington no longer possesses a towering fiscal advantage over the state and local governments. Thus, federal, state, and local governments must now compete head on for the political and fiscal support of federalism's ultimate arbiters—the voters/taxpayers. Over the last decade, states and localities have fared better in this competitive struggle than most students of federalism would have predicted a couple of decades ago.

The current state of competitive federalism is not without its sharp critics. Those critics with a liberal point of view emphasize the equity problem—that fend-for-yourself federalism does poorly by those who are least able to fend for themselves—poor people and poor governments. Many federalists (joined by many state and local officials) paint a grim scenario of things to come—a constitutionally unconstrained but financially strapped Congress is likely to be pushed by special interests to make ever-increasing use of unfunded mandates and in this process transform elected state and local officials into Washington's hired hands.

Neither concerns about inequities nor fears of power grabs can obliterate a striking reality: A deregulated Congress has not created a highly centralized national state—the Orwellian outcome that many had predicted. On the contrary, 50 years after the collapse of most of the constitutional and political constraints on the Congress, the resilient states and localities are very much alive, and most of them are doing quite well. It is the national government that is experiencing a considerable degree of fiscal distress—a chronic budgetary ailment caused by Washington's habit of biting off more expenditure commitments than its revenue dentures can chew.

16 / State and Local Governments Go International

John Kincaid

Though long seen as almost exclusively the domain of the federal government, international affairs increasingly involve state and local governments as active players. John Kincaid discusses ten ways in which the lower levels have become more involved in the international arena, and marvels that the change has come about with little federal–state conflict.

The growing involvement of state and local governments in international affairs, especially world commerce, is one of the remarkable changes occurring in our federal system. This change poses challenges and opportunities for both federalism and international relations. Indeed, the expanding international activities of constituent governments elsewhere—such as Canadian provinces, German *Länder*, Japanese prefectures, Soviet republics, and Swiss cantons—suggest that "international" relations may be a misnomer. Today, it might be more accurate to speak of global intergovernmental or interorganizational relations.

Some federations have constitutional provisions that expressly allow their constituent states to engage in international activities. In the United States, however, we have tended to think of foreign affairs as virtually an exclusive province of the U.S. government. Yet, states, counties, municipalities, townships, school districts, and many special districts are addressing global issues in many ways. These initiatives are generally compatible with our constitutional system and often beneficial for federalism and the national economy.

To see how this is so, we can look at the ten ways in which state and local governments are actually plugged into foreign affairs.

1. Partners in Foreign Policy Development
The U.S. Constitution makes states direct partners in foreign policymaking through their representation in the Congress, particularly the Senate. The

framers of the Constitution viewed treaty-making as central to foreign policy. To protect the interests of the states, including their different economies and foreign-country sympathies (e.g., the Francophiles vs. the Anglophiles), especially since treaty law supersedes conflicting state law, the Constitution requires treaties to be ratified by two-thirds of the Senators present. In addition, ambassadors must be appointed by the President with the advice and consent of the Senate.

Given that the Senate, according to James Madison, is the more confederal chamber than the House, which is the more national chamber, it is clear that federalism and state interests were uppermost in the framers' minds when they provided for the exercise of the union's normal foreign policy powers. Moreover, the framers of the Constitution provided that Senators be selected by their state legislatures, thus reinforcing the institutional base of state representation in foreign policymaking. The Senate, then, was to be the main arena for reconciling the interests of the union as a sovereign nation in world affairs with the interests of the states as co-sovereign partners in the federal union.

However, the most drastic foreign-policy action—a declaration of war—is reserved exclusively to the Congress, both houses. Here, the framers were unwilling to leave decisionmaking to the President and the Senate, neither of which was to be chosen directly by the people. The framers brought the House into the picture because its members were to be elected by the people directly, and at the youngest age permitted by the Constitution for elected U.S. offices, thus presumably putting House members more closely in touch with the sentiments of the young people called on to fight wars.

Local governments are not directly represented in the Congress, but they are indirectly represented in both houses, and more finely so in the House. Constitutionally, the House does not have much of a direct role in foreign affairs, but given that all revenue bills must originate in the House and that treaties require implementing legislation, the House in fact has a sizable role in foreign affairs. Thus, the House is another arena in which state and local governments can try to shape foreign policy.

Given that the President is chosen through the electoral college, the states, especially large states and big cities, have periodic electoral opportunities to influence presidential foreign policymaking. Recognizing that large states and big cities would be the economic powerhouses of the union, perhaps the framers wanted to give them a slightly enhanced voice in international relations through the presidency, especially since the framers wanted American foreign policy to be dominated by commercial concerns, not by wars and colonial empire-building.

Just how foreign policy is to be shared between the President and the Congress, especially the Senate, has been debated since 1789. Clearly, most of the framers wanted an energetic President, not a clerk. The constitutional provisions suggest that the President, not Congress, is empowered to speak officially for the nation in world affairs and to conduct foreign relations on a day-to-day basis, but that the President must do so within basic rules established by Congress through treaty and statutory law, over which the President also has influence through his authority to negotiate treaties and veto legislation. It is through this matrix of power, then, that the diverse interests of the states and their citizens must be melded into coherent foreign policies for the federal union as a sovereign nation.

2. Pressure Points in Foreign Policymaking

In addition to the formal avenues of representation in the Congress, state and local officials, like other pressure groups, lobby and supply information to the Congress, the White House, and executive branch agencies. There is no constitutional barrier to this kind of activity. Indeed, in *Garcia* (1985) and *South Carolina* (1988), the U.S. Supreme Court seemed to say that such activity is necessary and essential if states are to protect their interests in the federal government's policymaking process.

Forty-some years ago, when state and local elected officials first set out in earnest to address issues in Washington, DC, they had domestic policymaking, especially federal grants-in-aid, at the top of their agendas. Today, with declining federal aid and rising globalization, foreign policy is an added and increasingly important agenda item. Furthermore, the line between domestic and foreign policy becomes less clear everyday. State and local officials must, therefore, straddle both policy fields, much like their congressional counterparts. State and local officials, however, must be especially attentive to the impacts on their jurisdictions of decisions made in both the national and international arenas.

The experience acquired by state and local officials in being intergovernmental diplomats to Washington has no doubt helped them to become competent international diplomats for their jurisdictions as well. Now, more and more state and local officials have direct contact with both worlds, contacts that require and allow them to address issues of national and international significance to their constituents.

3. Self-Governing Political Communities

States and localities are self-governing political communities in their own right, having a full range of constitutional powers for domestic governance. Through their powers of taxation, regulation, service provision, and law enforcement, state and local governments create climates in their jurisdictions that encourage or discourage a wide range of internationally related activity, especially trade, tourism, and investment. As such, state and local governments have substantial and direct influences on many matters of international significance. Furthermore, states enforce and implement many provisions of U.S. law, including treaty law. Thus, state and local governments are constitutionally well equipped to act in the global arena, although all are not fiscally or politically well equipped to do so.

It is in this area of direct state action, however, that we are likely to see heightened debate over federal and state powers. For example, one controversy over state and local powers has involved divestiture policies with respect to

South Africa. Given the huge size of state and local pension funds and other investments, as well as the sizable purchases of state and local governments, state and local fiscal policies targeted at specific nations or sectors of the world economy can have very tangible consequences that can run counter to or parallel with U.S. policy. Small states that engage in this kind of activity perhaps can make a dent in foreign economic affairs, but a few large states acting at the same time can produce much more than an economic fender bender.

As co-sovereign partners in the federal union, then, just how far can state powers be extended into the global arena so that states can meet their domestic constitutional obligations to their citizens? In turn, how far can federal powers be extended into the state-local arena so that the federal government can meet its domestic and foreign constitutional obligations? Some observers argue, for example, that globalization and the emergence of such regional economic organizations as the European Community require significant preemptions of state and local authority in order to create a more open and uniform national market. Others argue that because of the diversity of state economies, needs, and preferences, and because of the diminishing ability of the federal government to insulate the national economy from international shocks, states need more, not less, power to maneuver in the global economy.

4. Promoters of Area Interests
Perhaps the international role for which state and local governments are best known is that of promoters of their own jurisdictions in foreign markets. Through aggressive advertising, trade missions, and foreign offices, state and local governments are seeking to promote exports of their constituents' products and to attract foreign investment and tourists. There has been a tremendous increase in these activities since the late 1970s, and there is every indication that they will continue to increase during the 1990s.

Controversies in this field are less likely to involve federal-state issues than interstate and intrastate issues. Although states and localities frequently cooperate on such matters as export promotion and tourism, the attraction of investment often involves keen competition. The public, moreover, is divided over the wisdom of attracting foreign investment ("the selling of America"), certain methods of attracting investment ("tax giveaways"), and state and local trade missions and foreign offices ("junkets and boondoggles"). One can expect, therefore, a certain amount of conflict between and within states as state and local governments expand and refine their promotional activities. The forging of equitable and efficient tools of interstate and interlocal competition in the global economy is an urgent challenge because every jurisdiction must compete with a growing number of very active and attractive jurisdictions around the world.

5. Proxies for the Nation
Although state and local governments cannot officially represent the nation abroad, elected state and local officials do, in effect, represent, in the

minds of others, what is best or worst about the United States. Sometimes state and local officials can also open doors in unofficial ways that would be awkward or impossible for the U.S. to do officially. In addition, state and local officials and their counterparts abroad can initiate discussions on issues of mutual concern, and then carry proposals back to their respective national governments. At times, state and local governments can also provide aid to equivalent governments in another country where it would be awkward for the U.S. to do so, or for the other national government to accept direct U.S. aid.

This role of state and local governments is not well developed, nor is it likely to be developed with much vigor—with two exceptions. First, if the democratization of authoritarian regimes continues to spread throughout the world, the federal government, as well as private foundations and international organizations, will be calling more frequently on state and local officials to lend their expertise to governmental reform in these countries. Second, as laboratories of experimentation, state and local governments are likely to serve increasingly as sources of ideas for national responses to globalization.

6. Parties to Agreements with Foreign Powers
The U.S. Constitution does not allow states to make treaties, join alliances, or enter confederations; however, states can make agreements and enter compacts "with a foreign power" with the consent of Congress and also without congressional approval so long as such agreements do not intrude on the federal government's prerogatives or give states attributes of true sovereignty in international affairs. Today, there are thousands of formal and informal agreements between state and local governments and "foreign powers." Most of these agreements, however, are with equivalent state or local governments abroad, such as Canadian provinces. Along the Canada-U.S. border, for example, many agreements involve housekeeping matters, such as roads and bridges, traffic, fire protection, and animal control. An occasionally hot issue is reciprocity in traffic-ticket enforcement.

As state and local governments' international activities expand, so does the scope of agreement making, both substantively and territorially. Most sister-city and sister-county programs, for example, used to be polite cultural affairs involving minimal government commitment. Today they are taken more seriously, involve a wider range of activities and substantive issues, and are viewed increasingly in the context of overall economic development strategies. Similarly, in addition to bilateral agreements, there is a growing number of multilateral agreements involving several states and several equivalent foreign governments.

Surprisingly, perhaps, there has been hardly any federal-state conflict over these agreement making activities. Constitutionally, the federal government has broad and express authority to regulate these activities and to abrogate agreements not to its liking; however, state and local governments have pretty much confined themselves to matters appropriate to their jurisdictional concerns.

7. Public Education and Opinion Forums

A major key to a successful economy today is a well educated workforce attuned to world events. Yet, it is local and state governments that have the primary responsibility for education. If Americans are to learn world geography, foreign languages, and international sensitivities, it will be largely through resources and encouragement provided by state and local institutions. Internationally relevant education, moreover, must go beyond the classroom. It must permeate the jurisdiction and be reflected in public and private sector activity, so that children can see its importance and adults can use their knowledge.

At the same time, it is clear that states and localities also have emerged as public-opinion forums on foreign policy. City councils and state legislatures pass resolutions on foreign policy; mayors, county commissioners, and governors speak out on foreign affairs; and more and more foreign policy propositions appear on state and local ballots, some of which are hotly contested and attract supporters and opponents from out of state. Although many of these legislative resolutions and ballot propositions criticize U.S. foreign policies, and although many citizens regard these resolutions as improper, there is no U.S. constitutional barrier to such expressions of opinion, and there is no sign that such activities will decline in the near future.

8. Problem Solvers on the World Scene

"Think globally, act locally" has become an attractive slogan in this era of interdependence and rising concern about the global effects of local behavior, such as environmental pollution. Here, state and local governments can demonstrate one of the virtues of federalism, namely, the ability to experiment with different solutions to public problems and, at the same time, actually do something constructive. If a jurisdiction is concerned about global warming, for instance, it can (if not preempted by the federal government) reduce or eliminate its production of the offending pollutants. By itself, a small jurisdiction cannot have much of an impact, but the point is to lead the way and get the ball rolling while still making some contribution.

State and local governments also can make useful contributions to easing border tensions and resolving cross-border problems. In so doing, they can help prevent manageable problems from becoming less manageable international controversies. This is less of a problem for the United States than it is for many other countries where border issues can be intense, but still, there are important issues to be dealt with, and often are dealt with, by state and local governments that share a border with Canada or with Mexico or, in the case of Alaska, a narrow waterway with the USSR.

9. Patrons of Democracy

If state and local governments are to capture more markets for their constituents' products, and if the Sunbelt states are to resolve their concerns about Latin America, then state and local governments will have to be attentive to the economic and democratic development needs of most countries around the world. State and local governments are uniquely qualified to help because they possess hands-on expertise, and because economic development and democratization require competent local and regional institutions of government that can provide essential services, unleash entrepreneurial energy, and stimulate citizen participation.

In numerous and generally quiet ways, many state and local governments, usually in cooperation with private and nonprofit organizations, are providing technical assistance, equipment, and other aid to various communities around the world. Exchange programs also have taken on more importance, and there has been a quantum leap in information sharing among state and local governments all over the world. In turn, American state and local officials have become more interested in learning lessons from abroad that can be applied at home. Furthermore, state university systems, which include some of the best universities in the world, are excellent vehicles for contributing to economic and democratic development.

10. Practitioners of Goodwill

Finally, but not last in importance, state and local governments have been playing significant roles in promoting goodwill abroad and improving cultural understanding between the United States and other nations. These activities are actually quite traditional for many state and local governments, and they predate the newer kinds of international involvements developed during the past two decades.

State and local governments are well suited for this role. Such activities are often best carried out on a small-scale, person-to-person basis so that participants can see how other people really live and think about things. State and local governments also can work closely with their private and nonprofit counterparts to build different kinds of bridges between peoples and assemble rich cultural and educational programs. State and local activities, moreover, are likely to show best the great cultural diversity of American life. In addition, state and local programs are less likely to be freighted with the ideological baggage and policy antagonisms that separate national governments, thus enabling state and local efforts to break through barriers that otherwise divide peoples.

Conclusion

The emergence of state and local governments as actors on the world scene can be characterized, thus far, as cooperative dual federalism. That is, state and local governments have, by and large, been carving out international niches for themselves, and by themselves, in the fashion of dual federalism. At the same time, the federal government has been largely tolerant and benignly cooperative, neither interfering in overt ways with state and local initiatives nor going out of its way to lend a helping hand. There are, of course, some direct points of cooperation as well as friction, but what is remarkable is that there has been so little federal-state conflict. The principal challenge is to continue carving out appropriate roles for the federal sector and the state-local sector so that each can do what it is best equipped to do, and the two sectors can coordinate and cooperate as necessary and appropriate.

17 / The Law of Appropriateness in Intergovernmental Relations

David J. Kennedy

The term *intergovernmental relations* refers to all *interactions* among units of government at the national, state, and/or local levels within American federalism.* David J. Kennedy, writing as a Minnesota state legislator, makes the case that there is a "law of appropriateness" that goes far in explaining the complex world of intergovernmental relations. Somewhat tongue-in-cheek, no doubt, he suggests that it always seems that one's own level is best suited to carrying out a program, and that some other level is best suited to paying for it.

During a number of years of studying and lecturing about the American federal system, I have been dismayed by the virtually total absence of any formalized statement of the principles underlying its inner workings. True, there has been no lack of published work on the subject of American intergovernmental relations—on the contrary one feels overwhelmed by its bulk—yet, most of the writing has been essentially normative, describing the structure without developing any basic rules about its controlling dynamics.

Noting that my concern was shared by a number of public administrators at the local, state, and federal levels of government, and encouraged by a number of successful investigations of related questions, I set about the task of formulating some rather easily observable axioms about intergovernmental relations with the hope that a general theory, or at least an approach to such a theory, would emerge. In doing so, I was fully aware of the appalling lack of statistical and other empirical evidence in the field and was quite prepared to treat the results of my investigation as preliminary to more extended research.

As is so often the case in scientific inquiry, the outlines of the basic law governing intergovernmental relations evolved more from insight rather than investigation. The development of its corollaries and related principles required the testing of innumerable applications of the law on case histories and hypothetical models. The ultimate truth of the body of doctrine must,

*See Wright, Deil S., *Understanding Intergovernmental Relations* (North Scituate, Mass: Duxbury Press, 1978, p. 8).—*Editor's Note.*

of course, await more complete demonstration, but it should be stated that in the work I have concluded thus far, the law has proved immutable, or nearly so.

The results of my study are presented in this article. Its title ambitiously refers to a "general theory" in the hope that it will be viewed as a working document for governmental administrators. On another level, it can be viewed as a philosophical statement about the *appropriateness* of the assignment of functions to various levels of government, and in this sense should be useful to politicians and political theorists. If neither administrators nor politicians find it particularly helpful, I will, of course, content myself with the knowledge that the discovery of truth, like virtue, is its own reward.

The Law of Appropriateness
The level of government most appropriate to deal with a given problem is that level by which one is presently employed.

Observers of the American federal system, beginning with de Tocqueville, have been uniformly impressed with its unique combination of decentralization and its ability to react in a unified way to a major problem. In their respective spheres of responsibility, the cities, the states, and the federal establishment operate with a large degree of independence and in an atmosphere of mutual mistrust; but under the stimulus of war, national disaster, or economic collapse, the three levels coalesce into a working whole that achieves results that are the envy of the world.

In the wake of one such catastrophic event, the depression of the '30's, a residual structure of relations between the levels of government emerged as the dominant characteristic of the system. Various euphemisms have been used to describe it—New Deal, Fair Deal, New Frontier, Great Society, Creative Federalism—and a number of metaphors (for the most part culinary in nature)—marble cake, layer cake, carrot and stick—have been employed to visualize it. Stripped of descriptive terminology, however, what remains is the vertical flow of funds and administrative regulations we know as the "federal grant-in-aid system."

In briefest terms, under this system the federal government decides policy and supplies money; the local governments face the problems; and the state government, if involved at all, reluctantly goes along with the whole thing.

On its face the intergovernmental system appears to be the result of conscious decisions at each level to cooperatively approach a given problem, with each level offering its own peculiar resources to achieve a solution. The resulting interrelationships of administrators in the form of meetings, memoranda, guidelines, accounting, and reports is seen as evidence of this cooperative venture. It is in demonstrating the fallacy of this view that the clarity of the basic law becomes apparent. What has actually occurred is that administrators at each level have decided that the level of government by whom they are presently employed is the most appropriate to deal with the problem.

A single example should suffice to illustrate this fundamental truth. Assume City A discovers an infestation of rats in a two-square block residential area near its center, and current funds are not sufficient to exterminate them. Two approaches are possible:

Case 1 (Ideal). City Manager X telephones Federal Admininistrator Y about his problem and is informed that funds under a health program Y administers may legitimately be used by the city for rat extermination. Y asks X to send him a letter request specifying the amount needed and a statement from a city attorney that under state law the city has the legal authority to accept the funds and expend them for that purpose. On its receipt he mails X a check for the amount requested. X then engages an exterminating company to destroy the rats.

Case 1 is idealized, since it depicts the three levels of government exercising only the authority necessary to accomplish the objective sought: the protection of public health by the elimination of rodents. Note that each level assumes the others to be competent, trustworthy, and exercising an appropriate role. Such conditions do not, of course, obtain in the present intergovernmental system.

Case 2 (Actual). Federal Administrator Y notes Manager X's request, but decides that no present authorization for funds of this sort exists. He then calls a meeting with administrators of other agencies who relate similar requests for assistance. It is decided collectively that rat infestation in central cities is a problem of national significance, and that at least $10 billion is necessary to mount an effective program. In due course Congress authorizes a $5 billion national rat control program embodying direct grants to cities to be administered by Y's agency. An actual appropriation of $1 million is made and Administrator Y must now decide between competing applications from a number of cities. To administer the program, a federal rat control division is established to prepare guidelines to insure that the funds are properly expended by the cities.

State B, in which City A is located, learns of the rat program when its commissioner of health, presenting his budget request to a legislative committee, is informed by his staff that an unidentified contingency item is actually to be used to match federal funds for a state plan for rat control, required by the congressional act. Subsequently, the state decides that the rat problem is not confined to City A, and that the state should establish a rat control program and demand that Congress convert the grant-in-aid to a "block" grant program for distribution according to state-determined priorities.

In the interim, City Manager X, vexed by what he considers outrageous conditions attached to the program by federal bureaucrats who know nothing of running a city, and convinced that the state intends to divert the funds to pocket gopher control, has not applied for the funds. By now the rats have infiltrated the central business district, requiring the establishment of a city rat control program requiring financial support equal to 50 times the original estimate.

Case 2 clearly delineates the actual dynamics of the intergovernmental system. It should be observed that administrators at each level of government have consciously decided that their level is the most appropriate one to deal comprehensively and effectively with rat infestation. Each views the other levels as incompetent, ill-equipped, or unwilling—or all three—to handle the problem. Each level has its own views as to which role in the program the others should appropriately perform; in each case a very narrow one indeed.

It can readily be seen that these independent decisions about "appropriateness" give rise to a number of administrative attitudes which may be viewed as corollaries or principles derived from the basic law.

1. *Other levels of government are basically untrustworthy and require constant supervision and observation.* A great deal of time and effort must therefore be expended in finding out "what they're up to," usually by meetings or other techniques of coordination.

2. *The decision about "appropriateness" does not include the willingness to assume the actual operational phase of the program, except at the local government level where no choice exists.* This phenomenon, properly termed "program sedimentation," results in the most difficult and unpleasant aspects of the program (killing rats, disposing of sewage, eviction of elderly home owners) descending to local government. Program sedimentation, however, should not be viewed as an exception to the basic principle, because if the choice were available to local government, it would return the operational responsibilities to another level ("program rebound"). An example of program rebound is occurring presently in a number of states in the field of public welfare. Most states charge county government with the duty of caring for the mentally ill and inebriate, and state, federal, and local funds support this activity: yet, the actual operation of those programs is inexorably drifting upward to regional organizations which are in effect state agencies. For reasons not yet completely clear, counties have a choice of allowing the operational aspects of local functions to move elsewhere.

3. *Duplication of program effort at various levels is not wasteful or inefficient but, rather is essential to the preservation of the intergovernmental system.* It is not accidental that each administrative level in Case 2 established a rat control program, but merely the basic rule at work. The concept of appropriateness, fully understood, involves a sense of responsibility and mission, which necessarily demands administration, to measure accomplishment if nothing else.

Thus, it can be seen that the assignment of responsibility for problem solving in the intergovernmental relations system is controlled by a basic principle based squarely on the position occupied by the administrators at the various levels of the system. The level of government most appropriate to deal with a given problem is that level by which one is presently employed. Once the rule's validity is assumed, significant insights about other operational factors in the system are perceived, and will be elaborated more fully presently.

Finance and Taxation in the Intergovernmental System—
The Doctrine of Appropriateness Extended

Finance—"Shifting the Burden"   We have seen that the issue of the appropriate level of government to solve any given problem is resolved by identifying one's position in the intergovernmental system. It is also reasonably clear, I hope, that the concept of appropriateness is flexible enough to accommodate and, in fact, to determine and perpetuate the American multilevel governmental structure.

But in resolving the issue of appropriateness, does not the administrator or decision maker run the risk of casting the entire financial burden of dealing with the problem on his own level of government, thus incurring the displeasure of the employer? In other words, does calling the tune necessarily result in paying the piper? On its surface the question appears to require an affirmative response, but on closer examination, it will be seen that this is not the case. How is it possible, for example, for the U. S. Corps of Engineers, with a congressional assist, to plan and execute public works projects, the cost of which in any given year usually far exceeds the Corps' annual appropriations? Or how can the Department of HUD contemplate the construction of 26 million housing units in ten years when such an expenditure by the federal government would likely precipitate a stunning depression and fantastic inflation?

The explanation lies in the operation of another principle in the general doctrine of appropriateness which may be stated as follows:

The level of government most appropriate to finance any given governmental program is a level other than that by whom one is presently employed.

The almost universal application of this principle is shrouded by a semantic thicket that can easily throw all but the most determined investigator off the track. It is said by local school administrators, for example, that state support of all costs of elementary and secondary education will have an "equalizing effect" and insure "equality of opportunity for quality education," irrespective of the wealth or poverty of individual school districts. In point of fact, the administrator's personal safety is threatened by outraged taxpayers; the rule of appropriateness for him ceases to be a convenient guideline and assumes the stature of holy writ.

Most if not all federal grant-in-aid programs contain generally overlooked (until it's too late) but significant provisions that their purpose is to "increase state capability" or to "improve the ability of urban areas" to deal with a problem. These are straightforward assertions that the federal level has no intention of financing any more than a portion of the program and that the state and local levels will be expected to take over the total financial commitment created within an unspecified but very short period of time.

Both state and federal levels employ more subtle techniques to insure that some other level actually finances the program. Common examples are:

1. *The matching requirement ("sandbag effect")*. Many grant-in-aid programs require the grantee (supplicant) level to furnish a portion of the cost of the program, which is then matched in varying proportions by the grantor (benefactor). Cash is not required: in fact,

services of grantee employees ("new effort") is preferred as match, since an administrative structure will have been created (directors, deputies, clerks, supplies, etc.) which the grantee will never be able to dismantle. Thus the entire financial burden of the program will be shifted to another level of government.

2. *Seed money ("Seminalis Pecuniae")*. This approach consists of a thinly veiled bribe by the grantor to induce grantee to take a flyer at some project that both know will come to nothing. If the seed should fall on good ground, however, the shift of financial responsibility will be accomplished with a minimal expenditure of money and effort.

3. *The demonstration grant ("Quid Pro Nihil")*. Under this technique the grantor offers grantee 100 per cent financing of some innovative and usually impractical problem-solving program. After six months the idea is abandoned, the consultant paid, and the affair closed and hushed up. Grantee believes he has truly obtained something for nothing, but grantor merely removes the amount of the demonstration grant from funds that would otherwise be available to grantee under other programs. Thus, the financial burden is successfully shifted to some other level.

4. *Package grants ("The Green Stamp Technique")*. Shifting the burden under this device is more involuted but equally effective as in other methods. Grantee is encouraged to "coordinate" by a sort of free association thought process, as many programs as he can to be "brought to bear" on "root causes" in "target areas." Grantor promises not only to finance a good portion of the necessary planning, but to come across with a large percentage of the capital costs of construction of facilities to be built as a bonus for doing such a good job. The promises are kept (within the limitations of available funds), but the grantor's commitment is minimal and transitory; the grantee's commitment is massive and continues for at least three generations.

The concept of shifting the financial burden while retaining control is central to understanding the intergovernmental system. The doctrine of "appropriateness by location in the system," embodied in the general rule and the above-stated corollary must be mastered by administrators at all levels if the system is to be preserved and one's position retained.

Taxation—"Maximizing Revenue—Minimizing Incidence" A full discussion of financing the intergovernmental system cannot avoid the troublesome business of how the needed revenue is to be raised, though adherence to the concept of appropriateness can significantly reduce the attendant discomfort. The basic principle is easily stated, and, though widely accepted as a kind of folk wisdom, its actual operation in the system is apparently not fully realized, and certainly not adequately studied. The adage that "the best tax is the one someone else pays" was first subjected to serious analysis by

Kittrick and Kalkbrunner in an unpublished bachelor's thesis.[1] Their work was exploratory, and had it not been cut short by the great war, we most certainly would be better equipped to deal with this important problem.

The value of the maxi-mini concept of taxation is easily illustrated. Let us suppose a meeting of local government officials seeking new sources of revenue for cities preferably: (1) to be imposed by the state (assignment of function), (2) to be used to finance a program of state operation of dog pounds (program rebound), and (3) not resulting in an increase in local property taxes (shifting the burden). Questions of appropriateness having been easily resolved, the ticklish problem of the actual tax measure to be employed confronts the group. After fruitless hours of uninformed discussion about the sales tax, income tax, wheelage tax, and various other exotic excises, City Manager A suggests a $.10 per pound tax on coffee. His logic is unassailable: virtually everyone in the state drinks coffee; the levy is small but the return significant; the coffee industry can easily pass the tax on to the consumer; and the administrative costs of collection would be minimal.

The suggested tax on coffee is, of course, soundly defeated by the committee. Why? Simply because everyone present is being asked to impose a tax on himself. The maxi-mini relationship is $+1$, or, as some have put it, the coefficient of incidence of the tax is $+1$, clearly an undesirable state of affairs. The tax would maximize revenue while maximizing incidence, and upon reflection Manager A would have seen the basic unacceptability of the proposal.

Next, suppose that Councilman B proposes that the group request the state to impose a motel tax with a substantial portion of the revenue returned to the cities where the motels are located. Logical arguments abound in favor of such a scheme, but as B sets them forth no one listens. They are quickly, but unknowingly, calculating the coefficient of incidence of the proposed tax which in this case works out to $-.9777$, that is, for every $1,000 of revenue produced by the tax, the personal (and local taxpayer) incidence is $.003, a very acceptable ratio indeed.

A good deal of rubric surrounds the present (and historic) dialogue about taxation—equity, regressivity, progressivity, and the like. Though the terms are useful in a proper setting, the student of intergovernmental relations should never allow them to distract him from the true principle of appropriateness of taxation in intergovernmental relations:

The most appropriate tax to finance a given governmental program is one imposed by another level of government which maximizes revenue while minimizing incidence. . . .

Too pat? Too nice? Too precious? Perhaps. I submit in defense of this brief analysis, however, that the most pervasive of principles governing the physical world, the concept of gravity, has only two variable factors, the mass of bodies and the distance between them. The concept of appropriateness may prove to be of equally simple beauty.

Note

1. Kittrick and Kalkbrunner, "Maximizing Revenue—Minimizing Incidence: A Personal View of Tax Policy," unpublished thesis, 1917.

CHAPTER FIVE

Civil Rights
and Civil Liberties

The history of civil rights and civil liberties in the United States has been primarily one of extension and expansion. Though a bill of rights was not included in the original wording of the Constitution, one was later promised as a means of securing ratification from several states that wished to extend to the national government their own established guarantees against government infringements. The first ten amendments were proposed in the first session of the new Congress in September 1789 and were ratified by December 1791. Ironically, a later amendment (the Fourteenth, ratified in 1868) would ultimately have the effect of requiring all of the state governments to comply with most of the national Bill of Rights.

Though (and perhaps because) the wording of the Bill of Rights seems at first to be quite simple and clear, there has been no shortage of debate on the exact meaning of each amendment. Are there really to be be no governmental limits placed on religion, or speech, or the press, or assembly (First Amendment)? *Unreasonable* searches and seizures are prohibited, but what is to be considered unreasonable (Fourth Amendment)? What is "due process of law," a "speedy trial," "excessive bail," "cruel and unusual punishment" (Fifth to Eighth Amendments)? By laws of Congress and decisions of the courts, working answers to these questions have been gradually developed. And as we will see in the following set of readings, a given question may have been answered in fundamentally different ways at different times by the same institution.

18 / *Plessy v. Ferguson*
163 U.S. 537 (1896)

One significant example of the Supreme Court's "changing its mind" in the area of civil rights involved a principle called "separate but equal." Since 1896, the principle had provided a judicial justification for racial segregation; the principle's demise in 1954 would herald the coming of a new era in which segregation would be rejected as offensive to "equal protection of the laws."

As a specified right, equality came late to the Constitution. It is guaranteed neither in the original document nor in the Bill of Rights. In fact, such a guarantee would have run contrary to the Constitution's own provisions for the continuation of slavery, and it was only after emancipation that equality found a place in the Constitution.

The Thirteenth Amendment (1865) abolished slavery; the Fourteenth (1868) prohibited the states from denying "to any person within its jurisdiction the equal protection of the laws." As might be expected, many questions developed as to the applicability of this "right" in specific cases, and efforts began in some quarters to maintain vestiges of slavery that would not be judged unconstitutional.

Among those efforts was institutionalized segregation of the type that Homer Plessy experienced on the East Louisiana Railway. In rejecting Plessy's claim that he had been denied equal protection, the Supreme Court (in *Plessy v. Ferguson*, 1896) established the principle that separate facilities (in this case, train cars) for blacks and whites were not unconstitutional if those facilities were "equal."

This was a petition for writs of prohibition and certiorari originally filed in the supreme court of the state by Plessy, the plaintiff in error, against the Hon. John H. Ferguson, judge of the criminal district court for the parish of Orleans, and setting forth, in substance, the following facts:

That petitioner was a citizen of the United States and a resident of the state of Louisiana, of mixed descent, in the proportion of seven-eighths Caucasian and one-eighth African blood; that the mixture of colored blood was not discernible in him, and that he was entitled to every recognition, right, privilege, and immunity secured to the citizens of the United States of the white race by its constitution and laws; that on June 7, 1892, he engaged and paid for a first-class passage on the East Louisiana Railway, from New Orleans to Covington, in the same state, and thereupon entered a passenger train, and took possession of a vacant seat in a coach where passengers of the white race were accommodated; that such railroad company was incorporated by the laws of Louisiana as a common carrier, and was not authorized to distinguish between citizens according to their race, but, notwithstanding this, petitioner was required by the conductor, under penalty of ejection from said train and imprisonment, to vacate said coach, and occupy another seat, in a coach assigned by said company for persons not of the white race, and for no other reason than that petitioner was of the colored race; that, upon petitioner's refusal to comply with such order, he was, with the aid of a police officer, forcibly ejected from said coach, and hurried off to, and imprisoned in, the parish jail of New Orleans, and there held to answer a charge made by such officer to the effect that he was guilty of having criminally violated an act of the general assembly of the state, approved July 10, 1890, in such case made and provided.

The petitioner was subsequently brought before the recorder of the city for preliminary examination, and committed for trial to the criminal district court for the parish of Orleans, where an information was filed against him in the matter above set forth, for a violation of the above act, which act the petitioner affirmed to be null and void, because in conflict with the constitution of the United States. . . .

The case coming on for hearing before the supreme court, that court was of opinion that the law under which the prosecution was had was constitutional and denied the relief prayed for by the petitioner. . .; whereupon petitioner prayed for a writ of error from this court, which was allowed by the chief justice of the supreme court of Louisiana.

Mr. Justice Brown, after stating the facts in the foregoing language, delivered the opinion of the court.

This case turns upon the constitutionality of an act of the general assembly of the state of Louisiana, passed in 1890, providing for separate railway carriages for the white and colored races. . . .

The constitutionality of this act is attacked upon the ground that it conflicts both with the thirteenth amendment of the constitution, abolishing slavery, and the fourteenth amendment, which prohibits certain restrictive legislation on the part of the states.

1. That it does not conflict with the thirteenth amendment, which abolished slavery and involuntary servitude, except as a punishment for crime, is too clear for argument. . . .

A statute which implies merely a legal distinction between the white and colored races—a distinction which is founded in the color of the two races, and which must always exist so long as white men are distinguished from the other race by color—has no tendency to destroy the legal equality of the two races, or re-establish a state of involuntary servitude. Indeed, we do not understand that the thirteenth amendment is strenuously relied upon by the plaintiff in error in this connection.

2. By the fourteenth amendment, all persons born or naturalized in the United States, and subject to the jurisdiction thereof, are made citizens of the United States and of the state wherein they reside; and the states are forbidden from making or enforcing any law which shall abridge the privileges or immunities of citizens of the United States, or shall deprive any person of life, liberty, or property without due process of law, or deny to any person within their jurisdiction the equal protection of the laws. . . .

The object of the amendment was undoubtedly to enforce the absolute equality of the two races before the law, but, in the nature of things, it could not have been intended to abolish distinctions based upon color, or to enforce social, as distinguished from political, equality, or a commingling of the two races upon terms unsatisfactory to either. Laws permitting, and even requiring, their separation, in places where they are liable to be brought into contact, do not necessarily imply the inferiority of either race to the other, and have been generally, if not universally, recognized as within the competency of the state legislatures in the exercise of their police power. The most common instance of this is connected with the establishment of separate schools for white and colored children, which have been held to be a valid exercise of the legislative power even by courts of states where the political rights of the colored race have been longest and most earnestly enforced. . . .

The distinction between laws interfering with the political equality of the negro and those requiring the separation of the two races in schools, theaters, and railway carriages has been frequently drawn by this court. . . .

. . . [I]t is also suggested by the learned counsel for the plaintiff in error that the same argument that will justify the state legislature in requiring railways to provide separate accommodations for the two races will also authorize them to require separate cars to be provided for people whose hair is of a certain color, or who are aliens, or who belong to certain nationalities, or to enact laws requiring colored people to walk upon one side of the street, and white people upon the other, or requiring white men's houses to be painted white, and colored men's black, or their vehicles or business signs to be of different colors, upon the theory that one side of the street is as good as the other, or that a house or vehicle of one color is as good as one of another color. The reply to all this is that every exercise of the police power must be reasonable, and extend only to such laws as are enacted in good faith for the promotion of the public good, and not for the annoyance or oppression of a particular class. . . .

So far, then, as a conflict with the fourteenth amendment is concerned, the case reduces itself to the question whether the statute of Louisiana is a reasonable regulation, and with respect to this there must necessarily be a large discretion on the part of the legislature. In determining the question of reasonableness, it is at liberty to act with reference to the established usages, customs, and traditions of the people, and with a view to the promotion of their comfort, and the preservation of the public peace and good order. Gauged by this standard, we cannot say that a law which authorizes or even requires the separation of the two races in public conveyances is unreasonable, or more obnoxious to the fourteenth amendment than the acts of congress requiring separate schools for colored children in the District of Columbia, the constitutionality of which does not seem to have been questioned, or the corresponding acts of state legislatures.

We consider the underlying fallacy of the plaintiff's argument to consist in the assumption that the enforced separation of the two races stamps the colored race with a badge of inferiority. If this be so, it is not by reason of anything found in the act, but solely because the colored race chooses to put that construction upon it. The argument necessarily assumes that if, as has been more than once the case, and is not unlikely to be so again, the colored race should become the dominant power in the state legislature, and should enact a law in precisely similar terms, it would thereby relegate the white race to an inferior position. We imagine that the white race, at least, would not acquiesce in this assumption. The argument also assumes that social prejudices may be overcome by legislation, and that equal rights cannot be secured to the negro except by an enforced commingling of the two races. We cannot accept this proposition. If the two races are to meet upon terms of social equality, it must be the result of natural affinities, a mutual appreciation of each other's merits, and a voluntary consent of individuals. As was said by the court of appeals of New York in *People v. Gallagher*, 93 N. Y. 438, 448: "This end can neither be accomplished nor promoted by laws which conflict with the general sentiment of the community upon whom they are designed to operate. When the government, therefore, has secured to each of its citizens equal rights before the law, and equal opportunities for improvement and progress, it has accomplished the end for which it was organized, and performed all of the functions respecting social advantages with which it is endowed." Legislation is powerless to eradicate racial instincts, or to abolish distinctions based upon physical differences, and the attempt to do so can only result in accentuating the difficulties of the present situation. If the civil and political rights of both races be equal, one cannot be inferior to the other civilly or politically. If one race be inferior to the other socially, the constitution of the United States cannot put them upon the same plane. . . .

The judgment of the court below is therefore affirmed.

Mr. Justice Harlan dissenting.

It was said in argument that the statute of Louisiana does not discriminate against either race, but prescribes a rule applicable alike to white and colored citizens. But this argument does not meet the difficulty. Every one knows that the statute in question had its origin in the purpose, not so much to exclude white persons from railroad cars occupied by blacks, as to exclude colored people from coaches occupied by or assigned to white persons. Railroad corporations of Louisiana did not make discrimination among whites in the matter of accommodation for travelers. The thing to accomplish was, under the guise of giving equal accommodation for whites and blacks, to compel the latter to keep to themselves while traveling in railroad passenger coaches. No one would be so wanting in candor as to assert the contrary. The fundamental objection, therefore, to the statute, is that it interferes with the personal freedom of citizens. "Personal liberty," it has been well said, "consists in the power of locomotion, of changing situation, or removing one's person to whatsoever places one's own inclination may direct, without imprisonment or restraint, unless by due course of law." If a white man and a black man choose to occupy the same public conveyance on a public highway, it is their right to do so; and no government, proceeding alone on grounds of race, can prevent it without infringing the personal liberty of each. . . .

The white race deems itself to be the dominant race in this country. And so it is, in prestige, in achievements, in education, in wealth, and in power.

So, I doubt not, it will continue to be for all time, if it remains true to its great heritage, and holds fast to the principles of constitutional liberty. But in view of the constitution, in the eye of the law, there is in this country no superior, dominant, ruling class of citizens. There is no caste here. Our constitution is color-blind, and neither knows nor tolerates classes among citizens. In respect of civil rights, all citizens are equal before the law. The humblest is the peer of the most powerful. The law regards man as man, and takes no account of his surroundings or of his color when his civil rights as guarantied by the supreme law of the land are involved. It is therefore to be regretted that this high tribunal, the final expositor of the fundamental law of the land, has reached the conclusion that it is competent for a state to regulate the enjoyment by citizens of their civil rights solely upon the basis of race.

In my opinion, the judgment this day rendered will, in time, prove to be quite as pernicious as the decision made by this tribunal in the Dred Scott Case....

The arbitrary separation of citizens, on the basis of race, while they are on a public highway, is a badge of servitude wholly inconsistent with the civil freedom and the equality before the law established by the constitution. It cannot be justified upon any legal grounds.

If evils will result from the commingling of the two races upon public highways established for the benefit of all, they will be infinitely less than those that will surely come from state legislation regulating the enjoyment of civil rights upon the basis of race. We boast of the freedom enjoyed by our people above all other peoples. But it is difficult to reconcile that boast with a state of the law which, practically, puts the brand of servitude and degradation upon a large class of our fellow citizens—our equals before the law. The thin disguise of "equal" accommodations for passengers in railroad coaches will not mislead any one, nor atone for the wrong this day done....

I do not deem it necessary to review the decisions of state courts to which reference was made in argument. Some, and the most important, of them, are wholly inapplicable, because rendered prior to the adoption of the last amendments of the constitution, when colored people had very few rights which the dominant race felt obliged to respect. Others were made at a time when public opinion, in many localities, was dominated by the institution of slavery; when it would not have been safe to do justice to the black man; and when, so far as the rights of blacks were concerned, race prejudice was, practically, the supreme law of the land. Those decisions cannot be guides in the era introduced by the recent amendments of the supreme law, which established universal civil freedom, gave citizenship to all born or naturalized in the United States, and residing here, obliterated the race line from our systems of governments, national and state, and placed our free institutions upon the broad and sure foundation of the equality of all men before the law.

I am of opinion that the statute of Louisiana is inconsistent with the personal liberty of citizens, white and black, in that state, and hostile to both the spirit and letter of the constitution of the United States. If laws of like character should be enacted in the several states of the Union, the effect would be in the highest degree mischievous. Slavery, as an institution tolerated by law, would, it is true, have disappeared from our country; but there would remain a power in the states, by sinister legislation, to interfere with the full enjoyment of the blessings of freedom, to regulate civil rights, common to all citizens, upon the basis of race, and to place in a condition of legal inferiority a large body of American citizens, now constituting a part of the political community, called the "People of the United States," for whom, and by whom through representatives, our government is administered. Such a system is inconsistent with the guaranty given by the constitution to each state of a republican form of government, and may be stricken down by congressional action, or by the courts in the discharge of their solemn duty to maintain the supreme law of the land, anything in the constitution or laws of any state to the contrary notwithstanding.

For the reason stated, I am constrained to withhold my assent from the opinion and judgment of the majority.

Later cases would extend the principle of "separate but equal" to educational facilities, and as late as 1950 (*Sweatt v. Painter*) the Court still allowed for the principle in a case involving separate Texas law schools for blacks and whites.

In 1954 the Court fundamentally changed its view of the validity of the "separate but equal" principle. *Brown v. the Board of Education of Topeka* involved a black child who was denied admission to an all-white public school. Because "equality" of the black and white schools was not at issue, the Court instead focused on "the effect of segregation itself on public education." The Court relied heavily upon social science findings in concluding that separation of black schoolchildren on account of race contributes to a feeling of inferiority that may seriously hamper the educational process for those children. Hence, "in the field of public education the doctrine of 'separate but equal' has no place." With those words, the Court in 1954, in effect, overturned the precedent-setting decision of *Plessy v. Ferguson* (1896) and established a precedent with far-reaching consequences of its own.

19 / *Brown v. The Board of Education* (1954 and 1955)

In *Brown v. the Board of Education*, the Court chose to separate its decision overturning the "separate but equal" principle from its decision on how desegregation should be implemented. The second decision was announced a year after the first. Rather than providing guidelines for immediate desegregation of the school systems involved in the cases at hand, the Court wrote a more general decision that left the actual implementation in the hands of the schools and the lower federal courts and that called for "all deliberate speed" in reaching the objectives.

Brown v. the Board of Education of Topeka 347 U.S. 483 (1954)
Mr. Chief Justice Warren delivered the opinion of the Court.

These cases come to us from the States of Kansas, South Carolina, Virginia, and Delaware. They are premised on different facts and different local conditions, but a common legal question justifies their consideration together in this consolidated opinion.*

In each of the cases, minors of the Negro race, through their legal representatives, seek the aid of the courts in obtaining admission to the public schools of their community on a nonsegregated basis. In each instance, they had been denied admission to schools attended by white children under laws requiring or permitting segregation according to race. This segregation was alleged to deprive the plaintiffs of the equal protection of the laws under the Fourteenth Amendment. In each of the cases other than the Delaware case, a three-judge federal district court denied relief to the plaintiffs on the so-called "separate but equal" doctrine announced by this Court in *Plessy v. Ferguson*, [1896]. Under that doctrine, equality of treatment is accorded when the races are provided substantially equal facilities, even though these facilities be separate. In the Delaware case, the Supreme Court of Delaware adhered to that doctrine, but ordered that the plaintiffs be admitted to the white schools because of their superiority to the Negro schools.

The plaintiffs contend that segregated public schools are not "equal" and cannot be made "equal," and that hence they are deprived of the equal protection of the laws. Because of the obvious importance of the question presented, the Court took jurisdiction. Argument was heard in the 1952 Term, and reargument was heard this Term on certain questions propounded by the Court. . . .

In the first cases in this Court construing the Fourteenth Amendment, decided shortly after its adoption, the Court interpreted it as proscribing all state-imposed discriminations against the Negro race. The doctrine of "separate but equal" did not make its appearance in this Court until 1896 in the case of *Plessy v. Ferguson* . . . involving not education but transportation. American courts have since labored with the doctrine for over half a century. In this Court, there have been six cases involving the "separate but equal" doctrine in the field of public education. In *Cumming v. County Board of Education* [1899], and *Gong Lum v. Rice* [1927], the validity of the doctrine itself was not challenged. In more recent cases, all on the graduate school level, inequality was found in that specific benefits enjoyed by white students were denied to Negro students of the same educational qualifications. *Missouri ex rel. Gaines v. Canada* [1938]; *Sipuel v. Oklahoma* [1948]; *Sweatt v. Painter* [1950]; *McLaurin v. Oklahoma State Regents* [1950]. In none of these cases was it necessary to re-examine the doctrine to grant relief to the Negro

*Actually, five similar cases were decided together in this one opinion.—*Editor's Note.*

plaintiff. And in *Sweatt v. Painter*. . .the Court expressly reserved decision on the question whether *Plessy v. Ferguson* should be held inapplicable to public education.

In the instant cases, that question is directly presented. Here, unlike *Sweatt v. Painter*, there are findings below that the Negro and white schools involved have been equalized, or are being equalized, with respect to buildings, curricula, qualifications and salaries of teachers, and other "tangible" factors. Our decision, therefore, cannot turn on merely a comparison of these tangible factors in the Negro and white schools involved in each of the cases. We must look instead to the effect of segregation itself on public education.

In approaching this problem, we cannot turn the clock back to 1868 when the Amendment was adopted, or even to 1896 when *Plessy v. Ferguson* was written. We must consider public education in the light of its full development and its present place in American life throughout the Nation. Only in this way can it be determined if segregation in public schools deprives these plaintiffs of the equal protection of the laws.

Today, education is perhaps the most important function of state and local governments. Compulsory school attendance laws and the great expenditures for education both demonstrate our recognition of the importance of education to our democratic society. It is required in tbe performance of our most basic public responsibilities, even service in the armed forces. It is the very foundation of good citizenship. Today it is a principal instrument in awakening the child to cultural values, in preparing him for later professional training, and in helping him to adjust normally to his environment. In these days, it is doubtful that any child may reasonably be expected to succeed in life if he is denied the opportunity of an education. Such an opportunity, where the state has undertaken to provide it, is a right which must be made available to all on equal terms.

We come then to the question presented: Does segregation of children in public schools solely on the basis of race, even though the physical facilities and other "tangible" factors may be equal, deprive the children of the minority group of equal educational opportunities? We believe that it does.

In *Sweatt v. Painter*. . .in finding that a segregated law school for Negroes could not provide them equal educational opportunities, this Court relied in large part on "those qualities which are incapable of objective measurement but which make for greatness in a law school." In *McLaurin v. Oklahoma State Regents*. . ., the Court, in requiring that a Negro admitted to a white graduate school be treated like all other students, again resorted to intangible considerations: ". . .his ability to study, to engage in discussions and exchange views with other students, and, in general, to learn his profession." Such considerations apply with added force to children in grade and high schools. To separate them from others of similar age and qualifications solely because of their race generates a feeling of inferiority as to their status in the community that may affect their hearts and minds in a way unlikely ever to be undone. The effect of this separation on their educational opportunities was well stated by a finding in the Kansas case by a court which nevertheless felt compelled to rule against the Negro plaintiffs:

"Segregation of white and colored children in public schools has a detrimental effect upon the colored children. The impact is greater when it has the sanction of the law; for the policy of separating the races is usually interpreted as denoting the inferiority of the negro group. A sense of inferiority affects the motivation of a child to learn. Segregation with the sanction of law, therefore, has a tendency to [retard] the educational and mental development of negro children and to deprive them of some of the benefits they would receive in a racial[ly] integrated school system."

Whatever may have been the extent of psychological knowledge at the time of *Plessy v. Ferguson*, this finding is amply supported by modern authority. Any language in *Plessy v. Ferguson* contrary to this finding is rejected.

We conclude that in the field of public education the doctrine of "separate but equal" has no place. Separate educational facilities are inherently unequal. Therefore, we hold that the plaintiffs and others similarly situated for whom the actions have been brought are, by reason of the segregation complained of, deprived of the equal protection of the laws guaranteed by the Fourteenth Amendment. This disposition makes unnecessary any discussion whether such segregation also violates the Due Process Clause of the Fourteenth Amendment.

Because these are class actions, because of the wide applicability of this decision, and because of the great variety of local conditions, the formulation of decrees in these cases presents problems of considerable complexity. On reargument, the consideration of appropriate relief was necessarily subordinated to the primary question—the constitutionality of segregation in public education. We have now announced that such segregation is a denial of the equal protection of the laws. In order that we may have the full assistance of the parties in formulating decrees, the cases will be restored to the docket, and the parties are requested to present further argument on Questions 4 and 5 previously propounded by the Court for the reargument this Term....

It is so ordered.

Brown v. The Board of Education of Topeka 349 U.S. 294 (1955)

Mr. Chief Justice Warren delivered the opinion of the Court.

These cases were decided on May 17, 1954. The opinions of that date, declaring the fundamental principle that racial discrimination in public education is unconstitutional, are incorporated herein by reference. All provisions of federal, state, or local law requiring or permitting such discrimination must yield to this principle. There remains for consideration the manner in which relief is to be accorded....

Full implementation of these constitutional principles may require solution of varied local school problems. School authorities have the primary

responsibility for elucidating, assessing, and solving these problems; courts
will have to consider whether the action of school authorities constitutes good
faith implementation of the governing constitutional principles. Because of
their proximity to local conditions and the possible need for further hearings, the courts which originally heard these cases can best perform this
judicial appraisal. Accordingly, we believe it appropriate to remand the cases
to those courts.

In fashioning and effectuating the decrees, the courts will be guided by
equitable principles. Traditionally, equity has been characterized by a practical flexibility in shaping its remedies and by a facility for adjusting and reconciling public and private needs. These cases call for the exercise of these
traditional attributes of equity power. At stake is the personal interest of
the plaintiffs in admission to public schools as soon as practicable on a
nondiscriminatory basis. To effectuate this interest may call for elimination
of a variety of obstacles in making the transition to school systems operated
in accordance with the constitutional principles set forth in our May 17,
1954, decision. Courts of equity may properly take into account the public
interest in the elimination of such obstacles in a systematic and effective
manner. But it should go without saying that the vitality of these constitutional principles cannot be allowed to yield simply because of disagreement
with them.

While giving weight to these public and private considerations, the courts
will require that the defendants make a prompt and reasonable start toward
full compliance with our May 17, 1954, ruling. Once such a start has been
made, the courts may find that additional time is necessary to carry out the
ruling in an effective manner. The burden rests upon the defendants to
establish that such time is necessary in the public interest and is consistent
with good faith compliance at the earliest practicable date. To that end, the
courts may consider problems related to administration, arising from the
physical condition of the school plant, the school transportation system,
personnel, revision of school districts and attendance areas into compact
units to achieve a system of determining admission to the public schools
on a nonracial basis, and revision of local laws and regulations which may
be necessary in solving the foregoing problems. They will also consider the
adequacy of any plans the defendants may propose to meet these problems
and to effectuate a transition to a racially nondiscriminatory school system.
During this period of transition, the courts will retain jurisdiction of these
cases.

The judgments below, except that in the Delaware case, are accordingly
reversed and the cases are remanded to the District Courts to take such proceedings and enter such orders and decrees consistent with this opinion as
are necessary and proper to admit to public schools on a racially nondiscriminatory basis with all deliberate speed the parties to these cases. The
judgment in the Delaware case—ordering the immediate admission of the
plaintiffs to schools previously attended only by white children—is affirmed
on the basis of the principles stated in our May 17, 1954, opinion, but the

case is remanded to the Supreme Court of Delaware for such further proceedings as that Court may deem necessary in light of this opinion.

It is so ordered.

For some school systems (and some federal judges), "all deliberate speed" apparently meant moving at the pace of a snail. In a number of cases beginning in the mid 1960s, and including the "school busing decisions" of 1971 (*Swann v. Charlotte-Mecklenburg County Board of Education*), the Court was more specific in prescribing remedies for some school districts that had a history of segregation.*

20 / Does Affirmative Action Mean Reverse Discrimination?

Glenn A. Phelps

Ten years after the "conceptual" *Brown v. the Board of Education* decision, Congress passed a monumental piece of legislation designed to come to grips with the obvious conflict between racial discrimination and equal protection: the Civil Rights Act of 1964. Title VI of that Act clearly states that no person is to be "subjected to discrimination under any program or activity receiving federal financial assistance." Many recipients of federal aid, including some institutions of higher learning, responded to this language by establishing "affirmative action" programs designed to recruit more employees and/or students from groups discriminated against in the past.

Ironically, or perhaps inevitably, the programs designed to deal with past discrimination would now themselves be challenged as merely implementing a new form of discrimination. Title VI, which outlawed discrimination against any person "on the basis of race, color, or national origin," would now serve as the basis of lawsuits from self-perceived victims of "reverse discrimination."

Allan Bakke, a white applicant denied admission to the medical school at the University of California–Davis, brought the first such suit to be decided eventually by the U.S. Supreme Court. In the following selection, Glenn A. Phelps considers the issues involved in the Bakke case and places the Court's decision in context. The decision itself, as presented by Justice Powell, follows Phelps's article.

Allan Bakke was not, at first glance, the sort of person whom one would suspect as likely to make a federal case out of anything. To most he seemed quiet, even shy. To say that Bakke was just an average guy would be a misstatement, however; he was in many ways exceptional. But nothing in his background indicated that he would instigate one of the most talked-about civil rights cases of the 1970s.

*One source of information on the *Plessy* and *Brown* cases, used by the editor as background for this section, is John Brigham, *Civil Liberties and American Democracy* (Washington: CQ Press, 1984, Ch. 6).—*Editor's Note.*

Those who knew Allan Bakke well were aware that he had a goal that bordered on obsession: he wanted to be a doctor. This realization had come to Bakke later in life than most. He had graduated from the University of Minnesota in 1962 with a degree in engineering. To fulfill his ROTC obligation he then served four years as an officer in the U.S. Marine Corps with a tour of duty in Vietnam. After his military service, he resumed his engineering career at the National Aeronautics and Space Administration (NASA), in the meantime obtaining a master's degree in engineering from Stanford University.

Vietnam changed many people in many ways. For Allan Bakke it was where he first realized he wanted to be a doctor. His association with medics and doctors there convinced him that he could serve his community more appropriately as a physician than as an engineer. That desire became an almost single-minded obsession on his return. He often worked early morning hours and evenings at NASA so that he would have time to commute to school, where he took the biology and chemistry courses needed as prerequisites for medical school. He also began working as a volunteer at the local hospital as an emergency room assistant. Those who know him there were struck by his dedication.

Among the medical schools to which he applied was the University of California at Davis (UCDMS). Ironically, at this point Bakke's greatest concern was about his age. He was thirty-two years old when he first applied to UCDMS, an age that many schools classified as too old for consideration due to the number of years that medical training requires. (Subsequent civil rights legislation now prohibits age discrimination.) Otherwise his credentials were impressive: a 3.5 grade point average combined with Medical College Admissions Test scores that were near the ninety-fifth percentile on three of the four tests. The admissions standards at Cal–Davis, though, were highly competitive for candidates seeking regular admissions. In 1973 2,173 applicants were vying for only 84 seats (an acceptance rate of one in twenty-six). Bakke's record, however, was sufficiently impressive to advance him to the interview stage, after which the five evaluators gave him a cumulative score of 468 (out of a possible 500). The benchmark score for advancing further in the admissions process was 470, so he was denied admission. In another curious turn to the story, had Bakke's application been received several months earlier, the record suggests that his score would have been sufficiently high for admission under the early consideration process, and *Regents v. Bakke* 1978 would have never occurred.

Bakke applied to UCDMS again in 1974, this time early enough to be considered in the rolling admissions process that he had missed the year before. Although there were 3,109 applicants (almost 50 percent more than in 1973), he again reached the interview process. This time six evaluators assigned him a score of 549 out of 600, marginally lower than in 1973, and he was rejected for a second time.

Bakke had discovered, however, that Cal–Davis had two admissions review processes: one for regular applicants, like himself, and one for special applicants. The special admissions process was intended to review carefully applicants who might in some way be considered "disadvantaged." On the surface, there was nothing to prevent a white male from being reviewed by this special process, perhaps because of poverty, physical handicaps, age, or some other factor that would make him personally "disadvantaged." In practice, though, the only persons offered admissions to UCDMS by the special review process were racial minorities. Of the sixty-three special admittees between 1971 and 1974, thirty were Hispanic, twenty-one were black, and twelve were Asian. The grade averages and MCAT scores for these special admittees were considerably lower than Bakke's.

Allan Bakke now found himself the odd man out in a conflict between two principles, each with an authentic civil liberties pedigree and each using the Equal Protection Clause of the Fourteenth Amendment for its justification. The antidiscrimination principle sees the Equal Protection Clause as asserting that race must not be a consideration when making public policy. U. S. history has been so fraught with infamies resulting from discrimination based on the race that that road ought to be singularly avoided. Accordingly persons ought to be judged by their individual talents, character, and abilities rather than by irrelevancies like race.

The second principle, "affirmative action," also anchors itself in the Fourteenth Amendment. In assessing the history of that Amendment, supporters of "affirmative action" note that the purpose of the Equal Protection Clause was to guarantee that the civil rights of blacks as a group were protected and promoted. To be satisfied with an end only to *de jure* discrimination would leave historically disadvantaged blacks to compete with historically advantaged whites, a competition many observers analogized to a foot race in which some runners are shackled at the beginning and then released to compete on an "equal" basis with those far down the track. Thus, government would be justified in seeking to remedy for past discriminations by encouraging "affirmative action" through various means including quotas, targets, and set-asides.

Cal–Davis chose to adhere to the "affirmative action" principle in its admissions policy by setting aside sixteen of the one hundred places in each medical school class for "disadvantaged" applicants. The university was concerned especially about the underrepresentation of blacks and other minorities in the medical professions. Who, they wondered, would serve the needs of those, often poor, minority communities? Allan Bakke, on the other hand, saw himself as a victim of "reverse discrimination." He believed he would have received one of the sixteen set-aside places had they been open to all candidates regardless of race. (In truth, his assertion was probably true only for 1973. His 1974 benchmark score was probably not within the highest one hundred applicants.)

The Court's resolution of the antidiscrimination versus "affirmative action" conflict raised by *Bakke* was eagerly anticipated because of the disappointing results of an earlier "reverse discrimination" case, *DeFunis v. Odegaard* (1974). Marco DeFunis was a white Jewish male who had applied for admission to the University of Washington Law School (UWLS). He, too, complained that he was a victim of "reverse discrimination": that thirty applicants from designated minorities were admitted despite having PFYA (predicted first-year average) scores significantly lower than his. Despite enormous public interest, however, the Supreme Court declined the opportunity to make a definitive ruling. The original trial court had ordered UWLS to admit DeFunis in 1971 as a temporary measure until the issue could be resolved; he was now about to graduate. Thus, the Court determined that the issue, at least in DeFunis's case, was moot.

No such opportunity for nondecision existed in *Bakke*, though. The result was one of the most curious decisions in the Supreme Court's history. Instead of a clear majority for one party or other, the Court offered a bizarre one-person plurality. Justice Powell wrote the opinion for the Court, but to do so he was compelled to negotiate an unusual 4–1–4 coalition between two diametrically opposed blocs.

One group of four justices (Brennan, White, Marshall, and Blackmun) accepted the "affirmative action" principle as decisive. While recognizing that discriminations based on race were "suspect" and merited "strict scrutiny," they noted that the Equal Protection Clause did not demand that racial classifications could *never* be constitutional. Rather, it was imperative that such classifications be both benign *and* essential for some legitimate state purpose. The "affirmative action four" were impressed with Cal–Davis's claims regarding the shortage of black and minority doctors and agreed that rectifying this situation, a result of past discrimination, was a legitimate state purpose. In addition, they asserted that the special admissions program was benign rather than invidious:

> Unlike discrimination against racial minorities, the use of racial preferences for remedial purposes does not inflict a pervasive injury upon individual whites in the sense that wherever they go or whatever they do there is a significant likelihood that they will be treated as second-class citizens because of their color.

Justice Marshall stated in his support for "affirmative action" even more passionately:

> It must be remembered that, during most of the past 200 years, the Constitution as interpreted by this Court did not prohibit the most ingenious and pervasive forms of discrimination against the Negro. Now, when a State acts to remedy the effects of that legacy of discrimination, I cannot believe that this same Constitution stands as a barrier.

The "anti-discrimination four" (Justices Burger, Stewart, Stevens, and Rehnquist), on the other hand, argued that race could not be used to discriminate against *anyone* in the allocation of public benefits. Moreover, they noted that the specific language of the Civil Rights Act of 1964 went beyond the Equal Protection Clause. Title VI of this act states that "race cannot be the basis of excluding anyone from participation in a federally funded program." To this bloc, Bakke was clearly excluded from consideration solely because of his race.

Powell carved out an interesting compromise position. His opinion was critical of the quota aspect of the UCDMS plan. Setting aside sixteen places for minorities only struck Powell as the kind of overt racial discrimination prohibited by both the Fourteenth Amendment and Title VI. Moreover, Cal–Davis had no institutional history of racial discrimination (the medical school opened in 1968, long after the official demise of race-conscious school systems), so its claims of remedying the effects of past discrimination were unconvincing. Thus, the Court commanded that Bakke be admitted.

But Powell did not go so far as to say that race could *never* be a consideration in the admissions process. Universities have long considered many factors other than grades and test scores in attracting a diverse student body. Scholarships can be offered to candidates with superior athletic ability, or to musicians, or to the needy, among others. Colleges may wish also to examine factors such as geographic distribution or socioeconomic class or veteran status. In this light, Powell argued that universities may consider race as *a* factor in the admissions process but only if it is considered as one among many such special factors. Powell thus concluded with an invitation to other interested parties to redesign their admissions process: quotas, no; affirmative action, yes.

The ambiguity of Powell's decision (accepting the antidiscrimination principle in part and the "affirmative action" principle in part) appeared Solomonlike, but it did not resolve the conflict. Both opponents and supporters of "affirmative action" hailed it as a victory. Shortly thereafter the Court decided that "affirmative action" in the private sector was constitutional (*United Steelworkers v. Weber*, 1979), as was a federal law requiring that 10 percent of all government contracts be allocated to minority businesses (*Fullilove v. Klutznick*, 1980).

21 / Regents of the University of California v. Bakke
438 U.S. 265 (1978)

Mr. Justice Powell announced the judgment of the Court.

This case presents a challenge to the special admissions program of the petitioner, the Medical School of the University of California at Davis, which is designed to assure the admission of a specified number of students from certain minority groups. The Superior Court of California sustained respondent's challenge, holding that petitioner's program violated the California Constitution, Title VI of the Civil Rights Act of 1964. . . and the Equal Protection Clause of the Fourteenth Amendment. The court enjoined petitioner from considering respondent's race or the race of any other applicant in making admissions decisions. It refused, however, to order respondent's admission to the Medical School, holding that he had not carried his burden of proving that he would have been admitted but for the constitutional and statutory violations. The Supreme Court of California affirmed those portions of the trial court's judgment declaring the special admissions program unlawful and enjoining petitioner from considering the race of any applicant. It modified that portion of the judgment denying respondent's requested injunction and directed the trial court to order his admission.

For the reasons stated in the following opinion, I believe that so much of the judgment of the California court as holds petitioner's special admissions program unlawful and directs that respondent be admitted to the Medical School must be affirmed. For the reasons expressed in a separate opinion, my Brothers The Chief Justice, Mr. Justice Stewart, Mr. Justice Rehnquist, and Mr. Justice Stevens concur in this judgment.

I also conclude for the reasons stated in the following opinion that the portion of the court's judgment enjoining petitioner from according any consideration to race in its admissions process must be reversed. For reasons expressed in separate opinions, my Brothers Mr. Justice Brennan, Mr. Justice White, Mr. Justice Marshall, and Mr. Justice Blackmun concur in this judgment.

Affirmed in part and reversed in part.

The language of §601, 78 Stat. 252, like that of the Equal Protection Clause, is majestic in its sweep:

> "No person in the United States shall, on the ground of race, color, or national origin, be excluded from participation in, be denied the benefits of, or be subjected to discrimination under any program or activity receiving Federal financial assistance."

The concept of "discrimination," like the phrase "equal protection of the laws," is susceptible of varying interpretations, for as Mr. Justice Holmes declared, "[a] word is not a crystal, transparent and unchanged, it is the skin of a living thought and may vary greatly in color and content according to the circumstances and the time in which it is used." *Towne v. Eisner*. . . (1918). We must, therefore, seek whatever aid is available in determining the precise meaning of the statute before us. . . . Examination of the voluminous legislative history of Title VI reveals a congressional intent to halt federal funding of entities that violate a prohibition of racial discrimination similar to that of the Constitution. Although isolated statements of various legislators, taken out of context, can be marshaled in support of the proposition that §601 enacted a purely colorblind scheme, without regard to the reach of the Equal Protection Clause, these comments must be read against the background of both the problem that Congress was addressing and the broader view of the statute that emerges from a full examination of the legislative debates.

The problem confronting Congress was discrimination against Negro citizens at the hands of recipients of federal moneys. . . . There simply was no reason for Congress to consider the validity of hypothetical preferences that might be accorded minority citizens; the legislators were dealing with the real and pressing problem of how to guarantee those citizens equal treatment.

In addressing that problem, supporters of Title VI repeatedly declared that the bill enacted constitutional principles. . . .

In the Senate, Senator Humphrey declared that the purpose of Title VI was "to insure that Federal funds are spent in accordance with the Constitution and the moral sense of the Nation." Senator Ribicoff agreed that Title VI embraced the constitutional standard: "Basically, there is a constitutional restriction against discrimination in the use of federal funds; and title VI simply spells out the procedure to be used in enforcing that restriction." Other Senators expressed similar views. . . .

In view of the clear legislative intent, Title VI must be held to proscribe only those racial classifications that would violate the Equal Protection Clause or the Fifth Amendment.

Petitioner does not deny that decisions based on race or ethnic origin by faculties and administrations of state universities are reviewable under the Fourteenth Amendment. . . . For his part, respondent does not argue that all racial or ethnic classifications are *per se* invalid. . . . The parties do disagree as to the level of judicial scrutiny to be applied to the special admissions program. . . .

En route to this crucial battle over the scope of judicial review, the parties fight a sharp preliminary action over the proper characterization of the special admissions program. Petitioner prefers to view it as establishing a "goal" of minority representation in the Medical School. Respondent, echoing the courts below, labels it a racial quota.

This semantic distinction is beside the point: The special admissions program is undeniably a classification based on race and ethnic background. To the extent that there existed a pool of at least minimally qualified minority applicants to fill the 16 special admissions seats, white applicants could compete only for 84 seats in the entering class, rather than the 100 open to minority applicants. Whether this limitation is described as a quota or a goal, it is a line drawn on the basis of race and ethnic status.

The guarantees of the Fourteenth Amendment extend to all persons. Its language is explicit: "No State shall. . . deny to any person within its jurisdiction the equal protection of the laws." It is settled beyond question that the "rights created by the first section of the Fourteenth Amendment are, by its

terms, guaranteed to the individual. The rights established are personal rights."
Shelly v. Kraemer. . . . The guarantee of equal protection cannot mean one
thing when applied to one individual and something else when applied to
a person of another color. If both are not accorded the same protection, then
it is not equal.

Nevertheless, petitioner argues that the court below erred in applying
strict scrutiny to the special admissions program because white males, such
as respondent, are not a "discrete and insular minority" requiring extraordinary protection from the majoritarian political process. *Carolene Products
Co.* . . . This rationale, however, has never been invoked in our decisions as
a prerequisite to subjecting racial or ethnic distinctions to strict scrutiny. Nor
has this Court held that discreteness and insularity constitute necessary preconditions to a holding that a particular classification is invidious. . . . These
characteristics may be relevant in deciding whether or not to add new types
of classifications to the list of "suspect" categories or whether a particular
classification survives close examination. . . . Racial and ethnic classifications,
however, are subject to stringent examination without regard to these additional characteristics. . . .

. . . Racial and ethnic distinctions of any sort are inherently suspect and
thus call for the most exacting judicial examination.

This perception of racial and ethnic distinctions is rooted in our Nation's
constitutional and demographic history. The Court's initial view of the Fourteenth Amendment was that its "one pervading purpose" was "the freedom
of the slave race, the security and firm establishment of that freedom, and
the protection of the newly-made freeman and citizen from the oppressions
of those who had formerly exercised dominion over him." *Slaughter-House
Cases,* . . . (1873). . . .

Although many of the Framers of the Fourteenth Amendment conceived
of its primary function as bridging the vast distance between members of
the Negro race and the white "majority," *Slaughter-House Cases, supra,* the
Amendment itself was framed in universal terms, without reference to color,
ethnic origin, or condition of prior servitude. As this Court recently remarked
in interpreting the 1866 Civil Rights Act to extend to claims of racial
discrimination against white persons, "the 39th Congress was intent upon
establishing in the federal law a broader principle than would have been
necessary simply to meet the particular and immediate plight of the newly
freed Negro slaves." *McDonald v. Santa Fe Trail Transportation Co.* . . .
(1976). . . .

Over the past 30 years, this Court has embarked upon the crucial mission of interpreting the Equal Protection Clause with the view of assuring
to all persons "the protection of equal laws," *Yick Wo.* . . , in a Nation confronting a legacy of slavery and racial discrimination. . . . Because the landmark decisions in this area arose in response to the continued exclusion of
Negroes from the mainstream of American society, they could be characterized
as involving discrimination by the "majority" white race against the Negro
minority. But they need not be read as depending upon that characterization

for their results. It suffices to say that "[o]ver the years, this Court has consistently repudiated '[d]istinctions between citizens solely because of their ancestry' as being 'odious to a free people whose institutions are founded upon the doctrine of equality.' " *Loving v. Virginia* . . . (1967). . . .

Petitioner urges us to adopt for the first time a more restrictive view of the Equal Protection Clause and hold that discrimination against members of the white "majority" cannot be suspect if its purpose can be characterized as "benign." The clock of our liberties, however, cannot be turned back to 1868. . . . It is far too late to argue that the guarantee of equal protection to *all* persons permits the recognition of special wards entitled to a degree of protection greater than that accorded others. "The Fourteenth Amendment is not directed solely against discrimination due to a 'two-class theory'—that is, based upon differences between 'white' and Negro." *Hernandez.* . . .

Once the artificial line of a "two-class theory" of the Fourteenth Amendment is put aside, the difficulties entailed in varying the level of judicial review according to a perceived "preferred" status of a particular racial or ethnic minority are intractable. The concepts of "majority" and "minority" necessarily reflect temporary arrangements and political judgments. As observed above, the white "majority" itself is composed of various minority groups, most of which can lay claim to a history of prior discrimination at the hands of the State and private individuals. Not all of these groups can receive preferential treatment and corresponding judicial tolerance of distinctions drawn in terms of race and nationality, for then the only "majority" left would be a new minority of white Anglo-Saxon Protestants. There is no principled basis for deciding which groups would merit "heightened judicial solicitude" and which would not. Courts would be asked to evaluate the extent of the prejudice and consequent harm suffered by various minority groups. Those whose societal injury is thought to exceed some arbitrary level of tolerability then would be entitled to preferential classifications at the expense of individuals belonging to other groups. Those classifications would be free from exacting judicial scrutiny. As these preferences began to have their desired effect, and the consequences of past discrimination were undone, new judicial rankings would be necessary. The kind of variable sociological and political analysis necessary to produce such rankings simply does not lie within the judicial competence—even if they otherwise were politically feasible and socially desirable.

Moreover, there are serious problems of justice connected with the idea of preference itself. First, it may not always be clear that a so-called preference is in fact benign. Courts may be asked to validate burdens imposed upon individual members of a particular group in order to advance the group's general interest. . . . Nothing in the Constitution supports the notion that individuals may be asked to suffer otherwise impermissible burdens in order to enhance the societal standing of their ethnic groups. Second, preferential programs may only reinforce common stereotypes holding that certain groups are unable to achieve success without special protection based on a factor having no relationship to individual worth. . . . Third, there is a measure of inequity in forcing innocent persons in respondent's position to bear the burdens of redressing grievances not of their making.

By hitching the meaning of the Equal Protection Clause to these transitory considerations, we would be holding, as a constitutional principle, that judicial scrutiny of classifications touching on racial and ethnic background may vary with the ebb and flow of political forces. Disparate constitutional tolerance of such classifications well may serve to exacerbate racial and ethnic antagonisms rather than alleviate them.... Also, the mutability of a constitutional principle, based upon shifting political and social judgments, undermines the chances for consistent application of the Constitution from one generation to the next, a critical feature of its coherent interpretation.... In expounding the Constitution, the Court's role is to discern "principles sufficiently absolute to give them roots throughout the community and continuity over significant periods of time, and to lift them above the level of the pragmatic political judgments of a particular time and place." A. Cox, The Role of the Supreme Court in American Government 114 (1976).

If it is the individual who is entitled to judicial protection against classifications based upon his racial or ethnic background because such distinctions impinge upon personal rights, rather than the individual only because of his membership in a particular group, then constitutional standards may be applied consistently. Political judgments regarding the necessity for the particular classification may be weighed in the constitutional balance..., but the standard of justification will remain constant. This is as it should be, since those political judgments are the product of rough compromise struck by contending groups within the democratic process. When they touch upon an individual's race or ethnic background, he is entitled to a judicial determination that the burden he is asked to bear on that basis is precisely tailored to serve a compelling governmental interest. The Constitution guarantees that right to every person regardless of his background....

We have held that in "order to justify the use of a suspect classification, a State must show that its purpose or interest is both constitutionally permissible and substantial, and that its use of the classification is 'necessary... to the accomplishment' of its purpose or the safeguarding of its interest." In re Griffiths... (1973).... The special admissions program purports to serve the purposes of: (i) "reducing the historic deficit of traditionally disfavored minorities in medical schools and in the medical profession," Brief for Petitioner 32; (ii) countering the effects of societal discrimination; (iii) increasing the number of physicians who will practice in communities currently underserved; and (iv) obtaining the educational benefits that flow from an ethnically diverse student body. It is necessary to decide which, if any, of these purposes is substantial enough to support the use of a suspect classification.

If petitioner's purpose is to assure within its student body some specified percentage of a particular group merely because of its race or ethnic origin, such a preferential purpose must be rejected not as insubstantial but as facially invalid. Preferring members of any one group for no reason other than race or ethnic origin is discrimination for its own sake. This the Constitution forbids. . . .

The State certainly has a legitimate and substantial interest in ameliorating, or eliminating where feasible, the disabling effects of identified discrimination. The line of school desegregation cases, commencing with *Brown*, attests to the importance of this state goal and the commitment of the judiciary to affirm all lawful means toward its attainment. In the school cases, the States were required by court order to redress the wrongs worked by specific instances of racial discrimination. That goal was far more focused than the remedying of the effects of "societal discrimination," an amorphous concept of injury that may be ageless in its reach into the past. . . .

Hence, the purpose of helping certain groups whom the faculty of the Davis Medical School perceived as victims of "societal discrimination" does not justify a classification that imposes disadvantages upon persons like respondent, who bear no responsibility for whatever harm the beneficiaries of the special admissions program are thought to have suffered. To hold otherwise would be to convert a remedy heretofore reserved for violations of legal rights into a privilege that all institutions throughout the Nation could grant at their pleasure to whatever groups are perceived as victims of societal discrimination. That is a step we have never approved. . . .

Petitioner identifies, as another purpose of its program, improving the delivery of health-care services to communities currently underserved. It may be assumed that in some situations a State's interest in facilitating the health care of its citizens is sufficiently compelling to support the use of a suspect classification. But there is virtually no evidence in the record indicating that petitioner's special admissions program is either needed or geared to promote that goal. . . .

The fourth goal asserted by petitioner is the attainment of a diverse student body. This clearly is a constitutionally permissible goal for an institution of higher education. Academic freedom, though not a specifically enumerated constitutional right, long has been viewed as a special concern of the First Amendment. The freedom of a university to make its own judgments as to education includes the selection of its student body. . . .

Ethnic diversity, however, is only one element in a range of factors a university properly may consider in attaining the goal of a heterogeneous student body. Although a university must have wide discretion in making the sensitive judgments as to who should be admitted, constitutional limitations protecting individual rights may not be disregarded. Respondent urges— and the courts below have held—that petitioner's dual admissions program is a racial classification that impermissibly infringes his rights under the Fourteenth Amendment. As the interest of diversity is compelling in the context of a university's admissions program, the question remains whether the program's racial classification is necessary to promote this interest. . . .

It may be assumed that the reservation of a specified number of seats in each class for individuals from the preferred ethnic groups would contribute to the attainment of considerable ethnic diversity in the student body. But petitioner's argument that this is the only effective means of serving the interest of diversity is seriously flawed. In a most fundamental sense the argument misconceives the nature of the state interest that would justify consideration of race or ethnic background. It is not an interest in simple ethnic diversity, in which a specified percentage of the student body is in effect guaranteed to be members of selected ethnic groups, with the remaining percentage an undifferentiated aggregation of students. The diversity that furthers a compelling state interest encompasses a far broader array of qualifications and characteristics of which racial or ethnic origin is but a single though important element. Petitioner's special admissions program, focused *solely* on ethnic diversity, would hinder rather than further attainment of genuine diversity. . . .

The experience of other university admissions programs, which take race into account in achieving the educational diversity valued by the First Amendment, demonstrates that the assignment of a fixed number of places to a minority group is not a necessary means toward that end. An illuminating example is found in the Harvard College program. . . .

In such an admissions program, race or ethnic background may be deemed a "plus" in a particular applicant's file, yet it does not insulate the individual from comparison with all other candidates for the available seats. . . .

This kind of program treats each applicant as an individual in the admissions process. The applicant who loses out on the last available seat to another candidate receiving a "plus" on the basis of ethnic background will not have been foreclosed from all consideration for that seat simply because he was not the right color or had the wrong surname. It would mean only that his combined qualifications, which may have included similar nonobjective factors, did not outweigh those of the other applicant. His qualifications would have been weighed fairly and competitively, and he would have no basis to complain of unequal treatment under the Fourteenth Amendment.

It has been suggested that an admissions program which considers race only as one factor is simply a subtle and more sophisticated—but no less effective—means of according racial preference than the Davis program. A facial intent to discriminate, however, is evident in petitioner's preference program and not denied in this case. No such facial infirmity exists in an admissions program where race or ethnic background is simply one element—to be weighed fairly against other elements—in the selection process. . . .

In summary, it is evident that the Davis special admissions program involves the use of an explicit racial classification never before countenanced by this Court. It tells applicants who are not Negro, Asian, or Chicano that they are totally excluded from a specific percentage of the seats in an entering class. No matter how strong their qualifications, quantitative and extracurricular, including their own potential for contribution to educational diversity, they are never afforded the chance to compete with applicants from the preferred groups for the special admissions seats. At the same time, the preferred applicants have the opportunity to compete for every seat in the class.

The fatal flaw in petitioner's preferential program is its disregard of individual rights as guaranteed by the Fourteenth Amendment.... Such rights are not absolute. But when a State's distribution of benefits or imposition of burdens hinges on ancestry or the color of a person's skin, that individual is entitled to a demonstration that the challenged classification is necessary to promote a substantial state interest. Petitioner has failed to carry this burden. For this reason, that portion of the California court's judgment holding petitioner's special admissions program invalid under the Fourteenth Amendment must be affirmed.

In enjoining petitioner from ever considering the race of any applicant, however, the courts below failed to recognize that the State has a substantial interest that legitimately may be served by a properly devised admissions program involving the competitive consideration of race and ethnic origin. For this reason, so much of the California court's judgment as enjoins petitioner from any consideration of the race of any applicant must be reversed.

With respect to respondent's entitlement to an injunction directing his admission to the Medical School, petitioner has conceded that it could not carry its burden of proving that, but for the existence of its unlawful special admissions program, respondent still would not have been admitted. Hence, respondent is entitled to the injunction, and that portion of the judgment must be affirmed.

That the constitutionality of affirmative action is not a simple, clearcut matter is evidenced not only in the Court's close vote in *Bakke* but also in the nature of its decisions over the next decade. In about a dozen related decisions through 1990, the Court overturned affirmative action programs in approximately half of them, allowing the programs to stand in the other half.* Given that these decisions also tended to be based on narrow majorities, many observers felt a few additional conservative apointments could position the Court more definitively against affirmative action in the future.

*From Wilson, James Q., *American Government*, Fifth edition (Lexington, Mass: D. C. Heath and Company, 1992, p. 541).—*Editor's Note*.

22 / Seventeen Words: The Quiet Revolution of the Fourteenth Amendment

Fred W. Friendly and Martha J. H. Elliott

In addition to guaranteeing equal protection under the laws, the Fourteenth Amendment also provided that no state shall "deprive any person of life, liberty, or property, without due process of law." Unlike the case of equality, however, due process provisions already existed in the Bill of Rights (in the Fifth Amendment). In this instance, the importance of the Fourteenth Amendment was in extending the due process protections to the states as well as the national government. Like the case of equality, though the history of the Supreme Court's decisions regarding due process has involved both extension and expansion of the concept.

In the following reading, Fred Friendly and Martha Elliott recount the expansion from a property-oriented interpretation of the Fourteenth Amendment's due process clause, through incorporation of limited individual rights, to what is now almost complete inclusion of the Bill of Rights. In the 1960s, the Court's decisions extended most of the "rights of the accused" (in the Fourth, Fifth, Sixth, and Eighth Amendments) to the states.* More recently, the Court has upheld individuals' claims to due process from other agencies outside the criminal process, including schools and welfare agencies.†

It took 44 years for the Supreme Court even to consider the question of whether the Bill of Rights applied to the states, and Marshall answered the question in the negative.‡ If *Barron* were still the ruling opinion, then the individual states might be free to censor newspapers or inflict cruel and unusual punishments or deny a person the right to a jury trial. Not only is this not the case, but the Supreme Court today spends more than half its time wrestling with questions related to the fundamental liberties guaranteed by the Bill of Rights. How, then, did the situation change so dramatically? The answer is a complicated combination of the Civil War, the Fourteenth Amendment, and the Supreme Court itself.

John Marshall never lived to see the Civil War or the subsequent passage of the Fourteenth Amendment and the gradual chiseling away of his *Barron* decision by the use of 17 words in that amendment: "nor shall any State deprive any person of life, liberty, or property, without due process of law."

---

*See Rossum, Ralph A., and G. Alan Tarr, *American Constitutional Law*, Third Edition (New York: St. Martin's Press, 1991, pp. 455–475).—*Editor's Note.*

†See Brigham, John, *Civil Liberties and American Democracy*, (Washington, D.C.: CQ Press, 1984, pp. 87–88, 109–124).—*Editor's Note.*

‡In *Barron v. Baltimore* (1833), the Court found that the Bill of Rights restricted only the national government, not the states.—*Editor's Note.*

The Fourteenth Amendment was a direct result of the Civil War, a war many statesmen had tried to avoid. Men such as Marshall on the Court and Daniel Webster and Henry Clay in the Senate had devoted their energies to preserving the Union. However, economics, free trade versus protectionism, states' rights, party politics, and especially that "peculiar institution" of slavery created a vortex of irreconcilable differences. Slavery was the "constitutional cancer" that could not be checked, and it was the spreading of slavery into the territories that posed the greatest threat to the Union. For each time a territory was organized or a new state wanted to be admitted, the balance of slave states versus free states was threatened. In 1820, the Northern states, where slavery was prohibited, had a clear majority in the House of Representatives with, on the basis of census, 105 members compared to 81 for the Southern states. However, an equilibrium existed in the Senate because there were 11 free and 11 slave states. The Southern states feared that if they lost their equal representation in the Senate, slavery might be outlawed by Congress. In 1820 Missouri, a territory situated north of the Mason–Dixon line of demarcation between free and slave states, applied for admission to the Union as a *slave* state. After heated debates, Missouri was admitted as a slave state with the compromise that in the future slavery was to be prohibited above the latitude of 36°30'. At the same time, Maine was admitted as a free state, keeping the Senate balance at 12 and 12. Yet the growing boundaries of the nation and the impetus to admit new states continually threatened that balance.

Dred Scott's Fight for Freedom
It might all have happened if there had been no slave called Dred Scott. It might have been any of the other two million descendants of Africans who had been dragged in chains to a new world to be sold and traded like mules, cows, or cotton gins. But Dred Scott is the name coupled with that of John F. A. Sanford (which the Court records mistakenly spelled as "Sandford") on that decision of 1857 which the later Chief Justice Charles Evans Hughes described as the Court's first "self-inflicted wound...a public calamity." Historian James MacGregor Burns described more specifically the decision's effect: "As a political decision it upset the delicate position between North and South, exacerbated antagonism between proslavery and antislavery, and destroyed that superb device of compromise."[1]

No one knows the real facts behind the Dred Scott case. Its history is so tangled in conjecture and myth that the facts are almost impossible to unravel. It's not even clear that Dred Scott was the slave's real name; some historians are convinced that for his first 30 years he was called "Sam." What is known is that Scott was probably born in Virginia around the turn of the nineteenth century and had been the property of Peter Blow. When the Blow family moved to St. Louis in 1830, Scott was taken along with five other slaves. Blow died two years later, and either just before or just after his death, Scott was sold to Dr. John Emerson. What happened after that was most significant: Dred Scott was taken out of a slave state to free soil. In December 1833,

Dr. Emerson reported for duty at Fort Armstrong in Illinois, a free state, and took his slave with him. In 1836, when the army vacated Fort Armstrong, Dr. Emerson was transferred to Fort Snelling, near what is now St. Paul, Minnesota. The "Wisconsin territory," as it was then called, was an area where slavery had been forbidden by the Missouri Compromise.

The cold, harsh Minnesota winters were too much for Dr. Emerson, who was continually complaining of ill health; he requested a transfer and was sent to Fort Jesup in Louisiana. Dred Scott and his wife, Harriett, remained in Fort Snelling as rented servants until February 1838, when Dr. Emerson married and apparently sent for his two slaves. But Emerson was not happy with the damp Louisiana climate either and requested yet another transfer. In his letter to the army requesting the change he listed some of the other difficulties he was having, including the fact that "even one of my negroes...has sued me for his freedom."[2] As Don E. Fehrenbacker points out in his masterful study of the case, "No record of this suit has been found and...it is not impossible that the slave in question was Dred, making an early abortive attempt to secure his freedom."[3] Certainly, even if the suit had been initiated by another slave, the process might have given Dred ideas about his own chances for freedom.

The Emersons and Scotts eventually returned to St. Louis via a brief stint in Fort Snelling. Dr. Emerson died in 1843, only one month after the birth of his daughter Henrietta. Mrs. Emerson then hired out Dred, first to her brother-in-law and in 1846 to a man named Samuel Russell. A few weeks later after being hired out to Russell, Dred and his family sued for their freedom on the basis that since they had resided in free territory, they were no longer slaves.

How the suit got started is the biggest mystery of all. Some historians have suggested that Taylor Blow, the son of Scott's original owners and still in St. Louis, financed the suit in order to help Scott. Others have suggested that Blow's primary motive was to win a big "test case" victory against slavery. Another theory is that the lawyers handling the case were looking for profit from a large settlement in back wages due to the Scotts. The Scotts might have gotten the idea from their extensive travels to free soil or from discussions with old friends such as the Blows. Each of the suggestions has merit; each also has some flaw due to a detail of fact. One hundred twenty-five years later, it seems unlikely that the answer will ever be completely clear.

Dred Scott spent 11 years on an odyssey toward emancipation. It was a complex judicial process with a series of cruel dead ends, a process characterized by legal maneuvers that frustrated Scott's attempts at freedom and now frustrate scholars who try to sort it all out. For Dred Scott and his family there were many defeats with only one small victory that was quickly reversed. Finally, in March 1852, Missouri's highest court ruled against Scott.

At about this time, the Scotts were sold to Mrs. Emerson's brother, John F. A. Sanford. Many historical accounts have characterized this as a contrived sale. Since *Dred Scott v. Emerson* had been decided by the state's highest court, it could have gone directly to the United States Supreme Court for review.

However, the suit Scott now instituted against Sanford was a new case against a "new master." Moreover, because Sanford was a resident of New York and Scott claimed Missouri residency, the case would this time wind its way through the federal system, as suits between citizens of different states fall into federal jurisdiction.

Meanwhile, during all this legal maneuvering the Supreme Court had issued a decision in 1851 that would be an important precedent for the Scotts' case. It involved three Kentucky slaves who were taken into the free state of Ohio by their master. They later escaped to Canada with the help of a man named Strader, and their former master sued Strader for damages. Chief Justice Roger Taney dismissed the case for lack of jurisdiction (there was no federal question involved), but he could not resist giving his opinion on the matter despite the Court's refusal to decide the case. His "non-decision decision" confirmed the doctrine of "reversion." In other words, no matter what effect the laws of Ohio might have had on the slaves while they were in the state, the slaves were reverted back to their former status when they returned to Kentucky, a slave state.

Taney, born to a Maryland plantation-owning family, had manumitted (legally granted freedom to) his own slaves, but remained a Southerner at heart. To Taney it was not slavery that was at issue, but the right of the states to regulate themselves. He had made this sentiment clear in his draft of Andrew Jackson's 1836 farewell address, which proclaimed that "each state has the unquestionable right to regulate its own internal concerns according to its own pleasure." This was a way of saying that slavery was an internal concern of the states and that the federal government should keep out. The speech continued, "all efforts on the part of people of other states to cast odium on their institutions [i.e., slavery] and...to disturb their rights of property...are in direct opposition to the spirit in which the Union was formed...."[4] It seems incredible that Taney wrote a speech for President Jackson after he had assumed the chief justiceship. Today, that sort of collusion between the executive and judicial branch would be viewed as a serious breach of ethics.

When the case finally reached the nation's highest court, it took two hearings and pressure applied by President James Buchanan, following his election in 1856, to get a decision in the tortuous case of Dred Scott. As president-elect, Buchanan wrote to some of the justices, pleading for a speedy and forceful answer in the case. Buchanan wanted the Court to decide that slavery could be extended to all United States territory and two justices did assure him that the Court would go along with his wishes. Then, in his inaugural address, Buchanan spoke of the impending decision and his intention to "cheerfully submit, whatever [the decision] might be."[5] And on March 6, 1857, just two days after the inauguration, Chief Justice Taney, once a towering figure, now at 80 bent with pain and palsied, read, his voice failing at times, the opinion that denied one man's freedom while protecting another man's property.

The Supreme Court could have avoided the large slavery question simply by asserting that it lacked jurisdiction, that since slaves were not citizens, they could not sue in federal court. Indeed, the chief justice began with that issue, "The question is simply this: Can a negro, whose ancestors were imported into this country, and sold as slaves, become a member of the political community formed and brought into existence by the Constitution of the United States, and as such become entitled to all the rights and privileges, and immunities, guaranteed by that instrument to the citizen?"[6] The Court's answer was a resounding "no."

Taney reasoned that when the Constitution was drafted, the Negro race "had for more than a century before been regarded as being of an inferior order; and altogether unfit to associate with the white race, either in social or political relations; and so far inferior, that they had no rights which the white man was bound to respect; and that the negro might justly and lawfully be reduced to slavery for his benefit." Because of this attitude, the Court now ruled that Negroes, emancipated or not, were not citizens of the United States and could not sue in federal court.

In addition, following the *Strader* case, the Court said that Dred Scott and his family were not citizens of Missouri. Under the doctrine of reversion once they had returned to Missouri, a slave state, its laws—not those of Illinois, a free state—were controlling. In Missouri no Negro slave could be a citizen.

However, the pressure from the White House and the loyalties of the five Southern justices led them to a further ruling, and it was this final conclusion of the Court that was most intolerable to the abolitionists and free soilers (those who wished to keep slavery out of certain areas of the nation). The Court ruled that the Missouri Compromise of 1820, which prohibited slavery north of the 36°30' line, was unconstitutional. Declaring that the rights of a United States citizen were the same in a territory as in a state, Taney reasoned:

> No one, we presume, will contend that Congress can make any law in a Territory respecting the establishment of religion, or the free exercise thereof, or abridging the freedom of speech or the press...thus the rights of property are united with the rights of person and placed on the same ground by the fifth amendment....
> And if the Constitution recognizes the right of property of the master in a slave, and makes no distinction between that description of property and other property owned by a citizen ... no tribunal acting under the authority of the United States ... has a right to ... deny to it the benefit of the provisions and guarantees which have been provided for the protection of private property against the encroachment of the Government.

Thus, Taney stated, the Missouri Compromise, "which prohibited a citizen from holding and owning property of this kind in the territory of the United States north of the line therein mentioned, is not warranted by the Constitution, and is therefore void."

Despite the practice of judicial review, never before had the Court over-turned a major act of Congress. And never before had there been such a "deep and widespread revulsion against a finding of the nation's highest judicial tribunal.... [The later Supreme Court] Justice Felix Frankfurter once re-marked that after the Civil War justices of the Supreme Court never men-tioned the Dred Scott case, any more than a family in which a son had been hanged mentioned ropes and scaffolds."[7]

For Dred Scott the decision meant that he remained a slave. However, a few weeks afterwards, he was manumitted by his owners. He died less than a year later.

For the nation the decision was another factor that would lead to a bloody civil war. Instead of settling the question of slavery, as President Buchanan had hoped, the decision had heightened antagonisms. His Democratic party—with Northern and Southern factions—was in splinters; soon the nation would be. Four years later, in March 1861, with the nation on the brink of war, Abraham Lincoln was sworn into office as the sixteenth presi-dent. It was Chief Justice Taney who administered the oath. "Did the lonely and frustrated Chief Justice standing there on that bleak Tuesday in March on the eve of war, recall the tragic part that he, more than any other, had played in starting that march to war?"[8] The words are those of Justice Robert Jackson, written almost a century after the *Dred Scott* decision.

The Postwar "Revolution"

When the military battles ended in 1865, the political battles continued in Congress, as the blueprints for reconstructing the Union were drawn up. The cessation of war and the passage of the Thirteenth Amendment had ended slavery but had not settled many of the complex and controversial questions that faced the nation. Under what conditions would the Confederate states be readmitted to the Union? How would the rights of the emancipated slaves be protected? What, if any, punishments would be meted out to the rebel leaders? It was an uneasy time, a time filled with hatred and with hope.

The radical Republicans—most notably Representative Thaddeus Stevens of Pennsylvania—did not approve of the provisional governments set up by Presidents Lincoln and Johnson and, in December 1865, they blocked the seating of the newly elected Southern senators and representatives. Congress set up a special joint committee on Reconstruction to handle the thorny ques-tion of how to deal with the postwar situation.

One special concern was the treatment of the emancipated slaves. The provisional Southern legislatures had drawn up "black codes," special laws "so harsh as to constitute thinly veiled attempts to reinstitute slavery."[9] Although the codes varied from state to state, "they specified that blacks might not purchase or carry firearms, that they might not assemble after sunset, and that those who were idle or unemployed should be 'liable to imprison-ment or hard labor, one or both ... not exceeding twelve months.' ... South Carolina forbade blacks from practicing 'the art, trade or business of an ar-tisan, mechanic or shopkeeper, or any other trade, employment or business.' "[10]

In reaction to these laws, Congress passed the Civil Rights Act of 1866, which stated that "all persons born in the United States . . . excluding Indians not taxed, are hereby declared to be citizens of the United States." The act provided further that "such citizens, of every race and color, without regard to any previous condition of slavery or involuntary servitude . . . shall have the same right, in every State and Territory in the United States, to make and enforce contracts, to sue, be parties, and give evidence, to inherit, purchase, lease, sell, hold, and convey real and personal property, and to full and equal benefit of all laws and proceedings for the security of person and property, as is enjoyed by white citizens."

Doubtful of the constitutionality of the act and at odds with the Republican leadership, President Andrew Johnson vetoed the law, but his veto was overridden. Even radicals such as Representative John A. Bingham of Ohio, himself a member of the joint committee on Reconstruction, had doubts about the new law's constitutionality because it would force the states to uphold liberties which under *Barron* they were not obliged to respect. Many feared that the legislation could later easily be repealed. (The readmission of the Southern states would give the South about 15 more representatives than before the war, as now the freedmen would be counted. Prior to the war only three-fifths of the slave population was counted for purposes of determining number of representatives.) The Republicans wanted to add constitutional strength to the legal safeguards for blacks, that is, to completely nullify what the *Dred Scott* decision stood for. What emerged from this effort was the Fourteenth Amendment of 1866, which stated that "All persons born or naturalized in the United States, and subject to the jurisdiction thereof, are citizens of the United States and of the State wherein they reside." The part of the Amendment that would eventually lead to the overturning of *Barron* was at the end of Section 1:

> No State shall make or enforce any law which shall abridge the privileges or immunities of citizens of the United States; *nor shall any State deprive any person of life, liberty, or property, without due process of law*; nor deny to any person within its jurisdiction the equal protection of the laws. (Emphasis added.)

It is impossible now to look back and conclusively prove what exactly the framers of the Fourteenth Amendment had in mind when they wrote those words. What did they mean by "privileges or immunities" or "due process of law" or "equal protection"? Twentieth-century legal scholars and historians have debated the intention of the authors, of the Congress, and of the states that eventually ratified the measure. On one side of the debate is the position of Justice Hugo Black, who wrote "[m]y study of the historical events that culminated in the Fourteenth Amendment, and the expressions of those who sponsored and favored, as well as those who opposed its submission and passage, persuades me that one of the chief objects that the provisions of the Amendment's first section . . . were intended to accomplish was to make the Bill of Rights applicable to the states."[11] He argues that the framers' express intention was to overturn the constitutional rule set in *Barron*. Justice Black felt that the due process clause "incorporated" or took in the entire Bill of Rights, making those rights a national standard enforceable on the states.

Professor Raoul Berger of Harvard Law School has a decidedly different point of view: "[T]he framers were content to bar discrimination, to assure blacks that they would have judicial protection on the same terms as whites, no more, no less. . . . [T]he due process clause was not meant to create a new, general criterion of justice. Like state laws at which 'equal protection' was aimed, state justice had to be nondiscriminatory. It was 'equal justice to all men and equal protection under the shield of law.' "[12] Berger sees no justification for Black's incorporation theory.

In between Black and Berger is the view of constitutional scholar Charles Fairman, who reminds us that the framers were not "concentered upon our nice constitutional question" but on burning political questions: "Whether the freedman should be given suffrage, what should be the new basis of representation in Congress and . . . how could the Confederate leaders best be excluded from the councils of the nation."[13] Fairman's detailed analysis of the debates in the Congress, the state legislatures, and the newspapers convinces him that Congress wished to "establish a federal standard below which state action must not fall." He concludes, "Brooding over the matter in the writing of this article has, however slowly, brought the conclusion that Justice Cardozo's gloss on the due process clause [written in an opinion in 1937]—what is 'implicit in the concept of ordered liberty'—comes as close as one can to catching the vague aspirations that were hung upon the privileges and immunities clause."[14]

Whatever their intent, the framers of the amendment could not have foreseen the impact that those 17 words of the due process clause would have on the Bill of Rights and the future balance of power between the federal and state governments. It was as if the Congress had held a second constitutional convention, and created a federal government of vastly expanded proportions. The concern of the framers in 1787 had been to protect the people and the states from intrusion by the central government, and the Bill of Rights had been drafted to insure protection of those fundamental liberties. The Fourteenth Amendment and its later interpretation by the Supreme Court changed that balance; now the federal government—and especially the judiciary—would protect the people from arbitrary action by state governments. It was the beginning of a new era in constitutional development, in which the federal government would play a much larger role.

Of course, this new era did not spring into being overnight. The changes took place over the next hundred years and involved hundreds of cases and tens of thousands of pages of constitutional opinions, many of them first written by dissenters.

Giving Meaning to the Fourteenth Amendment

In 1871, three years after the Fourteenth Amendment was ratified, Congressman Bingham, its primary architect, had an opportunity to explain what the amendment's framers had intended. In a debate on a bill designed to enforce the amendment, Bingham attempted to convince his fellow congressmen that the amendment had been designed to "vest in Congress a power to protect the rights of citizens against the States, and individuals in States, never before granted." Bingham said that he had written the first section with the counsel of John Marshall "who, though departed this life still lives among us in his immortal spirit, and still speaks to us from the reports of the highest judicial tribunal on earth." He explained that in February of 1866 he had reread Marshall's decision in *Barron* and "apprehended as I never did before certain words in the opinion." Bingham told his colleagues that Marshall had been powerless to enforce the Bill of Rights in the state of Maryland. As Marshall had said, if the framers of the Bill of Rights "intended them to be limitations on the State governments, they would have . . . expressed that intention."[15] In other words, since the Bill of Rights amendments did not specify that their guarantees of rights applied against the states, Marshall felt he could not read that interpretation into them.

Bingham explained that he considered that problem seriously when writing the language of the Fourteenth Amendment. He wanted to make sure that his intention to grant those protections against the states was absolutely clear. Although he did not mention the due process clause in his oration to his colleagues, Bingham did assert that the privileges and immunities of a citizen were defined in the first eight amendments. He had, he claimed, tried to give the Supreme Court the power it didn't have at the time of *Barron*: the power to apply the Bill of Rights to the states.

Whatever Bingham had intended when he drafted the amendment, his explanation was planting a new idea—that the Constitution as now amended went beyond setting up the federal government and protecting citizens from the potential abuses of the central government. It was the beginning of an era in which, ever so slowly, the federal government would begin scrutinizing the activities of state governments—although initially in areas involving property, not individual rights.

Bingham's sentiments were echoed in 1873 by the plaintiffs' attorneys in the *Slaughterhouse Cases*.[16] That litigation began when the carpetbag Louisiana state legislature passed laws that gave the exclusive privilege to operate slaughterhouses to one butcher firm. The adversely affected butchers sued, alleging that their "privileges and immunities" as citizens—specifically the right to operate a business—had been violated. In a 5 to 4 vote, the Supreme Court disagreed, and with that decision the "privileges and immunities" clause of the Fourteenth Amendment was all but nullified.

However, Justice Field's dissent argued for the absolute right of a man to be engaged in a given business or profession. Field insisted that the Fourteenth Amendment protects "the citizens of the United States against the deprivation of their common rights by state legislation." He explained that the amendment had been enacted "to place the common rights of American citizens under the protection of the national government." Those rights, he stated, were "inalienable rights, rights which are the gift of the creator; which the law does not confer, but only recognizes."

Thus, although the Court had reaffirmed the notion put forth in *Barron* that the Bill of Rights did not apply to the states, Justice Field's dissent was the beginning of the concept that liberty had, with the Fourteenth Amendment, taken on a new constitutional and national meaning. Under that broader definition, states must meet a national standard in their legislation and administration of justice, and the federal government had the duty to see that the standard was enforced.

Field's view of the Fourteenth Amendment would not be the prevailing sentiment of the Supreme Court for some time. However, it lived on in dissenting opinions. In 1884, Justice John Marshall Harlan took a slightly different tack, advocating the incorporation of the entire Bill of Rights via the due process clause of the Fourteenth Amendment. In his dissent in *Hurtado v. California*[17] Harlan argued that Joseph Hurtado's murder conviction was unconstitutional because he had been indicted by "information" rather than by a grand jury. Harlan felt that the lack of a grand jury proceeding was a violation of the due process guarantees in the Fifth and Fourteenth Amendments. Subsequently, Harlan never failed "in appropriate cases—of which there really were not very many—to write impassioned opinions in dissent, urging his associates to accept the principle of the nationalization of the Bill of Rights."[18]

While Harlan argued for personal liberties, a majority of the Court developed this broader concept of liberty into a legal framework designed to protect property. It was an outgrowth of an era of laissez-faire economics in which business and industry resisted the efforts of government to regulate the economy. Known as "substantive due process," the theory held that the Fourteenth Amendment's due process clause incorporated the protections of property vested in the Fifth Amendment's guarantee that no person shall "be deprived of life, liberty, or property without due process of law." Due process came to mean more than a procedural guarantee—that a person would have his day in court. It came to mean that the substance of an act of a legislature could in and of itself be a violation of rights. Thus legislation was now scrutinized not just in terms of *how* it was administered, but *what* it was controlling. Out of the substantive due process theory came the notion of "liberty of contract" or "Lochnerizing," as it was called, through which the Court overturned progressive economic legislation enacted by the states. The Lochner case of 1905 is an example of this process.

Lochner, a bakery owner, was convicted of violating a New York State law that limited the hours of bakery workers to 10 hours a day and 60 hours a week. He appealed, and the Supreme Court overturned his conviction and voided the statute because the state of New York had engaged in "meddlesome interferences with the rights of the individual." The Court explained, "The general rights to make a contract in relation to his business is part of the liberty of the individual protected by the Fourteenth Amendment of the Federal Constitution."[19] If bakery workers wanted to work more hours—or perhaps if their employers demanded it—the state could not interfere. Child labor was another area which the Supreme Court, in 1905, felt could not be regulated.[20]

However, it was also in the Lochner case that Justice Holmes first blasted the notion of a constitutionally guaranteed "liberty of contract": "This case is decided upon an economic theory which a large part of the country does not entertain.... But a constitution is not intended to embody a particular economic theory, whether of paternalism ... or of *laissez faire*."[21]

The principle of substantive due process prevailed throughout the first quarter of the twentieth century, but it slowly fell into discredit when economic conditions, worsened by the Depression, called for more experimentation by the states in economic legislation.

From Contracts to Fundamental Liberties

First in dissents, Justices Holmes and Brandeis maintained a steadfast and pervasive pressure against the concept of substantive due process, viewing it as a subversion of the original purpose of the Fourteenth Amendment by the very institution charged with its preservation, the Supreme Court. At the same time these justices were willing to use the Amendment as a vehicle to nullify state laws that they believed fettered essential individual rights of political expression. In this way, the Court began to give closer scrutiny to those liberties which were written into the Bill of Rights. And as the membership of the Court gradually changed, its view of what the Fourteenth Amendment meant shifted.

Starting, in 1925, with the free speech guarantee of the First Amendment,[22] the Court began to accept the Harlan–Brandeis–Holmes theory that many of the fundamental liberties written into the Bill of Rights were enforceable on the states. In a piecemeal fashion began another phase of constitutional interpretation, in which certain personal liberties were taken under the protective umbrella of the Constitution. From freedom of speech to freedom of press to the right to counsel, the list grew.

Finally, in 1937, Justice Benjamin Cardozo spelled the Court's position on the relationship between the Bill of Rights and the states in *Palko v. Connecticut*.[23] Frank Palko had been tried for killing two policemen and convicted of second-degree murder with a sentence of life imprisonment. The state of Connecticut had appealed the verdict and sentence, and after a new trial, Palko was convicted of first-degree murder and sentenced to death. He appealed on the ground that his second trial was an instance of double jeopardy, prohibited by the Fifth Amendment.

Although Cardozo rejected Palko's claim that his Fifth Amendment rights against double jeopardy could not be violated by the state, the Justice did set up an "Honor Roll" of rights. In Cardozo's view there were certain rights enumerated in the Bill of Rights which were "the very essence of a scheme of ordered liberty" and must be protected from state infringement. Others were not ranked as being fundamental; "justice would not perish" without them. Double jeopardy, the right to trial by jury, the right of indictment by grand jury were not part of "the concept of ordered liberty." Freedom of speech and press and religion, in contrast, did fall within that framework.

Thus by the time of Palko, the role of the federal government through the judiciary had undergone another metamorphosis; it was now to protect actively certain fundamental civil liberties of the citizens of the states against state action. This mandate was expressed a year later in a famous footnote written in an otherwise insignificant case, *United States v. Carolene Products Company*.[24] While first asserting that economic legislation would be given less constitutional scrutiny (and thus signaling the end of "liberty of contract"), Justice Harlan Fiske Stone announced a new double standard of what legislation the court would give close attention. Laws that threatened basic liberties were to receive a close scrutiny by the Court; economic legislation would not.

For much of the last half century, the Court has been spending the majority of its time on questions concerning the Fourteenth Amendment and its relationship to the Bill of Rights. Some justices have relied on the Cardozo concept; others, such as Justice Hugo Black, have insisted that the entire Bill of Rights must be incorporated. Another judicial interpretation of the Fourteenth Amendment, known as "selective incorporation plus," would guarantee that states must not violate most of the rights specified in the first eight amendments as well as certain other fundamental rights. Under this interpretation, the Court has recognized a "right of privacy" and other "natural" and "fundamental" rights. It was this theory that led to the Court's ruling on abortion.

Thus, in this century the Supreme Court has given new meaning to the Bill of Rights, a meaning probably never imagined by John Marshall or James Madison or Thomas Jefferson. This new meaning traces back to a slave called Dred Scott and a case that caused first a bloody war and then a quiet revolution of constitutional proportions.

Notes

1. James MacGregor Burns, *The Vineyard of Liberty*, p. 577.
2. Don E. Fehrenbacher, *The Dred Scott Case*, p. 275.
3. Ibid.
4. Speech of Andrew Jackson, December 7, 1836, *Messages and Papers of the Presidents*, ed. J. D. Richardson, pp. 1513–1514, 1516.
5. Burns, *Vineyard*, p. 576.
6. *Dred Scott v. Sandford*, 19 How. 393, 403 (1857).
7. John A. Garraty, ed., *Quarrels That Have Shaped the Constitution*, pp. 88–89.
8. Robert H. Jackson, *The Struggle for Judicial Supremacy*, p. 327.
9. Hans L. Trefousse, *The Radical Republicans*, p. 321.
10. Bernard Bailyn, ed., *The Great Republic—A History of the American People*, 2d ed., vol. II, p. 537.
11. *Adamson v. California*, 332 U.S. 46, 71–72 (1946) (Black, J., dissenting).
12. Raoul Berger, *Government by Judiciary*, p. 211.
13. Charles Fairman, "Does the Fourteenth Amendment Incorporate the Bill of Rights?" 2 *Stan. L. Rev.*, 5, 8 (Dec. 1949).
14. Ibid., pp. 138–139.
15. March 31, 1871, *Congressional Record*, 42nd Cong., 1st sess., pp. 83, 84, 85.
16. *Slaughterhouse Cases*, 16 Wall. 36 (1873).

17. *Hurtado v. California*, 110 U. S. 516 (1884).

18. Henry J. Abraham, *Freedom and the Court*, p. 48.

19. *Lochner v. New York*, 198 U. S. 45 (1905).

20. *Atkins v. Children's Hospital*, 261 U. S. 394 (1923).

21. *Lochner*, p. 75 (Holmes, J., dissenting).

22. *Gitlow v. New York*, 268 U. S. 652 (1925).

23. *Palko v. Connecticut*, 302 U.S. 314 (1937).

24. *United States v. Carolene Products Company*, 304 U. S. 144 (1938).

23 / Gideon v. Wainwright
372 U.S. 335 (1963)

We have already noted that most of the "rights of the accused" in the Bill of Rights have now been extended by the Supreme Court to the states. All of these rights were not included at once under the Fourteenth Amendment umbrella, however, but instead were gradually incorporated on a case-by-case basis. The "public trial clause" and "notice clause" of the Sixth Amendment were incorporated in 1948, for instance; the "unreasonable search and seizure clause" of the Fourth Amendment was incorporated in 1949. Most others were included during the 1960s*, including the Sixth Amendment's "right to counsel" in the landmark *Gideon v. Wainwright* decision in 1963.

Clarence Gideon had been accused of committing an offense that was a felony under Florida state law. In the trial court, he indicated that he did not have funds to hire an attorney and asked the judge to appoint one for him. The judge refused, noting that Florida law allowed for appointment of attorneys only for those accused of capital offenses (that is, offenses punishable by death), and Gideon did not fit in that category. Gideon defended himself, was convicted and imprisoned, and eventually appealed his conviction all the way to the Supreme Court of the United States.

In the request for review, which he wrote himself in the prison library, Gideon argued that the Sixth Amendment, which promises that "in all criminal prosecutions, the accused shall enjoy the right . . . to have Assistance of Counsel for his defense," had been violated in his case.

The words seemed clear enough to Gideon. However, the Court had, in the past, seen limits to the application of the right to counsel in state court proceedings. In 1932 (in *Powell v. Alabama*), the Court had held that the right to court-appointed counsel for indigents does apply in all capital offenses, but as late as 1942 (*Betts v. Brady*), a majority had concluded that such a right exists in noncapital cases only if certain "special circumstances" exist. Gideon made no claim to any such circumstances.

---

*For a complete listing, see Rossum, Ralph A. and G. Alan Tarr, *American Constitutional Law*, Second Edition (New York: St. Martin's Press, 1987, p. 429). The "Grand Jury clause" (Fifth Amendment) and "Excessive fines" (Eighth Amendment) have not been incorporated.—*Editor's Note.*

The Court does not have to hear a case like Gideon's; it can simply deny the appeal. Given the strong similarities between the 1942 case and Gideon's, it would have seemed reasonable if the justices had simply denied the appeal outright. Instead, they appointed a famous Washington attorney (Abe Fortas, who himself later became an Associate Justice) to make Gideon's argument to the Court. In the decision, which follows here, it is clear why the Court acted as it did. It was ready to overturn *Betts v. Brady.*

Mr. Justice Black delivered the opinion of the Court.

Petitioner was charged in a Florida state court with having broken and entered a poolroom with intent to commit a misdemeanor. This offense is a felony under Florida law. Appearing in court without funds and without a lawyer, petitioner asked the court to appoint counsel for him, whereupon the following colloquy took place:

> "The Court: Mr. Gideon, I am sorry, but I cannot appoint Counsel to represent you in this case. Under the laws of the State of Florida, the only time the Court can appoint Counsel to represent a Defendant is when that person is charged with a capital offense. I am sorry, but I will have to deny your request to appoint Counsel to defend you in this case.
>
> "The Defendant: The United States Supreme Court says I am entitled to be represented by Counsel."

Put to trial before a jury, Gideon conducted his defense about as well as could be expected from a layman. He made an opening statement to the jury, cross-examined the State's witnesses, presented witnesses in his own defense, declined to testify himself, and made a short argument "emphasizing his innocence to the charge contained in the Information filed in this case." The jury returned a verdict of guilty, and petitioner was sentenced to serve five years in the state prison. Later, petitioner filed in the Florida Supreme Court this habeas corpus petition attacking his conviction and sentence on the ground that the trial court's refusal to appoint counsel for him denied him rights "guaranteed by the Constitution and the Bill of Rights by the United States Government." Treating the petition for habeas corpus as properly before it, the State Supreme Court, "upon consideration thereof" but without an opinion, denied all relief. Since 1942, when *Betts v. Brady,* [1942] . . . was decided by a divided Court, the problem of a defendant's federal constitutional right to counsel in a state court has been a continuing source of controversy and litigation in both state and federal courts. To give this problem another review here, we granted certiorari.... Since Gideon was proceeding *in forma pauperis,* we appointed counsel to represent him and requested both sides to discuss in their briefs and oral arguments the following: "Should this Court's holding in *Betts v. Brady,* 316 U. S. 455, be reconsidered?"

I

The facts upon which Betts claimed that he had been unconstitutionally denied the right to have counsel appointed to assist him are strikingly like the facts upon which Gideon here bases his federal constitutional claim. Betts was indicted for robbery in a Maryland state court. On arraignment, he told the trial judge of his lack of funds to hire a lawyer and asked the court to appoint one for him. Betts was advised that it was not the practice in that county to appoint counsel for indigent defendants except in murder and rape cases. He then pleaded not guilty, had witnesses summoned, cross-examined the State's witnesses, examined his own, and chose not to testify himself. He was found guilty by the judge, sitting without a jury, and sentenced to eight years in prison. Like Gideon, Betts sought release by habeas corpus, alleging that he had been denied the right to assistance of counsel in violation of the Fourteenth Amendment. Betts was denied any relief, and on review this Court affirmed. It was held that a refusal to appoint counsel for an indigent defendant charged with a felony did not necessarily violate the Due Process Clause of the Fourteenth Amendment, which for reasons given the Court deemed to be the only applicable federal constitutional provision.... Treating due process as "a concept less rigid and more fluid than those envisaged in other specific and particular provisions of the Bill of Rights," the Court held that refusal to appoint counsel under the particular facts and circumstances in the Betts case was not so "offensive to the common and fundamental ideas of fairness" as to amount to a denial of due process. Since the facts and circumstances of the two cases are so nearly indistinguishable, we think the *Betts v. Brady* holding if left standing would require us to reject Gideon's claim that the Constitution guarantees him the assistance of counsel. Upon full reconsideration we conclude that *Betts v. Brady* should be overruled.

II

The Sixth Amendment provides, "In all criminal prosecutions, the accused shall enjoy the right . . . to have the Assistance of Counsel for his defence." We have construed this to mean that in federal courts counsel must be provided for defendants unable to employ counsel unless the right is competently and intelligently waived. Betts argued that this right is extended to indigent defendants in state courts by the Fourteenth Amendment. In response the Court stated that, while the Sixth Amendment laid down "no rule for the conduct of the States, the question recurs whether the constraint laid by the Amendment upon the national courts expresses a rule so fundamental and essential to a fair trial, and so, to due process of law, that it is made obligatory upon the States by the Fourteenth Amendment." . . . In order to decide whether the Sixth Amendment's guarantee of counsel is of this fundamental nature, the Court in *Betts* set out and considered "[r]elevant data on the subject . . . afforded by constitutional and statutory provisions subsisting in the colonies and the States prior to the inclusion of the Bill of Rights in the national Constitution, and in the constitutional, legislative, and judicial history of the States to the present date." . . . On the basis of this historical data the Court concluded that "appointment of counsel is not a fundamental right, essential to a fair trial." . . . It was for this reason the *Betts* Court refused to accept the contention that the Sixth Amendment's guarantee of counsel for indigent federal defendants was extended to or, in the words of that Court, "made obligatory upon the States by the Fourteenth Amendment." Plainly, had the Court concluded that appointment of counsel for an indigent criminal defendant was "a fundamental right, essential to a fair trial," it would have held that the Fourteenth Amendment requires appointment of counsel in a state court, just as the Sixth Amendment requires in a federal court.

We think the Court in *Betts* had ample precedent for acknowledging that those guarantees of the Bill of Rights which are fundamental safeguards of liberty immune from federal abridgment are equally protected against state invasion by the Due Process Clause of the Fourteenth Amendment. This same principle was recognized, explained, and applied in *Powell v. Alabama*, [1932] . . ., a case upholding the right of counsel, where the Court held that despite sweeping language to the contrary in *Hurtado v. California*, [1884] . . ., the Fourteenth Amendment "embraced" those . . . " 'fundamental principles of liberty and justice which lie at the base of all our civil and political institutions,' " even though they had been "specifically dealt with in another part of the federal Constitution. " [1884] . . . In many cases other than *Powell* and *Betts*, this Court has looked to the fundamental nature of original Bill of Rights guarantees to decide whether the Fourteenth Amendment makes them obligatory on the States. Explicitly recognized to be of this "fundamental nature" and therefore made immune from state invasion by the Fourteenth, or some part of it, are the First Amendment's freedoms of speech, press, religion, assembly, association, and petition for redress of grievances. For the same reason, though not always in precisely the same terminology, the Court has made obligatory on the States the Fifth Amendment's command that private property shall not be taken for public use without just compensation, the Fourth Amendment's prohibition of unreasonable searches and seizures, and the Eighth's ban on cruel and unusual punishment. On the other hand, this Court in *Palko v. Connecticut*, [1937] . . . refused to hold that the Fourteenth Amendment made the double jeopardy provision of the Fifth Amendment obligatory on the States. In so refusing, however, the Court, speaking through Mr. Justice Cardozo, was careful to emphasize that "immunities that are valid as against the federal government by force of the specific pledges of particular amendments have been found to be implicit in the concept of ordered liberty, and thus, through the Fourteenth Amendment, become valid as against the states" and that guarantees "in their origin . . . effective against the federal government alone" had by prior cases "been taken over from the earlier articles of the federal bill of rights and brought within the Fourteenth Amendment by a process of absorption.". . .

We accept *Betts v. Brady*'s assumption, based as it was on our prior cases, that a provision of the Bill of Rights which is "fundamental and essential to a fair trial" is made obligatory upon the States by the Fourteenth Amendment. We think the Court in *Betts* was wrong, however, in concluding that the Sixth Amendment's guarantee of counsel is not one of these fundamental rights. Ten years before *Betts v. Brady*, this Court, after full consideration of all the historical data examined in *Betts*, had unequivocally declared that "the right to the aid of counsel is of this fundamental character.". . . While the Court at the close of its *Powell* opinion did by its language, as this Court frequently does, limit its holding to the particular facts and circumstances of that case, its conclusions about the fundamental nature of the right to counsel are unmistakable. Several years later, in 1936, the Court reemphasized what it had said about the fundamental nature of the right to counsel in this language:

> "We concluded that certain fundamental rights, safeguarded by the first eight amendments against federal action, were also safeguarded against state action by the due process of law clause of the Fourteenth Amendment, and among them the fundamental right of the accused to the aid of counsel in a criminal prosecution." *Grosjean v. American Press Co.*, [1936]. . .

And again in 1938 this Court said:

> "[The assistance of counsel] is one of the safeguards of the Sixth Amendment deemed necessary to insure fundamental human rights of life and liberty. . . . The Sixth Amendment stands as a constant admonition that if the constitutional safeguards it provides be lost, justice will not 'still be done.' " *Johnson v. Zerbst*, [1938]. . .

In light of these and many other prior decisions of this Court, it is not surprising that the *Betts* Court, when faced with the contention that "one charged with crime, who is unable to obtain counsel, must be furnished counsel by the State," conceded that "[e]xpressions in the opinions of this court lend color to the argument. . . ." The fact is that in deciding as it did—that "appointment of counsel is not a fundamental right, essential to a fair trial"— the Court in *Betts v. Brady* made an abrupt break with its own well considered precedents. In returning to these old precedents, sounder we believe than the new, we but restore constitutional principles established to achieve a fair system of justice. Not only these precedents but also reason and reflection require us to recognize that in our adversary system of criminal justice, any person haled into court, who is too poor to hire a lawyer, cannot be assured a fair trial unless counsel is provided for him. This seems to us to be an obvious truth. Governments, both state and federal, quite properly spend vast sums of money to establish machinery to try defendants accused of crime. Lawyers to prosecute are everywhere deemed essential to protect the public's interest in an orderly society. Similarly, there are few defendants charged with crime, few indeed, who fail to hire the best lawyers they can get to prepare and present their defenses. That government hires lawyers to prosecute and defendants who have the money hire lawyers to defend are the strongest indications of the widespread belief that lawyers in criminal courts are necessities, not luxuries. The right of one charged with crime to counsel may not be deemed fundamental and essential to fair trials in some countries, but it is in ours. From the very beginning, our state and national constitutions and laws have laid great emphasis on procedural and substantive safeguards designed to assure fair trials before impartial tribunals in which every defendant stands equal before the law. This noble ideal cannot be realized if the poor man charged with crime has to face his accusers without a lawyer to assist him.... The Court in *Betts v. Brady* departed from the sound wisdom upon which the Court's holding in *Powell v. Alabama* rested. Florida, supported by two other States, has asked that *Betts v. Brady* be left intact. Twenty-two States, as friends of the Court, argue that *Betts* was "an anachronism when handed down" and that it should now be overruled. We agree.

The judgment is reversed and the cause is remanded to the Supreme Court of Florida for further action not inconsistent with this opinion.

Reversed.

In 1972 (in *Argersinger v. Hamlin*), the Court extended the right to assistance of court-appointed counsel to misdemeanor cases where imprisonment was possible. In 1979 (*Scott v. Illinois*), review of this right was limited to cases where imprisonment had actually been imposed.

24 / Equal Justice under Law: The Supreme Court and Rights of the Accused, 1932–1991

David J. Bodenhamer

That the meaning and impact of the Fourteenth Amendment's "due process clause" were not crystal clear at the time of its adoption is one of the few things that can be stated about it without engendering debate. What the clause would and should mean for the rights of persons accused of crime has been the subject of much, often heated debate throughout the period covered in this selection by David J. Bodenhamer.

From the 1930s through 1950s the Supreme Court moved cautiously in incorporating a few such rights. Then during the 1960s the Court moved to the center stage of political discussion with a string of decisions (including, of course, *Gideon v. Wainwright*) amounting to a "due process revolution." According to Bodenhamer, the expected counter-revolution may not have occurred under Chief Justice Burger, but the Rehnquist Court is all but certain to bring an end to the revolution that the Warren Court began.

When the Warren Court bound states to follow the criminal procedures of the Bill of Rights during the 1960s, commentators aptly termed it a "due-process revolution." In decision after decision, the justices overturned long-standing precedents by declaring that the various provisions of the Fourth, Fifth, and Sixth Amendments applied to state law enforcement practices. For the first time in United States history, the rights of the accused became truly national. The guarantee of due process for criminal defendants no longer depended upon accidents of geography.

Americans divided sharply over the decisions. Liberals who distrusted exclusive local control of criminal justice applauded the new direction. The Court's actions promised equal justice under law through national protection for the rights of the accused. Conservatives cast a darker interpretation on the changes: the revolution portended an increase in crime and disorder by hampering the ability of local police and courts to protect citizens and property. Also at issue was the threat to democratic process and the federal system. Appointed judges had usurped the legislative function, conservatives argued, and their newly proclaimed power threatened the constitutional balance between the states and the central government.

By 1968 the Supreme Court stood at the storm center of national politics in a way not seen since the sectional crisis of the late 1850s, and the rights of the accused became a central issue in the presidential election. Republican nominee Richard Nixon and third-party candidate George Wallace campaigned on "law and order" themes, pledging to restore a conservative cast to the federal judiciary, especially the Supreme Court. Nixon's election and his subsequent appointment of Warren E. Burger as Chief Justice in 1969 redeemed that promise and foreshadowed an attempt to undo much of what the liberal Warren Court had accomplished.

But there was no counterrevolution in the fights of the accused. The Burger Court essentially continued and consolidated major Warren Court doctrines, even though it refused to extend them except in the area of capital punishment. One reason was because the Warren Court decisions were not as radical as critics maintained. In many instances, the logic of rights stemmed from cases that predated the 1960s. The decisions appeared more revolutionary because the majority justices abandoned the Court's traditional deference to the states and the legislative process and actively pursued its own solutions to these constitutional issues. Yet if the Burger court did not reverse the trend toward greater protection for the rights of the accused, the actions of the Rehnquist Court suggest that the justices now may be marking the end of the due-process revolution.

Until the mid-twentieth century, state constitutions were the primary source for the rights of the accused, and state courts were responsible for their enforcement. The U.S. Supreme Court had ruled repeatedly that Bill of Rights' guarantees applied only in violations of federal criminal law, a position that contrasted sharply with the Court's decision on the First Amendment. Here, early in the twentieth century, the justices extended federal protection against state interference to the freedoms of speech, religion, press, and assembly. These rights, the Court decided, were fundamental to liberty and applied to all citizens through the Fourteenth Amendment, adopted in 1868. The rights of the accused, on the other hand, were not so essential; freedom, the justices concluded, could exist under a wide variety of criminal procedures.

From the 1930s to the 1950s the Court slowly incorporated some rights of the accused into the Fourteenth Amendment's guarantee of due process to all citizens. The catalog of nationalized rights—provisions of the Bill of Rights binding on the states—was quite extensive by the end of the three decades, especially given the previous absence of such guarantees; but the list pales when compared to current practice. Fundamental rights included limited protection against illegal searches and seizures (Fourth Amendment) and coerced confessions (Fifth); public trial, impartial jury, and counsel (Sixth); and protection against cruel and unusual punishments (Eighth). Other rights considered central by later Courts were not included: prohibition of double jeopardy, protection against self-incrimination, and guarantee of jury trial, among others.

The nationalization of the Bill of Rights traveled an uncertain course prior to 1960 because the justices lacked a sure theoretical foundation for their decisions. There was no consensus on principles to guide interpretation of the amendments, in part because of the novelty of the idea that defendants' rights needed protection against state misconduct. Few judges doubted that injustice could—and did—occur in state criminal trials, but even many enlightened jurists accepted the traditional argument that classical federalism, with its curb of central power, offered the best security for individual liberty. Well into the twentieth century, courts accepted the states' authority in criminal matters and the primacy of state constitutions in guaranteeing the rights of the accused.

Powell v. Alabama (1932), the so-called Scottsboro case, first breached the jurisdictional wall separating state and federal authority in criminal procedure. In response to the inadequate representation provided to eight black youths who were sentenced to death for the alleged rape of two white girls, the U.S. Supreme Court ruled, 7–2, that the right to counsel was part of the due process clause of the Fourteenth Amendment and thus binding on the states. But this right was only similar to, not identical with, the same right guaranteed by the Sixth Amendment. The distinction permitted the Court to fashion a guide through the thicket of claims made by defendants anxious to secure federal protection for their rights. Five years later, in *Palko v. Connecticut* (1937), the justices decided that the Fourteenth Amendment required states to accept rights essential to a "scheme of ordered liberty." Rights received constitutional protection, Justice Benjamin Cardozo wrote for the majority, if their denial imposed "hardships so shocking that our polity will not endure it" or if the actions of government violated the "fundamental principles of liberty and justice which lie at the base of all our civil and political institutions."

In criminal matters, the guarantee of fair trial alone was fundamental to liberty. States could employ widely different procedures without denying fair treatment. The fair trial test meant that the Court would decide case-by-case which rights of the accused enjoyed constitutional protection. It also suggested that the values of individual judges would determine which state procedures created such hardships or so shocked the conscience that they denied fair treatment. Yet the test also provided a method for modernizing the Bill of Rights by inviting justices to extend liberties if modern conditions required it.

Some members of the Court accepted such judicial discretion as inescapable, but other justices distrusted any approach that allowed judges to substitute their personal notions of fairness for an objective standard. Chief among those who sought more definitive criteria was Justice Hugo Black. He urged his colleagues to acknowledge that the framers of the Fourteenth Amendment intended to incorporate the Bill of Rights into the due-process clause and to apply these rights as limits upon state action. This position, often called total incorporation, had considerable appeal. It was easy to express, simple to apply, and embraced a conviction that individual rights should not vary from state to state....

...But it also would radically change the nature of the federal system; and it was on these grounds that the Court engaged in a debate that shaped the rights of defendants for the next few decades.

The argument for total incorporation was unpersuasive to Justice Felix Frankfurter. The Fourteenth Amendment's due-process clause, he argued, called for "an exercise of judgment upon the whole course of the proceedings" to determine "whether they offend those canons of decency and fairness which express the notions of justice of English-speaking peoples" (*Malinski v. New York*, 1945). Due process incorporated fundamental values, one of which was fairness, and judges could dispassionately discover and apply these values to claims of injustice. Frankfurter also believed that imposing the Bill of Rights on the states would alter irrevocably the federal division of governmental power, a basic principle of American constitutionalism. And it would undermine popular government, which demanded judicial deference to the judgment of elected representatives. Even in the area of civil liberties, legislative actions should be respected unless they flagrantly defied the community's sense of values.

...Due process, after all, was not solely a federal standard. It was a concept that expressed local values arising from different historical and practical considerations. These divergent circumstances should be recognized insofar as they did not conflict with traditionally accepted Anglo-Saxon principles of justice.

The dispute between Black and Frankfurter was symptomatic of the Court's deep divisions in the 1940s and 1950s concerning nationalization of the Bill of Rights for criminal defendants. No one denied the importance of guaranteeing fair procedures. If anything, the rise of European and Asian police-states intensified the Court's sense of responsibility for careful evaluation of the administration of justice. But beyond a general concern for fairness in state trials, the justices could not agree on what their role should be. In case after case, the Court found itself deeply divided, first upholding a national standard and then, in similar circumstances, rejecting it as an infringement of state authority. . . .

The Court's decisions . . . produced only the most nebulous standards to guide law officers. Increasingly, it became more difficult to predict with certainty which actions of police, prosecutors, and judges were subject to constitutional limitations and which were not. The changing composition of the Court undoubtedly created some of the confusion: thirty men occupied seats on the bench from 1930 to 1960. So, too, did indecision elsewhere in the central government on issues touching the nationalization of rights. During World War II and the early part of the Cold War, both Congress and President hesitated to extend individual rights by statute or otherwise, because to do so might restrain the campaign against subversion and disloyalty. The nascent civil rights movement also led to unresolved tensions as southern whites raised the banner of state sovereignty in response to black demands for equal protection. . . .

By the late 1950s, four Justices—Warren, Black, Douglas, and Brennan—were ready to abandon the fair-trial approach to the Fourteenth Amendment. The 1960s witnessed their triumph. Too much had changed nationally to permit continuation of an interpretation that defined rights of the accused in terms of state boundaries. Prosecutors and police officers alike had grown weary of a tribunal in distant Washington deciding long after trial that state practices used to convict were at odds with the U.S. Constitution. Law schools and bar associations, too, desired more uniform standards. Increasingly, commentators and legal scholars questioned why the Fourth, Fifth, Sixth, and Eighth Amendments were not equally as fundamental to national citizenship as economic liberties or the freedom of speech and of the press, rights long since subject to national jurisdiction.

Suddenly, in a rush of Supreme Court cases during the 1960s and 1970s, the Bill of Rights became the national code of criminal procedure. Leading the due-process revolution was Chief Justice Earl Warren, a former California district prosecutor, attorney general, and governor whose appointment represented President Eisenhower's repayment of a political debt. Nothing marked Warren as a man of judicial temperament. He was instead an experienced politician; the judiciary scarcely figured in his pre-Court calculus of proper government. No wonder the conservative Eisenhower felt betrayed when Earl Warren led the Court through an extraordinarily controversial period, one that witnessed the triumph of judicial liberalism, the nationalization of the Bill of Rights, and an unprecedented expansion of the rights of criminal defendants.

Warren's tenure signaled a shift in judicial style from restraint to activism. As Chief Justice, he rejected the canons of judging that prescribed reference to legislative actions, respect for federalism and its diversity of state practice, and reliance upon neutral decision-making based upon narrow case facts rather than broad constitutional interpretation. His philosophy emerged from political experience. Warren specifically dismissed as "fantasy" the notion that justices should be impartial: "as the defender of the Constitution, " he wrote, "the Court cannot be neutral. " He also sought a broad role and active stance for the high bench: the "Court sits to decide cases, not to avoid decision." More important, cases must reach the right result, a condition defined by ethics, not legal procedures. Warren firmly believed the Constitution embodied moral truths which were essential to enlightened government. It was the Court's duty to apply these principles, even if doing so contravened the expressed wishes of the legislature, and to champion the individual, especially citizens without a meaningful political voice....

By the 1960s the Court was ready to embrace Warren's activist stance. Acting with unprecedented boldness during the 1960s, the majority justices of the Warren Court promoted liberal policies they deemed essential to a just society. The reforms came so swiftly that many commentators proclaimed them revolutionary—and in a sense, they were.... But no judicial reforms were as bold as, or more protest than, the landmark cases involving criminal process.

Between 1961 and 1969 the Warren Court accomplished what previous courts had stoutly resisted: it applied virtually all of the procedural guarantees of the Bill of Rights to the states' administration of criminal justice. Adopting the strategy of selective incorporation, the justices explicitly defined the Fourteenth Amendment phrase, due process of law, to include most of the rights outlined in the Fourth, Fifth, and Sixth Amendments. The result was a nationalized Bill of Rights that dimmed the local character of justice by applying the same restraints to all criminal proceedings, both state and federal. The majority justices did not seek to diminish states' rights; they desired instead to elevate subminimal state practices to a higher national standard. But in the process, the Court reshaped the nature of federalism itself.

The first breakthrough occurred early in the decade as the Court extended the Fourth Amendment fully to the states. Previous to 1960 there were two exceptions to constitutional protection against unreasonable searches. First, prosecutors could use illegally gained evidence to secure a conviction. The Fourth Amendment prohibition of unreasonable searches applied equally to state and federal officials, but state courts were not required to adopt the federal exclusionary rule. Second, even federal courts, under the so-called silver platter doctrine, might permit the use of evidence obtained illegally by state officers in searches which involved neither federal participation nor federal direction. By 1961 the Court had removed both exceptions, initially discarding the silver platter doctrine and then applying the exclusionary rule to state criminal trials.

In *Mapp v. Ohio* (1961) the Court, 5–4, extended the federal exclusionary rule to state criminal procedure. To hold otherwise was to grant the rights , under the Fourth Amendment but deny the remedy. Any other decision was also harmful to healthy federal-state relations. The lack of an exclusionary policy in many states only encouraged federal officers to disobey constitutional standards by delivering illegally seized evidence to local police and prosecutors.... The decision would not impede effective law enforcement, but, if it did, the Constitution was more important....

The barrier against selective incorporation of the criminal safeguards of the Bill of Rights had fallen. The margin was slim, but the abandonment of the fair-trial interpretation of constitutional guarantees was unmistakable. Dissenting justices recognized the shift and in defeat raised an objection that accompanied subsequent advances in the due-process revolution: the Court had exceeded its authority. . . .

The Court had acted uncharacteristically, although in a manner symbolic of future cases. Not only did the majority justices abruptly jettison an interpretive posture that had guided decisions since 1937—and discard an even earlier doctrinal separation of state and federal criminal power—they openly fashioned the decision on their sense of a right result. . . . Liberal judicial activists, despite their trenchant criticism of earlier attempts to legislate social and economic policy from the bench, were in turn vulnerable to the same charge.

The next year, 1962, the Court employed the same tactic in extending the Eighth Amendment to the states. . . . The states too were bound by the prohibition of cruel and unusual punishments. . . . It was becoming apparent that an activist majority controlled the Court, one intent on expanding the catalog of defendants' rights and applying it uniformly across the nation.

This new direction became certain one year later when the Court unanimously declared that the Sixth Amendment right to counsel in criminal cases applied to the states under the due process clause of the Fourteenth Amendment. Reflecting upon *Gideon v. Wainwright* (1963) after his retirement, former chief justice Warren viewed it as one of the most important decisions made during his tenure. Few scholars would disagree. Its significance was two-fold: it extended an important federal guarantee to state criminal defendants; and it marked the triumph of the incorporationists over fair-trial advocates in determining the meaning of the Bill of Rights.

The *Gideon* decision employed fair-trial rhetoric but only to ensure a unanimous Court. The opinion clearly represented a major victory for incorporationists. What made this conclusion inescapable were twenty-three *amicus curiae*, or friend-of-the-court, briefs from state attorneys general asking the justices to impose a uniform rule on state and federal courts alike. For more than two decades the prevailing fair-trial view had justified the case-by-case determination of due process and the resulting diversity of state practice as a necessary requirement of federalism. Now the states' chief lawyers wanted the Court to mandate the assistance of counsel in all serious criminal cases. Their assessment of the fair-trial approach to defendants' rights was damning. It had resulted only in "twenty years' accumulation of confusion and contradictions" that failed totally "as a beacon to guide trial judges."

The next year, 1964, the incorporationist majority added the Fifth Amendment protection against self-incrimination to the growing list of criminal procedures applied to the states through the Fourteenth Amendment. *Malloy v. Hogan*, decided 5–4, reversed another long-standing precedent: *Twining v. New Jersey* (1908) had determined the right against self-incrimination to be only a valued rule of evidence, not an essential part of due process.... "[I]t would be incongruous," Justice Brennan wrote for the majority, "to have different standards" for state and federal courts. The Fourteenth Amendment did not extend a "watered down, subjective version of the Bill of Rights" to the states....

...The incorporationists now commanded a majority on the Court, thanks to new appointments to the bench. Eventual nationalization of defendants' rights seemed inevitable.... The next year, 1965, in *Pointer v. Texas*, the Court ruled that "the Sixth Amendment right of an accused to confront the witnesses against him is a fundamental right and is made obligatory on the States by the Fourteenth Amendment."

The liberal majority had chosen a course of selectively incorporating the procedural guarantees of the Bill of Rights, but by what rationale? Although the incorporationist justices never advanced a systematic theory, Justice Goldberg's concurring opinion in *Pointer* offered an explanation. The fair-trial approach, rather than preserving federalism as its defenders maintained, had actually subverted healthy relations between the states and the central government because its case-by-case decisions invited "haphazard and unpredictable intrusions by the federal judiciary in state proceedings." Yet much more was at stake than the federal principle.... States might properly experiment in socioeconomic policy without harm to the nation, Goldberg asserted. This characteristic was a virtue of the federal system. But there could be no "power to experiment with the fundamental liberties of citizens." Diversity here was unacceptable because it failed to ensure equal justice.

A surprisingly muted public response greeted these early decisions. News coverage of the landmark cases was limited, and, except for the exclusionary rule, few commentators made the changes an issue for extended discussion. The civil rights movement, and the cases resulting from it, made far more dramatic claims on public attention....

The scant public attention given to the nationalization of defendants' rights disappeared abruptly in 1966 when the Court tackled the politically controversial task of reforming the states' pretrial procedures. *Miranda v. Arizona* ignited a firestorm of criticism. At issue was the admissibility of confessions obtained during police interrogations in which the suspect had not been told of his right to consult an attorney or to remain silent. There were several relevant precedents. The Court in 1936, in *Brown v. Mississippi*, held that a coerced confession brought about by police torture was a violation of the due process clause of the Fourteenth Amendment. More recently, *Escobedo v. Illinois* (1964) had invalidated confessions gained as a result of extended police questioning without the suspect's attorney being present. The ruling in *Escobedo* especially—that police could not deny access to an attorney—pointed directly to the result announced in *Miranda*: the Fifth Amendment protection against self-incrimination extended to suspects under interrogation by the police.

Chief Justice Warren's opinion for the Court was a classic expression of his ethically based, result-oriented jurisprudence. The opinion first detailed the unfair and forbidding nature of police interrogations.... This imbalance between interrogator and suspect did not belong in a democratic society. "The prosecutor under our system," he commented later, "is not paid to convict people [but to] protect the rights of people. . .and to see that when there is a violation of the law, it is vindicated by trial and prosecution under fair judicial standards." The presence of a lawyer and a protected right of silence created a more equal situation for the accused; thus, these conditions were essential to the constitutional conception of fairness.

By far the longest part of the opinion was a detailed code of police conduct, created and prescribed by the Court. The new rules quickly became familiar to anyone who watched crime dramas on television: the suspect must be informed that he has the right to remain silent; that anything he says can and will be used against him in court; that he has the right to have counsel present during questioning; and that if he could not afford an attorney, the court will appoint a lawyer to represent him. These privileges took effect from the first instance of police interrogation while the suspect was "in custody at the station or otherwise deprived of his freedom in any significant way." And the rights could be waived only "knowingly and intelligently," a condition presumed not to exist if lengthy questioning preceded the required warnings.

Policemen, prosecutors, commentators, and politicians were quick to denounce the *Miranda* warnings. Critics charged that recent Court decisions, culminating with *Escobedo* and *Miranda*, had "handcuffed" the police. This claim found a receptive audience among a majority of the general public worried about rising crime rates, urban riots, racial conflict, and the counterculture's challenge to middle-class values. Politicians eager to carry votes joined the chorus of protest. "Support your local police" became a familiar campaign slogan for candidates who sought electoral advantage in opposing the Court's reforms of pretrial procedure. . . .

The police response to *Miranda* was predictable but exaggerated. Numerous studies have since demonstrated that the decision, like the ones in *Mapp* and *Escobedo*, did not restrain the police unduly and, in fact, had little effect on the disposition of most cases. . . .

There was indeed a rapid growth in the incidence of reported crime, but the Supreme Court did not cause it. Rather, the baby boom generation had come of age. Young males, ages 15–24, traditionally account for most violations of law, and this group now comprised a larger-than-usual percentage of the nation's population. *Miranda* rules or not, there would be more crime. Police critics of the Court, frustrated by public demands to do something, simply found the Supreme Court a convenient scapegoat.

Although controversial, the *Miranda* decision—and to some extent the *Mapp* and *Escobedo* cases which preceded it—gradually brought needed improvements in police practices. Police procedures came more fully into public view, resulting in heightened awareness of official misconduct and greater expectations of professionalism. In response, many police departments raised standards for employment, adopted performance guidelines, and improved training and supervision. The Court's actions had begun to bear fruit, much in the manner desired by the majority justices who believed that hard work and respect for the law, not deception or lawbreaking, were the requirements of effective law enforcement. . . .

The Court, ever aware of public criticism, did make concessions to ensure more widespread acceptance of its actions. Most important was its decision not to apply new rulings retroactively. Prisoners convicted under older, discredited procedures would not be granted new trials simply because the Court now found those policies unconstitutional. The justices acknowledged that applying rules to future cases alone might benefit some defendants, while denying equal treatment to prisoners convicted under abandoned procedures. But they admitted candidly that wholesale release of prisoners was politically unacceptable.

The Court also hesitated to restrict the police unduly. In 1966, the same year as the *Miranda* decision, it upheld the government's use of decoys, undercover agents, and hired informers to gain evidence of crime. The justices further approved the admissibility of information secured by wiretaps. The next year the Court accepted as constitutional a warrantless arrest in a narcotics case based upon the word of an informer whom the prosecution refused to identify in a pretrial hearing. And in a Fourth Amendment case the justices sustained the right of police "in hot pursuit" of a suspect to search a house and seize incriminating evidence without a warrant.

These moderating decisions failed to quiet the Court's critics, but mounting pressure did not deter the justices from making further reforms in state criminal procedures. *In re Gault* extended certain due-process requirements of the Bill of Rights to juvenile courts. Several important decisions incorporated the remaining Sixth Amendment guarantees—specifically, the rights to compulsory process, speedy trial, and trial by jury—into the due process clause of the Fourteenth Amendment, thus creating new restraints on state criminal process. The Court continued to insist that poverty should be no impediment to justice by requiring the state to furnish transcripts to indigent defendants. And it maintained its long-established position that confessions be truly voluntary.

These later cases brought only scattered protest. Evidently most people accepted the premise that the rights of the accused were national in scope and that the Supreme Court should oversee the criminal process. Far more controversial were decisions like *Miranda* which defined these rights by proscribing certain police practices. Several cases in 1967 brought especially bitter criticism from "law and order" advocates. The justices struck down a New York eavesdropping law under which police could obtain permission to tap or bug conversations without identifying the crime suspected or the evidence sought. The decision, based on the Fourth Amendment's prohibition of unreasonable searches, undermined similar laws in other states and, according to law enforcement officials, deprived them of yet another valuable crimefighting tool.

The charge that the Court was coddling criminals gained momentum when, on the same day, it extended the right to counsel to suspects in a police lineup. And in another case, *Katz v. United States* (1967), the justices reversed a gambler's conviction based on evidence gained by the warrantless bugging of a public telephone booth. . . . Forgotten in the rush to criticize the Court were other decisions which endorsed law enforcement values, such as several 1968 cases upholding a police officer's right to stop and frisk a suspect, admittedly a personal search within the Fourth Amendment meaning, and even to seize evidence without a warrant, so long as the officer's actions were reasonable under the circumstances.

The activist justices could not long ignore this shift in support for their reform of criminal justice. But first, in 1969, the Warren Court completed its due process revolution by reversing, fittingly, the landmark case that had justified state experimentation with criminal procedures: *Palko v. Connecticut.* The issue, as it had been in 1937, was double jeopardy. The question: did the Fifth Amendment prohibition restrain the states? Again, the answer was yes. The majority opinion in *Benton v. Maryland* thoroughly rejected the premise that a denial of fundamental fairness rested on the total circumstances of a criminal proceeding, not simply on one element of it. Once the Court decides a particular guarantee is fundamental, then failure to honor that safeguard is a denial of due process. Equally important, these essential protections applied uniformly to all jurisdictions. The rights of the accused did not vary from state to state; they were truly national rights.

In a dual sense, the *Benton* case signaled the end of an era: it concluded the Warren Court's nationalization of the Bill of Rights, and it marked Earl Warren's retirement. The Chief Justice and his associates left an undeniable legacy. Never before had a group of judges championed so vigorously the rights of social outcasts—racial minorities, dissidents, the poor, and criminal defendants. Never before had the Court given such substantive meaning to the time-honored ethic of equal justice under law. No longer did the expression and application of rights depend so much on accidents of geography. In 1961 only eight of twenty-six provisions of the Bill of Rights restrained both federal and state governments; by 1969 nineteen guarantees had been incorporated into the Fourteenth Amendment.

Most of the safeguards nationalized under decisions of the Warren Court were rights of the accused. In a brief eight years, the liberal majority had revolutionized the concept of criminal due process. But the expansion of rights was highly controversial, especially among state and local officials charged with law enforcement. The 1968 election of a conservative law-and-order candidate, Richard Nixon, as President foreshadowed an attempt to undo much of what the liberal justices had accomplished. Now the question was, would the revolution hold?

The new Chief Justice, Warren Earl Burger, previously on the Court of Appeals for the District of Columbia, had little sympathy for the Court's due process revolution. His appointment redeemed candidate Nixon's pledge to restore a conservative cast to the nation's highest bench, especially when a few years later three other appointees replaced Warren Court justices. But contrary to expectations, there was no counterrevolution in the law governing defendants' rights. Upon Burger's retirement in 1986, the major criminal-procedure decisions of the Warren Court remained intact.

The lasting influence of the due-process revolution owed little to the new Chief Justice. Burger did not share his predecessor's concern for rights of the accused. He had often attacked the Court's procedural reforms while on the appellate bench, at one point claiming that recent decisions made guilt or innocence "irrelevant in the criminal trial as we flounder in a morass of artificial rules poorly conceived and often impossible of application." His announced goal was to limit the Court's rulemaking intrusions into areas more properly reserved for the federal and state legislatures and to manage the Court's large caseload more efficiently.

Under Burger's leadership, the Court declined to expand further the rights of the accused. Instead, it was more tolerant of police behavior than the Warren Court had been. Symbolic of the change was the Court's treatment of the Fourth Amendment's requirement for a search warrant. The conservative majority denounced "mere hypertechnicality" in warrant affidavits and applied a much less restrictive interpretation to the probable-cause requirement for granting a search warrant; accepted a warrantless search as voluntary, based on all the circumstances of the case rather than on an individual's knowledgeable consent; and permitted illegally seized evidence to be presented to a grand jury even though it was inadmissible at trial. The justices also approved the "stop and frisk" practices of state and local police and allowed law officers broad latitude to search automobiles, even accepting in a narcotics case evidence seized from the car's passenger compartment without a warrant.

Not only did the Court lower the threshold requirements for a valid search, it redefined the exclusionary rule. The justices in 1974 characterized the rule as a "judicially created remedy designed to safeguard Fourth Amendment rights generally through its deterrent effect." It was not a "personal constitutional right," and its use presented "a question, not of rights but of remedies"—one that should be answered by weighing the costs of the rule against its benefits.

For a decade the Court invoked its new cost-benefit analysis cautiously, declining to apply it fully and directly to criminal prosecutions. But in 1984 the justices decided in *United States v. Leon* that evidence produced by an officer's reasonable or good-faith reliance on the validity of a search warrant was admissible in court, even if the warrant later proved defective. The "good faith" exception to the exclusionary rule rested explicitly on a balancing of the costs and benefits involved: using evidence captured innocently under a defective warrant exacted a small price from Fourth Amendment protection when compared to the substantial cost society would bear if an otherwise guilty defendant went free....

The Burger Court shifted the direction of Fourth Amendment decisions, but it did not abandon entirely a concern for the rights of the accused. The justices declared unconstitutional a New York law permitting police to conduct a warrantless search of a private home in order to make a felony arrest.

It also prohibited a warrantless search of an automobile luggage compartment and required law officers to show probable cause of crime to check driver's licenses and auto registrations, although a later case lowered this threshold to "only a probability or substantial chance of criminal activity." More important, the new conservative majority left undisturbed the Warren Court's signal contribution on search and seizure issues, namely, that Fourth Amendment standards applied equally to state and federal jurisdictions.

In most other areas of criminal procedure, the Court maintained but did little to advance the rights of the accused that had been extended during the Warren era. Arguing that the law requires only a fair trial, not a perfect one, the Court upheld a conviction even though the police, when giving the required *Miranda* warnings, neglected to tell the defendant of his right to appointed counsel if he could not afford one. It also allowed admissions secured without the required warnings to be used to impeach the defendant's credibility, though not to obtain his conviction, if he took the stand on his own behalf. In Sixth Amendment cases the Court guaranteed the right to counsel to all trials that could lead to imprisonment, but following the lead of Congress in the Omnibus Crime Control Act of 1968, it refused to grant the protection to unindicted suspects in a police lineup. Similarly, the justices extended the guarantee of a jury trial to include all petty misdemeanors punishable by six months or longer imprisonment, yet allowed states to experiment with the size of juries and less than unanimous verdicts in non-capital cases.

Only in cases involving the death penalty did the Burger Court move beyond the Warren Court's conception of defendants' rights. All federal and state courts in the 1960s accepted capital punishment as constitutional, but late in the decade there was obvious judicial concern over its implementation. In 1968 the Supreme Court prohibited states from excluding opponents of executions from service as jurors in capital cases, although the justices otherwise refused to label the death penalty as cruel and unusual punishment. The Court of Appeals for the Fourth Circuit ruled in 1970 that the death penalty for rape was excessive, a position supported by recommendations from the National Commission on Reform of Federal Criminal Laws and the Model Penal Code. One year later the Califomia Supreme Court decided, 6–1, that the death penalty violated the state's constitutional injunction against cruel or unusual punishments.

The next year, 1972, in *Furman v. Georgia*, a 5–4 majority of the Supreme Court set aside the death penalty for three black defendants, two convicted of rape and one of murder. There was no majority opinion: each of the five concurring justices reached the decision by separate routes. Only Justices Marshall and Brennan concluded that the death penalty was cruel and unusual punishment within the meaning of the Eighth Amendment. Justices Douglas, Stewart, and White objected on more limited grounds: the death penalty was arbitrary and capricious punishment; it discriminated against the poor, blacks, and other groups at the margins of society; and it failed to deter violent crime.

Although the decision did not hold the death penalty unconstitutional, it nullified the capital laws of thirty-nine states. It also forecast a new interpretation for the Eighth Amendment. All nine justices agreed that the death penalty was morally repugnant, and they concurred that the amendment must be interpreted flexibly and in light of contemporary values. For executions to be constitutional, the Court implied, they must be administered consistently and fairly, without discriminatory intent or effect. Sentencing juries must be given objective standards to guide their choice of life or death. Above all, the punishment must be rational and reliable.

Significantly, the decision reflected the influence of the Warren Court's result-oriented view of criminal justice. Punishment by death was qualitatively different from any other sanction: the penalty was unique; mistakes were irreversible. The decision to execute required not only strict adherence to objective and reliable rules but also strong assurance that it was proper in light of the crime, the defendant, and the patterns of punishment for similar crimes. At least in capital cases, equal justice joined fair procedure as a requirement of due process.

Guided by these standards, numerous states adopted mandatory death sentences for certain crimes, while other states established special post-trial hearings to determine whether to impose the death penalty.... To pass constitutional muster, the justices implied, courts must apply capital punishment equally yet fit the penalty to the circumstances of individual cases.

By the 1980s the inherent contradiction between equal justice and individual treatment became unacceptable to a majority of the justices. Although the Court intended the *Gregg* decision to make the process of punishment more rational, the effect was to involve the Court more deeply in the supervision of capital convictions. Every inmate on death row sought a high court review, often repeatedly on different issues. Both state prosecutors and the general public viewed the years required to settle an appeal as a denial of justice, not a necessary delay to ensure fairness. Wearied by the issue, the Court retreated. Unable to accept the proposition that death was by definition cruel and unusual punishment, the justices abandoned the quest for reliability and settled instead for assurance that the process was not wholly arbitrary....

Appeals in capital cases commanded less of the Court's attention during the last half of the 1980s. And decisions in this area became decidedly more favorable to the state. In *Tison v. Arizona* (1987), for example, the justices accepted as constitutional those statutes allowing capital punishment for anyone convicted of a felony in which a death occurred, whether or not they actually participated in the killing. And in 1991 the Court sharply limited the number of federal appeals that death row inmates could make. One result was a steady increase in the number of executions. By 1990 there were more than 2,700 inmates on death row, most of them black men, and executions averaged twenty-five per year. Yet there were few demands for the justices to reconsider their course.

In other areas of criminal procedure, the Rehnquist Court generally declined to extend the rights of the accused beyond the limits established in earlier cases, and in some instances it restricted protections already granted. Law officers gained greater latitude in applying the *Miranda* rule when, in *Colorado v. Connelly* (1986), the justices adopted a less strict standard to determine whether or not a confession was truly voluntary. Police cannot fail to give the required *Miranda* warnings and must stop all questioning if a suspect demands a lawyer, but they can use nonthreatening tactics, such as pretending to sympathize with the suspect, to secure a valid confession. The Court also concluded in 1991 that illegal confessions would not necessarily taint a conviction if other evidence exists to prove the defendant's guilt. Clearly, these cases were far removed in spirit and effect from the decisions of the Warren Court two decades earlier.. . .

Even with the more conservative judicial stance during recent years, the legacy of the Warren Court remains substantially intact. The rights of the accused are now truly national, no longer dependent upon accidents of geography for their expression. Court decisions in large measure have redressed the imbalance of power that inevitably occurs in criminal proceedings when the state accuses an individual of wrongdoing. In restraining the hand of government, the Warren Court refused to heed ill-founded fears of disorder, and honored instead the older American tradition of limiting power to promote liberty. The Court led by Chief Justice Burger did not abandon the new understanding of rights, despite widespread political demands to reverse the most controversial decisions. The justices concerned themselves more with finding the practical meaning of these safeguards in individual cases than with rejecting either in whole or in part the advances of earlier Courts.

It is too early to know what modifications or new interpretations the Supreme Court in the 1990s will make in the rights of criminal defendants. But almost certainly the due process revolution is over. Under the leadership of Chief Justice William Rehnquist the Court has more often favored the prosecution than the defense. This trend will undoubtedly continue. And it will gain sustenance from legitimate concerns about continuing threats to public safety, including a startling increase in the rate of violent crime. But to date, the legacy of the Warren Court is secure. The justices have not abandoned their role to oversee the criminal process or to ensure equal justice, nor are they likely to do so, and for good reason. The nineteenth-century constitutional order is past; it cannot be recreated. Constitutional safeguards gain meaning from experience, and now a large part of our experience includes the due process revolution of the 1960s, and the new legal world it formed.

25 / Development of the Right of Privacy

John Brigham

It is a truism that while the Supreme Court was established to interpret law, its Justices—in the process of interpreting—do "make policy." And from time to time they change the policies made by others who sat on the Court at an earlier time. We have read here about two instances where the Court "changed its mind" with dramatic, far-reaching consequences. Of course, the "Court" does not really have a mind; it is merely an institution wherein the justices of the moment try to reach a collective opinion on some case before them. It is hardly surprising that as the personnel change, so may some of the collective opinions. The cases of *Brown v. the Board of Education* and *Gideon v. Wainwright* vividly demonstrate the Court's ability to change "its" mind as its personnel change over time. While such dramatic changes of mind have not been a regular occurrence in the Court's history, they have served to remind us that the Court is a human institution, and therefore changeable.

Brown and *Gideon* involved claims to rights that were clearly grounded in the original Constitution or its amendments; the "room for interpretation" was found in the exact wording and context of those expressed rights. Not all rights protected by the Court are easily found in the words of the Constitution. They are "inferred," sometimes from several different places in the original document and/or the amendments. Such is the case for the "right of privacy," that is, the "right to be let alone" to make your own decisions free from governmental intrusion.

In the following article, John Brigham traces the development of the privacy right from introduction in a law review article in 1890, through a gradual process of conceptualization, to full recognition as a constitutional right in 1965, and then to its use as the basis for a landmark abortion decision in 1973.

One hundred years ago, there was no right to privacy as such in the Constitution. The constitutional right to privacy emerged as a consequence of the twentieth century preoccupation with this value. Privacy has been an object of debate throughout this century, with legal arguments, judicial dissents, and ultimately majority opinions finding their way into constitutional interpretation. As the century progressed, the right became attached to the due process clause of the Fourteenth Amendment (Rubin, 1982:63), until by the early 1970s, the Supreme Court ". . . recognized that a right of personal privacy, or a guarantee of certain areas or zones of privacy, does exist under the Constitution. . ." (*Roe v. Wade*, 1973). The change in the ordinary or common law concept of privacy with its introduction into the Constitution reveals the structure of that body of law and its conceptual significance. Privacy in the Constitution is not simply the common law right with a different reference point; it is a different right in important respects.

Privacy has been institutionalized by the opinions of the Court. It has become a part of the common understandings to such an extent that it now has a stature comparable to some of the specific procedural protections in the Bill of Rights. Without a particular doctrinal reference, like that for double jeopardy, people know what it means to refer to constitutional protection for privacy. Creative developments of this sort tell us something about constitutional discourse. They reveal where the boundaries are and how they change. A concept can enter the domain of the Constitution and become intelligible. We see this in the way privacy is referred to, even by those who do not like its implications. In *Roe v. Wade,* Justice William Rehnquist claimed ". . . a difficulty in concluding, as the Court does, that the right of 'privacy' is involved in this case. . ." (*Roe,* 1973), but he certainly knew what the majority was talking about in this landmark abortion case. He acknowledged the existence of a right, if not its particular application, where no right had existed less than a century before. We begin our discussion of constitutional privacy by showing where the concept of privacy has come from and how it entered the constitutional frame.

A "Right to Be Let Alone"
Judge Thomas Cooley, an influential state judge and law professor, provided the seed, and distinctive phrasing, in articulating a right "to be let alone," in 1888. Advocacy of this notion as a "right to privacy" by Samuel Warren and Louis Brandeis in 1890 launched the concept. These advocates anticipated that "political, social, and economic" forces would suppport the inclusion of a new right in the common law. They concluded that "the right to liberty secures the exercise of extensive civil privileges, and the term 'property' has grown to comprise every form of possession—intangible, as well as tangible." These proper Bostonians were responding to a new technology, the instantaneous photography then becoming available to mass circulation newspapers. The traditional limitations existing in the law of libel and slander were too limited. Seeking a broader right "to demonstrate the extent to which thoughts, sentiments and emotions will be communicated," Warren and Brandeis argued in their article that:

> The principle which protects personal writings and all other personal productions, not against theft and physical appropriation but against publication in any form, is in reality not the principle of private property, but that of an inviolate personality (Warren and Brandeis, 1980:141).

They hoped to establish the "right to be let alone." Their successful law review article is closer to being the source of this legal concept than any judicial opinion. Prior to the article's publication, the right was not recognized in English or American law. By taking concepts from property and other rights, the authors established as a fundamental principle "the inviolability of an individual's privacy."

The first reference to the article by a higher court came early in the century in a New York case, *Roberson v. Rochester Folding Box Co.* (1902). The issue of compensation for humiliation arose when a young woman from New York had her picture used to market flour—without her consent. She sued and she lost because the courts of New York found there was no common law right to privacy. This was not a popular decision. On August 23, 1902, the *New York Times* editorialized against the New York State Court of Appeals for holding that "the right to privacy is not a right which in the State of New York anybody is bound to respect." The editorial resulted in a New York State statute directed against the commercial use of personal information and images. The right, developing at the turn of the century, was a new one.

Between 1890 and 1960, the individual's right to privacy developed into an accepted principle of American law. It was recognized in 31 states, and over 300 cases relating to privacy were decided in the appellate courts (Westin, 1967:347). The only resistance came on "the general grounds that it deals with a state of mind and recovery is difficult." Whether it was due to the "social status" that Warren and Brandeis are said to have given to it or because of "its compelling social attractiveness," privacy became a very popular legal claim (Davis, 1959:7). Although not all commentators could find a single tort or legal wrong (Prosser, 1960; O'Brien, 1979:7-10), among the claims associated with privacy, the right had become part of American law.

The concept has roots in the ideology of American politics. It is compatible with individualism, limited government, private property (Westin, 1967), and the specific protections in the Bill of Rights, all of which gave support to the developing interpretation of the constitutional right to property. Alan Westin viewed the ideological basis for privacy as evidence that it is not a modern legal concept:

> Thus, the notion put forward by legal commentators from Brandeis down to the present—that privacy was somehow a "modern" legal right which began to take form only in the late nineteenth century—is simply bad history and bad law (Westin, 1967:337).

Yet, there is no reference to "privacy" as a legal right prior to the end of the nineteenth century. There are differences in the ideological and the legal spheres of discourse. The notion of privacy is implicit in the ideology, the American tradition, and even in the common law. But, its articulation as common law or as a statutory right is a modern contribution. Like tort law, which owes much to the Industrial Revolution (Friedman, 1973:409), the law of privacy may be laid at the door of the technological revolution. From telephone and instantaneous photography through the intrusions of wiretaps and bugging devices, the concept of privacy has advanced along with the technology that has redefined the nature of American social life. Indeed, it was eavesdropping, sensing devices, and later data banks, that prompted the Committee on Science and Law of the Association of the Bar of the City of New York to study the relationship between modern technology and privacy.

Constitutional Development

A statutory right to privacy thus appeared in the last century in America. Rooted in the ideology of liberalism and reflected in the common law, the right developed as a protection against technological threats to private life. In its form and content, the articulation of these concerns accompanied privacy into the constitutional setting. In that sphere official commentary determined the sort of right that constitutional privacy would become. Judge Cooley's conception of privacy was evident in a decision of the Supreme Court in 1891 (*Union Pacific v. Botsford*). In that case, it was decided that a plaintiff in an injury claim did not have to submit to surgical examination on the basis of "the right of every individual to the possession and control of his own person" (*Botsford*, 1888:251). Potential indignity was considered "an assault and a trespass." The Court's references were to the common law and Cooley's interpretation. Although it introduced privacy to Supreme Court deliberations, this case did not lead to privacy being considered a claimable constitutional right.

Beyond the Procedural Protections. The constitutional right to privacy required a conceptual integration into the Constitution's framework, a conjunction of the protection against "intrusions" in the Fourth Amendment and the immunity from "disclosure" or self-incrimination in the Fifth Amendment. In his dissent in *Olmstead v. United States* (1928), Justice Louis D. Brandeis suggested the path to be followed in order to bring privacy into the Constitution. The case itself was closely associated with developing technology since it involved electronic taps on telephone lines. Since there was no trespass in appropriating the conversations, the issue was whether the Fourth Amendment protections applied (O'Brien, 1979:51). A majority of the justices did not believe wiretaps violated the protections in the Constitution against searches and seizures. Justice Brandeis, on the other hand, saw the wiretaps as evidence of the "subtler and more far-reaching means of invading privacy that have become available to the government," and he argued that the Founders had provided a protection against the government in ". . . the right to be let alone." This, for Brandeis, was "the most comprehensive of rights and the right most valued by civilized men" (Olmstead, 1928:473). In his opinion, Justice Brandeis thus expanded on the concept he had introduced in his seminal law review article almost 40 years before.

As important as this conceptual link to the law review article was an authoritative link to the constitutional past. Justice Brandeis's opinion in *Olmstead* relied on an 1886 decision that ". . . the Fourth and Fifth Amendments run almost into each other" (*Boyd v. United States*, 1886). By this reference, Brandeis was able to add significantly to his contribution by joining the protections against warrantless searches with those for self-incrimination. Until this time, the privilege against self-incrimination had been limited to criminal prosecution, and attempts to expand its reach to the protection of "reputation or private affairs" had failed (*Brown v. Walker*, 1986).

Building on the conceptual foundation provided by Brandeis, Justice Frank Murphy took constitutional privacy a step further in 1942 in *Goldman v. United States*. The case involved use of a detectaphone by federal agents investigating a lawyer's conspiracy to defraud creditors in a bankruptcy case. The device allowed conversations to be heard through a wall without "intrusion." Murphy's dissenting opinion recognized that physical entry was no longer necessary for a search ". . . for science has brought forth far more effective devices for the invasion of a person's privacy." Justice Murphy advocated capturing the essence of traditional protection, whether or not the doctrine seemed to apply literally. He cited Brandeis's 1890 law review article and indicated that "one of the great boons secured . . . by the Bill of Rights is the right of personal privacy guaranteed by the Fourth Amendment" (*Goldman*, 1942:136). Justice Murphy's opinion thus linked concern over searches and seizures in the Bill of Rights with the conception of privacy being introduced into the Constitution.

Justice Felix Frankfurter was a subsequent contributor to the development of this right when he described privacy as a constitutional liberty. Privacy, he said, was part of the conception of liberty through which the Bill of Rights could be incorporated. He wrote:

> security of one's privacy against arbitrary intrusion by the police— which is at the core of the Fourth Amendment—is basic to a free society. It is therefore implicit in the "concept of ordered liberty". . . (*Wolf v. Colorado*, 1949).

Reliance on privacy and its relation to things fundamental, like ordered liberty, had become commonplace.

In *Frank v. Maryland* (1959) Justice Frankfurter acknowledged "the right to be secure from intrusions into personal privacy," but he considered it insufficient to preclude a search where there was no threat of prosecution. The opinion in *Frank* contains a review of the protection afforded by the Fourth and Fifth Amendments, and Frankfurter's conclusion that "giving the fullest scope to this constitutional right to privacy, its protection cannot be here invoked" (*Frank*, 1959:366). Justice Douglas's dissent in *Frank* attacked the requirement of criminal proceedings as a limitation that was inconsistent with the American tradition outside the constitutional sphere. Douglas had indicated his sympathy with the Brandeis position some years before. When a lower court held radio programs on federally supervised buses to violate the "liberty protected by the Fifth Amendment," in that they constituted "forced listening," Douglas supported the decision, writing:

> The case comes down to the meaning of "liberty" as used in the Fifth Amendment. Liberty in the constitutional sense must mean more than freedom from unlawful governmental restraint; it must include privacy as well . . . (*Public Utilities Commission v. Pollak*, 1952:467).

On this basis, the Supreme Court came up with "a new concept of constitutional privacy" between 1956 and 1966 (Westin, 1967:330). The Warren and Brandeis article was mentioned three times during this period; each time the reference was to the common law roots of privacy and each time there was a push to expand the concept into a constitutional right. The article was first referred to in a dissent by Justice Douglas to an unsuccessful birth control appeal (*Poe et al. v. Ullman*, 1961). Then the article was cited in a concurrence, as support for the proposition that "the philosophical foundations" of privacy are rooted in the common law (*Gibson v. Florida*, 1963). Finally, the article was mentioned by Justice Brennan in 1963 in *Lopez v. United States*, when Brennan criticized what he saw as the Court's encouragement of electronic searches and seizures. "The right of privacy would mean little," he argued, ". . . if it were limited to a person's solitary thoughts" (*Lopez*, 1963:449). The reference to privacy had again united protection from "disclosure" with that of "intrusion" by means of electricity.

The last structural dimension to the constitutional development of the concept of privacy involved freedom of expression. The First Amendment freedoms expanded privacy related concerns beyond tbe criminal process, but protection associated with freedom of expression cut two ways. It was a source of strength to the new right with serious limitations. With regard to the common law right, the First Amendment impinged on the "right to be let alone" since it fostered and protected an aggressive press corps. The First Amendment, however, also protected political privacy (*Watkins v. United States*, 1957) and the related "right of associational privacy" (*NAACP v. Alabama*, 1958), which was far more positive in its orientation than the common law right. These aspects of the right to privacy prohibited the government from interfering with the private space that was also protected by common law privacy.

Thus, the foundations for constitutional privacy lay in creative adjudication incorporating protection against warrantless searches and seizures, self-incrimination, and providing for freedom of expression. The result was a right that went well beyond any of these and took on quite a different character from the common law roots to which it can be traced.

Polite Penumbras. Except for the limited Fourth Amendment holdings and a few connected with the First Amendment, constitutional privacy claims were not successful until 1965. Yet, privacy had become a possible claim well before it received authoritative support from a majority of the Supreme Court. Acceptance of the right by the Court is only the most obvious evidence that a concept is intelligible, that the idea "has arrived." *Griswold v. Connecticut* (1965) was that benchmark in which the constitutional right to privacy was recognized. In this case concerning a statute which limited the use of contraception in Connecticut, the majority opinion by Justice Douglas was grounded in constitutional privacy. The case involved "likely invasions of the privacy of the bedroom" (Ely, 1973). Although Douglas referred to "penumbras, formed by emanations" from the First, Third, Fourth, Fifth, and Ninth

Amendments (*Griswold*, 1965:484), the Connecticut contraceptive use statute was held to be unconstitutional by the Supreme Court on the grounds that to enforce it would require prying into the privacy of the home. The basis for the decision was thus a more limited right to marital privacy, "a right of privacy older than the Bill of Rights..." (*Griswold*, 1965:486). Justice Black dissented from the opinion of the Court because he desired the holding to be based on "some specific constitutional provision." In his opinion, Black paid homage to early collaborative efforts of Samuel Warren and Louis Brandeis, but objected to the elevation of the phrase "right to be let alone"— from the law review article—to the level of a constitutional rule. The view was consistent with Black's general disdain for more flexible interpretation. In his reaction to the holding, Black saw a larger development than that undertaken by Douglas, who limited the right to marital privacy.

A great deal of legal commentary subsequent to Griswold was directed toward the new right (Dixon, 1971). Constitutional privacy had become the point of contention (Emerson, 1971:37). In the decade that followed, privacy was often appealed to as an independent constitutional right (*Paris Adult Theater v. Slaton*, 1973), but this appeal was successful only where it was applied to the search and seizure context (*Katz v. U.S.*, 1967), the privacy of the home (*Stanley v. Georgia*, 1969; *United States v. Reidel*, 1971), or to the realm of sexual or marital privacy (*Eisenstadt v. Baird*, 1972). In short, the successes were all linked very closely to the elements of privacy that had brought the right to its constitutional status.

The development of the constitutional right to privacy is an example of conceptual change that has continuing doctrinal significance. In 1896 and for nearly half a century thereafter, the justices could not have ruled that prohibitions on abortion violated a constitutional right to privacy. There are many reasons for this, but the most dramatic was the absence of privacy as a constitutional right at that time....

References

Davis, Frederick. 1959. "What Do We Mean By Right to Privacy?" *South Dakota Law Review* 4:1.

Dixon, Robert G. 1971. *The Right of Privacy*. New York: DaCapo Press.

Ely, John Hart. 1973. "The Wages of Crying Wolf. A Comment on *Roe v. Wade*." *Yale Law Journal* 82:920.

_____. 1980. *Democracy and Distrust: A Theory of Judicial Review*. Cambridge, Mass.: Harvard University Press.

Emerson, Thomas Irwin. 1970. *The System of Freedom of Expression*. New York: Vintage Books.

_____. 1971. "Nine Justices in Search of a Doctrine." In *The Right of Privacy*, ed. R. Dixon. New York: DaCapo Press.

Friedman, Lawrence M. 1973. *A History of American Law*. New York: Simon and Schuster.

O'Brien, David M. 1979. *Privacy, Law, and Public Policy*. New York: Praeger.

Prosser, W. 1960. "Privacy." *California Law Review* 48:383.

Rubin, Edward L. 1982. "Generalizing the Trial Model of Procedural Due Process: A New Basis for the Right to Treatment." *Harvard Civil Rights and Civil Liberties Law Review* 17:61.
Westin, Alan F. 1961. *The Supreme Court: Views from Inside.* New York: W. W. Norton.

26 / *Roe v. Wade*
410 U.S. 113 (1973)

Over several decades, members of the Court had contributed to the development of a right not specified in the Constitution, but which could now be employed as though it were. In striking down Texas' criminal abortion statutes in *Roe v. Wade*, the Court's opinion was based primarily upon its view that the "right of privacy...is broad enough to encompass a woman's decision whether or not to terminate her pregnancy." Interestingly, Justice William Rehnquist, even in dissenting from the Court's opinion, accepted the existence of a right to privacy. Both Justice Harry Blackmun's decision for the Court and Justice Rehnquist's dissenting opinion follow.

The Texas statutes that concern us here are Arts. 1191–1194 and 1196 of the State's Penal Code. These make it a crime to "procure an abortion," as therein defined, or attempt one, except with respect to "an abortion procured or attempted by medical advice for the purpose of saving the life of the mother."...

...On the merits, the District Court held that the "fundamental right of single women and married persons to choose whether to have children is protected by the Ninth Amendment, through the Fourteenth Amendment," and that the Texas criminal abortion statutes were void on their face because they were both unconstitutionally vague and constituted an overbroad infringement of the plaintiffs' Ninth Amendment rights....

The usual rule in federal cases is that an actual controversy must exist at stages of appellate or certiorari review, and not simply at the date the action is initiated....

But when, as here, pregnancy is a significant fact in the litigation, the normal 266-day human gestation period is so short that the pregnancy will come to term before the usual appellate process is complete. If that termination makes a case moot, pregnancy litigation seldom will survive much beyond the trial stage, and appellate review will be effectively denied....

We, therefore, agree with the District Court that Jane Roe had standing to undertake this litigation....

The principal thrust of appellant's attack on the Texas statutes is that they improperly invade a right, said to be possessed by the pregnant woman, to choose to terminate her pregnancy. Appellant would discover this right in the concept of personal "liberty" embodied in the Fourteenth Amendment's Due Process Clause; or in personal, marital, familial, and sexual privacy said to be protected by the Bill of Rights or its penumbras...; or among those rights reserved to the people by the Ninth Amendment.... Before addressing this claim, we feel it desirable briefly to survey, in several aspects, the history of abortion, for such insight as that history may afford us, and then to examine the state purposes and interests behind the criminal abortion laws.

It perhaps is not generally appreciated that the restrictive criminal abortion laws in effect in a majority of States today are of relatively recent vintage.... [T]hey derive from statutory changes effected, for the most part, in the latter half of the 19th century....

It is thus apparent that at common law, at the time of the adoption of our Constitution, and throughout the major portion of the 19th century, abortion was viewed with less disfavor than under most American statutes currently in effect. Phrasing it another way, a woman enjoyed a substantially broader right to terminate a pregnancy than she does in most States today. At least with respect to the early stage of pregnancy, and very possibly without such a limitation, the opportunity to make this choice was present in this country well into the 19th century. Even later, the law continued for some time to treat less punitively an abortion procured in early pregnancy....

Three reasons have been advanced to explain historically the enactment of criminal abortion laws in the 19th century and to justify their continued existence.

It has been argued occasionally that these laws were the product of a Victorian social concern to discourage illicit sexual conduct. Texas, however, does not advance this justification in the present case, and it appears that no court or commentator has taken the argument seriously....

A second reason is concerned with abortion as a medical procedure. When most criminal abortion laws were first enacted, the procedure was a hazardous one for the woman.... Thus, it has been argued that a State's real concern in enacting a criminal abortion law was to protect the pregnant woman, that is, to restrain her from submitting to a procedure that placed her life in serious jeopardy.

Modern medical techniques have altered this situation. Appellants and various *amici* refer to medical data indicating that abortion in early pregnancy, that is, prior to the end of the first trimester, although not without its risk, is now relatively safe. Mortality rates for women undergoing early abortions, where the procedure is legal, appear to be as low as or lower than the rates for normal childbirth. Consequently, any interest of the State in protecting the woman from an inherently hazardous procedure, except when it would be equally dangerous for her to forgo it, has largely disappeared. Of course, important state interests in the areas of health and medical standards do remain.... [T]he State retains a definite interest in protecting the woman's own health and safety when an abortion is proposed at a late stage of pregnancy.

The third reason is the State's interest—some phrase it in terms of duty—in protecting prenatal life. Some of the argument for this justification rests on the theory that a new human life is present from the moment of conception. The State's interest and general obligation to protect life then extends, it is argued, to prenatal life. Only when the life of the pregnant mother herself is at stake, balanced against the life she carries within her, should the interest of the embryo or fetus not prevail. Logically, of course, a legitimate state interest in this area need not stand or fall on acceptance of the belief that life begins at conception or at some other point prior to live birth. In assessing the State's interest, recognition may be given to the less rigid claim that as long as at least *potential* life is involved, the State may assert interests beyond the protection of the pregnant woman alone.

Parties challenging state abortion laws have sharply disputed in some courts the contention that a purpose of these laws, when enacted, was to protect prenatal life. Pointing to the absence of legislative history to support the contention, they claim that most state laws were designed solely to protect the woman. Because medical advances have lessened this concern, at least with respect to abortion in early pregnancy, they argue that with respect to such abortions the laws can no longer be justified by any state interest. There is some scholarly support for this view of original purpose. The few state courts called upon to interpret their laws in the late 19th and early 20th centuries did focus on the State's interest in protecting the woman's health rather than in preserving the embryo and fetus. Proponents of this view point out that in many States, including Texas, by statute or judicial interpretation, the pregnant woman herself could not be prosecuted for self-abortion or for cooperating in an abortion performed upon her by another. They claim that adoption of the "quickening" distinction through received common law and state statutes tacitly recognizes the greater health hazards inherent in late abortion and impliedly repudiates the theory that life begins at conception.

It is with these interests, and the weight to be attached to them, that this case is concerned.

The Constitution does not explicitly mention any right of privacy. In a line of decisions, however, going back perhaps as far as *Union Pacific R. Co. v. Botsford* [1891]. . ., the Court has recognized that a right of personal privacy, or a guarantee of certain areas or zones of privacy, does exist under the Constitution. In varying contexts, the Court or individual justices have, indeed, found at least the roots of that right in the First Amendment, *Stanley v. Georgia* [1969]. . .; in the Fourth and Fifth Amendments, *Terry v. Ohio* [1968]. . ., *Katz v. United States* [1967]. . ., *Boyd v. United States* [1886]. . ., see *Olmstead v. United States* [1928]. . .; in the penumbras of the Bill of Rights, *Griswold v. Connecticut*. . .; in the Ninth Amendment, *id.*, at 486. . .; or in the concept of liberty guaranteed by the first section of the Fourteenth Amendment, see *Meyer v. Nebraska* [1923]. . . . These decisions make it clear that only personal rights that can be deemed "fundamental" or "implicit in the concept of ordered liberty," *Palko v. Connecticut* [1937]. . . are included in this guarantee of personal privacy. They also make it clear that the right has some extension to activities relating to marriage, *Loving v. Virginia* [1967]...; procreation, *Skinner v. Oklahoma* [1942]...; contraception, *Eisenstadt v. Baird*...; family relationships, *Prince v. Massachusetts* [1944]...; and child rearing and education, *Pierce v. Society of Sisters* [1925]..., *Meyer v. Nebraska, supra.*

This right of privacy, whether it be founded in the Fourteenth Amendment's concept of personal liberty and restrictions upon state action, as we feel it is, or, as the District Court determined, in the Ninth Amendment's reservation of rights to the people, is broad enough to encompass a woman's decision whether or not to terminate her pregnancy. The detriment that the State would impose upon the pregnant woman by denying this choice altogether is apparent. Specific and direct harm medically diagnosable even in early pregnancy may be involved. Maternity, or additional offspring, may force upon the woman a distressful life and future. Psychological harm may be imminent. Mental and physical health may be taxed by child care. There is also the distress, for all concerned, associated with the unwanted child, and there is the problem of bringing a child into a family already unable, psychologically and otherwise, to care for it. In other cases, as in this one, the additional difficulties and continuing stigma of unwed motherhood may be involved. All these are factors the woman and her responsible physician necessarily will consider in consultation.

On the basis of elements such as these, appellant and some *amici* argue that the woman's right is absolute and that she is entitled to terminate her pregnancy at whatever time, in whatever way, and for whatever reason she alone chooses. With this we do not agree. Appellant's arguments that Texas either has no valid interest at all in regulating the abortion decision, or no interest strong enough to support any limitation upon the woman's sole determination, are unpersuasive. The Court's decisions recognizing a right of privacy also acknowledge that some state regulation in areas protected by that right is appropriate.... [a] State may properly assert important interests in safeguarding health, in maintaining medical standards, and in protecting potential life. At some point in pregnancy, these respective interests become sufficiently compelling to sustain regulation of the factors that govern the abortion decision. The privacy right involved, therefore, cannot be said to be absolute. In fact, it is not clear to us that the claim asserted by some *amici* that one has an unlimited right to do with one's body as one pleases bears a close relationship to the right of privacy previously articulated in the Court's decisions. The Court has refused to recognize an unlimited right of this kind in the past. *Jacobson v. Massachusetts* [1905]...; *Buck v. Bell* [1927]....

We, therefore, conclude that the right of personal privacy includes the abortion decision, but that this right is not unqualified and must be considered against important state interests in regulation.

We note that those federal and state courts that have recently considered abortion law challenges have reached the same conclusion....

Although the results are divided, most of these courts have agreed that the right of privacy, however based, is broad enough to cover the abortion decision; that the right, nonetheless, is not absolute and is subject to some limitations, and that at some point the state interests as to protection of health, medical standards, and prenatal life, become dominant. We agree with this approach.

The District Court held that the appellee failed to meet his burden of demonstrating that the Texas statute's infringement upon Roe's rights was necessary to support a compelling state interest.... Appellant, as has been indicated, claims an absolute right that bars any state imposition of criminal penalties in the area. Appellee argues that the State's determination to recognize and protect prenatal life from and after conception constitutes a compelling state interest. As noted above, we do not agree fully with either formulation.

A. The appellee and certain *amici* argue that the fetus is a "person" within the language and meaning of the Fourteenth Amendment. In support of this, they outline at length and in detail the well-known facts of fetal development. If this suggestion of personhood is established, the appellant's case, of course, collapses, for the fetus' right to life would then be guaranteed specifically by the Amendment. The appellant conceded as much on reargument. On the other hand, the appellee conceded on reargument that no case could be cited that holds that a fetus is a person within the meaning of the Fourteenth Amendment.

The Constitution does not define "person" in so many words. Section 1 of the Fourteenth Amendment contains three references to "person." The first, in defining "citizens," speaks of "persons born or naturalized in the United States." The word also appears both in the Due Process Clause and in the Equal Protection Clause. "Person" is used in other places in the Constitution.... But in nearly all these instances, the use of the word is such that it has application only postnatally. None indicates, with any assurance, that it has any possible pre-natal application.

All this, together with our observation, *supra*, that throughout the major portion of the 19th century prevailing legal abortion practices were far freer than they are today, persuades us that the word "person, " as used in the Fourteenth Amendment, does not include the unborn....

B. The pregnant woman cannot be isolated in her privacy. She carries an embryo and, later, a fetus, if one accepts the medical definitions of the developing young in the human uterus. See Dorland's Illustrated Medical Dictionary [24th ed. 1965].... The situation therefore is inherently different from marital intimacy, or bedroom possession of obscene material, or marriage, or procreation, or education, with which *Eisenstadt* and *Griswold, Stanley, Loving, Skinner,* and *Pierce* and *Meyer* were respectively concerned. As we have intimated above, it is reasonable and appropriate for a State to decide that at some point in time another interest, that of health of the mother or that of potential human life, becomes significantly involved. The woman's privacy is no longer sole and any right of privacy she possesses must be measured accordingly.

Texas urges that, apart from the Fourteenth Amendment, life begins at conception and is present throughout pregnancy, and that, therefore, the State has a compelling interest in protecting that life from and after conception. We need not resolve the difficult question of when life begins. When those trained in the respective disciplines of medicine, philosophy, and theology are unable to arrive at any consensus, the judiciary, at this point in the development of man's knowledge, is not in a position to speculate as to the answer....

With respect to the State's important and legitimate interest in the health of the mother, the "compelling" point, in the light of present medical knowledge, is at approximately the end of the first trimester. This is so because of the now-established medical fact that until the end of the first trimester mortality in abortion may be less than mortality in normal childbirth. It follows that, from and after this point, a State may regulate the abortion procedure to the extent that the regulation reasonably relates to the preservation and protection of maternal health....

This means, on the other hand, that, for the period of pregnancy prior to this "compelling" point, the attending physician, in consultation with his patient, is free to determine, without regulation by the State, that, in his medical judgment, the patient's pregnancy should be terminated. If that decision is reached, the judgment may be effectuated by an abortion free of interference by the State.

With respect to the State's important and legitimate interest in potential life, the "compelling" point is at viability. This is so because the fetus then presumably has the capability of meaningful life outside the mother's womb. State regulation protective of fetal life after viability thus has both logical and biological justifications. If the State is interested in protecting fetal life after viability, it may go so far as to proscribe abortion during that period, except when it is necessary to preserve the life or health of the mother.

Measured against these standards, Art. 1196 of the Texas Penal Code, in restricting legal abortions to those "procured or attempted by medical advice for the purpose of saving the life of the mother," sweeps too broadly. The statute makes no distinction between abortions performed early in pregnancy and those performed later, and it limits to a single reason, "saving" the mother's life, the legal justification for the procedure. The statute, therefore, cannot survive the constitutional attack made upon it here.

To summarize and to repeat:

1. A state criminal abortion statute of the current Texas type, that excepts from criminality only a *life-saving* procedure on behalf of the mother, without regard to pregnancy stage and without recognition of the other interests involved, is violative of the Due Process Clause of the Fourteenth Amendment.

(a) For the stage prior to approximately the end of the first trimester, the abortion decision and its effectuation must be left to the medical judgment of the pregnant woman's attending physician.

(b) For the stage subsequent to approximately the end of the first trimester, the State, in promoting its interest in the health of the mother, may, if it chooses, regulate the abortion procedure in ways that are reasonably related to maternal health.

(c) For the stage subsequent to viability, the State in promoting its interest in the potentiality of human life may, if it chooses, regulate, and even proscribe, abortion except when it is necessary, in appropriate medical judgment, for the preservation of the life or health of the mother.

2. The State may define the term "physician," as it has been employed in the preceding paragraphs. . .of this opinion, to mean only a physician currently licensed by the State, and may proscribe any abortion by a person who is not a physician as so defined. . . .

This holding, we feel, is consistent with the relative weights of the respective interests involved, with the lessons and examples of medical and legal history, with the lenity of the common law, and with the demands of the profound problems of the present day. . . .

Mr. Justice Rehnquist, dissenting.

. . .I have difficulty in concluding, as the Court does, that the right of "privacy" is involved in this case. Texas, by the statute here challenged, bars the performance of a medical abortion by a licensed physician on a plaintiff such as Roe. A transaction resulting in an operation such as this is not "private" in the ordinary usage of that word. Nor is the "privacy" that the Court finds here even a distant relative of the freedom from searches and seizures protected by the Fourth Amendment to the Constitution, which the Court has referred to as embodying a right to privacy. *Katz v. United States* [1967]. . . .

If the Court means by the term "privacy" no more than the claim of a person to be free from unwanted state regulation of consensual transactions may be a form of "liberty" protected by the Fourteenth Amendment, there is no doubt that similar claims have been upheld in our earlier decisions on the basis of that liberty. . . . [t]he "liberty," against deprivation of which without due process the Fourteenth Amendment protects, embraces more than the rights found in the Bill of Rights. But that liberty is not guaranteed absolutely against deprivation, only against deprivation without due process of law. . . . The Due Process Clause of the Fourteenth Amendment undoubtedly does place a limit, albeit a broad one, on legislative power to enact laws such as this. If the Texas statute were to prohibit an abortion even where the mother's life is in jeopardy, I have little doubt that such a statute would lack a rational relation to a valid state objective under the test stated in *Williamson, supra.* But the Court's sweeping invalidation of any restrictions on abortion during the first trimester is impossible to justify under that standard, and the conscious weighing of competing factors that the Court's opinion apparently substitutes for the established test is far more appropriate to a legislative judgment than to a judicial one.

The Court eschews the history of the Fourteenth Amendment in its reliance on the "compelling state interest" test. . . . But the Court adds a new wrinkle to this test by transposing it from the legal considerations associated with the Equal Protection Clause of the Fourteenth Amendment to this case arising under the Due Process Clause of the Fourteenth Amendment. Unless I misapprehend the consequences of this transplanting of the "compelling state interest test," the Court's opinion will accomplish the seemingly impossible feat of leaving this area of the law more confused than it found it.

. . .The decision here to break pregnancy into three distinct terms and to outline the permissible restrictions the State may impose in each one, for example, partakes more of judicial legislation than it does of a determination of the intent of the drafters of the Fourteenth Amendment.

The fact that a majority of the States reflecting, after all, the majority sentiment in those States, have had restrictions on abortions for at least a century is a strong indication, it seems to me, that the asserted right to an abortion is not "so rooted in the traditions and conscience of our people as to be ranked as fundamental," *Snyder v. Massachusetts* [1934]. . . . Even today, when society's views on abortion are changing, the very existence of the debate is evidence that the "right" to an abortion is not so universally accepted as the appellant would have us believe.

To reach its result, the Court necessarily has had to find within the scope of the Fourteenth Amendment a right that was apparently completely unknown to the drafters of the Amendment. As early as 1821, the first state law dealing directly with abortion was enacted by the Connecticut Legislature. . . . By the time of the adoption of the Fourteenth Amendment in 1868, there were at least 36 laws enacted by state or territorial legislatures limiting abortion. While many States have amended or updated their laws, 21 of the laws on the books in 1868 remain in effect today. Indeed, the Texas statute struck down today was, as the majority notes, first enacted in 1857 and "has remained substantially unchanged to the present time.". . .

There apparently was no question concerning the validity of this provision or of any of the other state statutes when the Fourteenth Amendment was adopted. The only conclusion possible from this history is that the drafters did not intend to have the Fourteenth Amendment withdraw from the States the power to legislate with respect to this matter.

For all the foregoing reasons, I respectfully dissent.

The application of the "right of privacy" to abortion decisions has not been without its critics in the legal community. As recently observed by Ralph Rossum and Alan Tarr,

> By declaring that "the personal right of privacy includes the abortion decision," *Roe*, together with the companion case of *Doe v. Bolton* (1973), generated a firestorm of controversy that has enveloped the Court ever since. . . . To begin with, critics have charged that *Roe* and *Doe* gave an entirely new meaning to the term *privacy*. . . . The Court has come to

understand the "right to be let alone" to protect not only against official intrusion but also against official regulation. This expansion of what
privacy is understood to secure could well render government itself problematic, were privacy to be regarded as an absolute right.*

Nonetheless, the Court tended to support and even reinforce *Roe* in later decisions, going so far in *Akron v. Akron Center for Reproductive Health* (1983) to declare
abortion itself to be a "fundamental right." But then in 1989, though stopping short
of actually overturning *Roe*, the Court demonstrated in *Webster v. Reproductive
Health Services* (1989) that it could be moving in that direction. In *Webster*, the
Court let stand a Missouri law that "declared in its preamble that human life begins
at conception and that 'unborn children have protectable interests in life, health,
and well-being,' . . . required medical tests to ascertain whether a fetus over twenty
weeks old was viable and prohibited the use of public employees and facilities
to perform abortions not necessary to save the life of the mother."** Furthermore,
what in *Akron* was a "fundamental right" to abortion was now seen as a "liberty
interest." In 1992, in *Planned Parenthood v. Casey*, the Court (in a 5–4 vote) allowed
a number of additional state restrictions to stand, but again stopped short of overturning *Roe*. While feeling it "imperative to adhere to the essence of Roe's original
decision" and concluding that *Roe* had resulted in a "rule of law and a component
of liberty we cannot renounce," the majority nonetheless let stand four restrictive
provisions of a Pennsylvania law that would not impose "undue burden" on the
right to abortion.

*Rossum, Ralph A. and G. Alan Tarr, *American Constitutional Law*, Third Edition (New York:
St. Martin's Press, 1991, pp. 690, 694)—*Editor's Note.*
**Rossum and Tarr, p. 692.—*Editor's Note.*

CHAPTER SIX

Political Values and Issues

The partisan "realignments" that have occurred approximately every thirty-six years in American politics (until 1932) have been, in large part, just behavioral reflections of fundamental changes in issue priorities that have followed roughly the same cyclical pattern. When the issues on which people make their partisan identifications and their electoral choices change in a dramatic way, as they did when social welfare concerns were moved from the back burner to the front during the Great Depression of the 1930s, it is reasonable to expect that citizens will reassess whether the "right" party for them on the old issues is still the right party given the new political agenda.

The issue changes themselves are often, if not always, practical reflections of changes in more abstract, underlying values. Among the most basic values in a democracy are those of equality, liberty, and physical security. Priorities among even those most basic values differ from person to person, however, and even from time to time for the same person. (See also the introduction to Chapter Twenty.) When fundamental value change affects a significant portion of the population, the effects on the political agenda may be profound. And even when change in the electorate may not amount to a realignment per se, there may be other important ramifications for the party system. For example, in those countries where concerns for the environment have grown to rival the emphasis on economic growth, new "ecology" parties have been formed, old parties have been forced to adjust to the new values, and the context for political discussion has been fundamentally, if not permanently, altered. And when, in the early 1970s in the social democracies of Scandinavia, a significant minority came to value low taxes and individual freedoms as (or more) highly than collective responsibility, anti-tax protests developed that have since become institutionalized threats to some of the most traditional of social democratic values (as well as to the existing political parties).

In spite of the lack of a classical nationwide realignment of the American electorate since the 1930s, other changes in partisan behavior have been documented over the past three decades, and *those* changes (including the signs of dealignment) have certainly occurred in the context of changing political values and issues. Evidence exists in new and renewed battle cries of the '70s, '80s and '90s: "Energy Independence!," "Women's Rights!," "Minority Empowerment!," "Pro-Life!" vs. "Pro-Choice!," and "Save the Planet!". At the same time, new support has been found for efforts to "cut taxes" and "get government off our backs." In part, the new issues and the changing values they reflect are a response to successes, excesses, or failures of past governmental programs. In part, they are a reflection of other changes that have occurred in a society that has graduated from "industrial" to "postindustrial," with all of the promises, problems, and challenges that entails. Regardless of the reasons, the fact is that the agenda for political discussion in America today is dramatically different from that of the 1930s, '40s, and '50s, with profound consequences for government and politics more generally.

The readings in this chapter deal with both change and continuity in American political values and issues in recent decades. Thomas and Mary Edsall provide evidence of rising support for "conservative" values in recent decades. Jane Mansbridge investigates the failure of the Equal Rights Amendment to gain ratification in the 1970s and early '80s, and finds a telling distinction between growing support for equal rights in the abstract and increasing concerns about the amendment's possible consequences in practice. Shifting from the mass level to the political elite, Alan Ehrenhalt suggests that there has been important change in the values motivating politicians to seek office, with belief in government becoming more important as material incentives have declined.

27 / Race, Rights, Taxes, and the Conservative Ascendance

Thomas Byrne Edsall
and Mary D. Edsall

From the 1930s through at least the mid-1960s, liberal attitudes seemed to prevail in American politics, whether toward redistributive programs or policies aimed at protecting and extending "rights." But by the middle 1970s, as documented here by Thomas Edsall and Mary Edsall, changing conditions in society were bringing significant changes in public opinion. Concerns over economic, political, and physical security have significantly affected not only how Americans think about politics today, but also how they vote.

In the aftermath of Richard Nixon's 1972 landslide victory over George McGovern, the investigation of the Republican break-in at the Democratic party headquarters—the scandal known as Watergate—provided the besieged forces of liberalism with an opportunity to stall the conservative ascendance. Watergate replenished forces on the liberal side of the political spectrum— the Democratic Congress, organized labor, civil rights groups, and the network of public-interest lobbying and reform organizations—supplying new leverage in what was otherwise rapidly becoming, in political terms, a losing ideological battle.

The central conflict between liberalism and conservatism since the late sixties had focused on the aggressive expansion of constitutional rights to previously disfranchised, often controversial groups. These included not only blacks, but others in relatively unprotected enclaves (mental hospitals, prisons, ghettos) as well as homosexuals (who increasingly resented being cast as deviant), ethnic minorities, and women—who had the strongest base of political support but whose movement, nonetheless, engendered substantial political reaction. Just as this expansion of rights had run into growing public and political opposition, the Nixon administration was itself caught flagrantly violating the core constitutional rights of "average" citizens—rights for which there was, in general, broad consensual support.. . .

The outcry against the actions of the Nixon White House effectively stifled for the moment public expression of the growing resentment toward the liberal revolution.. . . .

For many liberal constituencies, Watergate provided the grounds to attempt to indict and convict the snowballing conservative counteroffensive. For Democratic members of Congress, and for the larger Democratic establishment, the procedural ruthlessness of the Nixon administration—the enemies lists, the attempts to use the IRS and Justice Department to harass political adversaries, the burglaries, and the illegal wiretapping—was part and parcel of a much broader and more threatening administration drive to assault the constitutional underpinnings of the liberal state.. . .

The Watergate-inspired re-invigoration of the left effectively choked off the growth of conservatism from 1973 through 1976, but the suppression meant that instead of finding an outlet within the political system, rightward pressure built throughout the decade to explosive levels. The Democratic party experienced a surge of victory in 1974 and 1976, while developments in the economy, in the court-enforced enlargement of the rights revolution, in the expansion of the regulatory state, in rising middle-class tax burdens, and in the growth of crime and illegitimacy were all in fact working to crush liberalism.

Watergate resulted in a political system out of sync with larger trends. A host of groups on the left of the spectrum—Democratic prosecutors, the media, junior congressional Democrats, new reform organizations, and traditional liberal interest groups—gained control over the political agenda just when a selection of other key indicators suggested that the power of the right should be expanding:

- Family income after 1973 abruptly stopped growing, cutting off what was left of popular support for government-led redistributional economic policies. Inflation (driven in part by the first OPEC oil shock) simultaneously pushed millions of working and middle-class citizens into higher tax brackets, encouraging them to think like Republicans instead of Democrats. As low and middle-income voters began to view the taxes deducted from their weekly paychecks with rising anger, the number of welfare and food stamp clients continued to grow at record rates, forcing a conflict between Democratic constituencies that would lead, by the end of the decade, to a racially-loaded confrontation between taxpayers and tax recipients.

- In courts across the country, the drive by a wide range of civil liberties organizations—from the ACLU to the Mental Health Law Project to the National Gay and Lesbian Task Force—reached its height. These organizations were committed to winning new rights for recreational drug users, the mentally ill, gays, American Indians, illegal aliens and the dependent poor. Their success produced not only benefits for targeted populations, but also conservative reaction in communities in every region of the country.
- Crime rates continued to surge, intensifying public discontent with liberal Democratic support of defendants' and prisoners' rights.
- The movement to liberalize abortion laws, which had been making substantial political progress in state legislatures, succeeded with the Supreme Court's 1973 decision, *Roe v. Wade*; that decision, in turn, produced a political counter-mobilization that rapidly became a mainstay of the conservative movement. Equally important, *Roe* reflected the growing dependence of liberalism on court rulings. The legal arena provided liberal interest groups with a host of victories through the mid-1970s. Court rulings frequently lacked the political legitimacy and support, however, that comes from public debate and legislative deliberation. Liberal court victories reduced incentives for the left to compete in elective politics to win backing for its agenda, while sharply increasing the incentives for the right—both social and economic—to build political muscle.
- The Arab oil embargo of 1973 resulted in gas lines across the country, intensifying in some sectors hostility toward liberal foreign-policy positions seen as supportive of Third World interests. Covert and explicit hostility towards Third World countries intensified and fueled, in some cases, a resurgence of domestic nativism, and even a degree of racism.
- Legislation passed in the civil rights climate of 1965, liberalizing previously restrictive, pro-European immigration policies, produced a surge of Hispanic, Asian, and other non-European immigration; created new competition for employment and housing; increased pressure for public services; and generated a revival of pressures to restore restrictions on immigration.
- The Justice Department, the Equal Employment Opportunity Commission (EEOC), and the Office of Federal Contract Compliance Programs (OFCCP) all capitalized on a sequence of legislative mandates, court rulings, and executive orders to sharply expand enforcement of affirmative action programs in the public and private sectors, increasing the saliency of the issue of quotas, an issue beginning to match busing in terms of the depth of voter reaction.

- Busing, in turn, by the early and mid-1970s, had become a legal remedy frequently imposed to correct school segregation in the North as well as in the South. The 1973 Supreme Court decision in *Keyes v. Denver School District No. 1* significantly increased the likelihood that a northern school system would be found guilty of illegal discrimination, and therefore subject to busing orders.
- In a number of major cities, black political gains were translating into the acquisition of genuine power. An inevitable outcome of the process of enfranchisement, the ascendancy of black politicians meant the loss of power for some white politicians, and in an increasing number of major cities competition for control of City Hall turned into racial confrontation. In 1967, Richard Hatcher and Carl Stokes won the mayor's offices in Gary, Indiana, and Cleveland, Ohio, respectively; in 1970, Kenneth Gibson became mayor of Newark; in 1974 Coleman Young and Maynard Jackson won in Detroit and Atlanta. These contests involved sharply polarized electorates (the only exception being the 1973 election of Tom Bradley, a black, in Los Angeles, where the mayoralty was won with more white than black votes). As Democratic black political power grew in the cities, Republican voting in white suburbs began to intensify, accelerating the creation of what political strategists would term "white nooses" around black cities.

There were forces at work in the 1970s, combining to produce an explosive mix—forces pitting blacks, whites, Hispanics, and other minorities against each other for jobs, security, prestige, living space, and government protection. As weekly pay fell, and as the market for working-class jobs tightened, government intervention in behalf of employment for minorities intensified; the doors opened for a wave of Latinos and Asians legally seeking jobs, at the same time that illegal immigration from across the Mexican border increased. Simultaneously, former civil rights lawyers and activists turned their attention to continuing the extension of rights to the ranks of the once-excluded.

This sequence of developments engendered a form of backlash within key sectors of the majority white electorate, backlash generating conservative pressures on an ambitious and threatening liberalism, conservative pressures which were only temporarily held in check by Watergate. The immediate political consequences of the investigation and prosecution triggered by the Watergate break-in lulled Democratic Party leaders into ignoring the outcome of the 1972 presidential election—into thinking that their majority party status was secure, and that the ability of the Republican Party to dominate presidential elections with a racially and socially conservative message had been washed away in the outcry for official probity and reform.

Politicians, academics, and the media remained largely ignorant of the direction the country would, in fact, take by the end of the decade. . .Everett Carll Ladd, a political scientist, expert in assessing the balance of power between the two parties, wrote in 1977:

[W]e are dealing with a long-term secular shift, not just an artifact of Watergate. The Republicans have lost their grip on the American establishment, most notably among young men and women of relative privilege. They have lost it, we know, in large part because the issue orientations which they manifest are somewhat more conservative than the stratum favors.... The [Republican) party is especially poorly equipped in style and tone to articulate the frustrations of the newer, emergent American *petit bourgeoisie*—southern white Protestant, Catholic, black and the like."[1]

In fact, it was the Democratic party that was continuing to lose its class-based strength. The forces pushing the country to the right exerted the strongest pressures on whites in the working and lower-middle class, and it was among these voters that Democratic loyalty was continuing to erode. Party leaders failed to perceive these trends because losses among low-to-moderate-income whites during the mid-1970s were compensated for by momentary gains among upper-income, normally Republican white voters who were most insistent on political reform in response to Watergate....

In effect, Democrats were winning in 1974 and 1976, just as the core of their traditional base among whites was crumbling. The party became dependent on upscale, traditionally Republican voters whose new found loyalty would disappear as economic and foreign-policy issues regained their saliency, and as the memory of Watergate faded.

In the buildup of conservative, anti-liberal sentiment in the electorate, the most important development was the fact that 1973, the year the Senate set up a special committee to investigate Watergate, was also the year that marked the end of a sustained period of post-World War II economic growth. Hourly earnings, which had grown every year since 1951 in real, inflation-adjusted dollars, fell by 0.1 percent in 1973, by 2.8 percent in 1974, and by 0.7 percent in 1975.[2] Weekly earnings fell more sharply, by 4.1 percent in 1974 and by 3.1 percent in 1975. Median family income, which had grown from $20,415 (in 1985 inflation-adjusted dollars) in 1960, to $29,172 in 1973, began to decline in 1974, when family income fell to $28,145, and then to $27,421 in 1975.[3]

Steady economic growth, which had made redistributive government policies tolerable to the majority of the electorate, came to a halt in the mid-1970s, and, with stagnation, the threat to Democratic liberalism intensified. In a whipsaw action, the middle-class tax burden rose with inflation just as the economy and real-income growth slowed. The tax system was losing its progressivity, placing a steadily growing share of the cost of government on middle and lower-middle-class voters, vital constituencies for the Democratic party. In 1953, a family making the median family income was taxed at a rate of 11.8 percent, while a family making four times the median was taxed at 20.2 percent, nearly double. By 1976, these figures had become 22.7 percent for the average family, and 29.5 percent for the affluent family.[4] In other words, for the affluent family, the tax burden increased by 46 percent from 1953 to 1976, while for the average family, the tax burden increased by 92.4 percent. Not only were cumulative tax burdens growing, but they were also shifting from Republican constituencies to Democratic constituencies. . . .

In political terms, the damage was most severe to the Democratic party. Democratic-approved Social Security tax hikes fell much harder on those making less than the median income, voters who had traditionally tended to vote Democratic by higher margins than those above the median. In 1975, for example, a worker with taxable income of $14,100 paid $825, or 5.85 percent of his income, to Social Security, while someone making $75,000 paid the same $825, or just 1.1 percent of income.[5]

These economic developments became one-half of an equation that functioned to intensify racial divisions within the traditional Democratic coalition. The other half of the equation was that taxpayer-financed welfare, food stamps, and other expenditures for the poor were growing exponentially. In the decade from 1965 to 1975, the number of families receiving benefits under Aid to Families with Dependent Children (AFDC), grew by 237 percent. Until that point, the national caseload had been growing at a *relatively* modest pace—from 644,000 households in 1950 to 787,000 in 1960 to 1,039,000 in 1965, an increase over fifteen years of 61 percent.

From 1965 to 1970, the number of households on welfare more than doubled to reach 2,208,000, and then grew again by more than one million, reaching 3,498,000 families in 1975.[6] The Food Stamp program, which was initiated on a small scale in 1961 and then greatly enlarged in 1970, provided benefits to 400,000 people in 1965, 4.3 million in 1970, and increased fourfold, to 17.1 million recipients in 1975.[7] Throughout the 1970s, the illegitimacy rate for both blacks and whites grew significantly, but for blacks, the decade saw illegitimate births begin to outnumber legitimate births. For whites, the illegitimacy rate rose from 5.7 percent of all live births in 1970, to 7.3 in 1975, to 11.0 in 1980; for blacks, the rate went from 37.6, to 48.8, to 55.2 percent in the same period.[8]

The tensions growing out of these economic and social trends were compounded by the substantial conflicts growing directly out of the expansion of the civil rights movement into the broader rights revolution. Lawyers who had been trained in the trenches of the South—often funded by liberal, tax-exempt organizations and foundations, just as civil rights litigation projects had been—moved, in the late 1960s and early 1970s, into the broader rights arena. They developed litigation strategies designed to remedy the long-standing denial of rights to groups in unprotected enclaves (psychiatric hospitals, immigrant detention camps, Indian reservations, jails), and also to social "victims" (homosexuals, the disabled, the indigent). Particularly powerful was the evolving idea that conditions of birth or chance—ranging from gender to race to skin color to sexual orientation to class origin to ethnicity to physical or mental health—should not place any American at a social or economic disadvantage, insofar as it was possible for the state to offer protection and redress. "The rights revolution was the longest-lasting legacy of the 1960s," writes Samuel Walker in his history of the ACLU. "Millions of ordinary people—students, prisoners, women, the poor, gays and lesbians, the handicapped, the mentally retarded and others—discovered their own voices and demanded fair treatment and personal dignity. The empowerment of these previously silent groups was a political development of enormous significance."[9]

The rights movement had already found political expression within the Democratic party, which had not only endorsed a broad spectrum of human rights at its 1972 convention, but which was granting specific recognition to a network of separate caucuses for blacks, women, and homosexuals within the Democratic National Committee. It was not until the mid-1970s, however, that the rights revolution reached its full power, changing some of the most fundamental patterns and practices of society. As these changes began to seep into public consciousness, the political ramifications slowly became felt throughout the majority electorate—an electorate under economic siege and rapidly losing its tolerance for the rapid redistribution of influence, as well for the redistribution of a host of economic and social benefits.

Just as the economy was beginning to stagnate, as oil producing countries were demonstrating their power to hold the energy-hungry United States hostage (with the price of imported oil rising from $1.80 a barrel in 1970 to $14.34 in 1979),[10] and as the shift from manufacturing to services was forcing major dislocations in the job market, the rights revolution assaulted the traditional hierarchical structure of society, and in particular the status of white men.

The strongest of the rights movements was, in fact, the drive for the equality of women, who were included as beneficiaries of the equal employment provisions of the original 1964 Civil Rights Act. Political support for women's rights remained strong, symbolized by the congressional approval in 1972 of the Equal Rights Amendment (ERA) and by a series of legislative victories throughout the 1970s. At the same time, the women's movement— in combination with financial pressures making the one-earner family increasingly untenable—produced a major alteration in family structure, as labor force participation among married women grew steadily, from 35.7 percent in 1965, to 41.4 in 1970, to 45.1 percent in 1975, to 50.7 percent in 1980.[11]

The changes that were taking place in the workplace, in family relationships, and in the balance of power between men and women were not cost-free. The number of divorces, which had remained relatively constant from 1950 through 1967, began to escalate sharply. In 1967, the divorce rate for every 1,000 married women was 11.2; by 1975, the rate had grown to 20.3; and in 1979, the divorce rate reached its height, 22.8—more than double the 1967 level.[12] At the same time, the annual number of children of parents getting divorced grew from 701,000 in 1967, to 1.12 million in 1975, to 1.18 million in 1979.[13]

The more outspoken leaders of the women's rights movement, many of whom cut their teeth in the civil rights and anti-war movements, adopted rhetoric and tactics that exacerbated the anxieties of a host of men already facing diminished job prospects, eroding family incomes, and a loss of traditional status in their homes. "Lesbian sexuality could make an excellent case, based on anatomical data, for the extinction of the male organ," Anne Koedt wrote in "The Myth of the Vaginal Orgasm," an essay subsequently reprinted in an estimated twenty different anthologies of feminist writings.[14]

The women's rights movement was reinforced by the Supreme Court in *Roe v. Wade*, as the Court took the expanded right to privacy established in *Griswold v. Connecticut*, a case involving the sale of contraceptives, and extended the reasoning to establish a woman's right to terminate pregnancy during the first trimester. The sum of these developments—the entry of women into the workforce, the rising divorce rate, and the doubling of the number of reported abortions, from 586,800 in 1972 to 1.2 million in 1976[15]—as well as the halving of the fertility rate between 1960 and 1975[16]—contributed to the building of a conservative response.

The anti-abortion movement and the massive growth of parishioners attending fundamentalist Christian churches during the 1970s were in many ways powerful reactions to the emergence of the women's rights movement. "[T]he danger signs are quite evident: legislation on the national level reflects widespread acceptance of easy divorce, abortion-on-demand, gay rights, militant feminism, unisex facilities, and leniency towards pornography, prostitution and crime. . . . In short, many religious leaders believe that America may soon follow the footsteps of Sodom and Gomorrah," wrote Tim LaHaye, organizer of fundamentalist Christian voters, in his book, *The Battle for the Mind*.[17]

The surge of women newly entering the job market, women now empowered with unprecedented control over their reproductive and sexual lives, coincided with the opening of the nation to another source of competition for employment and, in the Southwest and West, for political power: Hispanic and Asian immigration. Legislation enacted in 1965, growing out of the general climate surrounding the civil rights revolution, ended the racially restrictive immigration policies that had been on the books since the Immigration Act of 1924. The 1965 law opened the door to a wave of new immigration, primarily from Mexico and the Caribbean. . . .

The drive to achieve equality for women and the abandonment of racially exclusionary immigration policies, in tandem with the civil rights movement, were consistent with the evolution of an egalitarian American political culture. But each evolutionary development contributed in turn to a growing conservative backlash or reaction, which was strengthened in turn by the increasing momentum of the more controversial rights movements. In 1974, the gay rights movement persuaded the American Psychiatric Association to remove homosexuality from its list of mental illnesses; between 1973 and 1975, the movement won approval of gay rights ordinances in eleven cities and counties, barring discrimination on the basis of sexual orientation; by 1989, the drive had produced legal prohibitions against discrimination against gays in housing, employment, and in the provision of other services in sixty-four municipalities, sixteen counties, and thirteen states. . . .[18]

Perhaps the most controversial of all the major rights movements identified with liberalism over the past twenty-five years were the initiatives in behalf of criminal defendants and prisoners. In a series of decisions between 1957 and 1966, including *Mallory v. United States, Gideon v. Wainwright, Escobedo v. Illinois, Mapp. v. Ohio,* and *Miranda v. Arizona,* the Supreme Court found criminal defendants, many of them poor and black—and some clearly guilty—entitled to a range of fundamental protections and rights in state as well as federal courts. These included protections against illegally obtained evidence, self-incrimination, deprivation of due process, and cruel and unusual punishment; and called for rights to counsel, to silence, and to a speedy trial. The prisoners' rights movement grew out of both the civil rights struggle and the Supreme Court decisions affirming defendant protections. Proponents of inmate rights took up the issues of prison overcrowding, restrictions within prisons on political activity and free speech, and the authority of prison officials to punish inmates.

The *Miranda, Gideon,* and *Escobedo* rulings, enlarging the rights of defendants and often restricting the activities of police and prosecutors, were issued just as the nation's crime rate began to shoot up. The reaction of much of the public, of the law enforcement community, and of a host of moderate to conservative politicians was intense—and almost invariably hostile....

What was widely seen as a judicial assault on the criminal justice system extended, in addition, to the prison system. In a precedent-setting decision, a federal district court found in *Pugh v. Locke* in 1976 that the entire Alabama prison system was in violation of the eighth amendment prohibition against cruel and unusual punishment. Judge Frank M. Johnson found that "prison conditions are so debilitating that they necessarily deprive inmates of any opportunity to rehabilitate themselves or even maintain skills already possessed."[19] By the late 1980s, thirty-seven states, the District of Columbia, Puerto Rico, and the Virgin Islands were operating prisons under court order, almost all because of overcrowding and inmate violence, lack of medical care, unsanitary conditions, and absence of rehabilitation programs.[20]

Following the reforms of the criminal justice system and at the beginning of the prisoners' rights movement, were a sequence of Supreme Court decisions that rendered the death penalty illegal. In three related 1972 cases, *Furman v. Georgia, Jackson v. Georgia,* and *Branch v. Texas,* the Court overturned all existing death penalty statutes on the grounds that there was a "wanton and freakish" pattern in their application; the decisions effectively took an estimated 600 people across the country off death row.[21] The prohibition against the death penalty stood until 1976, when the court in *Gregg v. Georgia, Profitt v. Florida,* and *Jurek v. Texas,* restored its use.

The expansion of defendants' rights, the prisoner rights movement, and the four-year prohibition on the death penalty coincided with a sharply increasing crime rate and ran headlong into increasingly conservative public opinion on crime—all of which had marked consequences for domestic politics and for race relations. Popular support for liberal policies on crime and rehabilitation had grown steadily from the mid-1930s, when polls were first taken, to the mid-1960s. At that juncture, public opinion shifted in a decisively rightward direction, as crime rates rose sharply. In 1965, a substantial minority of survey respondents, 36 percent, said that the courts treated criminals "about right" or "too harsh[ly]," while 48 percent said the courts were not harsh enough. By 1977, the percentage describing court treatment of criminals as too harsh or about right had fallen to a minimal 11 percent, and those who said the courts were not harsh enough had risen to 83 percent....[22]

The criminal rights and the prisoner rights movements strengthened the linkage between the rights revolution and one of the most emotionally charged areas of American life: crime. The crime rate, which had surged in the 1960s, continued to grow in the 1970s....

The sharp rise in reported violent crime had major consequences for both politics and race relations across the country. There are a number of ways to measure differences between crime rates for blacks and whites—the three most common being 1) an annual victimization survey conducted by the Department of Justice from 1973 to the present; 2) FBI arrest rate statistics from 1965 onward; and, 3) the makeup of the prison population.[23] All three show a much higher crime rate among blacks than whites, with the ratio significantly higher for violent crime (murder, robbery, assault, and rape) than for property crimes (larceny, motor vehicle theft, burglary). From 1960 to 1986, the prison population shifted from 38 percent to 43.5 percent black.[24] In terms of the victimization surveys, which suggest lower rates of crime for blacks than does the FBI compilation of arrest rates, and are thus less subject to charges of racial bias, the 1974 survey found that while blacks made up 11 percent of the total U.S. population,[25] victims of aggravated assault said 30 percent of their assailants were black, victims of robbery said 62 percent of their attackers were black, and victims of rape said 39 percent of the offenders were black.[26]

The gap between the races has consistently been widest of all for robbery, (muggings, stick-ups, purse-snatches), one of the most threatening and most common of the violent crimes. It is threatening because it is the crime committed most often by strangers; it involves the use of force or the impending use of force; and it is the crime that occurs most often where the victim feels most vulnerable, outside of the home, on the streets and sidewalks.... The annual criminal victimization surveys conducted by the Department of Justice consistently show that more robberies are committed by blacks than whites.

The robbery figures throughout the 1960s, 1970s, and 1980s reflect at the extreme the challenge posed to Democratic liberalism by rising rates of social disorder in the wake of civil rights legislation and following upon substantial growth of federal expenditures in behalf of the poor. This is a dilemma that the Democratic party and liberals have been reluctant to address, a reluctance motivated by compassion, by fear of provoking backlash, and by the desire to preserve a basis for more effective policy interventions. This reluctance, no matter how understandable, has nonetheless eroded the political credibility of liberalism and of the Democratic party.

For many members of the black leadership class, and for much of the white liberal community, examination of divisive racially freighted issues has been seen as having the potential to produce damaging results. These include the encouragement of a racist and "victim blaming" analysis of black poverty; a disproportionate focusing on black dysfunction, downplaying white criminality and white drug abuse; and failure to recognize the emergence of white underclasses in other highly industrialized and competitive societies, including a largely white underclass in England.[27] A focus on so-called social pathology or on a "culture of poverty" among the most disadvantaged, some liberals argue, can be used to shift the burden of responsibility for institutionalized discrimination from the perpetrators to those who suffer social and economic ostracism at society's hands; to shift to blacks blame for an aberrant culture, rather than holding accountable their historic victimizers. A focus on "social deviance" or on an underclass subculture leaves unaddressed, according to this perspective, the oppressive economic and social structures which make inevitable the set of behavioral responses then labeled pathological. Finally, a number of liberals feel that the public naming of patterns of social disorder, including the use of the word "underclass,"[28] draws undue attention to such patterns, attention which can be manipulated by conservative ideological antagonists for political gain. The successful election in 1989 of Republican State Representative David Duke in Louisiana, the president of the National Association for the Advancement of White People, whose campaign stressed with striking success black crime, illegitimacy, and welfare dependency, and Duke's 44 percent vote in the 1990 Louisiana senatorial primary, can be seen as a confirmation of these fears.

Conversely, pointed liberal avoidance of these issues has its own liabilities. First of all, these issues are inescapably in the political arena: voters are seeking a resolution to the violence and social disorder expressed in crime, drug use, and illegitimacy. Secondly, the failure of the left to address such issues has permitted the political right to profit from explicit and covert manipulation of symbols and images relying upon assumptions about black poverty and crime—as in the Republicans' 1988 campaign focus on the death penalty, Willie Horton, and the "revolving prison door" television commercials.

The liberal failure to convincingly address increasingly conservative attitudes in the majority electorate, attitudes spurred in part by crime and welfare rates, has damaged the national Democratic party on a variety of counts. Perhaps most important, it has signaled a failure to live up to one of the chief obligations of a political party: to secure the safety and well-being of its own constituents, black and white. Secondly, self-imposed Democratic myopia has in no way prevented the majority public from forming "hard" opinions on crime, drug use, chronic joblessness, and out-of-wedlock births—nor from judging the national Democratic party as excessively "soft" in its approach to contemporary social issues—nor from voting for politicians whose conservative attitudes on crime and social disorder more completely mirror its own.

Notes

1. Everett Carll Ladd, Jr., *Transformations of the American Party System* (New York: Norton, 1978), 258–59.
2. *Economic Report of the President, 1987* (Washington, D.C.: U.S. Government Printing Office), 292.
3. Ibid., 278.
4. Robert Kuttner, *The Revolt of the Haves* (New York: Simon and Schuster, 1980), 211–12. Ladd, *Transformations*, 220.
5. *Statistical Abstract of the United States, 1987*, Table 586, p. 348.
6. Dept. of Health and Human Services, *Social Security Bulletin*, Annual Statistical Supplement, 1986, (Washington, D.C.: GPO, 1986) Table 204, p. 282.
7. Henry Owen and Charles L. Schultze, ed., *Setting National Priorities: The Next Ten Years*, (Washington, D.C.: The Brookings Institution, 1976), 340.
8. *Statistical Abstract of the United States, 1987*, 61.
9. Samuel Walker, *In Defense of American Liberties: A History of the ACLU* (New York: Oxford Univ. Press, 1990), 300.
10. *Data supplied by the American Petroleum Institute, by phone, July 18, 1990.*
11. *Statistical Abstract*, 1987, 382.
12. Department of Health and Human Services, National Center for Health Statistics, *Advance Report on Final Divorces, 1986* (Washington, D.C., 6 June 1989), 4.
13. Department of Health and Human Services, National Center for Health Statistics, *Children of Divorce* (Washington, D.C., January 1989), ser. 21, no. 46, p. 14.
14. Anne Koedt, "The Myth of the Vaginal Orgasm," as quoted in Irwin Unger and Debi Unger, *Turning Point: 1968* (New York: Scribner's, 1988), 441.
15. *Statistical Abstract of the United States, 1987*, 67.
16. Bureau of the Census, *Statistical Abstract of the United States, 1989*, (Washington, D.C., 1989), 64.
17. Tim LaHaye, *The Battle for the Mind* (Old Tappan, N.J.: Fleming H. Revell, 1980). Material quoted from the interior cover of the book.
18. Arthur S. Leonard, *Gay & Lesbian Rights and Protections in the U.S.* (Washington, D.C.: National Gay and Lesbian Task Force).
19. *Congress and the Nation* Vol. III, 255–56.
20. Ibid., 311.
21. Elder Witt, ed., *Guide to the Supreme Court* (Washington, D.C.: Congressional Quarterly, 1979), 576–78.
22. Richard G. Niemi, John Mueller, and Tom W. Smith, *Trends in Public Opinion: A Compendium of Survey Data* (New York: Greenwood Press, 1989), 136.
23. There is a large body of data and literature on the subject of racial disparities in crime rates. The Deparment of Justice annually releases a survey, "Criminal Victimization in the United States," based on large polls of 40,000 or more households. The FBI issued in June 1988, a report called "Age-Specific Arrest Rates and Race-Specific Arrest Rates for Selected Offenses 1965–1986," and provides on request data for more recent years. . . .
24. Gerald David Jaynes and Robin Williams, *A Common Destiny: Blacks and American Society* (Washington, D.C.: National Academy Press, 1984), 461, and cf. footnote 7, Chapter One.
25. The black percentage of the U.S. population has grown from 9.9 percent in 1950, to 11.1 percent in 1970, to 12.2 percent in 1987. *Statistical Abstract of the United States, 1987* Table 18, p. 16.

26. Michael J. Hingelang, "Race and Involvement in Common Law Personal Crimes," *American Sociological Review* (Febraury 1978), 100.
27. Charles Murray, "The British Underclass," *The Public Interest* (Spring 1990): 4–28.
28. Herbert J. Gans, "Deconstructing the Underclass: The Term's Danger as a Planning Concept," *American Planning Association Journal* (Summer 1990): 271–77.

28 / How the ERA Was Lost

Jane J. Mansbridge

Within approximately one year of being proposed by Congress in March of 1972, the Equal Rights Amendment was ratified by thirty states, just ten short of adoption. But only five more states joined by 1977, and then no more by the extended deadline of 1982. In her analysis of what happened between the early successes and the final failure, Mansbridge provides evidence that while attitudes toward equal rights in the abstract were increasingly supportive, growing concerns over the proposed amendment's possible consequences for other deeply held values contributed to its downfall.

A Very Brief History

The major women's organizations were able to persuade two-thirds of the states to approve women's suffrage in 1920. In the same year these organizations began to discuss an Equal Rights Amendment. Alice Paul and her militant National Woman's Party had gained national notoriety by picketing the White House and staging hunger strikes for women's suffrage. Now the same group proposed a constitutional amendment, introduced in Congress in 1923, that read: "Men and women shall have equal rights throughout the United States and in every place subject to its jurisdiction. Congress shall have power to enforce this article by appropriate legislation."[1]

From the beginning, "equal rights" meant "ending special benefits." An ERA would have made unconstitutional the protective legislation that socialists and social reformers like Florence Kelley, frustrated by the lack of a strong working-class movement in America, had struggled to erect in order to protect at least women and children from the worst ravages of capitalism. Against Kelley and women like her, the National Woman's Party leaders, primarily professional and upper- or upper-middle-class women,[2] argued that "a maximum hour law or a minimum wage law which applied to women but not to men was bound to hurt women more than it could possibly help them." Kelley in turn dubbed the ERA "topsy-turvy feminism," and declared that "women cannot achieve true equality with men by securing identity of treatment under the law."[3]

After a 1921 meeting between Alice Paul, Florence Kelley, and others, the board of directors of the National Consumers' League voted to oppose the Equal Rights Amendment. The League, a powerful Progressive organization of which Kelley was general secretary, thereafter made opposition to the ERA a consistent plank in its program.[4] The strong opposition of Progressive and union feminists meant that when the Equal Rights Amendment was introduced in Congress in 1923 it was immediately opposed by a coalition of Progressive organizations and labor unions. And although the Amendment was introduced in every subsequent Congress for the next twenty years, opposition from this coalition and from most conservatives ensured its repeated defeat.

During the 1930s, the National Association of Women Lawyers and the National Federation of Business and Professional Women's Clubs (BPW) decided to sponsor the ERA, and in 1940 the Republican party revitalized the ERA by placing it in the party's platform. In 1944, despite strong opposition from labor, the Democratic party followed suit.[5] Nonetheless, the ERA never came close to passing until 1950 and 1953, when the U.S. Senate passed it, but with the "Hayden rider," which provided that the Amendment "shall not be construed to impair any rights, benefits, or exemptions now or hereinafter conferred by law upon persons of the female sex."[6] In both years the House of Representatives recessed without a vote. Because the women's organizations supporting the ERA knew that special benefits were incompatible with equal rights, they had tried to block the amended ERA in the House and were relieved when their efforts succeeded.[7]

Support widened during the 1950s—primarily among Republicans, although among the Democrats Eleanor Roosevelt and some other prominent women dropped their opposition to the ERA in order to support the United Nations charter, which affirmed the "equal rights of men and women."[8] In 1953 President Dwight Eisenhower replaced the unionist head of the Federal Women's Bureau with a Republican businesswoman who, having sponsored Connecticut's equal pay law, moved the bureau from active opposition into a neutral position regarding the ERA. In later speeches Eisenhower also stressed the pro-ERA planks of both parties and stated his support for "equal rights" for women.[9] In 1963, however, labor struck back when President John Kennedy's Commission on the Status of Women—created under labor influence partly to siphon off pressure for an ERA—concluded that "a constitutional amendment need not now be sought in order to establish this principle [equal rights for women]."[10]

The crucial step in building progressive and liberal support for the ERA was the passage of Title VII of the Civil Rights Act of 1964, which prohibited job discrimination on the basis of sex. Title VII had originally been designed to prevent discrimination against blacks, but a group of southern congressmen added a ban on discrimination against women in a vain effort to make the bill unacceptable to northern conservatives. Initially, Title VII had no effect on "protective" legislation. Unions, accordingly, continued to oppose the ERA because they thought it would nullify such legislation. In 1967, when the newly formed National Organization for Women (NOW) gave the ERA first place on its Bill of Rights for Women, several union members immediately resigned.[11] But by 1970 both the federal courts and the Equal Employment Opportunity Commission (EEOC) had interpreted Title VII as invalidating protective legislation, and had extended most traditional protections to men rather than removing them for women. With their long-standing concern now for the most part made moot, union opposition to the ERA began to wane.[12]

In 1970, the Pittsburgh chapter of NOW took direct action. The group disrupted Senator Birch Bayh's hearings on the nineteen-year-old vote, getting Bayh to promise hearings on the ERA the following spring.[13] This was the moment. Labor opposition was fading, and, because few radical claims had been made for the ERA, conservatives had little ammunition with which to oppose it. In April, the United Auto Workers' convention voted to endorse the ERA.[14] In May, Bayh began Senate hearings on the ERA, and for the first time in its history the U.S. Department of Labor supported the ERA.[15] In June, Representative Martha Griffiths succeeded in collecting enough signatures on a discharge petition to pry the ERA out of the House Judiciary Committee, where for many years the liberal chair of the committee, Emanuel Celler, had refused to schedule hearings because of the persistent opposition by labor movement traditionalists. After only an hour's debate, the House of Representatives passed the ERA by a vote of 350 to 15.

The next fall, the ERA came to the Senate, which, after several days of debate, added by a narrow majority a provision exempting women from the draft.[16] This provision eliminated the only consequence proponents claimed for the ERA that might not have received support from a majority of Americans. However, having consistently insisted on bearing the responsibilities of citizenship as well as the rights, the women's organizations promoting the ERA had decided that women must be drafted. Because an ERA amended to exempt women from the draft was not acceptable to any of the organizations promoting the ERA, Senator Bayh did not bring it to a vote. Instead, without consulting those organizations, he proposed a new wording for the ERA that mirrored the words of the Fourteenth Amendment: "Neither the United States nor any State shall, on account of sex, deny to any person within its jurisdiction the equal protection of the laws." Bayh described his new wording as "recognizing the need for a flexible standard" and "meeting the objections of [the ERA's] most articulate critics,"[17] and he said in a subsequent press interview that the new wording would permit excluding women from the draft.[18] Fearing, on the basis of these remarks, that Bayh would be too flexible in his interpretation of this new wording, the major women's organizations told him that this substitute was not acceptable to them.[19]

In the spring of 1971, the House Judiciary Committee returned to the original 1970 wording of the ERA but adopted the "Wiggins amendment," which said that the ERA would "not impair the validity of any law of the United States which exempts a person from compulsory military service or any other law of the United States or any state which reasonably promotes the health and safety of the people."[20] The women's organizations supporting an ERA concluded, correctly, that the standard of "reasonably" promoting health and safety was no more stringent than the standard the Supreme Court was already using to judge constitutional many laws discriminating against women. Accordingly, they opposed the Wiggins amendment, and under their urging the House rejected it, voting 354 to 23 to adopt the original ERA.

Having passed the House, the ERA went to the Senate, where the Subcommittee on Constitutional Amendments, chaired by ERA opponent Senator Sam Ervin, adopted another substitute: "Neither the United States nor any State shall make any legal distinction between the rights and responsibilities of male and female persons unless such distinction is based on physiological or functional differences between them."[21] A majority of the full Committee on the Judiciary, chaired by Senator Bayh, rejected this attempt, so similar to the previous two, and adopted the original wording of the ERA in its definitive March 1972 report.

In the immediately ensuing Senate debate, Senator Ervin introduced eight amendments to the ERA relating to draft and combat, marital and family support, privacy, protections and exemptions, and homosexuality. His goal was twofold. First, he hoped to tempt a majority in the Senate into adopting one or more of the amendments, which would have divided the ERA proponents and at the very least would have delayed the ERA's passage. Second, if the ERA did pass in the Senate, he hoped to focus the upcoming debates in the states on the potentially unpalatable substantive consequences of the ERA. According to Catherine East, an active participant in these events, "proponents could not accept any amendment, even innocuous ones, since an amended ERA would have had to have gone to conference, where hostile House Committee members would most likely have killed it. (Senator Ervin knew this.)"[22] Bayh succeeded in persuading a majority to vote down all the Ervin amendments. On March 22, 1972, the ERA passed the Senate of the United States with a vote of 84 to 8.

As soon as the Senate voted, a secretary in the office of the senator from Hawaii contacted the Hawaii legislative reference bureau, and within twenty minutes the president of the Hawaii state senate presented a resolution to ratify. Five minutes later the resolution, unanimously passed, came before the Hawaii house, receiving equally quick and unanimous treatment.[23] Thus on the very day that the U.S. Senate passed the ERA, Hawaii became the first state to ratify. Delaware, Nebraska, and New Hampshire ratified the next day, and on the third day Idaho and Iowa ratified. Twenty-four more states ratified in 1972 and early 1973. The very earliest states to ratify were all unanimous, and in the other early states the votes were rarely close.....

By late 1973, however, the ERA's proponents had lost control of the ratification process. While the national offices of the various pro-ERA organizations could relatively easily coordinate their Washington activities to get the ERA through Congress, they were slow in organizing coalitions in the states. At the end of the 1973 state legislative sessions, only a few states even had active ERA coalitions.[24]

Moreover, in 1973 the Supreme Court decided, in *Roe v. Wade*, that state laws forbidding abortion violated the "right to privacy" implicit in the Constitution. Although the ERA had no obvious direct bearing on whether "abortion is murder," the two issues nonetheless became politically linked. The *Roe* decision took power out of the hands of relatively parochial, conservative state legislators and put it in the hands of a relatively cosmopolitan, liberal U.S. Supreme Court. The ERA would have done the same thing. Furthermore, both were sponsored by what was at that time still called the "women's liberation" movement. Traditionalists saw the "women's libbers" both as rejecting the notion that motherhood was a truly important task and as endorsing sexual hedonism instead of moral restraint. The *Roe* decision seemed to constitute judicial endorsement for these values. Since NOW was not only the leading sponsor of the ERA but the leading defender of abortion on demand, conservative activists saw abortion and the ERA as two prongs of the "libbers' " general strategy for undermining traditional American values. Unable to overturn the *Roe* decision directly, many conservatives sought to turn the ERA into a referendum on that decision.[25] To a significant degree, they succeeded. The opponents began to organize and convinced the first of several states to rescind ratification—a move that had no legal force but certainly made a political difference in unratified states.

Three more states ratified in 1974, one in 1975, and one—Indiana—in 1977, bringing the total to thirty-five of the required thirty-eight. No state ratified after 1977 despite the triumph of ERA proponents in 1978 in getting Congress to extend the original 1979 deadline until 1982.[26] In 1982 this extension ran out, and the Amendment died. Alabama, Arizona, Arkansas, Florida, Georgia, Illinois, Louisiana, Mississippi, Missouri, Nevada, North Carolina, Oklahoma, Utah, and Virginia had not ratified. All were Mormon or southern states, except Illinois, which required a three-fifths majority for ratifying constitutional amendments and which had a strongly southern culture in the third of the state surrounded by Missouri and Kentucky.[27] . . .

Rights versus Substance

Why did the states stop ratifying in 1973? Why did public support in the unratified states begin to decline? The campaign against the ERA succeeded because it shifted debate away from equal rights and focused it on the possibility that the ERA might bring substantive changes in women's roles and behavior. In this era, the American public, though changing in its outlook, still objected to any major changes in traditional roles of men and women. To the degree that the opposition could convince people that the ERA would bring about such changes, it eroded support for the ERA.

Much of the apparent support for the Equal Rights Amendment in surveys came from a sympathetic response to the concept of "rights," not from a commitment to actual changes in women's roles. In 1977, exactly half-way through the campaign for ratification, the National Opinion Research Center's General Social Survey (GSS) asked a representative sample of Americans both whether they favored or opposed the ERA (question V, table A1) and how they felt about women's roles. Among the people who claimed to have heard or read about the ERA, a strong majority—67 percent—favored it, while 25 percent were opposed, and 8 percent had no opinion. Yet . . . many in the same sample also had quite traditional[28] views about women's roles, especially in the economic sphere. Two-thirds of the sample thought that preschool children were likely to suffer if their mothers worked, 62 percent thought married women should not hold jobs when jobs were scarce and their husbands could support them, and 55 percent thought it more important for a woman to advance her husband's career than to have one of her own. The sample was about evenly divided regarding abortion on demand and women in politics. Only on questions about a wife's right to refuse to have children or voting for a woman Presidential candidate—questions that raise libertarian issues of personal privacy and equal opportunity—did a sizable majority take a "feminist" position. This pattern held for both men and women.

These traditional attitudes are not surprising. The surprise is that in almost every case a substantial majority of those who took traditional positions on women's roles *favored* the ERA. . . . Among the majority who disapproved of a married woman working when jobs were limited, for example, 67 percent still favored the ERA. Even among the diehard 20 percent who could look a female interviewer in the eye and tell her that they would not vote for a qualified woman their party had nominated for President, 49 percent favored the ERA. This pattern had not changed appreciably by 1982. . . . [29]

In the period 1972–1982, Americans were highly ambivalent regarding the appropriate role for women. The percentage of women in the paid work force had risen steadily after 1950 . . ., and attitudes toward women in business and government had changed correspondingly. More Americans have become willing to vote for a qualified woman for President if their party nominated her . . ., and more had come to approve of married women earning money in business or industry. . . . The women's movement that took shape in the late 1960s and legitimated itself in the 1970s also brought important changes in public attitudes toward women. . . . If we had more long-term data on attitudes toward women's roles, we would probably find that most attitudes followed the same pattern as willingness to vote for a woman for President: a gradual change after World War II, a dramatic change after the women's movement began to get national publicity in 1969, and some leveling off toward the end of the 1970s.

. . . [W]hen the Equal Rights Amendment went to the states for ratification in 1972, attitudes toward women were in the midst of rapid change. As a consequence, positions were not firmly held and much depended on the wording of a question. When a survey organization worded a question so as to stress freedom of choice, this greatly increased the proportion of "feminist" responses. Asked to agree or disagree with the statement, "There is no reason why women with young children shouldn't work outside the home if they choose to," 84 percent of the American public agreed in 1981. Superficially, this response seems to *favor* mothers of young children working. But given the statement, "A woman with young children should not work outside the

home unless financially necessary" —a statement that did not stress free choice
and provided a useful "unless" escape clause—76 percent of the public again
agreed, thus taking almost the opposite position and seeming to come out
against mothers of young children working.[30]

In the same way when a survey worded a question so as to stress general
principles rather than substantive role changes, it usually produced more
egalitarian responses. In one 1980 survey, 62 percent of American men said
they favored "an equal marriage of shared responsibility in which the husband and wife cooperate on work, homemaking and childraising."[31] But in
the same year, 69 percent of American men said they disapproved of the
changes in women's traditional roles that they had observed, primarily because
"the husband has to spend more time on household chores he doesn't like."[32]
Because people had acquired their new "egalitarian" attitudes recently and
had not worked them into a stable set of rules to live by, egalitarian principles could coexist with traditional sexist expectations about how the world
should run from day to day.

This tension between support for the principle and opposition to the practice helps explain how Harris generated its 1982 leap in support for the ERA.
Survey questions that told people what the Amendment actually said—a statement of principle regarding equal rights—always produced greater approval
than questions that simply identified the ERA as an Amendment to the Constitution or suggested possible consequences of its passage. This pattern was
not confined to the Harris poll. Even in Mormon Utah, a bastion of anti-
ERA sentiment, 58 percent endorsed the words of the ERA when these words
were read and not identified with "the Equal Rights Amendment." But only
29 percent of the same sample approved of the Equal Rights Amendment
as an actual constitutional amendment.[33] The same pattern appeared in
Oklahoma.[34]

Americans have always favored "rights" in the abstract. The principle
that government should not deny anyone "equal rights" commands widespread
approval. But citizens who approve this principle are often conservative in
practice. They support the principle of "equal rights" only insofar as they
think it is compatible with the status quo. Focusing on the principle, by
reading the extremely general words of the ERA, therefore produced much
more support than asking people, either without a prelude or with "balanced"
arguments on both sides, whether they wanted the Constitution of the United
States to be amended....

...The men and women of America approved the principle of equal
rights only so long as it did not change much in practice. But ERA proponents had something more substantive in mind. They wanted real changes
in the lives of both men and women. Admitting women to an all-male
organization like the Boy Scouts, for instance, would be a "right" for women
but would change the character of the male organization. A woman's "right"
to take a combat job in the armed forces would change the military and,
eventually, the way men and women acted toward one another in everyday
life.

The tension between rights and substance was particularly strong from 1972 to 1982, because the Supreme Court had recently applied many principles enshrined in the Constitution of the United States in controversial ways. The cases legalizing pornography that began in 1957,[35] the decisions beginning in 1961 that set convicted criminals free if the police had not conformed to certain standards in arresting them,[36] the 1963 decision against school prayer,[37] the school busing decisions that began in 1969,[38] and the abortion decisions that began in 1973[39] had all evoked strong liberal support and strong conservative opposition. Their crucial feature, however, was that they reinforced the popular view that federal judges could and would use superficially innocuous principles to achieve substantive results that many conservative and middle-of-the-road citizens opposed. If "equal protection" could mean busing white children to black neighborhoods, if "due process" could bar punishing people who everyone agreed had committed serious crimes, and if the "penumbra" of the Bill of Rights gave women a right to abortions, one did not have to be a certifiable paranoid to suppose that guaranteeing men and women "equality of rights under the law" might turn out also to have substantive consequences that legislators who supported the Amendment had not anticipated and that many of them would have opposed....

. . . Unlike other recent amendments to the Constitution, the ERA spelled out a broad statement of principle, in language much like that of the First, Fifth, or Fourteenth Amendments—those amendments on which the civil liberties of the nation largely rest. But many mainstream legislators had been burned too often by the Court's interpretation of the broad principles incorporated in those amendments. While it was not true, as opponents often claimed, that the ERA would give the Supreme Court a "blank check," it was true that the Supreme Court had used other seemingly unexceptional principles to generate highly unpopular substantive results. It seemed, then, that the ERA would give the Court another set of words to work with. By calling the ERA a "Pandora's Box" the opponents used imagery that captured the way many state legislators already felt about the First, Fifth, and Fourteenth Amendments. Given the relative ease with which a determined minority can block a constitutional amendment in America, the analogy was fatal.

Notes

1. *S.J. Res. 21* and *H.J. Res. 75*, 68th Cong., 1st sess.
2. Eleanor Flexner, *Centuries of Struggle: The Women's Rights Movement in the United States* (Cambridge, Mass.: Harvard University Press, 1959), p. 328.
3. Josephine Goldmark, *Impatient Crusader: Florence Kelley's Life Story* (Urbana: University of Illinois Press, 1953), pp. 182, 183. See also Mary Van Kleek, "Women and Machines," *Atlantic Monthly* 127 (February 1921): 250–260....
4. Clement E. Vose, *Constitutional Change: Amendment Politics and Supreme Court Litigation since 1900* (Lexington, Mass.: D. C. Heath, 1972), p. 254. See also Esther Peterson, "The Kennedy Commission," in Irene Tinker, ed., *Women in Washington* (Beverly Hills, Calif.: Sage, 1983), p. 24; and Kathryn Kish Sklar, "Why Did Most Politically Active Women Oppose the ERA in the 1920's?" in Joan Hoff-Wilson,

ed., *Rights of Passage: The Past and Future of the ERA* (Bloomington: Indiana University Press, 1986).

5. In response, twenty-seven national women's organizations and unions formed the National Committee to Defeat the Un-Equal Rights Amendment (Katherine Kraft, "ERA: History and Status," *Radcliffe Quarterly* 68 [1982]: 4).

6. Marguerite Rawalt, "The Equal Rights Amendment," in Tinker, ed., p. 53. [See Note 4.]

7. Rawalt, p. 55.

8. Kraft, p. 5. [See Note 5.]

9. Rawalt, pp. 54–55. See also Gilbert Y. Steiner, *Constitutional Inequality: The Political Fortunes of the Equal Rights Amendment* (Washington, D.C.: Brookings Institution, 1985), p. 10.

10. Marguerite Rawalt, past president of the National Federation of Business and Professional Women (BPW) and later a founding member of the National Organization for Women (NOW), managed to persuade the commission to add the word "now" to its conclusion, so that in the end the phrase became "need not now be sought" (President's Commission on the Status of Women files, Esther Peterson Papers, Schlesinger library, cited by Kraft, p. 15).

11. Marguerite Rawalt indicates that NOW was founded by a group of women dissatisfied at the Interstate Association of State Commissions on the Status of Women for rejecting a resolution endorsing the ERA (Rawalt, p. 59). For the NOW Bill of Rights, see Robin Morgan, ed., *Sisterhood Is Powerful* (New York: Random House, 1970), pp. 512–514. For the union members' walkout, see the Minutes of the NOW annual meeting, November 19–20, 1967, Schlesinger Library, reported in France Kolb, "How the ERA Passed the Congress," *Radcliffe Quarterly* 68 (March 1982): 11. See also Judith Hole and Ellen Levine, *Rebirth of Feminism* (New York: Quadrangle Books, 1971), p. 68.

12. Peterson, p. 31. . . . For the union position as of 1967, see Mary O. Eastwood, "Constitutional Protection against Sex Discrimination: An Informal Memorandum Prepared for the National Organization for Women Regarding the Equal Rights Amendment and Similar Proposals" (unpublished MS. in the files of Mary Eastwood).

13. Kolb, p. 11. [See Note 11.]

14. Marguerite Rawalt, Testimony, Equal Rights Amendment Hearings before the Committee on the Judiciary, Subcommittee no. 4, U.S. House of Representatives, March 25, 1971, p. 205.

15. Hole and Levine, p. 56. [See Note 11.] See also Rawalt, Testimony, p. 204.

16. The vote on this provision, proposed by Senator Ervin, was 36–33. A 50–20 majority also added a school prayer amendment, presumably intended to kill the ERA. The Amendment's supporters did not fight the school prayer amendment because they "felt that with the passage of the Ervin amendment we'd had it" ("Snarl in Senate All But Kills Women's Rights Amendement," *Washington Post*, October 14, 1970, p. 1).

17. *Congressional Record*, (hereafter *Cong. Rec.*), October 14, 1970, p. 36863.

18. Senator Birch Bayh, press interview, "Men's Lib Pending," *Washington Daily News*, October 15, 1970, p. 25.

19. See Catherine East, "The First Stage," *Women's Political Times* (September 1982), p. 9. . . .

20. Janet K. Boles, *The Politics of the Equal Rights Amendment: Conflict and the Decision Process* (New York: Longman, 1979), p. 39.

21. East, "The First Stage," p. 10.
22. Ibid.
23. Boles, *Politics*, p. 142.
24. Ibid., p. 72. See also pp. 62–66, and passim.
25. [For example,] In Decemer 1974, Schlafly's banner headline proclaimed, "ERA Means Abortion and Population Shrinkage," *Phyllis Schlafly Report* 8, no. 5 (December 1974)....
26. I have taken this account largely from Boles, *Politics*, passim, and her table 1.1, pp. 2–3.
27. The states that refused to ratify were also relatively poor....
28. Although I have labeled these positions "traditional," a feminist could quite easily hold some of them. Given the state of day-care arrangements in the United States, a feminist could certainly argue that a preschool child is likely to suffer if his or her mother works. Given both the kinds of socialization men and women receive the character of politics in the United States, a feminist could argue that most men are better suited emotionally for politics than most women. It is likely, however, that most people who gave what I have called "traditional" responses to these questions in fact held traditional values in these areas....
29. Only four of these questions were available for analysis in the 1982 NORC General Social Survey. As one might expect, in 1982 the percentage of the sample taking the traditional position on women's roles had in most cases decreased slightly: on women's emotional unfitness for politics (question 6), a decrease from 42 to 35 percent; on leaving running the country to men (question 7), a decrease from 37 to 26 percent; and on refusing to vote for a woman for President (question 9), a decrease from 20 to 13 percent. Regarding allowing legal abortion (question 5), there was a nonsignificant increase from 48 to 49 percent. However, a majority of the "traditional" group still supported the ERA in 1982 as in 1977 (63, 61, and 56 percent, respectively, in questions 5, 6, and 7), except, as in 1977, among the tiny minority who would not vote for a qualified woman for President, 38 percent of whom supported the ERA in 1982. Although by 1982 the percentage of the anti-abortion group favoring the ERA had declined from 68 to 63 percent, this decline is what one would expect given the opposition's increasing stress on the connection between the ERA and abortion as the decade progressed....
30. The first survey in this paragraph was conducted by the Roper Organization, *Roper Report*, January 10–24, 1981, pp. 81–82; second survey by Research and Forecasts, Inc., for Connecticut Mutual Life Insurance Company, September 1–November 15, 1980, p. 156. Both are reported and compared in *Public Opinion* (August/September 1981): 32. In reporting survey research, I will sometimes use the word "public" to mean "representative sample of the public."
31. Research and Forecasts, Inc., *The Connecticut Mutual Life Report* (Hartford: Connecticut Mutual Life Insurance Company, 1981), pp. 182. 151 (survey dated September 1–November 15, 1980). Note: In this survey only 29 percent of the sample preferred "a traditional marriage in which the husband is responsible for providing for the family and the wife for the home and taking care of the children....
32. Doyle Dane Bernbach, *Soundings*, no. 6 (September 1980): 2,4.
33. In the spring of 1980, the Bardsley and Haslacher Survey Organization asked a sample of 615 Utah voters: "From what you heard, would you favor or oppose the State of Utah passing the Equal Rights Amendment?" Favor 29%, Oppose 65%, Undecided 6%. (Members of the Mormon church were more heavily

opposed: Favor 18%, Oppose 76%, Undecided 6%. Members of other denominations had a majority in favor of the Amendment: Favor 57%, Oppose 37%, Undecided 6%.)

The organization then asked respondents how they would vote on this measure: "Equality of rights under the law shall not be denied or abridged by the United States or by a state on account of sex." Favor 58 percent, Oppose 32 percent, Undecided 10 percent.... Source: J. Roy Bardsley, "Voters Opposed to ERA, But Support Its Concept," *Salt Lake Tribune*, May 11, 1980, p. Al.

34. On January 11 and 12, 1982, the *Daily Oklahoman* conducted a survey of 400 voting-age Oklahomans "designed by an independent polling service so that it has 95 percent reliability and no more than a 5 percent sampling error." Asked, "Do you agree with the statement, 'Equality of rights under the law shall not be denied or abridged by the United States or any state on account of sex?' " 81 percent of the sample agreed. Only 9 percent disagreed, and 11 percent were either uncertain or wouldn't say (percentages sum to 101 due to rounding). However, asked, "Should Oklahoma approve the ERA?" only 44 percent agreed, 39 percent disagreed, and 17 percent were uncertain or wouldn't say. *Daily Oklahoman*, January 14, 1982, pp. 1, 53. (Note: the 17 percent is composed of 15.1 percent "uncertain" and 2.0 percent "wouldn't say.". ..)

35. *Roth v. U.S.*, 354 U.S. 476 (1957).
36. *Mapp v. Ohio*, 367 U.S. 643 (1961); and *Miranda v. Arizona*, 384 U.S. 436 (1966).
37. *School District of Abington v. Schempp*, 374 U.S. 203 (1963).
38. *Green v. County School Board of New Kent County*, 391 U. S. 430 (1968).
39. *Roe v. Wade*, 410 U.S. 113 (1973).

29 / New Values in the Pursuit of Office

Alan Ehrenhalt

In this assessment of changes in the values that motivate politicians to seek congressional office, Alan Ehrenhalt argues that as the job has become more difficult to do and to attain, and as related material incentives have effectively declined, another motive has become increasingly important: "sheer enjoyment." And the level of enjoyment, not surprisingly, tends to be associated with a positive attitude toward the role of government in society.

Thinking about Politicians
One thing we can say with confidence is that seeking and holding office take up more of a politician's time than they did a generation ago. It is much harder now to combine politics and a career in private life.. . .

As recently as the 1950s the U.S. Congress could reasonably be described as a part-time institution. Its members arrived in Washington on the train in January and left in the summer, when heat and humidity made the city uncomfortable. When they returned home upon adjournment in July or August, these politicians had enough time left in the year to practice law or sell insurance or do whatever they had done before they were elected.

Since the early 1960s Congress has essentially been in session year-round. It recesses for a month in August during the odd numbered years and adjourns for campaigning a month or so before each national election, but the rest of the time it is conducting business. A member can return home virtually every weekend if he chooses, and there are half a dozen week-long recesses scattered throughout the average congressional year, but there is no sustained opportunity to pursue any career at all in private life. When someone is elected to Congress, he gives up his "regular job," assuming he did not give it up months earlier to campaign. He returns to it—assuming it still awaits him—only when he leaves office. . . .

Millions of words have been written about the advent of year-round legislating, most of them warning that it leads to too many unnecessary laws and to legislators isolated from the people they represent. We can leave that argument aside. My point is a simpler one: Full-time jobs in Congress and in legislatures attract people who want to devote most of their waking hours to politics. There is no reason to suppose that this is the same set of people who would want to do politics in their spare time. . . .

If it is more demanding to hold office in America than it was a generation ago, it is also far more demanding to seek office. Campaigning at any level these days is almost certain to be a time-consuming, technologically complicated, physically strenuous form of work.

To win a seat in Congress now is frequently to do what Bill Schuette did in Michigan in 1984: devote the better part of a year to meeting people and raising money seven days a week. Schuette was, as of 1984, the state of the art in congressional campaigning. "Amateur night is over in this district," he proclaimed one afternoon, more than six months before the election, as he drove from one campaign stop to another in the middle of a day crowded with political appearances. Schuette was on his way to spending nearly $900,000 on a successful campaign that included a meticulous month-by-month game plan, a summer rehearsal, and a headquarters full of computers. Running for Congress for the first time at the age of thirty, Schuette was essentially the proprietor of a small business.

It is perfectly possible to spend $900,000 on a congressional campaign and lose it badly; people do that every year. But as the enterprise becomes more complex and more sophisticated, those who want to stay in business have little choice but to move with it. There is no reason in principle why congressional campaigns have to last a year and cost a fortune. But candidates who do the things Bill Schuette did rarely lose to opponents who campaign casually and run on a shoestring. . . .

Politics in the 1990s is for people who are willing to give it vast amounts of their time. It is also for people who are not particularly concerned about making money. Time and money are related. If state legislatures met for one week every year, it would not be difficult to find a wide assortment of people willing to serve for very little pay, or even for free. But a job that is apt to require six months or more of full-time work every year is measured against a different standard.

Any time members of Congress receive a pay increase, they are assaulted by complaints from constituents who do not understand why a public servant cannot live on an annual wage several times higher than the median in every community in the United States. An annual wage of more than $90,000 (the congressional salary at this writing) seems lavish to them. But if you or I were pondering a campaign for Congress, the crucial question, of course, would not be whether we could make more than our plumber does. It would be whether a member of Congress makes more than we could make staying home and doing something else. And the answer, for most people with the capacity to win election to Congress, is that they can make considerably more money in private life. . . .

There is nothing particularly new about this. Nobody ever became rich on his salary as a public official. Candidates for public office have always had to accept that fact as a condition of political life. Until recent years, however, politics offered many ambitious young people another incentive—a route to prestige and social acceptance that was unavailable to them in the private world. As recently as a generation ago, no Italian-American college graduate, however talented, could reasonably expect to become president of Yale or chief executive officer of Ford or Chrysler. There was no Bart Giamatti or Lee Iacocca to influence ethnic career decisions. There was, however, Fiorello La Guardia. Politics was an outlet for the ambitions of bright young people who were rightly suspicious of how far merit alone might carry them in a prejudiced private realm.

Prejudice has not disappeared from the world, but even the skeptic must concede that careers in all fields are, to an unprecedented extent, open to talent across ethnic and racial lines. Nobody today needs to become a politician because he fears his roots will make him unacceptable as a political scientist, or a doctor or lawyer.

A political career in America in the 1990s, to summarize, is not easy, lucrative, or a particularly good route to status in life. This places increased importance on one other motive for entering politics: sheer enjoyment. You pretty much have to like the work.

You also have to be good at it. Almost as important as the question of what sorts of people want a political career is the question of what sorts of people possess the skills to do it well. Here too there is no reason to assume that the answers are the ones that would have applied earlier in this century, or even earlier in the postwar years.

The skills that work in American politics at this point in history are those of entrepreneurship. At all levels of the political system, from local boards and councils up to and including the presidency, it is unusual for parties to nominate people. People nominate themselves. That is, they offer themselves as candidates, raise money, organize campaigns, create their own publicity, and make decisions in their own behalf. If they are not willing to do that work for themselves, they are not (except in a very few parts of the country) going to find any political party structure to do it for them.

At one time in American politics, parties represented the only real professionalism that existed. A century ago, when defenders of "good government" complained that public life was being usurped by professional politicians, they did not mean candidates. They meant bosses—the people who chose the candidates. Legislators came and went, in Congress as they did at lesser levels. The institutions of professionalism were the party machines: New York's Tammany Hall, the Republican organization of Pennsylvania, the Cook County Democratic Central Committee. The leaders of these machines were the lifelong political practitioners who reaped the rewards of power and graft that the system offered.

Today's professional politicians are less imposing figures, even to those who do not like them. Their influence as individuals is modest, and their opportunities for graft are few. In most cases they do not control anyone's election but their own. Their ties to any political party are limited. They are solo practicioners. It is a different brand of professionalism altogether. . . .

. . .Candidates do not win because they have party support. They do not win because they have business or labor support. They win because they are motivated to set out on their own and find the votes that will make a majority. Group support helps. But it is almost never enough. The candidate who possesses every attribute needed for victory except the willingness to thrust himself forward is a losing candidate nine times out of ten.

Who sent us the political leaders we have? There is a simple answer to that question. They sent themselves. And they got where they are through a combination of ambition, talent, and the willingness to devote whatever time was necessary to seek and hold office.

In the age of the entrepreneurial candidate, character traits that used to be helpful turn out to be counterproductive. When Alfred E. Smith entered politics in Manhattan in the early years of this century, the one crucial trait he had to exhibit to win nomination was loyalty—uncomplaining devotion to the organization and leaders who placed him in the state assembly. If his loyalty to Tammany Hall had been less than total, he would not have been rewarded with a seat in the legislature, and if his loyalty had declined when he assumed office, he would have been dumped. But the people who have represented Smith's old territory in Congress or in the New York legislature in recent years have not been there because of loyalty. There has been no organization, even in the old machine strongholds, worth a pledge of allegiance. The quality that nourishes political careers today, in Manhattan as elsewhere, is independence.

Most candidates who succeeded on the basis of loyalty did not have to be especially articulate. Political organizations required spokesmen, but they did not require that all their officeholders be capable of playing a visible public role. A genial young man blessed with the support of the party organization did not need to express himself vigorously on the issues of the moment.

That is no longer true. A candidate for virtually any office has to know how to talk. Voters may not make their choices very often on the basis of public policy, but they do not like to vote for candidates who seem uncomfortable expressing themselves. More than in the old days, campaigns for all offices are exercises in communication: in town meetings, in door-to-door canvassing, on television, in direct-mail literature that the candidate has to write himself. Even if it does not matter a great deal what the candidate says, it makes an enormous difference how he looks and sounds saying it. The politics of the 1990s, unlike the politics of earlier generations, is an enterprise in which the inarticulate have no place to hide. When candidates are left to themselves to orchestrate campaigns and do their own communicating with the voters, it is only natural that the glib will survive and the tongue-tied will be drawn toward other lines of work....

Politics is, then, more than in the past, a job for people who prefer it to any other line of work. About these people one more important point should be made: They tend not only to enjoy politics but to believe in government as an institution. The more somebody is required to sacrifice time and money and private life to run for the city council, for the state legislature, or for Congress, the more important it is for that person to believe that government is a respectable enterprise with crucial work to do.

That principle comes through in interviews with people at all levels of the political system. Ron Mullin expressed it one day in 1987, as he trudged down the streets of Concord, California, campaigning door to door all afternoon in 95-degree heat, an incumbent mayor seeking reelection to the city council. "If I believed government wasn't an institution beneficial to society," he said, "I wouldn't give a tinker's dam about politics. I wouldn't waste my time on it." Robert Torricelli expressed similar sentiments a few years earlier, in the midst of his successful Democratic campaign in New Jersey against an incumbent Republican congressman. "People who believe government should be doing less," Torricelli declared, "should not vote for me." Those are the sorts of words one hears from people who succeeded in politics in the 1980s, people whose zest for the game is reinforced by a conviction that they need not apologize for what they are doing.

Occasionally one hears the opposite. Randy Kamrath was elected to the Minnesota Senate as a Republican in 1981 at age twenty-five and almost immediately began pondering his retirement from a profession whose value he questioned. "If a politician likes his job," Kamrath mused one summer morning, as he drove his tractor across his southwest Minnesota farm, "then I don't think I like the job he's doing." Kamrath was in his second legislative term then, seeking a third, yet he worried that the Minnesota legislature was no place for an honest conservative. The next year the voters solved Kamrath's problem for him; they unseated him and put in a liberal Democrat, freeing him to do the farming he regards as honest work.

There are people like Randy Kamrath at all levels of the American political system—people who are highly suspicious of government yet persuade themselves to run for office, or who hate government but find themselves addicted somehow to politics as a game. But it is hard to find enough of them, in most places, to make a majority on a city council, or in a legislature, or in a congressional delegation.

In another sort of political environment, one in which parties made the important decisions, or in which it did not take much time or trouble to serve in office, belief in government might not be a crucial point. People who disliked government might become candidates and win elections in large numbers whether they found the work exciting or not. But in the current environment belief matters a great deal. Indeed, it is critical....

. . . Political office today flows to those who want it enough to spend their time and energy mastering its pursuit. It flows in the direction of ambition—and talent. To recognize this fact is to begin to solve perhaps the oddest riddle of American politics in recent years: the ability of the Democratic party to thrive at so many levels of the political system in the face of a national conservative tide that has elected Republican presidents five times in the last six elections, overwhelmingly in the last three. How could it be, in the era of Ronald Reagan and George Bush, that Democrats prolonged their control of the U.S. House into its fourth uninterrupted decade; reestablished a comfortable majority in the U.S. Senate after a short Republican interlude; controlled as many as thirty state legislatures, compared with fewer than ten for the Republicans; and consistently elected more than 60 percent of the 7,412 people who serve in ninety-nine state legislative chambers nationwide?

Most of the efforts to answer this riddle have fallen back on psychological examination of the electorate. We vote for Democrats below the presidential level, it is said, to place a check on the Republicans to whom we entrust control of the White House. Or, somewhat more plausibly, we split our vote because we have different expectations about different offices. Republicans win the presidency by offering an ideology that the majority of the country feels comfortable with. Democrats win further down by delivering the personal services and generating the governmental programs that voters, on a day-to-day basis, refuse to give up.

There may be some truth to these answers, but in the end they are answers to the wrong fundamental question. Once we drop beneath the level of presidential politics, there is no reason to believe that voters are trying to tell us much of anything. They are responding in an essentially passive way to the choices placed in front of them. The best candidates and the best campaigns win. It is not really a matter of demand. It is a matter of supply. Over the past two decades, in most constituencies in America, Democrats have generated the best supply of talent, energy, and sheer political ambition.

Under those circumstances it has not been crucial for them to match the opinions of the electorate on most of the important national issues of the day.

It should be clear, of course, that we are talking about large numbers of elections. We are talking about a distinction which, over time, enables Democrats to win an extra 10 percent of the seats in a state legislature, or an extra two or three seats in a congressional delegation. It adds up. It does not predict the outcome of an individual campaign. Republicans win their share of elections on the basis of talent all over the country, every election year. They just do not win an equal share.

None of this guarantees the Democratic party majority control of any legislative body anywhere in the system. But it does mean that any party, faction, or interest that wants to compete on equal terms must meet the demands of present-day political life. And doing that requires generating large numbers of people to whom politics is more important, or more rewarding, than money, leisure, or privacy. It is not absolutely necessary that these people believe in government as the ultimate social problem solver. It is helpful if they believe rather strongly in something—something sufficiently compelling to generate the sacrifice involved. . . .

Thinking about Power

[M]ost elections in America do not turn on party or ideology. It does not make very much difference to the outcome of elections for the U.S. House of Representatives, let alone elections to a state legislature or a city council, what either of the two major parties thinks about the vital issues of the day. What matters most . . . is ambition. Political careers are open to ambition now in a way that has not been true in America in most of this century. Those with the desire for office and the ability to manipulate the instruments of the system—the fundraising, the personal campaigning, the opportunities to express themselves in public—confront very few limits on their capacity to reach the top. The bosses and party leaders who used to pass judgment on political careers have just about all departed the scene. They are no longer a significant barrier to entry.

The real barriers are the burdens that a political career has come to impose on people who pursue it—the burdens of time, physical effort, and financial sacrifice. Politics is a profession now, not just in Congress but in many state legislatures and in countless local governments, where a casual part-time commitment used to suffice. Many people who would be happy to serve in office are unwilling to think of themselves as professionals, or to make the personal sacrifices that a full-time political career requires.

And so political office—political power—passes to those who want the jobs badly enough to dedicate themselves to winning and holding them. . . . [T]hey do not come come in one standardized model of personality or temperament. I wouldn't argue that, as individuals, they are emotionally healthier or less healthy than those who choose not to run for office. Any attempt to prove this is bound to be spurious. It is possible, of course, to be consumed with politics to the point of pathology. But that is true of any preoccupation in life.

So I don't have any simple generalization to make about the inner workings of the people who have chosen to devote their lives to politics in the last quarter of the twentieth century. They are different people in different places. They are drawn to political careers for different reasons. What stands out, though, is that for most of them the commitment to a political life has been accompanied by a positive attitude toward government itself as an instrument for doing valuable work in American society. There is nothing very remarkable about that. Government is the product that politics produces; hostility toward it is bound to rob many people of their enthusiasm for full-time political work.

The baby boom Democrats who took over Concord, California, in the 1980s; the civil rights and antiwar protesters who eventually became the Democratic leadership in Wisconsin; the teachers who moved in to fill the vacuum of power in Alabama; the skillful professionals who now dominate the U.S. House of Representatives—all of them think positively about government, and that conviction has helped them cultivate the skills for a political career and sustain that career over a number of years.

In some places we met people who were motivated to enter politics more by skepticism about the role of government than by any willingness to expand it. That was true of the fundamentalists at Bob Jones University in Greenville, and the conservative activists who worked a revolution in the Colorado legislature at the end of the 1970s. Still, those are exceptions in the modern American political system. By and large, faith in the possibilities of government to do good has been one of the underlying values of the professionals who have come to dominate that system in the last two decades.

There are others. Equality is a crucial one. The modern political generation believes in equality not just as an abstract social principle but as a way of organizing political institutions. This is the generation that has turned legislative bodies all over the country into egalitarian places in which even the most junior members are entitled to the full privileges of participation, and no one is obliged to defer to the Speakers and presidents pro tempore and committee chairmen who used to be the figures of authority.

Next to equality is individualism—the freedom of the officeholder to go his own way, even when that conflicts with the goals of the caucus or faction or political party to which he nominally belongs. This is the generation of Louis LaPolla, the Utica mayor who says, "I answer to no one, only the electorate," and of Shaun McNally, the Connecticut legislator who says, "It should be possible to be part of the process without being part of the team." It is the generation in which U.S. senators serve entire terms and scarcely know one another, so committed are they to their own projects and schedules in an institution that was once supposed to be like an exclusive men's club.

The third value is openness. Most of the political professionals who have been coming into office and influence in recent years grew up in an atmosphere of closely held political power. They were raised at a time when true political leaders, people like John Bailey in Connecticut and Rufus Elefante in Utica, New York, were frequently unelected and rarely obliged to discuss their decisions with the public or even with the nominal officeholders who were expected to carry them out. When today's politicians came to maturity in the 1970s, they reacted against this system, propelled in large part by Vietnam, Watergate, and the suspicions of secrecy and power that those events created.

Equality, individualism, and openness are the crucial values of American politics in the 1990s. They are the values of the participants—the people who, having helped to discredit old-fashioned hierarchical leadership, have taken advantage of the absence of that leadership to nominate themselves to office and begin immediately to govern.

The government that these politicians have generated has not always been the government that their constituents would have created had they voted on it by referendum. . . .

But if the policies of the professionals have often been out of step with the political instincts of the passive electorate. . .one has to admit that these people's careers have been consistent with many of the changes taking place in our society beyond the borders of the political process. In building their political lives around the principles of equality, openness, and individualism, the new political leaders have been moving government along the same road that all of our important social institutions have been traveling. . . .

. . . For all our ignorance as voters and inattentiveness as citizens, we have a politics that is, in the end, appropriate to its time and place.

PART TWO

Sources of Inputs

CHAPTER SEVEN

Mass Participation

The debates at the Constitutional Convention covered not just how governmental institutions should be structured, but also how much of a role should be provided for "participation" of the citizenry in political decisions (as demonstrated in the selection from Madison's Notes in Chapter One). When the framers debated whether, and how, to implement "government by the people," it was generally assumed that the "governance" would be indirect, by voting for elected officials, and that "the people" would actually be limited to particular categories of adults. Although individual citizens have had other means by which they could attempt to influence policy (such as writing letters to officials, working in campaigns, or even participating in demonstrations or other forms of protest), voting has remained the type of mass participation that is most widespread and the most closely identified with the United States version of participatory democracy. The concept of "the people," however, has been greatly expanded over time.

Under the Articles of Confederation, members of the unicameral Congress were selected by their state legislatures.* Debate at the Constitutional Convention would eventually focus on whether at least one house in the new Congress should be selected by vote of "the people." The decision, of course, was in the affirmative, but definition of which people would actually be allowed to vote was left up to the individual states. Initially, most states limited their voters to white, male, property owners. Over many decades, through changes of state law, amendments to the U.S. Constitution (specifically, the Fifteenth [1870], Twentieth [1933], and Twenty-Sixth [1971]), adoption of a national Voting Rights Act (1965), and numerous demonstrations on the streets and decisions in the courts, the suffrage was eventually extended to almost all citizens over the age of eighteen. Perhaps the most important change in mass participation in the United States has been this tremendous expansion in the "potential" national electorate.

And although the "actual" electorate (that is, eligible voters who do vote) has always been much smaller than the potential electorate, the specific size and the nature of the actual voting public have also changed over time. Each significant extension of the potential electorate, of course, also altered the makeup of the actual electorate. As we will read in Chapter Eight, significant changes in the "issue agenda" of American politics have occurred at regular intervals throughout most of the nation's history, and with those changes have come equally significant changes in the patterns of party attachments within the electorate. Recent research has shown that, just since the 1950s, *potentially* important changes have once again occurred in American voting behavior. The following selection by Michael Gant and Norman Luttbeg documents those changes and analyzes their cumulative importance. Then Margaret Conway assesses the impact of the news media on citizens' attitudes and political participation.

---

*In each of the states, though, at least one house of the state legislature was elected by popular vote.—*Editor's Note.*

30 / Change in American Electoral Behavior: 1952–1988

Michael M. Gant and
Norman R. Luttbeg

Michael Gant and Norman Luttbeg summarize evidence concerning a number of changes in the electorate since the 1950s—including declining partisanship, increased defection from party voting, increased issue voting, declining turnout, and increasing political distrust. While finding evidence of these specific changes, the authors warn that "the magnitude of change in these trends should not be exaggerated," and in fact they conclude that "stability rather than change best characterizes the American electorate over the period 1952–1988."

The Pattern of Change in the Electorate

As we reflect on trends in American electoral behavior, it is clear that the electorate of the 1980s is different from those studied in the 1940s and 1950s. There are fewer ardent partisans now than then. Issues play a more important role in voters' evaluations of candidates. Americans are increasingly inclined to avoid the polls on election days, and while not as pervasive as in the 1970s, distrust and alienation are still substantially higher than in the 1950s and 1960s. With respect to congressional elections, the incumbency advantage is stronger than ever. But despite the obvious fact that the electorate has changed in some regards,...the magnitude of change in these trends should not be exaggerated. We are a different electorate today but not greatly different in most respects.

Despite the absence of sweeping change in American electoral behavior, some political scientists persist in their concern about many...trends.... [T]his concern stems from a belief that certain trends may be the harbinger of an era of social and political upheaval. A rather substantial body of political theory supports this belief by arguing, for example, that a govermnent cannot remain stable without the trust and confidence of its citizens. Furthermore, professional interest in the patterns of change in American electoral behavior points to possible interrelationships between several trends, interrelationships that might accelerate or render irreversible the most feared trends.... [W]e have examined interrelationships among five of these trends in an effort to determine whether they individually or collectively merit our continued concern. We have analyzed the following trends:

1. Declining partisanship
2. Increased defection from party voting
3. Increased concern with issues

4. Declining voter turnout
5. Increasing political distrust and alienation

Our reasons for examining relationships among these trends are several. If declining turnout, increased defection, increased independency, and declining trust are the common result of a frustrated electorate that is not satisfied with the alternatives afforded by the major political parties, we cannot be optimistic about America's future. Some voters may become receptive to demagogues offering quick solutions to our nation's problems. Others could come to violate the laws and norms of our society as their disenchantment grows.

If there is an ever-increasing number of Americans impatient with government's failure to adopt certain solutions to the problems faced by our society, and if this impatience makes them less disposed to accept government policy decisions, government may be burdened with higher costs to gain public compliance. Furthermore, these citizens may become receptive to substantial changes in the political process that could disrupt the stability we have enjoyed for over 200 years. Such voters, for example, may press to make political parties illegal or circumscribe sharply what government can do by supporting legislation like California's tax-cutting Proposition 13.

[We have] sought to determine whether there is evidence of a substantial group of issue oriented, less partisan, distrusting citizens refusing to participate in the existing political process. Our analysis has turned on an assessment of the five changes in the electorate noted above and their possible interrelation. We have used what we think are the best measures available, National Election Studies survey questions asked in conjunction with each presidential election since 1952. We think each group of questions straightforwardly and validly assesses relevant attributes of the electorate.

The importance of using identical measures to assess trends and change cannot be overstated. As some of the studies cited herein have demonstrated, different data can result in different conclusions. Had we used different questions in different years, the wording of the questions, instead of actual changes, could very well have produced the results we would have observed. Certainly, even minor changes in the wording of survey questions can alter the response patterns of respondents.

We have measured partisanship and independence from political parties with survey questions in which respondents were asked to express their willingness to identify with a political party or even to admit leaning toward one. Defection was measured by simply comparing survey respondents' votes with their political party identification; defectors do not vote for the candidates of their party. Issue voting was appraised by survey respondents' statements about what would cause them to vote for or against the major political parties' presidential candidates. We have [found] that the candidate evaluations of some people reflect more concern with issues and ideology, causing us to label them ideological or issue oriented evaluators. Others' judgments are less sophisticated. We have called these voters group-benefit, partisan, image, or no-content evaluators based on their particular responses to the candidates. Voting has been measured by self-reports of respondents. And finally, political alienation has been measured by two survey questions that assess beliefs about individual influence on government and perceptions of the responsiveness of public officials.

These measures confirm many of the trends, although there have been some discontinuities and even reversals in certain trends. Independents have become more numerous, comprising 11 percent of the electorate in 1988 versus 5 percent in 1952, and 8 percent in 1956. Alienation has also increased, with 36 percent of the SRC/CPS sample classified as alienated in 1976 versus 20 percent in 1952. The trend reversed in 1980, however, when only 26 percent of those interviewed could be classified as alienated, and the percentage has remained at this level since. The quality of candidate evaluations has changed, too. Low quality evaluations based solely on candidate image have declined from 62 percent in 1952 to only 8 percent in 1984, with a small increase noted in 1988. Issue oriented evaluations and defection have fluctuated over the last ten elections. Voting turnout has dropped in a steady fashion since 1960, but we observed that current turnout levels are not much worse than those which occurred in the 1940s and 1950s.*

Our analysis of the interrelationships among the five trend variables yields little support for concern that they are related and comprise a potential danger for our society. The quality of a respondent's candidate evaluations does relate to participation and to alienation, but not in a way consistent with what we might expect. Instead of the issue oriented evaluators being less participant and more alienated, it is the no-content evaluators that prove distinctive. Typically, less than half of those saying nothing in evaluating presidential candidates vote in presidential contests. No-content evaluators also have been consistently the most alienated group of citizens.

The quality of the electorate's evaluation of presidential candidates is often at the root of explanations of how the trends in participation, partisan voting, and alienation are related. This explanation does not appear to be adequate because while improvements in candidate evaluations can be noted, relationships with participation, partisan voting, and alienation are weak or nonexistent. The pattern of relationships we have found is compatible with the depiction in *The American Voter*† of those marginally involved in politics as being uninformed, nonparticipant, and least likely to identify strongly with a political party or to vote consistently with party identification.

While independents did not prove to be distinctive in terms of candidate evaluations, they are somewhat more numerous in contemporary society and less likely to vote than before. In 1952 only 6 percent of all nonvoters were independents, but in 1988 they comprised 17 percent. But independents prove to be no more alienated than either strong or weak partisans. Issues are no

---

*This was written prior to the 1992 election, when turnout increased to 54 percent.— *Editor's Note.*

†Angus Campbell, Philip E. Converse, Warren E. Miller, and Donald E. Stokes, *The American Voter* (Chicago: University of Chicago Press, 1960).—*Editor's Note.*

more pivotal to the candidate assessments of independents than they are to those of partisans, and the declining participation of independents is unrelated to their greater alienation. So neither issue orientation nor alienation accounts for the declining participation of independents.

By defining the alienated as those respondents believing that "officials do not care what people like me think," and that they personally have "no say in what government does," we found some ties with other political behavior but no consistent patterns. Based on 1988 data that compare alienated and nonalienated Americans, the alienated are less likely to vote for president but are slightly less likely to defect from the political party with which they identify to vote for the opposition party's candidate. Further, alienation is not related to issue or ideological evaluation of a candidate or to independency.

Thus we end up with three clusters of atypical types of citizens: (1) those who have nothing to say when evaluating the candidates, who consistently fail to participate, and who are alienated, (2) the increasingly nonparticipant independents, and (3) the alienated who are consistently less participant and more likely to defect. Each of these groups is a minority when contrasted with the largest group of citizens—the trusting, partisan voters.

Other Changes in the Electorate

Two other changes can be noted in the American electorate since the 1950s, in addition to the trends discussed previously. Both of these changes involve significant demographic changes in the electorate. First, Americans are increasingly better educated. Census Bureau figures indicate that the median school years completed for the adult population (twenty-five years of age and older) increased from 10.6 years in 1960 to 12.5 in 1980. There has been an even greater increase in the percentage of the population attending college. In 1960, only 16 percent of the adult population had completed one year or more of college. By 1988, nearly 40 percent had completed one or more years of college. Thus, the exposure of the electorate to college has more than doubled in just two decades.

Second, changes in the birth rate since 1940 have had and will continue to have an impact on the age distribution of the electorate. The first major change in the birth rate occurred after World War II when veterans, in particular, married in extraordinary numbers and produced what is now known as the "baby boom" generation. Great numbers of these post-World War II babies became eighteen during the 1970s. Their entrance into the electorate was hastened by the Twenty-sixth Amendment to the U.S. Constitution, enacted in 1971, which lowered the minimum voting age from twenty-one to eighteen years of age. The net result of these events was a lowering of the median age of the electorate. The baby boom cohort will continue to influence the age distribution of the electorate by increasing the median age as its members pass into their middle and elderly years. This is because the birth rate has dropped almost every year since 1960, meaning new voters will comprise a smaller and smaller percentage of the electorate for several years to come, while the baby boom generation will comprise a larger and larger percentage.

Why are these demographic trends—increased education and a declining birth rate—so important? They are important because education and age are possibly related to some of the other major trends we have discussed. What is confusing, however, is that some political attitudes and behaviors have not moved in the direction that we would expect, given the simultaneous changes in demographics. Changes in voter turnout illustrate this puzzle. As we have observed, turnout has declined steadily since the early 1960s. The change in turnout is perfectly consistent with the change in the age distribution of the electorate. Young citizens vote less frequently than their elders, and given that young people have made up an increasingly greater percentage of the voting age population since 1960, we would expect turnout to decline. Educated citizens, however, are more likely to vote than the less educated; as we have a better educated populace now, turnout should have increased. But it has not, constituting a rather intriguing puzzle.

In order to assess the relationship between these two demographic trends and the other trends . . ., we have divided age and education into three and four categories, respectively. The analysis of age divides the population into three groups: those eighteen to twenty-nine years of age in 1988, those thirty to forty-nine, and those fifty and over. The analysis of education divides persons into four categories: less than high school education, high school, some college, and college degree or more.

Our analysis of data collected in 1988 confirms much that we learned in previous elections about the relationships between these demographic variables and electoral behavior. In 1988, those between eighteen and twenty-nine years of age constituted only 22 percent of the electorate but represented 29 percent of all "pure" independents, 26 percent of leaning independents, and 35 percent of nonvoters. The relationship is strongest between age and nonvoting as 49 percent of respondents between eighteen and twenty-nine reported not voting in 1988, compared with about 30 percent for the CPS sample as a whole. When one combines the impact of youth and nonpartisanship, the effect on abstention is heightened: only 26 percent of young (eighteen to twenty-nine years old) independents reported voting in 1988.

Our youngest category of potential voters, those between eighteen and twenty-nine years of age, also proved modestly different than other age groups on other measures in 1988. While 55 percent of this group gave issue based or ideological evaluations of the presidential candidates, as compared to 58 percent of those between 30 and 49 years old, and 52 percent of the oldest members of the electorate, the youngest voters led all age groups in having nothing to say about the candidates (23 percent no-content, versus 14 percent of the middle-aged group and 12 percent of the oldest segment). The youngest age cohort is the most likely to defect from partisan voting but is less likely to be alienated than those over 30 years of age.

Our analysis of the relationship between education and electoral behavior suggests that all but one of the trends we have discussed have been affected by the increased education of the electorate. The lone exception is the trend in partisan defection. We find that in 1988 the educated tended to be slightly more partisan, equally likely to defect, considerably more likely to have reported voting, less alienated, and more likely to use issues and ideology in evaluating candidates. Persons in the college-educated sector of society are less likely to call themselves independents (6 percent among the college educated versus 12 percent among others). Thus, without increasing education, independents would be slightly more common.

The impact of education on partisan defection at the ballot box reveals very little difference in defection rates among the various education categories. Differences were apparent for political alienation, however, as only 20 percent of those with some college education were alienated in 1988 compared with 33 percent of the other respondents. It seems that political alienation would be less common if the public were better educated. In truth, however, education can scarcely account for the changes in alienation inasmuch as the educational level of Americans has not changed to the same degree, nor in the same fashion, as has alienation over the last three decades.

The college educated are also more likely to have reported voting; 85 percent of the college educated voted in 1988, compared with 58 percent of those with less education. Thus the decline in turnout has been retarded by education. Finally, education has affected candidate evaluations. In their evaluations of Bush and Dukakis, the college educated were clearly more likely to use ideology and issues than were those with no college education. Twenty-eight percent of the less-than-high-school education category used image or no-content evaluations of Bush and Dukakis, compared to 17 percent of those with at least one year of college. Thus, at least some of the increase in issue oriented evaluations noted earlier can be explained by the improving education of the American electorate.

In conclusion, we can say that education has *inhibited* certain politically relevant changes in American society. Were American society to be no better educated today than was the case in the 1950s, participation and partisanship would probably be lower, and alienation and image oriented evaluations of political candidates would be more common.

Conclusion

At this point it is fair to ask whether any substantial conclusions can be noted about the changes in the American electorate. We believe that four conclusions are justified. The first conclusion is that, overall, stability rather than change best characterizes the American electorate over the period 1952–1988. While the American electorate is changing, for example becoming more likely to evaluate presidential candidates in terms of issues, this evolution is quite gradual at best and erratic and patternless at worst. In many ways the 1988 election was more like elections in the 1950s than any election in the interim. If one were forced to pick between the polar adjectives, *changed* and *unchanged*, the electorate seems unchanged.

This lack of change is most apparent in the impact of partisanship on voting: party identification remains highly predictive as to how people will vote. While the number of independents has more than doubled since 1952, 89 percent of the electorate still identifies with a political party, and 85 percent of these voted for their party's nominee in 1988, rather than defecting. Thus, at least three quarters of all votes for major party candidates for president in 1988 can be explained by partisanship in the electorate, whatever the source of partisanship might be.

The impact of party identification on voting in congressional elections is attenuated somewhat by the effects of incumbency. Higher rates of partisan defection are observed in elections for the House of Representatives than for the presidency, with most defectors voting for the incumbent. This helps us understand why the Democratic party has such a strong hold on the House. Republicans are loyal in presidential voting but often vote for the incumbent in House contests. Given that the incumbent is most likely to be a Democrat, partisan defection and continued Democratic control of the House of Representatives result.

Second, even today there remains a very substantial minority of persons so peripherally involved in politics that even the noisy trappings of the presidential campaign gives them nothing to say about the candidates. Such persons also typically fail to vote. It is far more common today, as it was in the 1950s, for nonvoters to be passive bystanders of the political scene rather than zealous proponents or opponents of policy who failed to find a choice among the presidential candidates. Nonparticipant bystanders, rather than nonparticipant zealots, while equally unfortunate for the goal of participatory democracy, are probably less threatening to the smooth performance of democracy.

Third, verbal assurances of trust for the political system and officials within it, which were common in the 1950s, do not appear as essential as suggested by David Easton and others. We have seen substantial distrust and alienation in the 1970s and 1980s among voters and nonvoters, defectors and partisan loyalists, issue evaluators and those unable to articulate any candidate attributes, and among independents and strong partisans. However, the alienated are much less likely to vote than are the non-alienated, suggesting that the increase in disaffection since 1964 has partially contributed to the decline in voter participation.

Fourth and finally, the forces affecting the electorate over time are not as simple as some theories would suggest. It is not sufficient to tie trends together, based on perceptions of an increasingly issue oriented electorate that sees little choice among the major political parties and is therefore rebelling into independency, nonvoting, and alienation. No doubt there are Americans who do follow this dynamic pattern, but our analysis suggests this simple theory does not account for the patterns of stability and change that are most notable within the electorate.

Despite these conclusions, there have been limits to our analyses. In our assessment of trends in the American electorate, we have used data from large national samples. This has necessarily meant that we are assessing the impact of national trends rather than more limited regional patterns of change. We have also limited our primary analysis to patterns of presidential and congressional voting. There is no systematic assessment of statewide elected office voting comparable to the National Election Studies we have used here. There is research, which must still be judged as tentative, that suggests that state- and local-level voting differ somewhat from the patterns found here.

It is beyond the scope of our effort to deal with these differences. The reader should be aware, however, that media coverage, public familiarity with the candidates, and participation are all less in such subnational elections. In most respects, presidential voting affords the electorate the greatest opportunity for obtaining information on the candidates and issues associated with an election. This greater, more dynamic, flow of information in presidential campaigns would seem to foretell greater change in future presidential elections than subnational contests.

Similarly, the reader should note that our assessment is limited to ten presidential elections. We cannot say with confidence which outcomes were the result of long-term changes in the behavior of the electorate and which were the one-of-a-kind results of unique combinations of presidential candidates. If we had data on many more presidential elections, we might be able to say something definitive about what happens when Democrats nominate a Southerner and the Republicans a Midwesterner, or when the Democrats nominate a liberal candidate rather than a moderate, or when Republicans nominate a conservative. Many of our figures show erratic changes over the ten elections. Were we to have many more elections, we might be better able to see underlying long-term changes that transcend these erratic short-term changes. In many ways our speculation, indeed anyone's speculation, about changes in the American electorate is like predicting whether a baseball team will have a good season after having watched its first ten games.

The presidential election of 1984 serves as a good example of the dangers associated with trying to use one election's results to predict future trends. Of course, in 1984 the minority party won the presidential election. This has been the rule during the time period we have studied. In fact, only in 1960, 1964, and 1976 has the majority party won the presidency. Many political observers interpreted Reagan's 1980 victory, given his ideological orientations, as a conservative mandate that continued and was reinforced in 1984 and 1988. Voters in the 1980s were seen by some as taking a new, more conservative, direction. We would urge caution in such an interpretation, especially given the lessons of the past. For example, Eisenhower's victory in 1952 and Nixon's in 1968 were also interpreted as signaling a dramatic restructuring of American politics, but these restructurings did not occur. More importantly, most public opinion polls in the late 1980s, including election studies, continue to show the American public to hold moderate, not conservative, policy positions.

As we have seen in the case of increasing alienation among Americans in the 1960s and 1970s, the limited perspective of even several presidential elections can be in error. Carter's victory in 1976, as well as Reagan's in 1980, can be interpreted as reflecting the public's alienation from the Washington establishment, in that the incumbent president was defeated; from this interpretation, it can be inferred that levels of alienation can impact election outcomes. In turn, alienation remained stable in 1988, while the prototypical establishment, Republican George Bush, was elected to the presidency. Shouldn't alienation have increased in 1988, in the face of two candidates who were such typical representatives of their respective parties? Or does alienation *not* contribute to election outcomes? These sorts of questions are most difficult to answer within the limited perspective of two or three, or even ten, presidential elections.

31 / The Mass Media, Political Trust, and Participation

M. Margaret Conway

Ideally, the role of the press and other news media in democracy would be that of educator of the public, equipping the electorate with what it needs to make rational decisions. Though there are probably few Americans today who would accept the idea that the role of mass media in politics is all positive, the evidence summarized in this reading leads Margaret Conway to conclude that the media do have an important impact on citizens' attitudes and on their participation in politics.

Effects of the Mass Media on Political Attitudes

The impact of the mass media on political participation is a subject of continuing dispute. One controversy concerns the depth of coverage of governmental activities. A majority of Americans rely on television for political news.[1] But most local television stations present only limited coverage of state and local government activities,[2] and much of national news coverage focuses on momentary controversies or on crisis events.[3] Television news tends to concentrate on events that can be presented dramatically; "talking heads" are considered to be relatively unappealing to the viewers. Thus, continuing coverage of less dramatic events is avoided, even if these may have greater importance in the long run.[4] For example, debates on budgetary allocations usually receive superficial coverage, although they can have a greater impact on citizens' lives than many of the fleeting but more dramatic political incidents that obtain greater coverage.

The style of media coverage, as well as the selection of stories, may foster negative perceptions and cynical attitudes about government and politics, and some scholars suggest that these perceptions and attitudes tend to reduce involvement with government to the extent that it is possible in a modern society.[5] Surveys conducted since the 1950s show that the growth of television coverage of politics has been accompanied by a decline in political trust. The proportion of citizens who can be said to "trust" the government declined from 76 percent in 1960 to 32 percent in 1982, increased to 44 percent in 1984, but fell to 40 percent in 1988.[6] In another series of surveys, 50 percent of those questioned in 1966 reported they had "a great deal" of confidence in "the people running" the Supreme Court, and 42 percent had a great deal of confidence in the people running the Congress; by 1981, the proportion reporting a great deal of confidence had dropped to 29 percent for the Supreme Court and 16 percent for Congress. The executive branch of government fared almost as badly: 41 percent had a great deal of confidence in 1966 and 24 percent in 1981.[7] More recently, however, confidence in political institutions has apparently begun to rise.

In a series of questions used by Gallup since 1973, the decline in confidence in the Congress, but not the Supreme Court, is evident. In 1973, Gallup reported that 44 percent of respondents expressed "a great deal" or "quite a lot" of confidence in the Supreme Court; by 1988, the percentage expressing that level of confidence had increased to 56 percent. In contrast, only 35 percent indicated that level of confidence in the Congress in 1988, compared to 42 percent in 1973. Confidence in Congress declined from 1973 to 1983 when it reached a low of 28 percent indicating "a great deal" or "quite a lot" of confidence in the Congress.[8]

Can these declines in trust and confidence that took place after 1966 be attributed to the mass media? Several researchers have concluded that they can be, and they place the principal blame on television. Analysis of data from a 1968 survey indicates that those who rely primarily on television as their main or only source of political news are more cynical and have less understanding of politics than those who use several sources, including print media. This difference remains, although at a reduced level, even when comparisons are made among persons with the same level of education.[9] A study of the effects of a controversial CBS television documentary, "The Selling of the Pentagon," led to the conclusions that reliance on television as a primary source of news increases "(a) social distrust, (b) political cynicism, (c) political inefficacy, (d) partisan disloyalty, and (e) third party viability."[10]

The print media also have an impact, with people's exposure to higher levels of political criticism in newspapers resulting in lower levels of political trust and efficacy. Newspaper stories that give relatively greater emphasis to political conflict and controversy stimulate greater political distrust and lower levels of political efficacy, although levels of trust appear to be affected more than efficacy.[11]

If both print media and television focus on conflict and controversy and present criticisms of political leaders, why do we assign to television more of the blame for the decline in the attitudes that are important in stimulating mass political participation? The reason apparently is that exposure to political stories on television is inadvertent; if one is watching a television news program, one sees whatever the television news editors have decided to present on that program. By contrast, print media can be selectively "edited" by readers themselves. If individuals wish to read only the sports section and the comics, or only stories about political issues and events, they can do so.[12]

Of course, the events unfolding since the development of television as a mass medium for the presentation of news in the 1950s also partly account for the decline in public confidence in political leaders and the political process. The assassinations of a president and of other prominent figures, the long and ultimately unpopular Vietnam War, the resignation of a president in disgrace, recurrent cycles of economic recession and recovery, and a continuing series of international economic and political crises—all have provided news that is not only controversial or unpleasant but often complex and confusing to the average citizen. That exposure to political news has a depressant effect on those attitudes, such as political efficacy and partisan loyalty, which are important in stimulating political participation is thus not surprising. Most content of the news media, however important or trivial, is presented as significant and usually in a context of controversy and crisis. Furthermore, good news and positive outcomes receive far less coverage than the bad and the negative. In short, both the content of the news and the style of news coverage have had an important impact on citizens' attitudes.

Effects of the Mass Media on Political Participation

The news media have a direct impact on one form of political participation—voter turnout. This comes about through the media's presentation of campaigns in news broadcasts, through candidate-sponsored advertisements, and through programs devoted to candidate debates or forums. The media also affect turnout through citizens' reactions to predictions of election outcomes before or on election day.

Editors make judgments about who are the more important candidates and how extensive the coverage of different candidates and contests should be. Reporters offer interpretations of candidates' actions and ideas that influence the electorate's perceptions and attitudes and ultimately their decisions about whether to vote and for whom. For example, potential presidential candidates must be considered "viable" by the media in order to get sufficient news coverage; if candidates are taken seriously by the media, they find it much easier to raise campaign funds and build an effective organization. . . .[13]

. . . Media coverage structures citizens' perceptions of the candidates and the issues, and these perceptions are interpreted within the context of existing attitudes and beliefs. If some citizens think that the need for a strong national defense is the most important problem facing the nation, and if one candidate is presented by the media as being more likely to support additional expenditures for national defense, that perception, structured by both what the candidates are saying and the media's coverage of the candidates, will affect those citizens' vote choices as well as their probability of voting....

The activities of candidates presented through the mass media can have an impact on citizens' familiarity with the candidates. In 1978, more than half the citizens in districts where an incumbent representative was seeking reelection reported having heard, seen, or read something about the representative in the mass media, while only 20 percent had personally talked with the incumbent or the incumbent's staff. While a vigorous challenger to an incumbent can help stimulate electoral participation, the challenger is usually much less visible. Such was the case in 1978, when four-fifths of those interviewed in a national study recognized the incumbent's name but only two-fifths recognized the challenger's. One-fifth of those surveyed reported having seen or read about the challenger in the mass media, so it appears that about half the recognititon received by a challenger is attributable to media coverage and campaign advertising.....[14]

Studies of the news coverage of political campaigns indicate that the press concentrates on who is winning and losing (the "horse race") and on the strategies pursued by various candidates, rather than on the candidates' issue stands and competence to govern.[15] If the election is predicted to be close, that prediction stimulates interest in it. The cost-benefit calculations of citizens are affected, as they perceive an increased probability that their votes will affect the outcome. That such calculations influence the decision to vote has been demonstrated by several studies.[16] Thus, predictions by the mass media about the closeness of a contest can have significant impact on election-day turnout.

Predictions of the election outcome are also made both during the campaign and on election day itself. The latter especially have become quite controversial. Formerly, outcome projections were based on surveys of samples of voters taken days or even weeks before the election. Now, however, they can be based on interviews with randomly selected voters as they leave the voting place (exit polls), and predictions of the outcome can be broadcast on television on election day before the polling places have closed in some areas.

Several studies have examined the effects of these election-day predictions. Three of them concerned the 1964 presidential election, when Lyndon Johnson won a landslide victory over Barry Goldwater. That outcome had been predicted long before election day, however, so the effects of the election-day predictions were probably minimal. One study reported no effects on turnout, a second reported a 1 percent change in choice of candidate, and a third reported a 3 percent change in choice.[17] While effects found in the latter two studies could have made a difference in a close presidential election, they had no impact on the outcome of the 1964 contest. A study of the 1968 election found that 4 percent of those surveyed in the east and 7 percent surveyed in the west changed their turnout intention after hearing the election outcome projections; 6 percent in the east and 7 percent in the west changed their choice of presidential candidate.[18] It should be noted that, aside from their effects on the presidential election, changes in the level of turnout can have an impact on the concurrent congressional contests. A study of the effects of election-day predictions in 1972 concluded that they reduced turnout by 2.7 percent in the Pacific coast states. That translates into 337,000 votes in California, for example, or an average of 7,800 votes per congressional district—enough to determine the outcome of a close congressional contest.[19]

Appraisal of the effects of election-day projections of the 1980 presidential contest also provides support for the view that they can have a small but decisive influence on voting participation. The projections that year, as well as President Carter's concession speech, both of them coming before the polls closed in many states, reduced turnout in both the east and the west below what was predicted on the basis of preelection interviews.[20]

Election-day projections probably have their greatest impact in those elections where a close race for president is expected, but instead an easy victory materializes for one of the candidates....

...The effects [of the projections] are seen not only in the vote totals in the presidential contest but also in the outcomes of elections for congressional and state offices being held at the same time....

What is the contribution of media coverage to rational voting decisions? One scholar has concluded that "the prevalence of negative information makes it seem that all of the candidates are mediocre, or even poor, choices. This negative case appears to be a major factor in many voters' decisions to stay home on election day." She continues:

> Although it would be unfair to blame low voter turnout in primary elections on inadequate election news, interviews with voters show that poor coverage plays a significant part. People find election stories interesting, but they do not feel that these stories prepare them adequately to make choices. Media images depict campaigns as tournaments where voters sit on the sidelines and watch the bouts, waiting to see who is eliminated and who remains. Winning and losing are all important, rather than what winning and losing means in terms of the political direction of the country in general or the observer's personal situation in particular. Taking its cues from the media, the audience accepts election news as just another story, rather than as an important tale about real life with very direct impact on its own welfare.[21]

Summary

...Political mobilization can be stimulated by the electoral context, including such factors as the perceived closeness of the contest for an office; the appeal of the candidates; the perceived importance of an issue; and the activities of party, candidate, and interest-group organizations. While the impact of these mobilization efforts may be small, it can have a significant effect in close elections, on legislative outcomes, and on the decisions of bureaucrats charged with implementing or enforcing a policy.

The mass media must also be recognized as a key element in the political environment. The development of television and changing patterns of print news accessibility have had a significant impact on citizens' perceptions of government, politicians, and the political process.

Notes

1. Alan R. Gitelson, M. Margaret Conway, and Frank B. Feigert, *American Political Parties: Stability and Change* (Boston: Houghton Mifflin, 1984), 239, table 10.1.
2. Graber found that local television news broadcasts mentioned state and local government in not more than 7 percent of their stories: Doris A. Graber, *Mass Media and American Politics*, 3d ed. (Washington, D.C.: CQ Press, 1989), 88, table 3-3.
3. Ibid., 83–84.
4. Ibid., 84–86.
5. Ibid., 172; and Austin Ranney, *Channels of Power* (New York: Basic Books, 1984), chap. 3.
6. This represents the proportion responding "always" or "most of the time" to the question "How much of the time do you think you can trust the government in Washington to do what is right?" *American National Election Studies, 1960 to 1982.*
7. Seymour Martin Lipset and William Schneider, *The Confidence Gap* (New York: Free Press, 1983), 48–49, table 2-1.
8. The Gallup Report, December 1988, #279, 30.
9. Michael J. Robinson, "American Political Legitimacy in an Era of Electronic Journalism: Reflections on the Evening News," in *Television as a Social Force*, ed. Douglass Cater and Richard Adler (New York: Praeger, 1975), 97–139.
10. Michael J. Robinson, "Public Affairs Television and the Growth of Political Malaise," *American Political Science Review* 74 (1976): 409–432.
11. Arthur H. Miller, Edie Goldenberg, and Lutz Ebring, "Type-Set Politics: Impact of Newspapers on Public Confidence," *American Political Science Review* 73 (1979): 67–84.
12. Shanto Iyengar and Donald R. Kinder, *News That Matters* (Chicago: University of Chicago Press, 1987).
13. See, for example, C. Anthony Broh, "Presidential Preference Polls and Network News," in *Television Coverage of the 1980 Presidential Campaign*, ed. William Adams (Norwood, N.J.: Ablex, 1983), 29–48.
14. M. Margaret Conway, "Mass Media Use, Candidate Contacts, and Political Participation in Congressional Elections" (paper delivered at the annual meeting of the Southern Political Science Association, November 6–8, 1980).
15. C. Anthony Broh, "Horse Race Journalism: Reporting the Polls in the 1976 Campaign," *Public Opinion Quarterly* 44 (1980): 514–529; and Thomas E. Patterson, *The Mass Media Election* (New York: Praeger, 1980), chap. 3.
16. Norman Frohlich and Joe A. Oppenheimer, *Modern Political Economy* (Englewood Cliffs, N.J.: Prentice-Hall, 1978), chap. 5; and Gregory Brunk, "The Impact of Rational Participation Models on Voting Participation," *Public Choice* 35 (1980): 549–564.

17. Kurt Lang and Gladys Enget Lang, *Voting and Non-Voting* (Waltham, Mass.: Blaisdell, 1968); Harold Mendelsohn and Irving Crespi, *Polls, Television and the New Politics* (Scranton, Pa.: Chandler, 1970), chap. 4; and Douglas A. Fuchs, "Election Day Radio-Television and Western Voting," *Public Opinion Quarterly* 30 (1966): 226–236.

18. Sam Tuchman and Thomas E. Coffin, "The Influence of Election-Night Television Broadcasts in a Close Election," *Public Opinion Quarterly* 35 (1971): 315–326.

19. Raymond Wolfinger and Peter Linquiti, "Tuning In and Turning Out," *Public Opinion Quarterly* 4 (1981): 57–58.

20. John E. Jackson, "Election-Night Reporting and Voter Turnout," *American Journal of Political Science* 27 (1983): 615–635.

21. Graber, *Mass Media and American Politics*, 181–183.

CHAPTER EIGHT

Campaigns and Elections

One of the more enduring elements of American democracy has been the great importance and attention given to elections to national office and the campaigns that precede them. However, the nature of campaigning has changed significantly over time, and many important changes have taken place within the past few decades. Modern campaign technology—especially campaigning by television—has led to astronomical increases in campaign costs and to development of a new profession of campaign management. Simultaneously, and not coincidentally, the reliance of both candidates and voters on parties has declined markedly. Some of the most important changes in campaigning, and their consequences, are discussed in the first two selections of this chapter. In "The Postmodern Election," Lance Bennett identifies a number of political, economic, and technological changes that he says have contributed to what are now presidential campaigns devoid of meaningful choices. And in "Selling of the President 1988," Nicholas O'Shaughnessy describes how professional consultants turned that presidential campaign into "an exercise in product marketing" consisting largely of packaging candidates for television.

Not only have campaigns changed over time, but voting patterns have as well. In fact, changes in voting alignments have occurred with such regularity that lack of change is sometimes viewed as an oddity. Students of American electoral history have recognized a pattern they refer to as the "cycles of 36 years." Approximately every thirty-six years from 1824 until at least 1932, "old" political issues were replaced by new ones, voters rethought their party allegiance on that basis, and many switched parties in what came to be called a period of "realignment." From 1860 until 1896, for instance, issues of reconstruction and states' rights dominated national politics. Then, around 1896, a realignment resulted from the rise of "new" dominant issues, including the government's role in regulating business and the country's role in world affairs. Around 1932 and "right on schedule," another realignment occurred, this time coinciding with the rise of "Depression era" issues involving the establishment of a modified social welfare state.* Most observers agree, however, that the realignment that might have been anticipated for 1968 (thirty-six years after 1932) did not take place. Instead, data for the new period seem to show that instead of switching parties, large numbers of voters were abandoning both parties in favor of seeing themselves as "independent" voters. This led some to refer to the period beginning around 1968 as a period of "dealignment."

Expectations that dealignment could not continue indefinitely (and indeed, the tendency toward larger numbers of independents has tapered off) have led political scientists to carefully examine each recent presidential election for signs that might indicate realignment, continued dealignment, or something else. In their selection in this chapter, Nelson Polsby and Aaron Wildavsky carefully analyze

*See Frank Feigert and Margaret Conway, *Parties and Politics in America* (Boston: Allyn and Bacon, 1976, Chapter 2).—*Editor's Note.*

evidence from the elections of the 1980s, in an effort to determine whether the long-awaited realignment may have taken place during that decade.

In the realignment of the 1930s, black voters were one group that contributed to the ascendance of the Democratic Party to majority status. Previously a source of support for Republican candidates, black voters' allegiance shifted dramatically to the Democratic Party during that realignment. Since then, the importance of the black vote to Democratic presidential candidates has been demonstrated in a number of elections. In "Black Politics and Presidential Elections," Lenneal Henderson identifies a set of conditions under which the black vote has actually been pivotal in some Democratic victories.

Finally, in the last reading of this section, Stephen Wayne considers one of the "continuities" of American politics: proposals for change in the electoral college system of selecting presidents. Although its flaws have been well documented over the years, this creation of the framers has managed to escape reformers' chisels and wrecking balls. Wayne holds out little hope of success for a number of proposals currently being discussed.

32 / The Postmodern Election

W. Lance Bennett

Are mudslinging and issueless campaigns something new, and what do they mean for the role of campaigns and elections in the future? The mudslinging is not totally new, says Lance Bennett, but what is new and particularly ominous is the lack of meaningful choices in recent elections. The increasing roles of money, television, and marketing strategy have contributed to this tendency, which reached the point in the 1988 campaign that Bennett calls that election the first postmodern election, marked by "all text and no context; all rhyme and no reason."

The Postmodern Election
. . . America's national political contests are moments of great opportunity for defining public problems, exploring new directions, evaluating the character of aspiring leaders, and dreaming about the future. Elections are the centerpieces of the civic culture. Yet these grand occasions for stock-taking, consensus-building, and renewal are being squandered on a regular basis. Instead of drawing people into the political arena and stimulating wide-open dialogue about the problems that threaten continued national greatness, candidates appear to be walking on eggshells. They not only hide from the press, but with the growing acceptance of image-making techniques, they even hide from themselves.

The decline of elections has been a long process, with the contests of recent years merely marking its completion. Pinpoint history, like surgical bombing, is an imprecise art. The argument here is not that before the 1980s and 1990s we were living in one political age and afterward we entered another. Rather, the last several elections cap a long process in which the very language of public life has been transformed to the point that most citizens can no longer find the sense in it. . . .

Signs of electoral foolery can be traced to much earlier periods in American history. . . . George Washington's campaign practices were anything but models of noble principle. And the likes of Thomas Jefferson, Andrew Jackson, and Abraham Lincoln were savaged by opponents in ways that make the negative campaigning of the present seem tame. William McKinley spent most of his election campaign in 1896 pandering to the media from his front porch in Canton, Ohio, mouthing such pithy sound bites as "McKinley and a Full Dinner Pail." Franklin Roosevelt's fireside chats were masterpieces of media manipulation. And few latter-day marketing feats can top the selling of the "new and improved" Richard Nixon in 1968.

The difference is that these contests of the past also contained historic choices. Perhaps they were not phrased as eloquently as intellectuals and language lovers would like, but at least there were choices. For example, there were the Jeffersonian battles over the Alien and Sedition Acts with their implications for the freedom of speech; the Jacksonian referendum on national monetary policy, and its impact on the growth of the frontier; the social and economic ordeal of the Civil War, and its legacy of industrial growth and the death of agrarian society; the birth of protective government in the New Deal; the promise of civil rights in the New Frontier; and the white conservative backlash that contributed to the Republican reformation in 1968.

Meaningful choices have been harder to find in recent years. Even the Reagan presidency could not deliver on its core promise of shrinking the federal government. Instead, it delivered a bloated national budget while handing off a long list of underfunded social and regulatory responsibilities to the states. In addition, the Reagan landslides of 1980 and 1984 were delivered by fewer than 30 percent of the eligible electorate. Perhaps most telling of all is the fact that majorities or near majorities in the opinion polls opposed virtually every major policy that made up the "Reagan revolution."

. . . [W]e have entered a political era in which electoral choices are of little consequence because an electoral system in disarray can generate neither the party unity nor the levels of public agreement necessary to forge a winning and effective political coalition. The underlying explanation is that the political and economic forces driving our national politics have created a system in which the worst tendencies of the political culture—the hype, hoopla, and negativity—have been elevated to the norm in elections, gaining a systematic dominance in campaign content as never before. Meanwhile, the best hopes for creative leadership are screened systematically out of the running by political and economic forces that are only dimly understood, when they are recognized at all.

The result is a new electoral system—one filled with paradox. As voters grow more discontented with elected officials, incumbents grow more likely to win reelection. This result is not accidental—it is systematic. Rather than brand discontented-but-seemingly-helpless-voters as fools, it makes as much sense to consider the choices they are given. Rather than dismiss declining turnouts as products of apathy, it may be that genuine anger is expressed in opinion polls, but it simply has few meaningful outlets. The disturbing possibility is that many voters have come to accept, whether angrily, cynically, or apathetically, an electoral system that grows more dysfunctional with each election. As society's problems grow in size and number, the political system generates fewer solutions and puts more issues "on hold." Society and politics move awkwardly together, as if in a dream that is all the more troubling because the citizenry cannot seem to awaken. In short, the voters are mad as hell, but they don't know how to stop taking it anymore....

The easiest explanation for the decline of political ideas is television.... What can politicians do but fashion their messages to this passive medium, leaving most of the challenging ideas on the cutting room floor? As New York governor Mario Cuomo put it, taking a stand on political principles these days "requires that you explain your principles, and in this age of electronic advocacy this process can often be tedious and frustrating. This is especially so when you must get your message across in twenty-eight-second celluloid morsels, when images prove often more convincing than ideas. Labels are no longer a tendency in our politics. In this electronic age, they are our politics."[1]

While Governor Cuomo may have perceived correctly the effects of our political transformation, identifying television as the cause of it all is a bit too easy. There is little doubt that television has changed the way we do politics, but it is not the sole, or even the major, source of our political decline; it is merely the most visible sign of it. Behind the television images lies a whole set of political and economic changes that limit what politicians say, how they say it, and to whom they can say it. These hidden limits make television the perfect medium for saying nothing, but doing it with eye-catching and nerve-twitching appeal....

In this upside-down world where Madisonian ideals have been traded for Madison Avenue methods, the political challenge is not to inspire and mobilize the great and diverse masses of people, as a romantic notion of democracy might lead us to hope. Rather, the challenge of contemporary politics is to isolate key groups (the smaller and more homogeneous, the better) who can be persuaded to go out and pull their levers in response to test-marketed images like wimpiness, competence, liberalism, prayerless schools, burning flags, tax-paid abortions, and weekend rapists on prison release programs. The nervous systems of target audiences seem to twitch more violently if the weekend rapist is black, and all these symbolic effects are enhanced when distracting "noise" is screened out of the communications between candidates and their chosen publics. "Noise" in this age of political unreason consists of things like serious proposals, programs, and spontaneous moments in which candidates act on their own instincts. Thus, our electoral process revolves around small but scientifically chosen segments of the public who are bombarded with images of candidates standing squarely behind flags, fetuses, bibles, and other market-tested and, therefore, politically unassailable symbols of the day.

Add to this mix of money and marketing the growing repertoire of techniques for keeping a growling press pack at bay, and voilà, a system emerges in which we witness celluloid candidates pronouncing suspect lines to listless voters while the managed media try to point out the absurdity with mixed success. . . .

Welcome to the Postmodern Election: Campaign '88

"Read my lips."

"Senator, you're no Jack Kennedy."

"Make my twenty-four-hour time period."

Just a few of the high—or low—points of Campaign '88, depending on one's view of political language and its proper uses.

For most scholars, commentators, and the majority of the American public, the presidential election of 1988 was the worst in memory. It was no easy last-place finish, considering the stiff competition in recent years. Evidence from polls, editorials, and academic studies suggests that, even by minimal standards, the most expensive contest in history failed to accomplish what an election campaign should do: introduce intelligent, well-reasoned, and occasionally inspiring debate into the voter choice process. Yet—and here's the rub—these superficial one-liners and telegenic sound bites seem to be what speech writers, consultants, and willing candidates aspired to achieve in their communications with the electorate.

Welcome to the first postmodern election: all text and no context; all rhyme and no reason. And meet the candidates: George Bush, Blade Runner; Mike Dukakis, Max Headroom; Dan Quayle, the Happy Camper; and Lloyd Bentsen, the first candidate who couldn't lose. . . .

Begin with the TV image. Looking at television gives us a rough picture of how political messages have been transformed over the last few decades but not much of an idea about what transformed them. . . . It is useful, however, to begin with this glassy surface of elections—the transparent screen through which most people experience their political reality.

For several elections, television has been the decisive factor in the reports of voters about how they make up their minds on a candidate. For reasons that will soon become clear, political advertising is often the most influential part of the TV picture. Yet the election of 1988 struck many observers as something of a capstone in the TV age—not so much for voters, who have already adapted to televised information, but for campaigns and candidates. After decades of experimentation and flirting with TV as a strategic weapon in election battles, Election '88 suggested that campaign managers had fully and unashamedly accepted the use of TV technology to reconstruct candidates. The subordination of communication between candidates and public to the dictates of "tele-campaigning" was revealed, among other places, in Democratic candidate Michael Dukakis' transformation during the campaign from traditional campaigner to a creature of television (albeit an unsuccessful one).

Many observers agree that something happened in 1988.[2] "Some invisible line has been crossed," said Marvin Kalb, a former network correspondent and, more recently, director of Harvard's Barone Center on the Press, Politics, and Public Policy.[3] That line, according to John Buckley, a media consultant who has worked for both the Republican party and CBS News, is between print and video, the word and the image: "This is the first election of a newly mature style of politics wherein it is accepted as absolute gospel by both sides that what you need to do is create...a message...that communicates itself on television.... There is no longer a value judgment on the need to tailor a message to television. It's now a matter of survival, not a matter of ethics or intellectual honesty."[4]

Like most historical changes, this realignment of our political discourse to fit the medium of television did not occur overnight. The first step over the electronic line probably occurred in 1960, the year Richard Nixon arguably won the presidential debate in print and on the radio but lost it, along with the election, on television. Goodbye *logos*, hello *logo*.

logos: reason as constituting the controlling principle of the universe, as manifested by speech

logo: short for logogram: the word replaced by the sign, or the visual image

Crossing the line from intellectual to anti-intellectual discourse has altered the ways in which we (are forced to) understand and participate in politics. The most fundamental change, as noted above, is the decline of the traditional political argument itself. A case in point is the now legendary incident in the 1984 campaign involving CBS correspondent Leslie Stahl's attempt to point out the logical inconsistencies between candidate Ronald Reagan's campaign appeals and the contradictory positions and policies Mr. Reagan advocated on the same issues as president. To her amazement Stahl received a thank-you call from the White House after the lengthy piece was aired. The reason for the thank-you was that the visual images of Reagan speaking, no matter what the contradictions in his speech, were more powerful than the argument that Stahl fashioned to go along with those images. The moral we can derive from this incident is that political ideas are no longer anchored in reason, logic, or history; political ideas as we may have known them once upon a time don't exist....

Crossing the rhetorical line to the bullier pulpit of television emboldened ABC News president Roone Arledge (president of ABC Sports at the end of the modern age) to pronounce the Democratic National Convention boring. He found it so boring, in fact, that he threatened to cut back coverage of the Republicans the following month.[5] Something must be going on when a threat like that is issued on the heels of a convention that offered its audience no fewer than four or five excellent speeches by prominent members of the party—speeches recalling a bygone era of rousing, thought-provoking, morally challenging rhetoric.

No matter. Speech of any caliber or length greater than a sound bite seems to be the problem. ABC's executive producer for the conventions dismissed the television coverage of these speech fests as a "dinosaur."[6] So, we witness the demise of what has been the most important rhetorical form at least since the time of Aristotle: The Speech. Welcome to the postmodern election.

Basking far too long in the fleeting electronic glow of his convention speech, Michael Dukakis finally woke up to the fact that he was losing the election, and was losing it badly. His midsummer dream lead of seventeen points dwindled to a dead heat following the Republican National Convention and then plummeted to a fifteen-point deficit in October.

Responding to the cries of state and local campaigns and the encouragement of liberal editorialists, the Democrats finally lifted a page from the Republican play book: think short, talk negative, get mediated. In the closing weeks, the Duke's handlers withdrew their candidate from informal contact (especially question–answer sessions) with the press corps and replaced his basic stump speech emphasizing competence and economic recovery with a positive–negative format emphasizing the profound message "I'm on your side. He's on theirs."

Meanwhile, the campaign went after Bush's "negatives" (another key word in the postmodern political vocabulary) with a vengeance. So negative was the closing Democratic campaign that its newly appointed advertising director estimated an even higher negative-to-positive ad content (60–40) than the Bush campaign's more "balanced" target ratio of 50–50.[7]

Although Dukakis still lost the election, and lost it convincingly, his rhetorical rebirth near the end of the campaign is significant. It suggests that what I propose to call "tele-rhetoric" has become the absolute gospel that media consultants proclaim it to be. One suspects that Dukakis did not bow easily to the new rhetorical doctrine. Much of his punishment at the polls and on the editorial pages may well have resulted from his stubborn resistance to the dogma of the electronic age. Yet, convert he did, even if too late.

Once the decision was made, and a new ad man was in place, the candidate went before the cameras with exhausting, if not shameless, determination. A *New York Times* "Campaign Trail" piece on his TV blitz began "H-e-e-e-e-r-e's. . . Michael." A splashy front page article the same week aptly summed up the tone now unifying the two campaigns: "TV's Role in '88: The Medium Is the Election." The author, Michael Oreskes, described the last weeks of the Dukakis campaign as an electronic whistle stop: "This is the electronic age's equivalent of the final whistle stop tour, seeking Nielsen ratings, not crowds at the tracks."[8]

Once all the candidates were on board, that rhetorical train moved rapidly down its electronic track. The average length of a TV sound bite plummeted to 9.2 seconds in 1988, down from a robust 14 seconds in 1984.[9]

As the very concept of sound bite indicates, the postmodern election comes complete with euphemistic and ambiguous jargon to help bridge the uneasy gap with more familiar and, one might add, meaningful, electoral realities past. It is hard to discuss the meaning of any 9.2 second slice of a text, particularly when such slices are constructed to stand alone, rendering the rest of the text something like a serving utensil. But in the new age, it is unnecessary to fret over meaning; meaning, as it were, is a pre-postmodern phenomenon.

The new language of postmodern politics is preverbal; it is anything but proverbial. It transcends easy distinctions between issues and candidate images, reason and feeling. May the Greeks forgive us, it throws out the classical categories of *logos, pathos,* and *ethos.* Indeed, it was when the Bush message, for all its rhetorical hubris, was universally declared effective, and the Dukakis message, for all its traditional tenacity, was pronounced a blur that Dukakis entered the new age.

What he found on the other side of the line was something the Republicans had known ever since they began winning the presidency on a regular basis. Mike Dukakis, meet Roger Ailes, the electronic guru who brought us Spiro Agnew, the "new" Richard Nixon, Dan Quayle, and the George Bush who parlayed his "wimp factor" into a "kinder, gentler" guy who "goes ballistic" only when he really has to. As Ailes put it, "There are three things that get covered: visuals, attacks and mistakes."[10] As a challenge, try to fit this typology into any of the traditional ways of thinking about argument, debate, or public speech.

The new political language is slippery by design. It is as if baseball legalized the spitball as a concession to pitchers and paid no mind to the inevitable declines in batting averages and fan interest in the game. And so, to pursue the analogy, the new political rhetoric comes as a welcome change only to the political pitchmen and the winning candidates. Despite the disapproval of spectators and journalists alike, the place of minimalist, ambiguous language seems secure in the postmodern campaign.

Assuring the marginality and ambiguity of language has become so important that campaigns these days employ people known in the new vernacular as spin doctors. These specialists come into play when a political pitch is released and heads too straight for the plate. The spin doctors rush out ahead of it, trying to influence or deflect the way reporters pass it along to the mass audience.

In 1988, the Democratic National Convention boasted a Spin Control Coordination Unit. In October of that year, when Bush's campaign chairman, the late Lee Atwater, made a rare appearance on the press plane, he was surprised with a chorus of boos and a chant for a "Spin Moratorium." Undaunted, he solemnly explained how Dan Quayle had done a splendid job in the debate. Initially pleased that everyone seemed to be taking him seriously, Atwater looked up to discover a sign being held above his head. It read: "The Joe Isuzu of Spin—He's Lying."[11]

Perhaps cartoonist Lynda Barry said more with a picture than these words can convey. Her cartoon version of Election '88 was titled "The Election from Hell." The devil was a journalist. . . .[12]

When things fall apart (as manifested in industrial decline, an emerging underclass, homelessness, health care costs, the disappearing dream of home ownership, etc.), people expect the election rhetoric to sharpen the issues, define the problems, and point to the solutions. Yet just the opposite occurred in 1988. An early warning for voters to disabuse themselves of their normal expectations came in June when two publications no less diverse than *The Nation* and *Time* agreed on what the coming contest held in store. In what may well have been a first, a *Nation* editorial cited *Time* as its source: "As *Time* aptly put it last week, 'The contest. . .will be less about ideas and ideologies than about clashing temperaments and styles.' "[13]

Perhaps it requires greater distance to appreciate the irony here. As Lynda Barry's cartoon cuts to the quick of it, so, too, did French television's response to the first debate (arguably the more "exciting" of the two). After no more than a few words had been exchanged, French viewers were whisked back to the newsroom where a deadpan newscaster pronounced judgment: "This debate is not too exciting. Let's go to the Olympics."[14] . . .

Toward an Explanation of Elections without Choices

Consider the possibility that tele-rhetoric is something known in academic circles as an epiphenomenon, or, in everyday parlance, as a symptom of something deeper. Television, after all, is a passive medium, having the capacity to show us everything from talking heads, the public affairs people, to Talking Heads, the rock band—everything from commentators trying to make sense of it all, to a rock concert video called "Stop Making Sense." . . .

Stepping back, we can view postmodernism in general as the product of deeper social forces. The whole syndrome: multiple realities, strange loopiness, power lunching, slam dancing, microwave meals, nostalgia for "Leave It to Beaver" reruns, the generalized loss of meaning, diminished concern for truth, the spinoff academic disciplines of deconstructionism and Foucault studies, and the pervasive social schizophrenia and collective amnesia that artists and writers have been trying to call to mind. All these things, including the emergence of the idea-less, choice-impaired election, may be traced to identifiable and quite palpable social, political, and economic forces.

As a first step toward identifying these forces in the electoral arena, consider the curious role of the political audience. Murray Edelman has argued that this is the age of the political spectator.[15] Citizen-spectators confronted with mass media spectacles may be entertained, dazzled, confused, or bored—the normal range of audience emotions. There is even a role for the audience to play: voting. Elsewhere, Edelman has argued that voting and elections are important mainly for legitimizing the governments that are installed in Washington..[16] . . .

The decline of voter interest and satisfaction suggests that even the symbolic meanings of electoral choices have become undermined in recent elections, raising questions about this legitimation function of elections and the stability of public support for any elected governments put in office. The main reason for the loss of voter involvement and the declining legitimacy of elected government is an interesting one. Unlike audiences of other spectator media— even television—the political audience is a captive of a political system with no competition. Political marketers have finally figured out the beauty of the captive political audience: voters are unable to command new programming when their lack of interest sends the ratings plummeting. To explore this point a bit further, there are, it seems to me, two important differences between political spectators and the audiences who respond to theatrical performances and other entertainment in various ways from buying tickets to laughing at the funny lines. First, spectator displeasure with the quality of the electoral performance, even to the extent of the spectator not voting, does not shut down or otherwise "condition" the spectacle itself—as lack of patronage conditions the content of both the fine arts and popular culture media. Second, the converse also holds true: those who choose to participate in the political audience do not do so because they necessarily enjoy or find meaning in the experience—as one expects audiences for music, theater, or film to connect with their chosen medium. Recall here that full satisfaction with electoral choices in 1988 was expressed by a tiny 9 percent of those planning to vote for the two candidates.

In most other spectator arenas, decline of patronage and rise of antipathy would be more consequential. Whereas other cultural forums are responsive to the marketplace of popular taste, elections seem relatively immune from the most important market forces of consumer dissatisfaction and outright withdrawal from the marketplace. This curious feature of elections helps us recast traditional thinking about candidate–audience communication. The easy assumption is that the effectiveness of electoral rhetoric turns on some sort of meaningful, positive, responsive exchange between communicator and audience. Throwing out this assumption raises the question of what does shape the content of electoral language these days.

Begin with Money...

Consider this possibility. Instead of competing with each other for audience approval, candidates increasingly compete for the support of a much more select and seldom recognized group: political campaign contributors. Presidential candidates spent more than $300 million in 1988. Although federal funding covers part of a candidate's immediate costs, campaigns must raise more than half these amounts from private backers. Competition for these staggering sums of money is stiff, and the nature of this offstage maneuvering does not reward those who expand the domain of issues and policy proposals. To simplify the point, a restricted range of political ideas makes backing a candidate a safer bet for big money interests. In fact, restricting the range of ideas enables backers to hedge their bets and support both candidates.

This is, of course, a bad thing for the health of democracy but a very good thing for those who invest their money in elections....

...The pull of interests this way and that simply erodes the abilities of most candidates (at presidential and congressional levels) to express broad policy programs or to join in stable political coalitions. After deducting the silent commitments made to the numbers of financial backers required for successful campaigning, candidates are left with little in the way of credible governing ideas to offer voters.

Next, Add Marketing...

This brings us to the second major constraint on campaign discourse: the wholesale use of marketing techniques and strategies to generate campaign content. Enter marketing experts into elections in a big way. Their task is to transform a product of diminished or dubious market value into one that wins the largest market share. The result is an emphasis on communication that short-circuits logic, reason, and linguistic richness in favor of image-making techniques. This means that candidates are not sold to a broad general public but to narrow slices or "market segments" of that public. These market segments need not understand the candidates; they need only vote for them. Thus, people are induced to vote for Candidate A over Candidate B much as soap buyers may favor Brand X over Brand Y without feeling they have established a meaningful relationship with their laundry detergent in the process. This further diminishes the importance of language, logic, and reason in the articulation of campaign issues....

In a classic commentary on the new political age, a Republican strategist ushered in the election of 1980 with these words: "I don't want everyone to vote. Our leverage in the election quite candidly goes up as the voting population goes down."[17] Borrowing this page from the Republican play book, the Democrats in the 1980s went after the narrow market segment of blue collar Republicans with a vengeance. Perhaps the most blatant example involved the Dukakis campaign's avoidance of anything resembling an overt appeal to Jesse Jackson's constituency. This market analysis, even though flawed, was followed to the end: the liberal Jackson wing of the party was not viewed as essential to victory, while the Reagan Democrats were. The constraints on campaign rhetoric and issue definition were equally clear: it was feared that anything said to liberal segments of the fragile voter market would send more conservative segments into the Republican camp. As it turned out, this feared pattern of conservative defection occurred anyway, owing in part to Dukakis' withering at the charge of being a "liberal" (the dreaded L-word), and in larger part to the inability of strategically hamstrung Democrats to compete rhetorically on remaining issues like prayer, patriotism, civil rights, and abortion. Such is political life without a credible rhetorical vision.

Now, Try to Control the News Media...

In the three-factor model proposed here, the above two constraints necessarily engage a third limiting condition operating on electoral communication:

the highly controlled use of the news media. The press, like the voters, generally regards issues and ideas as the most important grounds for electoral
choice. Idea-less elections antagonize reporters searching for meaningful differences between the candidates to write home about. An aroused press can
be expected to assume an adversarial role, leaping on inconsistencies, making much of candidate slips and blunders, seizing on anything inflammatory
in the absence of much to say about policy positions. As a result, campaigns
tend to isolate their candidates from the press corps, and stick to a tightly
controlled and carefully scripted daily schedule....

It is by now well accepted that good media strategy entails three requirements: keeping the candidate away from the press; feeding the press a simple,
telegenic political line of the day; and making sure the daily news line echoes
("magnify" may be the better word) the images from campaign ads, thus blurring the distinction between commercials and "reality."[18] Candidates and their
"handlers" vary in the ability to keep the press at bay, but when they succeed,
reporters are left with little but an impoverished set of campaign slogans to
report. As ABC reporter Sam Donaldson said on an election-week news analysis program in a tone that resembled that of the coroner disclosing an autopsy
result: "When we cover the candidates, we cover their campaigns as they
outline them."[19] Thus, a willing, if unhappy, press becomes a channel for much
the same meaningless tele-rhetoric that emerges from the interplay of advertising strategy and the concessions made to campaign contributors....

One might think the press would do something bold to elevate election
news content above the intellectual level of political commercials. For example, the various news organizations could separate themselves from the pack
mentality and develop a thoughtful agenda of important issues (based, if need
be, on opinion polls) and score the candidates on how well they address these
issues. But that is not very likely. A news executive vetoed out of hand a very
modest version of this suggestion. When asked why the media did not make
more of George Bush's well-documented connections to the Iran–Contra arms
scandal and the CIA hiring of Panamanian dictator Manuel Noriega, the producer of one of the three network evening newscasts explained simply, "We
don't want to look like we're going after George Bush."[20]

Despite this reluctance to tackle candidates on the issues, it is apparently appropriate to go after them on grounds of health (Thomas Eagleton in
1972), character (Edmund Muskie, 1972), gaffes and malapropisms (Gerald
Ford, 1976), family finances (Geraldine Ferraro, 1984), extramarital sex (Gary
Hart, 1988), or hypocrisy and gall (Dan Quayle, 1988). However, the press
draws the line when it comes to pursuing issues beyond where the candidates
are willing to take them.

Never mind the resulting decline in the quality of campaign discourse
and citizen interest in politics (not to mention public faith in the press), the
media seem determined to steer a safe course of "objectivity." Elaborating
the doctrine behind Sam Donaldson's earlier words, the ABC vice president
in charge of campaign coverage in 1984 and 1988 said: "It's my job to take
the news as they choose to give it to us and then, in the amount of time that's

available, put it into the context of the day or that particular story.... The evening newscast is not supposed to be the watchdog on the Government."[21]

This self-styled impression of what the media are "supposed to be" has changed about 180 degrees from the hallowed role of the press defined by the likes of Peter Zenger and Thomas Jefferson. The new norm of press passivity enables increasingly profitable and decreasingly critical mass media to chase political candidates in dizzying circles like cats after their own tails. To wit, two-thirds of the coverage in 1988 was coverage of coverage: articles on the role of television, news about campaign strategy, and updates on voter fatigue in response to meaningless media fare. As the irrepressible French social critic Jacques Ellul said about the contemporary mass communications industry: "The media refer only to themselves."[22]

Each of these related constraints on political communication imposes a substantial limit on what candidates say to voters, creating, in turn, important limits on the quality of our most important democratic experience. Taken together, these limiting conditions go a long way toward explaining the alarming absence of meaningful choices and satisfied voters in recent elections. These restrictions on political speech also explain the mysterious elevation of tele-rhetoric to gospel standing in contemporary campaigns. With ideas safely out of the way and the press neutralized, television has little use other than as a medium for turning a seemingly endless election process into the world's longest running political commercial without programmatic interruption.

Other puzzles about the contemporary election scene also become less baffling. Take the rise of negative campaigning, for example. Because of the severe content restrictions imposed by the three limits outlined above, candidates suffer the marketing problem of appearing unattractive (i.e., negative). In this strange world, victory goes to the candidate who manages to appear the least unattractive or negative. The easiest strategy is to play up the opponent's negatives, in an effort to look less negative by comparison. (One can hardly hope to look positive in this context.) Hence, the obsession with the opponent's negatives, as emphasized in commercials and played up in news sound bites spoon-fed to the press.

All of the above—the rhetoric without vision, the telegenic sound bites, and commercialized advertising and news production—happen to play best (or, in keeping with the new spirit, less offensively) on television. In the words of a leading campaign consultant commenting on a race in California, "A political rally in California consists of three people around a television set."[23]

Considering the magnitude of these forces working against the traditional forms and contents of political communication, it is not surprising that candidates say so little these days. One marvels that they are able to say anything at all....

The Final Analysis: It's Up to the People
One can only hope that Americans will convert their anger about a failing government into action. But how can the right reforms get started? There

are signs that citizens are stirring around the land. The important question, however, is whether those stirrings will become focused on the right problems and find the right ways to address those problems. For example, there is something of a groundswell around the country to limit terms in office, and even to seek passage of a constitutional term limit amendment at the national level. However, before too much time and energy are consumed in this effort, it would be wise to reflect on whether term limits would solve *any* of the problems outlined in this book. As an angry signal to politicians, term limits may be a start, but as a full-blown substitute for more basic reforms, they are way off the mark.

Similarly, it may be a mixed blessing that a number of third-party initiatives are in the wind these days. There has been talk in recent years of a women's party, a labor party, a consumer party, a "green" party, and perhaps a coalition of such groups in a revitalized rainbow party. Such efforts are doomed to splinter and fail unless they all recognize that their respective issues must be subordinated, first, to the broader issue of campaign reform. Perhaps a reform party with a set of election reform proposals heading its platform would make a difference and win support among discouraged voters. If nothing else, a reform party would provide a focal point (and more importantly an organizational base) for the kind of sustained social movement that will have to emerge in the next decade if Americans are to have any hope of regaining control of their government.

The prospects for a social movement are reasonably good—particularly with a third party as its beacon. Indeed, American history can be viewed as a succession of social movements (the frontier movement, transcendentalism, abolitionism, populism, the progressive movement, the suffrage movement, prohibitionism, labor, civil rights, feminism, the counterculture, born-again Christianity, etc.). In this view, social movements are the noninstitutional, "hidden hand" of change in American life. The time is ripe for another one. The stakes have never been higher: all lesser issues, interests, and groups are affected by the governing crisis. Without a grass-roots movement aimed squarely at regaining popular, idea-based control of the government, democracy may well become an electronic echo in a marketing jingle or a nostalgic image of times gone by. Now is the time for electoral reform while there is still reason to govern.

Notes

1. This quote can be found in Kathleen H. Jamieson, *Eloquence in an Electronic Age: The Transformation of Political Speechmaking* (New York: Oxford University Press, 1988), p. 248.
2. See, for example, R. W. Apple, Jr., "Old Pros Appraise the '88 Campaign," *New York Times*, November 6, 1988, Sec. 1, p. 18.
3. Quoted in Michael Oreskes, "Talking Heads: Weighing Imagery in a Campaign Made for Television," *New York Times*, October 2, 1988, Sec. 4, p. 1.
4. Ibid.

5. Jeremy Gerard, "Convention Coverage: Endangered Species?" *New York Times*, July 23, 1988, Sec. 1, p. 9.

6. Ibid.

7. Michael Oreskes, "TV's Role in '88: The Medium Is the Election," *New York Times*, October 30, 1988, Sec. 1, p. 10.

8. Ibid., p. 1.

9. NBC Nightly News, March 26, 1989. See also Marvin Kalb, "TV, Election Spoiler," *New York Times*, November 28, 1988, Sec. 1, p. 19.

10. Quoted in ibid.

11. On the Democrats, see Philip Weiss, "Party Time in Atlanta," *Columbia Journalism Review* (September/October 1988) 29. On the Republicans, see "Campaign Trail," *New York Times*, October 10, 1988, Sec. 1, p. 10.

12. Lynda Barr, "The Election from Hell," 1988.

13. Editorial, *The Nation*, June 25, 1988, p. 1.

14. William Echikson, "Difference between Bush, Dukakis Lost on French," *Christian Science Monitor*, November 2, 1988, p. 10.

15. Murray Edelman, *Constructing the Political Spectacle* (Chicago: University of Chicago Press, 1988).

16. Murray Edelman, *The Symbolic Uses of Politics* (Urbana: University of Illinois Press, 1964).

17. Paul Weyrich quoted in Thomas Ferguson and Joel Rogers, "The Reagan Victory: Corporate Coalitions in the 1980 Campaign," in Ferguson and Rogers, eds., *The Hidden Election: Politics and Economics in the 1980 Presidential Campaign* (New York: Pantheon, 1981), p. 4.

18. See, for example, Mark Hertsgaard, *On Bended Knee: The Press and the Reagan Presidency* (New York: Farrar, Straus and Giroux, 1988).

19. "This Week with David Brinkley," ABC, November 6, 1988.

20. Unnamed source, cited in Mark Hertsgaard, "Electoral Journalism: Not Yellow, but Yellow-Bellied," *New York Times*, September 21, 1988, p. A15.

21. Ibid.

22. Jacques Ellul, "Preconceived Ideas about Mediated Information," in Everett M. Rogers and Francis Bolle, eds., *The Media Revolution in America and Western Europe* (Norwood, N.J.: Ablex Publishing Co., 1985), p. 107.

23. Robert Shrum, quoted in R. W. Apple, Jr., "Candidates Focus on Television Ads," *New York Times*, October 19, 1986, p. A16.

33 / The Selling of the President, 1988

Nicholas J. O'Shaughnessy

Do presidential elections provide a choice between two competent leaders offering different options on important issues facing the country? Or do they offer merely a choice between two carefully packaged "products" whose meaningful differences, if there are any, cannot be seen through the artfully designed wrapping? The latter more accurately captures the essence of the 1988 campaign, as described here by Nicholas O'Shaughnessy. With professional campaign consultants calling the shots, both candidates were packaged as products to be offered to the "consumers" that we used to call voters.

Bush the Underdog: Those Bluefish Are Dead Meat

The Bush campaign began abysmally. This was not deliberate, but it was an invaluable asset in his merchandising. It meant that core Republican supporters and contributors were galvanised out of their apathy. It meant that the public wearied of the press baiting of Bush: he attracted the sympathy of the fighting underdog, an important symbol in American myth.

The position was bleak. Opinion polls suggested that Bush had the highest negatives of any Republican since Goldwater.[1] After the Atlanta Democratic convention 50 per cent of voters claimed to be voting for Dukakis and 33 per cent for Bush.[2] Then, his vote began to rise. How Bush and his consultants achieved their turnabout will ever rank as the superlative case of political merchandising.

At the beginning of August the Bush epitaph seemed already to have been written:

> He tends to appear grim and unsmiling before the cameras, as though seized by an air of defeat.[3]

The contrast with Reagan was often noted:

> Too much of what he is saying sounds only like a rewarmed version of what came, more gloriously, before.[4]

By contrast people were talking about Dukakis showing the 'charisma of a winner'.[5] Many began to dismiss Bush. For Paul Weyrich, Bush was bound to lose because 'You can't beat something with nothing'.[6] No one knew where he stood, or what he felt strongly about. Doonesbury depicted him as an invisible bubble. The communications objective was therefore clear: to define his position with blazing clarity, and to articulate his passion. The jokes about him—a man born with a silver foot in his mouth who reminded women of their first husband and always had a white-haired woman (his mother?) at his side—were endless. His 'talent for just plain seeming silly'[7] made him a target of satire. One correspondent thus described Bushese: Bush's vernacular has created its own little world: a place called 'Tension city' where George catches 'the dickens from friends', tells ocean bluefish they're 'dead meat' and searches for the 'vision thing' while trying to avoid stepping in deep doo-doo.[8]

. . . Running through all the ridicule at this stage was an obsession with George Bush's social class:[9]

> Reagan is western boots and chopping wood to Bush's Lacoste shirts and tennis shoes . . .

[Reagan] makes all those in the lumpen electorate who also went to a mediocre college feel better. Then along comes George Bush, who is everything they're not—Greenwich, Andover, Yale, captain of the Yale baseball team, elitist clubman—and because he cannot be identified with any issues, people focus on the manners of his class.

Yet Bush was able to rise from this position of unique derision. In marketing similarity—the first basis of attraction—is often used to sell. There could be none of that here: Bush seemed to inhabit a private world that spoke its own peculiar hothouse preppie jargon. He could not be democratised. Yet commentators erred in dismissing him as too elitist for the tastes of American democracy. The President of the United States is a monarch; an elite background gives credence to this role and echoes similarly patrician figures in American history. Moreover democratic publics do not detest inherited privilege. They feel ambivalent about it. Part of ambivalence is a feeling of attraction as well as rejection. In addition, personal style is not the exclusive basis of attraction: shared values are another and perhaps a more important one. All Bush had to do was to show he shared majority values and they would be with him, however distancing his style. The pundits did not understand this distinction. Bush's consultants did.

Bush Turnaround

How was the Bush turnaround achieved? There had to be a 'new' Bush: the negative could be cosmeticised, new attributes of personality could be laid bare to counter them.

Bush had scored one notable hit early on with the Dan Rather incident: 'how would you like it if I judged your career by those seven minutes when you walked off the set in New York'. Like almost everything else in the campaign this was not spontaneous but the result of conscious packaging: a media ambush prepared by the political consultant Roger Ailes; and the beginning of a disciplined effort to change public perceptions.

The core of this effort was to emphasise shared values, with their emotive charge, as distinct from the managerial emphasis of Dukakis. Inevitably the result of such grand strategy would be that the Republican emerged as the more human candidate. Republicans chose symbolic acts to express their 'values', and emotive rhetoric; they underwrote this with a vehemently negative advertising campaign which sought to expose Dukakis as alienated from these values and by implication un-American, in that to be American is to laud such values. In the autumn campaign Bush successfully played two roles:

He can, at the same time, appear as Dirty Harry the enforcer—his Texas persona—while also coming over as Bush the wistful advocate of a kinder, gentler nation.[10]

The touchstone for the strategy was a few obscure acts by Dukakis as Governor of Massachusetts, which—paraded, inflated, decorated in savage colours—could be used to expose the 'real' (i.e. liberal) Dukakis, and damage his cultivated centrist image. The amazement of the campaign was Dukakis's failure to counterattack, and to a competitive society like the US this would be inexplicable.

Moreover any counterattack would have forced Dukakis to stress illiberalism, something he could not in conscience do, to participate in an auction as to who was the most hard right. Roger Ailes, in his usual way, expressed Republican strategy bluntly: 'That little computer heart from Massachusetts isn't going to know what hit him'.[11]

Partly the fight was at the level of speechifying rhetoric—the renowned, lush 'sound bites' that were articulated in some sort of memorable regional or social setting against a backdrop of delirious supporters. Thus Bush would speak 'at length of a problem of values in America and the need for self-discipline, courage, character, support for family and faith in God and one's self'.[12] Bush ridiculed the 'competence' unique selling proposition in his convention speech:

> a narrow ideal that makes trains run on time but doesn't know where they're going, the creed of the technocrat who makes sure the gears mesh but doesn't for a second understand the magic of the machine.[13]

He turned his reserve into an asset:

> I may sometimes be a little awkward but there's nothing self-conscious in my love of country. I am a quiet man, but I hear the quiet people others don't—the ones who raise the family, pay the taxes, meet the mortgage. I hear them and I am moved, and their concerns are mine.[14]

Now he was fighting and the door was yielding.

Complementing the rhetorical strategy was a more unbuttoned public posture: Americans are a relaxed people, primness annoys them, so to approximate their style more closely it was necessary to enact events such as when 'the would-be first couple broke out in a gushing display of "lovey-dovey" in a CBS television interview, right down to the Vice-President administering a sharp slap on Mrs Bush's derrière.'[15]

Then there was the purchased advertising. This echoed the themes of the sound bites, but it was coarser. Most outrageous of all was the Willie Horton commercial: the weekend release of this homicidal rapist, when he raped and wounded again, played on America's subterranean rage. It was a high risk strategy that worked...: legions of eerily silent prisoners were shown walking through a revolving door. This commercial hit American liberalism at its most vulnerable point: its ideologically conditioned inability to sound determined on crime, even though that is now a central choice criteria for American political consumers.

Then there was the 'Boston Harbor' commercial. Democrats have always been more believable on some of the 'quality of life' issues, particularly the environmental ones. To convict them here would seem to reduce much of their public posturing to cant and humbug. So film of noxious Boston harbour was repeatedly shown. This helped to challenge Dukakis's assumption of the moral highground: the remembrance of that image could make his sermonising tone seem merely ridiculous.

Then there were the symbolic appeals. Dukakis, on legal advice, had not assented to a bill committing teachers to the pledge of allegiance. This peripheral fact was made a Republican cause celèbre. It was ideal propaganda material. In a country as diverse as America the flag is an important unifier, an emblem of identity that commands intense emotional adherence: thus Dukakis's patriotism—and how could we have a President who was unpatriotic?—was questioned, the fact that he was only a second-generation immigrant darkly hinted. So Bush took to leading Republican audiences in pious theatrical pledges of mass allegiance, like a scandalised schoolmarm.

Bush had another, priceless, asset. He was—or could be made to seem—happy. He smiled, and seemed to relish living. To a nation that prizes its optimism this was wise. Dukakis by contrast often wore a look of accusation, and when he smiled it was more the worn, casual flash of an elevator operator than the projection of a man who has drunk richly of life, and found it fun: behind that look there seemed to lie an eternity of tiring days, of statistics studied, meetings chaired, memorandums written: of forever breathing the scentless air of bureaucratic culture.

The Retreat of Michael Dukakis

It is easy now to forget, so complete was the Republican villification of Dukakis, how strongly he once appeared. In part, this was due to the centricism of his message: never recently had a Democrat presidential candidate appeared so uninterested in ideology.

The communications objective of the Republicans was therefore to 'expose' this as a sham, to discover and merchandise the 'evidence' that really Dukakis was an unreconstructed liberal of the pattern American voters feared and had consistently rejected. The onus would be then on Dukakis to 'prove' his innocence of the charge, and thus be on the defensive.

The Dukakis strategy was vaguer: to appeal to 'competence', an appeal that is intrinsically difficult to sell since it cannot be dramatised or made glamorous. According to the Dukakis thesis, Reaganite prosperity was an illusion created by borrowing[16]: a difficult theme to communicate, since prosperity for many was a fairly tangible thing. For 'competence' to work as a sales pitch, there has to be a considerable degree of consumer dissatisfaction: they had to be convinced (a) that there was gross incompetence and (b) that such incompetence was highly dysfunctional to their group interests. On neither point was Democrat propaganda sufficiently convincing.

The story of the Dukakis career is now well known—and 'career' is the apposite word, with its implications of an ordered, managerial approach to life. Dukakis made his administration of Massachusetts the selling patter. However, there were many doubts about whether the Massachusetts experience could be replicated elsewhere. Nor was the recent history of the state reassuring: in 1988 it had a large revenue shortfall.

Dukakis, as all the world now knows, had a fundamental problem. He bored people. Stories abounded about his pedantry—how, for example, he spent a vacation studying Swedish land use.[17] They told about his stinginess, the terraced house, the bargain hunting and changing of dollars[18] 'so that he does not have to leave too big a tip'.[19] Like George Bush, then, Dukakis had a problem in communicating a rounded personality. Observers remembered Mr. Hart's words, that 'he liked people as a concept'.[20]

Clearly attractiveness as well as credibility is important in any communications process. Surely the failure of Dukakis to express this did mean something more than a lack of sympathy with the triteness of modern campaigning. Underpinning this failure, according to his political enemies, was a technician's view of life itself. Certainly modern Democrats have failed to make moral zeal exciting: the consequence of a party culture that has become privatised and introspective, that—conscious of its moral greatness—reproves others as it admires itself. It was the great achievement of Republicans in this campaign to allege such an element in Dukakis's make-up: how far different then from their hero: 'Kennedy [at least the buoyant, witty, graceful myth the public celebrates] was able to make altruism seem fun'.[21]

The major deficiency with Dukakis as a 'product' was his detachment. Americans are a passionate people. They show their emotions. They discuss them. Dukakis violated a cultural norm: in so doing he neglected the first principle of attractiveness, which is similarity. He was not 'similar' because he could not communicate outrage; Bush, dissimilar in background and style, united himself to people by affecting to share their emotions. That is why he came to be perceived as 'likeable'.

Are such criteria irrelevant? Communication skill must be the essence of the US presidency. The idea that administrative skill is an adequate substitute is erroneous: it is merely a desirable attribute, not a necessary one. The presidency is many roles—monarch, uncle, tribune of the people, high priest of national values, national totem—all of them have a common theme, the ability to project personality feelingly. Dukakis could do none of these things. He failed in the key job specification. His personality seemed to owe more to New England than sunlit vistas of Greece: his heritage more Cotton Mather than Demosthenes—or Melina Mercouri. A moralising, provincial damp seemed to have seeped into his soul: for all the world as if he would spring forth a wide white ruff and a high black hat.

This of course is merely the personality as it was projected, not necessarily as it really was, which is a very different thing. Moreover it was the personality as the Republicans wished us to see it, the overlay of their propaganda contributing mightily to the shaping of this perception. It was a perception which evolved through the campaign—that is to say, we began to receive a new interpretation of the known facts of the Dukakis personality. Originally then his frugal living seemed to signify an honest, self-disciplined character: later it seemed to suggest a ponderous dullness. His ethnicity appeared at first romantic: later just another empty political pose. By contrast, Bush made a journey in the opposite direction. This success cannot be attributed simply to the packagers. Whatever the panache of men like Roger Ailes, they must have responsive material to work with: moreover, humble material. For a consultant to successfully rework a candidate, the politician has to admit deficiency. Dukakis was just unwilling to change. Secondly, political packagers often claim that they simply allow the real man to speak, by enabling him to manage the artificial distortions of television. If they are right—and that is simply a matter of opinion—then the 'wimp' Bush was the distorted image, and 'likeable' Bush the proximate truth.

Above all else, it was the law and order issue which betrayed Dukakis. This is by tradition conservative territory: Dukakis like many Democrats chose to ignore it, or say of the causes of crime 'We all know them: the lack of jobs and opportunity'.[22] This led to the most pathetic memory of the whole campaign, Dukakis's bloodless response when asked if he would reconsider the death penalty were his own wife raped and murdered. As one observer commented, Dukakis's stance missed the fact that the law and order issue was less about keeping the streets safe, than about revenge.[23]

Then, in the words of one commentator, 'the body twitched'.[24] Dukakis Mark II was a reborn 'class war populist'.[25] Republicans were delighted. Their 'exposure' strategy had ostensibly succeeded.

Packaging for the Free Media

Image management is an operation of quite remarkable subtlety. Completely unintentional nuances can easily be conveyed, and this is where the intuitive and tactical insights of the political consultants are most needed.

In the case of Quayle it almost seems to have been a case of life imitating art: apparently as a student he concluded after watching Redford's *The Candidate* that he was better looking than Redford and with the aid of consultants would excel in politics.[26] Quayle became an instant legend for his mediocrity— his startled doe expression, his answers 'waffle—a disjointed, meaningless and unknowledgeable ramble'.[27] Still, the packagers managed to silence him.

There was another reason why image should be central in this election: for the Reagan epoch had redefined our conception of presidential leadership; melodrama was now part of the job specification:

> The candidates were auditioning for the first time for the role of replacing Ronald Reagan each evening on the news for at least the next four years.[28]

Increasingly the election seemed to have become a game between rival political consultants. Contexts, the visual setting chosen to perform in, assumed a high importance.[29]

The 'Snoopy' incident, as well as displaying the amateurism of the Democrat team, also illustrates the difficulties of 'packaging' for the free media.... The 'Snoopy' incident was described thus by Charles Bremner:

> On ABC News Sam Donaldson, the star reporter, relished the fun. 'Who is this?' Donaldson asked. 'Is it General Abrahams? Is it General Patton? No', he said, as the camera zoomed in to the Snoopy-like figure on top of the speeding tank, 'it is the governor of Massachusetts'.[30]

...By contrast, the packaging of Bush was often flawless: in the end all spontaneity was excised:

> His advisers now intend to keep him in a hermetic seal for the final three weeks. They plan not a single press conference. Every detail has been mapped out, including each day's photo-opportunity and one-line message for the voters.[31]

Such 'packaging' is currently the only way a candidate can manage. It may be too stilted for the life of a democracy: but its defenders would argue that given the piranha appetites of the American press, it is the only way to engage. Is it, as we suggest elsewhere, a necessary antidote to the adversarialism of the American press?

But even the Democrats had managed to package their convention, so strong were electorate expectations of a visually exciting political 'product' with a resounding message and contextual colour. Speeches were rehearsed by a speech consultant, with speakers on a dummy rostrum.[32] Reporters sat on the podium, delegates were relegated, 100 press assistants operated. Liberal motions were very firmly rejected.[33] Packaging—up to a point. There was a figure more difficult for merchandisers to control, Jesse Jackson. He plays a central role in this campaign, as much by his absence as by his presence. The tension between black and white was a 'hidden persuader' in the election.

Television Commercials

...Advertising on both sides during the general election interpreted the truth about the opponent flexibly, even if it did not exactly lie. Candidates, especially Bush, could remain 'nice', and the poison be carried by purchased persuasion which, being a commercial, somehow did not stigmatise the candidate who had sanctioned it. One-quarter of the electorate claimed to be influenced by the advertising, which was often repeated on the news. Moreover, there was the black propaganda, running across the campaign like a scrawl of obscene graffiti. In Illinois, pamphlets proclaimed that murderers, rapists and child molesters in Massachusetts would vote for Dukakis.[34] Maryland material referred to the 'Dukakis/Horton team'. They constructed a nightmare world which the central campaign could, of course, disown while harvesting the benefits.

Dukakis's advertising tried to avoid sounding liberal, and to humanise their man. Bland themes were picked. Thus Dukakis confided to viewers how much harder it is to be a young parent today: 'that's not a Democratic concern. That's not a Republican concern. That's a father's concern'. Dukakis's negative advertising focussed on the wrong victims, seeking to ridicule Bush's image makers, a target too esoteric for voters.

The political merit of Republican advertising, most especially on the Horton issue, was that it gave the debate flesh and bones: no longer could murder be an abstraction when perpetrators and victims were singled out. Was the tactic unethical? Massachusetts apparently was 'the only state to give weekend passes to first degree murderers facing life without parole'.[35] A cogent ethical defence can be made in that the release signified an entire corpus of attitudes to crime and punishment which many Americans reject, and that the attitudes of the future President were of central, not tangential, importance to voters. Was it, therefore, wrong of the Republicans to 'run' Willie Horton as a kind of anti-candidate? Many would say 'yes' on the grounds that the advertising constituted a covert racism—an argument the Republicans deny.

Another objective of the Bush purchased advertising was to expose Dukakis as a naive provincial. A still of Bush and Gorbachev was accompanied with the words 'This is no time to train somebody in how to meet with the Russians'.[36] Naturally, Bush's advertisers featured the martial Dukakis tank perambulation, illustrating the fast-responsive, hard hitting capacity of the purchased advertising: it added that Dukakis opposed 'virtually every defence system we developed...America can't afford that risk'.[37]

One Republican commercial was a straight lift from the Saatchi advertising for the British conservatives—the misery of life under the old regime (in this case Carter), with inflation, sneering foreigners, unemployment.[38]

Targetted advertising played a notable part in this campaign. Thus Bush's consultants dealt with the 'gender gap' by targetting specifically women voters. These advertisements repeated Bush's call for a kinder, gentler America— featuring his domesticity, cooking and petting his grandchildren—and were often shown on daytime soap operas, etc. By September the 'gender gap' had ceased to exist.[39] Jackson commercials went on exclusively black media, with anti-drug pro-Dukakis messages.[40] Dukakis was anti-gun in advertising on black radio, yet in Texas could denounce gun control in Bush's very distant past. Bush's daughter-in-law advertised to Hispanic voters.

Giving and Spending
It is significant that both the candidates who won their parties' nominations were blessed with masterful financial organisations. No Democratic candidate had been more cash laden; the reception that began the Dukakis campaign in 1987 garnered $2.2 million (three times the total for any previous Democratic event). By March 1981 the campaign chest was $20 million, twice that of any party rival: thus Dukakis was in a position to invest heavily in television advertising. There is no better illustration of the intimate connection between financial organisation and campaign success.[41]

It was estimated that a total of $400 million would be spent in the 1988 election, with the winner spending around $75 million. Television advertisements themselves could easily cost $500,000 per week for those pursuing national or major state office in the later stages of their campaigns. An individual poll surveying a state could cost $30,000 and direct mailing came at 50 cents per shot. Dukakis spent some $70 million on television commercials. Final nominees would get $46.75 million apiece from the federal government. Additionally each state had spending limits for primaries—limits which all the candidates managed to pervert in ingenious ways, such as by buying time on television channels beamed from other states.[42]

During this election season pressure group activity was as strong as ever: but conservative forces were no longer dominant. Others had learnt the same tune. The AFL-CIO purchased a $13 million advertising campaign, an exercise in image surgery for unions; and commercials of the garment workers referred to the national trade imbalance. Corporate America also strode directly into the election, with Kodak hiring political consultants to help make manufacturing industry an issue, and Drexel Burnham Lambert incorporating election images—housing, child care, factory closings—into its advertising.[43] . . .

Organisation

At the organisational level, the Dukakis campaign was amateur and, for a long time, complacent. They closed their California office in June. Their key personnel were 'high minded neophytes'.[44]

This demonstrates that the Democrats are still not up to the businesslike demands of merchandised political communication. Their party culture is still too introspective and besotted with dated individualism. By contrast, the Republicans, being more of a managerial culture, are better suited to the marketing-led, market-arbitered style of modern campaigning.

Competence versus Values

For John O'Sullivan 'attitudes and the values they express *are* the real issues, far more so than the technical economic arguments that the media affect to respect'.[45] O'Sullivan's point is fundamental to the modern presidential campaign, yet the Democrats had still not grasped it or—as the Snoopy–tank affair showed—understood it at only a superficial level. And according to the pollster Richard Wirthlin:

> You move people's votes through emotion, and the best way to give an emotional cut to your message is through talking about values. Bush has to do that. He has to touch the values of family, self-esteem, hope, opportunity, security![46]

Things we care about have meaning for us and reflect our values. We want them to be endorsed by others, particularly the powerful. . . .

Just as the consumer looks for indicators of likely future performance of a product, the electorate looks for signs that appear significant. Such signs are symbols. The Bush campaign was run on symbols—the flag, Horton, Boston Harbour, etc. If the country was in a bad state it is unlikely that this would have worked.

Dukakis put too much exclusive stress on economic and technical matters. This does not exploit emotions unless accompanied by pictures of soup kitchens, ghostly regiments of the unemployed, etc.... If a candidate can...parade the symbols of the things people cherish, the reaction is more emotional support. Bush was the leader here even though personally his own attractiveness and credibility were not high.

Why Are American Presidential Candidates So Boring?

Why are American Presidential candidates—indeed, American politicians—so boring? The question is not a trivial one: excitement, given the leadership and symbolic pseudo-monarch functions of the US Presidency, is not a frivolous thing to demand. By 'boring' I mean that a man is inarticulate, unable to express a vision, and provincial—he cannot think in the large, and his political consciousness hums with the minor concerns of the moment and the locality. This campaign saw two boring individuals emerge from a field of forgettable candidates....

American campaigns are now constructed almost exclusively for television. The average American spends three hours per night viewing, and political events must compete with other forms of entertainment. At the Democrat convention 'visibility whips'[47] roamed the hall and 'bite patrols' —baseball hatted teams of speech writers—were on hand; demonstrators were relegated to the 'protest pen', a car park. It is not surprising that politicians come to resemble the actors with whom they compete for air time, and that indeed sometimes they are actors. The American election process is now designed to 'produce professional campaigners and amateur presidents'; in the words of J. M. Burns, America has 'the worst top leadership recruitment system in the democratic societies of the world'.

Much of the harm is done by a conscious conceptualisation of American campaigning as an exercise in product marketing. It is a demand-led kind of politics in which real leadership is impossible. Consultants' invisible hand is behind almost everything we see in American politics. Senator Quayle was chosen on their advice, the ultimate exercise in identikit politics, a plastic mannequin who filled the specifications charted by market research. On the advice of their consultants American politicians struggled to be charismatic: Dukakis's laboured ethnicity, Bush's sudden predilection for chromium diners and the company of truck drivers. Consultants would be better advised to work within and not against the limits of the candidate's personality.

Finally, the veneration of market values tends to devalue the perceived worth of public service so that the best seek distinction elsewhere, in the professions and business. A country that places the commercial ethos on a pedestal will have little tolerance for the stillness and reflection and erudition that enable leadership to reach its classical forms: a Roosevelt, for example, now seems the leisured creation of a bygone age. Ultimately great leaders cannot emerge when politicians are expected simply to reflect, not direct or modify, popular will, and where truth is assumed to be what the majority of people think. In Andrew Bonar Law's words, 'I must follow them, I am their leader'.

Conclusions

On the basis of this campaign the advice for any future presidential candidate is as follows:

(1) The candidate should connect with majority values. He does not need to have been born in a log cabin: he must show, however, that he experiences common emotion with uncommon intensity. So he will play on whatever suburban anxieties happen to be uppermost, especially fear of disorder and delinquency, and he needs to project a fierce patriotism.

(2) Such concern about values should not be merely enunciated through traditional speeches, but also via symbolic appeals, which can both avoid polarising issues such as abortion, and make a notation in the elector's mind such as mere argument never can. The memorable image, significant setting or symbolic rite will therefore articulate the values the candidate has laid claim to.

(3) In general a point-scoring debating style is ill-suited to the needs of modern campaigning. But if debate means less, rhetoric means more: a kinder, gentler sound bite.

(4) Candidates must conceive the campaign in strategic marketing terms, with full integration of advertising and free media. An entirely consumerist approach is adopted, with prior market research discovering the winning themes and candidates listening reverently to their packagers.

(5) This campaign also established the importance of a sureness of touch with the free media, and therefore the need for a pedantic attention to the visual. However, the point needs qualification: the staged symbolic event can backfire.

(6) The candidate should purchase wholesale a negative strategy, especially if personally somewhat vacuous, creating fear and proposing himself as the antidote. He must press the emotive buttons, particularly anger. He will expose his opponents' key vulnerabilities, pervert them, magnify them. Underlying the overt strategy will be the covert strategy involving black propaganda. Voters will claim to deride the negativity, but they will listen.

(7) The candidate who is villified must counter-attack eloquently and even brutally. He must have every conceivable aspect of his record manicured for the agnostic light of public scrutiny. In one sense a campaign is a simulated anticipation of the political confrontations of the real world, national and international, and whatever we might mean by strength, the candidate must communicate the signals that indicate strength.

(8) In all this, the role of the consultant becomes critical. Therefore novices, academics, etc., should be jettisoned from the campaign. Candidates should only employ seasoned campaigners, those at the top of their trade.

None of this style is however any replacement for the substance of moral worth, intellectual depth and a demeanour most sublime. Stature cannot be manufactured, but will it ever return to transcend the exhaustions and triviality of the campaign trail? America's problem is the imagining that it once experienced a golden age. And indeed, from time to time in the history of the Republic giants have ascended the stage, so that their successors, tedious and grey, seem toiling lilliputians beside the past masters. Americans suffer a bereavement syndrome, the remembrance of great ones who came and, seizing their bewitched partner, took it on a grand and terrible journey.

Notes

1. *Sunday Times*, 14 August 1988.
2. *Time*, 8 August 1988.
3. *The Times*, 14 August 1988.
4. Michael Binyon, *The Times*, 9 August 1988.
5. Michael Binyon, *The Times*, 17 February 1988.
6. *Economist*, 2 July 1988.
7. *Newsweek*, 1 August 1988.
8. *Newsweek*, 22 August 1988.
9. Gail Sheely, *Sunday Times*, 14 August 1988.
10. *New York Times*, 29 September 1988.
11. *Newsweek*, 22 August 1988.
12. *The Times*, 9 August 1988.
13. *The Times*, 20 August 1988.
14. *The Times*, 29 August 1988.
15. *The Times*, 10 August 1988.
16. Charles Bremner, *The Times*, 18 October 1988.
17. *Sunday Times*, 21 February 1988.
18. Ibid.
19. *The Times*, 17 February 1988.
20. Michael White, *Guardian*, 7 November 1988.
21. Joe Klein, *Sunday Times*, 9 October 1988.
22. Joe Klein, *New York*, 24 October 1988.
23. Simon Hoggart, *Observer*, 16 October 1988.
24. David Blundy, *Sunday Telegraph*, 6 November 1988.
25. *Economist*, 29 October 1988.
26. Charles Bremner, *The Times*, 14 October 1988.
27. Christopher Thomas, *The Times*, 26 September 1988.
28. John Buckley, *New York Times*, 29 September 1988.
29. Charles Bremner, *The Times*, 18 October 1988.
30. Ibid.
31. Simon Hoggart, *Observer*, 16 October 1988.
32. *Newsweek*, 1 August 1988.
33. *Economist*, 23 July 1988.
34. *Economist*, 29 October 1988.
35. Joe Klein, *New York Times*, 24 October 1988.
36. *New York Times*, 19 October 1988.
37. Ibid.
38. *The Times*, 16 August 1988.

39. Simon Hoggart, *Observer*, 16 October 1988.
40. William Safire, *New York Times*, 13 October 1988.
41. Richard L. Berke, *New York Times*, 21 March 1988.
42. *The Times*, 17 February 1988.
43. *New York Times*, 21 May 1988.
44. Simon Hoggart, *Observer*, 16 October 1988.
45. *Sunday Telegraph*, 6 October 1988.
46. *Newsweek*, 22 August 1988.
47. *Newsweek*, 1 August 1988.

34 / The 1980s: Realignment at Last?

Nelson W. Polsby and Aaron Wildavsky

Although concluding that there has been no nationwide, classic realignment in the electorate since the 1930s, Nelson Polsby and Aaron Wildavsky do cite evidence of an "elite realignment," reflected in increased party polarization, and of deeper regional realignment in the South.

. . . In the 1950s and 1960s, the Republicans seemed doomed to a permanent minority status. Then in 1980 something happened—or so it appeared. The Republicans did so well in electing Ronald Reagan over Jimmy Carter that it was widely assumed that at long last a party realignment was about to occur.[1]

This assessment proved to be quite wrong as 1988 once again demonstrated, but it was understandable that such an idea should have arisen. After all, virtually every presidential election brings with it something anomalous, unusual, novel, and hence interesting in the way events sort themselves out. Afterward, pundits and political analysts set about patting and palpating the body politic, trying to discover what, if anything, has really changed. Usually, the correct answer is not much. The political habits of voting Americans, while subject to mood swings, are pretty stable on the whole. The same old parties—Democrats and Republicans since 1860—divide up most of the political offices. Every once in a great while, however—the 1860s, the 1890s, and the 1930s are examples—for one reason or another the very terrain shifts and recontours itself under the political parties, and we have a significant party realignment: new, more or less permanent, majorities and minorities, a new sort of ideological consensus, new participants in politics, or all three.

Partisan realignments are such intellectually stimulating events that it is no wonder that political observers are awaiting the next one with some impatience. And so, of course, are hopeful beneficiaries of the new dispensation. So it should come as no surprise even to the most casual follower of American politics that the 1980 election, like so many of its predecessors, would provoke at least a few political analysts to announce a party realignment, and that the definitive demise of the party system dominated by the New Deal coalition was finally at hand. All those doomsaying prophets who hoisted their umbrellas in vain way back during the Eisenhower years, waiting for the sky to fall on the Democrats, could at long last hear the pitter-patter of something or other just above their heads.

An elected incumbent president, for the first time since Herbert Hoover in 1932, had been defeated for a second term of office. And, even more surprisingly, the Senate, after twenty-six years, had a Republican majority. "For the first time in a generation," David Broder wrote in the *Washington Post*, "it is sensible to ask whether we might be entering a new political era—an era of Republican dominance."[2]

The sort of answer one might give to such a question is not wholly devoid of significance in the world of partisan politics. If it can plausibly be argued that a realignment has taken place, then presumably it can be claimed that the legislative program of the president is, as an attempt to fulfill an electoral mandate, the most accurate available translation into law and public policy of an authentic majority sentiment among the people at large. This programmatic mandate is something grander and more impressive than merely the entitlement to hold office: that sort of entitlement is something a president gets by winning the election, by whatever margin, in the Electoral College. The winner of a programmatic mandate, on the other hand, has a talking point of considerable weight in the continuing process of persuasion that goes on as the president interacts with the people whose cooperation he needs to accomplish his goals. Armed with a mandate, a president can speak with a stronger voice in setting the terms for the consideration of legislative alternatives. Without a secure mandate, presidents must give ground to other elected officials, to the claims of tradition, of expertise, of political expediency.

So the discussion of mandates in the 1980 election carried some political freight along with it. The beliefs of political actors about the proper interpretation of the electoral results color the ways in which they treat one another in Washington. The impressive legislative victories won by President Reagan during his first year in office suggested that more than a few politicians were convinced that the 1980 elections had indeed produced what the president's poll taker, Richard Wirthlin, labeled "a political Mount Saint Helens."[3] Steven V. Roberts of the *New York Times* located the legislative successes of President Reagan's first year in his "overwhelming electoral victory, and the outpouring of public support for his policies generated by a politically savvy White House."[4]

The evidence for the emergence of a new majority backing the president's program was, however, extremely thin. It was based on three considerations:

(1) the size of Mr. Reagan's victory, (2) the results in the Senate, and (3) the results in the House of Representatives. None of these could stand much scrutiny as a basis for believing that the 1980 election created a policy mandate.

While it is true that Governor Reagan defeated President Carter for the presidency by an overwhelming landslide in the Electoral College, 489 votes to 49, the actual numbers of voters for the two candidates—43.9 million to 35.5 million—were much closer, or, as percentages of the two-party vote, 55 percent to 45 percent. The electoral vote landslide was the third biggest in the twentieth century, but in percentage of the two-party vote ten other twentieth-century presidential elections gave their winners more impressive majorities.

In the end, 46 percent of the age-eligible population did not vote for president, a percentage of stay-at-homes larger than in any election since 1948. And there was a sizable third-party vote, constituting 4.4 percent of the age-eligible population, or 5.7 million votes. Thus, as a proportion of all age-eligible voters, 27 percent voted for Ronald Reagan for president, while 73 percent did not. This impaired President Reagan's right to govern not one whit, but it did, of course, bear significantly on the resources of popularity on which he might expect to draw.

The next ground for the belief that the 1980 election constituted a significant break with past policies was the fact that the United States Senate changed hands and brought in a Republican majority. Because Republican presidential landslides have generally failed to resonate farther down the ticket, as in 1972 and 1956, the fact that at the senatorial level the Republicans did well in 1980 takes on significance. Nine Democratic incumbents lost in the general election to Republicans, and no Republican incumbent lost to Democrats. Out of nine open seats, seven went Republican. There was a Republican gain in the Senate of twelve seats, for an overall majority of fifty-three to forty-seven seats.

Some of the defeated senators were well-known liberals: Frank Church of Idaho, Birch Bayh of Indiana, John Culver of Iowa, George McGovern of South Dakota, and Gaylord Nelson of Wisconsin were all beaten by conservative Republican members of the House running strongly conservative campaigns. This led David Broder to comment:

> The election was plainly more than a repudiation of Jimmy Carter.... [W]as there an ideological message in the 1980 vote? There sure was.... [Y]ou had to be dense to miss...a flat-out repudiation of basic economic, diplomatic, and social policies of the reigning Democratic liberalism.[5]

Yet the fact is that the change in the ideological and party balance of the Senate indicated no great surge at the level of voters. By aggregating the vote totals for thirty-three Senate seats, and excluding the vote for Democratic incumbent Russell Long of Louisiana, who ran unopposed, we discover that 3 million more votes were cast for Democratic than Republican candidates.

How can this have happened? Senatorial electorates, following state boundaries, are of greatly unequal size. On the whole, Republicans won the closely contested races, and won in some very small states . . . while Democrats won most of the senatorial landslides, notably in California. . . .

The Reagan landslide failed to overturn the Democratic majority in the House of Representatives, but it did reduce that majority by thirty-three seats, from 276 Democrats to 243 out of 435 seats. The party balance in the House reverted to the identical number—243 Democrats to 192 Republicans—as occurred after the Nixon hairbreadth 1968 victory over Hubert Humphrey, which few mistook for a realignment. That was just one Democratic seat less than was produced by the 1972 Nixon landslide against McGovern, which was also not a realignment. In the midterm elections of 1970 and 1974, the Democrats picked up twelve and forty-seven seats, respectively. In the 1976 presidential election, the old New Deal coalition elected Jimmy Carter president and 292 Democrats to the House. As Robert Axelrod's research showed:

> For the Democrats, the New Deal Coalition made a comeback in 1976. For the first time since the Johnson landslide of 1964, the Democrats got a majority of the votes from each of the six diverse majorities which make up their traditional coalition: the poor, blacks, union families, Catholics, southerners, and city dwellers.[6]

In the context of the previous few elections, what the House electoral results of 1980 showed was a set of outcomes well within normal expectations, not anything remotely approaching a realignment.

We have so far considered evidence favoring the proposition that the 1980 election was the occasion of a fundamental party realignment in which President Reagan received a programmatic mandate. We must conclude that this evidence is weak if not contradictory to that argument.

If ever there were presidential election results that looked like they conferred a mandate, 1984 should have been the year. President Reagan's 525 electoral votes (lacking only those of Walter Mondale's home state of Minnesota and the District of Columbia) constitute a modern record. More votes were cast for him than for any other candidate in history. Outside of New England, the upper Midwest and the upper Far West, Reagan received more than 57 percent of the vote everywhere with large sections giving him over 62 percent. Why, then do we still doubt there was anything like a mandate?

To be effective, a presidential mandate must carry over to Congress. In 1984, the Democrats won the close Senate races. Consequently, Democrats gained two seats. Whatever claim the president might have laid to a new mandate was challenged by the power of incumbency—among the 15 senators running for reelection, eight received over 70 percent of the vote, four got over 60 percent and only three (two Republicans and one Democrat) were defeated by tiny margins.[7] Not only did they hold their own in the Senate in 1984, the Democrats gained control of the Senate in 1986. In 1984 the House results followed the usual pattern in connection with huge Republican presidential majorities: Republicans gained only fourteen seats, not nearly enough for a majority. . . . Not much to carry out a mandate here.

It is not change, in fact, but continuity that is the main story of the 1984 elections for the House of Representatives as it was for the Senate. Among the 254 Democrats running for reelection, 240 won, a 94.4 percent success rate. The Republican success rate was an astounding 98.1 percent (151 out of 154). . . .

Despite his lower vote in 1980, there was more reason for Reagan to make a claim to a mandate in that year than in 1984. Although voters differed with Reagan on social issues, from ERA to abortion, they did want more spent on defense, less spent on welfare, and lower taxes. And that, in Reagan's first term, is more or less what they got. But by 1984, voters had turned moderate on these matters, wishing neither a return to the pre-1980 situation, nor to go as far as the president.[8] The lesson here is twofold: first, an American presidential election is ordinarily limited to a choice among candidates, and is not an issue referendum; second, in thinking about candidate and issue preferences, voters may decide they want a candidate even if they do not wish to endorse his policies.

Since 1937 or thereabouts, public opinion polls have been asking voters about their party affiliations. The long-term stability of the responses has been notable. There seems to be no room for doubt that over the four-and-a-half-decade period for which such figures exist, persons claiming identification with the Democrats have outnumbered Republicans in the general population, and, until recently, by large numbers. This would surprise nobody who has been attentive to election results over this same stretch of years. Only twice in the entire generation since Franklin Roosevelt's first election in 1932—after the elections of 1946 and 1952—have the Republicans controlled both houses of Congress. When landslides have favored Democrats—for example, in 1934, 1936, 1958, 1964, and 1974—massive Democratic majorities have resulted in Congress, and shock waves have been felt farther down on the ticket, for example, in state assemblies. After the 1980 elections, however, looking at the system from the bottom up, the Republicans got no such advantage. Although Republicans gained some seats, the Democrats were still comfortably ahead, with 4,497 state legislative seats, compared with 2,918 for the Republicans. And Democrats controlled sixty-three state chambers, compared with thirty-four controlled by Republicans.

At the beginning of 1984 there were 7,363 state legislators of whom 4,624, or 63 percent, were Democrats. Newspaper reports said that the Republicans gained around 300 legislative seats in the elections of 1984. So, 4,324 out of 7,363 means the Democrats held 59 percent of the seats after the Republican landslide. Or, to quote the outgoing Republican governor of Delaware, Pierre du Pont, "Of the 6,243 state legislative seats contested in 1984, Republicans lost 58 percent of them."[9] After the election the Republicans controlled thirty-two out of ninety-eight legislative chambers, or one-third. Before Reagan's 1984 landslide, there were thirty-five Democratic governors, fifteen Republican governors. After the landslide, there were thirty-four Democratic governors, sixteen Republican governors. Over the thirty-two years from Dwight D. Eisenhower's first election until 1984, 7,392 congressional elections were held, and the Democrats won 4,372 of them, or 59 percent. Over the same period, 587 senatorial elections took place. There have been 331 Democratic winners, or 56.4 percent.[10]

The election of 1984, far from constituting a sharp break with the past, actually followed a rather stable pattern that has been more or less well established over the last fifty years. During these last five decades we have had fourteen presidential elections. Ten of them—two-thirds—have been part of what we could call a "landslide sequence.". . . In the first election in the sequence a candidate is elected president. The second time around he wins a resounding personal triumph, in an enormous landslide. This happened to Roosevelt in 1936, to Eisenhower in 1956, to Johnson, standing in for Kennedy, in 1964, to Nixon in 1972, and to Reagan in 1984. Seen in this context, 1984 does not seem so unusual.

The pattern of Democratic benefit further down the ticket from landslides is also well established.[11] It is a little hard to see this in 1936, because Roosevelt came into the election with sixty-nine Democrats out of ninety-six Senators, and 333 Democrats out of 435 House members. This was the result of the 1934 election, the only midterm election in the twentieth century when the president's party gained seats. Even so, in 1936 the Democrats bumped up against the ceiling of possibility, winning eleven more House seats and six more Senate seats to go with Roosevelt's advantage of 515 electoral votes and 24 percent of the popular vote. In 1964, Johnson's margin over Barry Goldwater was 23 percent of the popular vote and 434 of the electoral votes. Democrats picked up two Senate and thirty-seven House seats. This is what Democratic landslide sequences look like: When the presidential candidate does well, the party does well.

Republican sequences follow a different pattern. Eisenhower's great popular victory in 1956 gave him a net advantage of 384 electoral votes and a 15 percent popular vote margin over Adlai Stevenson. There were no net gains for Republicans in the Senate and a net loss of two Republican seats in the House. In 1972 Nixon's margin was 503 electoral votes and 23 percent of the popular vote, yet Republicans picked up only seven seats in the House and Democrats gained two Senate seats.

Reagan's 1984 victory was like that: an 18 percent margin in the popular vote, and 512 in electoral votes, and yet the Democrats gained two Senate seats and suffered a net loss of only fourteen seats in the House. In 1980, when Reagan's personal margin was only 10 percent, the Republicans picked up twelve seats in the Senate (mostly by very small margins) and thirty-three House seats. But there was no realignment, nor even much of a mandate, as we all discovered at the 1982 midterm election when the Democrats bounced back with a net gain of twenty-six House seats.

Nobody viewed the 1988 election as a realigning election. Although it is extremely unusual for a vice president directly to succeed a president of his own party, the rest of the 1988 election results fell well within normal expectations. It is worth reciting the 1988 numbers: Bush led Dukakis by eight points in the popular vote, 53 percent to 46 percent. He had a winning margin of 315 electoral votes. Yet there was no change at all in the Senate and the Democrats actually picked up two House seats. . . . [A]n eerie silence descended on the Democrats a year before the 1992 contest.[12]

Split Results

How is it possible to maintain a political system in which Republicans do extremely well in presidential elections and Democrats do extremely well otherwise? Such a phenomenon is clearly impossible in a system lacking a separation of powers, giving voters no chance to make the disparate choices that add up to this peculiar pattern of results. But the separation of powers, long ballots, and a large array of electoral choices all exist in the American political system. And Americans take advantage of the opportunity to diversify their political portfolios. . . . But the fact that a formal opportunity exists for voters to split their tickets does not require them to do so. . . .

. . . If people are becoming more Republican, why does this show up decisively only in the voting for president? Is there any reason why grass-roots realignments should start at the top of the ticket? Perhaps there is a reason: the great visibility of the presidential race as compared with other races on the ballot. But if this is how a modern realignment works, it works through a mechanism that focuses on candidates, not parties, and helps Republican presidential candidates, not Republicans generally. The weight of evidence seems to be against the proposition that realignment has gone further than the presidency, except in the South. There we can see ample evidence of realignment as northern migrants have combined with native converts to greatly strengthen the Republican party. . . . [I]n a thirty-year period, the number of Republicans representing the old Confederacy in Congress has risen steeply. All this has been at the expense of conservative Democrats; the prospects of liberals in the Democratic parties of the South are at worst unchanged.[13] . . .

Other Partisan Changes

It is not only the evidence of the 1980s, but the far stronger evidence of trends since 1972, that enables us to conclude that there has been a considerable internal reshuffling of activists within the Democratic and Republican parties. This process has unfolded slowly. It constitutes a meaningful change, even though it is not the classic realignment of voters that definitively changes the parties so that the majority becomes the minority and vice versa. Instead we observe a deepening and intensification of preexisting positions— Democrats becoming more liberal and Republicans more conservative, and an increase in the coverage of these positions over a much wider range of issues, from defense spending to foreign policy to ecology to various matters concerning social behavior. Thus there has been a polarization of the major party activists consisting in part of the conversion of southern conservative Democrats to the Republican party and of some liberal Republicans to the Democratic party.[14]

Party identifiers in the general public have either become a little more Republican or not changed very much, leaving the Democratic party with a clear but diminished advantage. Among party identifiers there is evidence of ideological consistency. Thus the opinions of identifiers cohere in the same directions as their respective party activists, though not as strongly. Identifiers are of course more interested in politics and public policy than the general public. Being loyal as well, identifiers are more likely to learn what stands they ought to take from their respective party activists and leaders. As party elites become more consistent in their views, therefore, party identifiers follow suit. And those who are at odds with their party—say, Democrats who favored war against Iraq or prayer in schools or Republicans who opposed the Strategic Defense Initiative or are permissive with respect to abortion—can expect to suffer more discomfort than in the past when party positions were fuzzier. As liberal comes more unequivocally to mean Democratic and conservative to mean Republican, people who identify with a given party for historical or habitual or traditional or other reasons unrelated to ideology will become more uncomfortable.

Yet the views of the public at large appear largely unchanged over the last decade or two. There is little evidence of anything except small movements in issue positions. Self-identifications as liberal or conservative have remained stable with conservatives consistently outnumbering liberals and a large number identifying as centrist or moderate. Nevertheless, when votes in the 1980s are related to voters' self-identifications and issue positions, the more conservative supported Republican candidates for president and the more liberal went for Democrats.[15] Whether these particular candidates generated an ideological response among voters or whether voters already felt that way is an open question.

If there has been a growth of both liberal and conservative ideology, then we can expect increased polarization among the major parties and heightened levels of conflict over public policy. If party activists and, to a much lesser extent, identifiers are becoming more polarized, but voters are not, the question must arise of whether there is room for a third party whose issue positions would be closer to those of the citizenry.

James Q. Wilson says: "The central change that has occurred in American party politics in the last twenty years has been the realignment of party elites."[16] Wilson notes that a sitting Democratic president, Jimmy Carter, was challenged for renomination in 1980 by a more liberal challenger, Senator Edward M. Kennedy, and an incumbent Republican president, Gerald Ford, was challenged in 1976 by a more conservative rival, Ronald Reagan. In 1956 Democratic delegates were close in issue positions to Democratic voters, while from 1972 on delegates of both major parties were fairly far from their party's voters. Twice as many Democratic delegates as rank-and-file Democrats called themselves liberal in 1980 according to a CBS News/*New York Times* poll, whereas in 1984 according to a *Los Angeles Times* survey that number had increased to four times. And where a third more Republican delegates than rank-and-file Republicans called themselves conservative in 1980, half did the same in 1984. These sharp liberal-conservative differences, Wilson maintains, ... show up in congressional votes, House and Senate, across a spectrum of issues. Democratic and Republican politicians are internally cohesive and differ substantially from each other.[17]

Wilson thinks that elite realignment may have made mass realignment—"a sharp enduring change in the coalitions supporting each party" —less likely. As party elites grow further from party voters, and from the general public, he reasons, they are less likely to select generally appealing candidates. Candidates who appeal to party leaders are less likely to appeal to voters.

Party polarization is not just a statistical artifact; it is observed by voters. Whereas from 1952 to 1976, 46 to 52 percent of the electorate saw important differences between the major parties, 58 percent did so in 1980 and 63 percent in 1984. "This greater public perception of philosophical differences between the parties," Martin Wattenberg suggests, "may well be one of the most long-lasting changes in the political system from the Reagan era."[18] We think that the Reagan era saw the continuing liberalization of the Democratic party as well as the growing conservatism of Republicans.

On the other hand, Wattenberg argues that candidate-centered nomination processes mean that party identification will come to mean less to most voters. He shows that while voters perceive more differences between the parties than formerly, they are also less likely to believe that one or the other party would do a better job on specific issues they find important. Thus party polarization may be less important than the declining relevance of party to voters. . . .

Notes

1. This analysis of the 1980 election draws extensively on Nelson W. Polsby, "Party Realignment in the 1980 Election," *The Yale Review* 72 (Autumn 1982), pp. 43–54.
2. David S. Broder, "Is It a New Era?" *Washington Post* (November 19, 1980).
3. David S. Broder, "Election '80 Called 'Blip,'" *Washington Post* (September 5, 1981).
4. Polsby, "Party Realignment in the 1980 Election," p. 42.
5. Broder, "Is It a New Era?"
6. Robert Axelrod, "Communication," *American Political Science Review* 72 (June 1978), p. 622.
7. Norman Ornstein, "The Election for Congress," in Austin Ranney, ed., *The American Elections of 1984* (Durham: Duke University Press, 1985), p. 268.
8. J. Merrill Shanks and Warren E. Miller, "Policy Direction and Performance Evaluation: Complementary Explanations of the Reagan Elections" (Paper delivered at the Annual Meeting of the American Political Science Association, New Orleans, August 29–September 1, 1985).
9. Pierre S. du Pont IV, "The GOP Isn't Doing Well Enough," *The Washington Post National Weekly Edition* (November 26, 1984), p. 24. See Iver Peterson, "Republicans Gain in State Legislatures," *New York Times* (November 11, 1984).
10. Commentators observe that in recent years Democratic state legislatures have rigged the boundaries of congressional districts so that small Democratic electoral majorities produce bumper crops of Democratic congressional seats.

Democrats have enjoyed an advantage in recent years in the conversion of votes to seats. In the Senate an opposite result, greatly favoring Republicans, prevails. Even so, over the thirty-year period, Democrats have dominated elections for both houses by almost exactly the same margin. See John T. Pothier, "The Partisan Bias in the Senate Elections," *American Politics Quarterly* 12 (January 1984), pp. 89–100. Norman J. Ornstein, in "Genesis of a Gerrymander, " *Wall Street Journal* (May 7, 1985), argues that turnout is characteristically lower in Democratic-held districts; consequently the charge that the Democratic majority in Congress is the result of a gerrymander is, in all probability, spurious.

11. This point is also made by Stanley Kelley, Jr., in *Interpreting Elections* (Princeton, 1983).
12. Rhodes Cook, "History a Tough Opponent for Democrats in 1992," *Congressional Quarterly Weekly Report* (April 14, 1990), pp. 1146–1151.
13. For evidence, see Nelson W. Polsby, *Consequences of Party Reform* (New York, 1983), pp. 110–113.
14. The most complete set of published data bearing out these observations is "Is It Realignment? Surveying the Evidence," *Public Opinion* 8 (October/November 1985), pp. 21–31.
15. Shanks and Miller, "Policy Direction and Performance Evaluation: Complementary Explanations of the Reagan Elections." See also Miller and Shanks, "Policy Directions and Presidential Leadership: Alternative Interpretations of the 1980 Presidential Election," *British Journal of Political Science* 12 (July 1982), pp. 299–356.
17. James Q. Wilson, "Realignment at the Top, Dealignment at the Bottom," in Ranney, Austin, ed., *The American Elections of 1984* (Durham: Duke University Press, 1985) "By an elite realignment, I mean a change in the identity and views of those persons who play important roles in the selection of the candidates, the writing of the platforms, the definition of the rules, and in conducting the affairs of each party." p. 300. See also John S. Jackson, III, David Bositis, and Denise Baer, "Political Party Leaders and the Mass Public: 1980-1984" (paper presented at the Annual Meeting of the Midwest Political Science Association, Chicago, April 19, 1987), who also argue that Democratic and Republican elites have become more polarized.
17. Wilson, "Realignment at the Top, Dealignment at the Bottom," pp. 301–302.
18. Martin P. Wattenberg, "The Hollow Realignment: Partisan Change in a Candidate-Centered Era," *Public Opinion Quarterly* 51 (1987), p. 61.

35 / Black Politics and Presidential Elections

Lenneal J. Henderson, Jr.

The importance of "the black vote" was demonstrated in the 1930s by a massive shift of black voting support from the Republican Party to the Democrats during the Great Depression. Since that time, as Lenneal Henderson documents in this reading, black support has been pivotal in a number of Democratic victories. Whether the black vote will be critical in a particular election, though, depends on the presence of three key conditions.

Both symbolically and substantively, American presidential elections are essential opportunities for black voters to exert national political influence. Black political activity, particularly since the civil rights and black power movements, is manifested most intensely in neighborhood, rural, municipal, and metropolitan politics. Sharp increases in the election of black state legislators and black Lieutenant Governors in Colorado, California, and Virginia within the last 10 years signal an emerging state-centered black politics. Presidential elections, however, provide blacks with a series of opportunities to:

1. influence party politics at the state level in presidential primaries
2. become party delegates and broker with fellow delegates in supporting presidential candidates for the party nomination most supportive of black policy preferences
3. express, pursue, and construct planks in the party platform prior to and during party national conventions in a presidential election year
4. influence national policy issues connected to the presidential campaigns of candidates they support or oppose
5. become party officials, including candidates or prospective candidates for the presidential or vice-presidential nomination
6. play major negotiating and brokering roles in both the campaign strategies of presidential candidates in the general election and in the formulation and projection of issues associated with those campaigns
7. influence U.S. senate and congressional elections associated with presidential elections
8. participate in the formulation and expression of political philosophy and ideology both within and outside mainstream party politics[1]

Taken together, these opportunities represent a range of political options blacks may pursue during a presidential election. What they actually pursue may be considered *a distribution of political choice*. For example, the highlight of the 1984 presidential election for blacks was not the landslide victory of President Ronald Reagan over former Vice-President Walter Mondale, but the ascendancy of Jesse L. Jackson as a serious contender for the Democratic party presidential nomination. Although Channing Phillips and Shirley Chisholm had been among the first blacks to receive some support for their presidential aspirations, Jesse Jackson was the first to seriously challenge other prominent aspirants for the Democratic party nomination.

The Jackson candidacy represented the exercise of an option in the politics of presidential elections never before seriously pursued by blacks. Moreover, the exercise of that option brought new meaning to the exercise of most other political options by blacks. In 1976, black voters were integral to Jimmy Carter's primary as well as general-election victories. In the general election, blacks gave Carter 90 percent of their vote. Assertions and hypotheses about "the pivotal role" of the black voter were frequently heard.[2] Conversely, Ronald Reagan could have triumphed in both the Republican primaries and the general election of 1980 without the black vote. In 1984, the ever-increasing black vote showed widespread dissatisfaction of blacks with the policies of President Reagan. This dissatisfaction, along with the well-publicized elections of black mayors in Philadelphia and Chicago, encouraged Jesse Jackson to become a candidate for the Democratic nomination for President. Jackson surprised and startled many who gave his candidacy little chance. He demonstrated that the black vote could be combined with other political ingredients to pose a serious presidential challenge in the Democratic primary.

In spite of Ronald Reagan's landslide victory in 1984, the Jackson candidacy demonstrates the significance of black presidential voting to the *political self-image* and *confidence* of blacks. The symbolic and substantive association of black voters with the Democratic party encourages blacks when Democrats win and discourages blacks when Democrats lose. But the Jackson candidacy projected new possibilities for black political action during a presidential election year that potentially transcend even the Democratic and Republican party polemics. These possibilities include increased brokering by prominent black presidential aspirants within political parties and the opportunity for a serious third party candidacy, lead by a charismatic black leader, to *influence public policy. Jesse Jackson demonstrated this point during his bid for the presidency* through his help in securing the release of Lieutenant Robert Goodman from Syria and through his policy proposals for Central America, Cuba, and South Africa.

Thus, the varying fates of black voters in the 1976, 1980, and 1984 presidential elections illustrate the agony and the ecstasy of black voting in presidential elections in both *the black political context* and in America as a whole....

The black presidential vote assumes a fourfold significance. First, many political leaders and analysts consider it *a barometer of political participation and influence,* particularly in national politics. Second, as a largely cohesive bloc vote, *it may be pivotal in close presidential elections.* Third, it represents *a symbolic and substantive expression of black values and preferences* through interest-group articulation and mobilization. And fourth, it is *an instrument of political brokering and bargaining by black leaders* seeking to advance black economic, political, and policy goals through the presidency.[3]

Black Presidential Voting and Concepts of Political Participation

Historically, the key issue in the participation of blacks in presidential elections was the acquisition and maintenance of the right to vote. The concept of political participation thus revolved around the vote....

Once blacks secured the right to vote through the Fifteenth Amendment [ratified in 1870], electoral as well as nonelectoral modes of participation in presidential elections became important. These modes included party registration and participation, participation as delegates to party conventions, party officeholding, and election or appointment to public office. Each of these kinds of participation became particularly critical during presidential election campaigns.

For instance, black party affiliation has switched from predominantly Republican from 1866 to 1934 to predominantly Democratic from 1934 to the present. This switch in party affiliation is particularly manifest in presidential elections. Levy and Kramer argue:

> Until 1934 the black vote in the U.S. was decidedly Republican. Those blacks who voted did so for the G.O.P. with the same singlemindedness as Southern whites went for the Democrats, and for precisely the same reason—the Civil War. The G.O.P. was the party of Lincoln and with the exception of his successor, Andrew Johnson, who vetoed a bill providing for black suffrage in the District of Columbia (Congress overrode the veto), the Republicans, perhaps by design, perhaps not, aided the black advance with popular executive orders and selective federal appointments during the succeeding 20 years.[4]

Paradoxically, the budding black influence in presidential campaigns was all but destroyed by a Republican presidential candidate. Rutherford B. Hayes promised to return control of the politics of race to the southern states in the presidential campaign of 1876 if the South promised him their vote. Both Hayes and the white South were victorious....

By 1934 the economic devastation of the Great Depression, black urbanization, and President Franklin Roosevelt's New Deal combined to turn the majority of the black vote to the Democratic party. This dramatic transition to the Democratic party underscored the increasing importance of the black presidential vote. When the 1942 off-year elections suggested that some black voters were returning to the GOP, some white and black Republican leaders predicted the Republicans would substantially reclaim many black votes in the 1944 presidential election. Two prominent black organizations, the Chicago Citizen's Committee of 1,000 and the National Negro Council, joined with the Republicans in opposing Roosevelt for a fourth term. But the 1944 general election only demonstrated the strength and resiliency of black support for Roosevelt. Blacks provided a key margin of victory for Roosevelt in Pennsylvania, Maryland, Michigan, Missouri, New York, Illinois, and New Jersey. These seven states contributed 168 electoral votes to Roosevelt's victory.[5]

Nevertheless, southern states and southern black voters were not pivotal in presidential elections prior to 1944. Seven months prior to the 1944 presidential election, the U.S. Supreme Court, in the case of *Smith v. Allwright*[6] declared the white primary unconstitutional, stimulating black voter registration. But not until the massive civil rights and voter registration efforts of the 1950s would the southern black vote become a factor in presidential elections. The focus was primarily on the black voter in large cities in the Midwest and North. Voting registration figures generated by the U.S. Commission on Civil Rights indicate that late in the 1950s, black voter registration in the South began to rise significantly....

In 1948, black support for President Harry Truman contributed to his victories in the key states of Ohio, Illinois, and California, accounting for 68 percent of his 115 electoral vote margin. Truman's Executive Orders 9980 and 9981, establishing a Fair Employment Board within the Civil Service Commission and outlawing segregation in the nation's armed forces, proved enormously popular with black voters.[7] There can be no doubt that black voters participated in the presidential contest with a keen rational self-interest and some political acumen.

Nevertheless, in the 1952 and 1956 presidential elections, some blacks defected to the Republican party candidate, Dwight Eisenhower. Also, a number of blacks perceived Democratic party candidate Adlai Stevenson's pursuit of an illusory black-southern Democratic coalition as a political setback. According to a Gallup poll in January 1957, black voting for Republican candidates rose 18 percentage points from 1952, when only 20 percent of the black vote went to Eisenhower. The poll also indicated that "of all the major groups of the nation's population, the one that shifted most to the Eisenhower-Nixon ticket last November was the Negro voter."[8] The southern black vote seemed particularly important to this trend....

What is also important about the slowly emerging influence of the black southern vote is its underlying nonelectoral participatory base. The Montgomery bus boycott of 1955, the desegregation crisis at Little Rock in 1957, the North Carolina Agricultural and Technical sit-ins of 1960, and other civil rights actions began to infiltrate themselves into the major issues that characterized the 1960 presidential election. Black voters in the North and South began to use events in the South as a method of evaluating prospective Democratic and Republican presidential candidates. Thus, although most civil rights actions in the South were aimed at influencing racial norms and mores, laws, and customs, they also influenced politicians and political systems. As will be discussed later in this chapter, black southern votes would be critical to presidential hopefuls in 1960, 1968, and 1976.

Testing the Pivotal Black Vote Thesis

The focus on voting as the key political resource in the acquisition and maintenance of black civil rights was dramatically illustrated in the 1960 presidential election. John F. Kennedy symbolized a youthful political genesis more sensitive to black goals and aspirations. Black votes substantially contributed to his 110,000-vote margin over Republican Richard M. Nixon. This pivotal role of the black vote in the 1960 presidential election elated civil rights leaders and notified political strategists that black votes were no longer of minor significance.

The 1964 and 1968 presidential elections seemed to argue *against* the pivotal black vote thesis. Although more than 90 percent of the black vote went to Democrat Lyndon Johnson, how critical were these votes to Johnson's victory margin of 434 electoral votes and 61.6 percent of the popular vote? In Louisiana, Mississippi, Alabama, Georgia, and South Carolina, electoral votes went to Republican Barry Goldwater in spite of civil rights activity and the emerging black southern vote. Although it is possible that the visibility of black politics in these states triggered the Goldwater vote, it is clear that the national and southern black vote were minor factors submerged in the Johnson landslide in 1964.[9]

The 1968 presidential election was a more distinctive and complex test for the pivotal black vote thesis. Both the 1964 Civil Rights Act and the 1965 Voting Rights Act were expected to combine with continued black voter registration to increase the strategic significance of the black vote in both the presidential primaries and the general election. Ghetto unrest, the emerging black power movement,[10] the Poor People's Campaign, and other civil rights actions maintained race as a controversial national issue. Moreover, several prominent hopefuls in the Democratic primary intensified interest in the campaign. Edmund Muskie, Hubert Humphrey, and Robert Kennedy all seemed viable presidential nominees at the Democratic convention. All seemed sensitive to civil rights and black needs.

Key circumstances, however, deprived black voters of the opportunity to become electoral arbiters in the 1968 presidential election. First, George Wallace's defection from the Democratic party and his show of political strength as the nominee of the American Independent party seriously weakened the regular Democratic party coalition, which included blacks. Wallace's candidacy was an antidote to emerging black voter strength. He symbolized reaction to increasing black political power. His 46 electoral votes and 9 million popular votes were captured in Arkansas, Louisiana, Mississippi, Alabama, and Georgia—states targeted by civil rights advocates.

Also, the assassination of Robert F. Kennedy during the Democratic primary eliminated the most popular black presidential choice and pitted civil rights against the Vietnam war as the principal issues in the general election. Black voters supported Robert Kennedy more than any other Democratic or Republican presidential hopeful. . . . His association with his brother John F. Kennedy, with civil rights advocacy, and with the liberal wing of the Democratic party made him attractive to many black leaders. His opposition to the Vietnam war distinguished him from Vice-President Hubert Humphrey. Had he become the Democratic party nominee, the Vietnam war would have been less a stigma than it became for Humphrey. Given the saliency of the war and the divisiveness of the Wallace campaign, blacks and civil rights could hardly have elected a President in 1968.

The 1972 presidential election was the antithesis of the 1964 election for the black vote. In spite of the visible role of black party leaders in George McGovern's nomination and the fact that almost 90 percent of the black vote went to McGovern, black voters could not reverse his landslide loss by 503 electoral votes and Nixon's capture of 60.7 percent of the popular vote. Black voters were as submerged in McGovern's loss in 1972 as they were in Johnson's victory in 1964.[11]

The role of the black vote in the 1976 presidential election revived and reinforced the pivotal black vote thesis. According to the Joint Center for Political Studies, the black vote proved to be the margin of Jimmy Carter's narrow 1976 victory in 13 states: Alabama, Florida, Louisiana, Maryland, Mississippi, Missouri, New York, North Carolina, Ohio, Pennsylvania, South Carolina, Texas, and Wisconsin. . . .[12] The Joint Center monitored election results from 1,165 predominantly black sample areas in 23 states. Their analysis is based upon careful manipulation of data from these sample areas.

Three elements seemed critical in the 1976 black presidential vote. The full impact of the 1965 Voting Rights Act, renewed in 1970 and 1975, seemed to be felt. . . . What is most critical to underscore is the substantial increase in black voter registration in Georgia, President Carter's home state. Black support for Carter in Georgia and Carter's "Georgiacentric" black politics can be largely attributed to this substantial increase in black voter registration in Georgia, as well as the visible and sophisticated black political infrastructure in the state.

In contrast to the 1960, 1964, 1968, and 1972 elections, black southern voters were indispensable to a winning presidential candidate in 1976. Cromwell points out that "with heavy support from black voters, Carter carried every southern state of the old confederacy except Virginia where President Ford won with a 23,906 vote margin. Without this massive black support, many political observers have noted, Carter would have lost his native South. A majority of whites voted for President Ford."[13]

What is somewhat paradoxical about the pivotal role black voters played in Carter's election is that they did so without as much influence in the Democratic party convention as they enjoyed in 1972 and with less overt support for Carter than either McGovern enjoyed in 1972 or Humphrey had in 1968. Once Carter captured the Democratic nomination, black politicians found themselves selling an unknown to black voters. This was particularly difficult because Carter often seemed ambiguous and elusive on major election issues, particularly those of concern to blacks.[14] This may suggest that party participation is less positively correlated with election outcomes than is commonly believed. Campaign issues, the characteristics of presidential contestants, televised debates between presidential candidates, and other variables may be more causal in presidential elections than are party participation variables.[15]

Thus, *external political events* and *internal black political organization* combined to make the 1976 black presidential vote pivotal. The lingering shadow of Watergate certainly favored Jimmy Carter. Ford's association with Richard Nixon reinforced Carter's anti-Washington-establishment image. Black voter mobilization, particularly through Operation Big Vote, stressed not only the necessity of a high black voter turnout but also the need to vote for more ethical and accountable elected officials.

The cumulative impact of internal black political organization began to be felt during the 1976 campaign. The Civil Rights Acts of 1960 and 1964, the Voting Rights Act of 1965, party reforms—particularly those preceding the 1972 Democratic National Convention—and coalitions of black political organizations bolstered the surge of black voters. Moreover, the sharp increase in the number, distribution, and visibility of black elected officials stationed elective leadership in many black communities during the 1976 presidential election. This increase in black elected officials, from little more than 600 in 1962 to 4,503 in 1978, symbolized both the need for and the result of more conscientious black voting behavior.

Despite this temporary rise in the influence of black presidential voting, blacks had yet to realize their full political potential in presidential elections. Of the 15.6 million blacks eligible to vote in 1976, only 9.2 million registered to vote and only 5.7 million (64.1 percent) actually voted. Thus just over one-third of the eligible black voting population actually voted in 1976. Although black voting has increased sharply over past trends, many black adults remain to be registered, and many have yet to vote.[16]

Thus, although the black vote has been numerically pivotal in the 1960 and 1976 presidential elections, whether it will continue to be pivotal is related to the following factors: (1) whether it is the margin of victory in a precinct, county, city, or state needed by a candidate to capture the popular and electoral vote; (2) whether the election is close enough to require a decisive bloc vote; (3) whether blacks contributed to the issues that were decisive in the election; (4) whether black primary votes in individual states and the aggregate primary vote secured the nomination for a candidate; and (5) whether blacks coalesced with other interest groups to contribute to the margin of victory for a candidate.

Ronald Reagan's election severely tests the pivotal black vote thesis. Reagan's victory margin was the second largest (behind that of Richard Nixon in 1972) attained by any Republican presidential candidate in the 20th century. Reagan acquired 43,267,462 popular votes, 489 electoral votes, and 51 percent of the popular vote, despite the 7 percent of the popular vote captured by Independent party candidate John Anderson.[17] Carter obtained 34,968,548 popular votes, only 49 electoral votes, and 41 percent of the popular vote. Approximately 16,967,000 blacks were eligible to vote in the 1980 presidential election, or 10.8 percent of the total voting-age population in America. According to the Joint Center for Political Studies, 61.3 percent of the eligible black votes actually voted, *2 percent more than turned out in the 1976 race.* Only 7 million, or 40 percent of the total black voting-age population, actually voted. The key element in the Joint Center's analysis is the relationship of Reagan's strongest regional support to the strongest regional black voting turnout.... Reagan's strongest electoral and ideological support came from the West and the South. Turnout by black registered voters, however, was highest in the Northeast (67 percent) and lowest in the South (60 percent). And although black voter turnout was relatively high in the West (64.1 percent), a much smaller percentage of black voters exists in the West than in the South or Northeast.[18]

What is particularly interesting is the comparison between black and Hispanic support for Carter. More than 80 percent of the black vote went to President Carter. But according to the *New York Times,* only 54 percent of the Hispanic vote went to Carter. More than 36 percent of the Hispanic vote went to Reagan. What this suggests is the weakening of the black-Hispanic coalition support for Democratic presidential candidates coupled with relatively weak black support for Reagan in strong Reagan regions. It is also evident that the southwestern and western configuration of the Hispanic population appeared to be influenced by strong Reagan support in those regions.

In brief, a number of preconditions for pivotal status eluded the black vote in 1980. There were few precincts, counties, cities, or states in which the black vote could have been the margin of victory for Reagan or Carter. National election results were not nearly close enough to make any racial or ethnic bloc vote decisive. Blacks were an unspoken but significant issue in national support for Reagan. Since only 2.7 percent of the Republican party delegates were black, black support in the Republican primaries was insignificant. And black coalitions with Hispanics, labor unions, Jews, and others were considerably weaker than in previous presidential elections.

The 1984 presidential election provided still another variant on the pivotal black vote thesis. Jesse L. Jackson's emergence as a contender for the Democratic party nomination suggested that *blacks are as pivotal to the nomination of the Democratic presidential and vice-presidential team as they are to influencing presidential general election outcomes.* Jackson won more than 400 delegates in the primaries and figured prominently in the selection of Walter Mondale's vice-presidential running mate, Geraldine Ferraro. However, some analysts argue that the Democratic party ignored the Jackson surge and that Jackson's influence peaked at the convention. If this is so, evidence for a pivotal black vote becomes even more difficult to identify.

Summary
...It is important to reiterate that black southern votes are growing in political influence in presidential elections. Unable to overcome racist third-party mobilization or the incursion of conservative Republicans into the South for

decades, black southern voters gave Jimmy Carter decisive support in southern states in 1976. Still, Reagan victories in these states in 1980 reminded black voters of the mobilization yet to be done and the limits of even maximum black voter mobilization.

Although the role of the black vote in 1976 illustrates how pivotal black presidential voting can become, the Reagan elections illustrate that the black vote is only pivotal when elections are close, when black votes help presidential candidates win key states, and when blacks forge effective coalitions with other groups whose support is indispensable to the presidential candidate....

Notes

1. See, for example, Michael B. Preston, "The 1984 Presidential Primary Campaign: Who Voted for Jesse Jackson and Why." University of Illinois, Institute of Government, November 1985; Ronald E. Brown, "Group-based Determinants of Campaign Participation in the 1984 Presidential Election." University of Michigan, Institute of Survey Research, 1985; Robert C. Smith and Joseph R. McCormick, "The Challenge of a Black Presidential Candidacy." *New Directions* 11, no. 2 (April 1984): 38–43; and Thomas E. Cavanagh, *Inside Black America: The Message of the Black Vote in the 1984 Elections* (Washington, D.C.: The Joint Center for Political Studies, 1985).

2. See Lucius Barker and Jesse McCorry, *Blacks in the American Political System* (New York: Winthrop, 1980).

3. Scholarly literature on blacks and presidential elections is surprisingly scarce. Among the key works are Henry Lee Moon, "The Negro Vote in the Presidential Election of 1956," *Journal of Negro Education* 26, no. 3 (Summer 1957): 219; Hanes Walton, Jr., *Black Republicans: The Politics of the Black and Tans* (Metuchen, N. J.: Scarecrow Press, 1975); Milton Morris, *The Politics of Black America* (New York: Harper and Row, 1975), chaps. 8 and 9; Hanes Walton, Jr., *Black Politics: A Theoretical and Structural Analysis* (Philadelphia: Lippincott, 1972), chap. 5; Eddie Williams and Milton D. Morris, *The Black Vote in a Presidential Election Year* (Washington, D.C.: Joint Center for Political Studies, February 1981); see also Ronald W. Walters, "Black Presidential Politics in 1980: Bargaining or Begging?" *Black Scholar* 11, no. 4 (March/April 1980): 22–31.

4. Mark R. Levy and Michael S. Kramer, *The Ethnic Factors: How America's Minorities Decide Election* (New York: Simon and Schuster, 1972), 38.

5. Henry Lee Moon, *Balance of Power: The Negro Vote* (Garden City, N.Y.: Doubleday, 1948).

6. *Smith v. Allwright*, 321 U.S. 649 (1943).

7. Ruth Morgan, *The President and Civil Rights* (New York: St. Martin's Press, 1970).

8. Quoted in Moon, "The Negro Vote in the Presidential Election of 1956," 219.

9. *Presidential Elections Since 1789* (Washington, D.C.: Congressional Quarterly Service, 1975).

10. Stokely Carmichael and Charles V. Hamilton, *Black Power: The Politics of Liberation in America* (New York: Vintage Books, 1967).

11. James A. Michener, *The Presidential Lottery* (New York: Random House, 1969).

12. *The Black Vote: Election '76* (Washington, D.C.: Joint Center for Political Studies, 1977); and Oliver Cromwell, "Black Impact on the 1976 Elections," *Focus*, November 1976, 4.

13. Cromwell, "Black Impact on the 1976 Elections," 5.

14. Lenneal J. Henderson, "Black Politics and the Carter Administration: The Politics of Backlash Pragmatism," *Journal of Afro-American Issues* 5, no. 3 (Summer 1977): 245.
15. A good discussion of sex and race differences in political participation may be found in Susan Welch and Philip Secret, "Sex, Race and Political Participation," *Western Political Quarterly* 34, no. 1 (March 1981): 3.
16. *The Black Vote: Election '76*, 31.
17. Anderson, a Republican, captured 5,588,014 votes as an independent candidate. He received only 1.49 percent of the black vote.
18. Williams and Morris, *Black Vote*, 229.

36 / Proposals for Reforming the Electoral College

Stephen J. Wayne

With some doubting the ability of "the people" to make a wise choice, and some seeing legislative selection as damaging to "separation of powers," the framers decided upon the electoral college as the means by which a small group of wise citizens, chosen by their states, would select a president for the country.* Although its actual role in the selection process has changed greatly, the electoral college remains part of the process today.

Throughout its history, the electoral college has been the object of proposals for reform. The most severe, and to many people the most logical, would eliminate the electoral college altogether, and replace it with direct election of the president. In the following reading, Stephen Wayne considers the direct election proposal and four other proposals. Each has notable advantages and disadvantages. But short of public outcry, the author concludes, Congress is unlikely to adopt any of these proposals.

. . . [The electoral college] has been criticized as undemocratic, as unrepresentative of minority views within states, and as potentially unreflective of the of the nation's popular choice. Over the years, there have been numerous proposals to alter it. The first was introduced in Congress in 1797. Since then, there have been more than five hundred others.

In urging changes, critics have pointed to the electoral college's archaic design, its electoral biases, and the undemocratic results it can produce. . . . In recent years, four major plans—automatic, proportional, district, and direct election—have been proposed as constitutional amendments to alleviate

---

*If no candidate receives a majority of electoral college votes, the selection of the president is to be made by the House of Representatives.—*Editor's Note*.

some or all of these problems. The following sections will examine these proposals and the impact they could have on the way in which the president
is selected.

The Automatic Plan

The actual electors in the electoral college have been an anachronism since
the development of the party system. Their role as partisan agents is not and
has not been consistent with their exercising an independent judgment in
choosing a president. In fact, sixteen states plus the District of Columbia prohibit such a judgment by requiring electors to cast their ballots for the winner of the state's popular vote. Although probably unenforceable because they
seem to clash with the Constitution, these laws strongly indicate how electors should vote.

The so-called automatic plan would do away with the danger that electors may exercise their personal preferences. First proposed in 1826, it has
received substantial support since that time, including the backing of
Presidents John Kennedy and Lyndon Johnson. The plan simply keeps the
electoral college intact but eliminates the electors. Electoral votes are
automatically credited to the candidate who has received the most popular
votes within the state.

Other than removing the potential problem of faithless or unpledged
electors, the plan would do little to change the system. It has not been enacted
because Congress has not felt the problem to be of sufficient magnitude to
justify a constitutional amendment. There have in fact been only eight faithless
electors, who failed to vote for their party's nominees—six since 1948.[1] Additionally, one Democratic West Virginia elector in 1988 reversed the order of
the nominees, voting for Lloyd Bentsen for president and Michael Dukakis
for vice-president.

The Proportional Plan

Electing the entire slate of presidential electors has also been the focus of considerable attention. If the winner of the state's popular vote takes all the electoral votes, the impact of the majority party is increased within that state
and the larger, more competitive states, where voters are more evenly divided, are benefited.

From the perspective of the minority party or parties within the state,
this winner-take-all system is not desirable. In effect, it disenfranchises people who do not vote for the winning candidate. And it does more than that:
it discourages a strong campaign effort by a party that has little chance of
winning the presidential election in that state. Naturally the success of other
candidates of that party is affected as well. The winner-take-all system also
works to reduce voter turnout.

One way to rectify this problem would be to have proportional voting.
Such a plan has been introduced on a number of occasions. Under a proportional system, the electors would be abolished, the winner-take-all principle would be eliminated, and a state's electoral vote would be divided in

proportion to the popular vote the candidates received within the state. A majority of electoral votes would still be required for election. If no candidate obtained a majority in the electoral college, most proportional plans call for a joint session of Congress to choose the president from among the top two or three candidates.

The proportional proposal would have a number of major consequences. It would decrease the influence of the most competitive states and increase the importance of the least competitive ones, where voters are likely to be more homogeneous. Under such a system, the *size* of the victory would count. To take a dramatic example, if the electoral votes of Vermont and New York in 1960 had been calculated on the basis of the proportional vote for the major candidates within the states, Richard Nixon would have received a larger margin from Vermont's 3 votes (1.759 to 1.240) than John Kennedy would have gotten from New York's 45 (22.7 to 22.3). Similarly, in 1968, George Wallace's margin over Nixon and Hubert Humphrey in Mississippi, which had 7 electoral votes, would have been larger than Humphrey's over Nixon in New York, which had 43.

While the proportional system rewards large victories in relatively homogeneous states, it also seems to encourage competition within those states. Having the electoral vote proportional to the popular vote provides an incentive to the minority party to mount a more vigorous campaign and establish a more effective organization. However, it might also cause third parties to do the same, thereby weakening the two-party system.

The proportional plan contains a pattern of biases far different from the one found in the electoral college.... [T]he electoral college benefits the very smallest and, to a greater extent, the very largest states. Within the larger and more competitive states, the system favors geographically concentrated groups with cohesive voting patterns. A proportional system, however, would advantage smaller, homogeneous states, disadvantage larger, heterogeneous ones, and would not benefit geographically concentrated groups nearly as much as the current system does.[2]

Finally, operating under a proportional plan would in all likelihood make the electoral college vote much closer, thereby reducing the president's claim to broad public backing for him, his new administration, and the policy proposals he has advocated during his campaign. George Bush would have defeated Michael Dukakis by only 43.1 electoral votes in 1988, Jimmy Carter would have defeated Gerald Ford by only 11.7 in 1976, and Richard Nixon would have won by only 6.1 in 1968. (See Table [1].)

In at least one recent instance, a proportional electoral vote in the states might have changed the election results. Had this plan been in effect in 1960, Richard Nixon would probably have defeated John Kennedy by 266.1 to 265.6. However, it is difficult to calculate the 1960 vote precisely because the names of the Democratic presidential and vice-presidential candidates were not on the ballot in Alabama and because an unpledged slate of electors was chosen in Mississippi.

Table 1   Voting for President, 1952–1988:
                    Five Methods for Aggregating the Votes

Year	Electoral College	Proportional Plan	District Plan	Direct Election (percentage of total vote)
1952				
Eisenhower	442	288.5	375	55.1%
Stevenson	89	239.8	156	44.4
Others	0	2.7	0	.5
1956				
Eisenhower	457	296.7	411	57.4
Stevenson	73	227.2	120	42.0
Others	0	7.1	0	.6
1960				
Nixon	219	266.1	278	49.5
Kennedy	303	265.6	245	49.8
Others	0	5.3	0	.7
1964				
Goldwater	52	213.6	72	38.5
Johnson	486	320.0	466	61.0
Others	0	3.9	0	.5
1968				
Nixon	301	231.5	289	43.2
Humphrey	191	225.4	192	42.7
Wallace	46	78.8	57	13.5
Others	0	2.3	0	.6
1972				
Nixon	520	330.3	474	60.7
McGovern	17	197.5	64	37.5
Others	1	10.0	0	1.8
1976				
Ford	240	258.0	269	48.0
Carter	297	269.7	269	50.1
Others	1	10.2	0	1.9
1980				
Reagan	489	272.9	396	50.7
Carter	49	220.9	142	41.0
Anderson	0	35.3	0	6.6
Others	0	8.9	0	1.7
1984				
Reagan	525	317.6	468	58.8
Mondale	13	216.6	70	40.6
Others	0	3.8	0	.7
1988				
Bush	426	287.8	379	53.4
Dukakis	111	244.7	159	45.6
Others	1	5.5	0	1.0

Source: Figures on Proportional and District Vote for 1952–1980 were supplied to the author by Joseph B. Gorman of the Congressional Service, Library of Congress. Calculations for 1984 and 1988 were completed by Mark Drozdowski and Erik Pages, respectively, on the basis of data reported in the Almanac of American Politics (Washington, D. C.: National Journal, 1985 and 1989).

The District Plan

The district electoral system is another proposal aimed at reducing the effect of winner-take-all voting. While this plan has had several variations, its basic thrust would be to keep the electoral college but to change the manner in which the electoral votes within the state are determined. Instead of selecting the entire slate on the basis of the statewide vote for president, only two electoral votes would be decided in this manner. The remaining votes would be allocated on the basis of the popular vote within individual districts (probably congressional districts). A majority of the electoral votes would still be necessary for election. If the vote in the electoral college were not decisive, then most district plans call for a joint session of Congress to make the final selection.

For the very smallest states, those with three electoral votes, all three electors would have to be chosen by the state as a whole. For others, however, the combination of district and at-large selection would probably result in a split electoral vote. On a national level, this change would make the electoral college more reflective of the partisan division of the newly elected Congress rather than of the popular division of the national electorate.

The losers under such an arrangement would be the large, competitive states and, most particularly, the organized, geographically concentrated groups within those states. The winners would include small states. Third and minority parties might also be aided to the extent that they were capable of winning specific legislative districts. It is difficult to project whether Republicans or Democrats would benefit more from such an arrangement, since much would depend on how the legislative districts within the states were apportioned. If the 1960 presidential vote were aggregated on the basis of one electoral vote to the popular vote winner of each congressional district and two to the popular vote winner of each state, Nixon would have defeated Kennedy 278 to 245 with 14 unpledged electors. In 1976 the district system would have produced a tie, with Carter and Ford each receiving 269 votes. (See Table [1]) In 1988, Bush would have defeated Dukakis, 379 to 159. The states of Maine and Nebraska are the only ones that presently choose their electors in this manner.

The Direct Election Plan

Of all the plans to alter or replace the electoral college, the direct popular vote has received the most attention and support. Designed to eliminate the college entirely and count the votes on a nationwide basis, it would elect the popular vote winner provided the winning candidate received a certain percentage of the total vote. In most plans, 40 percent of the total vote would be necessary. In some, 50 percent would be required.[3] In the event that no one got the required percentage, a runoff between the top two candidates would be held to determine the winner.[4]

A direct popular vote would, of course, remedy a major problem of the present system—the possibility of electing a nonplurality president. It would better equalize voting power both among and within the states. The large, competitive states would lose some of their electoral clout by the elimination of the winner-take-all system. Party competition within the states and perhaps even nationwide would be increased. Turnout should also improve. Every vote would count in a direct election.

However, a direct election might also encourage minor parties, which would weaken the two-party system. The possibility of denying a major party candidate 40 percent of the popular vote might be sufficient to entice a proliferation of candidates and produce a series of bargains and deals in which support was traded for favors with a new administration. Moreover, if the federal character of the system were changed, it is possible that the plurality winner might not be geographically representative of the entire country. A very large sectional vote might elect a candidate who trailed in other areas of the country. This result would upset the representational balance that has been achieved between the president's and Congress's electoral constituencies.

The organized groups that are geographically concentrated in the large industrial states would have their votes diluted by a direct election. Take Jewish voters, for example. Highly supportive of the Democratic party since World War II, Jews constitute approximately 3 percent of the total population but 14 percent in New York, the state with the second largest number of electoral votes. Thus the impact of the New York Jewish vote is magnified under the present electoral college arrangement.[5]

The Republican party has also been reluctant to lend its support to direct election. Republicans perceive that they benefit from the current arrangement, which provides more safe Republican states than Democratic ones. While Republican Benjamin Harrison was the last nonplurality president to be elected, Gerald Ford came remarkably close in 1976. On the other hand, Richard Nixon's electoral college victory in 1968 could conceivably have been upset by a stronger Wallace campaign in the southern border states.

A very close popular vote could also cause problems with a direct election. The winner might not be evident for days, even months. Voter fraud could have national consequences. Under such circumstances, large-scale challenges by the losing candidate would be more likely.

The provision for the situation in which no one received the required percentage of the popular vote has its drawbacks as well. A runoff election would extend the length of the campaign and add to its cost. Considering that some aspirants begin their quest for the presidency many years before the election, a further protraction of the process might unduly tax the patience of the voters and produce an even greater numbing effect than currently exists. Moreover, it would also cut an already short transition period for a newly elected president and would further drain the time and energy of an incumbent seeking reelection.

There is still another difficulty with a contingency election. It could reverse the order in which the candidates originally finished. This result might undermine the ability of the eventual winner to govern successfully. It might also encourage spoiler candidacies. Third parties and independents seeking the presidency could exercise considerable power in the event of a close contest between the major parties. Imagine Wallace's influence in 1968 in a runoff between Humphrey and Nixon.

Nonetheless, the direct election plan is supported by public opinion and has been ritualistically praised by contemporary presidents. Gallup Polls conducted over the last three decades have consistently found the public favoring a direct election over the present electoral system by substantial margins.[6] Carter and Ford have both urged the abolition of the electoral college and its replacement by a popular vote.

In 1969 the House of Representatives actually voted for a constitutional amendment to establish direct election for president and vice-president, but the Senate refused to go along. Despite this support, it seems unlikely that sufficient impetus for such a change that requires a constitutional amendment will occur until the issue becomes salient to more people. It may take the election of a nonplurality president or some other electoral crisis to produce the public outcry and political momentum needed to change the electoral college system.

The difficulty of generating change speaks to the resiliency of the electoral college system and perhaps also to its perceived success in choosing the president. Despite the complaints that are ritualistically voiced during the election period that the candidates are no good, that there is very little difference between them, and that the campaigns are mean, superficial, and irrelevant, the electorate has not demanded that its congressional representatives change the system beyond extending suffrage to all citizens. Similarly, the reforms in finance laws and party rules have been designed to achieve the democratic goals of encouraging more people to support the candidates and to participate in their campaigns. The electoral system may not be perfect, but it has functioned with public support for over 200 years, a significant achievement in itself. This achievement is cited by those who oppose changing it on the grounds that "if it ain't broke, it don't need fixing."

Summary
... [T]he equity of the electoral college has ... been challenged, but none of the proposals to alter or abolish it, except by the direct election of the president, has received much public support. With no outcry for change, Congress has been reluctant to alter the system by amending the Constitution and seems unlikely to do so until an electoral crisis or unpopular result forces its hand.

Does the electoral process work? Yes. Can it be improved? Of course. Will it be changed? Probably, but if the past is any indication, there is no guarantee that the changes will produce only, or even, the desired effect. If politics is the art of the possible, then success is achieved by those who can adjust most quickly to the change and turn it to their advantage.

Notes

1. There is some controversy whether three other electors in 1796 might also have gone against their party when voting for president. They supported John Adams although they were selected in states controlled by the Democratic-Republicans. However, the fluidity of the party system in those days, combined with the weakness of party identification, makes their affiliation (if any) difficult to establish.

2. Lawrence D. Longley and James D. Dana, Jr., "New Empirical Estimates of the Biases of the Electoral College for the 1980s," *Western Political Quarterly* 33 (1984): 172–73.

3. Abraham Lincoln was the only plurality president who failed to attain the 40 percent figure. He received 39.82 percent, although he probably would have received more had his name been on the ballot in nine southern states.

4. Other direct election proposals have recommended that a joint session of Congress decide the winner. The runoff provision was contained in the resolution that passed the House of Representatives in 1969. A direct election plan with a runoff provision failed to win the two-thirds Senate vote required to initiate a constitutional amendment in 1979.

5. John Kennedy carried New York by approximately 384,000 votes. He received a plurality of more than 800,000 from precincts that were primarily Jewish. Similarly, in Illinois, a state he carried by less than 9,000, Kennedy had a plurality of 55,000 from the so-called Jewish precincts. Mark R. Levy and Michael S. Kramer, *The Ethnic Factor* (New York: Simon and Schuster, 1972), p. 104.

6. A 1980 Gallup Poll found 67 percent favoring direct election over the present system, with only 19 percent opposed and the rest undecided. In Gallup surveys dating back to 1966, similar majorities have supported direct election and the elimination of the electoral college. George H. Gallup. *The Gallup Poll* (Wilmington, Del.: Scholarly Resources, 1981), pp. 258–260.

CHAPTER NINE

Nominating Presidential Candidates

Every four years, come November, American voters go to their polling places to choose among candidates for president. Though many names may appear on the ballot, for most voters the real choices normally boil down to two, the Democratic and Republican candidates. How did those two names end up on the general election ballot? How were they chosen from among the many Democrats and Republicans who wanted the honor? The answer today, of course, is that these two individuals were the winners in a game that began many months before the general election, and which involved running separate expensive and exhausting campaigns in numerous caucus and primary states, all to secure enough delegates' votes to be declared the party's sole presidential nominee at its national convention. The history of the development of this system is an interesting one, from the framer's preference for non-partisan elections, to the selection of the first parties' nominees by congressional caucuses and others by state parties, to the centrality of a national nominating convention whose delegates were often selected by means other than democratic, to what we have today.

For those concerned that the nominating system should be "open," the changes must be considered a success; a process once dominated by a small number of the "party elite" now involves literally millions of citizens! But is the new system an improvement on other dimensions? Gone may be the visions of deals cut in smoke-filled rooms, but in their place are images from long and often nasty nominating seasons. For all of the faults of previous systems, the new one seems designed to highlight a party's divisions rather than its commonalities. And whether inherent in the design or not, the new nominating battleground seems littered with victims of unfounded accusation and character assassination, often over matters of little relevance to presidential leadership.

If presidential campaigns today emphasize symbols over issues, image over reality, and character over effectiveness, then many observers suggest that the nominating process is a major factor. In this chapter, Elaine Kamarck assesses the changed role of nominating conventions and their delegates in the primary-dominated system, and Wayne Shannon evaluates the new nominating system more generally from a "governance" perspective.

37 / Structure as Strategy: Presidential Nominating Politics in the Post-Reform Era

Elaine Ciulla Kamarck

If one of the intentions of reformers of the nominating process was to make it less private and more "public," then according to Elaine Ciulla Kamarck's analysis, at least that objective has been reached. The change has affected not only the strategies of would-be nominees, but also the very nature of the parties' national conventions. The conventions, says Kamarck, have lost their original functions, and it is doubtful whether they can hold onto their new ones.

Imagine for a moment that Franklin Delano Roosevelt, Dwight D. Eisenhower, and John F. Kennedy were to join us once again. Furthermore, imagine that they found themselves in the middle of a political strategy session for a presidential campaign. Strategy for the general election would be quite familiar to them. It would revolve around winning the majority of electoral votes. Each state would be categorized as safe for one party or the other, as a lost cause, or as a possible battleground. Candidates and their surrogates would move around the country giving speeches and holding rallies in an attempt to win the crucial battleground states. Much about the general election would be different, of course, but the underlying strategy for accumulating a majority of electoral votes would be very much the same as it had been in their day.

Suppose, however, that our three returned presidents were to find themselves in the midst of a strategy session for the Democratic or Republican nomination. The goal would be the same as it had been for them—to accumulate enough delegates to win the nod at their party's nominating convention. Beyond that, however, the similarities would end, for the strategy for achieving that goal is very different today from what it was in their time.

Imagine Franklin Roosevelt's bewilderment at the use of the term *momentum.* In his day this term was used to describe activity in the convention hall; now it refers to the boost in attention that a candidate gets from primaries and caucuses that take place months before the convention even opens. Imagine Eisenhower's surprise upon hearing that Senator Howard Baker (R-TN) had given up both his job as majority leader of the Senate and his Senate seat *four years* before the presidential election in order to run for president full time. Ike spent the years before the 1952 Republican Convention in Europe with NATO, arriving home in June to campaign for his nomination in July. Imagine Kennedy's puzzlement over the decision made by Walter Mondale, a former Democratic vice-president and favorite of the Democratic party establishment, to enter every single presidential primary. In his day a candidate avoided presidential primaries unless, like Kennedy, he was young, untested, and eager to prove himself to the party establishment.

What our three returned presidents would soon realize is that the strategies for winning the nomination have changed dramatically as the result of underlying changes in the structure of the nominating system. Until the early 1970s, winning the nomination of a major political party was essentially an inside game. Presidential candidates worked at winning the allegiances of the major party leaders, who controlled the minor party leaders, who in turn became delegates to the nominating convention. Presidential primaries were sometimes important, especially if a candidate had to demonstrate vote-getting ability; but to do that he had to keep favorite sons out and draw other national candidates in, a task that was often very difficult. More often than not, the public portion of the nomination campaign—presidential primaries—was not very important to the eventual outcome.

What was important was the semi-public search for delegates—a search that was difficult to observe and often downright mysterious even to careful observers of the process. The nomination system prior to 1972 was, to use Nelson Polsby's term, "a mixed system" (Polsby, 1983:185). The first stage was public and took place in a few contested presidential primaries. The second stage was semi-public at best and involved intense negotiations between serious national candidates and powerful party leaders. James Reston described this stage as follows: "This presidential election is being fought on several levels. The most important of these, so far as nominating candidates is concerned, is the least obvious. . . the underground battle for delegates" (*New York Times*, June 24, 1968, p. 1). Usually the "underground" battle for delegates was fought in the proverbial smoke-filled rooms. Another political reporter, W. H. Lawrence, described the 1960 nomination race as follows: "With the end of the contested presidential primaries, the struggle for the nomination has moved from Main Street to the backrooms of individual party leaders and state conventions dense with the smoke of cheap cigars" (*New York Times*, June 8, 1960, p. 6E).

This process, of courting powerful and not so powerful party leaders in search of a convention majority, was hard to observe and impossible to quantify until the convention itself assembled and started to vote. Thus the race for the nomination used to be very visible during the weeks leading up to and including the convention. More recently, however, the race for the nomination is visible at least a year before the nominating convention and is usually over well before the convention itself ever convenes.

The Post-Reform Nomination System

The presidential nomination system that exists today is the result of two reform movements that occurred at approximately the same time in American politics. Between 1968 and 1972 the Democratic party adopted a series of changes in the process by which delegates to its nominating conventions were chosen. This movement began as a reaction to the contentious 1968 Democratic convention; newcomers opposed to the Vietnam war felt that the party establishment had unfairly thwarted their attempts at participating in the nominating process (Polsby, 1983). At the time, few people (including party professionals) anticipated how profoundly these changes would affect the way that Democrats *and* Republicans elected delegates (Shafer, 1983). Even though the Republican party did not undergo anything even remotely like the reform movement in the Democratic party, so many Democratically dominated state legislatures had to change their laws to comply with the new dictates of the Democratic National Committee that the state Republican parties, more often than not, were inadvertently reformed as well.

The other reform movement began in 1971 with passage of the Federal Election Campaign Act. This law was amended in 1974 as part of the post-Watergate reforms designed to decrease the influence of money in politics, and again in 1979 when it became clear that the law was having unintended negative effects on party activity. The campaign finance reform laws affected both political parties and, like the reforms in delegate selection, had far-reaching implications for the conduct of presidential elections, particularly primary elections.

The effect of these two reform movements was to transform the nomination system into a totally public system where activity at every step of the process could be observed and quantified. In the post-reform system, the search for delegates was conducted in public primaries or caucuses (which became the "functional equivalent" of highly visible primaries), and the search for money took place under the new election law. By limiting the amount of money that any one individual could contribute to a candidate, the new law transformed the quest for money from a quiet search for a few "fat cats" to a public search for thousands of small- and medium-sized contributions. Changes of this magnitude in the underlying structure of the nomination process eventually affected the strategies of presidential hopefuls seeking their party's nomination, but before we can understand these strategies we must understand the structure of the new nominating system.

Primaries and Their "Functional Equivalents"   In the pre-reform era fewer than half of the convention delegates were elected in primaries contested by the major national candidates. In the post-reform era, however, nearly all delegates are elected as the result of contested primaries. A famous quote by former Vice-President Hubert Humphrey sums up the attitude of many presidential hopefuls in the pre-reform era: "[A]ny man who goes into a primary isn't fit to be President. You have to be crazy to go into a primary. A primary now, is worse than the torture of the rack" (quoted in Polsby, 1983:14, and originally, in White, 1961:104).

No one who has watched candidates undergo the grueling process of the modern post-reform nomination process would be surprised to hear Walter Mondale, George Bush, or Michael Dukakis express these sentiments. But for these modern candidates, skipping the primaries is akin to skipping the whole ball game.

The Democratic reformers who made up part of the famous McGovern-Fraser Commission did not set out to increase the number of presidential primaries, but just such an increase was the most immediate and dramatic result of the new rules they had proposed for delegate selection to the 1972 convention.[1] In 1968 there were sixteen states that held some form of presidential primary; in 1972, twenty-three states; in 1976, thirty states; in 1980, thirty-five states; in 1984, thirty states; and in 1988, thirty-four states.

Most observers of the nomination process focus solely on the increase in the number of primaries that followed in the wake of the reform movement—but the increase in *number* is not nearly so important as the change in the *nature* of these primaries. The reform rules' requirement that delegates from a state "fairly reflect the division of preferences expressed by those who participate in the presidential nominating process in each state" greatly increased the importance of each primary by linking a presidential candidate's performance in the primary to the number of delegates that he could get from the state (Democratic National Committee, 1972:12).

. . . During the former period, primaries did not always dictate which presidential candidate the delegates from that state should support; in other words, if presidential candidates decided to put their names on the ballot (and they more often did not), they could win the primary and not necessarily get any delegates from that state because the primaries were nonbinding (i.e., advisory). In 1952 Senator Estes Kefauver won the most primaries and yet Governor Adlai Stevenson, who did not enter even one, got the nomination. In 1968, too, Vice-President Hubert Humphrey won the nomination without entering a single primary.

In the modern era, however, if a presidential candidate wants delegates who will vote for him at the convention, he must run in all the primaries that are held. Not only did the number of presidential preference polls increase, but the vast majority became binding on the selection of delegates. By 1980 more than half of all states had a binding presidential preference poll on their ballot.

The reason there were so few presidential preference polls in the pre-reform era is that most presidential primaries were held for the sole purpose of electing delegates to the national convention and these delegates were often not identified as to their presidential preference. Ordinary voters who were not knowledgeable about the politics of the local party members running as delegates had no way of knowing how the people they were voting for were going to vote at the convention. But as the number of primaries with binding presidential preference polls increased, two things happened: The practice of electing delegates directly on the ballot became less popular . . . , and the practice of allowing delegates to run unidentified by their presidential preference disappeared.

Thus the linkage between presidential primaries and delegate selection is far more important in shaping the structure of the post-reform nominating system than the simple increase in the number of primaries. The results of the presidential primary may or may not tell us who will be attending the nominating convention as a delegate (in many states the actual delegates are elected after the primary), but it *will* tell us exactly how many delegates each presidential candidate on the ballot will get. Hence presidential candidates must now either compete in every primary or risk having no delegates. Indeed, as the primaries have become more important to delegate selection, more and more presidential candidates have begun to compete in them....

When delegates to national conventions are not elected in primaries, they are elected in caucus systems. In a caucus system, people meet at the local level and elect representatives to the next level—usually the county level. At the county level, the people elected locally meet and elect representatives to the state convention. The state convention then meets to select those who will attend the presidential nominating convention.

Traditionally, many state parties have held conventions to elect delegates to the presidential nominating convention. These conventions used to be closed; that is, only individuals who already held party office could participate in the selection of delegates. But the party reform movement turned these systems of delegate selection into smaller versions of presidential primaries.[2]

Three new requirements—that party meetings having to do with delegate selection be open to anyone who wished to be known as a Democrat; that every participant in the process as well as every candidate for delegate declare his or her presidential preference; and that all first-tier caucuses (i.e., those at the precinct level) be held on the same day—effectively abolished the party caucus and began the process of turning the caucus system itself into the "functional equivalent of a primary."[3]

In the pre-reform era, many party meetings were not open to the public; they were attended by previously elected party officials such as precinct captains or county chairmen. Opening up local meetings to all who called themselves Democrats meant that the local party leaders could often be overruled by newcomers drawn into the party out of enthusiasm for a particular presidential candidate. That's what happened in caucus after caucus in 1972, when the old-time party regulars were beaten by supporters of George McGovern—that is, by young people who were drawn into the party by virtue of McGovern's opposition to the Vietnam War. In 1984 Walter Mondale spent more than $500,000 organizing the state of Maine and won the endorsement of every major Democratic politician in the state. But Senator Gary Hart, riding the momentum of his surprise victory over Mondale in New Hampshire, won the Maine caucuses handily as a brand new group of Democrats turned out to support him. And in 1988 the Reverend Pat Robertson beat sitting Vice-President George Bush in the Iowa caucuses by organizing hundreds of evangelical Christians who had never before participated in the Republican party.

In the pre-reform nominating system, the job of convention delegate was more often than not a reward for long and loyal service to the party. Convention delegates were elected first and expressed their presidential preferences later. In the new nominating system everyone, at every stage of the process, is required to state his or her presidential preference, and the selection of representatives to the next level must reflect the presidential preferences of the people who show up. This means that the most loyal party workers can be bypassed if they have chosen the wrong presidential candidate—which is just what happened in 1972 and 1976, when supporters of outsiders George McGovern and then Jimmy Carter surprised the party establishment in state after state.

Finally, the requirement that first-tier caucuses be held at the same time and on the same day meant that the delegate-selection system, the impact of which had heretofore been difficult to gauge, could now be treated like a primary. When precinct caucuses or county conventions were spread across several weeks or months, most reporters—especially those connected with the national news media—had to wait until the state convention met in order to see which presidential candidate would win the most delegates. Simultaneous precinct caucuses, the requirement that everyone present announce their presidential preference, and, or course, the use of computers and telephones to aggregate lots of data quickly meant that national reporters could descend upon a state such as Iowa and turn their hitherto-ignored precinct caucuses into a primary. . . .

Thus, in a relatively short period of time, the process of delegate selection in both political parties was transformed from a process understandable to only the most astute of political observers—and then only toward the end of the process—to a process that was easily quantifiable and therefore accessible to reporters from the earliest moments.

Money and the Need for an Early Start Reform of the delegate-selection system shifted the focus of attention from the convention to the seven or eight months of primaries and caucuses before the convention; reform of the campaign finance laws shifted attention to the year before the primaries even began. Without going into detail on campaign finance reform, I will say simply that, like delegate-selection reform, it transformed the search for money from a private (or at best a semi-public) undertaking to a highly public, easily quantifiable one.

The reasons are simple. In the pre-reform system a few very rich people could and did bankroll entire campaigns. Sometimes the public knew who these people were; often they did not. After campaign finance reform, the most that any one person could contribute to a presidential nomination campaign was $1,000. Thus candidates had to hold countless cocktail parties, dinners, luncheons, and other events in order to amass the millions of dollars needed to run in every caucus and primary in the country.

Another part of the campaign finance reform bill provided that any contribution up to $250 would be matched by the federal treasury. This meant that large numbers of small contributions suddenly became very valuable, especially if they could be raised through the use of direct mail. But in order for direct mail to work well, the presidential candidate signing the letter had to be well known. With money in lots of fairly small chunks doubling in value (due to the federal match), presidential candidates therefore sought ways to become visible and to appear that they were doing well as early as possible—usually one full year prior to the beginning of the primaries and caucuses.

Another provision of the new campaign finance reform laws required that all presidential candidates make quarterly reports of the money they had raised and spent. These quarterly reports, which are made public, have occasioned news stories on how each presidential candidate is doing. A candidate who raises lots of money begins to be taken seriously, whereas a candidate who raises little money tends to get left out of television stories, newspaper columns, and all the other free press that is so important in campaigns. Media coverage then generates more money, and more money generates more media coverage, and so on and on in a self-fulfilling circle.

This is not to say that money equals success. In 1984 Gary Hart tended to win those contests in which he spent a little bit of money and to lose those contests in which he spent a great deal (Polsby and Wildavsky, 1988:50). But early money not only makes a candidate look like a winner; it also allows him to withstand early disappointments once the nomination season begins. George Bush had $10 million in the bank when he placed third in the Iowa caucuses. Losing so early in the season was clearly a disappointment, but he had plenty of resources with which to withstand a loss. In contrast, a candidate like former Arizona Governor Bruce Babbitt on the Democratic side had such meager cash reserves that his 1988 campaign was over when he failed in Iowa....

Conventions in the Post-Reform Era

The Four-Day Television Commercial   Why is it so important to wrap up the nomination before the convention? Because the post-reform convention has a new role. With rare exceptions, it is no longer the place where the nomination is won. As we have seen, the nomination is won in the primaries and in the caucuses, and the nominee is almost always known prior to the convention. In the pre-reform era, the weeks between the last primary and the opening of the convention were times of intense activity as the leading candidates sought to pin down the votes of delegates who were not already pledged to a presidential candidate.... During the [pre-reform] period, an average of 38 percent of the delegates remained to be wooed in the weeks prior to the convention; during the [post-reform period] that number generally dropped significantly.

Another way to look at the same phenomenon is to compare the delegate count for the eventual nominee at the end of the primary season with the first ballot vote for the nominee at the convention. In the pre-reform years, the nominee had barely 50 percent of what he needed to get nominated by the end of the primary season; in the post-reform years, the count at the end of the season tends to be a pretty good predictor of the vote on the first ballot....

In the modern nominating system, therefore, the actual nomination function is all but gone from the convention; suspense about the identity of the nominee is a thing of the past. It has been many years since either political party has had a convention that went past the first ballot, so effectively have the primaries and caucuses displaced the convention as the place where the most important decision is made. Other matters of importance still go on at conventions—the party platform and party rules are debated and adopted, for instance—but the big decision is generally made weeks if not months before the convention ever opens.

In the post-reform era, then, the convention has become the place where the general election campaign begins. Byron Shafer, whose book *Bifurcated Politics: Evolution and Reform in the National Party Convention* is an excellent treatment of the post-reform convention, sums up the changes as follows: "[T]he role of the convention in inaugurating the general election campaign grew enormously as the nomination receded.... [N]ational news media, especially as embodied in full and national coverage, became the means by which public presentations at the convention could be turned explicitly to the task of advertising the candidate, his party, and their program" (Shafer, 1988:152–154).

Anything that detracts from the party's ability to put its best foot forward—platform fights, rule fights, and ongoing tensions such as those between Ford and Reagan in 1976, Kennedy and Carter in 1980, Hart and Mondale in 1984, and Dukakis and Jackson in 1988—is seen as a major impediment to the use of the convention to begin the general election.

Whereas political parties have become more and more adept "managing" their conventions, network news executives, under pressure to cut the huge costs involved in covering a convention, have become increasingly reluctant to cover events that are little more than four-day-long advertisements for the party and its nominee. Conventions used to be covered "gavel to gavel," or from the time they opened until the time they closed. In the 1950s and 1960s, in fact, television coverage actually exceeded the amount of time that the convention was in session.

Beginning in 1980, however, coverage by all three networks declined dramatically (Shafer, 1988:276–280). When NBC News announced a plan to cut from its prime-time coverage of the Democratic convention to a "convention without walls" that it was producing itself, there was a predictable outcry from party officials. Joe Angotti, executive producer of the news, said that "[o]ur first and primary responsibility is to cover the news. I'd like nothing better than to throw all this out and cover a real breaking story" (Kamarck, 1988). Threats by the networks to dramatically scale back coverage in the future have become more and more common.

Thus the nominating convention, devoid of its old functions, may have a hard time hanging onto its new functions. The political parties and nominees want to stage the entire affair so as to put the best light on their party, whereas the networks want to cover real news. If some balance is not struck, the conventions could go the way of the electoral college and become a vestigial part of the body politic.

Prospects for Change

The basic characteristics of the post-reform nominating system are not likely to change. For the foreseeable future the nominating process will be dominated by highly visible public contests for money and delegates. Though flawed, this system does have one advantage: People perceive it to be fair and open. When polled on the subject, the public has continually favored more primaries (usually national primaries), not fewer primaries. Any attempt to go back in time and give significantly more power to party officials would most likely be perceived as illegitimate by large numbers of voters accustomed to open presidential primaries.

Aside from Congress, which has traditionally been reluctant to get involved in the nomination process, the only agent of change would be the Democratic party, given that the Republicans do not believe in dictating delegate-selection systems to state Republican parties. Having preached the virtues of openness and wide participation for nearly twenty years, the Democrats, no matter how unhappy they are with the results of their recent nominating contests, can ill afford to return the process to smoke-filled rooms.

But the Democrats have made changes that, at the least, will put some checks and balances into the nomination system. One recent change was to make all major party elected officials (especially governors, senators, and members of Congress) automatic voting delegates to the convention. This change was necessary because one of the consequences of party reform was that elected officials, reluctant to compete with constituents for delegate slots, had dropped out of the convention picture.

The "Super Delegates" have not exercised an independent voice in the nomination process thus far. In 1984 many of them endorsed Mondale early, and in 1988 many members of Congress started out with their fellow House member Richard Gephardt and then switched to Dukakis when Gephardt failed in the primaries.

But the inclusion of the Super Delegates remains popular with the Democratic party for several reasons. Some see them as a centrist force that can serve as a counterbalance to the more ideologically extreme activists who tend to dominate the platform and other forums. Others want them there just in case the primaries fail to produce a winner one day and the nomination actually gets decided on the floor of the convention—an unlikely but still possible scenario. In that case the Super Delegates would be expected to exert a leadership role in bringing the convention to a decision, much as they did in the pre-reform era. And, finally, the Super Delegates can provide an element of "peer review" that the primary voters and ordinary delegates cannot provide, inasmuch as many of them will have known and worked with potential presidential candidates.

Another set of changes that are talked about but have not been incorporated into the Democratic party thus far involve deregulating the party rules. Some students of the rules (this author included) believe that the current rules dictate too many details of the delegate-selection process and that in some instances they have become examples of regulation for the sake of regulation.

Indeed, there is no real reason to force every state to elect delegates in exactly the same way so long as the process in each state is clear, open, and easy to participate in. If the Democrats allowed for variations among states, one state could check and balance another, and they could all avoid the unanticipated consequences that have ensued every time they have attempted to "reform" the process by writing yet another rule.

Changes in the nomination process should not be tied to an attempt to recapture some prior moment in history, when nominations were decided in the smoke-filled rooms of party leaders. To the extent that changes do occur in the future, they should be made with the goal of building checks and balances into the current system so that it can work to produce the best nominees—of both parties.

Notes

1. The first and most famous of the party reform commissions was the Commission on Party Structure and Delegate Selection, which met from 1969 to 1972 and was chaired initially by Senator George McGovern and then by Representative Donald Fraser; hence it is known as the McGovern-Fraser Commission. The work of delegate-selection reform was continued in 1972–1973 by the Commission on Delegate Selection and Party Structure, chaired by then Baltimore City Councilwoman Barbara Mikulski. The next commission, the Commission on Presidential Nomination and Party Structure (1975–1978), was chaired by Michigan Democratic Party Chairman Morley Winograd; it was followed by the Commission on Presidential Nomination, chaired by North Carolina Governor James Hunt from 1981 to 1982. The last of the delegate-selection commissions appears to be the Fairness Commission, chaired by former South Carolina party chairman Donald Fowler in 1985–1986.

2. In his book on the reform movement, Byron Shafer (1983:387) makes the following point: "Despite its status as the device by which the largest share of delegates to national party conventions in all of American history had been selected, the party caucus was abolished by rules which were not assembled in any one guideline, which were not presented in the order in which they had to be assembled, and which did not at any point claim to be making actual, aggregate, institutional impact."

References

Germond, Jack W., and Jules Witcover, 1985. *Wake Us When It's Over: Presidential Politics of 1984.* New York: Macmillan.

Kamarck, Elaine Ciulla, 1988. "Who Will Control Coverage of the Convention," *Newsday*, July 11.

Polsby, Nelson W., 1983. *Consequences of Party Reform.* New York: Oxford University Press.

Polsby, Nelson W. and Aaron Wildavsky, 1984, 1988. *Presidential Elections.* New York: Charles Scribner's Sons.

Shafer, Byron E., 1988. *Bifurcated Politics: Evolution & Reform in the National Party Convention.* Cambridge: Harvard University Press.

White, Theodore H., 1961. *The Making of the President, 1960.* New York: New American Library.

38 / Evaluating the New Nominating System: Thoughts from a Governance Perspective

W. Wayne Shannon

In 1968, with new forces in the Democratic party demanding a voice in party affairs, that party's national convention gave every appearance of still being "controlled from the top," ultimately giving the presidential nomination to a candidate (Vice President Hubert Humphrey) who had not entered one primary election. For television viewers at home, the images of chaos both in the convention and on the Chicago streets overwhelmed the more normal but very important business of the convention itself.

In the aftermath of their "Chicago disaster," the Democratic party led the way toward "opening up" the nomination process through a series of reforms. The result, suggests Wayne Shannon, was replacement of the old "Party Game" by the "Primary Game" still in place today. Evaluating the new system after 1988 according to five criteria, Shannon concludes that it has seriously weakened the ability of the parties to perform vital roles for the electorate.

Evaluating the Nominating System

What should we expect from a good nomination system? What criteria can we employ to evaluate the performance of the old system as it worked under the rules of "The Party Game" and the new system as it has operated since 1972?* I propose five criteria:

1. Insofar as possible, the system should produce candidates whose experience and temperament equip them to fulfill the high expectations of the modern presidency. The imperatives of the presidency call for extraordinary personal performance. We should expect the nominating system to put forward those who are best qualified to do the job.

2. The system should promote coalition building in the parties rather than magnifying existing intraparty divisions or creating divisions that otherwise would not exist. It should encourage a view of national governance as cooperative rather than individualistic.

3. The system should assist the parties' aggregation or "packaging" functions so voters better understand the broad options offered for future policy. The system should help to lower the information costs that citizens have to pay in order to link their preferences to decision-making in Washington.

*For details of the reforms and the "new system," see the previous reading by Elaine Kamarck.—*Editor's Note.*

4. The system should encourage the selection of candidates in both parties who can make a broad appeal to the national electorate.
5. The system should encourage participation in party affairs at all levels. It should certainly not discourage or foreclose participation on the part of any class or category of citizens. But it should not contribute independently to the weakening of political parties as organizations.

. . .The practiced eye will see that my criteria are greatly influenced by the arguments of those who favor a strong role for political parties in American politics. . . .

My criteria for evaluating the nominating process assume that political parties must play a strong role in the democratic process and that they must be understood as organizations of activists who perform specific political functions, such as formulation of programs, selection of candidates, and conduct of election campaigns. Two lines of reasoning underlie this perspective. The first involves the realistic limits on citizen participation in a large-scale polity. The second stems from the problem of generating leadership and support for national governance through the presidency—a unique American problem posed by the architectural features of our Madisonian Constitution. . . .

The thrust of this argument is not that party organizations need to be "machines," or that they must be motivated principally by patronage considerations, but rather that they are organizations with specific functions to perform. Insistence on very high levels of citizen participation in candidate selection and on procedures designed to make all party organizational activities internally democratic in effect denies this functional specificity and raises the danger that the parties' unique contribution to the democratic process will be weakened or lost. . . .

The second line of reasoning underlying the criteria proposed here concerns a specifically American problem—how leadership, direction, and coherence can be generated, given the unique Madisonian architecture of the Constitution. It is commonplace for students of comparative government to observe that no other democratic constitution so divides, checks, balances, and fractures the authority of government. This constitutional design, derived from the framers' desire to limit and control the dangerous power of the state, has proved itself a superb instrument for accomplishing that purpose, but it has always begged the question of how a national government so divided could achieve the direction or coherence required to govern.

As the functions of national government have expanded exponentially in this century, we have constantly inflated our expectations of presidential leadership, but in recent years "The Party Game" on which we have relied to support it has seemingly come apart. . . . [Prominent] students of the American party system thought a generation ago that presidential selection provided the "glue" or centripetal force necessary to counter the conflict and stasis inherent in our constitutional design. [They] saw the nominating convention as a central element of this process. Perhaps they were mistaken. At any rate, we need now to reconsider their logic. The criteria that I propose for evaluating the nominating system are meant to encourage a concern with governance. We should look at the nominating system in terms of its ability to bring direction, coherence, and accountability to national government.

Getting the Right Person: Experience and Personality

A frequent criticism of the present nominating system is that it does not bring forward the most qualified candidates. In every election since 1972 the complaint that "surely we can do better than this" has been widely voiced with respect to the nominees of one or both of the parties. Throughout the 1988 nomination cycle, the press called attention to the "lightweight" quality of the Democratic contenders by dubbing them "the seven dwarfs."

Is there merit to this argument? If it is possible to demonstrate that the nomination system in place since 1972, "The Primary Game," has systematically put forward candidates less fit for the presidency by their experience and personalities than one or more of the earlier systems, there would be good reason to condemn it on this ground. What does the evidence suggest?. . .

Let us look first at the question of experience. We possess little if any reliable knowledge about the relationship of experience or apprenticeship to presidential success. . . .

. . .There is no evidence that those regarded as "great" presidents have come from any particular background. Nor do the clearest cases of failure or those in-between fit any clear pattern of experience or apprenticeship.

Nevertheless, it is still possible to ask whether our nominating systems have systematically produced candidates with different kinds of experience or apprenticeship for the presidency. The answer is that only the system of congressional caucus nomination used from 1800 to 1824 has reliably produced candidates with a particular kind of background. That system, the only one that has operated more or less like the candidate selection procedures of the world's parliamentary democracies, chose insiders with predictable apprenticeships in national government. In an almost British way, that system chose eminent party men who had "ministerial" experience. Perhaps it is no accident that the congressional system fit poorly with the emerging political culture of American democracy. To a growing host of critics it seemed elitist and class-tinged, and for that reason it lost its legitimacy well before its demise in 1824. Oddly enough, it was the only American nominating system that would require presidential candidates to have national executive experience. The lack of such a requirement has always seemed curious to European observers of presidential selection (King, 1985), but the American presidency is a unique institution, very different from its prime-ministerial counterparts throughout the world. Ronald Reagan is only the most recent in a long string of relatively successful presidents who have done without it.

The evidence seems quite clear that the nomination system of "The Party Game" from the 1840s to the late 1960s and its successor, "The Primary Game," have brought forth candidates from a much wider range of backgrounds than the caucus system, but in general there does not seem to be any pronounced difference in the qualifications of the candidates they have produced. John Aldrich, who has done a careful analysis of the period between 1876 and 1984, concludes that "presidential candidates look remarkably similar" over this period (Aldrich, 1987: 156).... Looking just at those nominated in their own right (without prior accidental succession) since 1945, it is not apparent that those nominated under the new system (McGovern, Carter, Mondale, Reagan, Dukakis, and Bush) are inferior in experience to those nominated in the last decades of the old system (Dewey, Stevenson, Eisenhower, Kennedy, Nixon, Goldwater, and Humphrey). All the latter but Eisenhower are stock characters from the familiar political backgrounds from which presidential nominees have been drawn since the demise of the caucus system in 1824—senators, governors, or, more recently, vice-presidents. It is difficult to conclude that the present nominating system has systematically produced candidates who are dwarfed by comparison with those nominated before 1972. The same holds for the "also-rans" of the two periods. There is nothing more dwarflike about Paul Simon or Albert Gore in 1988 than about Estes Kefauver in 1952 or Stuart Symington in 1960.

Going back farther in time would seem, if anything, to make a stronger case on the average for the apprenticeship qualifications of candidates nominated in recent years, but that would hold for both nominating systems that have operated since World War II. Anyone nostalgic for the remote past should be reminded of the harsh judgment rendered by two of our best historians on the nominees of the old "Party Game:"

> Since 1840 successful presidential candidates have not been prominent and experienced statesmen, but military heroes or relatively obscure men who have not had time to make enemies. Only by inadvertence, as in the case of Lincoln or the Roosevelts, did the president prove to be a man of outstanding ability. (Morrison and Commager, 1930)

...Oddly enough, the present system, which is often accused of bringing forth "outsiders" with little or no political apprenticeship, has not yet nominated any such person. In the convention system many outsiders were selected in the hundred years between William Henry Harrison and Wendell Willkie. Our conclusion must be that, whatever else may be the shortcomings of the new nominating system, it cannot fairly be faulted for producing candidates less experienced than those produced in the hundred or so years of "The Party Game."

This brings us to the question of personality, character, or temperament. There is much to be said for the argument that, however conceptualized, presidents' psychological attributes influence their behavior in office. Because the presidency is uniquely personal and comparatively uninstitutionalized, personality conditions any incumbent's relationships with the public, subordinates, adversaries, and the press....

Of course, there is little or no evidence that the nomination system in place from the 1840s to the late 1960s—a much more elite-dominated system—could do personality or character analysis any better. Many presidents produced by the old nominating system were "wrong" for the office, according to Barber: Wilson, Hoover, Eisenhower, Johnson, and Nixon. The best conclusion is not that one nomination system has performed better than the other in this respect but that we have found no reliable way to produce candidates of "extraordinary temperament." . . .

The conclusion must be that "The Primary Game" cannot be fairly faulted on the grounds that is has produced candidates less qualified for the presidency than its predecessors. On the whole, the candidates nominated under the present system and the old convention system look remarkably similar. If they fall short of the ideal qualifications called for in the presidential literature, the fault would seem to lie more in our unrealistic expectations than in failures of the nominating system.

One final point on experience and personality criteria needs to be made. Although it is often said that "The Primary Game" discourages the best-qualified candidates from running, it seems far from clear that this is so. To be sure, the new system requires early entry in the campaign and bars the convention from drafting a reluctant candidate. From my perspective, there are unfortunate features of the new system, but it is not easy to believe that those who have held back since 1972 are cut from essentially different cloth than those who have entered the race. If, indeed, such potential Democratic candidates in 1988 as Sam Nunn and Mario Cuomo stayed out of a race they saw as too long, expensive, punishing to their families, subject to unfair media scrutiny, or whatever, it is not clear that they would have seemed better qualified than the "seven dwarfs" had they decided to run. They would almost certainly have been revealed to be ordinary mortals if they had joined the others in the field.

Something about the dynamic of the new system makes people look better simply by virtue of their not being candidates. If "The Primary Game" does not actually produce inferior candidates, it does seem often to diminish the stature of those who choose to run—to make them *seem* less able than they are. Accordingly, the system can at the same time produce nominees who are capable individuals but fail to generate support for them. The problem, then, would not be that we have a faulty mechanism for selecting individuals but that the nominating system is no longer capable of generating the support on which successful governance depends.

Coalition-building and Cooperation

A governance perspective directs our attention to how the nominating process, other things being equal, promotes or hinders the development of a sense of common purpose inside each of the parties and an understanding that governing the nation is a cooperative enterprise. It calls attention to the difficult problem of generating support for presidents and their programs. Key, Schattschneider, Rossiter, and most other students of the American party system a generation ago, just before the old nominating system was swept away, considered the national convention of state and local party leaders as attractive for precisely this reason; it operated, they thought, as a unifying, centralizing force in a policy characterized by extremely divided formal authority and decentralized political parties. It served as a mechanism to mediate the internal quarrels among the parties' heterogeneous sectional and social followings and the diverse policy perspectives to which they gave rise. . . .

What Americans . . . have had trouble seeing is that primaries as a normal system of presidential nomination are *by definition* divisive and individualistic. Clearly they appeal to deep individualistic and participatory strains in American political culture, or else we alone among the world's democracies would not have come to rely on them so extensively. Nevertheless, we ought to see more clearly than we do the dangers they pose for the party system. Everywhere else in the world it is regarded as obvious that inviting a large number of copartisans to compete with one another over a long period of time in public over whose personal qualifications and ideas are best is divisive and potentially threatening to a party's ability to unite in the general election and function afterward as a more-or-less cooperative entity in government. Parties everywhere have leadership-selection fights arising from ideological and policy disagreements and personal rivalries. Mainly, however, they deal with them as quickly and quietly as possible behind closed doors. The American system of selecting presidential candidates by national nominating convention after the 1840s was always recognized by European observers as an unusually open and participative system. The addition of "advisory" presidential primaries in the early 1900s made it much more so. "The Primary Game" in place since 1972 has institutionalized openness to an extreme degree. It virtually requires that intraparty policy disputes and personal nomination campaigns be fought out under the glare of the communications media's lights over a period of more than two years. The nominating system as it now operates literally manufactures personal rivalries and individualistic policy positions among copartisans. It inevitably encourages a candidate-based rather than a party-based politics.

In following this line of reasoning we need not idealize the old convention system. The historical evidence is clear that it was sometimes a forum for bruising intraparty battles over both policy differences and personal rivalries. When either party was severely split on policy grounds, the convention offered no guarantee of successful compromise. Hopelessly divided parties are incapable of pulling themselves together, winning elections, and governing under any nominating system.

The question of what kind of nominating system *best* facilitates intraparty agreement and cooperation in the ongoing contest for national power is better put when the parties have real but less severe internal policy differences and when several candidates want a nomination that can go only to one. In this situation, the preponderance of the evidence favors a convention of party leaders and officeholders over the present primary-dominated system of party activists bound to particular candidates. Ironically, the

Democrats seem to have been most adversely affected by the new system—one that would not have been invented in the first place had it not been for their bitter internal divisions in the late 1960s. But the system has had negative governance-related effects on the Republicans as well, despite their much greater unity in recent years....

Looking back over...five nominating rounds of the new system, it is difficult not to believe that a delegate-selection system much less radically altered after 1968 (and one that would not have triggered a sudden state legislative movement to create new primaries) would have better served the Democrats as a presidential party. Someone more like Muskie than McGovern would have been nominated in 1972; the election would most likely have been lost in any case, but it would have been more strongly contested. Someone other than Jimmy Carter would probably have been selected in 1976, and would have had a good chance to win the presidency with or without Watergate. Whoever had won as a Democrat would have been better off in those difficult years by virtue of having a greater measure of respect and support from other Democrats in Washington. No Democratic president would have had to fight off a strong primary challenge to renomination. Whatever would have happened after 1980, it would not have been likely that a Gary Hart would ever have so effectively labeled a Democratic front-runner as the "candidate of special interests" or that any other candidate would have depicted a Gephardt as a flip-flopping waffler in negative television ads. Women and blacks would surely have come to play a greater role in party affairs, although a less dramatic one without *de facto* quotas in national party rules. Jesse Jackson, of course, would have had no opportunity to run his long campaigns of 1984 and 1988, but other black politicians with more party and electoral experience would have staked their claims to power in a more traditional and less party-dividing manner....

It was certainly not helpful to Gerald Ford's presidency and his uphill struggle for a term of his own to have been set upon by Ronald Reagan in 1976. There can be no doubt that his reelection prospects were seriously damaged by Reagan's nearly successful challenge, which persisted right down to the convention. No such damaging attack on a president from the ranks of his own party had been launched since Theodore Roosevelt's assault on Taft in 1912, and it is difficult to believe that it would have occurred had the inviting new machinery of "The Primary Game" not been in place.

In 1980, the strongly fought campaign between Reagan and Bush in the early primary season established "voodoo economics" as a household expression and thereby made it more difficult for Reagan to convince the general electorate that he was not an extremist. In 1988, the personal, negative attacks that Bush and Dole inflicted on one another in the first weeks of the primaries left wounds that were very difficult to heal on two rivals who would subsequently need to cooperate as president and leader of the president's party in the Senate. Nowhere else in the world is there anything remotely comparable to the present nominating system's propensity to set copartisans against one another. The system is *inherently* subversive of party unity. Even the

Republicans, now perhaps more unified ideologically than any other major American party has ever been, are divided by it.

To make matters worse, it seems abundantly clear [from] five rounds of the new nominating system that what the primaries take apart the convention cannot put back together. The convention in the age of "The Primary Game" is a nearly hollow shell of its former self—an institution ill equipped to perform *any* of the functions once thought so important in achieving party unity and generating support for presidential candidates. . . .

The candidates, not institutional party actors, now control the delegates. Whatever deals are struck are determined by the candidates and their campaign staffs. If the long, public campaign has created hard feelings among them (as it has for the Democrats for years), party officials and officeholders have little capacity to provide conciliation. That being the case, the enthusiastic symbolic showing of partisan spirit and unity at the start of the general-election campaign—the "rallying" function for which the old convention was often notable—is now feebly performed at best. . . .

In general, the conclusion must be that the basic structure of "The Primary Game" is deficient as a mechanism for promoting the capacity of the American party system to build and maintain presidential coalitions. It detracts from the parties' ability to generate support for candidates and for presidents, who must rely on the cooperation of copartisans in order to govern. It has encouraged assaults on two presidents from the ranks of their own party. By requiring that copartisans engage in long campaigns against one another, the system serves to magnify existing intraparty divisions and to generate divisions and antagonisms that would not otherwise exist. No one would intentionally create such a system with governance ends in mind.

Clarifying Options: Helping Voters to Understand

A few years ago, ordinary Americans needed to pay scant attention to presidential politics until after the conventions met in the summer of the election year. The presidential campaign, already long, took place between the conventions and the election in November. The voter's job was relatively simple—to choose between the Democratic and Republican "packages" of candidates and issues, both independently important in the American presidential system. Even so, the American system of divided powers and federalism made demands on citizens that ran well in excess of those in parliamentary systems, in which voters could opt for one or another broad direction in national government by simply voting for a member of parliament, and that mainly on the grounds of party preference. Even in the much simpler world of the late nineteenth century, European observers like Lord Bryce thought American elections demanded too much of ordinary citizens. In more modern language, Bryce thought the information costs facing American voters were too high; voters were expected to know too much about too many things. In this context we need to ask whether we are better or worse off for having decided, in effect, that functions formerly performed by party organizational elites and officeholders ought to be performed directly by the electorate.

...[T]he tasks facing ordinary voters in the new system are formidable indeed. First, the presidential campaign has been greatly lengthened. By the most conservative definition, the nomination phase alone now runs for well over a year. Unless they are to abandon what the new system expects them to do—directly select the presidential nominees and determine the issue orientation of the parties in the general election—voters are required to be attentive during a much longer campaign. Second is the much larger roster of players in the new game, perhaps as many as twenty on both sides in a year like 1988, when both parties' nominations are open. Every candidate on both sides is a potential personality and issue conundrum for voters. Since intraparty processes cannot be structured for voters according to partisan symbols, the candidates have to be understood as individuals—not as Democrats or Republicans.... From the "exhibition season" through the election, a massive new "elections industry" churns out coverage of virtually every aspect of the presidential race—the candidates, their organizations, fundraising, strategies, personalities, issues, poll standings, predictions, and so on. It is asking a great deal to expect ordinary voters to cope with such a barrage of information and somehow to sift out of it the essentials for making informed decisions on candidates and issues....

...There is simply no way that the mass electorate can master the complex information necessary for the active role that ordinary citizens are expected to play in the new system....

...During the general election, strong partisans, at least, can be expected to attend to such stuff with a certain amount of satisfaction. During a long nomination contest, though, it is simply too much of a bad thing. Most people tune it out.

The new nominating system does little to help citizens understand broad options for the future direction of public policy. Ideas and claims of leadership ability are a dime a dozen inside both parties as candidates have at one another, but few of these ideas and claims help ordinary citizens link their private concerns to the world of national politics. In this partyless politics the voter is in the position of the southerner in the erstwhile one-party Democratic primaries described by Key (1949). The candidates were so numerous, the gimmicks so outlandish, and the rhetoric so cacophonous that the voter had little chance of making any sense of it all. This, of course, was why Key and others of his era considered *party* politics so important. It had a capacity to clarify, instruct, and mobilize—to create effective linkages between the private concerns of everyday life and the public order. It would be absurd to lay the entire blame for the weakening of this linkage on "The Primary Game," but it should certainly be seen as a significant part of the problem.

Strong Candidates and Broad Electoral Appeal

The traditional logic of the American party system is that two moderate parties, operating in the centrist space of our unique political spectrum, compete for control of the White House by making as broad as possible an appeal to their own partisans, independents, and some of the opposition's partisan followers as well.... [W]hen we structure the nominating system to achieve such values as openness, representativeness, and popular participation, we should take care not to hinder the parties' ability to produce strong, attractive candidates with broad appeal to voters across the nation.

While the old convention system did not always produce such candidates, most often the party leaders who dominated it tried to find presidential nominees who had the best chance to win the election. How does the new system fare by this standard? The evidence after five nominating rounds is that it comes off much better than we might have supposed after 1972. There is no good reason to fear now that the system is loaded to produce Democrats so far to the left or Republicans so far to the right that presidential politics will become ideologically polarized. No candidate nominated since 1972 except George McGovern has been so ideologically removed from the center of the American spectrum that his defeat was a foregone conclusion. Carter would almost certainly have failed to win the Democratic nomination under a convention system, but not for reasons of ideology. He artfully staked out a centrist position that served him well with the national electorate in 1976. He simply would not have seemed a proper choice to party regulars and office holders. Mondale and Dukakis, on the other hand, are exactly the sort who appeal to "professional" party peers. Both came to be seen as liberal ideologues by a large portion of the electorate, but, of course, they were not; both were experienced politicians, medially located in their party. Ford—an accidental president who finally patched together the delegates he needed in 1976—as well as Reagan and Bush are all garden-variety Republicans.... None of this merits an indictment of the new system on the grounds that it has produced candidates ill equipped to make a strong national appeal.

Still, it is interesting to ask why, as long as the new system has been in operation, we have so often heard the lament, "Surely, we can do better than this!" To return to a point discussed earlier, there is something about the new nominating system that makes people who are well suited to carry their party's standard in the presidential election *seem* lacking. It is especially curious that people like Mondale, Dukakis, Dole, and Bush—who are as smart, well apprenticed in government, and seasoned in party politics as the best people put forth in the era of the modern presidency by the old nominating convention—now seem so unimpressive. Why do those who stay out of the race nearly always seem to be better? Although there is no way to prove the proposition, I suspect that the culprit is the long intraparty squabble that lies at the heart of the new system. It requires candidates to toot their own horns endlessly and to undermine their partisan colleagues at every turn by hook or by crook. Much of this activity is inherently demeaning. The rules of this game virtually guarantee that the stature of the players will be diminished. Although it was not designed to do so, it seems to dwarf even those of substantial accomplishment.

In the old convention system, and especially in the more remote days of "The Party Game," presidential candidates suddenly emerged from the nomination process clothed in the robes of partisan symbolism. The victorious individual could not but look more impressive than the ordinary run of mere mortals for having been anointed by one of the tribes to which most people belonged. The candidates in the new system, by contrast, undergo a long and demanding process of public scrutiny during which they face the constant glare of the electronic media and their inherently skeptical commentaries on the "horse race." There is no way to win in this system, except by advancing themselves and creating all manner of doubts about their opponents. No candidate can be expected to emerge from this process unscathed. Someone will always win in such a system, but it is not a system likely to ennoble the nominee. Even the moment of victory does little to magnify the nominee's stature, since, as we have seen, the functionally hollow modern convention has little partisan glory to bestow. In an atmosphere of weakened partisanship, the nominee in the new system seems less the leader of invigorated party legions than a mere individual who has won the game. For this, again, we must not indict the nominating system alone; nevertheless, we should recognize it as an important component of an institutional setting that has weakened partisan linkages that once bonded us more effectively to presidents and thereby generated the support that successful governance in our system of divided powers requires.

Participation, Representativeness, and Party Organizations
The final standard for evaluating the nominating system holds that it should encourage participation by citizens in party affairs, and that the parties' activities should be open to all who desire to participate, but that it should not weaken parties as institutions. Broad participation in party affairs is a worthy goal. It is not, however, one that ought to be pursued single-mindedly without consideration for other goals, such as maintaining the health of institutional partisan organizations at the state and local levels. Here we need to recognize the strong possibility of trade-offs. As we seek greater participation and representativeness, we are likely to diminish the ability of party organizations to perform their traditional structuring functions for the electorate.

Most of the impetus to create a more participatory and socially representative party system has come from the Democrats. After the debacle in Chicago in 1968, the McGovern-Fraser Commission drafted rules designed to open decision-making at all levels to rank-and-file Democrats, to increase representation of blacks, women, and other underrepresented categories of Democratic followers, and to guarantee wide participation in the delegate-selection process (Shafer, 1983)....

What has been gained since 1968 by way of participation and representativeness?... We can be certain that the Democrats' rules changes have made their convention much more representative of two groups of their identifiers in the electorate, blacks and women.... [B]oth parties' delegates are now much more educated and affluent than their followers in the electorate, but it is very likely that this has always been the case....

The gender, racial, and social-class composition of the convention delegates is important but is much less closely related to the functional performance of the party system than the delegates' ideological and policy orientation. Before the post-1968 reforms, survey data indicated that both parties' convention delegates were more ideological than their followers or the general public. In the 1950s the Republican delegates were the ones who seemed to be out of step. They were so far to the right that Republican followers were much closer to Democratic activists than to activists in their own party. Studies done after the reforms suggest a general pattern in which both parties' delegates have become consistently much more ideological than their followers in the electorate. The main change since 1968 seems to be that the Democratic delegates have moved sharply to the left to mirror the position that the Republican delegates had earlier occupied at the other end of the political spectrum.

Is this amount of ideological polarization excessive? The answer is not clear, but from the perspective of this chapter, it must depend largely on whether the "principled amateurs" of the new system have the ability to package candidates and issues in such a manner that presidential majorities can be constructed and maintained. Both parties' convention delegates now seem to need the counsel that institutional party leaders on both sides often gave their more ideological colleagues in the old convention system. The party leaders' function was to keep them from becoming too unrepresentative of the parties' identifiers in the electorate and the broader electorate from which support was needed if elections were to be won....

While no one clearly intended the result, the movement to primaries between 1968 and 1972 created a presidential nominating politics largely unmediated by those with the greatest interest in the long-term ability of the parties to compete successfully for the presidency. The "principled amateurs" who in the new system have to do the job that party organizations used to do are certainly not pure ideologues, but they are much less skilled than the organization leaders they have supplanted in framing the essential structure of the presidential race. Both parties still need an institutional concern with "electability" that cannot be provided by citizen activists motivated by personal attachments to particular candidates or by policy or ideological preferences. Such concern is sorely lacking in the current nominating system.

Conclusion: A Flawed System

By the evaluative standards introduced above, "The Primary Game" does not fare well. The problem is not that it puts forth individual candidates less well suited by virtue of their experience or personal attributes than prior nominating systems did. Nevertheless, the system generates less support for nominees than they need in order to contest national elections vigorously and govern effectively if they win. In several ways it has contributed to the weakening of political parties in the presidential election, the central electoral drama of American democracy. The system magnifies existing intraparty cleavages, and—worse still—contributes to the creation of new ones in the course of its normal operation. It has not helped the parties perform the important function of clarifying broad policy options for the electorate. Rather, it has made matters worse by confusing and boring voters for months on end. It has little of the capacity of the old convention system to forge party unity and create enthusiasm before the general election campaign. The new system has needlessly weakened state and local party organizations. Since 1968 they have been almost entirely displaced from the central action in selecting the party's presidential nominee and shaping the issues on which the campaign is to be fought.

Would anyone with the benefit of what we now know about this system of nomination have chosen to create it? I do not think so.[1] Had the events of 1968 not generated such uncontrollable passions, we would not likely have set in motion the forces that transformed a central part of the venerable machinery of American government. Nominating politics might well have continued in the form we knew in the mid-1960s—the convention of delegates selected state by state in many different ways, with the primaries playing a very strong role in an age of national electronic communication. Would we be better off if that were the case? I think so. Why, in the face of the accumulated evidence, would we want to continue year after year to employ such a flawed nominating system? It is not easy to see why we continue to tolerate it. . . .

Our flawed nomination system is only a part of a broader trend toward party decomposition in this country that has undermined the governance capacity of the contemporary Washington community. Weaker presidents, a more individualistic Congress, divided government, and a House of Representatives all but divorced from the issue-related dynamic of the national election process are all parts of the big picture. Very few whose experience in Washington goes back to the period before Vietnam think we are better off now than we were then. Most believe that we now have less ability to sustain a more-or-less coherent process of national governance, and a wealth of evidence indicates that citizens are less effectively linked to national government than they were then. Electoral participation has fallen off sharply. For an alarmingly large segment of the public, Washington is out of sight and out of mind. The underlying dynamic seems to be a general weakening of political parties in American politics. The welcome evidence of the Reagan years that this process is not inevitable should not lull us into complacency but should encourage us to do whatever we can to re-create a vigorous party system.

Could "The Primary Game" be changed if we wanted to change it? Of course it could. The first steps are to understand that it does not work well and to understand that incremental tinkering with it (superdelegates, Super Tuesdays, and so on) will not help. From there, many other steps are possible. It is often said that we "can't go back to the smoke-filled room." That is true. But we could go back to selecting convention delegates as Democratic and Republican state organizations would wish if they wanted to make a larger role for themselves in the nomination process. Both national parties could encourage state parties to alter state statutes again in order to regain their place in the selection process. Or, if we wish to retain elements of "The Primary Game," we might design a preprimary convention system that would allow institutional party actors to play a larger role in candidate selection subject to review by party followers in later elections.[2] Perhaps there are other means to the end, but whatever we do, we should now try to find a way to restore the ability of state and local organizations to influence both candidate selection and the platform on which the national election is fought. . . .

National governance has always been difficult to attain in the United States for reasons that have been present since the founding: our extremely partitioned system of separated powers with its Madisonian logic of "ambition against ambition," the deep distrust of central government from which this system was derived, the centrifugal tendencies of a vast and heterogeneous nation, and political parties "decentralized to the point of anarchy." Decomposition of the party system in recent years has made our ongoing quest for national leadership and accountability through our unique formula of presidential government more difficult. A good first step toward arresting this ominous trend would be to repair the flaws in the unfortunate nominating system that we stumbled into after the disasters of 1968.

Notes

1. Even Benjamin Barber agrees that the new nominating system is no improvement over the old (Barber, 1984: 206). [Benjamin Barber, *Strong Democracy: Participatory Politics for a New Age*, Berkeley: University of California Press.]
2. My colleague at the University of Connecticut, David RePass, a thoughtful student of American elections, has drawn up a preliminary plan for a national preconvention system.

References

Aldrich, John H. 1987. "Methods and Actors: The Relationship of Processes to Candidates." In *Presidential Selection*, ed. Alexander Heard and Michael Nelson. Durham, N.C.: Duke University Press.

Key, V.O., Jr. 1949. *Southern Politics*. New York: Alfred A. Knopf.

_____. 1964. *Politics, Parties and Pressure Groups*. 5th ed. New York: Crowell.

King, Anthony. 1985. "How Not to Select Presidential Candidates: A View from Europe." In *Analyzing the Presidency*, ed. Robert E. DiClerico. Guilford, Conn.: Dushkin.

Morrison, Samuel Eliot, and Henry Steele Commager. 1930. *The Growth of the American Republic* I. New York: Oxford University Press.

Reiter, Howard. 1985. *Selecting the President: The Nominating Process in Transition*. Philadelphia: University of Pennsylvania Press.

Shafer, Byron E. 1983. *Quiet Revolution: The Struggle for the Democratic Party and the Shaping of Post-Reform Politics*. New York: Russell Sage.

CHAPTER TEN

Political Factions in American Politics

Special-interest politics is not new in the United States. It is neither a new phenomenon nor a new concern. In *Federalist* no. 10, James Madison argued that controlling special interests ("factions"), while allowing them a voice in the system, was a major reason for adopting the republican form of government. In 1797, retiring president George Washington warned his fellow citizens of the "baneful, divisive effects of faction," and emphasized that common goals must take precedence over geographical or other self-interests that could pull the new nation apart.

Despite Washington's warning, organized interests have always played an important role in American politics. For a long time, large political parties were clearly the most important organized political groups. More recently, politics has become increasingly splintered as thousands of interest groups play on the national stage. The following words of retiring president Jimmy Carter in 1981 provide an interesting base for comparison with Washington's earlier warning:

> Today, as people have become ever more doubtful of the ability of the government to deal with our problems, we are increasingly drawn to single-issue groups and special interest organizations to ensure that whatever else happens our own personal views and our private interests are protected.
>
> This is a disturbing factor in American political life. It tends to distort our purposes because the national interest is not always the sum of all our single or special interests. We are all Americans together—and we must not forget that the common good is our common interest and our individual responsibility.

The two readings of this chapter are extracts from Madison's *Federalist* no. 10 and Washington's Farewell Address. It should be noted here that modern, electoral parties such as exist in the United States today were only beginning to form at the time Washington delivered his Address. Hence, both Madison's use of the term *faction* and Washington's use of *party* should be taken as applying to political interest associations more generally, perhaps including both political parties and interest groups today.

39 / Federalist Paper no. 10

James Madison

Whether as large parties or small interest groups, "interests" have, throughout American history, organized to express their various needs and/or views to the government. Though the framers, obviously including Washington, wished aloud that special interests would simply go away, it is unlikely that any of them thought it would happen. (In fact, in the following readings, Madison refers to the latent causes of factions being "sown in the nature of man" and Washington sees the spirit of party as being "inseparable from our nature.") So, instead of constitutionally prohibiting the formation of organized political groups, the framers tried to design a means for controlling their effects.

In *Federalist* no. 10, James Madison argues that one major benefit of the new Constitution is that, in establishing a large republic, it would provide the means for countering the negative effects of factionalism in a pluralistic society. It would not do this by squelching the liberty necessary for expressing special interests,* but rather by controlling the effects of factional appeals. Because faction was considered a political disease by many in early American society, Madison clearly felt that any prescription for cure should be welcomed.

Number 10

To the People of the State of New York: Among the numerous advantages promised by a well-constructed Union, none deserves to be more accurately developed than its tendency to break and control the violence of faction. The friend of popular governments never finds himself so much alarmed for their character and fate, as when he contemplates their propensity to this dangerous vice. He will not fail, therefore, to set a due value on any plan which, without violating the principles to which he is attached, provides a proper cure for it. The instability, injustice, and confusion introduced into the public councils, have, in truth, been the mortal diseases under which popular governments have everywhere perished; as they continue to be the favorite and fruitful topics from which the adversaries to liberty derive their most specious declamations. The valuable improvements made by the American constitutions on the popular models, both ancient and modern, cannot certainly be too much admired; but it would be an unwarrantable partiality, to contend that they have as effectually obviated the danger on this side, as was wished and expected. Complaints are everywhere heard from our most considerate and virtuous citizens, equally the friends of public and private faith, and of public and personal liberty, that our governments are too unstable, that the

---

*In fact, the guarantees of freedom of speech and of assembly given in the Bill of Rights would provide constitutional protections for the development of political groups.—*Editor's Note.*

public good is disregarded in the conflicts of rival parties, and that measures are too often decided, not according to the rules of justice and the rights of the minor party, but by the superior force of an interested and overbearing majority. However anxiously we may wish that these complaints had no foundation, the evidence of known facts will not permit us to deny that they are in some degree true. It will be found, indeed, on a candid review of our situation, that some of the distresses under which we labor have been erroneously charged on the operation of our governments; but it will be found, at the same time, that other causes will not alone account for many of our heaviest misfortunes; and, particularly, for that prevailing and increasing distrust of public engagements, and alarm for private rights, which are echoed from one end of the continent to the other. These must be chiefly, if not wholly, effects of the unsteadiness and injustice with which a factious spirit has tainted our public administrations.

By a faction, I understand a number of citizens, whether amounting to a majority or minority of the whole, who are united and actuated by some common impulse of passion, or of interest, adverse to the rights of other citizens, or to the permanent and aggregate interests of the community.

There are two methods of curing the mischiefs of faction: the one, by removing its cause; the other, by controlling its effects.

There are again two methods of removing the causes of faction: the one, by destroying the liberty which is essential to its existence; the other, by giving to every citizen the same opinions, the same passions, and the same interests.

It could never be more truly said than of the first remedy, that it was worse than the disease. Liberty is to faction what air is to fire, an aliment without which it instantly expires. But it could not be less folly to abolish liberty, which is essential to political life, because it nourishes faction, than it would be to wish the annihilation of air, which is essential to animal life, because it imparts to fire its destructive agency.

The second expedient is as impracticable as the first would be unwise. As long as the reason of man continues fallible, and he is at liberty to exercise it, different opinions will be formed. As long as the connection subsists between his reason and his self-love, his opinions and his passions will have a reciprocal influence on each other; and the former will be objects to which the latter will attach themselves. The diversity in the faculties of men, from which the rights of property originate, is not less an insuperable obstacle to a uniformity of interests. The protection of these faculties is the first object of government. From the protection of different and unequal faculties of acquiring property, the possession of different degrees and kinds of property immediately results; and from the influence of these on the sentiments and views of the respective proprietors, ensues a division of the society into different interests and parties.

The latent causes of faction are thus sown in the nature of man; and we see them everywhere brought into different degrees of activity, according to the different circumstances of civil society. A zeal for different opinions concerning religion, concerning government, and many other points, as well of speculation as of practice; an attachment to different leaders ambitiously contending for preeminence and power; or to persons of other descriptions whose fortunes have been interesting to the human passions, have, in turn, divided mankind into parties, inflamed them with mutual animosity, and rendered them much more disposed to vex and oppress each other than to cooperate for their common good. So strong is this propensity of mankind to fall into mutual animosities, that where no substantial occasion presents itself, the most frivolous and fanciful distinctions have been sufficient to kindle their unfriendly passions and excite their most violent conflicts. But the most common and durable source of factions has been the various and unequal distribution of property. Those who hold and those who are without property have ever formed distinct interests in society. Those who are creditors, and those who are debtors, fall under a like discrimination. A landed interest, a manufacturing interest, a mercantile interest, a moneyed interest, with many lesser interests, grow up of necessity in civilized nations, and divide them into different classes, actuated by different sentiments and views. The regulation of these various and interfering interests forms the principal task of modern legislation, and involves the spirit of party and faction in the necessary and ordinary operations of the government.

No man is allowed to be a judge in his own cause, because his interest would certainly bias his judgment, and, not improbably, corrupt his integrity. With equal, nay with greater reason, a body of men are unfit to be both judges and parties at the same time; yet what are many of the most important acts of legislation, but so many judicial determinations, not indeed concerning the rights of single persons, but concerning the rights of large bodies of citizens? And what are the different classes of legislators but advocates and parties to the causes which they determine? Is a law proposed concerning private debts? It is a question to which the creditors are parties on one side and the debtors on the other. Justice ought to hold the balance between them. Yet the parties are, and must be, themselves the judges; and the most numerous party, or, in other words, the most powerful faction must be expected to prevail. Shall domestic manufactures be encouraged, and in what degree, by restrictions on foreign manufactures? are questions which would be differently decided by the landed and the manufacturing classes, and probably by neither with a sole regard to justice and the public good. The apportionment of taxes on the various descriptions of property is an act which seems to require the most exact impartiality; yet there is, perhaps, no legislative act in which greater opportunity and temptation are given to a predominant party to trample on the rules of justice. Every shilling with which they overburden the inferior number, is a shilling saved to their own pockets.

It is in vain to say that enlightened statesmen will be able to adjust these clashing interests, and render them all subservient to the public good. Enlightened statesmen will not always be at the helm. Nor, in many cases, can such an adjustment be made at all without taking into view indirect and remote considerations, which will rarely prevail over the immediate interest which one party may find in disregarding the rights of another or the good of the whole.

The inference to which we are brought is, that the *causes* of faction cannot be removed, and that relief is only to be sought in the means of controlling its *effects*.

If a faction consists of less than a majority, relief is supplied by the republican principle, which enables the majority to defeat its sinister views by regular vote. It may clog the administration, it may convulse the society; but it will be unable to execute and mask its violence under the forms of the Constitution. When a majority is included in a faction, the form of popular government, on the other hand, enables it to sacrifice to its ruling passion or interest both the public good and the rights of other citizens. To secure the public good and private rights against the danger of such a faction, and at the same time to preserve the spirit and the form of popular government, is then the great object to which our inquiries are directed. Let me add that it is the great desideratum by which this form of government can be rescued from the opprobrium under which it has so long labored, and be recommended to the esteem and adoption of mankind.

By what means is this object attainable? Evidently by one of two only. Either the existence of the same passion or interest in a majority at the same time must be prevented, or the majority, having such coexistent passion or interest, must be rendered, by their number and local situation, unable to concert and carry into effect schemes of oppression. If the impulse and the opportunity be suffered to coincide, we well know that neither moral nor religious motives can be relied on as an adequate control. They are not found to be such on the injustice and violence of individuals, and lose their efficacy in proportion to the number combined together, that is, in proportion as their efficacy becomes needful.

From this view of the subject it may be concluded that a pure democracy, by which I mean a society consisting of a small number of citizens, who assemble and administer the government in person, can admit of no cure for the mischiefs of faction. A common passion or interest will, in almost every case, be felt by a majority of the whole; a communication and concert result from the form of government itself; and there is nothing to check the inducements to sacrifice the weaker party or an obnoxious individual. Hence it is that such democracies have ever been spectacles of turbulence and contention; have ever been found incompatible with personal security or the rights of property; and have in general been as short in their lives as they have been violent in their deaths. Theoretic politicians, who have patronized this species of government, have erroneously supposed that by reducing mankind to a perfect equality in their political rights, they would, at the same time, be perfectly equalized and assimilated in their possessions, their opinions, and their passions.

A republic, by which I mean a government in which the scheme of representation takes place, opens a different prospect, and promises the cure for which we are seeking. Let us examine the points in which it varies from

pure democracy, and we shall comprehend both the nature of the cure and
the efficacy which it must derive from the Union.

The two great points of difference between a democracy and a republic
are: first, the delegation of the government, in the latter, to a small number
of citizens elected by the rest; secondly, the greater number of citizens, and
greater sphere of country, over which the latter may be extended.

The effect of the first difference is, on the one hand, to refine and enlarge
the public views, by passing them through the medium of a chosen body of
citizens, whose wisdom may best discern the true interest of their country,
and whose patriotism and love of justice will be least likely to sacrifice it
to temporary or partial considerations. Under such a regulation, it may well
happen that the public voice, pronounced by the representatives of the people, will be more consonant to the public good than if pronounced by the
people themselves, convened for the purpose. On the other hand, the effect
may be inverted. Men of factious tempers, of local prejudices, or of sinister
designs, may, by intrigue, by corruption, or by other means, first obtain the
suffrages, and then betray the interests, of the people. The question resulting
is, whether small or extensive republics are more favorable to the election
of proper guardians of the public weal; and it is clearly decided in favor of
the latter by two obvious considerations:

In the first place, it is to be remarked that, however small the republic
may be, the representatives must be raised to a certain number, in order to
guard against the cabals of a few; and that, however large it may be, they
must be limited to a certain number, in order to guard against the confusion
of a multitude. Hence, the number of representatives in the two cases not
being in proportion to that of the two constituents, and being proportional-
ly greater in the small republic, it follows that, if the proportion of fit
characters be not less in the large than in the small republic, the former will
present a greater option, and consequently a greater probability of a fit choice.

In the next place, as each representative will be chosen by a greater
number of citizens in the large than in the small republic, it will be more
difficult for unworthy candidates to practise with success the vicious arts by
which elections are too often carried; and the suffrages of the people being
more free, will be more likely to centre in men who possess the most attractive merit and the most diffusive and established characters.

It must be confessed that in this, as in most other cases, there is a mean,
on both sides of which inconveniences will be found to lie. By enlarging too
much the number of electors, you render the representative too little acquainted
with all their local circumstances and lesser interests; as by reducing it too
much, you render him unduly attached to these, and too little fit to comprehend and pursue great and national objects. The federal Constitution forms
a happy combination in this respect; the great and aggregate interests being
referred to the national, the local and particular to the State legislatures.

The other point of difference is, the greater number of citizens and extent of territory which may be brought within the compass of republican
than of democratic government; and it is this circumstance principally which

renders factious combinations less to be dreaded in the former than in
the latter. The smaller the society, the fewer probably will be the distinct
parties and interests composing it; the fewer the distinct parties and interests,
the more frequently will a majority be found of the same party; and the
smaller the number of individuals composing a majority, and the smaller
the compass within which they are placed, the more easily will they concert and execute their plans of oppression. Extend the sphere and you take
in a greater variety of parties and interests; you make it less probable that
a majority of the whole will have a common motive to invade the rights of
other citizens; or if such a common motive exists, it will be more difficult
for all who feel it to discover their own strength, and to act in unison with
each other. Besides other impediments, it may be remarked that, where there
is a consciousness of unjust or dishonorable purposes, communication is always
checked by distrust in proportion to the number whose concurrence is
necessary.

Hence, it clearly appears, that the same advantage which a republic has
over a democracy, in controlling the effects of faction, is enjoyed by a large
over a small republic,—is enjoyed by the Union over the States composing
it. Does the advantage consist in the substitution of representatives whose
enlightened views and virtuous sentiments render them superior to local prejudices and to schemes of injustice? It will not be denied that the representation of the Union will be most likely to possess these requisite endowments.
Does it consist in the greater security afforded by a greater variety of parties,
against the event of any one party being able to outnumber and oppress the
rest? In an equal degree does the increased variety of parties comprised within
the Union, increase this security? Does it, in fine, consist in the greater
obstacles opposed to the concert and accomplishment of the secret wishes
of an unjust and interested majority? Here, again, the extent of the Union
gives it the most palpable advantage.

The influence of factious leaders may kindle a flame within their particular States, but will be unable to spread a general conflagration through
the other States. A religious sect may degenerate into a political faction in
a part of the Confederacy; but the variety of sects dispersed over the entire
face of it must secure the national councils against any danger from that
source. A rage for paper-money, for an abolition of debts, for an equal division of property, or for any other improper or wicked project, will be less
apt to pervade the whole body of the Union than a particular member of
it; in the same proportion as such a malady is more likely to taint a particular
country or district, than an entire State.

In the extent and proper structure of the Union, therefore, we behold
a republican remedy for the diseases most incident to republican government.
And according to the degree of pleasure and pride we feel in being republicans,
ought to be our zeal in cherishing the spirit and supporting the character
of Federalists.

Publius

Note that when people in Madison's time expressed concern about the potential for "tyranny of the majority," the *majority* normally referred to those without wealth. In other words, Madison was appealing to the minority of "wealthy" to see in the Constitution a means of protecting their interests from a tyrannical, nonwealthy majority.*

40 / Washington's Farewell Address

George Washington

Retiring after serving two terms as his nation's first president, George Washington wrote a farewell address to his fellow citizens. In the address, which was actually written with the help of James Madison and Alexander Hamilton,† Washington warned of the terrible effects of factionalism, and called for common purpose to be placed above self-interest. (Note that when Washington used the term *party* any "small but artful and enterprising minority of the community" would apparently qualify.)

Friends and Fellow-Citizens:

. . .a solicitude for your welfare which can not end but with my life, and the apprehension of danger natural to that solicitude, urge me on an occasion like the present to offer to your solemn contemplation and to recommend to your frequent review some sentiments which are the result of much reflection, of no inconsiderable observation, and which appear to me all important to the permanency of your felicity as a people. . . .

Interwoven as is the love of liberty with every ligament of your hearts, no recommendation of mine is necessary to fortify or confirm the attachment.

The unity of government which constitutes you one people is also now dear to you. It is justly so, for it is a main pillar in the edifice of your real independence, the support of your tranquillity at home, your peace abroad, of your safety, of your prosperity, of that very liberty which you so highly prize. But as it is easy to foresee that from different causes and from different quarters much pains will be taken, many artifices employed, to weaken in your minds the conviction of this truth, as this is the point in your political

*See Janda, Kenneth, Jeffrey M. Berry, and Jerry Goldman, *The Challenge of Democracy* (Boston: Houghton Mifflin, 1987, pp. 92–93).—*Editor's Note.*
†Harold C. Syrett, ed., *American Historical Documents* (NY: Barnes and Noble, 1960, p. 139).—*Editor's Note.*

fortress against which the batteries of internal and external enemies will be most constantly and actively (though often covertly and insidiously) directed, it is of infinite moment that should properly estimate the immense value of your national union to your collective and individual happiness; that you should cherish a cordial, habitual, and immovable attachment to it; accustoming yourselves to think and speak of it as of the palladium of your political safety and prosperity; watching for its preservation with jealous anxiety; discountenancing whatever may suggest even a suspicion that it can in any event be abandoned, and indignantly frowning upon the first dawning of every attempt to alienate any portion of our country from the rest or to enfeeble the sacred ties which now link together the various parts.

For this you have every inducement of sympathy and interest. Citizens by birth or choice of a common country, that country has a right to concentrate your affections. The name of American, which belongs to you in your national capacity, must always exalt the just pride of patriotism more than any appellation derived from local discriminations. With slight shades of difference, you have the same religion, manners, habits, and political principles. You have in a common cause fought and triumphed together. The independence and liberty you possess are the work of joint councils and joint efforts, of common dangers, sufferings, and successes.

But these considerations, however powerfully they address themselves to your sensibility, are greatly outweighed by those which apply more immediately to your interest. Here every portion of our country finds the most commanding motives for carefully guarding and preserving the union of the whole.

The *North*, in an unrestrained intercourse with the *South*, protected by the equal laws of a common government, finds in the productions of the latter great additional resources of maritime and commercial enterprise and precious materials of manufacturing industry. The *South*, in the same intercourse, benefiting by the same agency of the *North*, sees its agriculture grow and its commerce expand.... The *East*, in a like intercourse with the *West*, already finds, and in the progressive improvement of interior communications by land and water will more and more find, a valuable vent for the commodities which it brings from abroad or manufactures at home. The *West* derives from the *East* supplies requisite to its growth and comfort, and what is perhaps of still greater consequence, it must of necessity owe the *secure* enjoyment of indispensable *outlets* for its own productions to the weight, influence, and the future maritime strength of the Atlantic side of the Union, directed by an indissoluble community of interest as *one nation.*...

While, then, every part of our country thus feels an immediate and particular interest in union, all the parts combined can not fail to find in the united mass of means and efforts greater strength, greater resource, proportionably greater security from external danger, a less frequent interruption of their peace by foreign nations, and what is of inestimable value, they must derive from union an exemption from those broils and wars between themselves which so frequently afflict neighboring countries not tied together by the same governments, . . . which opposite foreign alliances, attachments, and intrigues would stimulate and imbitter. Hence, likewise, they will avoid the necessity of those overgrown military establishments which, under any form of government, are inauspicious to liberty, and which are to be regarded as particularly hostile to republican liberty. In this sense it is that your union ought to be considered as a main prop of your liberty, and that the love of the one ought to endear to you the preservation of the other. . . .

Is there a doubt whether a common government can embrace so large a sphere? Let experience solve it. To listen to mere speculation in such a case were criminal. . . . It is well worth a fair and full experiment. . . .

In contemplating the causes which may disturb our union it occurs as matter of serious concern that any ground should have been furnished for characterizing parties by *geographical* discriminations—*Northern* and *Southern*, *Atlantic* and *Western*—whence designing men may endeavor to excite a belief that there is real difference of local interests and views. One of the expedients of party to acquire influence within particular districts is to misrepresent the opinions and aims of other districts. You can not shield yourselves too much against the jealousies and heartburnings which spring from these misrepresentations; . . .

To the efficacy and permanency of your union a government for the whole is indispensable. . . . Sensible of this momentous truth, you have improved upon your first essay by the adoption of a Constitution of Government better calculated than your former for an intimate union and for the efficacious management of your common concerns. This Government, the offspring of our own choice, uninfluenced and unawed, adopted upon full investigation and mature deliberation, completely free in its principles, in the distribution of its powers, uniting security with energy, and containing within itself a provision for its own amendment, has a just claim to your confidence and your support. . . . The basis of our political systems is the right of the people to make and to alter their constitutions of government. But the constitution which at any time exists till changed by an explicit and authentic act of the whole people is sacredly obligatory upon all. The very idea of the power and the right of the people to establish government presupposes the duty of every individual to obey the established government.

All obstructions to the execution of the laws, all combinations and associations, under whatever plausible character, with the real design to direct, control, counteract, or awe the regular deliberation and action of the constituted authorities, are destructive of this fundamental principle and of fatal tendency. They serve to . . . put in the place of the delegated will of the nation the will of a party, often a small but artful and enterprising minority of the community, and according to the alternate triumphs of different parties, to make the public administration the mirror of the ill-concerted and incongruous projects of faction rather than the organ of consistent and wholesome plans, digested by common counsels and modified by mutual interests. . . .

Toward the preservation of your Government and the permanency of your present happy state, it is requisite not only that you steadily discountenance irregular oppositions to its acknowledged authority, but also that you resist with care the spirit of innovation upon its principles, however specious the pretexts.... In all the changes to which you may be invited remember that time and habit are at least as necessary to fix the true character of governments as of other human institutions; that experience is the surest standard by which to test the real tendency of the existing constitution of a country; that facility in changes upon the credit of mere hypothesis and opinion exposes to perpetual change, from the endless variety of hypothesis and opinion; and remember especially that for the efficient management of your common interests in a country so extensive as ours a government of as much vigor as is consistent with the perfect security of liberty is indispensable. Liberty itself will find in such a government, with powers properly distributed and adjusted, its surest guardian. It is, indeed, little else than a name where the government is too feeble to withstand the enterprises of faction, to confine each member of the society within the limits prescribed by the laws, and to maintain all in the secure and tranquil enjoyment of the rights of person and property.

I have already intimated to you the danger of parties in the State, with particular reference to the founding of them on geographical discriminations. Let me now take a more comprehensive view, and warn you in the most solemn manner against the baneful effects of the spirit of party generally.

This spirit, unfortunately, is inseparable from our nature, having its root in the strongest passions of the human mind. It exists under different shapes in all governments, more or less stifled, controlled, or repressed; but in those of the popular form it is seen in its greatest rankness and is truly their worst enemy....

It serves always to distract the public councils and enfeeble the public administration. It agitates the community with ill-founded jealousies and false alarms; kindles the animosity of one part against another; foments occasionally riot and insurrection. It opens the door to foreign influence and corruption, which find a facilitated access to the government itself through the channels of party passion....

There is an opinion that parties in free countries are useful checks upon the administration of the government, and serve to keep alive the spirit of liberty. This within certain limits is probably true; and in governments of a monarchical cast patriotism may look with indulgence, if not with favor, upon the spirit of party. But in those of the popular character, in governments purely elective, it is a spirit not to be encouraged. From their natural tendency it is certain there will always be enough of that spirit for every salutary purpose; and there being constant danger of excess, the effort ought to be by force of public opinion to mitigate and assuage it. A fire not to be quenched, it demands a uniform vigilance to prevent its bursting into a flame, lest, instead of warming, it should consume....

CHAPTER ELEVEN

Political Parties

As we have already seen in the readings on *Political Factions in American Politics*, some of the framers were so concerned about the domination of government and politics by organized interests that they spoke and wrote strongly against them. At the Constitutional Convention, the prevailing intent was to design a set of representative governmental structures that would make parties—not just political parties, but organized interests in general—unnecessary. To the extent that they developed anyway, their effects would be controlled by the large republican form of government (as argued by Madison in *Federalist* no. 10).

Importantly, in not mentioning parties in the Constitution, the framers did not outlaw them.* Differing interests did exist in early American society (as noted in the earlier readings from Madison and Washington), and they eventually would seek expression through organized parties. Ironically, political parties as we know them today were to become an American invention, introduced here within a decade after ratification of the Constitution. Despite the framers' deeply felt concerns about the effects of "party," the two-party system was to become one of the most important political institutions in American politics.

Over the past few decades, however, observers have noted a decline in the influence of parties on both voters and candidates. This has occurred as the role of media in politics has expanded (see Chapter Thirteen), as campaigns and voting have become more "personalized" (see Chapter Eight), and as the number and influence of interest groups have increased (see Chapter Twelve). In the first reading of this chapter, Stephen Salmore and Barbara Salmore document changes in the parties' importance for the electorate, candidates, and officeholders since the 1950s. Although party decline has been the tendency over at least three decades, there is, as discussed by Salmore and Salmore, some recent evidence that the tide may be turning. Nevertheless, the authors conclude that it is too early to proclaim that the era of party decline has passed.

In the second selection, Kenneth Godwin considers how the availability of one technology-dependent approach—direct marketing—has affected the two major parties. In this instance, Godwin concludes, the Republican Party has more successfully adapted the new tool for its purposes than have the Democrats, resulting in a major financial advantage for the Republicans.

In the final reading of this chapter, Gary Orren considers several models of party politics, and suggests that while centralized, ideologically cohesive parties might not "fit" with the United States' political environment, it may not be necessary to continue to accept the weak partisan, limited-issue, and personalistic politics that are currently in place. Instead, he suggests that it may be possible to develop stronger but still pragmatic parties, with the consequence of more effective government.

*Development of parties would actually find constitutional protection in the guarantees of the freedom of speech and of assembly given in the Bill of Rights.—*Editor's Note.*

41 / The Decline and Possible Resurrection of Parties

Stephen A. Salmore
Barbara G. Salmore

In the following article, Stephen A. Salmore and Barbara G. Salmore document the decline of the American parties over recent decades, as individual candidates came to replace parties as the central focus of campaigns for national office. The authors also consider recent evidence that the decline may have been halted and the parties reinvigorated, but caution that it is too early to conclude that the parties will be "resurrected."

A summary of recent trends in American political campaigning would begin like this: Since about 1950 American political campaigns have become increasingly candidate-centered. All aspects of a campaign—its organization, fundraising techniques, polling, and media messages— exist for the sole purpose of electing a particular candidate to a particular office. Appeals to voters communicate an "image"—a combination of a candidate's personal characteristics and his or her issue positions. Campaigns are organized and directed by "hired guns"—people who have performed the same specialized tasks in other campaigns in the past. They know what information should be gathered in polls at various stages, what kinds of media messages are required at various points in the campaign, which sorts of direct mail lists will produce the most contributions, and so on. Organizational efforts are directed at identifying, and bringing to the polls, those voters who might favor the candidate.

This description will sound banal to anyone who came to political maturity in the television age. Yet for a century or more . . . American political campaigns were party-centered, not candidate-centered. The appeals of campaigns were to party identification and loyalty; the campaign organizations were party organizations. Party domination extended beyond campaigns; for a long period parties largely controlled the nomination and election processes as well. Throughout the nineteenth century, candidates were chosen in party caucuses and conventions rather than in primary elections, and voters cast their ballots on forms provided by the parties, not by nonpartisan election boards. Clearly, this was a very different kind of politics. . . .

The Decline of Parties

In the 1960s and 1970s scholars became disturbed by the apparent decay of the American parties in all their aspects. Their concern stemmed from the implications of party decline for the democratic process. One observer warned, "When parties are absent or . . . have become Cheshire cats of which very little is left except the smile, pathologies multiply."[1] The presumed pathologies included a state of affairs in which political debate was "more negative and bitter, and policy compromises are much harder to come by."[2] Scholars observed signs of party decay everywhere, pervading all its roles.

Within the electorate parties seemed increasingly unable to structure the voters' choices of candidates.[3] . . . [T]he electorate's psychological identification with the parties steadily weakened. Not only were fewer voters partisan identifiers, but those who did identify with a party reported weaker attachments.

Perhaps most damning was the voters' lack of interest in the parties. From 1952 to 1980, the percentage of the electorate that had no opinions about America's parties—either good or ill—rose from slightly less than one-tenth to somewhat more than one-third. More than two-thirds opposed the idea of voters registering as partisans, and almost as many rejected a proposal for a party lever on voting machines.[4] The parties, more and more, were not supported or rejected but were considered irrelevant. By a margin of 45 percent to 37 percent, the American public in 1983 believed that "organized special interest groups" spoke to their concerns better than the parties did.[5]

The decline of the parties' organizational role as the vehicle for nomination and election is [also clear]. Local party organizations and their vaunted machines have almost passed into history. Little more than one-tenth of all Democratic and Republican county organizations now have permanent headquarters; even fewer have paid staff.[6] State party strength rebounded a bit from its nadir, but . . . "the evidence is not overwhelming."[7]

At the national level, traditionally the weakest link in the party chain, growth was impressive. The fact remained, however, that the direct primary robbed the parties of their monopoly on nominations, just as the advent of television and computerized direct mail robbed them of their monopoly on campaign communication. In the late 1980s two-thirds of the public declared themselves in favor of primaries as the vehicle for choosing candidates rather than "open meetings of party activists"; 59 percent favored doing away with the national party conventions entirely and having voters select presidential candidates directly.[8] Campaign finance laws made it impossible for candidates to obtain from the parties the large amounts of money required to wage campaigns. Candidates turned to alternative sources such as political action committees, the candidates' personal resources, and direct solicitation of the public.

The parties' role in government suffered as well. Traditionally, parties were able to structure government policy because one party usually controlled both major policy-making institutions—the presidency and the Congress. Until the turn of the century, the president's party controlled the Senate almost 90 percent of the time, and the House more than two-thirds of the time. Most of the rare victories of the out-party occurred in midterm elections. Only twice in more than a hundred years—in the disputed Hayes-Tilden election of 1876 and the second election of Grover Cleveland, in 1892—did the president fail to carry both houses in a presidential election year. Between 1900 and 1954, despite the Populist and Progressive crusades against party control, the trend grew even stronger. The president's party controlled the Senate better than 90 percent of the time and the House more than 80 percent of the time. Not once in all the presidential elections between William McKinley's second campaign and Dwight D. Eisenhower's first campaign did the presidential party fail to bring in both houses of Congress.

Events changed dramatically in the 1950s. Between 1954 and 1990 the president's party would control the Senate barely half the time and the House only a third of the time. Furthermore, party control meant less and less, as both John Kennedy and Jimmy Carter found to their chagrin. Despite majorities in both houses, neither president was able to enact major components of his program. Lyndon Johnson, the only other president of the period to have party control of both houses, was more successful at first, but his accomplishments owed much to the powerful emotions generated by Kennedy's assassination.

Officeholders who appealed to an increasingly nonpartisan electorate to gain victory, often achieving it without any significant reliance on the party for assistance, had no compelling reason to vote a party line. For them, as for voters, the parties were becoming irrelevant. A member of the Democratic party leadership in the House observed:

> Nobody in the United States Congress ever talks about the Democratic or Republican party.... I have never heard a member of the Congress refer to a colleague and urge a vote for him because he was in the same party. Most Democrats and Republicans could not recall three items on the platform of their party.... We have 435 parties in the House.[9]

The result of these developments was, as the 1980s began, that the parties were weaker than they had ever been. The candidate-centered campaigns had their most negative effect on the parties' organizational role, but they impinged on other party functions as well. Campaigns that presented candidates to the public as individuals rather than as partisans hastened the decline of party identification as a means of structuring voters' choice: "The voters did not decide all of a sudden that parties were bankrupt political institutions and mandate their decline. Rather, voters reacted gradually over the last quarter of a century *to the way in which politics was presented to them*."[10]

Candidates for executive office—presidents and governors—appealed to the voters on the basis of leadership and competence, while legislators emphasized their service to their constituencies. Voters responded to these appeals as they heard them; they punished Jimmy Carter for the state of the nation and rewarded Ronald Reagan. At the same time they reelected the vast majority of legislators in both parties, in approval of the way incumbents fulfilled their stated roles and without regard to whether they shared either the partisanship or the policy preferences of successful or unsuccessful presidents.

Officeholders who were voted in as the result of candidate-centered campaigns emphasized electoral considerations in their decision-making calculus. Describing the culture of the House, a top staffer for the Democratic leadership distinguished between the "street-corner guys" and the "Atari guys." The former, a dying breed epitomized by former House Speaker Tip O'Neill and his Republican counterpart, minority leader Robert Michel, came to Congress originally through strong local party organizations. Their major career goal was to achieve seniority and thus important positions in the party leadership. Their orientation was hierarchical; when faced with a tough question, their response was to find out what the chairman or the leader thought about it.

In contrast, the Atari guys of the candidate-centered era arrived in Washington through their own efforts. Many represented areas that had been traditional strongholds of the other party. Many seemed supremely uninterested in their committee assignments; they sought rather to become national spokespersons for the "big issues" and were often notably nondeferential to the House establishment.[11] The same House staffer mused on the behavior of this new breed in their officeholding roles:

> They talk about issues, but little gets accomplished. They just talk. They don't care about bills or chairmen; they just care about sending messages. When they vote, they think, "What kind of ad can they run against me?" The biggest turnout at the caucus meetings is never for legislative discussions but to see the new party TV ads. They say, "Wow! This is great—I can save myself with this ad!"
>
> The only committees they care about getting on are Budget and Ways and Means so they can talk about the big macroeconomic issues, or Defense so they can talk about the big foreign policy issues, or Energy and Commerce so they can get PAC money. The Budget Committee is great because . . . they don't have to make hard program choices, they can just debate the macroeconomic issues.
>
> What do they want? They want to be famous. For the old guys, friendships crossed party lines. For these new guys, it's message sending that crosses party lines.

California's Vic Fazio, a Democratic House member and exemplar of the Atari guys, confirmed this view: "People think you're important so they listen to you. The media want to hear from members of the Budget Committee."[12]

No wonder that through most of the 1970s party cohesion in both House and Senate, as measured by the number of votes on which a majority of legislators of one party opposed a majority in the other party, continued to decline.[13] Increasingly, executives and not parties set the legislative agenda; increasingly, legislators decided whether to support this agenda based largely on an electoral calculus.

Was the party's declining role in the electorate, as organization, and in government permanent and irreversible? So it seemed. In 1982 the American

Political Science Association commissioned a set of papers to assess the state of the discipline. In the paper on political parties, Leon Epstein, a distinguished scholar of parties, asked his colleagues, "Are professional students of politics now champions of a lost cause, trying with words to roll back a tide of American antipartyism?"[14]

The Parties Resurrected? Maybe

In the past few years some of the political scientists who exhibited the most pessimism about the future of the parties (and with it the broader American future) have seen signs of party renascence. One who argued in the 1970s that the weakened parties "may eventually bring the nation to a free floating politics in which prediction is hazardous, continuities are absent, and governmental responsibility is impossible to fix,"[15] was more optimistic by the 1980s: "There is still hope and time available. The need for stronger parties is becoming evident."[16] Another student of party decline had second thoughts by 1984: "It is not inconceivable that the decline of political parties could begin to reverse in the near future."[17] The same year a third well-known scholar argued:

> The two parties show signs of strength as great, if not greater, than they have at any time in the past fifty years. It should be clear by now that the grab bag of assumptions, inferences, and half-truths which have fed the decline of party thesis is simply wrong.[18]

This substantial shift in tone was occasioned by a series of events, occurring mostly around and after the election of President Reagan in 1980, that apparently signaled the reversal of the decay of the party in all its major roles.

Party in the Electorate   There was, first, the matter of party identification within the electorate. Although approximately a third of the voters stubbornly continued to call themselves independents, the proportion of Republicans crept upward, mainly at the expense of the Democrats—some indication that Reagan's admirers were extending their commitment beyond the titular leader of the party to the party itself. Between 1984 and 1988 in twenty-eight states that required party registration, Democrats lost 107,000 adherents, while the Republicans gained 2.1 million:[19]

There were other signs that Reagan's strong leadership polarized the electorate in a partisan way. Ticket splitting for House and Senate races dropped 7 percent between 1980 and 1982, and the percentage of survey respondents who could find no way to characterize the two parties, either positively or negatively, dropped eight points in the same period. The president himself polarized partisans in a truly dramatic fashion. Harris polls charting every president since Kennedy had found that Democrats and Republicans tended to disagree fairly modestly in their assessment of presidential performance in office. Most, for example, agreed that Jimmy Carter was not doing a very good job—only ten percentage points separated the assessments of the two groups of partisans. Richard Nixon held the previous record for polarization, with a twenty-seven-point difference between Democrats and Republicans. In October 1983, however, the partisan discrepancy in views of Reagan was a full thirty-four points, and a September 1984 CBS News/*New York Times* poll charted an unprecedented gulf of fifty-six points.[20] Thus there were modest signs that the electorate might finally be realigning toward the Republicans, a shift that had previously been "akin to waiting for the Second Coming—much discussion, not much happening."[21]

Party as Organization   The strengthening of the party organizations at the national level continued apace. Both parties' congressional campaign committees engaged in extensive candidate recruitment and "nursing" activities. Fred Asbell of the National Republican Congressional Committee estimated that his organization was involved in a "major way" with sixty to sixty-five House candidates, or almost half of all NRCC-targeted districts in 1984. Martin Franks, director of the Democratic Congressional Campaign Committee, put the figure for his committee at thirty to thirty-five, "up from zero in 1980."[22]

There were signs that these efforts were bearing fruit. Analysts pointed to a sharp drop over time in the number of uncontested House seats; it began about 1960 but escalated in 1980 and 1982. They attributed this growing competition at least in part to the strengthened parties.[23] At lower levels there were reports of increasing state party activity in areas such as coordinated polling, media production, and mailings for legislative candidates. State party subsidies in many states extended to the level of county office. Thus at all levels there were new signs of life. The literature decrying the death of the parties was replaced by a new spate of books hailing their organizational revitalization.[24]

Party and Governance   Finally, dramatic shifts were apparent in the legislative behavior of officeholders. We referred earlier to the falling levels of party voting in both the House and the Senate. The Reagan administration, however, seemed to polarize legislators in much the same way that it polarized voters. In 1987 a majority of House Democrats opposed a majority of Republicans on 64 percent of all recorded votes—an all-time high.[25] Additionally, there was a strong ideological cast to the partisan divisions, with the Republican members becoming more conservative across all major issue areas (social policy, foreign policy, and the economy) and the Democrats becoming more liberal.

The strength of these partisan divisions cut across all regions. Even though Republican legislators from the East were more liberal than the rest of their party, and southern Democrats were more conservative than other Democrats, no Republican regional group was more liberal than any Democratic group. As a group, eastern Republicans were still more conservative than southern Democrats.[26]

If "the ultimate test of party linkage is the behavior of the party member in government,"[27] the signs seemed to indicate that in the 1980s officeholders were finally passing that test. Some analysts saw the increased party voting in the legislature as a direct consequence of the party's organizational activity. They speculated that the stepped-up party efforts that produced similar campaigns and similar issues across the country were responsible for the parties' more like-minded legislators. The campaign committees were seen as having a nationalizing and centralizing effect.[28]

The parties appeared to be regaining some of their lost effectiveness in all their roles. And if party meant more, it would follow that candidate-centered campaigns would mean less.

The Parties Resurrected? Maybe Not

Although the evidence for revitalized parties seems impressive, the old saying "One swallow does not a summer make" applies powerfully in this case. Short-term changes do not always become long-term trends. Party identification among the electorate has been notably unstable throughout the 1980s. Identification with the Democrats ranged from an eighteen-point lead in the depths of the 1982 recession to a fourteen-point lead in the early fall of 1988 and, in the immediate afterglow of the 1988 presidential election, a seven-point lead. After the election of 1984, there was a virtual tie.[29] Two surveys that monitored party identification over twenty-two weeks during the 1984 campaign found frequent and substantial shifts during that election season. Analysts of these data concluded, "When we find that a campaign can move partisanship, we do not have proof that such changes will outlast that campaign."[30]

The effects of party organizational activity were also difficult to quantify. The Republicans' position in the states showed little overall improvement in the 1980s. Despite the massive efforts of the Republicans to elect candidates to Congress and to the state legislatures, George Bush entered the White House in 1989 as the twentieth-century president with the fewest fellow partisans in the House.[31]

Campaign committee staff members were at best tentative in agreeing with some academics that their work might influence the voting behavior of the legislators they supported.[32] They recognized that even grateful challengers, once elected, became incumbents able to command contributions from nonparty sources. A cautious political scientist noted, "Once in office, members of Congress may be invulnerable to party pressure based on past or prospective allocations of party campaign resources." Observing that the Republican party bureaucracy "has not developed substantial influence over policymaking by Republican officeholders," he went on to say, "Indeed, influence tends to run the other way."[33]

The party's influence on PAC contributions was also limited. A survey found that directors of PACs were most likely to seek information and take contribution cues from their largest and most influential colleagues. Corporate and trade associations looked for guidance more to the Business-Industry Political Action Committee (BIPAC), labor committees to the AFL-CIO's Committee on Political Education (COPE), and liberal ideological groups to the National Committee for an Effective Congress (NCEC) than any of them did to the political parties.[34]

Heavy contributions by business-oriented PACs to Democratic incumbents made Republican congressional leaders particularly irate. A contingent led by Senate minority leader Bob Dole called a Washington meeting of business PAC directors in September 1988 and threatened to support legislation limiting PAC activity. House minority leader Robert Michel and NRCC chairman Guy Vander Jagt followed up in October. In a letter to top corporate officials, they wrote that it was "disturbing to see so many contributions going to members who consistently oppose the interest you and other business leaders advocate."[35] PAC leaders were unimpressed. They were more interested in protecting their access to Democratic committee chairs and other incumbents, particularly after the failure of Republican challengers to gain seats in 1986 and 1988. . . .

Finally, the effect of party activity on competition levels was erratic. Although the number of uncontested congressional seats had, as we have noted, dropped sharply after 1960, particularly in presidential years, it suddenly rose dramatically in 1984 to a level more than twice that of 1980. Of the fifty-three uncontested seats in 1984, forty-four were held by Democrats. Twenty-six of those were in the South, despite the resources the Republican party could offer challengers and its much improved southern performance. This pattern continued in 1988, when eighty House seats went uncontested by one of the major parties; sixty-one of those seats were held by Democrats.

It is also necessary to keep in perspective the high levels of party cohesion in congressional voting. Although it is true that the Democrats were more unified in their opposition to the Republicans during the Reagan administration than at any time since 1908, it was also the first time they had found themselves on the defensive against an activist and ideological president. Their behavior was similar to the Republicans' reaction to Democratic activists John Kennedy and Lyndon Johnson in the 1960s. In Reagan's final year in office, party voting dropped back to the levels of 1979.[36]

Much of the time, even during the Reagan years, the percentage of party votes in which a majority (more than 50 percent) of Democrats opposed a majority of Republicans was less than half the total number of votes. In 1988 only 23 percent of House roll calls and 12 percent of those in the Senate resulted in as many as three-quarters of Democrats and Republicans opposing each other. True party-line votes, where at least 90 percent of those on opposite sides of the aisle were in disagreement, numbered only 7 percent of House votes and a mere 3 percent in the Senate. Thus on the majority of roll call votes, most legislators of both parties voted the same way, or partisans distributed themselves more randomly.[37]

Nonparty votes were often cast on the classic pork barrel issues that legislators point to when they run for reelection as constituency ombudsmen. If we use the loosest definition of party unity (that is, votes in which at least 50 percent of Democrats and Republicans oppose each other), legislation dealing with appropriations of funds comprised less than one-tenth of the 1988 party votes in both the House and the Senate. If we use the strict criterion of 90 percent of opposing partisans in disagreement, not a single appropriations vote could be characterized as a true party-line vote. For constituency-minded legislators, pork barrel issues loomed larger than their votes on national security and foreign policy matters, which were relatively speaking much more likely to have a strong partisan cast.[38] One congressional observer noted: "Rhetoric is one thing, but when it comes down to who gets what, you pay attention to how they act, not how they talk. That's where partisanship falls apart."[39]

The overall note we sound in this section, therefore, is one of caution. Many of the trends of the last decade may be transitory; others are subject to the classic debate over whether a glass is half-empty or half-full. It appears to us that the political environment still contains many more forces that impel candidates away from parties and party discipline and toward the continuation of candidate-centered campaigns and what they imply for the behavior of voters and of candidates who become officeholders.

Notes

1. Walter Dean Burnham, "Foreword," in Martin P. Wattenberg, *The Decline of American Political Parties*, (Cambridge, Mass.: Harvard University Press, 1984), xii.
2. Wattenberg, *Decline of American Political Parties*, 128. This argument is further discussed later in this chapter.
3. See Norman H. Nie, Sidney Verba, and John R. Petrocik, *The Changing American Voter* (Cambridge, Mass.: Harvard University Press, 1976).
4. Wattenberg, *Decline of American Political Parties*, 63; Larry J. Sabato, *The Party's Just Begun* (Glenview, Ill.: Scott, Foresman, 1988), 224, 225.
5. Larry J. Sabato, *PAC Power: Inside the World of the Political Action Committees* (New York: Norton, 1984), 163.
6. David E. Price, *Bringing Back the Parties* (Washington, D.C.: CQ Press, 1984), 25.
7. Leon Epstein, "The Scholarly Commitment to Parties," in *Political Science: The State of the Discipline*, ed. Ada W. Finifter (Washington, D.C.: American Political Science Association, 1983), 142.
8. Sabato, *Party's Just Begun*, 207; Media General/Associated Press poll of 1,204 adults, April 29-May 8, 1988.
9. Democratic representative Thomas Foley, quoted in Austin Ranney, *The Referendum Device* (Washington, D.C.: American Enterprise Institute, 1981), 70.
10. Wattenberg, *Decline of American Political Parties*, 125. (Emphasis added.)
11. Burdett Loomis, *The New American Politician: Ambition, Entrepreneurship and the Changing Face of Political Life* (New York: Basic Books, 1988), is an extended study of the "new breed." An earlier important treatment is Robert Salisbury and Kenneth Shepsle, "U.S. Congressman and Enterprise," *Legislative Studies Quarterly* 6 (November 1981): 559-576.
12. *Congressional Quarterly Weekly Report*, September 13, 1986, 2135.
13. See the data on party cohesion in David W. Brady, Joseph Cooper, and Patricia A. Hurley, "The Decline of Party in the U.S. House of Representatives, 1887-1968," *Legislative Studies Quarterly* 4 (August 1979): 381-408; *Congressional Quarterly Weekly Report*, January 9, 1982, 61-64.
14. Epstein, "Scholarly Commitment to Parties," 147.

15. Gerald Pomper, "Impacts on the Political System," in *American Electoral Behavior*, ed. Samuel Kirkpatrick (Beverly Hills, Calif.: Sage, 1976), 137.
16. Gerald Pomper, *Party Renewal in America* (New York: Praeger, 1980), 15.
17. Wattenberg, *Decline of American Political Parties*, xvi.
18. Joseph Schlesinger, "The New American Political Party," *American Political Science Review* 79 (December 1985): 1152.
19. *National Journal*, December 3, 1988, 3097.
20. These data appear in Martin P. Wattenberg, "The Reagan Polarization Phenomenon and the Continued Downward Slide in Presidential Popularity," *American Politics Quarterly* 14 (July 1986): 219-246; Wattenberg, *Decline of American Political Parties*, xvii; John Kenneth White and Dwight L. Morris, "Shifting Coalitions in American Politics: The Changing Partisans," paper presented at the annual meeting of the American Political Science Association, Washington, D.C., August 30, 1984-September 3, 1984; the CBS News/*New York Times* polls of September 12-16 and November 8-14, 1984; and the ABC News/*Washington Post* poll of September 7-11, 1984.
21. White and Morris, "Shifting Coalitions," 5.
22. Transcribed remarks at the Roundtable on National Recruitment of Congressional Candidates: Trends and Consequences, annual meeting of the American Political Science Association, Washington, D.C., August 31, 1984.
23. Schlesinger, "New American Political Party," 1160.
24. For example, David E. Price, *Bringing Back the Parties*; Cornelius Cotter et al., *Party Organizations in American Politics* (New York: Praeger, 1984); Xandra Kayden and Eddie Mahe, *The Party Goes On* (New York: Basic Books, 1985); Paul S. Herrnson, *Party Campaigning in the 1980s* (Cambridge, Mass.: Harvard University Press, 1988).
25. *Congressional Quarterly Weekly Report*, November 19, 1988, 3334.
26. Calculated by *National Journal*, April 2, 1988, 873-899.
27. Schlesinger, "New American Political Party," 1168.
28. Gary C. Jacobson, "The Republican Advantage in Campaign Finance," in *The New Direction in American Politics*, ed. John Chubb and Paul Peterson (Washington, D.C.: Brookings Institution, 1985), 143-174; Sabato, *Party's Just Begun*, 99.
29. Carolyn Smith, ed., *The 84 Vote* (New York: ABC News, 1984), 43-44; George Gallup, Jr., "GOP Strength Declines," *Polling Report*, November 9, 1987, 2; George Gallup, Jr., and Alec Gallup, "Democratic Edge at 14 Points," *Polling Report*, August 22, 1988, 8; *New York Times*, November 10, 1988, B6.
30. Dee Allsop and Herbert F. Weisberg, "Measuring Change in Party Identification in an Election Campaign," *American Journal of Political Science* 32 (November 1988): 1014.
31. *Congressional Quarterly Weekly Report*, November 12, 1988, 3299, reviews state legislative results over the decade.
32. From transcribed remarks by Fred Asbell of the NRCC and Martin Franks of the DCCC at the Roundtable on National Recruitment of Congressional Candidates, August 31, 1984.
33. David Adamany, "Political Parties in the 1980s," in *Money and Politics in the United States*, ed. Michael J. Malbin (Chatham, N.J.: Chatham House, 1984), 111, 114.
34. Sabato, *PAC Power*, 46.
35. *Congressional Quarterly Weekly Report*, November 19, 1988, 3367.
36. *Congressional Quarterly Weekly Report*, November 19, 1988, 3335.

37. "Universalistic" votes—those on which 90 percent of House members vote the same way—hovered at or above 30 percent of all roll calls between 1965 and 1980, a level unmatched in any prior congressional sessions since 1921. Melissa Collie, "Universalism and the Parties in the U.S. House of Representatives," *American Journal of Political Science* 32 (November 1988): 869.
38. *Congressional Quarterly Weekly Report*, November 19, 1988, 3335-3337.
39. *Congressional Quarterly Weekly Report*, January 16, 1988, 106.

42 / The Impact of Direct Marketing on Political Parties

R. Kenneth Godwin

Computers, of course, have had tremendous impact on American society, affecting a wide variety of dimensions including politics. As just one important example, computers—and the large mailing lists they make so accessible—have made it possible for candidates, parties, and PACs to directly solicit funds from literally millions of citizens. This practice has grown to the point that an old adage can now be expanded: the *three* things that are certain in life are death, taxes, and a fundraising letter from some politician.

Kenneth Godwin reviews the growth in the use of direct marketing over the past few decades, and assesses the different impacts this phenomenon has had on the two major parties.

Direct mail emerged as an important political weapon as early as 1952 when Dwight Eisenhower ran as the Republican candidate for President.[1] Eisenhower entered the race unsure of which issues he should emphasize. An innovative staff member, one who probably had a good background in new product promotions, suggested that the best way to choose among issues would be to try several topics or themes at the same time. To do this, the campaign sent a different fund-raising letter to ten groups of 10,000 persons— each letter stressing a different issue. The letter that discussed the Korean war received the biggest response, raised the most money, and indicated to Eisenhower that this was the issue he should use to become the next President of the United States...

Between 1964 and 1984, direct mail emerged from a little-used method for special situations to the dominant means of political fund raising. The most successful of all political direct mailers, the national committees of the Republican party, raised over $200 million for the 1984 electoral campaign, almost six times the amount collected by their Democratic counterparts[2]... The huge sums of money, tremendous Republican advantage, and generous contributions of PACs have changed dramatically the role of the national parties, the personnel who work for them, and campaign funding for candidates. This [reading] examines these changes and their effects on politics in the United States.

The Republican Advantage

Although Dwight Eisenhower was the first Republican presidential candidate to use direct mail effectively to raise funds and determine which issues he should stress in the 1952 presidential election, the Republican party's current direct-mail program began with Barry Goldwater in 1964. The Goldwater campaign mailed over 12 million letters, raised $4.7 million, and created a list of over 221,000 contributors.[3] The Republican National Committee (RNC) used this list to begin a direct-response program that continues intact today.

Senator Goldwater's direct mailings appealed to persons who felt disenfranchised by both the national political system and their own party. His letters combined an emotional appeal and a threatened good—"Extremism in the defense of liberty"—and gave his supporters an opportunity to feel politically efficacious. These mailings argued that if the conservatives did not win in 1964, they might never have another chance; liberals would dominate both parties. But if conservatives supported Goldwater's candidacy, they could achieve an important victory. This blend of emotion, threat, and appeal to political efficacy reflected Goldwater's own beliefs; it was also the perfect recipe for successful direct mailing.[4] This fortuitous correspondence accounts for much of the Republican party's current direct-mail success.

Between 1976 and 1984, the RNC increased its contributions from direct mail by more than 1000 percent and tripled its house list of contributors. By 1980, the combined direct-marketing receipts of the three national committees—the RNC, the Republican National Senatorial Committee (NRSC), and the National Republican Congressional Committee (NRCC)—exceeded $100 million; in the 1981-82 electoral cycle, this total reached over $130 million and represented 77 percent of the party's receipts.[5] By 1984, the RNC had built a house list that peaked at over 1.1 million contributors and in the 1985-86 electoral cycle raised $201 million.[6] The three committees currently send over 30 million pieces of mail annually and work continuously to broaden the party's basis of support.[7]

Democratic national committees have not been nearly as successful as their Republican counterparts. Their three national committees raised only $31.4 million for the 1982 elections, or about 16 cents for each Republican dollar.[8] Herbert Alexander, a leading expert on money and politics in the United States, found that from 1976 to 1980, the Democratic National Committee (DNC) raised only $8.3 million through direct mail, less than one-third the amount the RNC received in response to its direct-marketing solicitations in 1980 alone![9] Only in George McGovern's campaign in 1972—a campaign that reflected a similar situation and appeal to the 1964 Goldwater campaign—and in the 1984 Senate race in North Carolina—where Governor

Hunt was able to capitalize on liberals' intense dislike of Jesse Helms—have the Democrats come close to matching the Republicans in direct-mail receipts.

How Party Elites View Direct Marketing

The directors of the Republican and Democratic direct-marketing programs suggest that a major cause of the imbalance between the two parties is the failure of the Democrats to identify a cohesive set of ideas or ideology to which recipients of direct mailings can respond.[10] While the GOP can appeal to fight the "Teddy Kennedy liberals," inflation, and the growth of big government, the Democrats do not have an easily identifiable enemy. Ronald Reagan [was] not the bogeyman to Democrats that Senator Kennedy is to Republicans, and the "fairness" issue [did] not threaten and mobilize upper-middle-class Democrats the way "big government" and "high taxes" activate Republicans. The success of Democratic mailings against Jesse Helms indicates, however, that Democrats can raise money through direct-response programs, if they find the right enemy and threat.

A second reason given by both Democrats and Republicans for the failure of the DNC to copy the success of the RNC is that, with the exception of McGovern, all Democratic presidential candidates are too moderate. Morris Dees, one of the leaders of McGovern's 1972 direct-mail drive, believes that direct marketing will not work for the current Democratic leaders because they lack the extreme appeal necessary for effective direct marketing.[11]

Although Teddy Kennedy is the ultimate liberal enemy to conservatives, he does not appeal to the more radical liberals McGovern reached. Democratic party leaders feel that part of this problem stems from the heterogeneity of their party.[12] If a candidate makes a radical appeal to one sector, he alienates another. This sentiment was echoed by David Adamany, who wrote that "mass-mail appeals appear to be most successful when pitched to ideological groups, the Democrats may find responses to their mass-mail fund raising limited to the party's liberal activists, but the party is so diverse that it includes important groups of moderates and conservatives as well. It would therefore risk alienating important constituencies if it pitched its financial appeals to one ideological group within the party coalition."[13]

The unenthusiastic attitude of liberal elites toward direct marketing also reduces the Democrats' success. A direct mailer for several liberal citizen action groups stated: "Most liberals fail to understand the advertising benefits of direct mail and only see it as a way of raising money." A direct-marketing specialist within the DNC argued that the Democratic party leadership neither understood the advertising benefits of mailings nor did it find the work that must go into effectively mining the membership as exciting as other aspects of politics. This opinion was repeated by Roger Craver, the leading direct-mail expert for liberal causes and the head of Governor Hunt's very successful direct-response program.[14]

A common explanation of Democratic and liberal respondents for the greater success of Republicans and conservatives was their more extensive use of extremism and emotionalism. Comparisons of the actual mailings of

Republicans, Democrats, conservatives, and liberals do not support this explanation; instead, the reverse is true.... Democrats are slightly, but not significantly, more likely to use extremism and emotionalism than Republicans; and liberals are more likely to utilize these techniques than are conservatives. Part of the reason that extremism by conservatives is a popular and plausible explanation is the visibility of the National Conservative Political Action Committee (NCPAC). This PAC's mailings score extremely high in fear and emotionalism, and between 1980 and 1984 NCPAC sent more mail than any political organization other than the Republican National Committee.

The earlier start of the Republicans and the budgetary constraints that have plagued the Democratic party in recent years provide final explanations of the differences in their direct-marketing success. The Republican direct-mail program began in 1964; the Democrats began almost a decade later, and their efforts were temporarily halted a number of times because of the party's massive debt problems. Because direct marketing requires a substantial initial investment and prospect mailings often lose money, an organization needs investment capital to mail effectively. The Republicans had the necessary capital, made the investment, and received substantial dividends. Even if the Democrats liked direct marketing, were more homogeneous, and had a readily identifiable national target, their late start and huge party debt would have placed them far behind the Republicans in direct-mail fund raising.

Although the political resources that direct marketing generates for the Republican party are much greater than those generated by the Democrats' direct-response program, the real question, as Elizabeth Drew points out, is not how well one group or another does with it, but how does this imbalance affect the political system? Does the inequality produce different kinds of candidates? Does it make effective government more difficult? Does it change public policy?[15]

Not surprisingly, the directors of the parties' direct-marketing fund raising efforts see the impact of *their* programs as a positive influence. They believe that the direct mail sent by the political parties educates the public, increases political interest and party loyalty, encourages more ideological parties, and makes politicians more responsive to the electorate. Not all direct-marketing and direct-mail experts within the two major parties see all of these positive things happening, but most believe that direct mail increases participation and democracy in America.

When asked whether direct mail generates more extremism in the political system, the directors of both parties' direct-marketing programs responded affirmatively. Each believed that because threat and a sense of urgency had to be created in every mailing, the number of extreme groups and individuals had increased. At the same time, however, the Republican leaders did not feel that direct marketing had polarized either the electorate or national politics. Instead, they saw direct mail from the parties as leading to a more responsible party system. They expected these beneficial consequences because party mailings impart information that helps the citizenry integrate issues into a coherent political ideology and alerts them to the party's positions on major issues. . . .

One significant characteristic of both Republican and Democratic party mailings is an absence of single issues. In our sample of party mailings the closest a Republican letter came to stressing a single issue was an appeal based on balancing the budget—an issue central to the Republican party platform under Ronald Reagan. Democratic mailings accentuated the traditional party issues of fairness in taxation and the failure of the Republicans to concern themselves with the poor.

All the party elites we interviewed reported that they intentionally stayed away from single issues and stressed instead loyalty, belonging, and traditional partisan issues. This decision not to use single issues was a pragmatic one, according to Phil Smith of the RNC. He stated that if there were single issues that the RNC could use, it would, but that contributors to the Republican party had not responded well to single issues in the past. Rod Smith of the National Republican Senatorial Committee pointed out that even if a single-issue prospect mailing had a good response, these persons did not make good house-list members because they had no loyalty to the ideals of the Republican party. They gave as a "knee jerk" response to a particular threat, but rarely gave again.

Partially because of their lack of success in direct marketing, Democratic party respondents were far more likely than their Republican counterparts to see direct mail as detrimental to the political system. The Democratic leadership believed that this political tool not only led to political extremism but also reduced opportunities for compromise among competing interests. As was true with Republican respondents, however, the Democrats we interviewed distinguished between direct marketing by the parties and that by single-issue citizen action groups and ideological PACS. In fact, a majority of the respondents from both political parties felt that some nonparty groups abused direct mail by emphasizing only negativism, extremism, and fear; and both Republicans and Democrats were likely to suggest that the mailings of Richard Viguerie and NCPAC were the worst offenders.[16] This perception by party elites that their mailings differ substantially from ideological PACs is correct. . . . [W]hen we combine the mailings of the parties into one category and those of both liberal and conservative ideological PACs into another, substantial differences emerge. Ideological PACs are more likely to stress fear and guilt, threatened values, and to use the propaganda techniques of card stacking and glittering generalities. Party mailings place much greater emphasis on citizen duty, political efficacy, and future values that a contributor can gain by donating to the party.

To summarize the perceptions of the party fund raisers, there was universal agreement that direct mail has helped the Republicans and conservatives much more than the Democrats and liberals, and a major reason for this was the absence of emotional issues that directly threaten potential Democratic and liberal contributors. There was close to complete agreement among interviewees from both parties that Democrats do not like direct marketing and that it will always be a better tool for the Republicans. And there was consensus among these party officials that the direct-marketing efforts of the political parties have had a positive impact on the political process. Although a consensus concerning the impact of other political direct mailers did not emerge, a majority of Democrats and Republicans felt that ideological PACs, particularly NCPAC, had hurt the political system through the use of extremism and negative independent expenditures.

The Changing Party Roles

Perhaps no set of events surprised political observers in the late 1970s as much as the emergence of the Republican party as a dynamic and effective institution. In 1975, for example, Joyce Gelb and Marian Palley wrote of American national parties:

> ...the national parties have little power vested in them and possess no real authority over state and local party organizations or elected officials.... [They are] little more than paper organizations during the years between presidential campaigns.[17]

...By the early 1980s, however, many political scientists had caught up with the reality of the Republican success and were writing of the rise of national parties and greater party ideology and power.[18]

Direct marketing was not the only factor in the emergence of the Republican national organizations; campaign finance laws also encouraged this process. The 1971 and 1974 campaign finance laws forced the centralization of presidential campaigns because of the many requirements related to the size and disclosure of contributions. Direct mail made the generation of large numbers of small contributions possible, and computer-readable numbers on return envelopes made the recording of contributions much simpler. The 1979 amendments to the campaign finance legislation accelerated the centralization process by allowing the national party organizations to fund the state and local party contributions to candidates and by permitting unlimited transfers of funds from the national parties to state and local organizations for use in voter registration, voter mobilization, and other grassroots activities.[19] These changes in election finance legislation, coupled with the development of the modern technologies of direct marketing and the importance of campaign polling, made the emergence of stronger national parties and the fund-raising domination by direct mail inevitable.

As might be expected, direct marketing has had different effects on the two parties. The Republican party has become more centralized, ideologically cohesive, and staffed by technical specialists in marketing, polling, and media presentations; the Democratic party has become more fragmented, state and local oriented, and centered on individual candidates. Local GOP parties and candidates have become increasingly dependent on national party assistance while local Democratic organizations and candidates have become increasingly independent of national party organizations and more dependent on nonparty organizations such as labor and citizen action groups.[20]

Bill Brock, chairman of the RNC, saw the opportunities that direct mail presented for the Republican party. He developed a strong national organization funded by direct mail and controlled by a centralized party that could assist state and local parties and individual political campaigns.[21] Brock's direct-mail program was a stunning success. In the 1977-78 electoral cycle, an expenditure of $7,973,000 brought a return of $25,128,000. In the 1979-80 cycle, an investment of $12.1 million returned $54.1 million.[22] The Republican party was so productive in its mailings that, contrary to other direct mailers, the overhead costs of direct mail were cheaper than all other kinds of party fund raising.[23]

Two factors stand out when comparing the national party organizations before 1970 and the national parties today. First, the characteristics of party professionals has changed dramatically. In the past, party officials were persons whose expertise was in generating money from large donors and in developing coalitions; today's professionals are skilled in computers, direct marketing, and public opinion polling. Second, the central bureaucracy of the Republican party has greater independence from contributors than any party in American history. The small donors who provide more than 70 percent of the national GOP's budget have little or no say in party decisions. Their contributions, however, sharply curtail the influence of large donors. David Adamany writes of this independence:

> Those who contribute the money to support the Republican party apparatus, largely in response to ideological appeals, have no direct voice in selecting party leaders or making decisions about party organization or activities. At most, they can withdraw their financial support if they become discontented.... As a consequence, the Republican party is able to maintain a professional bureaucracy that directs vast resources and activities that are largely insulated from state and local party organizations.[24]

Despite its ability to ignore state and local parties, the RNC has chosen not to do so. Instead, the RNC hired full-time regional coordinators to coordinate and encourage state and local inputs and established extensive training programs for state and local party elites. The national party organizations, however, did begin to exert substantial control over state and local party organizations through contributions to their treasuries and candidates at all levels and by directly hiring campaign consultants for candidates. In the 1984 elections, for example, the GOP national committees gave an average of almost $27,000 in either direct or coordinated expenditures to candidates for the House of Representatives, a figure that represented 10.5 percent of the candidates' total expenditures. In sharp contrast, Democratic candidates received less than 3 percent of their campaign funds from their party.[25]

Contributions and coordinated expenditures represent only a portion of what the Republican national party has been able to do for its candidates. The party committees employ a permanent staff of pollsters, media specialists, direct-mail advisers, and advertising specialists who train party workers and prepare sophisticated campaign packages. In addition, the party finances national advertising campaigns with common themes, provides press releases, and polls local districts to determine issues on which Democratic incumbents might be vulnerable.[26] During the 1980 elections the RNC staff wrote more than 700 computer programs for candidates and state party organizations, surveyed data from 175,000 precincts, and handled more than 20 million names for get-out-the-vote drives.[27]

The national Republican political action committee that assists local and state GOP candidates, GOPAC, raised $2.64 million for state races in 1984 and almost doubled that amount in the 1986 elections. In 1985, the RNC made cash grants totaling $400,000 to 214 key counties to assist county organizations in changing voters' registrations from Democratic to Republican, mailed 1.2 million pieces of mail to registered Democrats, and spent $350,000 on a media campaign as part of this same project.[28] In October 1985, the RNC chairman, Frank Fahrenkopf, announced his 1991 plan, which included funneling $1.4 million to state parties to assist their fund-raising efforts. Obviously none of these activities would be possible in the absence of the tremendous influx of funds that the GOP derives from its direct-response campaigns.

As the above paragraphs suggest, the thrust of the Republican national committees is unmistakable: They are encouraging more modern technology in all sectors of party activities and a more ideological approach to politics. The national organizations are dominated by technicians who have taken over almost all the functions traditionally filled by volunteers and local party regulars. Even in the area of voter mobilization, direct mail has taken charge. Xandra Kayden writes of this transformation:

> changes in communication technology . . . have eliminated the need for door-to-door activities: direct mail and paid media enable the party . . . to communicate directly and fully with voters in a far more sophisticated and complete manner than volunteer message carriers, however well-trained and articulate.[29]

The Republican national organizations have far outdistanced their Democratic counterparts. While the Republican organizations were becoming stronger, more centralized, and increasingly dominated by direct-marketing professionals and other technicians, the national Democratic organizations were actually becoming weaker.[30] Plagued by debt, the Democrats were unable to invest heavily in direct marketing. Even the Democratic national telethons, the party's major direct-marketing fund raiser in the 1970s, lost money in its most recent effort and deprived the Democratic National Committee of the major source of revenue that it previously used to assist state and local party organizations.

For the Democrats, this absence of national party strength has meant the rise of candidate organizations and increasing reliance on nonparty groups. Although the national organizations cannot afford to hire the necessary media, direct-marketing, and polling specialists, strong candidates can; but they must raise the necessary funds from sources not traditionally associated with Democratic party support and ideology. The most significant of these new sources are corporate and trade association PACS. These PACs increased their contributions to Democratic incumbent candidates for the House from an average of $33,800 in 1980 to $72,500 in 1984, more than ten times the amount the average candidate received from his or her party.[31]

At local and state levels, Democratic party organizations have fared better. Although the GOP strategy to capture state offices is heavily influenced by the national party and its resources, the local Democratic parties utilize not only the small contributions from the national committees but from many nonparty organizations such as the National Committee for an Effective Congress, the American Federation of State, County, and Municipal Workers, and labor unions. As John Bibby points out, the Republican and Democratic strategies at state and local levels clearly reflect the differences in the parties' strengths and orientation. The GOP effort is a party effort directed from the national level; the Democratic endeavors are joint operations with nonparty groups, with the latter in control of many major responsibilities.[32]

In the long run, the reliance of state and local Democratic organizations on nonparty institutions may strengthen the party. The Republicans' dependence on paid professionals and the national committees reduces opportunities for providing solidary benefits to local workers. Although the number of volunteers is declining in both parties, and this decrease has occurred not only because of increasing professionalism within the parties but also because of major social changes,[33] many nonparty organizations continue to offer the solidary and purposive incentives that can tie individuals to the parties if they see their organization's goals as partisan issues....

Summary

...[T]he increased use of direct marketing has affected political parties.... [T]he Republican party has a distinct advantage over Democrats. Republicans raise more than four times as much money through direct mail as Democrats do, and these funds—and the independence from large contributors that direct mail makes possible— have led to an increasingly powerful national Republican party....

Notes

1. The use of political direct mail actually predates the Eisenhower campaign. Woodrow Wilson used direct mail to campaign for President, and other candidates used it sporadically.
2. Interviews with direct response program personnel of the three Republican national committees. For data on previous years see Herbert Alexander, *Financing the 1980 Election* (Lexington, Mass.: Lexington Books, 1983); Larry Sabato, *PAC Power: Inside the World of Political Action Committees* (New York: Norton, 1984); and Gary C. Jacobson, "The Republican Advantage in Campaign Finance," in

The New Direction in American Politics, ed. John Chubb and Paul Peterson (Washington, D.C.: Brookings Institution, 1985).

3. Herbert Alexander, *Financing the 1964 Election* (Princeton, N.J.: Citizens' Research Foundation, 1966), 71.

4. Constance Cook, in her article "Participation in Public Interest Groups: Membership Motivations," *American Politics Quarterly* 12 (1984): 409-30, found that the single most important reason persons joined these groups was to increase their personal political efficacy.

5. Xandra Kayden and Eddie Mahe, Jr., *The Party Goes On* (New York: Basic Books, 1985), 81.

6. The GOP committees' house lists have fallen substantially since 1984. Leah Geraghty, finance chairman of the RNC, reports that its house list has fallen from 900,000 in 1984 to 700,000 in 1986. This drop appears to be the result of a saturated market. It currently costs the RNC 35 cents for every dollar it receives compared with 22 cents in 1980. Cited in Janet Novack, "The Gold Mine Is Playing Out," *Forbes Magazine*, 6 April 1987, 146-47.

7. Interviews with direct-response program personnel of the three national committees.

8. David Adamany, "Political Parties in the 1980s," and Gary Jacobson, "Money in the 1980 and 1982 Congressional Elections," in *Money and Politics in the United States: Financing Elections in the 1980s*, ed. Michael Malbin (Chatham, N.J.: Chatham House, 1984). Marjorie Hershey, *Running for Office: The Political Education of Campaigners* (Chatham, N.J.: Chatham House, 1984), 122.

9. Herbert Alexander, *Financing Politics: Money, Elections, and Political Reform*, 3d ed. (Washington, D.C.: CQ Press, 1985), 70-74.

10. Unless otherwise noted, comments from Republican and Democratic party leaders come from interviews with the direct-response program staffs of the two national parties. The first set of interviews were carried out by Margaret Latus and a follow-up set of interviews were conducted by the author in 1986.

11. Cited in *Newsweek*, 6 November 1978.

12. While 56 percent of Republican party identifiers classify themselves as conservative, Democrats are much less cohesive. Twenty-seven percent describe themselves as liberal, 38 percent as moderate, and 29 as conservative. Harris survey, *Boston Globe*, 11 November 1984. Cited in Kayden and Mahe, *The Party Goes On*, 177.

13. Adamany, "Political Parties in the 1980 Election."

14. Quoted in the *National Journal*, 10 October 1984, 1983.

15. Elizabeth Drew, *Politics and Money: The New Road to Corruption* (New York: Macmillan, 1983).

16. The perception among party elites that ideological PACs are detrimental to the political system has been prominent since Richard Richards was director of the RNC. Richards believed that the elimination of extremist groups, especially NCPAC, would be in the best interest of the political system. *White House Weekly*, 20 July 1981, 3.

17. Joyce Gelb and Marian Lief Palley, *Tradition and Change in American Party Politics* (New York: Crowell, 1975), 211.

18. See A. James Reichley, "The Rise of National Parties," in *The New Direction in American Politics*, ed. John Chubb and Paul Peterson (Washington, D.C.: Brookings Institution, 1985); Kayden and Mahe, *The Party Goes On*; Christopher Arterton, "Political Money and Party Strength," in *The Future of American Political Parties*, ed. Joel Fleishman (Englewood Cliffs, N.J.: Prentice Hall, 1982); John

Bibby, "Party Renewal in the National Republican Party," in *Party Renewal in America: Theory and Practice*, ed. Gerald Pomper (New York: Praeger, 1980); and Gary Orren, "The Changing Styles of American Party Politics," in Fleishman, *The Future of American Political Parties*.

19. Reichley, "The Rise of National Parties," 73; and Gary Jacobson, *The Politics of Congressional Elections*, 2d. ed. (Boston: Little Brown, 1987), 68–73.

20. John F. Bibby, "Political Party Trends in 1985: The Continuing but Constrained Advance of the National Party," *Publius* 16 (Summer 1986): 79-91.

21. James Reichley argues that the most important decision Brock made as chairman of the Republican National Committee was to emphasize direct-mail fund raising. In an interview with Reichley, Brock indicated that the decision was an easy one: "There was really no other way to build an effective national party." Quoted in Reichley, "The Rise of National Parties," 187.

22. Ibid.

23. Xandra Kayden, "Parties and the 1980 Election," in Campaign Finance Study Group, *Financing Presidential Campaigns* (Cambridge, Mass., John F. Kennedy School of Government, Institute of Politics, Harvard University, 1982), II. Even with the increase in overhead costs of the GOP's direct mailings, direct mail is still much cheaper per dollar generated than other fund-raising efforts.

24. Adamany, "Political Parties in the 1980s," 108.

25. The national and state party organizations are limited by the FECA as to how much they can contribute directly and spend in behalf of candidates. State organizations, however, rarely have sufficient funds to make significant expenditures. The GOP has taken advantage of a loophole in the FECA that allows the national party to give funds to the state party which in turn can contribute these funds to candidates or use them in coordinated expenditures. By 1986, the total limits on party contributions to House candidates had risen to $73,620. Jacobson, *Politics of Congressional Elections*, 69.

26. Ibid., 71-72.

27. "Chairman's Reports" Republican National Committee, Washington, D.C., 1981 and 1985.

28. Bibby, "Political Party Trends," 90.

29. Kayden, "Parties and the 1980 Presidential Election," 613.

30. James Gibson, Cornelius Cotter, John Bibby, and Robert Huckshorn, "Whither the Local Parties? A Cross-Sectional Analysis of the Strength of Party Organizations," *American Journal of Political Science* 29 (February 1985): 139-60.

31. Federal Election Commission press release, December, 1985.

32. Bibby, "Political Party Trends," 88.

33. These changes would include the increasing participation of females in the workforce, the more isolated living patterns within neighborhoods, and alternative organizations (e.g., health clubs) for meeting people.

43 / The Changing Styles of American Party Politics

Gary R. Orren

In 1950 the condition of the American political party system was critically evaluated by a committee of experts from the American Political Science Association (APSA). The committee found the system to be deficient in a number of ways, and suggested changes designed to result in much stronger, more cohesive, and more ideological parties.* Although some of the recommended changes have been adopted by one or both of the parties, most have not, and the American parties still bear little resemblance to the committee's ideal. Nevertheless the committee's report did serve an important function by focusing attention on the question of whether parties, by changing their ways, could better serve the broader political system.

In this reading, Gary R. Orren considers the APSA Committee's ideal of a "responsible party system" as one of four general models of political parties. He concludes that while the responsible parties model is not well suited for American politics, a more pragmatic version of strong parties would be preferable to the weak parties and personalistic politics of recent years.

Our point of departure is with the two most fundamental polarities in our political system: the clash between ideological and coalitional politics, the division between strong and weak partisanship.

Throughout American history, academics and politicians have debated the virtues and limitations of the ideological and coalitional styles of party competition. The former involves offering clearly defined, often highly principled, alternative policies, usually based in divisive issues, designed to capture the allegiance of a particular part of the electorate regardless of the ultimate cost in overall support. The coalition style of party competition, on the other hand, represents an attempt to attract the maximum cross section of the electorate by appealing to all voters as potential supporters. This strategy uses noncontroversial, nondivisive issues which will appeal to the broadest range of voters without necessarily driving away any support at all. Note that what is referred to here is not the substance or direction of ideology, but rather the decision of whether or not to emphasize it and make it a central element in one's political arsenal. There are liberal and conservative ideologues, just as there are coalition-oriented politicians on both sides of the spectrum. . . .

A second polarity in our electoral system is the clash between strong partisanship and weak (or even anti) partisanship. In a sense, this is the oldest issue in the American party system, since the republic was born in a climate

---

*American Political Science Association Committee on Political Parties, "Toward a More Responsible Two-Party System," *American Political Science Review* 44, September 1950, supplement.—*Editor's Note.*

of antipartisanship, and antipartisanship has been an important theme running throughout American political history. Madison warned that the first objective of republican government must be the search for the "methods of curing the mischiefs of faction." A century later, the Progressives advocated antipartisan principles and championed reforms to curb the power of the political parties of their day. Recent movements for party reform, particularly in the Democratic party, have advanced the ideals of antipartisanship. Even in the best times, Americans have been ambivalent and uneasy about political parties, treating them as "unavoidable evils.". . .

Previous studies have drawn a useful distinction between two general political styles. They have called attention to the differing approaches of politicians who rely heavily on issue appeals ("purists" or "amateurs") and those who avoid or underplay such appeals ("professionals"). Amateurs or purists, according to this view, are portrayed as candidates who rely on what we have called an ideological *and* a weak partisan style, while professionals display more of a coalitional *and* partisan style.

However, the twofold distinction does not capture the full range of styles employed by politicians and parties. Take, for example, the battle for the Republican nomination in 1952. Robert Taft was clearly an ideological-style candidate, in the sense that the term is used here. He was an outspoken, highly principled conservative. However, at the same time, he was also a strong partisan professional—one, in fact, who was referred to as "Mr. Republican." His opponent for the nomination, Dwight Eisenhower, clearly was not an ideological candidate, nor was he a strong partisan. He made a very personalistic appeal, stressing coalitional and nonpartisan themes. Taft was both a purist and a professional; Eisenhower was neither.

Cases such as these suggest the utility of keeping the ideology versus coalition and strong versus weak partisan dimensions separate so that we can identify four categories of party competition (see Figure 1). These four categories are "ideal types" of party competition since none exists in pure form. . . .

With this important qualification in mind, I shall refer to four types of party competition. Each of these quadrants describes a political history.

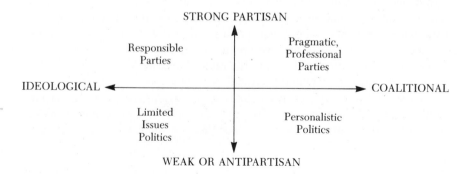

Figure 1. Types of Party Competition.

It is important to note that each quadrant also represents an argument about the best method for organizing party politics.... The typology will serve as a convenient framework for summarizing the past and assessing the likely future of American political parties.

The Antiparty, Coalition Style: Personalistic Politics
During the colonial period and the first few decades of the American republic, antiparty sentiment was nearly universal in the United States.... Most of the American founders were determined to keep the spirit of party out of American politics....

Antiparty sentiment took at least three forms in the early decades of the republic. According to the first view, the United States had achieved a consensus on all important issues. This approach might be called Washington since George Washington himself personified this unity. Politics was to be carried on not by partisans but by experienced gentlemen and financial managers who took their bearings from the established consensus.... Party organizations that tried to bring the electorate directly into such decision making would impede rational, dispassionate policy making and threaten to destroy social consensus. This version of antipartyism has been the most durable. In fact, several presidential campaigns in the nineteenth century invoked Washington's name to legitimate their own efforts to rise "above party."

The second antiparty position was Madison's.... As his argument in *The Federalist* (No. 10 and No. 51) shows, he encouraged a multiplicity of factions, each competing for its own advantage, but each unable to win singlehandedly. Factions would be tolerable as long as they were multiple....

The third antiparty view is that of Jefferson, the great party builder. Although Jefferson used party as a strategic organizational weapon, he never completely accepted party government or the idea that the alternating rule of political parties was legitimate. The Republican party was a temporary expedient required to bring the country back to its original principles.... The fight between Republicans and Federalists could only end in the death of one of the two parties. Once the "great" Federalist party was dead, the Republican party could disband. The ordinary politics of gentlemanly discussion on the basis of social consensus—the Washingtonian politics described earlier—could continue....

As the franchise expanded, indirect elections dwindled, and deference to the gentry (especially the Virginia dynasty) lessened, it became more difficult for candidates to win elections without relying on partisan or ideological appeals. For better or worse, "personal" politics, at least as it could advance a career on the national level, seemed to disappear. But there have remained candidates who maintain that a political consensus does exist in the United States and that they personify that consensus....

Recently, the opportunities afforded this brand of politician have increased. Television permits direct, personal appeals to the electorate and creates "personalities" in a way newspapers never could. At the same time, the large increase in the number of primaries has made it necessary for candidates to build organizations loyal to themselves alone, not to the party. The decrease in the availability of party patronage has increased the importance of candidates' ability to attract a following based purely on personal loyalty. Whether this loyalty is based on charisma and sex appeal or an image of competence and integrity, it belongs to the candidate, not to the party or a policy program.

The Proparty, Coalitional Style:
Pragmatic and Professional Parties

By the 1830s and 1840s, professional politicians were strongly entrenched in American politics. This "second generation" of leaders used party organization as a resource for combating the politics of deference and personal faction. . . .

The party professionals who dominated nineteenth-century politics have been much described and much maligned. . . . They saw parties purely as a device to build coalitions capable of winning the Presidency and other offices. Once parties had lost their stigma, the electoral success motive was sufficient to attract these professionals to a party. Not until the turn of the century did writers begin to fashion a justification for coalitional parties and their professional leaders. Lawrence Lowell and Henry Jones Ford, for example, . . . stressed the need for political parties to overcome the fragmentation of power caused by federalism and the separation of powers. But they warned that ideological parties could become class parties, pitting the wealthy against the poor and capitalism against socialism. Coalitional parties preserved the fragile American consensus, they argued, thereby protecting vulnerable individual rights. . . .

According to this argument, the major choice the parties can offer is that between the "ins" and the "outs." Since power in the United States is fragmented, it is often hard to fix responsibility for public policy. Separating political actors into two distinct groups gives the "out" group the corporate identity and incentives to criticize the "ins." The "ins" are thus forced to take responsibility for and to defend their policies and programs. This competition focuses public debate and gives the electorate a chance to "throw the rascals out." Without strong parties, politics becomes a proliferation of issues and personalities. Candidates find few incentives for stressing their records or those of their opponents. Without parties, or with very weak ones, the tendency to avoid or confuse issues is even greater than with coalitional parties.

. . . Parties can divide the electorate so as to form a governing majority, but they can also provide the invaluable service of integrating new voters into the political mainstream. American parties may not win academic beauty contests, but they are the best we have—or can hope to have. Or so runs the argument of those who defend a type of party system which, ironically, is weakening—just as its defenders become more respectable.

Strong Party, Ideological Style:
The "Responsible" Party Ideal

Despite the apparent power of the party professionals in the nineteenth century and the increasing respectability of their parties, party professionals and their academic supporters have continually faced strong challenges from advocates of more ideological parties. This struggle has taken place on two fronts, one political and one scholarly.

On the political front, opposition to coalitional party politics has come primarily from the policy purists who want parties to present coherent and well-integrated programs, principles, and world views. It is safe to say that the United States has never had what the purists hope for, namely, two principled parties which offer the electorate a clear policy choice every four years. While the purists have occasionally gained control of a major party, their candidates usually lose (e.g., the Democrats in 1896, the Republicans in 1964, and the Democrats in 1972). The major exception to this pattern is the Republican victory in 1860, but, given the Civil War, this is not an example most purists relish. . . .

While moralistic Whigs, pietistic Republicans, reformist Progressives, and their political progeny have devoted themselves to increasing the ideological purity of their own particular parties, only scholars have been sufficiently removed from party loyalties to argue for a system of opposing principled parties over a system of specific principles or programs. Woodrow Wilson was among the first American writers to hold up the British "responsible parties" as models for us. He argued that only unified, principled parties could accumulate the power fragmented by the Constitution, centralizing the government to the point where it could institute consistent policies. From Wilson to the American Political Science Association's (APSA) 1950 report "Toward a More Responsible Two-Party System," Liberals have had vague sympathy for responsible parties because such parties, unlike coalition ones, would bring centralization, direction, and thus "progress."

The clearest arguments for responsible, ideological parties have come from those who claim that the apparent consensus in American politics hides a real and serious divergence of interests between the haves and have-nots. . . .

. . . Despite the appeal of this theme, ideologies have had great difficulty controlling the major political parties. Academic recommendations on responsible parties, such as the APSA report, have been greeted with deafening silence. One reason for this reaction has been that divisive issues do not separate the American electorate into two or three neat subdivisions. Ideologues have been hard pressed to articulate programs and principles which can unite a majority of voters.

Another reason for the failure of the responsible party model involves the loyalty of the ideologues themselves. Their loyalties are divided between principles and party. . . . [P]arty loyalty often conflicts with their desire for ideological purity and their demands for internal democracy. This leads many ideologues to drop out of politics altogether and prompts others to turn to a weak or nonpartisan ideological style which we will here call "limited-issue politics."

The Antiparty Ideological Style: Limited-issue Politics

Major American political parties nominate candidates for a vast array of offices and claim to be capable of winning elections and convincing a majority of voters that their approach to governmental issues is practical and desirable. Ideologues may reject such parties for one or both of two reasons. First, they may believe that political issues are best treated individually instead of being lumped together in a package of party programs. This attitude usually stems from the perception that one issue overrides all the rest: slavery, civil rights, the Vietnam war, or abortion, for example. A second reason for deserting parties is the ideologues' despair of ever making them "principled." The ideologue who rejects parties for the latter reason does not necessarily reject the idea of party competition altogether. Principled parties may be possible once the ideologue, working outside the major parties, is able to awaken the "silent majority." Those who believe this can happen may campaign on the outskirts of established parties (as George Wallace and Eugene McCarthy have done). Or they may form third parties dedicated to revolutionizing the political consciousness of the electorate. . . .

In the United States, marginal parties which try to present a coherent world view have had little success. Ideological pressure groups marginally affiliated with parties have shown more strength. But the most successful ideological, nonpartisan groups have been those which have concentrated their attention on a narrow range of issues. Such associations, if they run candidates at all, usually run a limited slate, as well as a slate which does not claim to take responsibility for the overall governing of the country or state.

From Tocqueville's day to the present, America has always had a large number of such narrow-gauge organizations. Some have actually made significant inroads in electoral politics by stressing one major issue, e.g., the Abolitionists, the Prohibitionists, and the Dixiecrats. Limited-issue organizations are encouraged not just by the separation of powers and federalism, but by the Progressive reforms of the early 1900s and the more recent weakening of party organizations as well. The Progressives, following their town-meeting ideal, sought to increase direct participation at the expense of indirect representative government. The referenda they instituted proved particularly likely to stimulate single- or narrow-issue organizations. Moreover, the increased use of direct primaries has given single-issue organizations great leverage over the parties' nominating procedures, and television, in its turn, has given spokesmen for such organizations a vast audience. As parties' respectability decreases, the status and power of narrow-gauge "public interest" organizations increase. . . .

This approach proceeds on the debatable assumptions that issues can be handled one at a time and that somehow the electorate will not have to elect representatives who must make decisions on a wide variety of problems. Against the backdrop of ordinary party politics and representative government, this style continues to have broad appeal. However, its luster may dim as it gradually destroys its major opponent and precursor, namely, stable party loyalty and organization. . . .

Factors Influencing Political Style

While external political factors do not determine a party's or politician's style, the incentives for relying on personal, partisan, or ideological appeals will

greatly affect their choice. Some environmental factors, especially the configuration of political issues which the party and candidate must confront,
are in constant flux and can perhaps only be appreciated in retrospect. It
is other factors—especially the constant decline in the loyalty of voters to
political parties and in the resources available to party organizations—that
are more predictable. Depending on their personal proclivities and their
strategic predictions, politicians can react in several different ways to this continuing weakening of party.

While the factors encouraging the personalistic politics of the eighteenth
century—deference, indirect elections, limited franchise, and lack of established national or state-wide associations—have disappeared, new forces are
now working in the same direction. Personal appeals have partly filled the gap
created by the decline in the efficacy of party appeals. The expansion of
primaries has made it necessary to resort to nonpartisan appeals. Television
has made it possible to make personal appeals to the electorate directly. Within
a primary, the candidate who wants to "go for the middle" and thus avoid
divisive, ideological issues must stress above all his integrity and technical
competence. Stressing belief in an established national consensus will allow
the candidate to win the support of weak partisans who vote in the primary
and to gain the support of independents in the general election. Direct personal loyalties may also prove to be an effective substitute for political patronage which is no longer available to help build campaign organizations. . . .

As party loyalty and party organizations weaken, even dedicated partisans have had to develop new types of appeals. The use of nonparty issue
appeals (what we have called a "limited-issue" style of politics) is obviously
of importance in primaries. . . .

So we have seen that numerous forces are pulling parties and politicians
toward a style of politics that relies on weak or antipartisan appeals, the bottom half of the diagram shown in Figure 1. Indeed contemporary politics
seems to revolve in an orbit around this weak-partisan pole, passing in turn
through two kinds of competition: an ideological style in which candidates
such as George McGovern or George Wallace or groups such as environmentalists or antiabortionists make limited-issue appeals, and a coalitional style
in which candidates such as Jimmy Carter make personal appeals to the voters.

If this type of politics—where voter choices are not guided so much by
partisan cues as by issue appeals or candidate personality—has become the
hallmark of recent American elections, we are left to wonder whether parties serve any valuable purpose and, if they do, whether they will again become
an important part of our system.

Parties do, in fact, serve a number of very important functions, both during elections and in the governing process between elections. In elections, parties add an important element of clarity and accountability to our electoral
choices. Compared to ephemeral candidate organizations or single-issue
groups, parties have long, collective memories. They provide voters with
reasonable expectations about how party candidates will behave in the future,
and give voters a convenient way to pass judgment on past party records.

Parties are potentially more important *after* a campaign than during it. The antipartisan, nonideological style which served Jimmy Carter so well in the 1976 campaign, especially in the primaries, proved ill-suited to the task of governing. His steadfast avoidance of any ideological categorization and his quest for a very broad, almost universal, coalition made his policy efforts seem "fuzzy" and provoked attack from both the right and the left. In addition, Carter's reluctance to discard his outsider image undermined the partisan loyalty and special interest support so vital to the success of his presidential initiatives.

Only political leaders with support in a party can hope to govern effectively. Where there is no sense of party loyalty or party discipline, political leaders find it difficult to get a legislative program through Congress. Our unique set of constitutional arrangements in the United States will only work effectively with the counterweight of political parties. Yet it remains to be seen just what *kind* of parties these may be....

Toward a More Responsible
Party System, Again?

The weak partisan limited-issue and personalistic politics of recent vintage are poor foundations for governing. To seek a sturdier foundation, we must look to the two remaining styles of party politics: strongly partisan-ideological "responsible parties" and strongly partisan but coalitional "pragmatic" parties.

Recently we have witnessed a revival of interest in more responsible-type parties. This newest yearning for more centralized, cohesive, and policy-oriented parties stems from two sources: the perception that it has become more difficult for the government to get its programs adopted and implemented, and the recent success of the Republican party in building the power of its national committee....

We *should* try to strengthen political parties, but this does not necessarily mean that we should strive to create parties which are more ideologically cohesive or more centralized, two key ingredients of responsible political parties. Both the feasibility and the desirability of that goal are questionable.

Forecasting the future of political parties requires a prophet's vision; finding lessons in the past is much easier. It has been no accident that ideological, coherent parties have typically died on the vine, and those factors that historically have inhibited their development are no less powerful today. The truth is that disciplined parties are doomed from the start: they run against the grain of America's institutional machinery and political culture....

An additional problem with ideological parties is their propensity to be dominated by single-issue or extremist groups. Historically, the American political system has always been characterized by an extraordinary penchant for utopian moralism. Americans like to dramatize their politics as a morality play between the forces of good and evil. Seymour Martin Lipset and others have traced this penchant to our nation's Protestant origins and the absence of a state church in America. But for whatever reasons, our system is vulnerable to extremists on both the left and the right (nativists, abolitionists, feminists, prohibitionists, progressives, anticommunists, and the moral majority). Pragmatic, professional parties with their tendency toward coalition and compromise are an important bulwark against moralistic and extremist politics....

Responsible parties are neither feasible nor particularly desirable in the United States. Yet they are sometimes offered as a remedy for a political system sorely in need of strong parties. Creating strong parties, however, is a different task from fashioning ideological ones. Strong partisanship means that party leaders and candidates emphasize party themes and symbols, that the endorsements and support of elected officials and professionals in the party are sought and publicized, that campaigns rely on the organizational apparatus and networks of the party, that candidates stress partisan issues, and that leaders exploit the allegiance of the party faithful....

Conclusion

...[T]he spirit of weak partisan or anti-partisan politics first contemplated by the Founding Fathers seems to have returned with a vengeance in the third century of this nation. The current oscillation between personalistic and limited-issue politics has severely impaired the art of governing. To begin with, these two styles of politics have given us a succession of unappealing leading candidates. Strongly partisan, coalitional candidates like Hubert Humphrey, Henry Jackson, Edward Kennedy, and Howard Baker have found it difficult to succeed in the party nomination process. Weak partisan and ideological candidates have fared much better: Barry Goldwater, George Wallace, George McGovern, and Jimmy Carter. Admittedly, these weak partisan candidates displayed certain strengths. For example, they were known for their honesty and forthrightness, and they exploited this public perception in their campaigns. Some projected integrity in highly personal terms, others in issue terms. In either case, the voters generally regarded them as more candid and trustworthy than their election opponents. Of course honesty is a desirable quality for public office, but other political and governing skills are crucial as well in our fragmented, divided government. Among the final victors in the presidential race, the candidate problem is even more acute: arguably, no two Presidents have been less prepared in terms of prior experience in national politics than ... Jimmy Carter and Ronald Reagan. Yet inexperienced candidates are just what antipartisan politics begets.

Of course, no party style *guarantees* good leaders or bad ones. The old system that gave us Abraham Lincoln and Franklin Roosevelt gave us James Buchanan and Warren Harding as well. Party styles and the election rules that support them cannot assure the quality of candidates. But they do affect the way that those candidates, once elected, will govern. If parties are not intimately involved in our elections, then winning candidates, be they good or bad, will ignore them once in office or treat them as a minor annoyance. This will make the already difficult task of governing impossible.

Over the last two decades, American governmental and political institutions have become increasingly fragmented, atomized, and, in a word, ungovernable. The decline of parties and the rise of personalistic and limited-issue styles of politics lie at the heart of this disheartening turn of events. Much of the fractionalization and recalcitrance of Congress can be traced to the decline of party discipline. It is the electoral connection that is the key here: congressional candidates have come to rely less and less on party ties and labels in their efforts to get elected and reelected. As a result, they are more and more resistant to appeals for party loyalty after they have taken office....

...I have maintained in this chapter that part of the solution to our current problem lies in the development of pragmatic, coalitional parties, for it is this sort of party that best fits this country's peculiar institutional and electoral constitution.* This style of party politics, like all the others, reflects a particular vision of what party government in the United States ought to be and ought to provide. But it is precisely these visions that must be defended and vindicated before the business of party reform may proceed.

---

*In addition, Orren states, "The key factor working for the coalitional strong partisan style of politics is the need of candidates—especially those running for President or governor—to find a method of organization for winning and maintaining majority support in the face of the heterogeneity and crosscutting cleavages of the electorate and despite the fact that most voters are moderate and nonideological. Party is a steady source of loyalty, supported by years of traditional affiliation. While issues and personalities come and go, parties remain."—Editor's Note.

CHAPTER TWELVE

Interest Groups

As political parties have declined in recent decades, the star of interest groups has been rising in American politics. Despite long-lasting fears of a few special interests gaining dominance by "purchasing" influence in Washington, many more Americans have turned to forming interest groups as a means of influencing the decisions of government officials. Of course, interest groups are far from being a *new* phenomenon in American politics. As Burdett Loomis and Allan Cigler note in their article in this chapter, an important role for organized political interests has been a "great continuity in our political experience," as has been the "ambivalence" with which many have viewed special interests, seeing at once their benefits and their costs for a democracy. Within these broad continuities many interesting and important changes have occurred in interest-group politics. Loomis and Cigler document several changes that have occurred over recent decades, including dramatic growth in the number of interest groups, more focus on the national level of government, and development of new "tools" of influence. Of special importance for the electoral process has been the tremendous increase in the number of new political action committees (PACs) since the 1970s.

PACs are "interest groups that collect money from their members and contribute these funds to candidates and parties."* Herbert Alexander documents dramatic growth in PAC spending during the 1980s, and attributes it directly to the campaign finance reforms of the 1970s.

With the growing role of interest groups in campaign finance have come growing concerns over the role of money in pressing interests upon government officials. In response, Michael Malbin argues that along with the possible "negatives," PAC campaign financing also offers some benefits for pluralistic democracy; he then suggests some reforms that would save the benefits while reducing the potential for problems.

According to Robert Salisbury, in the final essay of this chapter, several factors—including the growth in the number of interest groups—have already led to an important change in the influence relationship with government. Where interest groups were once "seen as the prime motive force pressing politicians to make policy decisions in their favor," Salisbury argues, "now the officials very often exploit the groups."

---

*Jack C. Plano and Milton Greenberg. *The American Political Dictionary.* 7th edition. (New York: Holt, Rinehart and Winston, 1985, p. 164).—*Editor's Note.*

44 / The Changing Nature of Interest Group Politics

Burdett A. Loomis
Allan J. Cigler

While noting that a role for interest groups in American politics is itself not new, Burdett Loomis and Allan Cigler identify ten major changes that have occurred in interest group politics over recent decades. These include an expanding number of groups, an increasing national focus, and the growth of citizens' groups. While parties have declined in the "postindustrial" environment, interest groups have thrived on the new issues and new technology.

From James Madison to Madison Avenue, political interests have played a central role in American politics. But this great continuity in our political experience has been matched by the ambivalence with which citizens, politicians, and scholars have approached interest groups. James Madison's warnings on the dangers of faction echo in the rhetoric of reformers ranging from Populists and Progressives near the turn of the century to contemporary so-called public interest advocates.

If organized special interests are nothing new in American politics, can today's group politics be seen as having undergone some fundamental changes? Acknowledging that many important, continuing trends do exist, we seek to place in perspective a broad series of changes in the modern nature of interest group politics. Among the most substantial of these developments are:

1. a great proliferation of interest groups since the early 1960s;
2. a centralization of group headquarters in Washington, D.C., rather than in New York City or elsewhere;
3. major technological developments in information processing that promote more sophisticated, timelier, and more specialized grass-roots lobbying;
4. the rise of single-issue groups;
5. changes in campaign finance laws (1971, 1974) and the ensuing growth of political action committees (PACs);
6. the increased formal penetration of political and economic interests into the bureaucracy (advisory committees), the presidency (White House group representatives), and the Congress (caucuses of members);
7. the continuing decline of political parties' abilities to perform key electoral and policy-related activities;

8. the increased number, activity, and visibility of public interest groups, such as Common Cause, and the Ralph Nader-inspired public interest research organizations;
9. the growth of activity and impact by institutions, including corporations, universities, state and local governments, and foreign interests; and
10. a continuing rise in the amount and sophistication of group activity in state capitals.

All these developments have their antecedents in previous eras of American political life; there is little genuinely new under the interest group sun. Political action committees have replaced (or complemented) other forms of special interest campaign financing. Group-generated mail directed at Congress has existed as a tactic since at least the early 1900s.[1] And many organizations have long been centered in Washington, members of Congress traditionally have represented local interests, and so on.

At the same time, however, the level of group activity, coupled with growing numbers of organized interests, distinguishes contemporary group politics from the politics of earlier eras. . . .

Contemporary Interest Group Politics

Several notable developments mark the modern age of interest group politics. Of primary importance is the large and growing number of active groups and other interests. The data here are sketchy, but one major study found that most current groups came into existence after World War II and that group formation has accelerated substantially since the early 1960s.[2] Also since the 1960s groups have increasingly directed their attention toward the center of power in Washington, D.C., as the scope of federal policy making has grown, and groups seeking influence have determined to "hunt where the ducks are." As a result, the 1960s and 1970s marked a veritable explosion in the number of groups lobbying in Washington.

A second key change is evident in the composition of the interest group universe. Beginning in the late 1950s political participation patterns underwent some significant transformations. Conventional activities such as voting declined, and political parties, the traditional aggregators and articulators of mass interests, became weaker. Yet at all levels of government, evidence of citizen involvement has been apparent, often in the form of new or revived groups. Particularly impressive has been the growth of citizens' groups—those organized around an idea or cause (at times a single issue) with no occupational basis for membership. Fully 30 percent of such groups have formed since 1975, and in 1980 they made up more than one-fifth of all groups represented in Washington.[3]

In fact, a participation revolution has occurred in the country as large numbers of citizens have become active in an ever-increasing number of protest groups, citizens' organizations, and special interest groups. These groups often comprise issue-oriented activists or individuals who seek collective material benefits. . . .

Third, government itself has had a profound effect on the growth and activity of interest groups. Early in this century, workers found organizing difficult because business and industry used government-backed injunctions to prevent strikes. By the 1930s, however, with the prohibition of injunctions in private labor disputes and the rights of collective bargaining established, most governmental actions directly promoted labor union growth. In recent years changes in the campaign finance laws have led to an explosion in the number of political action committees, especially among business, industry, and issue-oriented groups. Laws facilitating group formation certainly have contributed to group proliferation, but government policy in a broader sense has been equally responsible.

Fourth, not only has the number of membership groups grown in recent decades, but a similar expansion has occurred in the political activity of many other interests such as individual corporations, universities, churches, governmental units, foundations, and think tanks.[4] ... The lobbying community of the 1990s is large, increasingly diverse, and part of the expansion of policy domain participation, whether in agriculture, the environment, or industrial development.

Governmental Growth

Since the 1930s the federal government has become an increasingly active and important spur to group formation. A major aim of the New Deal was to use government as an agent in balancing the relationship between contending forces in society, particularly industry and labor....

The proliferation of government activities led to a mushrooming of groups around the affected policy areas....

Decline of Political Parties

In a diverse political culture characterized by divided power, political parties emerged early in our history as instruments to structure conflict and facilitate mass participation. Parties function as intermediaries between the public and formal government institutions, as they reduce and combine citizen demands into a manageable number of issues, enabling the system to focus upon the society's most important problems.

The party performs its mediating function primarily through coalition building—"the process of constructing majorities from the broad sentiments and interests that can be found to bridge the narrower needs and hopes of separate individuals and communities."[5] ... Party organizations dominated electoral politics through the New Deal period, and interest group influence was felt primarily through the party apparatus.

Patterns of partisan conflict are never permanent, however, and since the 1940s various social forces have contributed to the creation of new interests and the redefinition of older ones. This has had the effect of destroying the New Deal coalition without putting a new partisan structure in its place and has provided opportunities for the creation of large numbers of

political groups—many that are narrowly focused and opposed to the bargaining and compromise patterns of coalition politics.

Taken as a whole, the changes of recent decades reflect the societal
transformation that scholars have labeled "postindustrial society," centering on

> several interrelated developments: affluence, advanced technological
> development, the central importance of knowledge, national com-
> munication processes, the growing prominence and independence
> of the culture, new occupational structures, and with them new
> life styles and expectations, which is to say new social classes and
> new centers of power.[6]

...The traditional political party system found it difficult to deal effectively with citizens' high expectations and a changing class structure. The
economic, ethnic, and ideological positions that had developed during the
New Deal became less relevant to parties, elections, and voter preferences....

There is some question about whether parties retain the capacity to shape
political debate even on issues that lend themselves to coalition building.
Although the decline of political parties began well before the 1960s, the
weakening of the party organization has accelerated in the postindustrial
age....

...The weakness of political parties has helped to create a vacuum in
electoral politics since 1960, and in recent years interest groups have moved
aggressively to fill it.

Growth of Interest Groups

Although it may be premature to formulate a theory that accounts for spurts
of growth, we can identify several factors fundamental to group proliferation in contemporary politics. Rapid social and economic changes, powerful
catalysts for group formation, have produced both the development of new
interests (for example, the recreation industry) and the redefinition of traditional interests (for example, higher education). The spread of affluence and
education, coupled with advanced communication technologies, further contribute to the translation of interests into formal group organizations. Postindustrial changes have generated a large number of new interests, particularly
among occupational and professional groups in the scientific and technological
arenas. For instance, genetic engineering associations have sprung up in the
wake of recent DNA discoveries.

Perhaps more important, postindustrial changes have altered the pattern of conflict in society and created an intensely emotional setting composed of several groups ascending or descending in status. Ascending groups,
such as members of the new professional-managerial-technical elite, have both
benefited from and supported government activism; they represent the new
cultural liberalism, politically cosmopolitan and socially permissive. At the
same time, rising expectations and feelings of entitlement have increased

pressures on government by aspiring groups and the disadvantaged. The 1960s and early 1970s witnessed wave after wave of group mobilization based on causes ranging from civil rights to women's issues to the environment to consumer protection.

Abrupt changes and alterations in status, however, threaten many citizens. Middle America, perceiving itself as downwardly mobile, has grown alienated from the social, economic, and cultural dominance of the postindustrial elites, on one hand, and resentful toward government attempts to aid minorities and other aspiring groups, on the other. The conditions of a modern, technologically based culture also are disturbing to more traditional elements in society. Industrialization and urbanization can uproot people, cutting them loose from familiar life patterns and values and depriving them of meaningful personal associations. Fundamentalist elements feel threatened by various technological advances (such as test-tube babies) as well as by the more general secular liberalism and moral permissiveness of contemporary life. And the growth of bureaucracy, both in and out of government, antagonizes everyone at one time or another.

Postindustrial threats are felt by elites as well. The nuclear arms race and its potential for mass destruction fostered the revived peace movement of the 1980s and its goal of a freeze on nuclear weapons. In addition, the excesses and errors of technology, such as oil spills and toxic waste disposal, have led to group formation among some of the most advantaged and ascending elements of society....

While postindustrial conflicts generate the issues for group development, the massive spread of affluence also systematically contributes to group formation and maintenance. In fact, affluence creates a large potential for "checkbook" membership. Issue-based groups have done especially well. Membership in such groups as PETA and Common Cause might once have been considered a luxury, but the growth in discretionary income has placed the cost of modest dues within the reach of most citizens. For a $15–$25 membership fee, people can make an "expressive" statement without incurring other organizational obligations. Increasing education also has been a factor in that "organizations become more numerous as ideas become more important."[7]

Reform groups and citizens' groups depend heavily upon the educated, white middle class for their membership and financial base. A 1982 Common Cause poll, for example, found that members' mean family income was $17,000 above the national average and that 43 percent of members had an advanced degree.[8] Other expressive groups, including those on the political Right, have been aided as well by the increased wealth of constituents and the community activism that result from education and occupational advancement.

Groups can overcome the free-rider problem by finding a sponsor who will support the organization and reduce its reliance upon membership contributions. During the 1960s and 1970s private sources (often foundations) backed various groups. Jeffrey Berry's 1977 study of eighty-three public interest organizations found that at least one-third received more than half of their funds from private foundations, while one in ten received more than 90 percent of its operating expenses from such sources.[9] Jack Walker's 1981 study of Washington-based interest groups confirmed many of Berry's earlier findings, indicating that foundation support and individual grants provide 30 percent of all citizens' group funding.[10] Such patterns produce many staff organizations with no members, raising major questions about the representativeness of the new interest group universe. Finally, groups themselves can sponsor other groups. The National Council of Senior Citizens (NCSC), for example, was founded by the AFL-CIO, which helped recruit members from the ranks of organized labor and still pays part of NCSC's expenses. . . .

Postindustrial affluence and the spread of education also have contributed to group formation and maintenance through the development of a large pool of potential group organizers. This group tends to be young, well educated, and from the middle class, caught up in a movement for change and inspired by ideas or doctrine. The 1960s was a period of opportunity for entrepreneurs, as college enrollments skyrocketed and powerful forces such as civil rights and the antiwar movement contributed to an idea-orientation in both education and politics. Communications-based professions—from religion to law to university teaching—attracted social activists, many of whom became involved in the formation of groups. The government itself became a major source of what James Q. Wilson called "organizing cadres." Government employees of the local Community Action Agencies of the War on Poverty and numerous VISTA volunteers were active in the formation of voluntary associations, some created to oppose government actions.[11]

Compounding the effects of the growing number of increasingly active groups are changes in what organizations can do, largely as a result of contemporary technology. On a grand scale, technological change produces new interests, such as cable television and the silicon chip industry, which organize to protect themselves as interests historically have done. Beyond this, communications breakthroughs make group politics much more visible than in the past. Civil rights activists in the South understood this, as did many protesters against the Vietnam War. Of equal importance, however, is the fact that much of what contemporary interest groups do derives directly from developments in information-related technology. Many group activities, whether fund-raising or grass-roots lobbying or sampling members' opinions, rely heavily on computer-based operations that can target and send messages and process the responses.

Although satellite television links and survey research are important tools, the technology of direct mail has had by far the greatest impact on interest group politics. With a minimum initial investment and a reasonably good list of potential contributors, any individual can become a group entrepreneur. These activists literally create organizations, often based on emotion-laden appeals about specific issues, from Sarah Brady's Handgun Control to Randall Terry's Operation Rescue.[12] To the extent that an entrepreneur can attract members and continue to pay the costs of direct mail, he or she can claim—with substantial legitimacy—to articulate the organization's positions on the issues, positions probably defined initially by the entrepreneur.

In addition to helping entrepreneurs develop organizations that require few (if any) active members, information technology also allows many organizations to exert considerable pressure on elected officials. The Washington-based interests increasingly are turning to grass-roots techniques to influence legislators. Indeed, by the mid-1980s these tactics had become the norm in many lobbying efforts.

Information-processing technology is widely available but expensive. Although the Chamber of Commerce can afford its costly investment in extensive television facilities, many groups simply cannot pay the cost of much technology, at least beyond their continuing efforts to stay afloat with direct mail solicitations. Money remains the mother's milk of politics. Indeed, one of the major impacts of technology may be to inflate the costs of political action, especially given group support for candidates engaged in increasingly expensive election campaigns.

Group Impact on Policy and Process

Assessing the policy impact of interest group actions has never been an easy task. We may, however, gain some insights by looking at two different levels of analysis: a broad, societal overview and a middle-range search for relatively specific patterns of influence (for example, the role of direct mail or PAC funding). Considering impact at the level of individual lobbying efforts is also possible, but even the best work relies heavily on nuance and individualistic explanations.

Although the public at large often views lobbying and special interest campaigning with distrust, political scientists have not produced much evidence to support this perspective. Academic studies of interest groups have demonstrated few conclusive links between campaign or lobbying efforts and actual patterns of influence. This does not mean, we emphasize, that such patterns or individual instances do not exist. Rather, the question of determining impact is exceedingly difficult to answer. The difficulty is, in fact, compounded by groups' claims of impact and decision makers' equally vociferous claims of freedom from any outside influence.

The major studies of lobbying in the 1960s generated a most benign view of this activity. Lester Milbrath, in his portrait of Washington lobbyists, painted a Boy Scout-like picture, depicting them as patient contributors to the policy-making process.[13] Rarely stepping over the limits of propriety, lobbyists had only a marginal impact at best. Similarly, Raymond Bauer, Ithiel de Sola Pool, and Lewis Dexter's lengthy analysis of foreign trade policy, published in 1963, found the business community to be largely incapable of influencing Congress in its lobbying attempts.[14] Given the many internal divisions within the private sector over trade matters, this was not an ideal issue to illustrate business cooperation, but the research stood as the central work on lobbying for more than a decade—ironically, in the very period when groups proliferated and became more sophisticated in their tactics. Lewis

Dexter, in his 1969 treatment of Washington representatives as an emerging professional group, suggested that lobbyists will play an increasingly important role in complex policy making, but he provided few details.[15]

The picture of benevolent lobbyists who seek to engender trust and convey information, although accurate in a limited way, does not provide a complete account of the options open to any interest group that seeks to exert influence. Lyndon Johnson's long-term relationship with the Texas-based construction firm of Brown & Root illustrates the depth of some ties between private interests and public officeholders. The Washington representative for Brown & Root claimed that he never went to Capitol Hill for any legislative help because "people would resent political influence."[16] But Johnson, first as a representative and later as a senator, systematically dealt directly with the top management (the Brown family) and aided the firm by passing along crucial information and watching over key government-sponsored construction projects.

> [The Johnson-Brown & Root link] was, indeed, a partnership, the campaign contributions, the congressional look-out, the contracts, the appropriations, the telegrams, the investment advice, the gifts and the hunts and the free airplane rides—it was an alliance of mutual reinforcement between a politician and a corporation. If Lyndon was Brown & Root's kept politician, Brown & Root was Lyndon's kept corporation. Whether he concluded that they were public-spirited partners or corrupt ones, "political allies" or cooperating predators, in its dimensions and its implications for the structure of society, their arrangement was a new phenomenon on its way to becoming the new pattern for American society.[17]

Subsequent events, such as the savings and loan scandal, demonstrate that legislators can be easily approached with unethical and illegal propositions; such access is one price of an open system. More broadly, the growth of interest representation in the late 1980s has raised long-term questions about the ethics of ex-government officials acting as lobbyists.

Contemporary Practices

Modern lobbying emphasizes information, often on complex and difficult subjects. Determining actual influence is, as one lobbyist noted, "like finding a black cat in the coal bin at midnight,"[18] but we can make some assessments about the overall impact of group proliferation and increased activity.

First, more groups are engaged in more forms of lobbying than ever before—both classic forms, such as offering legislative testimony, and newer forms, such as mounting computer-based direct mail campaigns to stir up grass-roots support.[19] As the number of new groups rises and existing groups become more active, the pressure on decision makers—especially legislators—mounts at a corresponding rate. Thus, a second general point can be made:

congressional reforms that opened up the legislative process during the 1970s have provided a much larger number of access points for today's lobbyists. Most committee (and subcommittee) sessions, including the markups or writing of legislation, remain open to the public, as do many conference committee meetings. More roll-call votes are taken, and congressional floor action is televised. Thus, interests can monitor the performance of individual members of Congress as never before. This does nothing, however, to facilitate disinterested decision making or foster statesmanlike compromises on most issues....

The government itself has encouraged many interests to organize and articulate their demands. The rise of group activity thus leads us to another level of analysis: the impact of contemporary interest group politics on society. Harking back to Lowi's description of interest group liberalism, we see the eventual result to be an immobilized society, trapped by its willingness to allow interests to help fashion self-serving policies that embody no firm criteria of success or failure. For example, even in the midst of the savings and loan debacle, the government continues to offer guarantees to various sectors, based not on future promise but on past bargains and continuing pressures.

The notion advanced by Olson that some such group-related stagnation affects all stable democracies makes the prognosis all the more serious. In summary form, Olson argued, "The longer societies are politically stable, the more interest groups they develop; the more interest groups they develop, the worse they work economically."[20] The United Automobile Workers' protectionist leanings, the American Medical Association's fight against FTC intervention into physicians' business affairs, and the insurance industry's successful prevention of FTC investigations all illustrate the possible linkage between self-centered group action and poor economic performance—that is, higher automobile prices, doctors' fees, and insurance premiums for no better product or service.

Conclusion
The ultimate consequences of the growing number of groups, their expanding activities both in Washington and in state capitals, and the growth of citizens' groups remain unclear. From one perspective, such changes have made politics more representative than ever before. While most occupation-based groups traditionally have been well organized in American politics, many other interests have not. Population groupings such as blacks, Hispanics, and women have mobilized since the 1950s and 1960s; even animals and the unborn are well represented in the interest group arena, as is the broader "public interest," however defined.

Broadening the base of interest group participation may have truly opened up the political process, thus curbing the influence of special interests. For example, agricultural policy making in the postwar era was almost exclusively the prerogative of a tight "iron triangle" composed of congressional committee and subcommittee members from farm states, government officials representing the agriculture bureaucracy, and major agriculture groups such as the American Farm Bureau. Activity in the 1970s by consumer and environmental interest groups changed agricultural politics, making it more visible and lengthening the agenda to consider such questions as how farm subsidies affect consumer purchasing power and how various fertilizers, herbicides, and pesticides affect public health.

From another perspective, more interest groups and more openness do not necessarily mean better policies or ones that genuinely represent the national interest. "Sunshine" and more participants may generate greater complexity and too many demands for decision makers to process effectively. Moreover, the content of demands may be ambiguous and priorities difficult to set. Finally, elected leaders may find it practically impossible to build the kinds of political coalitions necessary to govern effectively, especially in an era of divided government.

This second perspective suggests that the American constitutional system is extraordinarily susceptible to the excesses of minority faction—in an ironic way a potential victim of the Madisonian solution of dealing with the tyranny of the majority. Decentralized government, especially one that wields considerable power, provides no adequate controls over the excessive demands of special interest politics. Decision makers feel obliged to respond to many of these demands, and "the cumulative effect of this pressure has been the relentless and extraordinary rise of government spending and inflationary deficits, as well as the frustration of efforts to enact effective national policies on most major issues."[21]

In sum, the problem of contemporary interest group politics is one of representation. For particular interests, especially those that are well defined and adequately funded, the government is responsive to the issues of their greatest concern. But representation is not just a matter of responding to specific interests or citizens; the government also must respond to the collective needs of a society, and here the success of individual interests reduces the possibility of overall responsiveness. The very vibrancy and success of contemporary groups help contribute to a society that finds it increasingly difficult to formulate solutions to complex policy questions.

Notes

1. Kay Lehman Schlozman and John T. Tierney, "More of the Same: Washington Pressure Group Activity in a Decade of Change," *Journal of Politics* 45 (May 1983): 351–377. For an earlier era, see Margaret S. Thompson, *The Spider's Web* (Ithaca: Cornell University Press, 1985).
2. Jack L. Walker, "The Origins and Maintenance of Interest Groups in America," *American Political Science Review* 77 (June 1983): 390–406; for a conservative critique of this trend, see James T. Bennett and Thomas Di Lorenzo, *Destroying Democracy* (Washington, D.C.: Cato Institute, 1986).
3. Walker, "Origins and Maintenance of Interest Groups," 16.
4. Robert H. Salisbury, "Interest Representation and the Dominance of Institutions," *American Political Science Review* 78 (March 1984): 64–77.

5. David S. Broder, "Introduction," in *Emerging Coalitions in American Politics*, ed. Seymour Martin Lipset (San Francisco: Institute for Contemporary Studies, 1978), 3.
6. Everett Carll Ladd, Jr., with Charles D. Hadley, *Transformations of the American Party System*, 2d ed. (New York: Norton, 1978), 182.
7. James Q. Wilson, *Political Organizations* (New York: Basic Books, 1973), 201.
8. Andrew S. McFarland, *Common Cause* (Chatham, N.J.: Chatham House, 1984), 48–49.
9. Jeffrey M. Berry, *Lobbying for the People* (Princeton, N.J.: Princeton University Press, 1977), 72.
10. Walker, "Origins and Maintenance of Interest Groups," 400.
11. Wilson, *Political Organizations*, 203.
12. Sarah Brady, wife of former White House press secretary James Brady, organized Handgun Control after her husband was seriously wounded in John Hinckley's 1981 attack on Ronald Reagan. Randall Terry formed Operation Rescue, which seeks to shut down abortion clinics through direct action (for example, blocking entrances), after concluding that other pro-life groups were not effective in halting abortions.
13. Lester Milbrath, *The Washington Lobbyists* (Chicago: Rand-McNally, 1963).
14. Raymond Bauer, Ithiel de Sola Pool, and Lewis Dexter, *American Business and Public Policy* (New York: Atherton Press, 1963).
15. Lewis A. Dexter, *How Organizations Are Represented in Washington* (Indianapolis: Bobbs-Merrill, 1969), chap. 9.
16. See Ronnie Dugger, *The Politician* (New York: Norton, 1982), 273; and Robert A. Caro, *The Years of Lyndon Johnson: The Path to Power* and *The Years of Lyndon Johnson: Means of Ascent* (New York: Knopf, 1982 and 1990, respectively).
17. Dugger, *Politician*, 286.
18. Quoted in "A New Era: Groups and the Grass Roots," by Burdett A. Loomis, in *Interest Group Politics*, ed. Allan J. Cigler and Burdett A. Loomis (Washington, D.C.: CQ Press, 1983), 184.
19. Schlozman and Tierney, "Washington Pressure Group Activity," 18.
20. Robert J. Samuelson's description in *National Journal*, September 25, 1982, 1642.
21. Everett Carll Ladd, "How to Tame the Special Interest Groups," *Fortune*, October 1980, 6.

45 / PACs and Campaign Finance

Herbert E. Alexander

Campaign finance expert Herbert Alexander documents substantial growth in spending by political action committees (PACs) during the 1980s, and attributes it to campaign finance reforms of the 1970s. Alexander also describes "bundling," a technique that allows a PAC to play a legal fundraising role beyond its own limited campaign contributions.

Trends in Giving since the 1970s Reforms

Ironically, the laws of the 1970s led to an institutionalization of the special interests political reformers sought to eliminate. Following enactment of the 1974 amendments, which imposed limits on the amounts individuals may contribute to candidates, the once key role of the large donor was replaced by that of the elite fund raiser. No longer could a W. Clement Stone contribute millions of dollars or a Stewart R. Mott hundreds of thousands, so candidates were forced to broaden their financial bases. Persons with access to networks of proven contributors or with mailing lists to be prospected for potential donors became increasingly important because they could help to raise big money in smaller sums. Elite solicitors who can bring in large amounts of money are few, direct mail fund raising is expensive and not feasible for most candidates, and the number of fundraising dinners and other events that donors will attend is not unlimited.

Political Action Committees

Political action committees helped fill the void created by loss of the "fat cat." Sponsored by corporations or labor unions or membership groups with political interests, PACs share two characteristics essential to fund raising: Access to large aggregates of likeminded persons and internal means of communication. PACs collect numerous small contributions that they combine into larger, more meaningful amounts that are then contributed to favored candidates— all at no cost to the candidates' campaigns. In this sense PACs can be considered solicitation systems, reaching out to thousands of corporate employees or union members whom candidates would find prohibitively expensive to ask for money from separately. PACs are willing to undertake the task because the money raised goes to candidates or party committees that support their causes.

The reforms of the 1970s sought, among other things, to tighten restrictions on the kinds of illegal contributions uncovered by Watergate-related investigations and to diminish the influence of special interest groups and wealthy contributors in the electoral process. While reducing the role of the large individual contributor, the changes, particularly the low contribution limits, served to increase—or at least to make more visible—the roles played by special interests. The establishment of political action committees was sanctioned by the 1971 and 1974 laws.

A PAC normally is organized by a business, labor, professional, agrarian, ideological, or issue group to raise political funds on a voluntary basis from members, stockholders, or employees for the purpose of combining numerous smaller contributions into larger, more meaningful amounts that then are contributed to favored candidates or political party committees. A PAC can contribute up to $5,000 per candidate per election (that is, $5,000 in a primary and another $5,000 in the general election) provided the committee has been registered with the Federal Election Commission for at least six months, has more than fifty contributors, and has supported five or more candidates for federal office.

The 1980s witnessed an explosive growth in registered political action committees. The number went from a total of 2,551 in 1980 to 4,172 in 1990—an increase of 64 percent. However, the number of PACs reached its peak in 1988, when the tally hit 4,268. The decline from 1988 to 1990 was largely a result of a reduction in the number of nonconnected or ideological committees, a category that had grown more rapidly in number than any other grouping of PACs in the early 1980s.. . .

A great surge in PAC spending also occurred in the 1980s. In the 1980 election cycle, PACs raised and spent more money and contributed more to federal candidates than in the two previous election cycles combined. PACs gave federal candidates a total of $60.2 million. Throughout the decade, PACs spent more in each succeeding federal election campaign, until leveling off in 1988 and 1990. PAC spending increased 28.9 percent between the 1981–1982 and 1983–1984 election cycles. Expenditures in 1985–1986 were 23 percent higher than the $113 million spent in 1983–1984. PAC gifts in 1987–1988 totaled 14 percent more than in 1985–1986. But in 1989–1990, PACs gave federal candidates $159.3 million, virtually the same amount they gave in 1987–1988—$159.2 million.[1]

No clear reasons exist for why PAC spending is slowing or why the number of PACs has diminished. Corporate mergers and buyouts have led to the combining of some PACS. Some suggest that PACs are victims of their own unreasonable expectations or that PACs already have fulfilled their potential and that the law of diminishing returns gives some PACS, particularly small ones, less incentive to stay involved in the political process. Others believe that media criticism, the so-called "PAC attack," has made sponsors and participants wary.

Correlating the number of PACs to productivity may be misleading. The top 100 PACs in the 1989–1990 cycle contributed $74.5 million to federal candidates, or 46.7 percent of the total given by all PACs.[2] Some 64 PACs reported at least $1 million in total receipts, while 669 raised $100,000 or more. However, 870 PACs had no dollar activity, and 1,054 spent $5,000 or less.[3] These figures indicate that large amounts of money are handled by relatively few PACs.

Because many PACs are tied to corporations, trade associations, and unions with legislative interests, critics charge that wholesale vote-buying is occurring. Studies of congressional behavior have indicated, however, that personal philosophy, party loyalty, and an aversion to offending voters are more influential factors than campaign contributions in determining positions taken by members of Congress.

PACs, however, have created public relations problems at a time when Congress already is held in low regard by the American public. If PACs have not spawned vote-buying, they have created a system in which money and access to legislators have become intertwined. Not only have reformers criticized PACs but also, in recent years, has the Republican congressional leadership. Furthermore, President Bush called for their elimination in his 1991 State of the Union address. The irony is that Republicans in the 1970s and early

1980s championed business PACs and encouraged their development. Not surprisingly, when business PACs started to give more to Democratic incumbents, Republicans reversed their position—at least in their rhetoric if not in practice.

PACs have their defenders, who maintain they merely represent competing interests inherent in the U.S. pluralistic system and are not nearly as monolithic as portrayed, and some cancel others out. Defenders note that at a time when many bemoan declining citizen involvement in the electoral process, PACs have increased participation by their rank-and-file. Finally, they contend that efforts to abolish PACs would be ineffective. PAC money would not disappear; instead it would be channeled into less visible, less traceable channels such as soft money and independent expenditures....

Bundling

In the 1980s, as criticism of PAC spending grew and limits on PAC and party gifts made campaign contributions lose value through inflation, certain PACs, political parties, and corporate executives turned to an alternative method of fund raising: "bundling" contributions. Bundling is a technique whereby contributions are collected from individuals who have made out their checks to a designated candidate. An intermediary or conduit is involved; it may be a PAC or a party committee that provides individuals with a list of suggested candidates for whom a contribution is encouraged. The committee will then send the collection of individual contributions to a candidate in a "bundle."

Although the bundled contributions technically are a collection of individual campaign gifts, candidates receiving them can identify the contributions as being from a particular PAC or industry.

Bundling is not new, but the extent to which it is now used is new to the election process. The technique was invented by the Council for a Livable World (CLW), an organization that raises funds for candidates opposed to nuclear proliferation. In 1962, CLW bundled contributions for George McGovern in his Senate race. The method was identical to those used today: CLW mailed campaign information to supporters and asked them to send the council checks payable to McGovern.[4] CLW is still actively bundling contributions and along with an adjunct, Peace PAC, funneled $1.4 million to Senate and House candidates for the 1990 campaigns.

PACs are not the only bundlers. Industry executives also raise considerable amounts of money for candidates. The technique carries less stigma than PAC gifts and, perhaps more significantly, if properly executed, can give higher amounts of money to political campaigns (no one individual can give more than $2,000 to a single candidate). A PAC is limited to giving any individual candidate $10,000, but, for example, thirty corporate executives can each give $2,000, for a total of $60,000....

Groups from all sides of the political spectrum...have adopted the technique of bundling. In the 1980s, the Associated Life Insurance Group National Policyholder Advisory Committee (ALIGNPAC) channeled money to selected members of the Senate Finance and the House Ways and Means committees at a time when both panels were considering various tax proposals that would affect the life insurance industry. The bundled funds included $150,000 to Oregon Republican senator Bob Packwood, who was chairman of the Finance Committee, and $50,000 to House Ways and Means Committee chairman Dan Rostenkowski, an Illinois Democrat.[5] ALIGNPAC's bundled contributions were controversial and were criticized by the press. "ALIGNPAC's money stands out because. . . it illustrates how easily special interest groups can get around election laws when they wish," wrote *Wall Street Journal* reporter Brooks Jackson.[6] . . .

Some advocates of campaign finance reform argue that bundling is just as bad as PAC contributions. Fred Wertheimer, president of Common Cause, believes that bundling is a deliberate attempt to evade PAC contribution limits and should, therefore, be outlawed. "It's a direct threat to the integrity of the system," he said. "If the contribution limits are to have any impact, you have got to stop bundling."[7] Bundling is legal, but several campaign finance reform proposals have called for outlawing the practice or tightening the restrictions to its use.

Notes

1. Federal Election Commission, "PAC Activity Falls in 1990 Elections," press release, March 31, 1991, 1.
2. "The Top 100 PACs of 1989–90: They Gave 46.7 Percent of All PAC Gifts," *PACs and Lobbies*, April 17, 1991, 3.
3. "Have PACs Entered the 'Twilight Zone'?" *PACs and Lobbies*, April 3, 1991, 1, 3–5.
4. H. Richard Mayberry, Jr., and Kristine E. Heine, "Bundling Makes Strange Bedfellows," *Campaigns and Elections* (July 1986): 76–78.
5. Mayberry and Heine, "Bundling Makes Strange Bedfellows," 77.
6. Quoted in Ibid., 78.
7. Sara Fritz and Dwight Morris, "Political Money by the Bundle," *Los Angeles Times*, July, 30, 1990.

46 / Proposals for Change in the Federal Election Campaign Law

Michael J. Malbin

According to Michael Malbin, an interest-group role in congressional campaign finance can be seen as beneficial for democracy, as an additional means by which citizens may have a voice in politics, and also as a source of badly needed campaign money. Malbin suggests that by increasing the role of parties and public finance in congressional campaigns, while allowing PACs to contribute as well, it would be possible to keep the benefits of interest-group involvement while reducing the problems.

... [C]ampaign finance reform has resulted ... in wide-ranging consequences for both electoral politics and government in the United States. Strategy and tactics have been altered in presidential, congressional, and state politics, with different legal provisions working to the advantage of some candidates and the disadvantage of others. Political parties, political action committees, and other politically influential organizations have also had their relative and absolute importance changed in foreseen and unforeseen ways....

Groups and the Purposes of Elections

...During the debate over the Bill of Rights in the First Congress, a motion was made by Thomas Tudor Tucker of South Carolina to add a clause to what is now the First Amendment that would have given people the right to instruct their representatives on specific issues. The motion was rejected then, as it was repeatedly over the next few decades, because it was based on the view that the ideal representative should mirror the wishes, feelings, and interests of his or her constituents. The alternative view, which prevailed, was that representation in an extended, diverse republic required members to come together and deliberate in a central place—talking directly to one another, sharing opinions, compromising, and thereby reaching a national consensus that would transcend the local concerns from which members would most likely begin. If the decisions displeased constituents, the constituents could change their representatives at the next election.

One assumption in the discussion of 1789 is striking for our purposes. The members of the First Congress, and most of the active Federalists in the two-year period before then, saw the national legislature as a place where members would be several steps removed from the clamor of special interests, most of which were assumed to have local bases. Today, in contrast, reformers yearn for a more locally based campaign finance system in the hope that this will help legislators escape a different sort of nationalized, interest-group clamor. The hope is fruitless. The only way to escape the current clamor would be to return to the government, policies, and environment of almost two hundred years ago. Failing that, a complex age calls not for nostalgia but for a sophisticated understanding of the multiple objectives that have to be balanced, and compromises that have to be made, to keep elections and representative institutions serving their purposes at least reasonably well.

The main purpose of elections, as mentioned, is to give voters a chance to react to government policy by replacing the people who govern them. As a corollary, elections should also serve to confer legitimacy upon those who assume office. Finally, an election system that works well should help facilitate the process of government—not necessarily by making governmental actions easier, as supporters of parliamentary regimes would wish, but by giving the elected members a sense of institutional and personal self-interest that helps each branch perform its proper function.

When we take this broad view, we can begin to see that the problems of campaign finance in the modern communications age do not lend themselves to easy solutions, for at least two reasons. First, there was always an inherent, and healthy, tension between the desire for accountability and the desire to preserve freedom for members of Congress to think about the national interest. The tension has been exacerbated in recent years. The complexity of government makes it all but impossible for voters to follow individual issues. In addition, a legislator who wants to serve the national interest cannot possibly learn about the potential effects of proposed legislation without the reaction of organized groups. In this situation, the wishes of groups should not be seen merely as nuisances. They also help confer and sustain support for people in government, and they help facilitate the process of both government and opposition by keeping the governors and governed informed.

If interest groups are not merely nuisances, neither had their proliferation been just a blessing. It may be important for people to organize on a national level, especially as the role of government expands. The proliferation of a multiplicity of interests also has some important benefits, as James Madison argued in *Federalist No. 10*. But I am not one of those twentieth-century pluralist misinterpreters of Madison who believes the public good is simply the sum of, or a compromise among, interest-group claims. Group conflict does sometimes produce legislative stalemate, and groups do sometimes win special benefits, at the expense of the general public, when the public is not looking.

It would be misleading, however, to treat campaign finance, or even lobbying, as if they were the fundamental causes of legislative outcomes. They do make a difference, but only at the margins. Lobbyists can win when their activities generally go along with what the public wants, when public opinion is divided, or when the public has no particular opinion. Lobbyists can also help lighten the burden of defeat when the public is against them. Campaign finance may modestly help reinforce the effects of lobbying. But to address the contemporary role of interest groups fully, in its most basic aspects, would force one ultimately to look broadly at the reasons institutional power has been decentralized and at the public philosophy elected members tend to believe or, at least, act upon. These considerations go well beyond the scope of this chapter. Suffice it for now to say that the problem *exists* because most people, in part of their souls, want the government to look after their special, intensely felt desires and needs. It is *perceived* as a problem by most of these same people, because, in another part of their souls, they want the government to listen to their more general, less intensely felt, needs and desires when they conflict with the special desires of others. Politically, there is no easy solution because, as Aaron Wildavsky has noted, the Pogo Principle applies: "We have seen the enemy and they are us."[1] All of us react strongly to our own particular concerns, and a fair number of us are likely to let those special concerns determine our vote. As long as that is true, organized interests will continue to play an important role in electoral politics, whatever the rules of campaign finance.

The second reason there are no easy solutions has to do with another by-product of modern government and communication: the advantages of incumbency, especially for members of the House. The communication resources available to incumbent members, the fractionalization of the congressional policy process, and the long-term weakening of the importance of party to voters all make it hard to defeat incumbents without spending a great deal of money. But a system within which a lot of private money is available almost assuredly is a system in which special interests will participate on an individual or group basis. Interest-group participation may not be all that bad, therefore, if it is a necessary condition for assuring there will be enough money in the system to make the threat of subsequent accountability real.

Proposals for Change

Having said this, we are now prepared to look again at some proposals for changing the law. The benefits and problems interest groups bring to the legislative process would not be affected greatly if groups could not contribute to candidates. The benefits they bring to elections would be lost, however, unless the money they provide challengers toward the end of a campaign could be replaced. In theory the job might be done by full public financing, if it were sufficiently generous to cover the country's most expensive districts. Such a form of public financing might eliminate whatever reinforcement contributions now give to lobbying, while substituting for the needed money that now comes from interested contributors. There are two problems with this approach. First, as was argued earlier in connection with presidential elections, eliminating direct contributions would not and could not eliminate the electoral role of interest groups. It would only introduce new forms of bias into the system. Second, even if the idea were good in theory, it would stand little chance of being adopted. Members of Congress are not likely ever to give their opponents enough money, solely from public funds, to permit serious challenges in expensive districts. Incumbents cannot be expected to think first about the system's need for electoral insecurity as they design the rules for their own reelection campaigns.

We return, therefore, to the real world of political practice, where some form of interest-group participation is accepted, however unhappily, as inevitable, and where the level of electoral competition and the fragmentation of the legislative process are both causes for legitimate concern.... To the extent that fragmentation is caused partly by the role of groups, but more basically by the splits within our selves, the institutional remedy logically seems to call for building up those political institutions and organizations that can counter our particularized interests in the name of our more general ones. In practical terms, this means increasing the role of parties.

Parties should not be considered panaceas. Excessively strong national committees could weaken Congress, as we saw. In addition, one cannot simply assume that turning all power back to the parties would weaken the power of interest groups. The strong parties of the late nineteenth century, and the national conventions of today, hardly leave one sanguine on that score. Instead of a lesser role for groups, a system in which parties were dominant could just mean better access for fewer groups. But parties are a long way from being dominant today. A great deal can be done to strengthen their role in elections without granting the unlimited spending authority Republicans might wish. Spending limits can be raised, and state and local party volunteer activities can be encouraged....

In addition, the government could reclaim some of the air time it now gives freely to federally licensed radio and television stations. The stations could then be required to make 60 minutes or so of free prime time available to each party to be used in blocks of at least five minutes. In some local areas, the parties might turn the time over to candidates. In most, however, they would probably increase their generic advertising. This advertising ... would make the parties more important for both candidates and voters, nationalizing the election in a manner that would go a long way toward countering the decentralizing effects of individualistic, candidate-centered campaigning. To the extent this happens, it would heighten the sense that elections produce mandates, adding weight to the inclinations of those members who want to resist particularized pressures in the name of a more general interest.

The second approach that deserves serious consideration is ... public financing unencumbered either by spending limits or limits on a candidate's PAC receipts. As noted, public financing without limits works to the benefit of challengers, especially challengers who have not yet managed to establish themselves as serious competitors. In this respect, it serves as a perfect complement to the existing finance system, in which PACs avoid commitments to challengers in the early stage, but flock to the most serious ones at the end.

Public financing without limits also would decrease the importance of PACs by giving candidates other places to look for their funds. Not all forms of public financing would be equal in this respect, however. Matching grants would do nothing to change the mix of private givers or their importance. Flat grants—whether in cash or in such in-kind forms as postal subsidies, the frank, or free media—would decrease the importance of private money but not the mix. Of all of the bills proposed so far, only a 100 percent tax credit or voucher would change the incentives for candidates in a way that would broaden the base of participants. Interest groups would continue to play an important role, but their proportionate influence would be reduced in a way that would also reduce, rather than increase, the biases inherent in the current system.

In short, many steps can be taken to reduce the costs of interest-group participation while preserving the benefits. Nothing can be done, however, with a strategy of limits that fails to recognize that the fundamental source of interest-group power has little to do with campaign finance. Interest groups are what they are in the United States because parties, governmental institutions, communications and human nature are what they are. Any attempt to deal with what is essentially a surface symptom, the contemporary electoral role of organized groups, solely through direct regulations and limits can do little more than shift group power around and weaken electoral competition. The supposed reforms might also make a few regulators feel good for a while— but only until they glance backward at the unintended consequences of some past reforms and realize that they are looking at their own future.

47 / The Paradox of Interest Groups in Washington—More Groups, Less Clout

Robert H. Salisbury

According to Robert Salisbury, two descriptors that clearly apply to interest groups in national politics over the past four decades are "growth" and "fragmentation." Partly as a result of those trends, but also due to changes in the environment within which the groups operate, it is probably accurate to say that no interest group has the influence today that a few of them had in earlier times.

One of the most startling events in the history of public policy in the United States was the Tax Reform Act of 1986.[1] It was startling not so much because of its content or its possible impact as, first, because it happened at all, contrary to the forecasts of all knowledgeable observers and, second, because it was fashioned and passed while virtual armies of lobbyists looked on in distress and frustration, unable to intervene to affect the outcome. The "Battle of Gucci Gulch" was fought by members of Congress, mindful, to be sure, of the needs and concerns of organized interests but operating in a context shaped mainly by broader policy, partisan, and institutional considerations. It seemed a heavy irony indeed that, just when the number and variety of organized interests represented in Washington were at an all-time high— with unprecedented numbers of lobbyists using high personal skill supplemented by elaborate modern technologies of analysis, communication, and mobilization—and in a policy area, taxation, that had acquired many of its bizarre existing contours from the pressures and demands of narrowly based interest groups, the ultimate decision process should largely screen out those interests.

This paradox of more interest groups and lobbyists wielding less influence over policy results does not manifest itself all the time, to be sure. The paradox, however, is substantially valid, if not in quite this stark form, then at least in more nuanced forms. In this [reading] I argue the case that the growth in the number, variety, and sophistication of interest groups represented in Washington has been associated with, and in some measure has helped to bring about, a transformation in the way much public policy is made and, further, that this transformed process is not dominated so often by a relatively small number of powerful interest groups as it may once have been.

I certainly do not want to be understood as saying that interest groups as a whole have weakened in the way, say, that party organizations have lost control over the nomination of candidates. Nor would I deny that in particular instances the old ways are still intact—the "veterans' system" comes to mind—with triangular symbioses linking groups, congressional committees, and executive agencies in nearly impregnable policy success. Moreover, policies such as social security may be quite rigid and largely beyond amendment, not so much because of organized group pressure as such as from the fear among policy makers that such pressure is potentially mobilizable and would soon follow any adverse policy revision. Still, I contend that a great many interest group representatives seek information more than influence, that in many ways they have become dependent on and are sometimes exploited by government officials rather than the other way around, and that much of what contemporary lobbyists do is to be understood as a search for order and a measure of predictability in a policy-making world that has been fundamentally destabilized by developments of the past twenty years.

Changes since 1960

The Explosion in Numbers. The number of organizations directly engaged in pursuing their interests in Washington, D.C., has grown dramatically since about 1960. We have no reliable base line of observation, but the following items suggest the magnitude of expansion in the interest group universe.

- The number of registered lobbyists increased from 3,400 in 1975 to 7,200 in 1985.
- The annual publication *Washington Representatives* managed to find and list more than 5,000 people in 1979; by 1988 it listed nearly 11,000.[2]
- The proportion of U.S. trade and professional associations headquartered in and around Washington grew from 19 percent in 1971 to 30 percent in 1982.[3]
- The number of lawyers belonging to the District of Columbia Bar Association (a requirement for practice in Washington) increased from 10,925 in 1973 to 34,087 in 1981.
- The number of business corporations operating offices in Washington increased from 50 in 1961 to 545 in 1982.[4]
- Some 76 percent of the citizens' groups and 79 percent of the welfare groups in Washington in 1981 had come into existence since 1960.[5]

The Shifting Composition. From Tocqueville to Truman and beyond, interest group scholarship focused almost exclusively on voluntary associations, organizations of members who joined together to advance some common purpose. Mancur Olson showed that the simple fact that people share some political values is not a sufficient basis for collective action.[6] But Olson and other scholars have identified a variety of factors, including the presence of political entrepreneurs, selective benefits, social pressure, philanthropic motives, coercion, and sheer uncertainty, that can account reasonably well for the substantial numbers of voluntary associations that exist and are active in the political arena. This large set exhibits considerable variety, however. Thus trade associations composed of corporations operate quite differently from citizens' groups, especially expressive groups where the problem of free riders is more difficult to control. Important changes have occurred among voluntary associations in both composition and relative importance. In addition, however, three other, rather different kinds of interest organizations inhabit the Washington community, each of which has attained a larger and more consequential place in recent years.

First are institutions. Individual corporations, universities, state and local governments, and religious denominations are active on their own behalf as well as often belonging to voluntary associations of similarly situated entities.[7] ... Although some have long been influential—large oil companies, for example—it seems likely that in the past two decades individual institutions have been of greater importance in affecting national policy and certainly have devoted greater effort to keeping track of the policy process than they did before the 1960s.

A second category of interested participant, once not nearly so important, is the think tank. The American Enterprise Institute, the Brookings Institution, the Heritage Foundation, the Urban Institute, the Institute for Policy Analysis, the Cato Institute, and a good many others have come to play a significant role in national policy making.... The principal mode of think tank operation ... is to publish and publicize policy analyses and recommendations.[8] Think tanks do not usually insist that policy makers adopt their recommended positions to placate some organized constituency they represent. Rather, they depend on the logical power of their arguments or the persuasiveness of their evidence and analysis. They often seek more to shape the broad agenda of policy action than to push for specific decision outcomes. These are only tendencies, to be sure, and there is considerable variation among these organizations; but it is important to include them in any comprehensive picture of the nongovernmental participants attempting to influence the policy-making process. Moreover, it is important to recognize not only that they are more numerous than, say, in 1960 but that they have become considerably more visible....

Third, Washington lobbying is carried on not only by organizations on their own behalf but by agents of various kinds retained to advance their interests. Thus many of the lawyers in Washington do not pursue much conventional law practice but concentrate on representing client organizations before federal regulatory agencies, assisting in the presentation of testimony before congressional committees, arranging for a discussion between a client and a high-ranking White House staff person, or approaching potential sources of campaign contributions to help a senator's reelection campaign.... To the roster of Washington lawyers in private practice must be added the very considerable number of consultants, of whom Michael Deaver, Lyn Nofziger, and a good many other peddlers of influence are notorious though perhaps unrepresentative examples, and public relations firms, a few of which, such as Hill and Knowlton, have become large enterprises offering clients a broad array of services, including lobbying but extending to many other forms of contact with the public....

The Fragmentation of Interest Sectors

In the "old days" —the 1950s, say—it was characteristic of many policy sectors for a few organizations, sometimes only one, to have hegemony. The American Medical Association (AMA) dominated health policy, the American Farm Bureau Federation (AFBF) was far and away the most influential group on agricultural matters, the American Petroleum Institute led the list of energy interests, and so on. In the late 1980s these are still substantial organizations, actively involved in making policy pronouncements and using the tactics of influence, but in most policy domains such quasimonopoly power has been undermined by a process of interest fragmentation that has greatly changed the distribution of influence.

This fragmentation process has two distinct components. First, the self-interested groups have increased in number, variety, and specificity of policy concerns. In agriculture the National Farmers Union gained a position as liberal Democratic rival to the conservative Republican AFBF, only to be challenged on specific issues by the National Wheat Growers Association, the Soy Bean Association, the Corn Growers Association, and dozens of commodity-based trade associations....

In the mid-1980s William P. Browne identified well over 200 interests involved in shaping farm legislation.[9] With this massive expansion of private interest group participants, it has been necessary since at least the late 1950s to construct quite elaborate coalitions of these groups to get the support necessary to enact major farm legislation. In agriculture the farm bills still take broad multipurpose form and are enacted for terms of three to five years, after which there is another round of negotiation. The complexity of these negotiations defies quick summary, but it is clear that the peak associations no longer guide the process.

A similar story can be told of the health policy domain.[10] There no single legislative enactment brings into focus the full extent of interest fragmentation, although efforts to achieve national health insurance and sometimes medical cost containment issues have come close. Issues concerning hospital construction, medical research, veterans' health care, and drug regulation, however, have long been treated separately. Whatever the question, the AMA, once so imperiously powerful, is no longer the dominant voice even of organized medicine. The hospital associations now speak with quite independent voices. So do many organizations of medical specialists. Medical insurance interests, medical schools, corporations engaged in medical technology research and manufacturing, and of course the drug companies all get involved. Again, complex coalitions among diverse interests are necessary to enact legislation and secure its continued funding.

. . . But the fragmentation process has a second component in addition to the proliferation of self-interested groups just described, which puts even these narrowly bounded islands of policy stability at risk. This component may be called the "invasion of the externality groups."[11]

A major category of growth among interest groups has been citizens' groups. This label is attached to a broad array of motivating concerns and points of view, but it applies to all those groups for whom self-interest, narrowly defined, is not the primary organizing appeal. Members of taxpayer groups and animal rights enthusiasts may thereby express some private desire to save money to protect their pets, but even for them the collective purposes of the group bear only an indirect connection to their personal situations. In any case, the rapid growth of citizens' groups has affected the policy process in important ways. . . .

The central importance of the newly prominent externality groups is that they further destabilize the policy-making process. The proliferation or fractionation of interests in particular policy domains has undermined the hegemony of peak associations in those domains, pushing some groups into small policy niches and forcing others into much more complicated coalitional efforts to secure their policy desires. To this has been added this further assortment, differing from one policy domain to another in their specific concerns but similar in their tendency to appeal to high moral principle as the only proper criterion for deciding who gets what, when, and how. Many of these groups have dubious political muscle in the usual sense, as measured by membership size, money, or even social status, although some are impressive in one or more of these respects. Regardless, however, of their ability to affect electoral prospects directly, these groups are assertive in their use of mass media and thereby make themselves felt regarding which items get on the agenda, forcing the recognition of values and concerns that might, if left to the traditional cozy triangles, receive little attention. Further, the externality groups often call into question the legitimacy of otherwise stable cozy relationships among self-interested groups and officials. The attacks on the so-called cozy or iron triangles have been mounted by reformers of both left and right, by think tanks and citizens' groups of diverse motives and persuasions; as these groups have grown more numerous, the arrangements they have challenged have become less cozy, less stable. Not only are policy processes more uncertain, they are more often contentious. Externality groups attract considerable hostility from the more self-interested institutions and associations, which doubt the seriousness of purpose or understanding of real world effects on the part of citizens' groups and assorted do-gooders.[12] . . .

Uncertain Structures of Power

The destabilization argument I have been developing affects the pattern of policy outcomes at two levels. In the formulation of legislation and the implementing of regulations it means that it is no longer accurate to account for outcomes by reference to the familiar metaphor of iron or cozy triangles wherein interest groups, congressional committees or subcommittees, and executive agencies operate in symbiotic interdependence.. . .

At a more highly aggregated level, destabilization challenges the value of what for two decades has been the dominant conception of most U.S. policy, interest group liberalism. Theodore Lowi's view, embraced in at least substantial part by most observers, was that in the United States, since the 1930s at least, the major thrusts of policy decision reflected the demands of particularistic groups, opposed weakly if at all by competitors and enacted without much reference to standards of judgment drawn from outside the interest-dominated arenas of politics.[13] In a destabilized world of fragmented interests and multidimensional challenges from externality groups it becomes impossible for policy makers to identify which interests, if any, they can succumb to without grave political risk. They find themselves with choice and discretion, able to select policy alternatives and take positions knowing that almost any position will have some group support and none can prevent opposition from arising. We can easily carry this interpretation too far, denying all policy effect to organized groups, and this would be quite unwarranted. Nevertheless, as was illustrated by the Gucci Gulch example I began with, the presumption has been significantly altered: where interest groups were seen as the prime motive force pressing politicians to make policy decisions in their favor, now the officials very often exploit the groups.

This partial reversal in the flow of influence is not simply a product of the expansion in size and fragmentation in purpose of interest sectors. It is also closely linked with changes in the institutional configurations of Congress and the executive branch. I need not detail these developments here but merely identify those that have especially affected the position and practice of interest group politics.

First has been the diffusion of power in Congress. The weakening of seniority, the empowering of subcommittees, and the expansion of congressional staffs have all contributed to the result that many members are in a position to participate actively and meaningfully on a much larger number of issues than once was possible. Specialization is not so much required to gain substantive expertise—and not so much deferred to by others in any case. On any particular set of policy concerns there are multiple points of potentially relevant access as groups seek support in the Congress, but the depressing corollary for the groups is that none of them is likely to carry decisive weight in shaping policy. Indeed, the position-taking and credit-claiming competition among these many focal points may well mean that ultimately no action is possible in any direction.

Diffusion of power within Congress has been accompanied by the widely remarked increase in the electoral success of incumbents. Incumbents' electoral safety further undermines dependence on interest groups.. . . As members of Congress today find themselves increasingly secure beneficiaries of pork, casework, and name recognition, they learn that they can afford to stand aloof from many interest groups. There are important exceptions, but my argument is that in the Congress of the late 1980s interest groups are virtually awash in access but often subordinate in influence.

In the executive branch the most significant development affecting established interest triangles has been the centralization of policy initiatives within the Executive Office of the President and particularly the White House staff. Interest group access in the past has been greatest and most productive with line agencies and independent commissions. The White House is a much more difficult target for lobbyists to reach, and even though White House decisions will necessarily favor some interests over others, it will rarely be, in any direct sense, because of the groups' skill or power.... The groups go where they can; but ever since Franklin D. Roosevelt executive authority has been brought more and more fully within the White House orbit, and most organized interests have been disadvantaged accordingly.

Summary

...Despite repeated efforts to reform them, the legal rules constraining the behavior of organized interests in Washington have remained essentially stable for several decades. Only in the area of campaign finance has the law undergone major revision since 1946. Yet the world in which interest groups must operate has changed profoundly. Growth and the changing composition of their ranks are part of this transformation; diffusion of power in Congress and concentration of initiative in the executive are another part; the increase in incumbents' security against electoral defeat has likewise been a factor. The result is that from the perspective of the private interests old patterns of access and influence cannot be depended on to suffice for policy representation needs. Relationships are often friendly but generally unstable, with new groups and new coalitions appearing and reforming while the officials become stronger, wealthier in campaign funds, and as autonomous as they choose to be vis-à-vis the multitude of supplicant interests....

Conclusion

I come back to the apparent paradox with which I began, to the Tax Reform Act of 1986 in which the members of Congress made the choices, excluding the scores of interest group representatives from the process and forcing them to wait outside until it was over. The interpretation I have offered suggests that, rather than being a paradox, this situation simply registered important changes that have been taking place. Many of the old symbioses have given way, destabilized as a result of expanded group participation, of greater electoral security, increased staff, and lessened need or inclination to specialize on the part of Congress, and of more centralized control of the executive branch, which leaves the specialized agencies less able to create their own triangular policy deals.

The uncertainty generated by this political destabilization is compounded by the problematic nature of policy interests. Organizations are often unsure which among the live policy options might be most to their advantage;

indeed, they are often in doubt about what the options are. They are engaged in a never-ending process of learning, assessment, and calculation; and timely information, much of it available only from government, is the sine qua non of this process. It would be too much to claim that interest group lobbyists have been wholly subordinated to public officials, but we would surely misread the American political process if we ignored the extent to which these groups have come to Washington out of need and dependence rather than because they have influence.

Notes

1. Jeffrey H. Birnbaum and Alan S. Murray, *Showdown at Gucci Gulch* (New York: Random House, 1987).
2. Arthur Close et al., eds., *Washington Representatives, 1988* (Washington, D.C.: Columbia Books, 1988).
3. Craig Colgate, ed., *National Trade and Professional Associations of the United States, 1982* (Washington, D.C.: Columbia Books, 1982).
4. David Yoffie, "Interest Groups v. Individual Action: An Analysis of Corporate Political Strategies," Working paper, Harvard Business School, 1985.
5. Kay Lehman Schlozman and John T. Tierney, *Organized Interests and American Democracy* (New York: Harper and Row, 1986), p. 76; see also Jack L. Walker, "The Origins and Maintenance of Interest Groups in America," *American Political Science Review*, vol. 77 (1983), pp. 390–406.
6. Mancur Olson, *The Logic of Collective Action* (Cambridge, Mass.: Harvard University Press, 1965).
7. Robert H. Salisbury, "Interest Representation: The Dominance of Institutions," *American Political Science Review*, vol. 78, pp. 64–76.
8. See Lawrence Mone, "Thinkers and Their Tanks Move on Washington," *Wall Street Journal*, March 15, 1988. Think tank lobbying is described in David Shribman, "Lobbying of Bush Transition Office Is Turning to Matters of Policy from Personnel Choices," *Wall Street Journal*, January 3, 1989. See also Martha Derthick and Paul Quirk, *The Politics of Deregulation* (Washington, D.C.: Brookings Institution, 1985).
9. William P. Browne, *Private Interests, Public Policy, and American Agriculture* (Lawrence: University of Kansas Press, 1988).
10. See Edward O. Laumann and David Knoke, *The Organizational State: Social Choice in National Policy Domains* (Madison: University of Wisconsin Press, 1987).
11. See my essay, "Washington Lobbyists: A Collective Portrait," in Allan J. Cigler and Burdett A. Loomis, eds., *Interest Group Politics*, 2d ed. (Washington, D.C.: Congressional Quarterly Press, 1986), pp. 146–61.
12. See Robert H. Salisbury, John P Heinz, Edward O. Laumann and Robert L. Nelson, "Who Works with Whom? Interest Group Alliances and Opposition," *American Political Science Review*, vol. 81, pp. 1217–34. The excellent essay by Jeffrey M. Berry, "Subgovernments, Issue Networks, and Political Conflict," stresses the importance of increased conflict as a destabilizing force. Berry's essay came to my attention after I had completed my own, but it is clear that our thinking has moved along closely related lines. His work appears in Richard Harris and Sidney Milkis, eds., *Remaking American Politics* (Boulder, Colo.: Westview Press, 1989), pp. 239–60.
13. Theodore Lowi, *The End of Liberalism* (New York: W. W. Norton, 1969).

CHAPTER THIRTEEN

Media

When the authors of the *Federalist Papers* wanted to promote their new document for ratification, they turned to newspapers as the medium. When the Bill of Rights was added to the Constitution, an important role for a free press in American politics was all but assured. Indeed, a relationship for news media and politics has been one of the continuities of American politics, although the nature of that relationship has changed greatly over time, and especially with the advent of television.

When television joined the other mass media (newspapers and radio) in the 1950s, it set off a chain of events with important repercussions throughout the political system. Not only has television affected the ways public opinion is shaped and the political agenda set, but its impact has also been felt in the way candidates are selected and the way officials govern. In their book, *Politics in the Media Age*, Ronald Beckman and Laura Kitch have summarized some of the most dramatic changes:

> The first political arena where the media had an identifiable impact was in the process of selecting candidates.... Those politicians who early recognized this growing power of the media to determine political success, sought means to influence the choices made by news organizations and methods to use the mass media technologies to promote their candidacies.... If the skilled use of the media could make the difference in an election, it was only a small step to conclude that the media could also be used as a tool to help an elected official govern and maintain a good public profile.... By the middle 1960s, political actors from other branches of the federal government and from state and local governments began to spend more time considering how to use the media effectively.... Now that politicians have legitimized the use of the media to wage a political campaign and to serve as an instrument of governance, the corporation is prepared to use the media as a legitimate means for political agitation. (1986, 13–14)*

The changes in the role of the media in the American political process have been so significant that it is often suggested that news media should no longer be viewed as outside observers of the process, but rather as some of its most important actors.

In the first two selections of this chapter, James David Barber considers the reasons why the news media have become so important in election campaigns, and Sig Mickelson documents the growing role of television in campaigns and assesses the consequences. Then, shifting to the impact of television on policy-making, David Gergen evaluates the role of "teledemocracy" in the making of foreign policy and concludes that limitations of television and public opinion as instruments of democracy are too often overlooked.

*Beckman, Ronald, and Laura W. Kitch, *Politics in the Media Age* (New York: McGraw-Hill Book Co., 1986).—*Editor's Note.*

48 / Journalism: Power by Default

James David Barber

James David Barber notes that because the campaign season now lasts at least two or three years, "for those who would take a serious part in it, prolonged attention and sustained action are required." That requirement applies to "the people," who watch the campaign at a distance and through the eyes of the media. The media have adapted to play an important role in the new style of politics. That is something that the parties have been unable to do.

As the histories to follow make clear, journalism's role in Presidential politics has been significant—sometimes perhaps even decisive—at least since the turn of the century. It is important to understand this history, because the journalists of today, like other professionals, inherit their mindsets from their mentors. The old teach the young; the new journalists adapt old story forms to new conditions. What is new is not mass communication as one of the major forces in politics, but rather its emergence to fill virtually the whole gap in the electoral process left by the default of other independent elites who used to help manage the choice. Their power is all the stronger because it looks, to the casual observer, like no power at all. Much as the old party bosses used to pass themselves off as mere "coordinators" and powerless arrangers, so some modern-day titans of journalism want themselves thought of as mere scorekeepers and messenger boys. Yet the signs of journalists' key role as the major advancers and retarders of Presidential ambitions are all around us.

Smart candidates recognize that power and hurry to adapt their strategies to it. They learn to *use* journalism, as journalism uses them. They and the journalists grapple in a reciprocal relationship of mutual exploitation, a political symbiosis. If the journalists are the new kingmakers, the candidates are the new storytellers, active plotters of dramas they hope will win for them.

Nowadays when a man sets out to be President, his first plan is a media strategy. His first major expenditure is likely to go for hiring a top-flight, high-priced professional media manager. When he goes to New York, he may call on Mayor What's-his-name, but not until he has wangled lunch with the big-time editors and publishers. Give him a choice between a spot on the "Today Show" and a gathering at national party headquarters and he will hardly pause over the choice. His schedule is built around media markets in the primary and caucus states. He goes where he goes and does what he does *mainly* to get his message into the newspapers, magazines, and television programs. By far the biggest burden in his budget is for commercial advertising through the mass media. His aides ponder through the night how to get him covered for free without shoving him over into some eccentricity the press will pick up as a "gaffe." In the early obscurity of his campaign, he seeks out the major reporters like a lonely bachelor in a singles' bar. If his wooing works and fame begins to gather to him, he finds himself trailing a vast horde of writers and picture-takers as he marches through various scripted and scenarioed spontaneous encounters. In short, the primary task a Presidential candidate faces today is not building a coalition of organized interests, or developing alliances with other candidates or politicians in his party, or even winning over the voters whose hands he shakes. If he has his modern priorities straight, he is first and foremost a seeker after favorable notice from the journalists who can make or break his progress.

At the other end of the media pipe, citizens are getting whatever they eventually get of the candidate from print and broadcast journalism. Few get to the rallies. Indeed, there are not many rallies to get to anymore. The thousands who experience some airport or shopping-center event with the candidate are massively outweighed by the millions who know of him only what journalists tell them.

To suppose that either the candidate or the citizen is putty in the hands of conniving communicators is absurd. Candidates are made up by their own histories long before the television make-up artist gets hold of them. The citizen also has a mind of his own. The journalist has to find news in the material available. He is significantly dependent on what he judges his audience wants to know and on what the candidate hands him to depict. But it is just that position as middleman that sets the journalist up as the new powerbroker, filling the gap vacated by yesterday's bosses.

There he stands, between people and President. Whether he knows it or not, the impressions he composes and conveys are now the blood of Presidential politics. The journalistic tyros of old—the Hearsts and Luces and Murrows, whose impact on politics was often personal and direct—are gone. The collective, loose-jointed journalistic fraternity of today is all the more powerful because its influence is pervasive and indirect and atmospheric, an element of the cultural air we breathe.

Nothing signals quite so clearly the rise of the journalist to political power as the righteous wrath that now descends upon him. Spiro Agnew had his reasons for spraying journalism with indignant alliterations. His protest was but a visible bubble in a great outpouring of criticism from left, right, and center. "Media critic" is now a recognized occupation. Wounded and slain politicians, once they have really decided to retire, blast the media as obsessed with their warts and blind to their beauties. Academics who deign to notice what is happening chime in with their analytic condemnations. Journalists themselves rail at one another for bias and hype and error. There is scattered evidence that some elements of the public, ahead of their time, are looking askance at the media they associate with recent dips in our political fortunes. Just as it happened years ago, when the new ethnic bosses took over from the old Wasp elites in the big cities, reformers and reactionaries join in castigating the new powerbrokers.

That might do some good, though righteous indignation as a teaching technique can be overrated. I think political journalism is improvable; with many journalists, I think the craft has often missed its promise.... The interplay of journalism and politics turns out to be crucial to the most important political choice we make, the choice of a President. How has that connection grown up in the American culture? What casts of mind do the contemporary composers of this drama inherit from their traditions? Why have we come to tell the Presidential story as we do?

A solid starting point is the evident fact that we have transformed a quadrennial event into a saga lasting at least two or three years. In the days of McKinley—not so long ago—candidates for President, however burning with ambition and whatever they might do behind the scenes, were not expected to campaign for their party's nomination. Indeed, even after the national convention named the nominee, he stayed quietly at home until the official committee of notification made its way to his doorstep, an occasion of considerable ceremonial moment. Touring and speechmaking, for a really proper candidate, began in a serious way only in September after Labor Day. The public's time of awareness was relatively brief, the process of deliberation and choice concentrated in a few months. Today, thanks to the invention of new opportunities for early testing—the caucuses, primaries, and public opinion polls, and the chance to qualify early for federal funds—the typical campaign is well under way the fall before election year and it is not unusual to find candidates in hot pursuit of the prize well before that. Thus the quest is stretched out to Odyssean dimensions; stages previously compacted in time are elaborated and elongated; the dash becomes a race, the race a marathon, even a crusade. Along that trail, the fortunes and prospects of the candidates rise and fall in an extended series of connected events. For those who would take a serious part in it, prolonged attention and sustained action are required.

Insofar as the people are concerned, their participation is almost entirely vicarious. Except when a primary vote or a poll or a candidate appearance happens their way, they watch and read. It is natural for them to sense the campaign as a developing, continuing story, unfolding a piece at a time through the seasons.

That sense could not suit the journalist better. For the journalist is, at the heart of his calling, a storyteller. His attention is attuned to notice, in the flux of facts, just those features that lend themselves to interesting, novel narrative. The idea of the reporter as blotter, passively soaking up the inchoate slop his perceptual organs get wet with, is too trivial and naive to give us pause. Reporters are sentient beings and thus selective perceivers. Whatever their political leanings or unique personal biases, their *professional* interest is strongly focused on extracting stories from events. They look in order to tell. As historians of the present, they look for the significant—that is, news that may affect their readers' future for good or ill. So any strung-out sequence of connected events with fateful implications is grist for the journalistic mill. The story must persuade the reader—from paragraph one—that the events reported *will* make a difference. Thus journalists are impelled to drama, not as mere decoration, but as a skill essential to the craft of communication. Day after day, journalists must approach their work with the juices of their own curiosity and creativity flowing, composing stories their busy readers will *want* to read.

Fortunately for journalists (and thanks in no small part to their doings) today's campaign saga is a profoundly human story—the struggle of persons for power. The concentration on the candidate as star traces to an institutional sea change in the Presidency itself. Back in Lincoln's day, cabinet members felt free to challenge the President in public. Over the years the President himself rose up so far out of the Washington crowd that today we name administrations by naming the Presidential incumbent. The President has become by far the most visible feature in the political landscape, the focus of the nation's political interest and emotion. The star system spread from the Presidency to the Presidential campaigns—the Eisenhower crusade, the McGovern movement, the Carter campaign. The new Presidency thus puts a person at the center of each campaign story, a person whose tragedies and victories grip the human imagination.

All these trends come together to dramatize the quest for the Presidency. The material is real. The form is dramatic. The drama of politics has been there since the first, and journalists have written it. What demands attention to the way they do that today is, first, the conjunction in our era of an enormous mass electorate who must be addressed through the mass media; second, the root and branch democratization of the process—traceable to mass political disillusionment—which has virtually removed other traditional middlemen from respect and authority; third, the opportunity a much longer campaign offers for dramatic development; and fourth, the emergence of the individual candidate—the potential President—as star of the story. To grasp what is happening in Presidential politics today, one must move past the analysis of the details of issues, regional voting alignments, and systems of party organization, to an understanding of how the Presidential story has been shaped and shared in the experience of American political culture.

The parties, as we inherited them, failed. Their giant ossified structures, like those of the dinosaurs, could no longer adapt to the pace of political change. Journalism *could* adapt. Attuned to change—owing its very existence to its ability to tune in to change—journalism took over where the parties left off. The vitality of a political system originally designed to roll with the punches of history found in journalism a flexible, sensitive organism ready and able to respond to the pulse of politics. . . .

49 / From Whistle Stop to Sound Bite

Sig Mickelson

Over just four decades, television moved from being one of the smallest of bit players in electoral politics to ranking among its most important actors. Sig Mickelson not only describes how this occurred, but also analyzes the role played by television in transforming campaigns into the collections of images, symbols, and sound bites that they are today. Though television could still become the medium for discussion of important issues that was originally envisioned in the 1950s, Mickelson finds little reason to expect that to occur.

The Triumph of Imagery

When New York advertising agency executive Rosser Reeves strode into a private dining room at the 21 Club one night in the summer of 1952, a new era in political campaigning was about to get under way. It was to be an era that would see television rapidly becoming a dominant and frequently controversial influence for winning public support for political candidates. Reeves, a creative specialist at the Ted Bates Agency in New York, an agency noted for hard-sell tactics, arrived with storyboards in hand. He was there to convince members of the Eisenhower for President high command that they should launch a spot commercial campaign on television stations across the country. His aim was to urge the Eisenhower leadership to supplement their traditional campaign methods with a novel approach that had no precedent in presidential elections.

The audience for the Reeves presentation included Walter Williams, the chairman of the Citizens for Eisenhower organization; Sidney Weinberg, an investment banker and treasurer of the campaign organization; two more investment bankers, John Hay Whitney and Ogden White; Walter Thayer, one of Whitney's closest associates; and Robert Mullen, who had been the campaign's public relations adviser. By the time the dinner was over, Reeves had his go-ahead. It was not wholly unexpected. Whitney was the host. He had scheduled the dinner after talking at length with Reeves about the plan. Mullen says that Whitney had "stars in his eyes" as he introduced Reeves and his revolutionary approach to winning the election. His enthusiasm was apparently contagious. Support was unanimous. Once the go-ahead decision was reached, Whitney assumed the responsibility for obtaining the required funding. Reeves himself would write the commercials and oversee production.[1] . . .

While political commercials of 60 seconds or less had no precedent on television, spot radio commercials had been employed 16 years earlier in 1936, to support Alf Landon's campaign for the presidency. Advertising agencies had been involved in politics as early as 1916. The George H. Batten Company of Buffalo, New York, a predecessor of BBDO, had placed print advertising in Charles Evans Hughes's campaign for the presidency. Advertising and politics had thus established a nodding acquaintance prior to 1952 but no firm relationship. With the advent of television that would change abruptly.. . .

Reeves and General Eisenhower collaborated on 50 one-minute commercials that were placed on stations across the country at a cost of $1.5 million—a substantial sum then, a pittance now. The Democrats were either too idealistic at that point to try their hand at commercial spots or were caught asleep at the switch. Late in the campaign they caught on to the impact of the Eisenhower announcements and produced a limited schedule of their own, but it was a matter of too little and too late. Their total bill by Election Day amounted to only $77,000, a little more than 5 percent of the GOP expenditure.. . .

Rosser Reeves and his precedent-breaking spot commercial campaign for General Eisenhower made use of the agency virtually indispensable. Producing spots was complicated enough, but placing them on television stations required the expert services of sophisticated media departments to determine the most effective outlets and to negotiate favorable times and prices. It was imperative to determine where the dollars spent would yield the most votes. As the use of spots skyrocketed in subsequent elections, pressures on media departments rose exponentially. The $1,577,000 spent on commercial spots by both presidential candidates in 1952 was a pittance compared with expenditures in subsequent elections. By 1972 the figure had multiplied by approximately 15 times, to $24.6 million. By 1984 the grand total of approximately $154 million was 100 times as high as in 1952.[2]

Producing and placing television commercials was clearly not the only service advertising agencies performed for candidates. They were still concerned with print advertising, booking paid time for speeches, producing major campaign events for radio and television, and in some cases consulting on campaign strategy, but spots soon absorbed a major part of the effort.

It was obvious to anybody who was observant that there cannot be that rapid an increase in production and exposure without a decline in standards and taste. The straight, low-key, and largely factual Rosser Reeves commercials of 1952 were too good to last. It was inevitable that hard sell would intrude as more agencies and more producers entered the field. With hard sell there would surely be more emphasis on show business and communications pyrotechnics.. . .

By 1960 a new phenomenon was beginning to appear on the campaign scene, the political consultant. Political consultants were old hat in California. The Whitaker and Baxter firm had been operating since the middle 1930s. California's old-time progressivism had led to liberal use of the initiative as a process for passing legislation by popular vote, thus bypassing or overruling the legislature. All-out, high-cost campaigns for or against initiatives became commonplace. Since party organizations were only peripherally involved, if at all, citizen groups and committees were formed to support or oppose the

initiatives. In many instances major corporations had large stakes in the outcome of the voting and were willing to pour vast sums into the campaigns
to protect their interests. Masses of dollars were available to win over voters. . . .

By 1964, producers of political spots for television, both agency personnel and independents, had discovered that the best route to the voter's reflexes
is not through his capability to reason but through his emotions, prejudices,
and lingering responses to previous experiences. By the end of the 1950s, critics
had begun to note that television was brilliantly effective in delivering images and symbols but was frequently striking out when it tried to convey information. The viewer was retaining the picture but quickly forgetting the
facts. The impression remained, but the accompanying information was lost.
Marshall McLuhan was observing that the "medium is the message." The plan-
ners and producers of spot commercials were discovering the importance of
the image and the symbol. They were coming to the conclusion that it was
futile to try to persuade by delivering facts and appeals to reason. They began
to apply new theories to persuasion by television, depending on images rather
than facts to convey messages designed to win voter support. This trend created
a made-to-order opening for consultants.

Before the 1964 campaign got under way, consultants were beginning
to carve out a niche for themselves. Television, they argued, posed problems
that only specialists in media manipulation were adept at solving. Advertising agency staffs could boast of high competence in producing commercials,
but as political campaign advisers they frequently came up short. They were
skilled at selling products but not necessarily effective at manipulating ideas.
Political advertising called for winning over minds to ideas, not creating impulses to buy products. . . .

The political consulting agency, whose main thrust extended as much
to public relations as to regular advertising, could in some part duplicate the
agency's efforts in paid media, but it had also sharpened its skills in creating
situations and events that television stations and networks would find it difficult to overlook. The free media exposure frequently yielded more valuable
results to the candidate than paid commercials. Free media and paid media,
harnessed in tandem, made a powerful team. Imaginatively staged free media
events, masquerading as hard news, were a boon to the news director. He
had a chance to send his crews out to cover ready-made stories that had visual
appeal, human interest, political significance, and controversy, and could be
delivered without taxing his staff's imagination. If it all worked well, the consultant would get his payoff. He would have succeeded in implanting in voters'
minds the image he had designed, and he had done so without paying for
the time. . . .

Television was not ready for so refined an approach in the 1950s, and
the media specialists were not yet ready to deliver it. Prior to 1964, network
news was limited to 15 minutes nightly and shorter segments on the morning
programs, a relatively limited target for an aggressive free media merchant.
Local stations were expanding their news operations rapidly, but the 15-minute
early evening program was still the norm rather than the 90-minute and

even 120-minute programs that became popular in the late 1960s, following the networks' expansion to the 30-minute format. Until the advent of the longer news program, there was hardly enough time available on the air for the consultant to make a viable business out of aiming at the small target.

By the late 1960s, however, television news was an irresistible target. National television receiver penetration was reaching a near saturation level, and during the winter season the combined early evening network news programs were reaching nearly half the television homes in the nation every night. Local stations were expanding their time for news, adding to staff, and reaching rating levels in their local communities frequently exceeding those of the network programs. They were often less sophisticated than their network counterparts, and consequently less likely to be skeptical of suggestions from outsiders and less inclined to apply traditional journalistic standards. They were more apt to cover uncritically an event that the network might consider too soft or too biased for consideration.

It was the perfect setup for the smart consultant. No longer would he have to rely solely on sending press releases to the media and hope that they would get some response. He could begin to control all his candidate's activities so as to eliminate any possibility of error, avoid negative impressions, and get the most favorable media response. In the 1972 campaign Richard Nixon virtually never appeared except in the most rigidly controlled situations. He obtained favorable exposure by participating in events that television news felt must be covered. Cameras and microphones, however, never got close enough to pick up any slip of the tongue or awkward movement. The camera was able to record only the moments that the consultants had planned in advance. And, in view of the importance of the event, there really was no alternative for the news organization than to be present and hope that some morsel of real news might escape the tight controls. The consultant exploited the journalistic principle that what the president did was news, no matter if it was simply riding down a Philadelphia street in an armored car out of sight of television cameras....

Television news is more susceptible to this kind of image making and symbol promotion than it was three decades ago. Gordon Van Sauter, when he was president of the CBS News division during the middle 1980s, encouraged his reporters and producers to look for memorable "moments" to spice up his news broadcasts. Memorable "moments"—many of them can be "sound bites"—are precisely what the image makers try to deliver, and they have acquired considerable skill in creating them. They have probed for and uncovered the soft spots in television news organizations, using the benefit of several years of experience and of methods forged out of trial and error. Television news has generally been a soft target. The dollar stakes have grown so high, the competition so fierce, the hours to fill so expanded, that the station news director and assignment editor are constantly looking for attractive material. The quadrennial national election is so important to the national welfare that no news organization can afford to take it lightly. If the only access to the candidate is through an event the consultant has arranged, the editor has only a limited option to reject it, and virtually none if the event is staged with enough imagination to make it a "must carry" item. . . .

There is not much room, if any, for interpretation or explanation regarding serious issues, or for questioning the candidate on the logic behind his positions. The brief time allotted to the sound bite does not permit it. There is little evidence that news directors, whether on the local or the network level, prefer greater length. They seem dedicated to the notion that the viewer's attention span is short and a great variety of items must be covered. Long, serious expository pieces justifying complex positions don't grab audiences— not unless the item reeks with human interest. This desire for brevity spares the candidate the burden of having to support a generalization with facts and explanation. He can make his point and keep it colorful, simple, and brief. There is no point, current political campaign theory goes, in wasting time and money on factual and argumentative approaches to issues, particularly if the medium lends itself better to a more subtle approach based on imagery and symbolism. . . .

The Frustrated Dream

The most disappointing aspect of the four decades of the politics-television relationship has been the shattering of the optimism of the 1950s, the subversion of the confident predictions that the nation was on the threshold of a new era in which television would help democracy function with unprecedented efficiency. The exhilaration that permeated CBS studio 51 on election night 1952 has turned into frustration. The promise that television would open up the electoral system, encourage candidates to be more candid with voters, increase the turnout at the polls, and create a more responsive democracy has collapsed in an era dominated by packaged campaigns and avoidance of issues.

Television cannot be charged with full responsibility for the erosion of standards used in appealing to voters, but most of the methods and devices used for projecting those appeals are television-related. The sound bite was born in the television newsroom, not in the fertile brain of a candidate handler. The handlers discovered what television wanted and delivered it to support their own ends. The packaging process was designed to conform to television's requirements. The objective was to create appealing programming for television while simultaneously building insurance that the candidate would avoid any gaffs that would damage his standing in the polls. . . .

The results of the uneasy relationship are not very salutary. After four decades in which politics and television have been somewhat uneasy bedfellows, there does not seem to be much clear evidence that elections are any more efficient at selecting the best candidates, that voters are any better informed or more interested, or that candidates are of a higher quality.

The form of political campaigning in the four decades of television has been undergoing astonishing change, and it is equally evident now that the substance has changed along with it. There is more stress on emotional issues that play well on the tube. Long expository statements or detailed arguments in favor of a given position have been largely supplanted by carefully prepared sound bites. Debate is one of those campaign devices that television popularized on a national scale, but the formats have become so restrictive that it is impossible to generate much response from the candidates regarding issues. Presidential candidates are still talking, as they have for decades, about taxes, national defense, foreign affairs, Social Security, farm policies, foreign trade, and the national debt. But in the television era the voter receives less pertinent information, shorter explanations, more labels, and very little interpretation or reasoning on which to base sound judgments. Most of the candidates' responses to issues are delivered in the form of commercial spots and sound bites. Even though the issues are the same, the output from the candidates is not very nourishing, surely less so than before television helped trivialize the process.

The effect on the viewer-voter of this symbiotic relationship does nothing to enhance the voter's capability to choose wisely at the ballot box. The campaign managers and consultants are knowledgeable enough about television to realize that to win voters, they must be concerned with effect rather than meaning, with emotional response rather than factual presentation, with easily digested morsels rather than big bites of heavy dough. The voter is happy because there is no strain on his thinking processes. The candidates have allowed themselves to be mechanized to the extent that they participate easily in the razzle-dazzle of product advertising and enjoy the glamour of being lionized in the news, but not much effort is being devoted to informing the voters on significant issues. . . .

It is ironic that the most popular communications device of the century, one that is found in more than 98 percent of American homes and commands more family time than any activity other than sleeping, should not have brought a new era to American politics. In its early days it tried hard enough. In fact, it is still trying. The time, money, and effort devoted to coverage of primary elections and political conventions over and above the intensive coverage of the final two to three months prior to the national election attest to the fact that both networks and stations are trying, but trying apparently is not enough. Too much of the effort is concentrated on entertaining, self-promotion, and striving for ratings. This effort consumes so much attention that not much is left for developing more effective methods for informing the electorate.

The results do not encourage much optimism for the future. The public simply appears less interested than it was in the past. In 1960, 62.8 percent of eligible American voters went to the polls on Election Day, the highest percentage in recent history. By 1976 the percentage had dropped to 53.5, and by 1984 to 53.3. Only 1932 and 1948 registered lower percentages: 52.4 and 51.1 respectively.[3] Nearly everyone who had access to a television receiver watched some part of the national conventions in 1952. In the 1980s, baseball games, game shows, and movies were frequently rating better than the conventions.

There must be a reason, and it cannot be simply a matter of having seen it all before. The novelty has obviously worn off. That can account for some of the decline. It is more likely that the reduced voter interest has been influenced by a variety of factors.

The growing complexity of issues that must be decided by government may drive some potential voters off. Deciding whether to support or oppose the Strategic Defense Initiative or "Star Wars," for example, can be a frustrating experience. It is easier to forget it and let someone else decide. Television might be able to help if it had any competence to explain complex issues in the brief time allotted in news broadcasts, but news executives are, of necessity, dedicated to delivering high ratings. Brief, memorable "moments" are more likely to win the audience than scholarly scientific explanations. Too much time spent trying to explain implications of foreign trade imbalances or proposed tax legislation results only in frustrated viewers.

The entertaining and emotionally charged vignettes that television provides are calculated to entertain and amuse, and even to win sympathy, but they are not likely to arouse voters' passions to the point that they will determinedly march to the polls. Television is more likely to be looked at as a game, a spectator sport, not one for participants. It is conceivably possible for a viewer to get as excited about a serious issue as he does about a Super Bowl or a World Series, but that is a pretty remote possibility; and even if he does, he has little reason to believe that there is a realistic opportunity for him to do anything about it. Election campaign coverage, for the most part, consists of a fleeting series of images that float by on the screen entertainingly but hardly passionately, at least not passionately enough to encourage a sufficient number of voters to go to the polls to make their views known. The images are there to entertain and to create a favorable climate of opinion, but only the most effective are likely to arouse. They lack the inspiration to get the voter to the ballot box. Even the spot commercials are produced to convey strong entertainment values. They are more useful in energizing the committed than in persuading the undecided.

It was once the political parties that assumed the responsibility for seeing to it that voters went to the polls. In the age of television, there is valid doubt whether the party retains much real power. Television may have replaced it. The old ward boss maintained constant personal contact with his constituents. He was their link with government, their advisor on issues. Before the era when entertainment could be brought into the home with a flip of the switch, the ward and county organizations provided diversion at low cost and simultaneously stimulated enthusiasm for both issues and candidates. Now the voter can sit at home, enjoy his game shows and sports events, and get his political information in sugarcoated capsules on the television screen. He no longer needs the political party.

The voter also may be bored by the seemingly endless duration of the campaign. State governments, seeking publicity and increased influence in the selection of national candidates, started their primaries and caucuses earlier and earlier, until Michigan retreated to the year prior to the national election to begin its candidate selection process. Television news follows the entire process. Interest appears to run high during the preliminary jousting in Iowa and New Hampshire but fades as more states come on stream. The national conventions once revived interest in midsummer, but when they became cut and dried, there was no stimulant remaining to resuscitate flagging enthusiasm. Strategically placed rallies or major speeches once pumped new life into a sagging campaign, but even they have faded away. All that remains is a constant bombardment of sound bites and spot commercials flowing in a monotonous pattern with little evidence of peaks and valleys. Efforts are made to energize campaigns at the local level through visits by candidates. Even though they are covered by both national and local television, there is little except for the carefully produced and staged sound bites to attract national attention. Polls extract all the suspense, and the potential voter is left with a formless gray mass—hardly an inducement to act.

The media, led by television, have contributed to ennui by removing emphasis from issues and putting it squarely on the horse race. Starting with the first caucuses, the first questions are Who is ahead? and What influence will this victory have on the next primary or caucus? Politics, as a result, becomes a game. The game is relatively simple for television to cover. All it takes is the ability to count and to speculate who will win the next round. Discussion of the issues becomes lost in calculating odds regarding possible winners. Interpretation and analysis have turned from consideration of the dominant issues to guessing which candidate has derived the most favorable public response from his approach to a specific matter of contention. It is probably unfair to pin sole responsibility on television, but certainly it must bear a large share of the blame. Its appetite for action and brevity, supported by reproduction and transmission equipment that can get an item on the air in minutes and its orientation to show business, have made it peculiarly vulnerable. . . .

John F. Kennedy was the first genuine television candidate. His campaign was skillfully directed and carefully planned, but not tightly controlled. He and his advisers had confidence in their own political skills and in Kennedy's ability to communicate on television. It is hard to conceive of Lyndon Johnson sitting still for a lecture on campaign techniques from an outside consultant. The first genuine image campaign planned for optimum television exposure was Richard Nixon's presidential campaign in 1968. That effort set the pattern for subsequent runs for the presidency and introduced the tactic of keeping the candidate under wraps except on those occasions when the environment can be rigidly controlled and any slip of the tongue prevented.

There were a number of prospective benefits expected to derive from television. One of the early optimistic predictions held that television would make it possible for the unknown candidate to achieve name recognition in weeks, if not days. It once seemed a realistic possibility. Adlai Stevenson was a virtual unknown when he was nominated by the Democrats in 1952. Television quickly gave him national status as a viable candidate. Unless there is a drastic change in the nominating process, though, it probably will never happen again. Campaigns have become so long and the primary so critical to nomination that the latecomer would face overwhelming negative odds if he tried to inject himself into the race at the last minute. It is virtually impossible that a sudden ground swell for an outsider could detach delegates from their long-standing commitments stemming from victory in the primaries. It is ironic that it is largely television's influence in focusing attention on the primaries that has made nomination of a dark horse virtually unthinkable. There has not been a dark horse candidate since Stevenson who stood a chance of nomination. Television gave the dark horse the opportunity and then stole it from him.

The current primary system, in large part a legacy of television, has forced candidates to plunge all the way into the race without any easy warm-up or stretching exercises. Once they are in the game, they are all the way in. There is no preseason schedule, no Grapefruit League. It is the race for the pennant from the opening announcement. The only escape is to drop out.

The power of the networks to dictate political fashions or to influence them declined rapidly during the 1980s. During the network heyday, from the early 1950s through most of the 1970s, network shares of sets in use during prime time consistently ran in the 90 percent-plus range. By the end of the 1980s they had fallen to the mid-60s, gradually eroded by the rising strength of independent, nonaffiliated stations, by cable, and by the swiftly increasing popularity of video cassettes.

Broadcast news departments in local stations, both affiliates and independents, were flexing the muscles provided by their new electronic equipment: all-electronic cameras and editing gear, short-range microwave relays, and longer-range transmission by satellites. They were discovering that they were no longer dependent on the networks for all but strictly local coverage. Satellite mobile units, owned by individual stations, were being banded together in cooperatives to furnish national and even international coverage competitive with or supplementary to that of the networks. No longer do cooperative pools organized for coverage of major events consist of just three television networks. Now there is a fourth, the Cable News Network. And a fifth, the Public Broadcasting Service, delivers a service more attuned to a smaller audience with a deeper interest in public affairs.

Does the decline of the networks foreshadow more revolutionary changes in political campaign methodology? The answer is "probably not." It was not the networks that brought about the revolution in campaign techniques. It was the introduction of a live medium combining picture, sound, and motion, delivered free of charge and at the speed of light, that initiated the change. Political news and coverage of major political events were distributed by the networks, liberally supported by big budgets, packaged in an environment dominated by attractive entertainment programs, and backed up by massive promotion. All the ingredients required for a quick incursion into covering political campaigns were present. The networks have now crested, but independent stations, cable television, and video cassettes are already taking up the slack. Their capabilities for reaching the viewer are almost identical. Only the technology they use is different. They will continue to program for a visually oriented audience, and candidates and consultants will continue to exploit the opportunities they offer.

We probably cannot hope for a radical transformation of media coverage of political campaigns. An intellectual campaign geared to explanation of governmental policy regarding budgets, taxes, national defense, foreign affairs, and the environment is probably too much to ask from commercial broadcasting. In 1960, during only the third national campaign covered by television, the Survey Research Center at the University of Michigan completed an intensive study of voter attitudes. The results are discouraging reading for anyone hoping that campaign rhetoric will ascend to new heights and that the visual media will be able to contribute to a more sophisticated electorate.

"For a large part of the public," the study found, "political affairs are probably too difficult to comprehend in detail." Even more discouraging is the conclusion that "Very few people seem motivated strongly enough to obtain the information needed to develop a sensitive understanding of decision making in government."[4]

. . . [I]t is possible to conclude from the findings of the Survey Research Center that voters are easy targets for the blandishments of the image merchants. By playing to their natural tendency to avoid the complicated and the difficult to comprehend, television and consultants together may be depreciating the level of understanding and interest, and debasing the electoral process. A new dedication to emphasis on issues, using the unique power of the picture tube, might at least bring campaigns back to the level of the 1950s and early 1960s.

It all seemed so easy on election night 1952. At long last the nation had access to a medium that would lead to a nation more interested in politics and more sophisticated regarding electoral issues. The four decades since then have done little to give substance to that dream. We can hope that there still may be the time and the will to turn television and the newer visual media to the dream's fulfillment.

Notes

1. Mullen described the scene to me in a conversation in January 1970. A tape recording of the interview is available in the files of the Wisconsin Historical Library in Madison. Martin Mayer, in *Madison Avenue, U.S.A.* (New York: Harper and Brothers, 1958), pp. 294–96, points out that there was one other significant player in the effort to place commercials on television. Alfred Hollender, a broadcasting station manager and later an advertising agency executive who had met General Eisenhower when he was serving in the radio propaganda effort during the war, had volunteered to work on the campaign. Subsequently, according to Mayer, he had convinced the general and his brother Milton of the value of televised commercials. This had occurred prior to the dinner at 21.
2. Figures supplied by Television Bureau of Advertising in New York and printed in *Broadcasting Magazine*, January 18, 1988, p. 76.
3. *The World Almanac and Book of Facts* (New York: Pharos Books, 1987), p. 305.
4. Angus Campbell, Philip E. Converse, Warren E. Miller, and Donald E. Stoker, *The American Voter* (New York: John Wiley, 1961), p. 543.

50 / Diplomacy in a Television Age: The Dangers of Teledemocracy

David R. Gergen

David Gergen evaluates the growing roles of television and public opinion in the making of foreign policy, and argues that there are dangers in teledemocracy that have too often been overlooked.

Since the early 1970s, it has been axiomatic that television constitutes an independent force in international affairs. President Richard Nixon carefully choreographed his visit to China for primetime viewing back home. President Jimmy Carter's administration engaged in "verbal ping-pong" with Tehran as the two sent messages back and forth through the channels of television; and President Reagan converted "photo ops" into a science in his foreign trips. And even President Bush, though lower-keyed, chose Malta as the site for his first Soviet summit, searching for the perfect visual effect.

The Television Revolution

Recognizing the camera's power, foreign leaders, diplomats and terrorists have all followed suit, tailoring their messages to television audiences in America and elsewhere. Egypt's Anwar Sadat was one of the first foreign leaders to hire American communication experts; the Sandinistas are only among the most recent. And who will soon forget the Chinese students in Tiananmen Square carrying aloft their Goddess of Liberty or the young men and women dancing atop the Berlin Wall, sending a euphoric message to television viewers across the world?

The stunning events of 1989 and 1990 have made the world understand how positive a force television can be in human affairs. Time and again, evidence has surfaced that televised pictures from the West were a catalyst for people in communist countries of the East to press for change and that, in turn, repressed people used the medium to build public support in the West. Were it not for modern communication technologies—from television to the fax machine—modern revolutions might never have occurred. The past two years have been the most triumphant in television's short history.

Yet there is reason to ask whether in the land that invented the cathode ray tube, the United States, public officials have learned that there are also limits to television and the role that it should play in a democracy. Too often in recent years, U.S. officials have substituted the power of television for the power of their own reasoning, believing that successful policies must first and foremost please the Great God of Public Opinion. This emphasis on teledemocracy marks a serious departure in American diplomacy. For most of U.S. history, diplomats have been guided by their own judgments and only later have worried about public reaction. Indeed, in the first twenty years after World War II, American diplomacy was conducted with the rather certain expectation that public opinion would support it. Daniel Yankelovich has found that whenever a President like Eisenhower spoke to the nation on television, half his audience would automatically grant him the benefit of the doubt on any foreign issue simply because of who he was and what his office represented. Congress also was a ready partner.

It is well understood that Vietnam shattered the postwar foreign policy consensus, leading Congress to become more obtrusive and causing the executive branch to become much more concerned with public support. It is less appreciated that changes were also taking place in television technology which brought the world more fully into American living rooms. During the 1970s, for example, television introduced the portable videotape camera (or minicam), which allowed editing shortcuts. Soon after, satellites were sent aloft and earth stations were built in most nations. By the end of the decade, American television was prepared to broadcast instantaneously from almost everywhere in the world. The "global village" was upon us.

Increasingly during the 1980s, government officials have shaped their policies with an eye toward generating positive and timely television coverage and securing public approval. What too often counts is how well the policy will "play," how the pictures will look, whether the right signals are being sent, and whether the public will be impressed by the swiftness of the government's response—not whether the policy promotes America's long-term interests.

Given the number of hours that Americans spend in front of their television sets and the degree to which they depend on it for information, such preoccupation with the power of the camera is understandable. The camera is an extraordinarily powerful instrument. No other technology in history has so influenced a culture. Nonetheless, there is no need for leading officials to be mesmerized or intimidated by television and public opinion.

Realities of Television
Before the world turned upside down in 1989, the charge most often hurled against the networks was that they regularly neglected international affairs in favor of domestic news, soft features and personalities. In fact, as Michael Mosettig, a former NBC producer now a writer for Public Television's "MacNeill-Lehrer Newshour," pointed out in the late 1980s, "The foreign news content of the evening programs has doubled and trebled since 1976.... Ten years ago U.S. network coverage consisted largely of canned film features; now it runs like a wire service, with morning and evening cycles of updated news and pictures." A study by James F. Larson of evening news broadcasts over the period of a decade (1972–81) found that on average the networks devoted ten of their twenty-two minutes—40 percent—to coverage of foreign affairs....

Moreover, the Larson study does not take account of the foreign affairs coverage by the networks, PBS, and CNN during non-evening hours.

"Nightline," for example, was born during the Tehran hostage crisis and continues to emphasize international issues such as apartheid. The morning news shows not only carry reports from overseas, but sometimes move their entire operations to countries such as China and South Korea. CNN has not only built a far-flung system of correspondents, but is broadcasting by satellite to elite audiences in many other countries. The problem, therefore, is not indifference to foreign news.

In fact, the problem with television inheres in the medium itself. By its very nature, television is an instrument of simplicity in a world of complexity. In a report of 80 seconds—150 words at most—a television reporter cannot provide context or background. No matter how many stories it devotes to international affairs, a thirty-minute news broadcast must essentially be a headline service. It cannot be educational, nor does it even attempt to be. A former network president and veteran of the industry was dismissive when I once asked him whether his network had a duty to enlighten. "We have a duty to tell people the news—period," was his response. As many old-timers in television admit, they see their task as asking each day two essential questions about the news: Is the world still safe today? Is my family still safe today? If everything is alright, they feel perfectly justified providing entertainment.

Another limitation is that television cannot and does not provide continuity in its coverage of international affairs. As a medium that depends on drama, it is drawn to conflict and crisis. It shuns the quiet periods in which most people live. For instance, in 1982, when El Salvador held a critical election, television crews descended on the country, turning it into a center of world attention. American senators and congressmen inundated the region. Within forty-eight hours of the election, however, the cameras had left to cover the Falklands War. It was as if the lights went out over El Salvador, and the country's subsequent struggle to preserve democracy disappeared from sight. Out of sight, it also passed out of mind for American viewers. Television loves sagas in which someone wins and someone loses. It abhors long, tedious, complex stories and will usually ignore them if possible.

It is also obvious that television has terrible blind spots. In his study, James Larson found that the major networks rarely cover Latin America, sub-Saharan Africa, South Asia or Australia. Canada was also lucky if it made the news. Instead, stories were heavily centered on Europe, the Soviet Union and the Middle East. The most egregious mistake made by television in the past concerned Cambodia. A study by William Adams found that during the height of the worst massacre in modern times, the networks' evening news coverage of Cambodia averaged only ten minutes a year. The carnage was virtually ignored until it was far too late to arouse world attention. Television was also slow to recognize the extent of famine in Africa. American television was eager to dramatize ethnic conflicts in Azerbaijan and Armenia, two hotspots in the Soviet Union; should similar trouble develop in Yugoslavia, it is doubtful they will attract one tenth the coverage.

To be fair, networks are often handicapped by government restrictions on movement and coverage. For example, the Soviet invasion of Afghanistan would have caused much more of a sensation if Western television had had early access to the fighting. Many African nations are reluctant to grant visas to journalists, and the Soviet Union until recently has been highly restrictive. Restrictions on television coverage have also spread to industrialized nations such as south Africa, Israel, and Britain. The pattern is alarming because it appears to work to the short-term political advantage of the censoring nation. Should it take hold, television's "window on the world" will be even cloudier than it already is.

Room for Improvement

There was a time when observers thought that the development of new technologies would make television more thorough and complete in its coverage of the world, but the most recent breakthroughs—mini-cams and satellites—have actually been a setback to the quality of coverage. Because it is now possible to fly a crew to the scene of a crisis and instantaneously send back information, television is even more addicted to "parachute journalism" than before. "Technology has ruined the life of the foreign correspondent," NBC's Richard Valeriani has said, underscoring the point that correspondents now seem to spend more time jetsetting than concentrating on a small handful of countries. Moreover, reporting in one time zone while feeding stories to New York on another can make for grueling eighteen-hour days, hardly a lifestyle conducive to reflective reporting as Valeriani and others have admitted.

The cost of maintaining a foreign news operation has skyrocketed as the dollar has declined in value overseas. Some news organizations have found that maintaining a correspondent in Tokyo requires more than $200,000 in supplemental expenditures to meet that city's high costs of living. Cutbacks in foreign staffs have already occurred in several organizations. Between 1985 and 1989, for instance, *Time* magazine's masthead showed a cut from thirty-six to twenty-six in the number of overseas correspondents. The number of journalists sent scrambling overseas increased sharply in 1989–90, but whether that same commitment to international coverage will remain after the world calms down is highly uncertain.

Television clearly serves many excellent purposes. Yet it is a mistake to expect too much of the medium. In particular, policy makers cannot assume that television alone will ever create a public informed and enlightened about international affairs. Television can awaken people's interests, but it does not yet have the capacity to educate them.

Realities of Public Opinion

Just as it is important for policy makers to accept television's limitations, it is equally important to understand and accept at least three hard truths about public opinion:

First, even though their exposure to foreign affairs has increased, Americans in general have an abysmal understanding of the world. A number of surveys over the years have shown a startling lack of knowledge among the mass public. In 1981, for example, a *Washington Post*-ABC national survey asked the question, "One of these two nations, the United States or the Soviet Union, is a member of what is known as the NATO alliance. Do you happen to know which country that is, or are you not sure?" Through random guessing—say, by flipping a coin—50 percent should have given the correct response. Only 47 percent actually answered the question correctly. In the same survey, the public was asked which two countries were involved in the SALT talks: only 37 percent knew the answer. Another poll during that period asked for the location of El Salvador; 25 percent knew the answer. Barry Sussman of the *Post* concluded: "Whether they realize it or not, people are intentionally turning away from public affairs. It is not a lack of brains that is involved here. The little poll quizzes do not measure intelligence; they measure the storage of bits of information. A person need not be bright to avoid telling an interviewer, as one did, that El Salvador 'is in Louisiana, near Baton Rouge.'"

Second, Americans show little appetite for increasing their understanding of the world. At the elite or opinion-maker level, there is a keen interest in gobbling up new information about the world, most recently about Japan. *The Economist*, for example, has experienced its most rapid sales growth in the United States and circulation here now outpaces that in the United Kingdom. But consider a recent experience of the three major American news magazines, *Time, Newsweek,* and *U.S. News & World* Report. These three magazines all featured on their cover the 1985 summit meeting in Geneva between President Reagan and General Secretary Gorbachev, a splashy event that attracted saturation coverage by television. Ordinarily, magazines featuring events that have received widespread television attention score well on the newsstands. Yet, for all three magazines, the Geneva cover was that year's worst-selling cover. Other covers on foreign affairs, unless they concern crises or Americans in trouble, share a similar fate. It is hardly surprising, therefore, that only a modest number of magazine covers are devoted to foreign affairs. Recent events in Eastern Europe provided further evidence that the public is not easily drawn into major international events: ratings for national news programs actually went down during the period when communism was collapsing. Polls suggested that the public felt too confused to watch closely.

Third, there is no reason to believe that public opinion will grow more informed. In early 1989, National Geographic published the results of a disappointing survey by the Gallup organization, showing that Americans know less basic geography than the citizens of Sweden, West Germany, Japan, France and Canada, and considerably less than they knew forty years ago. More distressing, eighteen- to twenty-four-year-old Americans knew less than their counterparts in any nine countries; America was, in fact, the only country where young adults knew less about geography than did adults aged fifty-five and over. There is, as Gilbert M. Grosvenor, president of the National Geographic Society, has reported, a shocking lack of geographic knowledge throughout this country. And several surveys have demonstrated that familiarity with foreign languages is also low.

These findings do not support the view that Americans are dumber than other people. It has been aptly said that while one should not overestimate the amount of information Americans have, one also should not underestimate their intelligence. On many occasions, Americans have demonstrated sound common sense. Recent polls, for example, show that while approval ratings for Gorbachev have shot upward in the United States, the public still urges caution in trusting the Soviets and in extending financial help. Clearly, the American public has not forgotten the lessons behind the failures of détente. Moreover, despite the fears expressed by some about conflict escalation, Americans supported recent government efforts in the Persian Gulf, correctly sensing that they were in the national interest.

Americans have also demonstrated that, if a strong case can be made, they are open to persuasion. The Carter administration, for example, was able to turn public opinion around on the Panama Canal treaty. The larger point, however, is that Americans do not pay close attention to foreign affairs, even if they are frequently exposed to them. As Walter Lippmann noted in the early 1920s, most citizens spend their time thinking about their jobs, their families, their neighbors and communities. They cannot and should not be expected to keep up with every twist and turn in a fast-changing world. That is the job of their elected representatives.

Lessons for Foreign and National Security Policy Making

From these realities one can draw certain obvious lessons about the formulation of foreign policy. Most important, policy decisions ought to be made with an eye first and foremost toward what is sound and in the national interest, not toward what is temporarily popular in the opinion polls or toward what will gain a quick, favorable notice on television. A government cannot make sound decisions about, for example, the use of military force based on a referendum or some theory of participatory democracy. The public simply does not know enough about the world to be able to render sound judgments on issues such as the Strategic Defense Initiative, the START negotiations, or the ABM treaty. Rather, it is entitled to expect its elected and appointed officials to act on these issues and then to have the chance to throw them out of office if they fail. Were foreign policy to be dictated solely by public opinion, several sound decisions would never have been taken. It is highly likely that the United States would long ago have canceled its foreign aid program, for instance, and it is very unlikely that we would have instituted a peacetime draft before World War II.

By the same token, it is a serious mistake for executive branch officials to make policy hastily in order to meet news broadcast deadlines. Policy makers should respect the power of television and learn how to utilize it in conducting policy. They should not be cowed by it. In retrospect, several key members of the Carter administration thought they were wrong to respond within hours to the Soviet invasion of Afghanistan, a decision based in part on a perceived need to make the evening news. A better U.S. policy would have resulted from larger deliberations inside the U.S. government. Similarly, some members of the Reagan administration believed it was a mistake to rush out with a full-scale condemnation of the Soviet shootdown of Korean Airlines flight 007. Some of the information that the administration had in hand at the time later turned out to be wrong. In retrospect, it would have been more effective to build an air-tight presentation over a period of days so that the credibility of the strong case against the Soviets could not be undermined. Officials sometimes argue that the American public demands fast answers from its government, especially in a television age. There is no evidence to support this view. On the contrary, the public seems to care more about results and consequences than about one-night headlines.

To sustain a policy, the executive branch must also have a clear rationale for what it is doing *before* it acts. It is not necessary to have public approval in advance, but if public support is needed after the fact, the government must have a persuasive case that will stand up over time. The Reagan administration blundered, for example, in failing to develop a clear rationale for sending marines to Lebanon. When there was no obvious mission that could be explained to the country, support for the exercise crumbled, and the marines eventually had to be withdrawn. Similarly, it is now clear that the administration's efforts to bolster the Contras were badly handicapped by the lack of a clear rationale for the policy. In this case, the public became confused because the administration kept shifting its argument. . . .

PART THREE

Governmental Institutions

CHAPTER FOURTEEN

Congress

Article One of the United States Constitution clearly establishes that Congress is to have primary responsibility for making laws, and that law-making is to be the primary function of the Congress. But it is also implicit in the structure and powers of Congress that it is to be more than *just* a legislative body. It is also to be concerned with representation, and to oversee the executive, among other "secondary" roles.

In virtually all of its roles, demands upon Congress have grown tremendously over time.* In recent decades alone, Congress and its members have faced increasing demands for new programs to solve the nation's complex problems, for day-to-day servicing of individual constituents' needs, for overseeing the president and his massive bureaucracy, and at the same time, for "opening up" the legislative process. In response, Congress has experienced what some have called a "revolution" of structural and organizational changes, which have coincided with important behavioral changes.

The selections in this chapter highlight some of the most important changes and explore some of their causes and consequences. Roger H. Davidson and Walter J. Oleszek document and explain the growing roles of Congress in constituency service and oversight, and consider whether the law-making function has suffered as a consequence. Former House Speaker Thomas P. "Tip" O'Neill, Jr., reviews a host of changes in Congress and its environment over its first two hundred years, and concludes with a challenge to restore the legislative branch to a place of equality with the president. Burdett Loomis examines the impact on the House of its unusually large "Class of '74" with their greater sense of independence and entrepreneurial style, and suggests that the 1974 election marked a "break point" in congressional politics. And finally, Lawrence Dodd and Bruce Oppenheimer argue that the period of decentralizing the power of the House committees in the 1970s has been followed by another period of change in which party leaders have become stronger and a new "committee oligarchy" has developed.

---

*Actually, data show that the legislative "workload" is down compared to several decades ago, but this does not account for the complexity of the legislation or the nature of the problems the legislators are asked to address. See Ornstein, Norman J., et al, *Vital Statistics on Congress,* 1984–1985 edition (Washington: American Enterprise Institute, 1984, p. 138), and William Keefe and Morris S. Ogul, *The American Legislative Process,* 6th edition (Englewood Cliffs, N.J.: Prentice-Hall, 1985, pp. 14, 22, and 139).—*Editor's Note.*

51 / Challenge and Change in the Two Congresses

Roger H. Davidson
Walter J. Oleszek

As government has come to be involved in citizens' lives in more ways, on a more frequent basis, there has been a tremendous increase in requests for members of Congress and their staffs to become constituents' personal problem-solvers in the nation's capital. Likewise, as the number of governmental programs has grown dramatically, especially since the 1930s, so has the workload of Congress in its role as "overseer" of the executive branch's administration of those programs. In considering the impact of these and other changes in the roles of "Congress as Politicians" and "Congress as Institution," Roger Davidson and Walter Oleszek suggest that Congress may no longer have sufficient time for careful deliberation in the legislative process, and they wonder whether "organizational tinkering" will be enough to make the framers' Congress relevant, effective, and efficient in coping with today's demands.

Congress has a persistent image problem. The other branches of government have nothing quite like the comic image of Senator Snort, the florid and incompetent windbag. Pundits and humorists—from Mr. Dooley to Johnny Carson, from Thomas Nast to Pat Oliphant—find Congress an inexhaustible source of raw material. The public seems to share this disdain toward Congress. Fewer than one-third of the respondents in a recent survey approved of the way Congress was handling its job.[1]

Serious commentators' views of Congress are often scarcely more flattering than the public's. In scholarly and journalistic writing there appears a stereotype of the "textbook Congress": an irresponsible and slightly sleazy body of people approximating Woodrow Wilson's caustic description of the House as "a disintegrated mass of jarring elements."[2] Legislators in their home states or districts often contribute to this shabby image by portraying themselves as gallant warriors against the dragons back on Capitol Hill: as Richard F. Fenno, Jr., puts it, they "run *for* Congress by running *against* Congress."[3]

Notwithstanding its reputation for inertia, Congress was dramatically reshaped in the era just past. Changes wrought in this period of political upheaval, roughly from 1965 through 1977, reached into virtually every nook and cranny of Capitol Hill—its members, careers, structures, procedures, folkways, and staffs. If those legendary leaders of the 1950s, Sam Rayburn and Lyndon Johnson, were to return to the chambers they served with such distinction, they would doubtless be astounded at the transformations that have occurred—even though both men had a hand in bringing them about.

In the 1980s Congress appears to have slipped into a period of relative quiescence, as if to absorb the broadscale changes that took place. Yet Congress—both the institution and its members—continues to be buffeted by external and internal pressures. And while recent responses have taken the form of marginal adjustments rather than fundamental changes, dissatisfaction with Congress persists almost as strongly as before the era of change. Perhaps the changes themselves, addressed to the prior generation's complaints, brought in their wake a whole new generation of problems. Perhaps, too, the level of frustration will have to build until the right set of political circumstances brings on another era of upheaval. As one old country politician put it, "Things is bad enough as they is, we can't afford no reforms now."[4] In short, things may have to get worse before they will get better.

What is the current state and what is the likely future development of Congress? [In addressing these questions, we will employ] our notion of the two Congresses: Congress-as-Politicians and Congress-as-Institution. Although analytically distinct, these two Congresses are inextricably bound together. What affects one sooner or later affects the workings of the other. What forces have affected the functioning of the two Congresses? What changes have occurred in them? What are the current problems of each, and what innovations are likely to be invoked in coming years to alleviate these problems?

Congress-as-Politicians

The first thing to be noticed about the men and women who serve in Congress is that most of them arrived on the scene during the period of upheaval we have noted. During that decade or so, a tide of new members came to Capitol Hill, following 20 years of uncommonly low turnover.

In the House, the turnover did not flow primarily from electoral competition. In the five congressional elections concluding with 1980, 213 representatives retired while only 150 were defeated in primaries or general elections. Of those members seeking reelection, 91 percent were successful. On the other side of Capitol Hill, defeat at the polls was more of a factor. Voters in the late 1970s seemed to fix their discontent on incumbent senators, and in 1976, 1978, and 1980, nearly half the incumbents went down to defeat.

Whatever the causes, the result was what journalist David S. Broder called "changing the guard."[5] The World War II generation showed impressive staying power. This was the generation of John F. Kennedy and Richard M. Nixon, of Tip O'Neill and Robert Michel, of Robert C. Byrd and Robert Dole. It is giving way to the "baby-boom" generation, nurtured on post–World War II prosperity and chastened by Vietnam, Watergate, and the loss of American hegemony in the world. As the 99th Congress convened in 1985, only 9 senators and 35 representatives antedated the reform era.

The average lawmaker today is better prepared and more sophisticated than the crop of a generation or more ago. True, some Congress-watchers yearn for a return of bygone days of strong leaders and committee "barons" of the stature of Sam Rayburn, Lyndon Johnson, Everett Dirksen, and Wilbur

Mills. But time has a way of expanding and distorting their deeds, and it is all too easy to forget the hordes of others who served in Congress, and whose talents were far below today's average. There is as yet no shortage of able men and women, it seems, who wish to serve in Congress.

Contemporary members, however, arise from a recruitment and career system that has been restructured in important ways. The decline of local party organizations, the complexity of constituencies, the advent of new campaign technologies, the restructuring of candidate financing—such factors shape members' priorities and activities. "The real difference between members today is whether they feel at home with the electronic media or not," remarked Rep. Thomas Downey, D-N.Y., elected in 1974 as a 25-year-old. "That's a sad comment, but that's the truth."[6] On Capitol Hill they are confronted with more demanding workloads, more committee assignments and other commitments, and a more complex institutional structure. In short, the daily lives of our legislators are quite different from their predecessors'.

Of all the factors affecting today's politicians, the most conspicuous is the ebbing of political party organizations and loyalties. In only a few areas do party organizations still serve as sponsors and anchors for political careers. Nor do voters depend as heavily as they once did on party labels to guide their choices. Hence, politicians are thrust into the role of individual entrepreneurs, relying on their own resources to build and nurture supportive constituencies. The stress on individualism could wane if the national parties encourage greater discipline in Congress, building on their capacity to funnel financial, technical, and campaign assistance to their partisans.

Rising constituency demands inundate individual legislators and their staffs. The average state now numbers about 4 million people, the average House district more than half a million. Educational levels have risen; communications and transportation are easier. Public opinion surveys show unmistakably that voters expect legislators to "bring home the bacon" in terms of federal policies and services, and to communicate frequently with the folks back home.[7] Nor are such demands likely to diminish in the future.

Elected officials have countered these claims by building personal machinery for communicating with constituents and cultivating reelection support. True, U. S. legislators have always been expected to run errands for constituents. In an era of limited government, however, there were fewer errands to run. In the past generation, the constituency service role has been quantitatively and qualitatively transformed. Responding to perceived demands, senators and representatives have set up veritable assembly lines for communicating with voters, responding to constituents' inquiries, and even generating requests through newsletters, targeted mailings, and hot lines. Staff and office allowances have grown, district offices have sprouted over the landscape, and recesses are called "district work periods." This apparatus extends legislators' ability to communicate with constituents, and it provides badly needed help for citizens for whom coping with the federal bureaucracy can be a bewildering and frightening experience.

Nor is constituency service the only aspect of officeholders' survival strategy. Coping with organized interests occupies much of a legislator's own time. This includes responding to organized lobbying and mailing campaigns, meeting with group delegations, speaking at meetings, and jockeying for financial support. If today's members are independent of traditional party ties, they are enmeshed in complex supporting networks of their own.

The new demands of congressional careers have fostered conflicts for individual politicians between their legislative and political roles. Indeed, expectations in both areas have risen. Findings from a 1976–1977 member survey in the House convey the distinct impression that members experience severe strains between these two roles. On the whole, members *want* to spend more time on legislation than they actually do. Typically, they rate legislative tasks as more important than constituency service. But legislators cannot escape constituency demands, even if they wanted to do so. When asked to compare the ideal and actual role of a member of Congress, fully half of the representatives interviewed in 1977 stated that "constituent demands detract from other functions"—the most frequently mentioned obstacle.[8]

Nor are public demands likely to abate. We are fast approaching the day when 90 percent of all adults will have received a secondary education and perhaps 50 percent a postsecondary education. Thus, political activity is likely to remain at a high level or even rise—not the old-style activity of the political party cadres, but dispersive involvement in myriads of special-purpose groups and causes. These activists will expect their elected representatives to be responsive. In a recent national survey, citizens expressed the most dissatisfaction with legislators' efforts at public education and communication. Nine respondents out of every 10 said that Congress should do more to inform the public about its activities.[9]

No less obvious is the impact of career-building activities on the institutional life of Congress. It is at least arguable that ever more demanding electoral and ombudsman functions have helped erode the legislative and institutional folkways identified by observers in the 1950s and early 1960s—especially the folkways of specialization, apprenticeship, and institutional loyalty. At the very least, it has placed added demands on members' time and energies. Although most ombudsman activities are actually carried out by staff aides rather than by members themselves, there are inescapable costs to members' schedules. Larger staffs, while helping lawmakers extend their reach of involvement, require supervision and have a way of generating needs of their own. And with high constituent expectations, there are inescapably many symbolic functions that cannot be delegated to staffs—situations that require members' personal intervention and face-to-face presence.

Today's political entrepreneurs have shaped Capitol Hill institutions in their own image. Not only the overlaying of staff resources, but the proliferation of work groups and veto points, marks today's Congress. If members are better equipped as individuals to reach decisions and exert influence, it is harder to achieve leadership and integration of viewpoints and policies. "There are 100 gauntlets and 1,000 vetoes on Capitol Hill," stated OMB Director (and former representative) David A. Stockman. "You simply can't sustain any kind of policy through that process."[10]

Congress-as-Institution

The fragmentation of the first Congress—the individual members—thus yields heightened challenges for the second Congress—the lawmaking body. Congress continues to be asked to resolve a bewildering range of public problems on behalf of an impatient public. Constituents are "not content to wait for the normal evolutionary process of debate, dialogue, compromise, resolution, and consensus," observed Rep. Thomas S. Foley, D-Wash.[11] Yet, when Congress fails to take action, it may be for very good reasons. The ideas may be poor and lack the support necessary for enactment. A further complication is that many issues (promoting growth and curbing inflation, for example) are shaped by circumstances beyond Congress's control, such as natural disasters or military conflicts or the behavior of the nation's trading partners.

Relative to these policy demands, resources for resolving them in politically attractive ways are severely limited. It is vexing enough to shape policies for an affluent society; in an era of limits the task is excruciating, especially when there are so many well-organized and competing interest groups. Rather than distributing benefits, politicians find themselves having to assign costs or cutbacks. This represents a shift from distributive to redistributive policies—a disconcerting prospect for policy makers because it means higher levels of conflict and disaffection.[12]

One response to workload demands has been to delegate more to House and Senate committees and subcommittees. In the 1980s there were about 350 Capitol Hill work groups—standing committees, special and select committees, joint committees, subcommittees, task forces, and so forth. Efforts to consolidate or realign these work groups have had limited success. The Senate cut its committees and member assignments by one-third in 1977, but the numbers began rising again, and a 1984 study found that more than half the senators were in violation of the assignment limits.[13]

Senators and representatives are spread thin. Virtually any day the houses are in session, most legislators face conflicts in their meeting schedules. Members are tempted to committee-hop, quorums are hard to maintain, and deliberation suffers. Committee specialization and apprenticeship norms have been diluted, casting doubt on the committees' continued ability to give in-depth consideration to detailed measures that come before them.

Jurisdictional competition among committees is endemic, resulting in member complaints about the need for tighter scheduling and coordination. Attractive issues often cause an unseemly scramble for advantage—sometimes breaking into open conflict, more frequently simply raising decision-making costs by necessitating complicated informal agreements or awkward partitioning of issues. One clue is the number of measures referred to two or more committees—a procedure that gets more people into the act but also frustrates action.

Congressional staffs have grown to cope with the burgeoning workload and to compete with executive-branch expertise. No visitor to Capitol Hill can fail to be impressed by the number of people employed there. About 15,000 staff aides now work for members and committees; counting supporting staffs in the two chambers and the four associated agencies (Congressional Research Service, General Accounting Office, Congressional Budget Office, and Office of Technology Assessment), the total is about 24,000.

The Capitol Hill bureaucracy has grown in ways that betray the character of Congress as a decentralized institution. Congress has begotten not one bureaucracy but many, clustered about centers of power and in a sense defining those centers. Efforts to impose a common framework on the staff apparatus have thus far been stoutly resisted.

Democracy is in full flower on the Hill. Formal posts of power remain, as do inequalities of influence. But the Senate boasts nothing like its bipartisan conservative "inner club" of the 1950s, which so vexed the little band of liberals, and the House has few if any "bulls" or "barons" to dominate its committees and floor debate.

The changes of the 1970s made the House and Senate more open, democratic bodies. What that generation of reform did not solve, however, is how to orchestrate the work of the disparate work groups into some semblance of a coherent whole. Indeed, the advent of subcommittee government may compound the task of congressional (and presidential) leadership.

Most critics agree that stronger central leadership is required to coordinate the activities of the scattered committees and subcommittees, schedule consideration of measures, and provide more efficient administrative services. Vigorous central leadership also might help Congress solve its image problem by giving the media and the public a handle for identifying what is to most people a confusing, faceless institution.

Today's congressional leaders are in fact stronger, on paper at any rate, than any of their recent predecessors, even the legendary Sam Rayburn and Lyndon Johnson. Speakers exercise significant new powers under the House rules. They can schedule and cluster floor votes; they can make joint, split, or sequential referrals of bills to two or more committees with jurisdictional claims. In addition, the Speakers are empowered to create ad hoc legislative committees to handle bills claimed by two or more committees. These powers are often called into play: in 1977 and 1978 approximately 1,241 measures were referred to more than one committee. Although these devices give Speakers certain leverage on committee scheduling, they have turned out to be a mixed blessing because they underscore the fragmentation and overlap that besets the committee system.

When they are Democrats, Speakers have added powers conferred by the Democratic Caucus. They chair the Democratic Steering and Policy Committee and appoint nearly half its members. They nominate all Democratic members of the House Rules Committee, subject to caucus ratification. For the first time since the days of Speaker Joseph Cannon at the turn of the century, in fact, the Rules Committee serves as a leadership arm in regulating the flow of measures to the House floor.

Still, the leaders' powers seem a weak reed against the profusion of work groups and centers of influence. With few sanctions against recalcitrant members, leaders must listen to all viewpoints, barter their prerogatives for support, and search for the least common denominator of consensus. Majority Leader Jim Wright, D-Texas, called leadership "a license to persuade—if you can."[14]

On the Senate side, leadership is even more fragile. Lacking the same power of scheduling enjoyed by the House majority leadership, Senate floor leaders often seem little more than traffic cops, stretching the floor schedule to adapt to senators' frenetic schedules and wheedling unanimous consent agreements to see that the business of the chamber proceeds. Recent leaders like Robert C. Byrd and Howard H. Baker, Jr., have been praised for their legislative skills, but both have voiced frustration with the jobs. Baker compared leaders to janitors: the first to arrive in the chamber, the last to leave, and all the time cleaning up other people's messes.[15]

Leaders seem not to know which way to turn. Often they appear reluctant to accept new prerogatives, preferring to rely on informal powers like those that formed the basis of the vigorous leadership of Rayburn and Johnson. Yet they sense that, although publicly held responsible for congressional performance, they lack adequate power to coordinate or schedule the legislative program. That is why virtually all leaders since Rayburn have supported reforms that promised to increase their leverage in the legislative process.

In the face of a workload expanding both in quantity and breadth of subject matter, Congress responded by restricting the depth of its involvement—mainly by concentrating on fewer but more complex issues, delegating more decisions to executive-branch agents, and shifting its own role to that of monitor, vetoer, and overseer. The proliferation of reporting requirements, legislative approval and veto provisions, and oversight activities testified to this strategic shift. Sometimes, as in the 1973 War Powers Resolution, the innovation takes the form of lending formal recognition to de facto shifts in the constitutional blend of powers.

Heightened dependence upon the executive did not occur without resistance from conscientious legislators and from those opposed to the drift of legislation. Congress countered by striving to regain control it sensed had been lost. In the wake of the Watergate and Vietnam crises, a vigorous reaction took place in which legislators proclaimed their loyalty to the concept of oversight, some even putting the concept into practice. This legislative "resurgence" has marked legislative-executive relations since the mid-1970s and has substantially restrained presidential leadership.[16]

Predictably, cries of congressional "meddling" are heard from the other end of Pennsylvania Avenue. For their part, legislators risk becoming entangled in their own efforts to maintain control: reporting requirements and veto provisions, not to mention more elaborate schemes such as mandated "sunset" for federal programs, could demand at least as much time and attention as drafting the original legislation.

More seriously, some critics worry that our government's energy and coherence—a perennial issue, by constitutional design—are placed in even greater jeopardy by post-Watergate Congresses' insistence on restricting and second-guessing executive actions. Interbranch rivalries are underscored by the prevalence of "divided government," in which the White House is controlled by one party and Congress by the other. (An exception was the Carter administration, 1977–1981, when the two branches nonetheless remained at arm's length.) In the 1980s the two chambers were themselves under divided control, a fact that exacerbated internal divisions and factionalism on the Hill.

Under such circumstances, presidential leadership may be even more difficult than the Founders intended. An influential group of observers, including former presidential counselors Lloyd N. Cutler and C. Douglas Dillon and former senator J. William Fulbright, D-Ark., believe that constitutional repairs should be made to enable presidents to "form a government."[17] To bring the two branches closer together, they advocate elements of parliamentary government—as they put it, incentives for presidents and legislators of the same party to cooperate in "forming a government." Alternatives include: allowing incumbent members of Congress to serve in the president's cabinet; establishing simultaneous four- or six-year terms for presidents and legislators alike; requiring voters to cast a single ballot not only for a party's presidential and vice presidential ticket, but also for the party's House and Senate candidates as a bloc; or authorizing the president or Congress or both to call for new elections when a stalemate becomes endemic—thus making it possible for a government to "fall."[18]

. . .The notion is that a group of officeholders ought to be capable of organizing the executive and legislative branches into a coherent, energetic, and effective government. . . .

The drawback of reforms designed to promote majoritarian government is that they do not fit the pluralistic American political culture. The multiplicity of groups and interests renders virtually impossible the kind of broad-gauged consensus that would have to underlie such a regime, and makes a fragmented, open system of decision-making arenas virtually inevitable. Moreover, citizens seem to approve of divided government, and for about the same reason given by James Madison: it checks possible excesses on the part of one or another elements in the system.

Nor does the fragmented structure of our government preclude vigorous, purposive action. Ironically, at the very moment that critics, reflecting on the weak presidencies of Ford and Carter, were lamenting the lack of leadership, Ronald Reagan was demonstrating that very kind of leadership with his 1981 economic package. Combining popular appeal with skillful strategy and tactics, Reagan was able to alter the government's revenue and fiscal priorities, perhaps with lasting results. Opportunities for interbranch coordination on such a scale are rare under our political system, but they are eminently possible with the right circumstances. At other times, Americans seem happy to leave the checks and balances firmly in place.

On to the Third Century

...The year 1987 [was] the bicentennial of the U.S. Constitution, and two years later the House and Senate celebrated their anniversaries. In 1991 we [honored] the centerpiece achievement of the historic 1st Congress, the Bill of Rights.

The bicentennial is not only an occasion for lauding the Founders' foresight and taking comfort from the resilience of our institutions. It is also an opportunity to reflect soberly on the continuing, and even mounting, challenges that confront our institutions....

Is mere survival enough? Our age has been called antiparliamentary, and this is surely because of the staggering, shifting challenges emanating from the larger political and social environment. These include pressing national problems, rising public expectations, fast-moving events, competing institutions, and an exploding workload. In country after country, parliamentary forms have been overrun by military dictatorships or bureaucratic regimes after failing to cope with rapidly changing events or escalating political demands. Almost alone among the world's legislatures, the U. S. Congress strives to maintain its autonomy by crafting its own legislation and monitoring the governmental apparatus. Yet many people question whether, realistically, Congress can retain meaningful control, given the complex, interdependent character of current problems....

Not a few people question whether representative assemblies remain relevant for our third century's problems. For one thing, such assemblies rest on the principle of geographic representation. This was natural in the eighteenth century when land was the basic productive resource; indeed, for much of our history, local and regional fissures were translated into political divisions. Today this is less so. Our divisions tend to be economic or social or intellectual or ideological, rather than based on geographic location.... [S]tates and districts are increasingly microcosms of the nation as a whole, in terms of the diversity of interests they embrace.

Second, we may have reached (or passed beyond) the limits of elected generalists to render intelligent judgments on the dizzyingly complex problems of governance....

When the first Congress convened, the United States had a tiny population, mostly rural and uneducated; its social and industrial structure was simple; changes occurred slowly; government tasks were few. Nothing could be farther from the contemporary situation. As one social critic put it:

> The Congress is so overloaded by conflicting demands and oceans of unsynthesized data, so many pressures and demands for instant response. The institution is creaking and overloaded and unable to churn out intelligent decisions. Government policymakers are unable to make high priority decisions or making them badly, while they make thousands of small decisions. When a major problem arises, the solution is usually too late and seldom produces the desired impact.[19]

Congress has answered such challenges with organizational adaptation, primarily more division of labor and more staff assistance. It may be, however, that the challenges are so fundamental that they cannot be met with organizational tinkering.

Finally, the very concept of national policy may be unrealistic and irrelevant. The foes of technology originally feared that radio, television, computers, and other advances would create a single mass society in which individuals, brought together and exposed to the same stimuli, would march in lockstep and lose their individuality. If anything, the opposite has occurred: technology has "demassified" society and fostered diversity. While erasing geographical isolation, technology serves all manner of other human diversities. Far from being a single mass society, we are increasingly "sliced into dozens of different geographic, economic, social, and cultural markets."[20] According to one source, roughly 55,000 different mailing lists of citizens are available for rental by marketers, politicians, or interest groups. . . .

Our society is being reshaped structurally by this splitting-apart process. . . . The growth of voluntary associations and interest groups—always a hallmark of our nation—has been so startling in recent years that commentators speak of a "participation revolution."[21]

In the light of all this buzzing profusion, the survival of a single national assembly composed of generalists elected by majority votes from geographical areas may seem anomalous indeed. Perhaps it badly mirrors the real-world "democracy of minorities [composed of] complex, multiple and transient minorities."[22]. . .

Some commentators urge that we shift our attention from historic representative forms—legislatures, adversarial courts, secret ballots—to . . . more varied methods of citizen participation in decision making. . . . Benjamin R. Barber's program for "strong democracy," for instance, stresses participatory models such as neighborhood assemblies, electronic civic-communications networks, national initiative and referendum processes, and selective experiments with voucher systems for schools, public housing projects, and transportation systems.[23] Needless to say, not all these proposals will be workable or desirable; some, like the national initiative and referendum, may yield even greater problems than the current system. More important than the content of the proposed remedies, however, is the challenge these critiques pose to traditional forms of representative government.

This is but the latest wave of challenges to representative assemblies. At their heart, such critiques probe the dual character of legislatures . . . the demands of wise policy making versus the requirements of political representation. Alas, we have no convincing solutions for this dilemma and so end our discourse with questions for the uncertain future.

Are the two Congresses ultimately compatible? Or are they diverging, each detrimental to the other? The burden placed on both Congresses is vastly heavier than it was a generation ago. Congress-as-Institution is expected to resolve all sorts of problems—not only in processing legislation, but also in monitoring programs and serving as an all-purpose watchdog. By all outward signs of activity—such as numbers of committees and committee assignments, hearings, votes, and hours in session—legislators are struggling valiantly to keep abreast of these demands.

At the same moment, Congress-as-Politicians is busier than ever. Partly because of the sheer scope of modern government, partly because of consti- tuents' keener awareness, citizens are insisting that senators and representatives communicate more often, serve their states or districts materially, and play the role of ombudsmen. It is a function legislators have accepted and prof- ited from, but not without misgivings and not without detriment to their legislative tasks.

The intensified demands upon the two Congresses could well lie beyond the reach of normal men and women. Reflecting on the multiplicity of presidential duties, Woodrow Wilson once remarked that we might be forced to pick out leaders from among "wise and prudent athletes"—a small class of people. The same might now be said of senators and representatives. And if the job specifications exceed reasonable dimensions, can we expect even our most talented citizens to perform these tasks successfully?

In the longer view, the question is whether an institution embracing so many disparate motives and careers can continue to function as a coherent whole. Can policies patched together out of so many discrete interests really guide the nation on its perilous course? Ever since 1787, people have wondered about these questions. History is only mildly reassuring, and the future poses new and delicate challenges for which the margin of error may be narrower than in the past. And yet, representative democracy itself is a gamble; the proposition that representation can yield wise policy making remains a daring one. As always, it is an article of faith whose ultimate proof lies in the future.

Notes

1. Louis Harris Associates, July 1984.
2. Woodrow Wilson, *Congressional Government* (Baltimore: Johns Hopkins Univer- sity Press, 1981), 210.
3. Richard F. Fenno, Jr., *Home Style: House Members in Their Districts* (Boston: Little, Brown, 1978), 168.
4. *New York Times*, May 9, 1983, A19.
5. David S. Broder, *Changing of the Guard: Power and Leadership in America* (New York: Simon & Schuster, 1980).
6. Quoted in *New York Times*, Dec. 9, 1984, E2.
7. Glenn R. Parker and Roger H. Davidson, "How Come We Love Our Congressmen So Much More than Our Congress?" *Legislative Studies Quarterly* (February 1979): 53–61.
8. House Commission on Administrative Review, *Final Report*, 2 vols., H. Doc. 95–272, 95th Cong., 1st sess., Dec. 31, 1977, 2: 875.
9. Ibid., 2: 844.
10. "Discussing the Bugs in the Machinery," *New York Times*, April 12, 1984, B14.
11. *Congressional Record*, daily ed., 94th Cong. 2d sess., Feb. 25, 1976, E832.
12. Lester Thurow, *The Zero-Sum Society* (New York: Basic Books, 1980).

13. Temporary Select Committee to Study the Senate Committee System, *Hearings*, S. Hrg. 98–981, 98th Cong., 2d sess., July 31, 1984, committee print, 1: 52.

14. Jim Wright, *Reflections of a Public Man* (Fort Worth: Madison Publishing, 1984), 89.

15. *Congressional Record*, 98th Cong., 2d sess., April 26, 1984, S4877. See also Roger H. Davidson, "Senate Leaders: Janitors for an Untidy Chamber?" in *Congress Reconsidered*, 3rd ed., ed. Lawrence Dodd and Bruce Oppenheimer (Washington, D.C.: CQ press, 1985), 225ff.

16. James L. Sundquist, *The Decline and Resurgence of Congress* (Washington, D.C.: Brookings Institution, 1982).

17. See, for example, Kevin Phillips, "An American Parliament," *Harper's*, November 1980, 14–21; and Lloyd N. Cutler, "To Form a Government," *Foreign Affairs* (Fall 1980): 126–143.

18. Lloyd N. Cutler and C. Douglas Dillon, "Can We Improve on Our Constitutional System?" *Wall Street Journal*, Feb. 15, 1983, 32.

19. Toffler, "Congress in the Year 2000," 44.

20. Robert J. Samuelson, "Cultural Salami," *National Journal*, Jan. 28, 1975.

21. Jack L. Walker, "The Origins and Maintenance of Interest Groups in America," *American Political Science Review* (June 1983): 390–406.

22. Toffler, "Congress in the Year 2000," 44.

23. Benjamin R. Barber, *Strong Democracy: Participatory Politics for a New Age* (Berkeley: University of California Press, 1984). See also Jane J. Mansbridge, *Beyond Adversary Democracy* (Chicago: University of Chicago Press, 1983).

52 / Congress: The First 200 Years

Thomas P. O'Neill, Jr.

Elected to the House of Representatives in 1952, Massachusetts Congressman Thomas P. "Tip" O'Neill served as Speaker of the House from 1977 until he retired in 1986. In the following reading, written as a prelude to Congress's 1989 bicentennial, O'Neill discusses the impacts of such changes as decline of the party system in recent decades, the growing "careerism" associated with longer tenures in office, and the expanding workload of members, including greater demands for constituency service. Finally, he focuses on change in the relationship—and in the perception of the relationship—between Congress and the president, a relationship that O'Neill argues is no longer as "coequal" as was originally intended.

As we [celebrate] the Bicentennial of the Constitution and the Congress it created, it is appropriate to consider how the legislative branch of our federal government has developed during its nearly 200 years of existence. It might be both interesting and useful to see how much Congress has turned out the way the Drafters of the Constitution conceived it, as well as how much of the evolution of Congress was not anticipated by them.

Take the development of political parties, for example. It is hard to imagine our government functioning without a strong two-party system. Yet the Continental Congress and the Articles of Confederation Congress existed without parties. The idea of political parties apparently never arose at the Constitutional Convention, either; a careful reading of James Madison's *Notes of Debates in the Federal Convention of 1787* does not reveal any indication that political parties were at all anticipated by the delegates.

Such a remarkable lack of prescience on the part of this talented and experienced group has had incredible consequences for the Congress and for the Nation. We normally consider the role of political parties in the House or the Senate only in terms of partisan votes on legislative issues or the means for selection of internal leadership positions. The existence of political parties, however, has changed dramatically the basic relationship between the Congress and the president in a way unanticipated in 1787.

Specifically, when the Constitutional Convention considered the method of electing the president, only one state delegation—Pennsylvania—felt that the president of the United States should be elected directly by the people. After much discussion and negotiation, the delegates decided upon indirect election of the president, using electors meeting in their separate states to cast their votes. Because of the lack of communications facilities at the time and the lack of nationally popular leaders other than George Washington, it was commonly assumed that the electoral vote generally would be indecisive. George Mason, one of the luminaries of the Revolutionary War period and a delegate to the Convention, guessed that "nineteen times in twenty" there would be no presidential majority in the electoral college.

How, then, did the delegates think that the president would be elected? The answer, found in Article II, Section 1 of the Constitution, is that the House of Representatives—each state delegation having one vote—would usually elect the president. The candidate with the majority of state delegations would become president. The second-place finisher would become vice president. If there were a tie for second, the Senate would choose the vice president. Coupled with modifications by the Twelfth Amendment to the Constitution, this is the arrangement today.

The two-party system completely wrecked this carefully wrought plan, for only twice (Thomas Jefferson in 1801 and John Quincy Adams in 1825) has the House been called upon to elect the president. This is not to say that the way things have developed is bad or wrong. On the contrary, I believe we have a much better system than anticipated. But the plan to make the president dependent upon the Congress for election in most instances was all part of the balance designed by the men who wrote the Constitution.

Delegates to the Convention seem to have anticipated that a candidate for president would have to forge an alliance with the House of Representatives in order to attain the presidency. Presidents would not assume office with what has been too often the case in recent years—a highly personal interpretation that they have been given a specific mandate by the American people to whip the Congress into shape and force it to respond to their own interpretation of what is best for the country. On the contrary, the Constitution does not give to the president alone the power to interpret and execute the popular will.

. . . [T]he party system has changed a lot, and some of these changes have hurt the ability of Congress to act effectively. When I first entered the House in 1953, it seemed that most of the members had worked their way up through the ranks to get to the House of Representatives. They had worked for their party on the local or state level and had served in some kind of local office, like mayor or alderman or city commissioner. Perhaps they had served in the state legislature, as I did, and they knew what it meant to follow the leadership and learn the art of legislation. There were not many members in those days who set out on their own with complete disregard for the party to which they belonged. They had some understanding of government and how it works.

The party system is much different today, and I believe it works to our detriment as a Congress. Men and women are elected to the House without having previously held elective office. They can get elected because they raise the money and hire a media consultant and get on television. Some of them do not care about what party they belong to, and they feel as if they owe the party nothing when they take office. The House has always been a difficult body to lead; I do not believe, though, that even Henry Clay, despite the many problems he had with John Randolph of Roanoke who brought his hunting dogs on the floor of the House, ever had to deal with as many independent members as are found in the modern House of Representatives. The result has been a breakdown of party discipline and a refusal to follow party leadership, which leads in turn to congressional paralysis and an inability to act coherently as a legislative body.

Other fundamental changes have occurred in Congress over the past 200 years. Congressional tenures, for instance, have become much longer. Most of the men—there were only men in the Congress in those days—who served in the first years of the Republic stayed for only a term or two. The custom was that a representative would leave his farm or business or profession and go to Washington for a few years. He would stay in a boarding house, eat his meals with other members of the House and Senate, and curse the insects, Washington's heat and humidity, and the open sewer that ran near the Capitol building.

For the first fifty or so Congresses, very few men made a career of service in the House or the Senate. Until about 1880, more than half the men elected to each Congress were first-termers. Service of long duration, like that of Nathaniel Macon (1791–1828), Samuel Smith (1793–1833), and William R. King (1811–16, 1819–44, 1848–52), was most unusual. As we passed into the twentieth century, elective office became more of a career than a temporary public service.

Concurrent with the longer tenure in office, seniority began to acquire greater significance in leadership assignments in the Congress. Throughout the first century or so in the House of Representatives, the Speaker switched committee chairmen as he wished, often naming large numbers of new ones at the beginning of each Congress. His power to do this was enhanced by the relatively short careers of most congressmen of the time. By 1900, when the trend toward longer service in Congress was well-established, it had become accepted practice in both the House and the Senate that a member would move up in seniority as he outlasted other members of his party on a particular committee. When he reached the top of the ladder, he would become the committee chairman, provided that his party had a majority in his branch of the Congress. It still works this way in the Senate.

The House, however, has . . . introduced an element of flexibility into the process of committee chair selection. The Democratic Caucus, whose rules control the House as long as the Democrats have a majority, adopted a series of reforms in 1974. These changes require a secret ballot election for committee chairmen at the beginning of each Congress and limit a member to one subcommittee chairmanship. As a practical matter, seniority is still quite important in deciding who will chair a House committee, but it is no longer the only consideration.

There are other developments in the Congress that would surprise the men who drafted the Constitution in 1787. The Constitutional Convention, for example, was able to get by with only one staff person to help with its work. The growth of federal responsibilities and activities over the past 200 years, however, has meant that every branch of the government has increased in size since the first years of the Republic. This is as true for the Congress, which began in 1789 with only ninety-one members and a minuscule staff, as for any other branch.

For their first fifty years, the House and the Senate were able to function without having staff for particular congressional committees. By 1891, the first year for which we have good data, a total of 103 persons worked full-time for congressional committees. This assistance helped ease the committee members' workload, and as committee responsibilities have increased over the past ninety years, the number of committee staff persons has grown to just over 3000. Until almost the end of the nineteenth century, however, there was no such thing as personal staff support for a member of Congress. By 1930, the total of these congressional staffs was some 1569 persons. Fifty years later, some 14,000 individuals served the Congress as personal or committee staff members, an eightfold increase. By comparison, the national budget, for which Congress is responsible, increased by more than 172 times during this same period.

It is not unreasonable to believe that Congress has required an increase in staff assistance to enable it to cope with the growth of the national budget and the increased complexity of the federal government as a whole. The president is able to obtain information and advice from the Office of Management and Budget, the White House staff, and the thousands of analysts, statisticians, and managers elsewhere in the executive branch of the government. If the Congress is to consider legislation, appropriate hundreds of billions of dollars, perform its oversight of executive branch operations, answer millions of letters, and act as ombudsman for harassed constituents, it needs a staff much greater than the one man who served the delegates to the Constitutional Convention in 1787.

Although the role of members of Congress has expanded greatly over the past 200 years, they still have a responsibility to their constituencies. The difference, however, is the scope of these duties. Just over 100 years ago (1882) a congressman from Michigan, Roswell G. Horr, placed in the record an account of the typical constituent-service duties and activities:

> ...I think it is safe to say that each member of this House receives fifty letters each week; many receive more.... Growing out of these letters will be found during each week a large number of errands, a vast amount of what is called department work. One-quarter of them, perhaps, will be from soldiers asking aid in their pension cases, and each soldier is clear in his own mind that the member can help his case out if he will only make it a special case and give it special attention.
>
> Another man writes you to look up some matter in reference to a land patent. Another says his homestead claim should be looked after and he wants you to learn and let him know why he does not receive his full title. Another has invented some machine and the department have [sic] declared his discovery to be already supplemented by some former inventor, and have [sic] refused his patent. He would like you to go through the Patent Office and look over the patent laws and see if great injustice has not been done in his case. Another has a son or brother in the Regular Army whom he would like to have discharged.
>
> Another has a recreant son whom he would like to get into the Regular Army or Navy. In conformity with these requests you are liable to be called upon, perhaps several times in one week, by these applicants in personam, and they will require you to go at once and exert your enormous powers.

Recall that the members who preceded Representative Horr, as well as those who came along many years after, performed all of these functions personally. The fifty letters a week received by Representative Horr, however, have become more than 5000 a week for the typical member of the House. All of this mail needs to be answered, even if it is only a simple acknowledgement.

Much of this incoming mail is issue-oriented, and the marriage of the computer to the high-speed printer enables a well-organized, well-financed interest group to generate literally millions of letters to Congress on a given topic. If members did not in turn rely upon their own computers and computer operators to respond to this mass-generated correspondence, they would slowly disappear beneath a sea of paper. The computer age is upon us, and for better or worse the Congress has had to adjust its way of doing business to reflect this reality.

Certain realities have not changed. Constituents need help with some agency or department of the executive branch. By the time someone writes his or her member of Congress, you can be fairly certain that a long and frustrating history has already taken place. Many citizens today feel with some justification that too much of government has become large and impersonal. When there is a problem with their Social Security benefits or their Veterans Administration benefits, the ordinary citizen often feels reduced to nothing more than a multidigit number, dealt with in an impersonal fashion. The member can step in, cut through the Gordian knot of bureaucracy, and see to it that the citizen receives his or her due. Members of Congress have been helping their constituents in this manner since the beginning of the Republic, and I cannot imagine that anyone today would suggest that this is not an appropriate role for the Congress.

Finally, I would like to consider the relationship of the Congress and the president, in its idealized state, as it actually exists, and as I believe it should exist. When most of us were going through what used to be called civics class, we were taught that there were three branches of government at the national level. The legislative branch, we were taught, makes the laws; the executive branch enforces the laws; and the judicial branch interprets the laws. In a general sense, this scheme is correct.

But the distinction between making and enforcing laws has become blurred over the years with the advent of executive branch regulation making and the congressional veto. Even the courts have gone far beyond merely "interpreting" the law and have been performing such executive functions as administering state prison systems and redrawing school district boundaries. I believe that this blurring of duties will continue for the foreseeable future, and no amount of railing for a return to the good old days will do one bit of good.

If I could accomplish one thing as Speaker of the House of Representatives, it would be to teach the American public that the Congress is a co-equal branch of the federal government, with its own set of powers and responsibilities. It is not the duty of the House or the Senate to accede to the wishes of the president, just because the president occupies the Oval Office. Indeed, the Congress and the president were intentionally set at cross-purposes by the men who drafted the Constitution. Sometimes a powerful president has been able to dominate the Congress; sometimes the Congress has run over a president. The locus of power in the government swings back and forth between these two branches.

In my own lifetime, the man who was most responsible for concentrating power in the presidency was Franklin D. Roosevelt. A dynamic individual, he knew how to make the Congress bow to his will. After him other presidents, regardless of party, were able to build on Roosevelt's legacy and increase the power of the presidency.

The growth of personal and committee staffs has certainly given the Congress a better chance to meet the president on an equal basis. There are also certain congressionally initiated statutes that have recently increased the power and influence of the House and Senate, specifically the War Powers Act and the anti-impoundment provisions of the Budget Act of 1974.

The War Powers Act was passed over President Richard M. Nixon's veto in 1973 by a Congress that was reasserting its constitutional primacy in the war area. Twice since 1950—in Korea and in Vietnam—the United States has found itself in a hot war without a specific congressional declaration of war. Some people might argue that the War Powers Act is too much of a restriction on the president, but I see it as a return to the intent of the Constitution. I see the same principle in the anti-impoundment law incorporated in the Budget Act of 1974, which was largely a reaction to President Nixon's refusal to spend certain funds that had been appropriated by Congress.

In 1972 alone, President Nixon refused to spend $2.5 billion for highway construction, $1.9 billion in defense funds, and $1.5 billion for such programs as food stamps, rural water and waste disposal, and rural electrification. The proper and constitutional way for him to object to these appropriations would have been to veto the appropriations bill. Such action would have given the Congress an opportunity to override him; impoundment—refusing to spend the money that had been appropriated—leaves the Congress high and dry with little means to protest effectively. I believe this law was greatly needed and helps restore a balance to the government. Parenthetically, I would point out that the much-discussed presidential line-item veto would undermine congressional power in the budget process and could result in the elimination of many programs, such as federal aid to libraries or museums, that are favored by a majority of the Congress but opposed by an administration. The anti-impoundment law is the sole protector of these programs today.

The biggest advantage a modern president has is the six o'clock news. Presidents can be on the news every night if they want to—and usually they want to. They can easily make themselves the focus of every major news report, because the president of the United States is unarguably the most powerful individual in the world. And it is precisely for this reason that the Congress has a duty and a responsibility to act to counterbalance this power. The Congress is composed of the collective wisdom of 435 members of the House and 100 members of the Senate, men and women who bring to the Nation's capital every conceivable combination of education and experience, 535 individuals who together represent the richness and diversity of our country. Who is to say that this group, this Congress, should bow to the wishes of any one individual, no matter who that individual may be? No, the Congress has its own role to play, and it has always been a difficult one.

One of my predecessors as Speaker, Nicholas Longworth, a Republican who served with a Republican president in a Republican Congress, spoke some sixty years ago of the public perception problem faced by the Congress. His words are humorous, but I do not feel they are exaggerated:

> I have been a member of the House of Representatives ten terms. That is twenty years. During the whole of that time we have been attacked, denounced, despised, hunted, harried, blamed, looked down upon, excoriated, and flayed.
>
> I refuse to take it personally. I have looked into history. I find that we did not start being unpopular when I became a Congressman. We were unpopular before that time....
>
> From the beginning of the Republic it has been the duty of every free-born voter to look down upon us, and the duty of every free-born humorist to make jokes at us.
>
> Always there is something—and, in fact, almost always there is almost everything—wrong with us. We simply cannot be right.
>
> Let me illustrate. Suppose we pass a lot of laws. Do we get praised? Certainly not. We then get denounced by everybody for being a "Meddlesome Congress" and for being a "Busybody Congress." Is it not so?
>
> But suppose we take warning from that experience. Suppose that in our succeeding session we pass only a few laws. Are we any better off? Certainly not. Then everybody ... denounces us for being an "Incompetent Congress" and a "Do-Nothing Congress."
>
> We have no escape—absolutely none.
>
> We have no chance—just absolutely no chance. The only way for a Congressman to be happy is to realize that he has no chance.

Speaker Longworth's words often seem as accurate to me today as when they were first published in the mid-1920s. I hope we can change this situation in the future. If we can use this Bicentennial to restore in the public mind the equality that was intended between the Congress and the president, then we will have accomplished something truly significant and historic. In so doing we offer the greatest possible tribute to those men who ... sat through a hot summer in Philadelphia and drafted the greatest Constitution the world has ever known, and we will have accomplished something that will have a lasting effect on our great nation long after we and this Bicentennial are only distant memories.

53 / The Class of '74 and the New Way of Doing Business

Burdett Loomis

In the aftermath of the Watergate scandal that shook the nation and its political establishment, there were signs in the 1974 congressional elections that the electorate might be ready for change—in personnel, if nothing else. One hundred and three new members were elected to the House of Representatives alone. But more important even than their large number was the fact that many of them seemed "different" from what had become the norm in the House. Burdett Loomis argues that with their greater independence and entrepreneurial style, the members of the "Class of '74" have helped to reshape the way that business is done in Congress. Whether the change is for the better is less clear.

From the *New York Times*, August 8, 1986:

> Campaigns for six Democrats running for the Senate stand to profit considerably from a $1 million Hollywood fund-raising party next month starring Barbra Streisand, who has not sung in public for six years, and Robin Williams, the television and film comedian. Tickets, available by invitation only, will cost $5000 a couple, for a limit of 400 people. Candidates sharing in the proceeds include. . . Bob Edgar of Pennsylvania and Tim Wirth of Colorado.[1]

How time flies when you're having fun. Scarcely a decade earlier Bob Edgar (D-Pa.) and Tim Wirth (D-Colo.) would have welcomed a five-dollar contribution. Fifty bucks would have been a windfall and five hundred dollars almost beyond hope. In 1974 Edgar won a seat in the U.S. House of Representatives for the bargain-basement price of $38,819. Wirth, an effective fund-raiser ever since his initial 1974 campaign, spent all of $134,000 to join him. In 1986 Edgar raised and spent more than one hundred times as much—$3,905,186—in his losing bid for one of Pennsylvania's two Senate seats. Running in Colorado, a state with a third of Pennsylvania's population, Wirth matched Edgar's funding, spending $3.8 million in his successful 1986 Senate race.[2]

. . .Edgar, Wirth, and a horde of other national politicians have shaped a new era in American political life. Weaned on the Kennedy presidency, the civil rights movement, Earth Day, Vietnam, and Watergate, this cohort has produced a new style of policy-based activism that emphasizes both a serious consideration of issues and a fresh approach to the traditional rules of the game. Publicity-oriented and independent, the post-Watergate political generation has restructured both the process and the results of American politics. By the same token, years of working on Capitol Hill have affected the "Watergate babies" as they have matured and risen to influential positions.

Writing in 1987, Chris Matthews, former press secretary to Speaker of the House Tip O'Neill (D-Mass.), concluded that

> the American electorate sent a "new breed" of legislator to Washington [in 1974]: young, brash, independent of its elders and their system. It was the year of Watergate. . . . Rejecting cronyism and parochialism, [voters] elected a slate of freshman candidates pledged to a new order of ethics and independence. . . . More than a decade later, those who campaigned against Watergate in 1974 and 1976 remain the new kids on the political block.[3]

However oversimplified Matthews's assessment may be, the results of the 1974 election continue to define—inside and outside the Congress—a break point in American politics.

. . . In 1984 *Congressional Quarterly* devoted eight pages to the Watergate babies—the House class of '74.[4] The *Wall Street Journal* offered a similar front-page article, commemorating the tenth anniversary of this group. . . . No other contemporary group of legislators has received this kind of continuing attention. The congressional class of '74 remains distinct, well over a decade after its arrival on Capitol Hill.

Although scholars continue to debate the overall impact of Watergate on the 1974 electoral results,[5] members of Congress, the media, and the Washington community view that election as a dividing line in national politics. Not only did the members of the heavily Democratic House "freshman class" serve immediate notice that they were a force to be reckoned with, but they also demonstrated the skills that allowed them to take advantage of the great opportunities that the decentralized Congress and high levels of membership turnover afforded them, both in the aftermath of the 1974 elections and throughout the 1970s.

The impact of this group, for the most part, has been due to the emergence of effective individual politicians, like a Senator Chris Dodd (D-Conn.) or a Congressman Henry Waxman (D-Calif.), who have sought creative ways to gain major policymaking roles. . . . The *New York Times*'s Martin Tolchin observes that the "new leaders are less patient, more pragmatic, and take greater risks than their counterparts of a decade or two ago," and they have moved into positions of power "by doing the heavy legislative lifting, tackling the onerous, time-consuming tasks."[6] . . .

Thus, John Glenn (D-Ohio) and Gary Hart (D-Colo.) first won their Senate seats in 1974, as did Dale Bumpers (D-Ark.) and Patrick Leahy (D-Vt.); current Senators Charles Grassley (R-Iowa), Paul Simon (D-Ill.), Chris Dodd, Max Baucus (D-Mont.), Larry Pressler (R-S.D.), Paul Tsongas (D-Mass.), and Robert Kasten (D-Wisc.) all entered the House of Representatives that year, on their way up the political ladder; so did the popular two-term Democratic governor of Michigan, James Blanchard. The House found in its ranks a host of issue activists whose interests ranged from the environment (Henry Waxman), to foreign policy (Stephen Solarz [D-N.Y.]) to abortion policy (Henry Hyde [R-Ill.]). As part of the Democratic majority, Waxman and Solarz, together with most of their party colleagues, would soon—through good fortune and substantial political skills—chair subcommittees and thus enter the increasingly important "middle management" that is central to running the contemporary Congress.

The Class of 1974: Movers and Models

Political observers, whether in journalism, academia, or government, are all too apt to label unusual events as watersheds of historic proportions. Within the Congress this is especially true, given the glacial pace of most legislative change. Nevertheless, the Congress does undergo an occasional fundamental transformation, which profoundly alters both its internal power structure and its external relationships (such as with the president and with home constituencies).

Although the 1970s produced no single confrontation as dramatic as the 1910 insurrection that removed Speaker Joseph Cannon and ushered in the era of a dominant seniority system, they did result in changes that profoundly transformed the politics of Congress and its members. Indeed, the abrupt ousting of three senior committee chairmen in January 1975 may well rival the successful challenge to Speaker Cannon's authority. As Tip O'Neill notes, "In all my years in the House, this was one of the few times when I was genuinely caught by surprise."[7]

With the 1974 election and the subsequent organization of the 94th Congress, the three key elements of Watergate-era changes—fresh personnel, the outside environment, and the internal distribution of power on Capitol Hill—came together to fashion a qualitatively different legislature and an altered set of career choices for legislators.

The class of '74 has made its mark in two related ways. First, the class itself, with 103 newcomers in 1974, has been a real force. Its size, long-term electoral success, and talents have ensured that many of its members have become important national political figures. Second, and perhaps as significant, is the impact of these politicians as models for succeeding congressional cohorts.

With only a few exceptions, the class of '74 was young. In a House where the mean age in 1974 was over fifty-three, the members first elected in 1974 were thirteen years younger. This striking youth has had a continuing impact within the House; as of 1986, the thirty remaining members of the 1974 group had an average age of forty-nine, as compared to the representatives first elected in 1986, whose mean age was forty-six. With youth came inexperience; considerably fewer than half of the 1974 class had any legislative experience, the lowest percentage in more than twenty-five years. As former Congressman Toby Moffett (D-Conn.) observes, "We were different . . . not only much younger for the most part, but much *newer* to politics.". . .

The arrival of large numbers of newcomers with little legislative experience allowed societal forces to exert great influence on the Congress. Not only did the class of '74 hold together as a group when voting on major reform issues, but its unified presence stood as strong testimony to the perceived need for institutional change. The newcomers created neither the agenda for reform nor the outside pressures for change. Rather, they served as messengers from the public to the Congress about how far reform might be pushed. More than a decade after their arrival, members of the class of '74 retain an identity with the institutional reforms that fundamentally altered the rules of the policy game. Lobbyist Daniel Dutko noted in 1987 that the 1974 entrants "had a charter to see to it that Congress didn't get run by muscle.... That started a move toward a development of a new way of doing things."[8]

...For all their reformist origins, the 1974 entrants have acted pragmatically in shoring up their local political bases. In fact, they discovered that their office resources could serve them both as policy activists and sensitive representatives of their districts.[9] To this end, many 1974 newcomers found that developing sophisticated local political enterprises could give them a great deal of flexibility in pursuing their policy goals on Capitol Hill.

No matter how large and cohesive a single entering legislative cohort may be, its members can have little lasting impact unless they profoundly affect their colleagues and the entire context of national policy making. The class of '74 meets these criteria. Its members have helped to alter radically the role of the rank-and-file legislator and have contributed to the public style of policy articulation, which emphasizes the importance of agenda setting to the point that the notion has become a cliché. House majority whip Tony Coelho (D-Calif.)...concludes that the class of '74 "set an example for other classes, by striking out as individuals and developing their own power centers. They became independent and they didn't become beholden to the leadership."[10]*

At the same time, they emphasized issues and understood them with a speed that impressed and puzzled their senior colleagues. Former Congressman Richard Bolling (D-Mo.), another keen observer of congressional talent, notes, "These guys understand the complex. They're comfortable with it. With computers, technology, and all that. They're a different breed of cat."

...As then Congressman Tim Wirth concluded in 1984,

> We were the children of Vietnam, not children of World War II. We were products of television, not of print. We were products of computer politics, not courthouse politics. And we were the reflections of JFK as president, not FDR. We were the first class that was like that, and now the whole place is.[11]

With such a talent for providing a summarizing set of quotes, it is no wonder that Wirth obtained a lot of press attention and eventually won a Senate seat. And there is a lot of truth in Wirth's assessment. Nevertheless,

*Congressman Coelho resigned his House seat in 1989.—*Editor's Note.*

it misses the sense of change within the class, and the way Congress molds its members, rather than the reverse. Congressman Tom Foley (D-Wash.), first elected to the House in the Johnson landslide of 1964, places the class in a somewhat different perspective. Sympathetically, yet with an unmistakable edge, Foley commented in 1982 that a lot of class of '74 members

> see themselves as the "new model" member of Congress—the first with style, with tailoring, with media awareness. The first who knew what an i.c. [integrated circuit] is. They see themselves as qualitatively removed from those who came before. We [in 1964] came in thinking we were building a new model too.

For the "middle management" members of the House and the Senate, most of whom arrived on Capitol Hill in the 1970s, the very predominance of this independent, policy-activist style causes continuing difficulties, as Foley points out: "At worst, these guys say in effect, 'It doesn't matter. I am my own party,' [and] they emphasize their personal qualities." Although the Congress is a permeable institution that responds to societal changes, it is also a mediating body that seasons the raw talents attracted to national politics. The real capacities of the Watergate generation can scarcely be questioned. Its members have generally survived and prospered, often against long odds. The outstanding problem for this group is whether its members can help the Congress overcome the independence that they have practiced and encouraged in others. As David Broder concedes, a "New Breed, they are. But there's still the old need . . . to find enough followers to allow anyone to lead."[12]

Entrepreneurs, Enterprises, and Ambition

On December 1, 1975, my first day at work on Capitol Hill, I quickly discovered how contemporary politicians operate at the national level. There I sat, in the overcrowded office of Congressman Paul Simon (D-Ill.), then a first-term member of Congress, drafting a letter to the newly created Federal Election Commission (FEC). My task was simple: to request an FEC opinion on the guidelines and limitations that applied to Simon's efforts to establish a "Draft Hubert Humphrey for President" committee.

Like a good staffer I "plowed right ahead" (to borrow one of Simon's favorite phrases), never really questioning what business a freshman congressman had in organizing an attempt to piece together a presidential draft. Rather, I wrote the letter, followed it up, and for four months served as the coordinator of a murky, ill-defined "Draft Humphrey" effort that collapsed mercifully after Jimmy Carter wrapped up the nomination in the last big set of June primaries.

Only upon reflection did the significance of this work dawn upon me. Simon was exhibiting key characteristics of a new political style that he and his colleagues have developed since the mid-1970s. First, he did not wait to be invited into the higher reaches of presidential politics. Rather, he acted as an entrepreneur to press his interests, which encompassed both candidate preferences and policy goals. Second, Simon understood that entrepreneurs need resources. Eager, optimistic, and enthusiastic, I represented a politically useful resource. Equally important, my modest stipends came from an American Political Science Association fellowship, not from federal funds, thus freeing me to work openly on partisan politics. So it was that I became part of the Simon "enterprise," which comprised his office staff, his campaign organization, and a host of former staff members and confederates.[13] Transcending any formal organization, it revolved totally around the person and the unfolding political career of Congressman Simon.

Ten years after entering the House of Representatives, Simon won a Senate seat. By then, Simon's enterprise had grown so large that his Washington, D.C., victory party occupied a large private club and spilled over onto the street outside, where legions of his supporters (many from Illinois) waited in long lines to congratulate the senator-elect. Scarcely missing a beat, Simon declared his candidacy for president in 1987, only three years after reaching the Senate, and his enterprise grew exponentially, if temporarily, through the presidential campaign season. In addition, three members of the class of '74— former Congressmen Berkely Bedell (D-Iowa), Bob Edgar, and Floyd Fithian (D-Ind.)—became prominent aides in the Simon presidential organization.

Despite being somewhat older and considerably more experienced than most recent entrants into the Congress, Paul Simon nevertheless embodies many of the central characteristics of a "new style" of national politician. Simon has consistently cared a great deal about a wide range of issues, from enforcing the Helsinki accords to obtaining black lung benefits for coal miners. Just as consistently, Simon, a former newspaper publisher, has sought publicity to promote both his favored issues and his involvement with them. In addition, he has grasped the importance of resources—of staff, funds, position, and information—that are essential for allowing him independence to pursue his own agenda, which may or may not mesh with the preferences of party or committee leaders. Finally, and of great importance, Simon's substantial (but not atypical) ambition, both for higher office and for policy influence, has provided the glue to bind together the disparate elements of his personal style.

Policy Entrepreneurs: Advocates and Brokers   More than any other single metaphor, that of the politician as entrepreneur captures the essence of how most top-level officials operate today, in or out of the Congress. Secretary of Education William Bennett is no less a policy entrepreneur than is Senator Bill Bradley (D-N.J.). What has changed within the Congress is a context that fosters more entrepreneurial behavior from more legislators than ever before.

Relatively few politicians have succeeded at both issue advocacy, the public side of entrepreneurial activity, and its more private face of brokerage among interests.[14] Few push for the acceptance of a truly new idea. Rather, they tend to endorse, repackage, or resurrect concepts and ideas that either come from the outside (for example, academia) or have previously circulated within the Congress. Policy entrepreneurs are often both patient and persistent as they reshape policy solutions to fit emerging political conditions. Again, Paul Simon offers an apt illustration.

In the late 1970s, then Congressman Simon became alarmed by the declining status of foreign language education in the United States. This problem affected both elites—such as foreign service officers, who often could not speak the language of the country where they were stationed—and the public at large, which was faced with severe reductions in language training in high schools and colleges. Simon was convinced that as a nation the United States was paying a growing price in trade, security, and culture for its increasingly monolingual approach to the rest of the world.

Ever the entrepreneur, Simon moved beyond the House of Representatives to publicize the issue. He successfully urged Jimmy Carter to appoint a presidential commission to study the question. With Simon as a member, the commission undertook more than a year of research and made its report in October 1979. In and of itself, establishing a commission meant little. "[On] Capitol Hill . . . most members of the House and Senate yawned," Simon notes. "[The report's] ultimate impact will not be clear for several years as its recommendations are analyzed, refined, debated, and—I hope—confronted."[15]

Not content to let one more presidential commission's recommendations sit on the shelf, Simon persisted in campaigning for major foreign language reforms. Drawing on commission findings and his own research, Simon wrote a book that put forth the case for revitalized language training and awareness. That effort, *The Tongue-Tied American*, was well received within the educational community. It received especially positive comments in the national press, often getting better play on the editorial page than in the book review section.

Inside the Congress, Simon kept a watchful eye for a legislative opening to enact at least some of the commission's recommendations. That window of opportunity appeared in early 1983, as national concern grew over a crisis in science and math education. As he attached foreign language provisions to a "can't miss" set of science and math proposals, Simon's role shifted from advocate to broker. From his strategic vantage point as a subcommittee chair on the Education and Labor Committee, Simon could help ensure that this package held together.

Although Simon has always kept his share of policy irons in the fire, the five-year campaign for foreign language policy change absorbed a great deal of his attention and effort. Sheer persistence is a crucial part of much entrepreneurial achievement.[16] Simon's efforts were notable in their almost complete success, but they differed only in degree from the activities of many, if not most, other legislators. Increasingly, individual members of Congress have developed the capacity to place their favored issues on the legislative agenda. With almost half the House Democrats chairing a committee or subcommittee and with virtually all majority-party senators occupying similar slots, even reluctant legislators have the opportunity to act as entrepreneurs.

In turn, this limits the influence of committee chairs. Within the Senate to-day, for example, such a position confers essentially "positive control" over items that chairs wish to place on the agenda, not the ability to obstruct their colleagues' major initiatives.[17]

Legislators as Enterprises   Whether for a fledgling congressman or a hard-ened veteran, the enterprise concept captures the mix of personal goals, substantive issues, and structure that grows up around almost all national politicians. Policy entrepreneurs need vehicles and resources to promote their activities. From one point of view, legislative activists can usefully be depicted as independent operators who attempt to affect agendas or bring coalitions together. To a certain extent this is true; a Richard Gephardt (D-Mo.), a Bill Bradley, or a Phil Gramm (R-Tex.) does act on his own, expecting to receive personal credit for his entrepreneurial work. Nevertheless, even the least staff-dependent policy entrepreneurs must rely on their legislative assistants and committee personnel for a wide range of information and services.

Once again, it is the Congress of the mid-1970s that serves as the cutting point between legislative eras. The growth of staffs and other congressional resources in the approximate 1960–75 period permits the consideration of all members of Congress, and especially policy entrepreneurs, as "the head of an enterprise—an organization consisting of anywhere between eight or ten to well over one hundred subordinates."[18] . . .

. . . For better or worse, the enterprise revolves around its principal, and the resources serve the goals, ambitions, and—on occasion—whims of that individual.

The Glue of Ambition   Ambition is as American as apple pie, yet we distrust it profoundly. On the one hand, ambition is "the fuel of achievement" that usefully prods individuals into persistent attempts to gain their ends.[19] . . . At the same time, Joseph Epstein notes, "A person called ambitious is likely to arouse anxiety, for in our day anyone so called is thought to be threaten-ing, possibly a trifle neurotic."[20] And dangerous, the Constitution's framers would add. . . .

Political institutions channel . . . ambitions by providing a "structure of opportunities" within which politicians operate.[21] From 1910 through 1970, the legislative structure of opportunities became increasingly restric-tive, largely due to the Congress's strict adherence to the seniority system. Representatives either ran for the Senate within their first four or five terms or hunkered down for the long, predictable journey toward major positions of power in the House.[22] In addition, only senators could realistically hope to seek the presidency from Capitol Hill. Thus, Richard Nixon and John Ken-nedy, members of the House class of '46, soon abandoned the lower chamber for the "presidential incubator" of the Senate.[23]

The opportunity structure has become increasingly fluid, as witnessed by the serious presidential candidacies of House members Morris Udall (D-Ariz.), in 1976, Jack Kemp (R-N.Y.) in 1988, and Richard Gephardt in 1988.

Both Kemp and Gephardt have passed up attractive (if difficult) Senate races to mount presidential bids. In a related vein, such House members as Paul Simon and Tim Wirth abandoned powerful subcommittee chairmanships to seek Senate seats. This exemplifies a kind of undifferentiated ambition that may steer a politician toward both insider openings, such as party and committee slots, and the obvious outside targets for advancement of the Senate and the presidency.

Political Change and National Institutions

At the heart of political change is a set of two to three thousand national politicians who must react to new technologies, altered power alignments, and shifting voting coalitions. Given the constitutional requirement that all House members and a third of the Senate must face the electorate every two years, the Congress is, almost by definition, especially responsive to changes in the society at large.[24] Such responsiveness does not always provide for happy or successful solutions to difficult policy problems, but few serious issues escape congressional scrutiny and action—regardless of how (or if) the legislature eventually chooses to act.

Within the complexity of the Congress and its political environment, the long-term impact of most off-year congressional elections—no matter how substantial the immediate results—is extremely limited. Even the 1946 Republican sweep was little more than a blip in the post-1933 congressional dominance by Democrats. The 1974 elections, however, constitute a major exception to this generalization.

The politics and results of the 1974 congressional elections represent the intersection of three major dimensions of political change. First were broad, secular trends that came to a head in the aftermath of the Vietnam War and Watergate. The political system had served the United States well neither internationally nor domestically, and although the sources of discontent ran deeper than just these two specific issues, the war and the ethical implications of the Watergate affair posed serious questions for all national politicians.[25] Questions about inflation, energy policy, the environment, and the overall role of government also demanded responses, regardless of who was elected in 1974. In addition, the public expressed very little faith in the ability of any political institution—particularly the Congress—to generate effective solutions to increasingly complex policy problems.[26]

Perhaps more immediately significant to members of Congress was the second dimension of change—the internal legislative developments of the 1969–75 period. The class of '74 entered a Congress dramatically different from the institution that a handful of senior party and committee leaders had dominated for the previous half century. Major procedural changes were in place by the mid-1970s entrance of the post-Watergate class.[27]

Finally, wholesale change rarely occurs in politics without substantial turnover—new faces who can infuse an institution with new ideas, different voting coalitions, and, in some cases, a profound sense of fear.[28] Many committed, careerist politicians, including veteran state legislators like California's

Waxman and Illinois's Simon, first won national office in 1974, but such professionals were the exception, not the rule, among the newly elected officials. To the contrary, it was the large proportion of amateurs and reformers that best characterizes this group.[29] While a Waxman or a Simon could bring the perspective of considerable governmental experience to his new job, a majority of 1974 entrants possessed no such mediating background. For them, electoral and legislative politics required extensive on-the-job training. In fact, even after more than a decade of congressional service, many members of the class of '74 continue to reject the idea that they are "professional politicians." . . .

A New Political Style

Beginning with the class of '74, a new generation of leaders rushed to the fore of American politics and brought with them a new way of doing business. In the late 1980s these individuals have come to shape the political landscape, for better or worse. They have established an issue-oriented, publicity-conscious style that differs dramatically from that produced within the seniority-dominated Congress of the 1950s. This style encourages politicians to reach out to national constituencies from a succession of legislative positions that range from subcommittees to party leadership slots and informal caucus chairs. The central elements of this new style include expertise and the willingness to work hard, often at the expense of comity, collegiality, and compromise.[30]

These traits—expertise and hard work—allowed post-1974 legislators to pursue the key proximate goals of (1) obtaining publicity; (2) setting the policy agenda; (3) participating fully within the Congress; and (4) establishing large enterprises that move well beyond personal office staff. These goals can be achieved by virtually all members of Congress, and they can provide some sense of achievement even if full-blown legislative victories are not forthcoming. Indeed, these proximate goals relate directly to the overarching objectives of most members of Congress: advancement, good policy, internal power, and reelection.[31] Unfortunately, the goal of producing good policy often becomes an orphan on Capitol Hill. The proximate goals are more easily translated into advancement, power, and reelection than they are into policy achievements. The jury remains out on whether a Congress of policy entrepreneurs can temper its members' independence with enough teamwork to produce coherent policies. So far, the outlook is far from promising.

Whatever happens, the Watergate babies and their colleagues have stood center stage since the 1970s. Given their number, relative youth, and talents, they will continue to shape the nature of national politics well into the next century.

Notes

1. "Washington Talk," *New York Times*, August 8, 1986, p. A18.
2. Alan Ehrenhalt, ed., *Politics in America: The 100th Congress* (Washington, D.C.: CQ Press, 1987), pp. 1279, 231.

3. Christopher J. Matthews, "The Old Breed Strikes Back," *New Republic*, March 2, 1987, p. 21.
4. Diane Granat, "Whatever Happened to the Watergate Babies?" *Congressional Quarterly Weekly Report*, March 3, 1984, pp. 498–505.
5. See Eric Uslaner and M. Margaret Conway, "The Responsible Congressional Electorate: Watergate, the Economy, and Vote Choice in 1974," *American Political Science Review* 79 (September 1985): 788–803.
6. Martin Tolchin, "Young Democrats on Rise in House," *New York Times*, November 4, 1981, p. A24.
7. Thomas P. O'Neill, *Man of the House* (New York: Random House, 1987), p. 284.
8. Quoted in Kirk Victor, "New Kids on the Block," *National Journal*, October 31, 1987, p. 2727.
9. See Burdett A. Loomis, "The Congressional Office as Small (?) Business," *Publius* 9 (Summer 1979): 55; see also Steven H. Schiff and Steven S. Smith, "Generational Change and the Allocation of Staff in the U.S. Congress," *Legislative Studies Quarterly* 8 (August 1983): 465.
10. Granat, "Whatever Happened?" p. 503.
11. Ibid., p. 498.
12. David Broder, "Democratic Illusion on Old Guard Seems Ready to Shatter," Lawrence (Kans.) *Journal-World*, March 24, 1985, p. A4.
13. See Robert Salisbury and Kenneth Shepsle, "U.S. Congressman as Enterprise," *Legislative Studies Quarterly* 6 (November 1981): 559–76.
14. John Kingdon, *Agendas, Alternatives, and Public Policies* (Boston: Little, Brown, 1984), p. 192; see also Robert Eyestone, *From Social Issues to Public Policy* (New York: John Wiley & Sons, 1978), p. 89.
15. Paul Simon, *The Tongue-Tied American* (New York: Continuum, 1980), p. 178.
16. Kingdon, *Agendas, Alternatives*, p. 90.
17. Barbara Sinclair, "Senate Norms, Senate Styles, and Senate Influence," paper presented at the annual meeting of the American Political Science Association, Washington, D.C., August 28–31, 1986, p. 29.
18. Salisbury and Shepsle, "U.S. Congressman as Enterprise," 559.
19. Jacob Epstein, *Ambition: The Secret Passion* (New York: E. P. Dutton, 1980), p. 1.
20. Ibid., p. 3.
21. See Joseph Schlesinger, *Ambition and Politics* (Chicago: Rand McNally, 1966).
22. David T. Canon and David J. Sousa, "Realigning Elections and Political Career Structures in the U.S. Congress," paper presented at the annual meeting of the American Political Science Association, Chicago, September 3–6, 1987.
23. Robert L. Peabody, Norman J. Ornstein, and David W. Rohde, "The United States Senate as a Presidential Incubator: Many Are Called but Few Are Chosen," *Political Science Quarterly* 91 (Summer 1976): 237–58.
24. See Heinz Eulau and Paul Karps, "The Puzzle of Representation: Specifying the Components of Responsiveness," *Legislative Studies Quarterly* 2 (August 1977): 233–54.
25. See generally James L. Sundquist, *The Decline and Resurgence of Congress* (Washington, D.C.: Brookings Institution, 1981).
26. Seymour Martin Lipset and William Schneider, *The Confidence Gap* (New York: Free Press, 1983), pp. 45–50.
27. See Leroy Rieselbach, *Congressional Reform* (Washington, D.C.: CQ Press, 1986).
28. See David Brady, "Congressional Party Realignment and Transformations of Public Policy in Three Realignment Eras," *American Journal of Political Science* 26 (May 1982): 333–60, among other works by Brady.

29. Eric Uslaner, "Policy Entrepreneurs and Amateur Democrats in the House of Representatives: Toward a More Party-Oriented Congress?" in *Congressional Reform*, ed. Leroy Rieselbach (Lexington, Mass.: Lexington Books, 1978), pp. 105–16.

30. Burdett A. Loomis, "The 'Me Decade' and the Changing Context of House Leadership," in *Understanding Congressional Leadership*, ed. Frank Mackaman (Washington, D.C.: CQ Press, 1982), p. 161; on comity, see Eric M. Uslaner, "The Decline of Comity in Congress," paper presented at the annual meeting of the Midwest Political Science Association, Chicago, April 9–11, 1987.

31. Richard F. Fenno, Jr., *Congressmen in Committees* (Boston: Little, Brown, 1973), pp. 1–14.

54 / Power in the Reform and Post-Reform House

Lawrence D. Dodd
Bruce I. Oppenheimer

In the post-Watergate, reform-minded era of the middle and late 1970s, Congress (and particularly the House of Representatives) underwent what many experts have called a "revolution" of change. The reforms had the intended effect of reducing the power of committee chairs and decentralizing the power of committees more generally. Lawrence Dodd and Bruce Oppenheimer review those reforms and their impact, but also argue that by the late 1980s the House was entering a new period marked by more centralized leadership within both the party apparatus and a new "committee oligarchy."

The 1980s confronted the House of Representatives with a dilemma. With the landslide victories of Ronald Reagan in 1980 and 1984, the Democratic House majority faced a president of the opposite party and a Republican Senate for six of Reagan's eight years in office. The House was the center of "loyal opposition" to the government and the institution most likely to provide visible leadership to opposition forces. But the members of the House had spent the previous decade instituting a highly dispersed system of subcommittee power, a system designed to provide specialized decision making rather than strong policy leadership. Thus, the dilemma: how could the House Democratic majority play a strong role in national governance despite Reagan and the subcommittee system.

The response to this dilemma, we argue, has been the consolidation of institutional power in a new House oligarchy composed of the majority party leadership and members of a few elite committees. This solution emerged partly through accident and partly through conscious efforts of party members. This essay describes and assesses the development of the new power structure, starting with a discussion of membership change and rules reforms over the past twenty years.

Membership Change

From 1971 to 1981 the House experienced significant membership turnover. The percentage of House "careerists," members serving in their tenth or greater term, declined from a record high of 20 percent at the start of the 92d Congress to 11 percent at the start of the 97th.[1] Naturally, there was a corresponding increase in junior members, those with three or fewer terms.... Their numbers grew from 150 in the 92d Congress to a high of 214 in the 96th.[2] That trend has been reversed. At the start of the 100th Congress, careerists numbered 69 (16 percent of the membership) and junior members were down to 159 (37 percent of the membership).

Why Has the Trend Reversed? The obvious reason for the change in the seniority trend in the House can be seen in the number of first-term members entering the House. The 1984 and 1986 elections, respectively, produced only thirty-nine and forty-eight new House members. By comparison, the previous five elections had resulted in an average of seventy-six freshmen. The two factors contributing to this low number of first-term members were few retirements and high rates of incumbent reelection. After six elections in which an average of more than forty-two members voluntarily retired from the House, the average from 1984 and 1986 dropped to thirty, about the same level the House experienced from 1946 to 1970. Although many of the conditions used to explain the high retirement levels in the late 1970s are still present, fewer members are choosing to leave.[3] In 1988 only twenty-three members of the 100th House are retiring.

Many of those who leave the House seek another office, and with some success. Of the eighty-three House members who retired in 1984, 1986, and 1988, forty-seven did so to run for another office, usually the U.S. Senate. At the start of the 100th Congress, eighteen of the thirty-six senators first elected since November 1980 had come directly from serving in the House. By comparison, only eighteen of the sixty-four senators first elected before November 1980 came directly from the House.

The high rate of incumbent reelection has had an even more dramatic effect than the low number of retirements on the House turnover rate. In the 1984 and 1986 elections combined, only twenty-seven incumbents were defeated in a primary or general election. Of those incumbents seeking reelection in 1986, a record high 98 percent were successful.[4] With neither a high number of retirements as in the late 1970s nor a sizable number of incumbents defeated as in the early 1980s, House membership appears to be entering a new phase of careerism....

With the decline in turnover, the trend toward a younger, more diverse House membership has been reversed. At the start of the 98th Congress, the average age of a House member was 45.5 years, a post-World War II low. By the start of the 100th Congress, the average age had risen to 50.7 years. Growth in the number of women and blacks in the House has slowed. The number of women House members in the 100th Congress, twenty-three, is only one more than the total for the 98th and 99th Congresses; and the number of black members in the 100th Congress—twenty-two—is only two more than the 98th and 99th. Without membership turnover, the opportunity for further diversification of the House is limited. . . .*

Democratic Party Control Continues   It is not surprising that low membership turnover means the continuation of a Democratic party majority in the House. Even with the Reagan landslide victories and with six years of holding a Senate majority, the Republicans did not come close to capturing the House. At the start of the 100th Congress the Democrats held 258 seats, slightly more than the mean number of seats they have held since the era of Democratic House control stabilized in the 1930s.[5]

Rules and Procedures

Because the House is a much larger institution than the Senate, it must rely more heavily on formal rules and explicit procedures than on norms. Norms such as reciprocity, courtesy, hard work, expertise, and the most hallowed of all, seniority, exist in the House.[6] But the rules of party caucuses, of committees, and the rules of the House itself are the primary guides to member behavior and the centers of contention in power struggles. In the early to mid-1970s, the period of increased turnover, the rules were subjected to their most extensive restructuring in sixty years, altering the formal power structure of the House in dramatic ways.

House Reforms   The reform movement of the 1970s really began in the late 1950s with the creation of the Democratic Study Group (DSG), an organization committed to liberal legislation and liberal control of the House.[7] Throughout the 1960s the group pushed for changes in House procedures and party practice. Liberals' efforts in the 1960s to bring about formal changes in House rules resulted in the 1970 Legislative Reorganization Act. That measure, passed by a coalition of House Republicans and liberal Democrats, liberalized and formalized parliamentary procedure in committees and on the floor of the House.

During the late 1960s, just when these formal rules changes were approaching ratification, liberal Democrats developed a new strategy. They shifted their attention to reform of the House Democratic party. In January 1969 the Democratic Caucus, which had been dormant for most of the century, was revitalized by the passage of a rule stating that a caucus meeting could be held each month if fifty members demanded the meeting in writing. Using the party caucus, liberals throughout the early 1970s pushed for the

*Substantial turnover has occurred since this selection was written, with 110 new members elected to the House in 1992 alone. The elections for the 103rd Congress produced a House membership with 47 women (up from 28) and 38 blacks (up from 25).—*Editor's Note.*

creation of committees to study the House and propose reforms of its structure and procedures.

Three reform committees were formed as a result of Democratic Caucus activity.[8] All were chaired by Julia Butler Hansen, D-Wash., and their proposals became known collectively as the Hansen Committee Reforms. The proposals of Hansen I were debated and passed in January 1971, Hansen II in January 1973, and Hansen III in 1974. Another reform effort initiated by Speaker Carl Albert, D-Okla., was the creation of a Select Committee on Committees headed by Richard Bolling, D-Mo. The Bolling Committee introduced its proposals in 1974, but they were defeated by the House, which chose instead to implement the proposals of Hansen III.[9]

These reform efforts had five particularly important consequences. First, they established a clear procedure for the Democratic Caucus to select committee chairs by secret ballot. This change in the traditional voting procedure provided a way to defeat renominations of incumbent committee chairs and bypass the norm of committee seniority. Second, the reforms increased the number and strength of subcommittees. Third, the House moved to open to the public virtually all committee and subcommittee meetings. Fourth, the reforms increased the power of the Speaker by giving the post considerable control over the referral of legislation. A fifth change, which was not actually part of these caucus reforms but stemmed from the overall reform movement, was the creation in 1974 of a new congressional budget process and a House Budget Committee. But, the defeat of the Bolling Committee provisions restructuring committee jurisdictions left the maze of overlapping committee and subcommittee jurisdictions relatively untouched.

Other reforms of the post-1973 period also were adopted. In the 94th Congress, House Democrats refined the procedure for nominating committee chairs and voted down several incumbents. The caucus also adopted a rule requiring nominees for Appropriations subcommittee chairs to be approved by similar procedures. This rule, which seemed in order because Appropriations subcommittees are in many cases more powerful than other standing committees, was employed in the 95th Congress to deny a subcommittee position to Robert Sikes, D-Fla., who had been reprimanded for financial misconduct. . . .

Trends in Reform The changes in House rules and procedures in the 1970s and 1980s evidence two trends: the decentralization of power within committees and the centralization of authority in the party caucus, the Speaker, and a new budget committee. The move toward centralization continued, although in a less extensive fashion, during the 98th Congress. Frustrated by efforts of minority members to stir up controversy and obstruct House business, the Democratic leaders tightened House rules. The most controversial change was a restriction on appropriations bill riders. (Riders are amendments that are extraneous to the subject matter of a bill.) Conservative members often used riders to force roll call votes on controversial issues, such as school busing and abortion, while avoiding normal legislative procedures in such matters.

The rules changes also increased the procedural authority of the Democratic leadership to avoid other types of nuisance votes. Other changes included efforts to strengthen limits on the number of subcommittees to which members can be assigned and the decision to elect the Democratic whip.

These various reforms demonstrate the significant changes that have occurred in the House during the postwar years. These formal reforms, however, have not been the only forces shaping the structure of committee politics or party leadership.

Committees

The reforms of the 1970s sought to decentralize power in committees and to weaken the power of committee chairs. These reforms proved immediately successful and produced a period of subcommittee government and weak committee chairs, starting in the mid-1970s. By the late 1980s, however, a new sort of committee politics was emerging, a centralized committee oligarchy that reversed the decentralization of the 1970s. The rise of this new committee oligarchy resulted from the Reagan presidency, particularly the effect of large deficits and tight spending. In the area of committee politics, as will be shown in the area of party leadership, an environment of scarcity tends to produce centralized leadership, regardless of formal rules and procedures.

Committee Decentralization   The effort to create committee decentralization grew out of the historic domination of the House by approximately twenty committee chairs. The era of committee government had begun in the 1920s and was characterized by brokerage politics: committee chairs, usually conservative, attempted, through bargaining and compromise, to aggregate the numerous competing policy interests within their committees' jurisdiction.[10] As liberals began to dominate the Democratic party in the House during the 1950s and 1960s, opposition to the existing structure of committee government escalated.

Aside from ideology, the opposition was fueled by other pressures. In particular, the increase in the number and complexity of federal concerns created the need for higher levels of legislative specialization, putting considerable pressure on the existing system and necessitating more meetings and investigations than could be handled by the standing committees. As reformers in the 1950s and 1960s looked for ways to deal with the workload, they strengthened the subcommittees. Their efforts resulted in the reforms of the 1970s, which had two major dimensions: the rise of subcommittee government and the decline of committee chairs.

Subcommittee government means that the basic responsibility for most legislative activity (hearings, debates, legislative mark-ups) occurs, not at a meeting of an entire standing committee, but at a meeting of a smaller subcommittee of the standing committee.[11] The decisions of the subcommittee are viewed as authoritative decisions, which are altered by the standing committee only when the subcommittee is seriously divided or when its decisions are considered unrepresentative of the full committee.

A measure of subcommittee influence is the growth in their number and staff. At the start of the 84th Congress (1955–1956), when the Democrats began their current streak as the majority party in the House, there were 83 standing subcommittees in the House; the 98th Congress had 135. Moreover, the chair and ranking minority members of each subcommittee were entitled to appoint at least one professional staff member. By comparison, in the 86th Congress, the first time the *Congressional Staff Directory* was published, only 57 of the 113 subcommittees had their own staffs.

With the rise of subcommittee government in the 1970s, basic responsibility shifted from approximately 20 standing committees to about 160 committees and subcommittees.[12] In the process, the *power of committee chairs* declined. Formal change in the power of committee chairs came in 1973 when the caucus passed rules that deprived them of their most potent weapon: their invulnerability to removal. The changes in the procedures and traditions surrounding the election of committee chairs, when combined with the other reforms of the early 1970s and the removal of three sitting chairmen in 1975, clearly altered their status and authority. The chairs lost the right to determine the number, size, and majority party membership of subcommittees. They lost the power to appoint subcommittee chairs, to control referral of legislation to subcommittees, or to prevent their committees from meeting. Finally, as a result of the growth of subcommittee activity, many were forced to defer to their subcommittee chairs in the management of legislation on the House floor.

The emergence of subcommittee government, together with the decline of committee chairs, altered considerably the character of House decision making.[13] It brought more members into the policy process, opened the possibility of policy innovation by a wider range of members, and probably increased legislative expertise in the House. But subcommittee government had its cost as well.

Most significantly, subcommittee government created a crisis of interest aggregation. It largely removed committees as arenas in which interests would be compromised, brokered, and mediated; and it led to increased dominance of committee decision making by clientele groups, to narrowly focused policy leadership, and to confusion in policy jurisdictions. These problems were not necessarily unmanageable; strong party leadership, for example, could have mitigated them. But by the early 1980s it was clear that the committee reforms of the 1970s had generated their own set of problems that would eventually need to be rectified.[14] Just as these problems were becoming clear, however, the structure of committee decision making again started to change, not as a result of conscious planning and rules reform by House members, but as a result of contextual change.

The Rise of a New Committee Oligarchy   Committee decentralization and subcommittee government grew out of the vast expansion of governmental services that occurred in the 1950s and 1960s. An activist government required many specialized working groups to investigate, legislate, and oversee new and expanded programs. This need, together with career ambitions of junior legislators and the desire to break the power of conservative chairs, fueled the committee reforms of the 1970s. Just as subcommittee government was becoming firmly entrenched, the nation elected Ronald Reagan. The president pushed through giant tax cuts without a concomitant reduction in spending, and the country suddenly faced massive federal deficits, which blocked new programs and new spending. Seemingly overnight, the rationale for subcommittee government was gone: without money to spend, there was less need for a highly specialized system of subcommittees.

Instead of the extensive legislative agenda of the past, the House moved to what many members refer to as the "four bill" system.[15] In an average year there may be only four important domestic legislative vehicles—the budget resolution, continuing appropriations, supplemental appropriations, and the reconciliation package of spending cuts that the budget dictates. A fifth bill to raise the federal debt limit is sometimes needed. Members who can influence one of these "must pass" bills are important players in the House; the rest are largely spectators. The result is a new *committee oligarchy* different from committee government earlier in the century. In the earlier system, power was vested in seniority, and the chairs of the standing committees were the oligarchs. In the new system, power is concentrated not in the chairs of all committees, but in the membership of a few elite committees, primarily those dealing with money.

The elite committees certainly include Appropriations. Its power derives from its role in drafting the continuing resolution, the bill that funds all programs for which regular appropriations bills have not passed when the new fiscal year begins October 1. Because so few money bills clear Congress by the deadline, the continuing resolution is essentially a budget. It is all but certain of presidential approval and so massive that there is little chance to question any item placed on it by an Appropriations member. Members of less fortunate committees, even very senior members, must persuade Appropriations members of whatever rank to help them out. In this sense being a junior Appropriations Committee member can be more significant than being a subcommittee chair on an authorization committee.

Ways and Means is also an elite committee in the new oligarchy, partly because of its role in writing tax bills and partly because of its jurisdiction over "must pass" federal debt ceiling legislation—a vehicle for scores of legislative initiatives that might not pass on their own. Ways and Means also plays a significant role in the reconciliation process because of its jurisdiction over hundreds of billions of dollars in spending for health, Social Security, and other social need categories. This jurisdiction gives it leverage in the reconciliation process over reductions in these areas; in making the cuts, it can reshape the programs.

Aside from Appropriations and Ways and Means, several other committees deserve consideration as part of the oligarchy. One is House Energy and Commerce, the one authorization committee that continues to play a strong policy role in the 1980s. Its influence is a testament to its broad jurisdiction, which touches major regulatory agencies, nuclear energy, toxic waste, health research, Medicaid and Medicare, railroad retirement, telecommunications, tourism, and commerce. Another committee that is part of the new oligarchy is Budget, which oversees the preparation of the congressional budget resolutions and the reconciliation process. The power that membership on this committee bestows does not stem from a member's influence over the immediate content of legislation; rather it comes from potential influence on the debate over the nation's long-term policy agenda. The final member of the oligarchy is the Rules Committee, where every major bill must stop before going to the House floor. Its responsibility is to draft ground rules for floor debate on bills, which allows it to block legislation, set the parameters of debate, limit or bar amendments, and, therefore, to affect the ultimate content of legislation.[16]

Another influential committee, although not in the same league as the committee oligarchs, is Armed Services. This committee regulates the debate on the defense budget, which spends more than sixty cents of every discretionary federal dollar. The importance of Armed Services was demonstrated by the recent dispute over the selection of its chair, which included the 1985 removal of Melvin Price, D-Ill., from the chair and the strong challenge in 1987 to Les Aspin, D-Wis., the sitting chair, by Marvin Leath, D-Texas. This contentiousness would seem to reflect not just personal jockeying for power but the importance that members attach to Armed Services—concerns so strong that members were willing to take part in an extensive reconsideration of a sitting chair.[17]

Currently, no such importance attaches to the other authorizing committees. In principle, these committees—the vast number of standing committees that draft legislation to create programs or alter them— should be the heart of the policy process in Congress. Yet, according to a report by House Republicans, these committees "are rapidly approaching irrelevance— squeezed out by the budget and appropriations processes, and caught up in jurisdictional infighting and subcommittee strangulation."[18] The problems associated with committee decentralization and with budget limitations have crippled these committees: there is little discretionary money to fund new programs, and any authorization, particularly liberal ones, faced a Reagan veto threat. In addition, the committees are constrained by jurisdictional conflicts among their subcommittees and with other committees. The new oligarchy, ironically, addresses some of the problems of interest aggregation that arose with committee decentralization, providing fairly centralized consideration of a broad range of policy concerns. But, for the average member, the system is frustrating.

Part of members' frustration comes from the difficulty they find in explaining their powerlessness to their constituents. During the period of committee government most of them could argue that the seniority system and the power of committee chairs made it difficult for them to accomplish their goals. With the demise of committee government, that explanation no longer works. An honest explanation of their powerlessness would "involve parliamentary distinctions and power relationships so complex that few members want to attempt it."[19] Members are hard pressed to make constituents aware of the reality of their committee work and of their political limitations. Perhaps most frustrating is that there is so little members can do about this new committee oligarchy, as it arose not from new rules but from a new fiscal context.

Consolidating Majority Party Leadership

The rise of a new oligarchy in the House means the consolidation of considerable power in the majority party leadership. Unlike the development of the committee oligarchy, the power of the leadership is grounded solidly in the rules reforms of the 1970s. Ironically, it took fiscal austerity and the Reagan presidency for the majority party leaders to use fully the powers given them by the reforms. While the Reagan revolution undercut the subcommittee reforms, it breathed life into the powers of the Speaker and party leadership.[20]

The Party Caucus   The reform process of the early 1970s occurred largely through the efforts of the Democratic Caucus, the organization of all House Democrats. During this period the Democrats expanded the powers of their caucus, particularly its power to approve the selection of committee chairs. Democrats also began to use the caucus to debate policy positions and to nurture personal careers. The activism of the caucus led to cries from some Republicans and conservative Democrats that "King Caucus" was running the House and overriding the wishes of its total membership. These dissidents called for opening meetings of the caucus in the hope that this would cripple its effectiveness.

The eventual opening of the caucus, together with the election of a Democratic president, did reduce its effectiveness in the mid- to late 1970s. The presidency of Jimmy Carter in particular defused the activism of the caucus by providing House Democrats with leadership and a program to support without extensive debate. The party caucus fell into disuse. Reagan's election confronted the Democrats with a Republican president and a conservative legislative program. In response, the caucus decided to meet again in closed session and to reclaim its position as the center of party debate. The caucus was successful enough for one of its chairmen, Richard Gephardt of Missouri, to use this post to launch his 1988 presidential race.

The long-term fate of the caucus is uncertain. So far it appears strong only when the opposite party controls the White House and when debates are held in private. Because of its size, the caucus may not be the best forum for handling strategic problems or making delicate party decisions. The caucus' Steering and Policy Committee may be the best arena for collective party leadership, and the Speaker remains the natural spokesperson for the party.

The Speaker   Throughout most of the twentieth century, parties in the House have been unwilling to invest power in their party leaders.[21] This reticence stems from early in the century when Speaker "Uncle Joe" Cannon, R-Ill., used the considerable authority of the speakership to dominate the House. The 1910 insurgency against Cannon stripped the speakership of many of its major powers, including control over committee appointments, the Rules Committee, private and minor House business, the Special Calendar, and the party caucus. The rules changes also limited the Speaker's discretionary parliamentary prerogatives. After Cannon's downfall and a short flirtation with party caucus government, the House turned to committee government and reliance on the seniority rule.

Efforts to revitalize the speakership began in the early 1970s when the House majority party, the Democrats, needed strong leadership and a more coherent strategy to thwart the efforts by the Republican president, Richard Nixon, to dismantle the Democratic Great Society. The move toward a stronger speakership took several years, with major reform efforts occurring in 1973 and 1975. These reforms activated the long dormant Steering and Policy Committee, gave it the power of the Committee on Committees (that is, the power to nominate committee members and committee chairs), and made the Speaker its chair, with the authority to select a number of committee members. In addition, the Speaker was also given the power to nominate the chair and Democratic members of the House Rules Committee, thus bringing that committee more clearly into the control of the Speaker and the party. These developments meant that, for the first time in decades, a Democratic Speaker had a direct and significant role in committee nominations and the nominations of committee chairs, with total control of the Rules nominations. Members of the party seeking committee positions or leadership roles had far more reason to listen to and follow the Speaker than in the past because the office, perhaps more than any other, is critical to successful candidacies.[22]

Other reforms likewise strengthened the Speaker. First, increases in the financial and staff resources of the party whip office and in the number of whips appointed by the party leadership resulted in a stronger, more active whip system to assist the leadership in efforts to pass legislation.[23] Second, the Speaker regained some of the ground lost by Cannon concerning control over the referral of bills. Third, the creation of the new budget process provided mechanisms through which a skillful party leadership could control it and coordinate budget making by House committees.

. . .The sum of the changes thus constitutes a true resurgence of the speakership and, although a move constrained by the Subcommittee Bill of Rights and other rules changes that protect members' rights within committees and subcommittees, a move back toward the power enjoyed by Cannon. . . .

The Majority Leader and Whip   The two other leadership positions within the majority party—and the Speaker's principal support team—are the majority leader and the whip. The majority leader is the party's point man on the floor of the House, ensuring that the party's daily legislative program flows smoothly while the Speaker presides over House deliberations. The majority leader also joins the Speaker in setting the legislative schedule and serving as party spokesperson. The majority whip is responsible for surveying party members on their policy positions and rounding up votes to pass party legislation. . . .

[Tony] Coelho [the first whip elected by the Caucus in 1986] had five serious rivals for the post. The liveliness of the contest indicates not only that members see the whip position as a route to the speakership but also that House leadership races have become marathons, with steering committees, campaign managers, and well-funded political action committees (PACs). This modern whip system is larger than that of the earlier twentieth century. The office Coelho heads is a large intelligence-gathering operation, a four-tier system that includes a chief deputy whip, seven deputy whips, more than thirty at-large whips, and more than twenty assistant whips. The expansion reflects both the growing independence of House members and the pressure on House Democrats to find a vote-gathering device that could offset the early successes of the Reagan administration. . . .

Conclusion

Since the early 1970s the House of Representatives has proven to be a remarkably fluid institution. Buoyed by an infusion of younger legislators dedicated to reform, the House overthrew a system of committee government that had dominated it for most of a century. In its place the members instituted a highly dispersed system of power in which subcommittees, assisted by the party leadership, were the emerging force. But in the 1980s, in response to the nation's altered fiscal and political environment, the role of subcommittees declined, and power became concentrated in a small number of committee oligarchs—particularly the money committees—and in a more assertive party leadership. By the late 1980s a number of senior, experienced legislators, many of whom had worked to pass the reforms of the 1970s, found little opportunity for political activism. As the 100th Congress drew to a close, power within the House was consolidated in a more centralized and concentrated manner than at any time since the days of Joseph Cannon.

Will the system of consolidated power last? The return to low membership turnover would suggest that the days of committee and party oligarchs are numbered: the increase in House careerists—all of whom want to exercise real policy-making power within their subcommittees and committees—should produce many frustrated legislators trying to reclaim their policy-making prerogatives. Pressure toward power dispersion is building up in the House, with the backing of House rules and procedures.

The power structure of the House, however, is not determined solely by its rules and procedures, the career interests of its members, or turnover patterns. The fiscal condition of the federal government, united versus divided party control of government, the character of the nation's policy agenda—these and related factors also determine the power arrangements within Congress. These factors are exceedingly difficult to predict. No one in the early to mid-1970s anticipated the Reagan tax cuts or massive federal deficits, but these developments probably had as much influence on power distribution in the 1980s as the new House organizational rules.

In the face of political and fiscal uncertainties, we can only suggest some alternative scenarios for the House. We expect the system of concentrated power to persist under conditions of continued fiscal scarcity and divided government. Even then, however, low turnover and high careerism could generate growing pressure for power distribution. Should fiscal pressures ease during a period of united government—and perhaps even in a period of divided government—the House could turn back toward subcommittee government and a significant but somewhat less powerful party leadership. United government and continued fiscal austerity—with the Democrats in power in the White House and Congress but with little new money to spend—would create an interesting new dilemma. Such a development would probably undercut the national visibility of the House party leadership, with a Democratic president replacing the Speaker as the party's visible policy agenda setter; it could also give renewed stimulus to subcommittee policy makers anxious to pursue a Democratic policy agenda. Yet, an aggressive Democratic party, constrained by deficits but committed to social spending, also might continue to work through the money committees to find the fiscal strategies to implement its domestic agenda, thereby continuing a degree of oligarchic control in the House.

Each of these scenarios is plausible, suggesting that the power arrangements of the modern House are subject to some very wide swings. Over the past decade, we have seen one of the most decentralized Houses of the twentieth century evolve into perhaps the most centralized power arrangement of the past seventy years. It seems possible that this centralized House might, before the next century, revert to a highly decentralized institution.

In sum, power in the House has been consolidated in a far more concentrated manner than would have seemed possible a decade ago, but there is no concomitant sense that power arrangements have become institutionalized—that a new governing system analogous to committee government has solidified. . . .

Notes

1. Charles S. Bullock III, "House Careerists: Changing Patterns of Longevity and Attrition," *American Political Science Review* 66 (1972): 1295–1305. Bullock's operational definition of a House careerist is a member elected to ten or more terms.
2. Norman Ornstein, Thomas Mann, and Michael Malbin, *Vital Statistics on Congress, 1987–1988* (Washington, D.C.: Congressional Quarterly, 1987), 17–18.
3. For an analysis of retirements, see Joseph Cooper and William West, "The Congressional Career in the 1970s," in *Congress Reconsidered*, 2d ed., ed. Lawrence C. Dodd and Bruce I. Oppenheimer (Washington, D.C.: CQ Press, 1981).
4. Ornstein, Mann, and Malbin, *Vital Statistics*, 56.
5. Bruce I. Oppenheimer, James A. Stimson, and Richard W. Waterman, "Interpreting U.S. Congressional Elections: The Exposure Thesis," *Legislative Studies Quarterly* 11 (May 1986): 227–248.

6. See Herbert Asher, "The Learning of Legislative Norms," *American Political Science Review* 67 (1973): 499–513.

7. See Mark F. Feber, "The Formation of the Democratic Study Group," in *Congressional Behavior*, ed. Nelson W. Polsby (New York: Random House, 1971), 249–267; and Arthur G. Stevens, Jr., Arthur H. Miller, and Thomas E. Mann, "Mobilization of Liberal Strength in the House, 1955–1970: The Democratic Study Group," *American Political Science Review* 68 (1974): 667–681. For a discussion of the reform efforts in the House and the initial role of the DSG, see Norman J. Ornstein and David W. Rohde, "Congressional Reform and Political Parties in the U.S. House of Representatives," in *Parties and Elections in an Anti-Party Age*, ed. Jeff Fishel (Bloomington: Indiana University Press, 1976).

8. For a more extensive chronological discussion of the reform processes, see *Congress Reconsidered*, 1st ed., ed. Lawrence C. Dodd and Bruce I. Oppenheimer (New York: Praeger Publishers, 1977), 27–32; see also Norman J. Ornstein and David W. Rohde, "Congressional Reform and Political Parties in the U.S. House of Representatives," in *Congress Reconsidered*, 1st ed.; and Leroy N. Rieselbach, *Congressional Reform in the Seventies* (Morristown, N.J.: General Learning Press, 1977).

9. For an excellent discussion of the Bolling Committee, see Roger H. Davidson, "Two Avenues of Change: House and Senate Committee Reorganization," in *Congress Reconsidered*, 2d ed.; and Roger H. Davidson and Walter J. Oleszek, *Congress Against Itself* (Bloomington: Indiana University Press, 1977).

10. See George R. Brown, *The Leadership of Congress* (Indianapolis: Bobbs-Merrill Co., 1922); Richard Bolling, *Power in the House* (New York: Capricorn, 1968); Richard F. Fenno, *Congressmen in Committees* (Boston: Little, Brown, 1973); and the essays by Ralph Huitt in *Congress: Two Decades of Analysis*, ed. Ralph K. Huitt and Robert L. Peabody (New York: Harper and Row, 1965).

11. On the growing importance of subcommittees, see Steven S. Smith and Christopher J. Deering, *Committees in Congress* (Washington, D.C.: CQ Press, 1984), 194–198.

12. David W. Rohde, "Committee Reform in the House of Representatives and the Subcommittee Bill of Rights," *The Annals* 411 (January 1974): 39–47; Norman J. Ornstein, "Causes and Consequences of Congressional Change: Subcommittee Reforms in the House of Representatives, 1970–1973," in *Congress in Change*, ed. Norman J. Ornstein (New York: Praeger Publishers, 1975), 88–114; and Lawrence C. Dodd and George C. Shipley, "Patterns of Committee Surveillance in the House of Representatives" (Paper delivered at the annual meeting of the American Political Science Association, San Francisco, Sept. 2–5, 1975).

13. For case studies that demonstrate the legislative impact of committee change, see Norman J. Ornstein and David W. Rohde, "Shifting Forces, Changing Rules, and Political Outcomes: The Impact of Congressional Change on Four House Committees," in *New Perspectives on the House of Representatives*, ed. Robert L. Peabody and Nelson W. Polsby (Chicago: Rand McNally, 1977). For a discussion of the impact of committee change on legislative oversight, see Lawrence C. Dodd and Richard L. Schott, *Congress and the Administrative State* (New York: John Wiley & Sons, 1979).

14. For a more extensive discussion, see Lawrence C. Dodd and Bruce I. Oppenheimer, "The House in Transition," in *Congress Reconsidered*, 3d ed., ed. Lawrence C. Dodd and Bruce I. Oppenheimer (Washington, D.C.: CQ Press, 1985).

15. *Congressional Quarterly Weekly Report*, Sept. 13, 1986, 2136.

16. Ibid., Aug. 24, 1985, 672; Jan. 3, 1987, 22.

17. Ibid., Jan. 17, 1987, 103; Jan. 24, 1987, 139; Jan. 10, 1987, 83; Jan. 12, 1986, 1564.
18. Ibid., Jan. 3, 1987, 23.
19. Ibid., Sept. 13, 1986, 2136. For the impact of explanation in district politics, see Richard F. Fenno, Jr., *Home Style* (Boston: Little, Brown, 1978).
20. For a discussion of different leadership strategies in the postreform era, see Barbara Sinclair, "Party Leadership and Policy Change" in *Congress and Policy Change*, ed. Gerald C. Wright, Jr., Leroy N. Rieselbach and Lawrence C. Dodd (New York: Agathon Press, 1986).
21. See Joseph Cooper and David W. Brady, "Institutional Context and Leadership Style: The House from Cannon to Rayburn" *American Political Science Review* 75 (1981): 411–425.
22. On the Rules Committee in earlier eras, see James A. Robinson, *The House Rules Committee* (Indianapolis: Bobbs-Merrill, 1963); on the new Rules Committee, see Bruce I. Oppenheimer, "The Rules Committee: New Arm of Leadership in a Decentralized House," *Congress Reconsidered*, 1st ed., 96–116.
23. On the whip system in an earlier era, see Randall B. Ripley, "The Party Whip Organizations in the U.S. House of Representatives," in *New Perspectives on the House of Representatives*, ed. Robert L. Peabody and Nelson W. Polsby (Chicago: Rand McNally, 1969); on the expanded whip system, see Lawrence C. Dodd, "The Expanding Roles of the House Democratic Whip System," *Congressional Studies* 6 (Winter 1979); and Barbara D. Sinclair, *Majority Leadership in the U.S. House of Representatives* (Baltimore: Johns Hopkins University Press, 1983).

CHAPTER FIFTEEN

Presidency

At the time the framers met in Philadelphia, they had recently experienced tyranny by a monarch, followed by an inefficient, ineffective national government with no separate executive at all. Although the exact structure was not determined until the meetings were under way, virtually all of the delegates went to Philadelphia with the intention of creating an executive office, but one whose range of action could be effectively checked by the Congress. After considering various options, they ultimately gave executive authority to a president whose powers they only vaguely defined. Feeling that Congress was being given sufficient powers to check this executive, and knowing that George Washington would certainly be chosen as the first president, they were willing to give him room to maneuver in designing the more specific duties of the office.

The broad outline of presidential authority in Article II has provided ample room for carrying on one of the great continuities in American politics, the debate over exactly how much power presidents can and should exercise. Although countless participants have contributed to the debate since before the Constitution was written, two of the most often cited have been presidents themselves. Theodore Roosevelt, the twenty-sixth president (1901–1909), and William Howard Taft, the twenty-seventh (1909–1913), came from the same party (Republican) but approached executive powers very differently. As former presidents, both expressed their strongly held views in print, and excerpts from their writings are among the readings in this section.

For his part, Roosevelt argued (and acted accordingly) that the president, as "steward" of the people, should "do anything that the needs of the nation demanded unless such action was forbidden by the Constitution or by the laws." Providing contrast to Theodore Roosevelt's view in both theory and behavior, Taft felt just as strongly that "the President can exercise no power which cannot be fairly and reasonably traced to some specific grant of power or justly implied and included within such express grant as proper and necessary to its exercise." Taft's "literalist" view of executive power would confine the presidency; Roosevelt's "stewardship" doctrine would fuel its expansion.

The fact that the majority of American presidents, and most of the recent ones, have thought more like Roosevelt than Taft helps to explain the expansion that has actually occurred in presidential powers, as documented elsewhere in this book (see Chapter Three, "Separation of Powers," especially the selection by Arthur Schlesinger). Of course, others outside the presidency have made the expansion possible. Especially since the 1930s, the "powers" of the presidency have been expanded by laws of Congress and decisions of courts, in addition to the actions of presidents themselves, first in international affairs and then in domestic policy as well.

Although presidents have been given more *powers*, meaning responsibilities, they have not been given coercive *power* to carry them out. Democracy, after all, rests on leadership, not coercive power. And presidential leadership requires bargaining with other institutions, groups, and individuals. The third selection in this chapter deals with the increased difficulties of bargaining in the modern American political system. Bert Rockman notes that this country's political culture and separation-of-powers system have always placed limits on strong leadership, but suggests that the recent breakdown of "strong intermediate organizations," including the political parties and congressional leadership, have made presidential leadership even more difficult by increasing the number and decreasing the influence of those with whom the president would bargain. In the final essay, James David Barber argues that the acceptance of Ronald Reagan's style of leadership, based on a rhetoric of feelings more than facts, was an indicator of the extent to which America had become a "distracted nation."

55 / The Stewardship Doctrine

Theodore Roosevelt

In the following excerpt from his autobiography, former president Theodore Roosevelt discusses his "stewardship" orientation to the presidency, which justifies expansion of the presidential role by presidents themselves, if it is done on behalf of the people's interests and does not violate the Constitution or existing laws.

My view was that every executive officer, and above all every executive officer in high position, was a steward of the people bound actively and affirmatively to do all he could for the people, and not to content himself with the negative merit of keeping his talents undamaged in a napkin. I declined to adopt the view that what was imperatively necessary for the nation could not be done by the president unless he could find some specific authorization to do it. My belief was that it was not only his right but his duty to do anything that the needs of the nation demanded unless such action was forbidden by the Constitution or by the laws. Under this interpretation of executive power I did and caused to be done many things not previously done by the president and the heads of the departments. I did not usurp power, but I did greatly broaden the use of executive power. In other words, I acted for the public welfare, I acted for the common well-being of all our people, whenever and in whatever manner was necessary, unless prevented by direct constitutional or legislative prohibition....

The course I followed, of regarding the executive as subject only to the people, and, under the Constitution, bound to serve the people affirmatively in cases where the Constitution does not explicitly forbid him to render the service, was substantially the course followed by both Andrew Jackson and Abraham Lincoln. Other honorable and well-meaning presidents, such as

James Buchanan, took the opposite and, as it seems to me, narrowly legalistic view that the president is the servant of Congress rather than of the people, and can do nothing, no matter how necessary it be to act, unless the Constitution explicitly commands the action. Most able lawyers who are past middle age take this view, and so do large numbers of well-meaning, respectable citizens. My successor in office took this, the Buchanan, view of the president's powers and duties.

For example, under my administration we found that one of the favorite methods adopted by the men desirous of stealing the public domain was to carry the decision of the secretary of the interior into court. By vigorously opposing such action, and only by so doing, we were able to carry out the policy of properly protecting the public domain. My successor not only took the opposite view, but recommended to Congress the passage of a bill which would have given the courts direct appellate power over the secretary of the interior in these land matters.... Fortunately, Congress declined to pass the bill. Its passage would have been a veritable calamity.

I acted on the theory that the president could at any time in his discretion withdraw from entry any of the public lands of the United States and reserve the same for forestry, for water-power sites, for irrigation, and other public purposes. Without such action it would have been impossible to stop the activity of the land-thieves. No one ventured to test its legality by lawsuit. My successor, however, himself questioned it, and referred the matter to Congress. Again Congress showed its wisdom by passing a law which gave the president the power which he had long exercised, and of which my successor had shorn himself.

Perhaps the sharp difference between what may be called the Lincoln–Jackson and the Buchanan–Taft schools, in their views of the power and duties of the president, may be best illustrated by comparing the attitude of my successor toward his secretary of the interior, Mr. Ballinger, when the latter was accused of gross misconduct in office, with my attitude toward my chiefs of department and other subordinate officers. More than once while I was president my officials were attacked by Congress, generally because these officials did their duty well and fearlessly. In every such case I stood by the official and refused to recognize the right of Congress to interfere with me excepting by impeachment or in other constitutional manner. On the other hand, wherever I found the officer unfit for his position, I promptly removed him, even although the most influential men in Congress fought for his retention. The Jackson–Lincoln view is that a president who is fit to do good work should be able to form his own judgment as to his own subordinates, and, above all, of the subordinates standing highest and in closest and most intimate touch with him. My secretaries and their subordinates were responsible to me, and I accepted the responsibility for all their deeds. As long as they were satisfactory to me I stood by them against every critic or assailant, within or without Congress; and as for getting Congress to make up my mind for me about them, the thought would have been inconceivable to me. My successor took the opposite, or Buchanan, view when he permitted and requested Congress to pass judgment on the charges made against Mr. Ballinger as an executive officer. These charges were made to the president; the president had the facts before him and could get at them at any time, and he alone had power to act if the charges were true. However, he permitted and requested Congress to investigate Mr. Ballinger. The party minority of the committee that investigated him, and one member of the majority, declared that the charges were well-founded and that Mr. Ballinger should be removed. The other members of the majority declared the charges ill-founded. The president abode by the view of the majority. Of course believers in the Jackson–Lincoln theory of the presidency would not be content with this town-meeting majority and minority method of determining by another branch of the government what it seems the especial duty of the president himself to determine for himself in dealing with his own subordinate in his own department.

56 / The Proper Scope of Presidential Powers

William Howard Taft

Writing as a former president, William Howard Taft presents his "literalist" view of presidential powers, which is that presidents are limited to exercising only powers that are clearly granted to the office in the Constitution or in laws of Congress.

The true view of the Executive functions is, as I conceive it, that the President can exercise no power which cannot be fairly and reasonably traced to some specific grant of power or justly implied and included within such express grant as proper and necessary to its exercise. Such specific grant must be either in the Federal Constitution or in an act of Congress passed in pursuance thereof. There is no undefined residuum of power which he can exercise because it seems to him to be in the public interest, and there is nothing in the Neagle case and its definition of a law of the United States, or in other precedents, warranting such an inference. The grants of Executive power are necessarily in general terms in order not to embarrass the Executive within the field of action plainly marked for him, but his jurisdiction must be justified and vindicated by affirmative constitutional or statutory provision, or it does not exist. There have not been wanting, however, eminent men in high public office holding a different view and who have insisted upon the necessity for an undefined residuum of Executive power in the public interest. They have not been confined to the present generation. We may learn this from the complaint of a Virginia statesman, Abel P. Upshur, a strict constructionist of the old school, who succeeded Daniel Webster as Secretary of State under President Tyler. He was aroused by Story's commentaries on the Constitution to write a monograph answering and criticizing them, and in the course of this he comments as follows on the executive power under the Constitution:

> The most defective part of the Constitution beyond all question, is that which related to the Executive Department. It is impossible to read that instrument, without being struck with the loose and unguarded terms in which the powers and duties of the President are pointed out. So far as the legislature is concerned, the limitations of the Constitution, are, perhaps, as precise and strict as they could safely have been made, but in regard to the Executive, the Convention appears to have studiously selected such loose and general expressions, as would enable the President, by implication and construction either to neglect his duties or to enlarge his powers. We have heard it gravely asserted in Congress that whatever power is neither legislative nor judiciary, is of course executive, and, as such, belongs to the President under the Constitution. How far a majority of that body would have sustained a doctrine so monstrous, and so utterly at war with the whole genius of our government, it is impossible to say, but this, at least, we know, that it met with no rebuke from those who supported the particular act of Executive power, in defense of which it was urged. Be this as it may, it is a reproach to the Constitution that the Executive trust is so ill-defined, as to leave any plausible pretense even to the insane zeal of party devotion, for attributing to the President of the United States the powers of a despot, powers which are wholly unknown in any limited monarchy in the world.

The view that he takes as a result of the loose language defining the Executive powers seems exaggerated. But one must agree with him in his condemnation of the view of the Executive power which he says was advanced in Congress. In recent years there has been put forward a similar view by executive officials and to some extent acted on. Men who are not such strict constructionists of the Constitution as Mr. Upshur may well feel real concern if such views are to receive the general acquiescence. Mr. Garfield, when Secretary of the Interior, under Mr. Roosevelt, in his final report to Congress in reference to the power of the Executive over the public domain, said:

> Full power under the Constitution was vested in the Executive Branch of the Government and the extent to which that power may be exercised is governed wholly by the discretion of the Executive unless any specific act has been prohibited either by the Constitution or by legislation.

In pursuance of this principle, Mr. Garfield, under an act for the reclamation of arid land by irrigation, which authorized him to make contracts for irrigation works and incur liability equal to the amount on deposit in the Reclamation Fund, made contracts with associations of settlers by which it was agreed that if these settlers would advance money and work, they might receive certificates from the government engineers of the labor and money furnished by them, and that such certificates might be received in the future in the discharge of their legal obligations to the government for water rent and other things under the statute. It became necessary for the succeeding administration to pass on the validity of these government certificates. They were held by Attorney-General Wickersham to be illegal, on the ground that no authority existed for their issuance. He relied on the Floyd acceptances in 7th Wallace, in which recovery was sought in the Court of Claims on commercial paper in the form of acceptances signed by Mr. Floyd when Secretary of War and delivered to certain contractors. The Court held that they were void because the Secretary of War had no statutory authority to issue them. Mr. Justice Miller, in deciding the case, said:

> The answer which at once suggests itself to one familiar with the structure of our government, in which all power is delegated, and is defined by law, constitutional or statutory is, that to one or both of these sources we must resort in every instance. We have no officers in this government, from the President down to the most subordinate agent, who does not hold office under the law, with prescribed duties and limited authority. And while some of these, as the President, the Legislature, and the judiciary, exercise powers in some sense left to the more general definitions necessarily incident to fundamental law found in the Constitution, the larger portion of them are the creation of statutory law, with duties and powers prescribed and limited by that law.

In the light of this view of the Supreme Court it is interesting to compare the language of Mr. Roosevelt in his "Notes for a Possible Autobiography" on the subject of "Executive Powers," in which he says:

> The most important factor in getting the right spirit in my Administration, next to insistence upon courage, honesty, and a genuine democracy of desire to serve the plain people, was my insistence upon the theory that the executive power was limited only by specific restrictions and prohibitions appearing in the Constitution or imposed by Congress under its constitutional powers. My view was that every Executive officer and above all every Executive officer in high position was a steward of the people bound actively and affirmatively to do all he could for the people and not to content himself with the negative merit of keeping his talents undamaged in a napkin. . . .
> I did not usurp power but I did greatly broaden the use of executive power. In other words, I acted for the common well being of all our people whenever and in whatever measure was necessary, unless prevented by direct constitutional or legislative prohibition. . . .

My judgment is that the view of Mr. Garfield and Mr. Roosevelt, ascribing an undefined residuum of power to the President, is an unsafe doctrine and that it might lead under emergencies to results of an arbitrary character, doing irremediable injustice to private right. The mainspring of such a view is that the Executive is charged with responsibility for the welfare of all the people in a general way, that he is to play the part of a Universal Providence and set all things right, and that anything that in his judgment will help the people he ought to do, unless he is expressly forbidden not to do it. The wide field of action that this would give to the Executive one can hardly limit. It is enough to say that Mr. Roosevelt has expressly stated how far he thought this principle would justify him in going in respect to the coal famine and the Pennsylvania anthracite strike in which he did so much useful work in settling. What was actually done was the result of his activity, his power to influence public opinion and the effect of the prestige of his great office in bringing the parties to the controversy, the mine owners and the strikers, to a legal settlement by arbitration. No one has a higher admiration for the value of what he did there than I have. But if he had failed in this, he says he intended to take action on his theory of the extent of the executive power already stated. . . .

There is little danger to the public weal from the tyranny or reckless character of a President who is not sustained by the people. The absence of popular support will certainly in the course of two years withdraw from him the sympathetic action of at least one House of Congress, and by the control that that House has over appropriations, the Executive arm can be paralyzed, unless he resorts to a coup d'état, which means impeachment, conviction and deposition. The only danger in the action of the Executive under the present limitations and lack of limitation of his powers is when his popularity is such that he can be sure of the support of the electorate and therefore of Congress, and when the majority in the legislative halls respond with alacrity and sycophancy to his will. This condition cannot probably be long continued. We have had Presidents who felt the public pulse with accuracy, who played their parts upon the political stage with histrionic genius and commanded the people almost as if they were an army and the President their Commander-in-Chief. Yet in all these cases, the good sense of the people has ultimately prevailed and no danger has been done to our political structure and the reign of law has continued. In such times when the Executive power seems to be all prevailing, there have always been men in this free and intelligent people of ours, who apparently courting political humiliation and disaster have registered protest against this undue Executive domination and this use of the Executive power and popular support to perpetuate itself.

The cry of Executive domination is often entirely unjustified, as when the President's commanding influence only grows out of a proper cohesion of a party and its recognition of the necessity for political leadership; but the fact that Executive domination is regarded as a useful ground for attack upon a successful administration, even when there is no ground for it, is itself proof of the dependence we may properly place upon the sanity and clear perceptions of the people in avoiding its baneful effects when there is real danger. Even if a vicious precedent is set by the Executive, and injustice done, it does not have the same bad effect that an improper precedent of a court may have, for one President does not consider himself bound by the policies or constitutional views of his predecessors.

The Constitution does give the President wide discretion and great power, and it ought to do so. It calls from him activity and energy to see that within his proper sphere he does what his great responsibilities and opportunities require. He is no figurehead, and it is entirely proper that an energetic and active clear-sighted people, who, when they have work to do, wish it done well, should be willing to rely upon their judgment in selecting their Chief Agent, and having selected him, should entrust to him all the power needed to carry out their governmental purpose, great as it may be.

57 / The Leadership Problem in America

Bert A. Rockman

In the following selection, Bert Rockman suggests that while problems with generating coherent national leadership are not uniquely American, a number of factors have contributed to the greater magnitude of the problem in this country. And while presidents have always found difficulty in leading the nation, the erosion of traditional pillars of support and legitimation have increased the problems. At a time when Americans may be more open to the symbols of presidential leadership, the system has undergone other changes that have made it increasingly difficult to lead.

Generating leadership, policy coherence, and direction in the United States is an especially tall order. Foreign commentators, even those who are admiring, are frequently mystified by just how the society is governed. One comments:

> Most British observers of American government. . . have a real difficulty in adjusting themselves to the huge, sprawling conglomerate that constitutes the governments (in the plural) of the United States. . . .
>
> In the United States government has perpetually to justify itself, to overcome a set of peculiar resistances . . . to maintain . . . its ascendancy over the competing elements in the dynamic life of a diverse and restless people.[1]

American government and American society are both abundantly complex and diverse. One reinforces the diversity of the other. Divided within itself at each level by the separation of powers and divided across levels by federalism, the system is thus fragmented both horizontally and vertically. Lacking a definitive center, but accessible at many points, the system spawns and reinforces a highly diverse set of grassroots movements and interest groups, and thus a highly diverse set of elites. One consequence of this is that whatever problems of leadership exist in the American system, they have little to do with the supply of entrepreneurial leaders. The problem, in fact, may more nearly have to do with their proliferation. Dispersed authority proliferates leaders, both governmental and nongovernmental, because dispersion multiplies both decision-making channels and interests seeking to influence decisions. The multiplication of leaders, however, is inherently inverse to the scope of authority and the writ of influence each possesses.

Issue leadership—that which provokes attention to new issues and new constituencies—is abundant in America, and consistent with an activist (if class biased) public as well as a loosely structured politics. Although such activism is clearly on the upswing in Europe, too, the American political structure is remarkably receptive and open to it. Indeed, one writer, believing that too little attention is expended on these issue leaders while too much is given to the president, warns that:

> One cannot remember any president who provided the vision, who seized the opportunity to be the educator, or who played a significant role as even a consciousness raiser. . . .
> If this is so. . . We shall have to look to those interest group leaders, citizen and social movement leaders and those unreasonable and often unelectable types who dream dreams of a more ideal world.[2]

The problem of special importance confronting governability in the American system, therefore, is not the absence of leaders but the generation of integrated policy making and the provision of mechanisms for enhancing it. The abundance of issue leadership in the United States provides remarkably innovative possibilities for public policy making. It promotes attention to new concerns and widens the scope of debate. Yet, however necessary this diverse leadership stratum is to the circulation of ideas, to the promotion of causes, and to the surfacing of grievances, its great diversity also poses significant challenges to the prospects of imparting direction and integration of policy. Leaders are not lacking in the system, yet *the system* is lacking in leadership, that is, in the capacity to impart and sustain direction.

Although the reins of government are hard to find in America, much less to hold, it is easy to overestimate the tautness with which they are held in other political systems. The problem is not exclusively American in kind, even if in its American version it is *in extremis*—perhaps intended that way. The problem of giving direction to government, however, is universal, and it is illuminating to listen to foreign scholars discussing these difficulties in their own countries. To the American listener, the shock of recognition ought to be, if nothing else, therapeutic.

In the Federal Republic of Germany, for instance, Renate Mayntz reports that in the executive:

> The dominant pattern is one of checks and countervailing powers. The need for consensus building and conflict resolution is correspondingly high; the result can be the neutralization of initiatives and a loss in governmental effectiveness. The pattern of executive leadership in the Federal Republic of Germany seems . . . to make more for a stable than for a very powerful government.[3]

Similarly, in Italy, Sabino Cassese claims that:

> The leadership exercised is more the result of mediation among factions, pressure groups, and parties, than the result of elaboration, promotion, and planning by responsible and expert ministry officials. . . . The Italian system is more suited to reaching agreement about problems as they gradually emerge than to ensuring positive guidance and direction.[4]

And in Norway, according to Johan Olsen:

> The major response to the problems of capacity, understanding, and authority, has been a political-administrative division of labor. . . . Consultation and anticipated reactions are more important forms of coordination than command. . . . The tendency toward specialization and segmentation and the tendency toward consensus and anticipated reactions partly counteract each other [in that] the system is probably more segmented in its behavioral patterns than in the substantive premises that enter into policy-making processes.[5]

Substantive consensus, as this quotation from Olsen's paper suggests, is a powerfully binding glue. It helps to promote a set of role expectations that produce tacit understandings and develop systemwide perspectives among actors otherwise engaged in their specialized tasks. It is a powerful, if not all-compelling, agent for overcoming the parochialism inherent in the specialized tasks that various agencies of government undertake. To turn specialized agendas into commonly shared ones is the great objective of leadership, and the conditions under which this can be done are more uncommon than common. But what is apparent from Olsen's discussion is that this task need not rest upon a command model of leadership, nor upon zealous efforts to exercise authority.

Still, political systems that have been based upon some form of segmentation—the consociational systems of the Low Countries and the corporatist ones of the Scandinavian countries—have not been immune from stalemate and paralysis. The increased difficulties of simply forming governments evidenced in both Belgium and the Netherlands within the past decade give pause to ideas about the discovery of simple formulas for producing governmental effectiveness. The squatters' riots in Amsterdam, for example, lend credence to the notion that the forging of elite consensus may come at the price of alienating those who are distant from the consensus that emerges. And in Sweden, the reputed "utopian" democracy of the 1960s, harsher rumblings have been heard in the 1970s and into the 1980s. Strikes, street disturbances, and increasingly rapid turnover of governments are signs that no simple formula exists for effective government. The relative deterioration in the pace of economic growth of most Western economies has had disquieting effects both in hastening social discontents and in lessening the slack that governments require to deal with problems whose solutions are as yet not visible. Consensus will be more necessary, yet harder to obtain.

The generation of political will, therefore, is not a problem of exclusively American origin. Yet coherent leadership is a topic of constant concern in the American system in part because it defies that which the system was structured to prevent. Not surprisingly, therefore, much attention is paid to the prospects for generating effective political leadership—indeed, it is often a passionate obsession.

Generating Direction

Four sources of the American leadership problem are identified here—culture, institutions, individuals, and intermediaries. Each represents a somewhat different level of analysis, and each also holds different prospects of being remedied.

The first source lies in the cultural resistances that have a longstanding basis in the American past, but which are reinforced by the localism of American politics and often inflamed by the populist rhetoric of its politicians. The culture does not as such diminish the thirst for leaders and inspired leadership, but it fails to generate respect for authority, institutions, and the public realm.

The second source lies in the lack of supporting tools for generating coherence from the center, the remedy for which is usually proposed in the form of British-style party government.

The third source lies in the difficulty of locating and electing from the pool of potential leaders those who can comprehend the system and the limits it imposes, bring knowledge to the substance of governing, and yet push the system to respond to their priorities. In short, from the standpoint of a president's leadership, "the worse the system's characteristics, the more [they need to be] . . . compensated for by his virtuosity."[6] Leaders, in other words, need to be resourceful entrepreneurs.

The fourth source is thought to lie in the breakdown of strong intermediate organizations and a more coherently organized Congress. Their restoration is sometimes offered as a means of regenerating a politics of bargaining and accommodation—a modulated pluralism of elites, each with something to deliver in a bargain. There would be, accordingly, less need for presidents to heed the call to "greatness" and more need for them to be squared with other institutional and organizational elites who, in turn, could provide political support.[7] The democratization of organizations and institutions, the pervasive penetration of mass media, the mobilization of key publics, and the splintering of interests and institutions apparently have eroded the foundations on which such pillars of support and legitimation could rest.

Cultural Resistances   If, as James MacGregor Burns writes, "great leadership requires greater followership,"[8] then the populist roots of the American political culture provide a ready antidote to the emergence of "great leadership." In a seminal essay on the American political culture, the British political scientist, L. J. Sharpe, argues that the American political tradition has paid scant attention to "the importance of functional effectiveness, the public interest, and public trust," and that, to a considerable degree, this results from "the revolutionary tradition from which stems the belief that all authority should derive from the people."[9] Sharpe concludes, in this regard, that these aspects of the American tradition of government are unlikely "to be sympathetic to the idea that government must have some autonomy."[10]

Yet another British social scientist claims that:

> The American liberal tradition is profoundly individualistic and anti-bureaucratic [yet] the effective exercise of public authority depends on a prior capacity to determine the public interest and the maintenance of public respect for government as beneficial: in other words, on a disposition to approve of collective action.[11]

According to still another writer from across the Atlantic, it is the American political class that most keenly promulgates the antistate culture.[12] ... For better or worse, the culture tends to deter the development of professionalism in the practice of politics and especially in the art of government. It encourages the emergence of an elite with a distinctly entrepreneurial and individualistic outlook. American attitudes about government and governing—especially because these attitudes are significantly represented among the elite—may be even more unusual than the distinctiveness of American political institutions.

Beliefs that proclaim government a burden and view politicians and bureaucrats as parasites regardless of its (and their) responsiveness are unlikely to be easily manipulated, and thus are unlikely to be easily remedied. Politicians who degrade political institutions and government itself offer scant hope for providing the adhesion necessary to constitute a political community. Governments may be made and altered (though not easily) by men and women, but societies and the values that radiate from them are shaped and transformed by a chain of historical causes that are mostly beyond manipulation. Rearranging the machinery of government requires prescience, but reconstituting the culture that fuels the machinery may require omnipotence.

Better Tools   Structures, however, can affect culture, and in adherence to this proposition lies both faith in the possibilities of great change and the commitment of would-be constitution makers. One would-be constitution maker argues, for instance, that

> The framers of the American Constitution laid the groundwork for political institutions that fragmented the electorate and multiplied "issues with a disparate local impact." *Attitudes supporting heterogeneity were greatly reinforced.* Small wonder that a welter of local interests should form and become politically entrenched.[13]

To rearrange the machinery of government and alter the structural terms of politics is at the very least to implicitly engage in constitution making. If constitutions are to endure, however, they must be based upon considerations larger than yesterday's symptoms. Constitutional designs need to be based upon what it is like to be out of power as well as to be in power. Giving direction to government inevitably sounds more appetizing when the direction is a preferred one. However crass it may sound, stalemate is a more appealing result when one is in opposition. Constitution making (and thus retooling the machinery) is a demanding task that must reconcile the need to govern with the opportunity to oppose.

Whereas cultural modification might predispose to a general strengthening of authority and to some alteration in the organization of politics, it would not necessarily predispose to any particular governmental form. But ideas about retooling the machinery of government, whether in incremental or comprehensive terms, have tended toward a president-centric orientation to the political system and the society. The American presidency, as much by evolution as by constitutional design, has come to represent the expected fulcrum of leadership—the one source of coherent will in a system that institutionalizes the diversity of wills. With the development of such expectations assuredly comes a craving for tools to enhance central authority commensurately with the rise in expectations. Although a broad range of tools has been proposed, most have focused upon producing party majorities with a stake in presidential programs: in other words, a quasi-parliamentary system with a presidential head.

Nearly forty years ago, in an environment of presidential-congressional cooperation (induced by the crisis of full-scale war), Don Price noted that America was a federation in the process of becoming a nation, and that the American constitutional system, unlike a parliamentary one, was far better equipped to "accommodate the interests of diverse areas and populations in a federal republic."[14] Thirty-seven years later, in less crisis filled but domestically more contentious times, Lloyd Cutler, counsel to a president noted for his legendary political troubles, wrote that the issues confronting government now were ones of an allocative nature which the present system with its multiple veto points could not effectively confront. The pressing need, as he saw it, was to alter the political machinery so as "to form a government."[15] The source for such authority lies in the belief that elections confer a special mandate. For this mandate to be effectively conferred, the electoral (and, thus, representational) process must be simplified so as to reduce the babble of tongues generated by the localized election of officials gathered together in Washington to serve different terms across different institutions. The obvious appeal of quasi-parliamentary government, as put forth by its proponents, is to redirect accountability from institutions to electorates. Instead of institutional checkmating, accountability would flow from electoral decisions. Direct accountability, therefore, presumes the power to enact an agenda and to be judged on it. Such straightforward expectations are inevitably followed by complicating considerations.

The principal complication lies in the assumption that in the United States majority governments could easily be formed under new constitutional conditions. It is not self-evident that the reputed incoherence of the existing parties (usually such reference is to the Democrats) would be easily relieved, Depending upon a good many other factors, either the parties might be large and quite factionalized, or there might be a larger number of smaller parties. The main effect, then, simply might be to alter the places where, and the actors with whom, agreements must be concluded. In any case, one can easily imagine tensions emerging as in Britain between members of Parliament and local party organizations, and between parliamentary and extra-parliamentary parties, or between the inner party elite and the legislative rank and file as in West Germany. Accommodations must be arrived at, and the programs that result are as much a reflection of these compromises as they are the will of any one authority. A quasi-parliamentary system might make the enactment of laws and certainly the legislative movement of broad-scoped agendas somewhat easier, but such agendas themselves will not have been the product of a single officeholder's ideas.

Effective government, as Hugh Heclo noted, is the product of political leadership and bureaucratic knowledge.[16] Spurring movement of an agenda through legislative enactments is only one part of the story, even though it is the element that is most visible to the naked eye. To go beyond that means necessarily to relate enactments to administrative operations, though that relationship must be a two-way street. Pushing change beyond existing organizational routines and practices requires more than loyal soldiers in the legislature. At the same time, absorbing lessons from the permanent government requires some recognition of the limits of change. As one study of Britain shows, while different parties have "controlled" the government, the impact of policy upon the performance of macroeconomic indicators has not been noticeable.[17] Party government, by itself, does not equal effective control of the implementation of policy, but even effective control of policy operations does not necessarily mean more effective performance.

In this regard, tools that would strengthen political discipline to produce a form of party government also might have the effect of producing political whiplash—sudden starts and stops. The elevation of temporary majorities to a more or less ruling status presents the potential of radically shifting from one direction to another at the cost of continuity.

To join together the fate of congressional majorities with that of the president is a key aspiration of would-be constitutional revisionists. Presumably, this would help generate more adhesiveness within the parties which in turn could provide the basis for successful programmatic direction from the president. There are a number of operational hurdles in the road of this wish— not the least of which is that it is still possible for the White House and Congress to be dominated by different parties. Thus the prospects of such change appear to be limited at least on the immediate horizon. Except among the rapidly growing legion of living ex-presidents, there is, as yet, no substantial social consensus on its behalf, and without this social consensus there can be, in the American system, no political-legal consensus. To would-be reformers, of course, this is the "Catch-22" of the American constitutional system. Assuming that the biases of the existing system thwart, for the foreseeable future, the designs of those who would seek to synchronize the electoral fates of members of Congress with the president, what then can be done to promote effective leadership?

Better Leaders   A short but not necessarily simple answer to the question of how better leadership can be produced is "to elect good men to the presidency."[18] But what qualities does "good" translate into? Where are such prospects for the presidency to be found? And, are they likely to be elected? Is a good president to be defined, as was fashionable in the immediate aftermath of the exposing of excesses in the Nixon administration, merely as someone who would be unlikely to provoke a constitutional crisis? Is "good," in other words, to be an aspect of a president's moral character? Alternatively, is good meant to refer to one's skills at statecraft? This definition of good, as a consequence of its reputed absence seemed especially to come into fashion during the Carter administration. Yet a third conception of good might well refer to a president's intellectual tools; his ability to grasp the policy issues confronting him and to measure carefully the alternatives.

The presidency of Richard Nixon obviously gave rise to concerns about the first definition, which emphasizes apprehending the virtues of constitutionalism. One might suppose that leaders imbued with such virtues are produced through a socialization process that screens out the overreachers, the overzealous, and the corrupt. The underlying assumption here is that the political game that is played must be conducive to moderation in the quest for power, and probity in standards of conduct. A secondary assumption is pyramided onto the first—namely that if the political game is played in the described manner, then presidents should clearly be recruited from among experienced game players.

The central issues seem to lie in the two assumptions stated above. Does the system help to produce leaders of moderate temperament or of outsized ambitions? Does the system generate a politics highly immunized from corruption or one considerably dependent upon the influence of private money? If the answers to the first parts of each of these two questions are yes, then it should be especially important to recruit presidents from among professional politicians. But if serious doubts exist about providing an affirmative answer, then "good" presidents would have to be found (as the Progressives thought) from outside the professional political arena. Moreover, there would still be significant doubt that "good" presidents could overcome a bad system.

The second definition of "good" emphasizes statecraft; in other words, the capacity of presidents to steer the political system toward outcomes that accord with their goals. For twenty years, Richard Neustadt's book, *Presidential Power*, has been the most celebrated rendition of the statecraft definition of "good."[19] Neustadt's is an especially sophisticated analysis precisely because of its conditional nature. It is predicated on the supposition that a system designed to frustrate the exercise of leadership requires exceptional leaders with finely honed political skills. Neustadt is not unmindful of the need for better tools, yet remains skeptical of the likelihood of their appearance.[20] In their absence, the individual selected will have to compensate for the supporting structures that remain to be erected. In 1960, Neustadt concluded that for our presidents to be effective they would have to be selected from among the especially small class of experienced politicians of extraordinary temperament.[21] They would have to be politicians with a nose for power, yet a capacity to avoid overcommitment.

Similar imperatives, somewhat more abstractly stated, are emphasized by James David Barber in his study of presidential character. Only one of four possible mixes of character types, "active-positives," are likely under Barber's formulation to yield "presidents who want most to achieve results."[22] Barber's formulation emphasizes having the right temperament rather than applying the right technique. Perhaps because Barber's theory is somewhat more behaviorally generalized than Neustadt's focus on the proper uses of the levers of influence, Barber gives us clear hints, methodological issues aside, as to how we should search for those presidential prospects whose passion for power is mitigated by their equal passion for the enjoyment of political life. We need to read with care life histories in order to detect clues about character.

For Neustadt, there is more complication. It is essential to find people with the right temperament, but they must also interact with the right techniques. If, however, the scent for power is as critical as ever, the prey being stalked has become more elusive, a fact well appreciated by Neustadt in the twenty-year interregnum between the first and most recent appearance of *Presidential Power*. In short, if the instinct for statecraft necessarily must be constant, the techniques of its application may have to be altered with changes in the political context. To be effective, Neustadt now concludes, the powers of persuasion may have to be beamed over the airwaves, and not just to other elites.[23] All of this comes at a price, however. To the extent that power is put in constructive pursuit of policy, presidents need to know more than how to project themselves through the media. To be president even of a private company, after all, is to be more than vice-president for sales, notwithstanding the importance of the latter officeholder to the survival of the former. As a corporate president must know his company and not just his potential customers, the president of the United States needs to know about the government of which he is a part, and not just the mass audience to which he must ultimately turn. He can, of course, overdo this.[24] But the successful achievement of policy goals requires attention to the less visible, if equally pertinent, side of the equation. Put bluntly by Neustadt: "The intricacies of motivating bureaucrats in complex organizations are likelier than not to have escaped the President with a talent for TV."[25]

The complexity of government itself increasingly bedevils successful statecraft. To successfully master both the arts of governing and those of mass persuasion is surely to achieve a prodigious, and perhaps improbable, feat. The paradoxes of leadership grow as the instincts necessary for statecraft have become increasingly polymorphous. The virtuosity of skills required of prospective presidents to be both persuasive and effective, Neustadt readily concedes, places great demands on would-be presidents.

Even aside from this perplexing dilemma, and the problem of where such virtuosi are to be found, there is a remarkable subjectivity to the standards employed for evaluating presidential statecraft.... [I]t is worth for the moment... to point to the case of Eisenhower, a president whose political savvy has been both ridiculed and revered. In Neustadt's analysis, Eisenhower was portrayed as a political innocent. As rendered by Fred Greenstein, twenty years later, however, Eisenhower is portrayed as an astute, judicious, and worldly political leader.[26] These differences in interpretation, I suspect, are less likely to be found in the data (though, to be sure, Neustadt did not have access to the Eisenhower files available to Greenstein) than in the different models of statecraft held by Neustadt and Greenstein. To the question, where can "good" presidents be found is added the even more fundamental question: who are "good" presidents?

A somewhat different and yet also related answer to this last question of what constitutes "good" has to do with a president's comprehension of policy options, and his capacity to handle with some agility matters of intellectual complexity. This is the third meaning of good. Since policy making involves asking the right questions as well as making the right choices, and since neither is reducible to simple aphorisms or political slogans, a president needs to know not only how to keep options open (statecraft), but also what the options consist of (intellect). Certainly a president whose only skill is in policy analysis is not apt to be a president for very long, as a recent example suggests. On the other hand, statecraft without policy analysis is government by sheer instinct.

To join constitutional virtue to statecraft and to intellectual ability is surely, by composite, to define "good." To produce such persons for the presidency with any degree of regularity is quite another matter. At the very least, it is much to ask of a political culture that denigrates politics and politicians, abjures professionalism in government if not, in fact, government itself, and denounces bureaucrats and intellectuals while, ironically, the system becomes increasingly dependent upon each.

Restoring Intermediaries   Generating leadership may require collectivizing it, not by diluting the formal powers of presidents but by recognizing that the power both to make things happen in the system and to legitimize such actions requires bargaining. In contrast to a presidency-centric system, in which a mandate for programmatic leadership is assumed to be exclusively given to the president, is a restoration of strong intermediate organizations—political parties, peak associations, and congressional leadership. Turning presidential attentions to reaching accommodations with other elites is seen as a means of reducing the potential for demagogic media appeals and, therefore, for rightfully elevating substance over style.[27]

A genuine pluralism of interests, in this view, requires a lessening of the present hyperpluralism. Effective bargaining requires partners with the capacity to deliver. A system predicated on bargaining, necessitated in large part by the structural features outlined in the American constitution, requires unity among the bargaining partners. For stable agreements to be reached, compromise necessitates stability at the top. Intermediate organizations have not disappeared, of course. In many respects, as with interest groups, they have multiplied, meaning that each carries with it a more narrowly focused constituency with less and less willingness to compromise because the focus of concentration is so circumscribed. In other environments, as well as in Congress, there has been internal splintering and diffusion of leadership. Party organizations have tended surprisingly to become both more centralized and purposive, while becoming increasingly hollow at the local levels where they must relate to voters. Some of what has happened in recent times to intermediate organizations possibly is reparable by legal changes. And some repair may be caused by the collective realization of the many newly empowered that the costs and inefficiencies of excessive splintering can be exorbitant. But much is likely to be irreversible. . . .

Whatever the virtues of governing by accommodation and bargaining (there are of course liabilities too), it is simply not clear, as E. E. Schattschneider so ably pointed out, that large interest aggregates could ever deliver as much as they were given credit for.[28] Nor is it clear that presidents could effectively bargain with congressional committee chairmen who were obdurately opposed to presidential proposals, even in, indeed most especially in, the era of powerful committee chairs. And though presidents were once beholden to a few strong local party leaders, a condition very unlikely to be recreated, they are more likely now to have had substituted in their place the mayors who imbibe at the federal trough. The burden of dependence in this regard has been reversed.

In short, the pluralist dance may never have been the stately minuet that it sometimes has been held to be. At the same time, it may not have devoted quite as fully into the frenetic whirling dervish it now sometimes is reputed to have become. Bargaining partners remain, and ad hoc bargains can be reached, in some respects perhaps more easily for presidents now than when committee chairs bottle up legislation. The past was no less full of logjams. It is just that there are more logs now. Bargains are still a necessary part of how the American political system works. But more agreements now have to be reached with more people who, in turn, each represent fewer.

Everywhere, it seems, there are more obstacles to than conduits for the capacity to move government in coherent directions. As compelling as the need for leadership often is, the resisters to its exercise—however variable the form of these resistances—are also powerful. In a constitutionalist system the key question regarding leadership is not simply how it can be imposed—a view at the source of several recent U.S. presidents' troubles—but, more important, how it can be both legitimate and effective, an obviously more complicated question. Like the setting sun on the horizon, then, the question of leadership seems perfectly formed in the distance. But getting a firm grip on it is much like reaching for the sun: in a word, impossible.

Though the resistances to leadership are increasingly inherent in the complexity of both government and society, they still loom larger in the United States—their sources more multiple, intertwining, and deeply rooted. Americans are often enchanted by the rhetoric of leadership, but the American system mostly operates to deny its possibilities.

Notes

1. H. G. Nicholas, *The Nature of American Politics* (Oxford, England: Oxford University Press, 1980), p. 1.
2. Thomas E. Cronin, *The State of the Presidency*, 2nd ed. (Boston: Little, Brown, 1980), p. 377. A similar point is made by Bruce Miroff. See his "Presidential Leverage over Social Movements: The Johnson White House and Civil Rights," *Journal of Politics* 43 (February 1981): 2–23.
3. Renate Mayntz, "Executive Leadership in Germany: Dispersion of Power or 'Kanzlerdemokratie'?" in *Presidents and Prime Ministers* ed. Richard Rose and Ezra N. Suleiman (Washington, D.C.: American Enterprise Institute, 1980), pp. 169–170.
4. Sabino Cassese, "Is There a Government in Italy? Politics and Administration at the Top," in Rose and Suleiman, pp. 201–202.
5. Johan P. Olsen, "Governing Norway: Segmentation, Anticipation, and Consensus Formation," in Rose and Suleiman, pp. 252–253.
6. The comment was actually made about the situation of higher level civil servants in New York, but it is equally appropriate for presidents. It was originally attributed to Frederick O'R. Hayes, former budget director of New York City, and is quoted in Donald P. Warwick with Marvin Meade and Theodore Reed, *A Theory of Public Bureaucracy: Politics, Personality, and Organization in the State Department* (Cambridge, Mass.: Harvard University Press, 1975), p. 215.
7. For excellent examples of this argument, see James W. Ceaser, "Political Parties and Presidential Ambition," *Journal of Politics* 40 (August 1978): 708–739, and Nelson W. Polsby, "Against Presidential Greatness," in *American Government: Readings and Cases*, 7th ed., ed. Peter Woll (Boston: Little, Brown, 1981), pp. 418–424.
8. James MacGregor Burns, "More than Merely Power: II," *New York Times*, November 17, 1978, p. A29, as quoted in Cronin, *The State of the Presidency*, p. 378.

9. L. J. Sharpe, "American Democracy Reconsidered: Part II and Conclusions," *British Journal of Political Science* 3 (April 1973): 156.
10. Ibid., p. 157.
11. Kenneth Dyson, *The State Tradition in Western Europe* (New York: Oxford University Press, 1980), pp. 271–272.
12. Anthony King, "Ideas, Institutions, and Policies: Part III," *British Journal of Political Science* 3 (October 1973): 409–423. And, for an analysis of why the American business elite holds antistatist views, see David Vogel, "Why Businessmen Distrust Their State: The Political Consciousness of American Business Executives," *British Journal of Political Science* 8 (January 1978): 45–78.
13. Charles M. Hardin, *Presidential Power and Accountability: Toward a New Constitution* (Chicago: University of Chicago Press, 1974), p. 168. Emphases are in the original. The quote within the quote is from Richard Neustadt.
14. Don K. Price, "The Parliamentary and Presidential Systems," *Public Administration Review* 3 (Autumn 1943): 334.
15. Lloyd N. Cutler, "To Form a Government," *Foreign Affairs* 59 (Fall 1980): 126–143.
16. Hugh Heclo, *A Government of Strangers: Executive Politics in Washington* (Washington, D. C.: The Brookings Institution, 1977), p. 7.
17. Richard Rose, *Do Parties Make a Difference?* Chatham, N.J.: Chatham House Publishers, 1980), pp. 106–140.
18. William S. Livingston, "Britain and America: The Institutionalization of Accountability," *Journal of Politics* 38 (November 1976): 894.
19. The book first appeared in 1960; it has been added to on three occasions, most recently in 1980. All references, unless otherwise specified, are taken from the 1980 additions.
20. Richard E. Neustadt, *Presidential Power: The Politics of Leadership from FDR to Carter* (New York: John Wiley, 1980), esp. pp. 241–243.
21. Ibid., p. 243.
22. James David Barber, *The Presidential Character: Predicting Performance in the White House* (Englewood Cliffs, N. J.: Prentice-Hall, 1972), p. 13.
23. Neustadt, *Presidential Power*, pp. 236–238.
24. Richard Rose, "The President: A Chief but Not an Executive," *Presidential Studies Quarterly* 7 (Winter 1977): 5–26.
25. Neustadt, *Presidential Power*, p. 240.
26. Fred I. Greenstein, "Eisenhower as an Activist President," *Political Science Quarterly* 94 (Winter 1979–80): 575–599.
27. For excellent examples of this argument, see Ceaser, "Political Parties and Presidential Ambition," and Polsby, "Against Presidential Greatness."
28. E. E. Schattschneider, *The Semi-Sovereign People: A Realist's View of Democracy in America* (New York: Holt, Rinehart and Winston, 1960), esp. pp. 47–61.

58 / The Actor President in the Age of Fiction

James David Barber

James David Barber, well known for his theory that the nature of a presidential administration is likely to reflect the psychological character of the president, here analyzes some of the character of Ronald Reagan. General acceptance of President Reagan's manipulative rhetorical style was, Barber argues, an indicator of the extent to which American society has come to value "feeling good" more highly than "facing facts."

I had lunch with [Reagan] once, when he visited Yale, and liked him fine. But on the day he was inaugurated, in an article in the Washington *Post*, I predicted that[:] . . .

> The *climate of expectations* would be dominated by "the tide of reaction against too long and hard a time of troubles, too much worry, too much tension and anxiety" through the Carter years. Reagan came on as "a friend, a pal, a guy to reassure us that the story is going to come out all right. . . . He is supposed to make it well again. That is very likely to prove difficult, if not impossible."
>
> Reagan's *power situation* would be fragile. His "best bet for popular support in darker months to come may well be the fury of the radical right, whose indignant disillusionment with Reagan will help him gain acceptance with moderates." He would need help winning the public, having "won in an election with the lowest turnout in 32 years." He had a modest Senate majority and conservative Democratic allies in the House. Inflation would be tough to beat and he had "no terrible social disaster going for him, such as the collapse that brought in Franklin Roosevelt, to put steam behind a burst of effective legislation in his first 100 or 200 days." After an initial romance, the media would play up "the inevitable 'performance gap' stories, featuring bobbles and corruptions on the road to Utopia."
>
> The Reagan Presidential *style* would be dominated by rhetoric, with "little interest in homework on the issues" and little taste for "the charms of personal negotiation. . . . particularly if they involve an element of disagreement or confrontation." Further, "his rhetoric is essentially ahistorical and apolitical. He is bound to contribute to the ever-widening gap in American politics between speech and meaning.". . .

. . . [T]he fundamental balance of the Reagan style persisted as predicted: the antipathy for homework, the overwhelming emphasis on rhetoric. Reagan the President not only revived the one page "mini-memo" as his favorite homework-avoider, he also eventually brought its inventor, William Clark, into the White House as his National Security Advisor—thereby underlining doubly his disdain for mastering information, since Clark, whatever else he may have been guilty of, was innocent of national security expertise. As for negotiation, Reagan held many a meeting with Congressmen and the like— and typically charmed the socks off them. But he left the dealing to his staffers. He liked to play host. Others could arrange the terms of legislation. What he spent by far the most time and energy on was speaking and getting ready to speak—honing his performance. It was there, within that rhetorical emphasis, that the essential impact of the Reagan persona was to be found. Nearly three years into his Presidency, *Time* drew a summary portrait of the Reagan Presidential style:

> Reagan is remarkably disengaged from the substance of his job. His aides no longer dismiss as glib the theory that Reagan has a movie-star approach to governing. "In Reagan's mind," says a White House advisor, "somebody does the lighting, somebody else does the set, and Reagan takes care of his role, which is the public role."[1]

. . .The connections linking Reagan's words with historical reality, on the one hand, and his own actions, on the other, were, to put it mildly, loosely knit. Yet his communicative ability was celebrated as extraordinarily powerful. What forces in the Reagan character sustain his rhetorical effectiveness? He may not be the last President whose style is significantly theatrical. What does that portend for the processes of persuasion and deliberation in a democracy?. . .

The Reagan Rhetoric

Reagan the "actor" is only part—the minor part—of Reagan the political dramatist. He is miscast as a man who [brought] Hollywood to Washington. Long before he became a professional actor, he had trained in pretending: that he really could see the blackboard, that his father was not really a drunk, that he really could play football, that he really did belong in the rich kids' crowd. Though the Great Depression stopped Jack Reagan in his tracks, he was for years a salesman, a man who talks people into buying things, and a wonderful Irish storyteller; Ronnie experienced that presence for a long time before he met the *Reader's Digest*. His mother put on little playlets right there in the living room. His favorite reading was Tarzan, his favorite activity talking ("an incredible talker," a writer said, meaning only that there was lots of it). And when he went off by himself to play, it was to enter "a make-believe world in which heroic deeds had the capacity to transform reality," as Cannon puts it.[2] Blessed with a tall, straight body, an attractive face and a winning smile, young Ronald Reagan was a natural for high school popularity and thus for student politics and drama club.

Thus when, much later, it came time for Hollywood to make an actor of him, no lessons were necessary—they persuaded him to let his crewcut grow out and to get rid of his shoulder-padded suits. But he played himself. Of his first seven movies, four portrayed him as a radio announcer, which is what he had been for years. Keenan Wynn, who knew him a long time, said that "Ronnie was not so much an actor as a performer who played versions of himself," in Laurence Leamer's paraphrase.[3] The years in Hollywood gave him skill in technique and an actor's interest in the arts of projection, but the Reagan range, in dramatic terms, ran from A to about D, no farther. To confuse him, then, with Lawrence Olivier or even Cary Grant—that is, to suppose Reagan's success springs from the deep art of *becoming* the part and the mesmerizing effect that can have on audiences—is, I think, a mistake. He was an actor, yes, and he did moderately well when he appeared at a particular and historical junction. The Second World War interrupted his progress; by the end of it he was already getting too old to play the "Ronald Reagan" he had epitomized: the Earnest Young Fellow Up Against Trouble. . . .

Acting was . . . secondary in his life history. After college, his job was sports broadcasting and, in particular, rapidly inventing baseball and football stories to go with the spare facts ("Herman grounds out.") the telegraph provided. It was essentially a literary occupation, not a thespian one. He did that so well that he progressed to a major station, made himself a regional celebrity, and won a trip to Hollywood for the excellence of his work. Again the range was narrow: the few facts set a framework and the rules of the game a boundary within which his minor variations could play—the gestures of a batter, the outfielder tossing away his cap. Reagan could handle that, much as he could master, for example, the Presidential walk to the helicopter—the stride, the pause, the smile, the upraised hand, the snappy answer to the shouted question. He became a quick study. For all his lackadaisical academic record, he had a ready intelligence and an imagination which enabled him to get his lines, imagine how they would go, and zing them out.

But as with other Presidents-to-be, predicting Reagan's style worked much better by tracing back to his first independent political success than by averaging out his various subsequent occupations. In the Reagan history, that style-shaping experience stands out starkly: appropriately, it was a single, dramatic event in which the young man, away from his family, first discovered his own special technique for winning his way with significant others.

That happened for Ronnie at an appropriately named little country college: Eureka (i.e., "I have found it"). In the autumn of his freshman year, the college trustees met to ponder the school's financial crisis and to assess their president's recommendation that a number of courses be cut and their professors fired. That plan agitated the campus, drawing together faculty members, whose livelihoods were threatened, with students who feared they would be left without the courses they needed to graduate. The trustees, perhaps hoping the students would go away, mulled the matter until midnight before Thanksgiving holidays, when they announced acceptance of the president's cutback plan. The college bell began to toll; the chapel began to fill with students and professors, an angered, tense crowd ready for action. The student committee, nine members, of whom Reagan alone represented the freshmen, huddled and set the agenda: first a basketball star senior, then the senior class president, then freshman Reagan. That meant he got to present the motion—a call to strike and bring down the president. By the time he got the floor, the pent-up fervor was straining the chapel like an overheated steam engine. He spoke, he demanded the strike, the crowd exploded in unanimous applause and standing affirmation—of the strike and, so he had to hear and see and feel it, of himself. It was a sweet victory. Just a few weeks earlier Ronnie had tried out for football with twenty-five other students; he had been the only one rejected. Now, suddenly, he was the most famous freshman on campus. The students struck for a week, the president resigned, and the faculty-firing plan was put on the shelf.

So it was political oratory that formed the experiential base for Reagan's subsequent adventures in radio and the movies and public speaking and, eventually, real politics. That crucial midnight meeting stuck with him as a mythological event he never tired of telling, in somewhat mythic form. The lesson he drew from it was this: "I discovered that night that an audience has a feel to it and, in the parlance of the theater, that audience and I were together." Read the audience, get on that wavelength and power follows: "It was heady wine. Hell, with two more lines I could have had them riding through 'every Middlesex village and farm'—without horses yet."[4] In his own life, Reagan said as he ran for President of the United States, his performance that night formed "a beginning link in a later pattern."[5] Speaking at Eureka in October 1980, he said "Everything good that has happened to me—everything—started here on this campus in those four years that still are such a part of my life."[6]

Years later, in 1984, Reagan explained how his link to the audience translated into a political career:

I never in my wildest dreams ever aspired to public service.
I loved that world that I was in, the entertainment world.
So, the very fact that I'd been blessed with some success and could attract an audience, I thought that it was only right that I should use that in behalf of causes that I believed in. So, I don't know what I could have done differently.[7]

By the time Reagan reached the stage of the White House, he had more experience pleasing audiences than any American politician since William Jennings Bryan. He had mastered the arts of dramatic performance on the stage, in radio sportscasting and commentary, in the movies, in television and in specialized and general platform oratory. No other candidate in 1980 or 1984 had anything like Reagan's professional experience in the modern media. And not since Harding had a happy-talk President's character and style fit together so nicely with the public's yearning for positive thinking in politics. The President had a terrific sense of humor, which he exercised regularly in what started out to be formal prep sessions by his staff. "Being dull," he said, "is very hard for me,"[8] and he loved Nancy especially for shielding him from boredom. He and Nancy let their emotions show: for all his general geniality, the Reagans are to be found weeping sentimentally on scores of occasions from one end to the other of the biographies.

The obvious combination of public personality and media talent made it surprising that it had taken so long for the Reagan type to appear in the age of media politics. Here was a man who, at his inaugural ball, could do the apparently impossible: "Ronnie and Nancy danced intimately while thousands watched."[9] He knew how to rehearse systematically for the apparently unrehearsed, spontaneous move, such as saying "There you go again" before giving one of his memorized responses (based on leaked Carter memos) in answer to Jimmy Carter in their campaign debate. He introduced the teleprompter to the English Parliament. He could steal FDR's finest lines— "rendezvous with destiny," for example—and make them sound his own. Painted by his opposition as a combination fool and knave, he knew how to turn those expectations to his advantage: he became one of those lucky politicians who get credit for being normal. As an entertainer/speaker at an Al Smith dinner he could surpass any Presidential candidate in sight, approximately as Rudolph Nureyev could surpass him at the polka. Reagan was specially adept at playing the injured innocent, the wounded bear, saying "I can't be angry..."[10] when assaulted by a critic. The minor tricks were part of his nature by then—for example, knowing how to look and move slightly but expressively when the television camera finds you listening to your opponent's answer.[11] To the television audience for Presidential addresses, he spoke simple English and even used such homely but effective props as a dollar bill and 36¢ in change to make his point. His staging was superb, from his tan and tieless performance in front of the Statue of Liberty during the campaign to his inaugural on the visually correct side of the Capitol Building, where he could gesture expansively at the monumental wonders of the Mall. The television networks followed him around like trained puppies, eager to put on the news shows good happy clips from Nancy's "surprise" birthday party for him on February 4, 1983, followed a few days thereafter by the President's foray into a drugstore to buy her a Valentine.[12] Even his administration's top people seemed to have been typecast as supporting players for the Reagan performance. Surrounded by such sober types, his mildly maverick manner makes him seen fresh and interesting....

...The modern Presidency is of necessity a performance—a media performance—and the modern arts of President-playing are to be celebrated, not disdained. They make politics interesting and thus encourage participation. They translate complexity into simplicity, which, in real-world politics, is a prerequisite for action. At their best they enliven and expand the national classroom, where the lessons have to do with life and death. The bright side of Presidential dramatics is inspiration.

The dark side is the power of drama to overwhelm reason: the lure of illusion, the fracturing of logic, the collapse of political conversation. The dark side is the drift into the swamp of fantasy and on over the brink of disaster. Drama offers interest, but it risks political insanity. That process begins with contempt for the facts.

Reagan seemed to love facts. Unlike politicians who take their stand on the landscape of generality, Reagan was forever citing statistics and telling

THE ACTOR PRESIDENT IN THE AGE OF FICTION

interestingly specific bits of history or biography. The trouble was that he very often said, with an air of resolute conviction, things that simply were not true. Reporters and opposing candidates collected the Errors of Ronald Reagan by the notebookful. Far from trivial, Reagan's counterfactuals bore directly on major problems of public policy. If trees cause air pollution, if oil slicks help cure tuberculosis, if welfare cheats are rampant, if the Shah of Iran was a "progressive," if the Soviet economy is about to collapse "because they've already got their people on a starvation diet of sawdust,"[13] if there is more oil under Alaska than under Saudi Arabia, if billions upon billions of federal expenditures are "fat"—then follow various highly significant directions for the relevant policies. Not that his perceptions were random; they suited his rich friends far better than his poor victims. Richard Cohen reported that Reagan, at one spring 1982 press conference, "said Social Security was not 'touched' when in fact it had been cut. He said programs for pregnant women had not been reduced, but merely merged with others. They were cut—by about $200 million. He said the overall poverty budget was increased. It wasn't. The new money went for defense."[14] But the frequency of Reagan's "slips" or "gaffes" or "bobbles" was in itself amazing, especially given the heat Jerry Ford and Jimmy Carter had had to endure for far less significant blunders. More interesting, though, was Reagan's own apparent attitude toward his "mistakes": he did not seem to mind. Though he sometimes waxed indignant over accusations of inaccuracy, he typically acted like an actor who, having blown a line, has to forge right ahead without worrying over it. When a reporter quoted one of his strange statements back to him, he shrugged and said he did not remember saying that, but that he had "probably just read something from a piece of paper that had been put in front of me."[15] Or he "would just smile pleasantly or shake his head in disagreement with his critics, as if mastery of provable fact were things on which gentlemen certainly could differ in goodwill."[16] The gaffe story had developed its plot to perfection in Presidential politics, from error to expiation—but Reagan would not play. He was, it seemed, literally shameless when it came to the question of factuality. As James Reston put it, "Give Mr. Reagan a good script, a couple of invisible TV screens and a half hour on prime time and he'll convince the people they have nothing to fear but the facts."[17]

Like his dramatic skills, that attitude was rooted in his own theatrical experience. Arriving in Hollywood, he remembered being "filled with all the star-struck awe of one who had from childhood been entertained in the house of illusion—the neighborhood theatre."[18] He missed completely the GI cynicism of World War II, dwelling instead through those years in another house of illusion—making mythic films of patriotic puffery and acting in a musical comedy about the war.[19] Fantasy in Reagan's life was not, as it might be for a reporter or historian, something to guard against, but rather a point of pride. The actor is meant to be an enthusiastic fantasist, a dreamer. "So much of our profession is taken up with pretending," he wrote, "with interpretation of never-never roles, that an actor must spend at least half his waking hours in fantasy."[20] Reagan especially liked Carl Sandburg's slant on dreaming: "The Republic is a dream. Nothing happens unless first a dream."[21] David Stockman summed up the White House system at one critical era: "Every time one fantasy doesn't work they try another one."[22] Another staffer left the Reagan White House saying, "The whole administration's a fantasy that they have the power to maintain and define as normal. . . . but they have no questions. It's an administration without questions."[23] To Reagan, accusations of fantasy translate easily into praise for having the courage to dream great dreams and not to let a lot of piddling little facts get in the way. His conscience is easy—he didn't lie, he just made things up.

For years, Reagan has been making up stories about himself—mythlets he seems to believe. "I'll never forget one game with Mendota," one such tale begins and goes on to describe how he lost a close football contest for Dixon High by confessing to the unseeing umpire that he deserved a penalty; though sorely tempted, "truth-telling had been whaled into me. . . . I told the truth, the penalty was ruled, and Dixon lost the game." But the fact is, as Cannon reports, that Dixon lost only one game that season—to Mendota by a score of 24–0.[24] . . . In 1983, Reagan told Hugh Sidey of a peak experience in his life—when, at Eureka, "I played Captain Stanhope in *Journey's End*. I never was so carried away in the theater in my life. I was in the war as far as that play was concerned."[25] He added details about the cast and his role. The trouble is, he did not act in the play at all. He saw it performed, when he was a freshman. Later he said that "in some strange way, I was also on stage."[26] That psychological identification had overwhelmed the facts and he had moved from his seat to the stage. "He is forever reinventing his past," as William Leuchtenburg writes, especially in juggling the history of his attitude toward Franklin Roosevelt to suit Reagan's current politics.[27] As David Broder noted, "It is apparently President Reagan's belief that words can not only cloak reality but remake it."[28] The past is raw material, to be shaped as needed for purposes of revealing dramatic truth.

Nor is Reagan's fantastic imagination devoted only to historical reconstructions. He thinks up stories he might act in in the future. After he lost to Ford in 1976, Betty Glad noted, Reagan fantasized about man-to-man confrontation with Leonid Brezhnev. As he told his son, Mike, after he lost to Ford in 1976:

> You know the real reason I'm upset? I was looking forward to sitting down with Brezhnev and negotiating the SALT II Treaty. I wanted to listen to the interpreter tell me for an hour and a half what Brezhnev wanted the President of the United States to give up in order to maintain friendship with Russia. Then, I was going to slowly get up, walk around the table and whisper in his ear, "Nyet." I really miss that. I don't think Brezhnev has ever heard that word before.[29]

. . .Nowhere does Reagan make this attitude clearer than in his story of how segregation ended in the armed services "in World War II . . . largely under the leadership of generals like MacArthur and Eisenhower": "When the Japanese dropped the bomb on Pearl Harbor there was a Negro sailor whose total duties involved kitchen-type duties. . . . He cradled a machine gun in his arms, which is not an easy thing to do, and stood at the end of a pier blazing away at Japanese airplanes that were coming down and strafing him and that [segregation] was all changed." A reporter told him segregation lasted at least until three years after the war when Truman ordered it stopped. Reagan replied: *"I remember the scene. . . . It was very powerful."*[30]

Reagan off-stage seemed to be engaged in creative fantasizing. Laurence Leamer notes that

> What was so extraordinary was Ronnie's apparent psychic distance from the burden of the Presidency. He sat in cabinet meetings doodling. Unless held to a rigid agenda, he would start telling Hollywood stories or talk about football in Dixon. Often in one-on-one conversations Ronnie seemed distracted or withdrawn. "He has a habit now," his brother, Neil, said. "You might be talking to him, and its like he's picking his fingernails, but he's not. And you know then that he's talking to himself."
>
> "If people knew about him living in his own reality they wouldn't believe it," said one White House aide. "There are only ten to fifteen people who know the extent, and until they leave and begin talking, no one will believe it."[31]

The uncoupling of the President from White House decision-making became a startling fact of life among his advisors. A former aide said that the President, facing a policy question, "will not go far into it because he is not really looking to make a decision. He is looking for lines to repeat when the time comes to sell. He thinks of himself not so much as the person who decides but rather as the person who markets." A current aide confessed how difficult it was to get the President to concentrate on policy specifics: "I have to prepare a script. Otherwise he will get me off the subject and turn what I have to say to mush. I have about six or seven minutes, and then he guides the conversation."[32] Similarly abroad: Joseph Kraft noted that "foreign leaders repeatedly come away from sessions with the president claiming he is a pussycat, too nice even to mention disagreeable subjects."[33]

The uncoupled quality came through also in public on those rare occasions when he spoke without a script. David Broder noted that "To hear him speak extemporaneously on domestic policy is to hold your breath in nervous anticipation of the unknown."[34] Lacking firm anchoring in the mind of the President himself, policy in the Reagan administration lurched from one accident to another. The supply-side hocus-pocus was but the most evident of a series of inventions in which the logic of politics fell apart in the presence of the logic of the theater. Theodore White saw that the Reagan budget "defied common sense—almost as much as the illusion that by sheer power alone, people can learn to slide uphill."[35] Stockman and Murray Weidenbaum slapped together figures from their "visceral computers"—their gut feelings.[36] The Reagan people had thought to propose a 5 percent rise in defense spending, but Carter proposed that figure in his final budget, so the Reaganites upped theirs to 7 percent, the President explaining that "worldwide, what we're doing in defense must be seen as different from Carter. It must be a symbol of a change in the climate as regards to defense."[37] Thus the figures had nothing much to do with actual guns and bullets, but with symbols, and so there was not much apparent need to get the figures right; the billions were tossed around with cheerful abandon. That was the dashing style in which much of the Reagan "program" got constructed, from governmental decentralization to missile development. One after another, the major new projects rolled out of the White House hangar: a new defense system, based in outer space, to turn back Soviet missiles, a new "zero option" aiming at total elimination of nuclear weapons, a new proposal for merit pay for school teachers—each enjoying its week or so in the sun before passing into the oblivion from which it had emerged. Cannon came to call the President "The Great Deflector."

Planned Distraction

It was not too long before a savvy White House aide picked up the method behind the madness and pushed planned distraction. Dick Darman proposed this list:

> Hype Federalism for as long as it will play.
>
> Develop and implement plans for minor (low cost) and symbolic actions for key constituencies—aged, Spanish-surnamed, white ethnics/blue collar, populist/rednecks, (other?).
>
> Distract attention from economic focus until the economy is clearly turning up—via a combination of foreign and domestic actions...[38]

In the summer of 1983, Federalism—delegating functions and their costs to the states—was virtually played out as an issue by the time the governors met to bemoan their losses of federal revenues. Step 2 of the Darman plan was in full force as the President, suddenly discovering that there were major complaints about his policies, dashed around doing his best to woo the disaffected blacks, women, Hispanics, unemployed, etceteras on his list with a good many "minor (low cost) and symbolic actions."...

But it was item 3 of Darman's memo that posed the greatest danger. Reagan succeeded wonderfully in distracting the nation's—and the world's—attention when in 1983 he dispatched to wartorn Central America a massive fleet and thousands of American troops, supposedly for maneuvers. A Soviet ship was stopped and asked about its cargo. Added to the troops the U.S. had spread over the Middle East, these soldiers and sailors stood at risk, not only from the types of surprise missile attacks Argentina had used, only a year before, to sink British ships in the area, but also from encounters with the various right- and left-wing armed bands pursuing each other over this strange terrain. Risk was evident also in the chaos at the top—the foreign policy equivalent of the chaos in economic planning Stockman had described. Observers who had breathed a sigh of relief at the departure of Haig and Richard Allen and their replacement by George Shultz and William Clark, in what the White House liked to call a "mid-course correction," choked up again when normally placid Shultz stormed into the Oval Office and told the President he had to be in on major foreign policy moves. He had learned about the dispatch of the fleet by reading it in the newspaper. That was only a symptom of the sprawling disorder endemic in the Reagan foreign policy collection in which power drifted and lurched from the Secretary of Defense to the United Nations Ambassador to the National Security Council chief to special Presidential envoys in Central America and the Mideast to the Secretary of State to, of all people, Henry Kissinger, previously Reagan's prime example of a defective part in the foreign policy machine, who was put in charge of a special commission designed to sidetrack dissent on Central American policy. The President floated along, blaming the press for the public's increasing skepticism.

The new military exercise was variously described as routine maneuvers or a massive show of force to encourage negotiations, which the Reagan administration had previously rejected. The land maneuvers were to be held in Honduras, from which a war against the Nicaraguan government was being waged with U.S. aid furnished "covertly," according to the administration, although pictures of it all appeared week after week in the news magazines. The purpose of the aid was described first as to stop Nicaragua from supplying arms to rebels in El Salvador and then as aiding Nicaraguan "freedom fighters" out to overthrow the government. In April 1984, it was revealed that the CIA, in violation of international law, had been laying mines in Nicaraguan harbors[39] and in October 1984 the press printed shocking excerpts from a CIA manual for revolution, recommending assassinations, blackmail, and other crimes.

But it was in Lebanon, in October 1983, that the Reagan military policies brought their first disaster, the worst since Vietnam. Two hundred and forty-one Marines died in Beirut, thanks to what a subsequent Administration Commission found to be a thoroughly botched mission—men virtually staked out and waiting for an accident to happen.[40] Having adamantly refused to pull them out, Reagan finally did so, but not before suggesting that advocates of withdrawal were treasonous. His own Minority Whip in the House, conservative Republican Trent Lott (R-Mississippi) complained that "You people are not in touch with reality."[41] A year later, in September 1984, another bomb in Beirut blew up at a U.S. embassy annex, killing two more Americans.

The Threat Ahead
Thus the Reagan administration lurched into international military adventure, the arena where the risk of tragedy loomed largest. In the White House the President's men muffled their tensions and struggled to manage his destiny

by managing his image. In the short run, which is all we may have, the major danger of the Reagan administration stood out starkly: not adamance, but drift; not ideological rigidity, but accident; not obsession, but distraction. Domestically, Reagan's erratic and ill-developed dashes hurt people he never meant to hurt—by the millions. Internationally, the sudden movements of masses of armed men and weapons posed enormous risks to the tenuous stability of a changing world. At the center of it all was a President continually in search of directors to tell him what to do.

Reagan continued the Presidential posture he inherited from his parade of predecessors. That is, a President cabined with "political" advisors, promoted from the top of his campaign staff, innocent of experience in the high arts of statesmanship. That is, a Presidency preoccupied with "crisis management"—reacting to one blow after another from an environment he was elected to shape, not merely respond to. That is, a President-centered government in which rational deliberation disappeared in the mystic clouds of manipulative rhetoric. On the obvious major challenges of the age—the institutionalization of peace, the establishment of the rudiments of justice in the world, and the management of world resources for the welfare of humankind—no progress whatever was evident. Instead, we continued the pattern of challengers and incumbents competing, with all the vigor and imagination at their command, to win the nation's highest authority only to realize, on the morning after, that they did not know what to do with it.

If nevertheless we survive for a longer run at the progress of the American democracy, we will look back on Reagan's presidency as marking a fundamental departure from the basic tradition. For democracy rests on a tacit social contract that the government will operate in the real world. As Freud understood, the alternative is enormously attractive: illusion beckons, luring not only the anxious or desperate individual, but also the distracted nation. We have seen in Naziism and in Communism how millions of people— including a good many smart ones—can be suckered into believing crazy theories as if they are factually founded. A true democratic "conservatism," unlike the brittle and frightened imitation by that name, would insist on genuine argument in politics—that is, on the systematic presentation of accurate information, to which the steady light of reason can be applied.

Judging by the forces arrayed against it, the defense of empiricism in democracy will take some doing. We exist in an era of history in which history itself is passe, an age of fictions, especially tales of the human heart, an age of feeling. Our literature is dominated by the novel, as literatures in ages past were dominated by theology or military science or the sagas of discovery. The boundaries between what really happened and what must have or might have or could have happened fade from vision. We seem less interested in testing facts than in savoring insights. Wit is popular, in political commentary as elsewhere. The anonymous and thus uncheckable source is the fashion in journalism. Our economics and, increasingly, our politics too, breathe the airs of speculation and the hope that wide agreement on an idea can somehow substitute for a demonstration of the truth of it. Our generation's contribution to communication, television, far prefers to probe for feelings than to test theories against facts. And our generation's contribution to politics, the endless campaign, still manages to throw down an iron curtain between the suppositions of running for President and the actualities of being one.

For these and other reasons, our politics is especially vulnerable to the Reagan dramatics. We do not seem to be able to pay attention very long and the attention we do pay is scant to start with. Yet that is democracy's scarcest and most valuable resource. Squander attention, or let fiction sop it up, and the democratic spirit sheds its practical incarnation and, wraithlike, sails out into the ether.

Notes

1. *Time*, February 6, 1984, p. 23.
2. Lou Cannon, *Reagan* (New York: Putnam's, 1982), p. 19.
3. Laurence Leamer, *Make-Believe: The Story of Nancy & Ronald Reagan* (New York: Harper & Row, 1983), p. 98.
4. Cannon, *Reagan*, p. 36, quoting from Reagan's autobiography.
5. Quoted in T. R. Reid, "Reagan: A Life Built on Performance," *Washington Post*, October 22, 1980.
6. Cannon, *Reagan*, p. 34.
7. *Time*, February 6, 1984, p. 22.
8. Laurence I. Barrett, *Gambling with History: Ronald Reagan in the White House* (Garden City, New York: Doubleday, 1983), p. 25.
9. Leamer, *Make-Believe*, p. 18.
10. Jack W. Germond and Jules Witcover, *Blue Smoke and Mirrors: How Reagan Won and Why Carter Lost the Election of 1980* (New York: Viking, 1981), p. 257.
11. Ibid., p. 278.
12. C. T. Hanson, "Gunsmoke and Sleeping Dogs: The President's Press at Midterm," *Columbia Journalism Review*, May/June 1983, pp. 27ff.
13. *World Press Review*, January 1982.
14. *Washington Post*, April 11, 1982.
15. Dom Bonafede, "The Press and the Hollywood Presidency," *Washington Journalism Review*, January/February 1981.
16. Germond and Witcover, *Blue Smoke*, p. 224.
17. *New York Times*, January 29, 1984, p. E19.
18. Leamer, *Make-Believe*, p. 97.
19. Leamer, *Make-Believe*, p. 123.
20. *Where's the Rest of Me?* Ronald Reagan & Richard G. Hubler, (New York: Dell Pub. Co., Inc., 1965), p. 10.
21. Quoted in Leamer, *Make-Believe*, p. 328.
22. Cannon, *Reagan*, p. 332.
23. Leamer, *Make-Believe*, p. 331.
24. Cannon, *Reagan*, p. 36.
25. *Time*, July 11, 1983, p. 16.
26. Cannon, *Reagan*, p. 36.
27. William E. Leuchtenburg, "Ronald Reagan's Liberal Past," *The New Republic*, May 23, 1983, pp. 18ff.

28. *Washington Post*, February 12, 1984.
29. Quoting *Newsweek*, July 21, 1980, p. 53. Betty Glad, "Black-and-White Thinking: Ronald Reagan's Approach to Foreign Policy," *Political Psychology*, Vol. 4, No. 1, 1983, p. 63.
30. Cannon, *Reagan*, 20. Emphasis added.
31. Leamer, *Make-Believe*, p. 344.
32. "How Reagan Decides," *Time*, December 13, 1982, p. 15.
33. *Washington Post*, January 10, 1982, p. B7.
34. Quoted in Leamer, *Make-Believe*, p. 352.
35. Theodore H. White, *America in Search of Itself: The Making of the President 1956–1980* (New York: Harper & Row, 1982), p. 422.
36. Barrett, *Gambling*, p. 142.
37. Barrett, *Gambling*, p. 178.
38. Quoted in Barrett, *Gambling*, p. 391.
39. *New York Times*, April 10, 1984, p. 1.
40. Robert Kaiser, *Washington Post*, January 15, 1984, p. D1.
41. *Washington Post*, February 12, 1984, p. A17.

CHAPTER SIXTEEN

Bureaucracy

In the American republic, those who are chiefly responsible for making and executing the policies of government are elected officials, but most government employees are appointed or hired rather than elected. These non-elected employees, who are necessary for operating government on a daily basis, are known as "bureaucrats," and, naturally, their numbers have grown substantially as the number of government programs has increased.

In 1848 President James K. Polk wrote in his diary (presumably without tongue in cheek), "I prefer to supervise the whole operations of government myself. . ., and this makes my duties very great."* Today, layers of bureaucrats supervise other layers of bureaucrats, and elected officials exercise direct supervision over very few of the actual operations of government.

As bureaucracy has grown in size, it has also grown in importance. How is a president to maintain control over five million employees (roughly 3.1 million civilian and 2.1 million military**)? The answer, of course, is that the president cannot; those unelected employees who exercise powers in the name of elected officials must be given some leeway to make decisions themselves. And therein lies an important tension between bureaucracy and democracy, as effectively argued in the first reading by David Nachmias and David Rosenbloom. In the second selection, Margaret Wyszomirski documents increasing reliance on administrative rather than political skills in making cabinet appointments, and concludes that while this may help presidents to "manage," it does not help them to "govern."

*In Richard Fenno, Jr., *The President's Cabinet* (Cambridge, Mass: Harvard University Press, 1959, p. 217).—*Editor's Note.*
**Numbers as of 1988.—*Editor's Note.*

59 / Democracy and the Growing Bureaucracy

David Nachmias
David H. Rosenbloom

During the twentieth century and especially since the 1930s, the national bureaucracy has experienced tremendous growth in both size and importance. David Nachmias and David Rosenbloom argue in the following selection that the requirements of bureaucracy consistently conflict with principles of democracy, such that democracy inevitably suffers as the power of bureaucracy increases.

The Organization of Bureaucracy

People often apply the word "bureaucracy" to incompetent organizations and administrative behavior. As a result the term has caused such confusion that some political scientists have seriously suggested avoiding using it even when they are studying bureaucratic institutions.[1] Ignoring the word, however, will not bring us any closer to an understanding of the organizational reality behind it. Some sort of definition is necessary. First let us say what bureaucracy is *not*. It should not be used in serious research as a synonym for inefficient organization or ineffective administration.* Efficiency and effectiveness can be found in virtually any setting; there is nothing to be gained by calling poor work "bureaucratic" and competent work "nonbureaucratic." There is a related tendency in the United States to call all public organizations "bureaucracies." This practice is not helpful either. Given the diversity in types of public organizations and organizational structures, and the fact that many private organizations can also legitimately be described as "bureaucratic," there is little reason to use the term as a synonym for the less confusing word "public."

Once these definitional approaches are discarded, it becomes possible to identify the core of structural features that constitute bureaucratic organizations:

1. *Hierarchy.* This is the hallmark of bureaucracy. It consists of a ranking of roles and a system of status. Those who are higher up in the organization are termed *superordinates;* those who are lower down are *subordinates*. Hierarchy carried to its logical extreme is pyramidal in shape, with one position at the head. Information flows up the hierarchy; direction and control flow

---

*Efficiency generally refers to the accomplishment of a task at the lowest feasible cost. Effectiveness concerns the attainment of objectives.—*Author's Note.*

downward. Generally, superordinates enjoy privileges unavailable to their underlings. While rank in a hierarchy may be attached to a person, in civilian public bureaucracies in the United States it is usually attached to the position itself. Where hierarchies are rigid, they condition virtually all human interaction within them. Indeed, some social scientists say that an individual's position in a hierarchy can modify his or her self-characterizations.

2. *Specialization* (differentiation). Bureaucratic organizations have a well-developed division of labor. Tasks and jurisdictions are parceled out among various offices. This enables officeholders to concentrate on limited spheres of activity. Consequently bureaucratic organization tends to produce high levels of expertise in narrow areas. Often, but not always, the duties of officials and bureaus are spelled out in detailed written form. (In the federal bureaucracy there is a position description covering each of its 2.8 million slots.) The multitude of specialized functions must be coordinated; typically this is the task of the hierarchy. There is an inherent tension, however, between the authority based on the specialist's knowledge and the formal organizational authority of superordinates. Those at the top find it difficult to control specialists throughout the ranks.

3. *Formalization.* Communication in bureaucracies tends to be in writing. Because the organizations are designed to continue even though individuals come and go, communication takes the form of memos written from one position or office to another. The memos are stored in files, whose maintenance and control are vital to the organization. In addition, many aspects of organizational life are set forth in formal written fashion: not only position descriptions but also aspects of the personnel's behavior such as the kinds of clothes and the hairstyles that may and may not be worn to work. The principal object of formalization is clarity. (Sometimes, however, the desire to specify what is to be done under all possible circumstances produces language that is gobbledy-gook even to the bureaucrat.) Formalization acts as a constraint on individual discretion by specifying what the organization demands in various situations. Sometimes formalization is the prime cause of "red tape," but by the same token it generally assures uniform treatment of identical cases.

4. *Merit and Seniority.* Bureaucratic organizations make use of the principles of merit and seniority in their personnel systems. Merit is the ability to perform tasks well and is supposed to be measured or estimated in some evenhanded fashion. Typically, merit is the primary criterion for entrance into a bureaucratic organization, with the "best"-qualified being selected first. Promotions may also be according to merit, but seniority commonly plays a role here as well. Although the achievement orientation

found in bureaucracies is second nature to us today, it is not the only value system in organizations. In the past, and even today in nonbureaucratic personnel systems, criteria such as kinship, race, and religion have been used to hire and promote people.

5. *Size.* In order to be fully bureaucratized, most organizations must be large. Anthony Downs suggests that an organization has reached the right size to become truly bureaucratic when the highest-ranking members know less than half of the other members.[2] Bigness reinforces the need for hierarchy and formalization and is likely to be associated with a high degree of specialization as well.

6. *Nonmarketable Output.* Typically the output of public bureaucracies is unassessable in the marketplace. They generally do not produce a product that can be freely bought and sold. Although price tags may be attached to bureaucratic services, they are not established by market mechanisms. They are really budgetary devices (as in the Department of Defense, for example) or monopolistic transactions (as in the Postal Service). Agencies may show surpluses or deficits, but these should not be confused with profit and loss. Hence a bureaucracy's output and efficiency cannot be evaluated by the simple question: does it make a profit? One consequence is that bureaucracies tend to judge themselves by the quantity rather than the quality of their work.

In order to be considered a true bureaucracy, an organization must have all six characteristics in this list. Although it can be useful to think of bureaucratization as a continuum on which some organizations are more and some less bureaucratic, it is important to distinguish between true bureaucracies and organizations that simply have a few bureaucratic qualities. Those that fulfill the six criteria tend to show similar forms of behavior. And this behavior makes them different in nature and in operations from other organizations.

The Growth and Dominance of Bureaucracy

One of the outstanding features of bureaucracy is that it tends to engulf and dominate an increasing number of social, economic, and political activities. For instance, citizens in contemporary America are involved with bureaucratic organizations throughout their lives. We are born, and often die, in hospitals—the larger of which are bureaucratic organizations. Our births and deaths must be officially registered. Knowledge and culture are transmitted to us through educational bureaucracies. Many of us work for bureaucracies. To people in almost any walk of life, the power position of bureaucracy is "overtowering."[3] Indeed, it has been said that bureaucracy has the same relation to nonbureaucratic organizations that the machine does to nonmechanical modes of production.[4] So pronounced has the trend toward bureaucracy been in the twentieth century that some social scientists have spoken of "the bureaucratization of the world."[5]

Why has bureaucracy spread so far so fast? Although we often think of bureaucracies as inefficient by definition, in reality they have technical advantages over other forms of organization. Hierarchy enables the bureaucracy to speak largely with one voice and to maintain a unified system of command. Some bargaining and compromise take place within the hierarchy, but nothing like the give-and-take that characterizes organizations where all members have an equal voice. Centralized command yields speed and projects unity. Moreover, since bureaucracies develop expertise through specialization, many decisions can be made without widespread consultation throughout the organization. Hierarchy, specialization, and formalization give bureaucracies a life of their own, apart from that of the individuals who staff them. Indeed, it has been said that individual bureaucrats are nothing more than "cogs" in a machine whose direction they cannot control.[6] Individuals enter and leave the organization, but it remains an entity with a "personality" and "culture."[7] Finally, the bureaucracy's formalization provides the great advantage of precision.

In turn, other forms of organization offer some advantages that bureaucracy lacks: for example, more participation, personal freedom, and individualism. It is reasonable to assume that different types of organizational structures are best suited to different kinds of tasks. Bureaucracies can process large numbers of cases with little deviation in routine. Thus they serve to reduce complexity and make modern life more manageable. The individual bureaucrat is directed through hierarchy, formalization, and specialization. The client is also constrained by the organizational rules and becomes a "case" that gets processed. If the client does not like the result, the case can be appealed. However, it is very difficult for a person to break through the standard bureaucratic process and transform the "case" back into the individual. Most people who are dissatisfied with a bureaucracy's treatment of their case eventually come to accept the result. This is the nature of rational-legal authority as exercised by public bureaucracies.

Bureaucracy is an organizational form well suited to regulating human behavior. The Internal Revenue Service (IRS), the motor vehicle departments, police forces throughout the country, the Department of Agriculture, . . . and so on all have a major impact on citizens' lives. Often their regulation is indirect, as in the case of rules that affect home owning, retirement, marriage, and divorce. Sometimes, as in the case of the police, control is direct, highly visible, and coercive. Ironically, bureaucracies are also service organizations. This paradoxical quality was expressed in the title of the old military draft bureaucracy, the Selective Service System. Indeed, the federal bureaucracy is often called the federal "service." Bureaucracies do render service, but we must remember that usually they are also engaged in regulation. So when we criticize them for giving us inefficient *service*, we may be overlooking the major part of their work. For instance, people who complain about the Postal Service usually speak as if its only duty is to handle first class mail. They do not consider the impact of its regulations on the mail order, advertising, and publishing businesses. . . .

Conclusion: Democracy and Bureaucracy   It has been evident since the earliest days of social scientific analysis of bureaucracy that it inherently and inevitably conflicts with democracy. As Weber observed, although middle-class dissatisfaction with aristocracy often brought both bureaucracy and democracy into being, eventually the bureaucratization of government and politics clashes with the idea of popular rule.[8] Indeed, in a fully developed bureaucratic political system, rule would be by bureaucratic organizations rather than by individual bureaucrats. The inherent tension between the two forms of organization is obvious when their requirements are compared:

Democracy Requires	*Bureaucracy Requires*
Plurality	Unity
Equality	Hierarchy
Liberty	Command
Rotation in office	Duration in office
Openness	Secrecy
Equal access to participation in politics	Differentiated access, based on authority
Election	Appointment

Given these divergencies, it is an open question whether bureaucracy and democracy can reach a harmonious accommodation.

The primary difficulty in integrating bureaucratic government into a democratic political framework is that control of public bureaucracies by elective and appointive political authorities is highly problematic. True, bureaucrats can be influenced, but it is virtually impossible to dominate all of them over a long period. Traditional notions about accountability and responsibility to political authorities are largely inappropriate in the modern bureaucratized state. For instance, the rapid unionization of public employees in the past decade is based on the idea that public employees are an independent group with whom the government must bargain. Similarly, budgeting and reorganizational schemes are not equal to the task of changing the bureaucracy. Budgetary approaches have succeeded more in reorganizing budget bureaus than in giving elective and appointive political authorities greater control over public bureaucracies. Likewise, reorganizations do not necessarily resolve problems of substance nor enable political authorities to exert greater influence over bureaucratic agencies. In addition, as Weber argues, bureaucratic specialization and expertise often place "the 'political master'. . . in the position of the 'dilettante' who stands opposite the 'expert,' facing the trained official who stands within the management of administration."[9]

If public bureaucracies cannot be made responsive to outside control by individuals, can they instead be held accountable to the rule of law? Not without difficulties. Statutes in the United States allow administrative agencies a great deal of discretion and thereby delegate authority and power to them. Why is this the case? In part it is due to electoral politics and the reluctance of elected officials to take clear-cut operational stands on controversial issues. But it is also due to the fact that bureaucratic agencies have a great deal of expertise which can improve the implementation of programs. In short, although bureaucracies are far from perfect, they often have the know-how that government requires. Individual bureaucrats can take a less partisan view of policy and act as impartial, expert judges. Moreover, any effort to try to legislate in such a way as to cover all possible contingencies in today's complex and fast-paced world of permanent crisis would be doomed to failure. The legislative process can only give broad direction to most governmental programs or else veto them entirely.

As the power of bureaucrats and bureaucratic organizations grows, the political influence of the general citizenry inevitably declines. Elections are still important, especially as a means by which the voters can pass judgment on government performance and contribute to the formulation of broad national objectives. But at best, elections can only indirectly influence the behavior of public bureaucrats, and at the federal level an election rarely provides the public with specific policy options. Paradoxically, since changing the elected officials does not normally lead to farreaching changes in the government bureaucracy, the citizen's most forceful legal protest against the bureaucratic polity may lie in *not* voting—that is, in refusing to legitimize the state of affairs with his or her vote. Thus the tension between bureaucracy and democracy goes beyond the relations among politicians and bureaucrats; it engulfs the citizenry and militates against their participation in political life....

Notes

1. Martin Albrow, *Bureaucracy* (New York: Praeger, 1970), p. 125.
2. Anthony Downs, *Inside Bureaucracy* (Boston: Little, Brown, 1967), pp. 24–25.
3. Max Weber, *Essays in Sociology*, trans. and ed. by H. H. Gerth and C. W. Mills (New York: Oxford University Press, 1958), p. 232.
4. Ibid., "Bureaucracy."
5. Henry Jacoby, *The Bureaucratization of the World* (Berkeley; Calif: University of California Press, 1973).
6. Weber, *Essays in Sociology*, p. 228.
7. Harold Seidman, *Politics, Position, and Power* (New York: Oxford University Press, 1970), p. 18.
8. Weber, *Essays in Sociology*, especially pp. 224–235.
9. Ibid., p. 232.

60 / The Waning Political Capital of Cabinet Appointments

Margaret Jane Wyszomirski

Presidents need help in managing their administrations, but they also need help in the "politics" of dealing with the rest of the government (and especially the Congress). In reviewing the history of presidents' appointments to their cabinets, Margaret Wyszomirski finds that presidents have increasingly come to name secretaries for their administrative rather than political skills. This may have contributed to making presidents better managers, but at the price of making it more difficult for them to "govern."

Cabinet appointments are publicly and politically regarded as the single most important action of a new president.[1] Cabinet appointees symbolically bridge the transition from election to administration, from the politics of campaigning to the politics of governance. Despite the actual as well as symbolic importance of cabinet recruitment, the cabinet as a political institution, exhibits little organizational coherence and only a tenous claim on presidential influence since it rests on the shifting sands of a "completely customary basis."[2]

The process of selecting presidential appointees (including cabinet members) has undergone important changes during the last half century. While cabinet recruitment has become part of a more institutionalized staffing system, it nonetheless retains strong idiosyncratic and personalistic aspects. While post-World War II presidents have developed (and increasingly relied upon) elaborate personnel recruitment and talent scouting systems to fill specialized administrative and sub-cabinet positions,[3] they continue to prefer managing the cabinet appointment processes more directly. Hence the process of cabinet-making is one of the most personal and least institutionalized aspects of presidential staffing. It is also one of the most variable since cabinet agencies vary considerably with regard to importance, whether judged in terms of size, age, complexity or programmatic responsibilities. Similarly, the members of the cabinet exhibit an array of origins, abilities, and loyalties. Furthermore, cabinet secretaries perform a variety of roles with varying degrees of proficiency and have had quite disparate relations with their respective presidents. Despite the cabinet's discontinuous and variegated character, one constant seems to prevail. A major purpose of the cabinet has been to provide presidents with political capital. Each president requires political capital if he is to fulfill his roles and responsibilities as executive, as legislator, as policy designer and advocate, and as preeminent democratic politician. Although the cabinet is surely not the sole source of a president's political capital, it is, nonetheless, an important source.[4]

In addressing its primary purpose, the cabinet (and its members) is called upon to act in the following capacities, either singly or in combination:

- political coalition representative
- political operations assistant
- departmental administrator
- expert policy adviser

The prospect for effective performance in each role can be associated with certain skills, experience, and other individual characteristics. If situational factors do not generate hindering or countervailing conditions, then cabinet appointees who possess such qualities and qualifications should be assets to the president, increasing his political capital in terms of policy expertise, administrative competence, political skills, and/or political support. Ideally, cabinet secretaries will be able to augment the president's resources on more than one of these dimensions. Certainly it is logical to assume that presidents might seek to maximize their capital accumulation by means of appointees who represent resources of more than one type.

It must be recognized that such political capital can be useful both in affirmatively advancing a president's agenda as well as in protecting his balance of resources from unnecessary depletion through error or mischance. Such "preventive assistance" would include using political skills to help keep Congressional-Executive relations cordial so as not to prejudice later prospects for positive cooperation. It would also include the use of administrative skills to conduct departments in such a way as to avoid unnecessarily taxing the president with managerial detail or with the political costs of scandals. These preventive contributions to the president's political capital are rather like tax exemptions— their impact is "measurable by contrast to what the consequences (or costs) might have been if the situation were otherwise."[5] . . .

A comprehensive analysis of patterns of presidential capital accumulation of all four types of capital during the last fifty years is beyond the scope of this paper, which will instead, focus on a selection of patterns pertaining to the most explicitly political types of political capital that cabinet appointees have represented.

Political Skills
One can think of such political skills—persuasion, negotiation, consensus formation, and coalition building—as possibly being directed at three types of "targets"—independent decisionmakers in other political institutions (e.g. congressmen, governors), public officials in ostensibly subordinate executive positions (e.g. bureaucratic administrators), or the public (either in general or in special interest constituencies). It seems logical that political skills are best acquired and polished through active engagement in public affairs. This may be done from authoritative bases or from informal ones. Authoritative bases may include tenure as the member of a legislature or as a political executive who has dealt with the legislature, such as a governor or a big city mayor

or as the director of a federal agency who has had extensive contact with Congress. Informal experience is most likely gained through experience as a lobbyist for an interest group or as congressional liaison staff for an executive agency. In their application, political institutions other than the presidency are those most likely to be of use in governance, while those applied to ostensibly subordinate public officials are of primary concern to administrative tasks. While political skills employed with regard to the public are a necessary and valuable support to governance functions, they are, first and foremost, indispensable to success in the campaign and electoral process.

Given the necessity for collaboration between the President and Congress, skills pertaining to the legislative process are highly valuable. It seems logical to assume that those who have acquired these skills via authoritative experience are likely to have additional qualitative advantages in that they have established reputational and social networks to draw upon and which enhance their credibility with other political officials. It therefore follows that Congressmen are a most valuable source of political skills, that the utility of non-federal elected executives may be limited by their relative unfamiliarity with the specifics of the national political scene, and that informal craftsmen (such as lobbyists or experienced congressional liaison staff) may have considerable skill but comparatively little independent legitimacy for its exercise.

Thus, to maximize their investment in political skills capital, presidents would be wise to recruit Congressmen and, secondarily, Governors. Furthermore, incumbent officials are likely to carry greater cachet than former officials, with the utility of their social networks and legitimacy declining in proportion to the length of time out of office and the circumstances under which they left office. Conversely it would increase according to their institutional position and seniority (e.g., as chairman of a congressional committee or as governor of a major state)....

During the past fifty years, Democratic presidents have sought political skills capital with more frequency than have Republican presidents. For example, in an unlikely pair, FDR and Carter made the greatest efforts to recruit individuals with reputations and skills in congressional affairs. FDR recruited Senate committee chairmen Cordell Hull and Claude Swanson in 1933. Later he brought in Henry Stimson and Jesse Jones—two highly respected federal executives known for their abilities to work with Congress. Carter initially recruited the chairman of the House Budget Committee (Brock Adams to Transportation) and later appointed Senator Edmund Muskie as a replacement Secretary of State. Additionally, Carter appointed one incumbent Congressman (Bob Bergland—Agriculture), one Governor (Cecil Andrus of Idaho to Interior), and later two big city mayors (Moon Landrieu of New Orleans to HUD and Neil Goldschmidt of Portland to Transportation).

Although other Democratic presidents sought to recruit politically skilled individuals, they followed less prestigious patterns. Truman generally settled for former Congressmen who had gone on to federal judgeships.... He supplemented these with the acquired skills of a number of experienced federal administrators. JFK mixed one relatively junior Representative . . . with three governors . . . and a big city mayor. . . . While these appointees were quite successful in terms of preventive political assistance, they were less able to move Kennedy's policies through Congress to enactment—a record reflecting not only their extra-Washington experience as well as the generally conservative and uncooperative mood of Congress at that time. Surprisingly, Lyndon Johnson paid scant attention to political skills amongst his cabinet personnel, retaining only two of Kennedy's original political appointees but recruiting none himself. Perhaps, given Johnson's own considerable legislative skills, he felt little need for additional political skills among cabinet members.

In contrast, Republican presidents have made fewer and weaker efforts to use cabinet appointments to increase their political skills capital. . . .

A possible explanation for the infrequency with which Republican presidents appoint members of Congress or Governors into their cabinets lies in the relatively small recruitment pool of such individuals. For the last 50 years the Republicans have been the minority party. As such, Republican presidents have fewer elected partisans to consider for possible executive appointment. . . . Paradoxically, because Republican presidents have so frequently faced Democratic controlled Congresses, their need for extra political capital of the political skills variety is likely to be more acute than that of Democratic presidents.

An alternative source of political skills has historically resided in the political parties. Indeed, party functionaries, even if they have never held elective office, are likely to be adept political operants. However, their practice in coalition-building has often been gained through activity in nomination and campaign politics rather than in governance. Virtually every president has recruited such political operants into the cabinet, with the campaign director, the party chairman, or the party campaign finance chairman being most frequently rewarded with cabinet office.

Historically, the Postmaster-generalship went to one of these party officials (e.g., James Farley-FDR, Robert Hannegan-HST, Arthur Summerfield-Eisenhower, and Lawrence O'Brien-LBJ), but with the conversion of the Post Office Department to a government corporation, this cabinet appointment is no longer available. Alternatively, modern presidents have sometimes appointed party leaders/campaign supporters to inner cabinet posts (e.g., Robert Lovett to Defense-HST, Robert Kennedy-JFK and Herbert Brownell-Eisenhower as Attorneys-General). One must, however, note that in a period of declining political parties and of increasingly individualized campaigning, the political value of political skills gained in party positions is likely to be particularly attuned to the mobilization of candidate-centered electoral coalitions and not as readily transferable to the task of assembling and maintaining governing coalitions.

Although the decrease and diminution of political skills capital in the cabinet has been erratic and subtle, the significance of this change is nonetheless apparent. A growing chorus of observers and critics have pointed to the difficulty presidents have in forming "a government"[6] or in converting their electoral coalition into a governing one.[7] While some attribute this problem to split partisan control of the institutions of Congress and of the presidency (e.g., during periods in the Truman, Eisenhower, Nixon, Ford and Reagan presidencies), it is equally true that Kennedy and Carter fared no better with solid Democratic party control of both Congress and the White House. Indeed, as the cases of Presidents Nixon and Carter demonstrate, even if politically skilled cabinet members are recruited, they may use those skills for other purposes than support of their president and his programs or else they may find themselves unconsulted and underutilized. Conversely, Presidents Truman and Eisenhower seemed to have dealt effectively with opposition controlled Congresses. Thus, awareness of a less politically efficacious presidency with regard to Congress seems to coincide with the noted decline in the political skills capital available in the cabinet. While not the sole cause of this worsening performance, changes in cabinet recruitment patterns certainly seem to be a contributory factor....

The development of the administrative presidency is another factor contributing to the apparent difficulties modern presidents seem to encounter in effectively capitalizing on politically skilled cabinet appointments. As postwar presidents have sought to realize bureaucratic control and assert political direction implied by the idea of an administrative presidency, they have exhibited increasing difficulty in tolerating, much less collaborating with, potent political allies within their "official family." As Colin Campbell has astutely observed, all modern presidents except Eisenhower and to some extent Ford and Truman, have regarded cabinet secretaries as "barons to be dealt with one-on-one or to be forced into passivity" rather than as allies or colleagues.[8] Thus, it would seem that in the quest for greater administrative control, presidents have diminished their ability to accumulate political capital through cabinet appointments....

Within the White House staff a special office for Congressional liaison was initiated by President Eisenhower and maintained and expanded by subsequent presidents. Thus it would appear that presidential staff agencies have become a locus of political skills capital rather than the cabinet. Such presidential staff resources are not, however, completely comparable substitutes for political allies in the cabinet. First, the skills of many such campaign assistants are geared to electoral politics rather than governance. Thus, the newer breed of political operants tends to be candidate-centered and politically dependent upon a specific president rather than its appointive alternative who were more politically independent and party-centered. Second, the White House Congressional Liaison Office, unlike cabinet politicians, seldom adds to a president's political capital; rather they assist him in utilizing already available resources when dealing with Congress. Indeed, the existence of such an office does not guarantee that it will function successfully. For example, President Carter's congressional assistants were notorious for their ineptitude and consequently for drawing-down the president's political capital.

Political Support

It is commonly held that "the chief significance" of the cabinet is that it "offers an opportunity for consolidating political strength through a coalition of leaders whose adherence brings the strength of their political following to the administration."[9] During the last 50 years, however, there has been a decreasing tendency to recruit actual political leaders who can command either partisan or constituency support. The decrease of partisan leaders is, in part, related to the declining incidence of former elected officials with their attendant political skills. But it is also related to the increasing tendency (and indeed necessity) of presidents to seek support both beyond their own party base and among special interest groups. Hence most modern presidents have deviated from the historic norm of partisan purity when appointing their cabinet.

Perhaps the most common strategy has been to appoint representatives of "opposition" party factions that have already begun to shift their allegiance. For example, FDR's appointments of Progressive Republicans, Henry Wallace and Harold Ickes, were meant to confirm both their personal and their constituency's support during the 1932 election campaign. Likewise Roosevelt's June 1940 appointment of former Republican Secretary of State Henry Stimson and former Republican vice presidential candidate Henry Knox were designed to attract bipartisan support both for an unprecedented third electoral bid and for the anticipated war effort. Similarly Eisenhower's appointments of Oveta Culp Hobby and Robert Anderson brought nominal Texas Democrats into his administration, while seeking to consolidate the electoral support of moderate Southern Democrats who had voted for Eisenhower in 1952 and 1956. Richard Nixon sought to appeal to the very same geographic constituency with his appointment of a Democrat and former Governor of Texas John Connally.

Again, a subtle shift in the potency of such partisan representative capital must be noted. Beginning with Eisenhower, the tendency has been to seek to appoint nominal members of the opposition party, rather than leaders within the opposition. Both Hobby and Anderson were active in Democrats for Eisenhower but this represented a candidate-centered group rather than an enduring partisan realignment. While Kennedy appointed registered Republicans, such as Douglas Dillon and Robert McNamara, these gentlemen were not party leaders or spokesmen, but rather symbolic representatives of the opposition party. Johnson's appointment of Republican foundation executive, John Gardner, was of a similar cast. Ford appointed not only symbolic Democrats like William Usery and F. David Mathews, but the avowed independent, Edward Levi. Finally, Carter appointed veteran Republican administrator James Schlesinger to serve as his first Energy Secretary. Thus presidents have retained the appearance of bipartisan coalition-building through appointments but have seldom enjoyed the additional partisan support that would attend actual, as opposed to merely symbolic, coalition partners. . . .

Aside from partisan representatives, political support capital can also be accumulated through the appointment of interest group representatives. Indeed this would seem particularly appropriate among the nominees to head the constituency-oriented departments of Agriculture, Commerce, Labor, and Education. Indeed there is strong precedent for the recruitment of just such representatives at Agriculture and Labor, although interest group leaders can be placed in any cabinet position. Here again it would seem that presidents have had an increasing tendency to discount the potential value of such appointments by selecting symbolic representatives or special interest administrators.

The trend toward special interest administrators rather than leaders is, perhaps, most clearly seen at two of the historic clientele departments. For example, while each Secretary of Agriculture is expected to own a farm and figuratively "to have dirt under his fingernails," Henry Wallace (FDR) may have been the last actual agricultural leader to head the department. Since then, the secretaries have generally been state or national agricultural administrators...or academic agricultural economists.... Occasionally a former congressman who had served on food or agriculture committees ... has been recruited to this post. While such appointees are usually acceptable to the farm constituency, it is clear that they function as the president's spokesman to farmers rather than as farm leader-as-member-of-the-administration....

Somewhat similarly, the Secretaries of Labor display a rather paradoxical pattern, with union leaders often recruited by Republican Administrations while Democratic presidents tend toward naming labor lawyers and mediators.... Thus, the Democrats, long identified as the party of the working man, have not appointed a single labor leader to head the Labor Department during the last fifty years.

...[W]ith the exception of gestures to demonstrate an "above politics as usual" style ... or to woo electoral support in an upcoming election ... the labor secretary has at best, been only a symbolic representative of his nominal constituency. As such, they could bring little additional political support capital to the presidents who appointed them. Conversely one might point to the succession of Labor Secretaries as evidence of the waning political clout of organized labor itself: a trend apparently reflected in the two most recent secretaries of Labor, William E. Brock, III and Anne McLaughlin, who demonstrate the tenuousness of labor's claim on a cabinet seat since neither evidenced any prior linkage to labor interests or issues.

Minority interests have also come to be represented in the contemporary cabinet, though these appointees have been scarce, tend to cluster in issue-area departments, and to occupy outer-cabinet influence status. During the past half century, nine women have been named to the cabinet, seven of these since 1975.... The incidence of female cabinet members is indicative of both the persistent under-representation of women in the highest councils of government as well as recognition of their growing political significance in modern American society.

Despite their symbolic importance, none of the appointees could be considered representatives of women in any politically organized sense. Rather, they were symbolic representatives of their gender constituency. As such, they added little in actual political support capital to the administrations for which they were recruited. Indeed, most were appointed for a complex of reasons and attributes of which their gender was a contributory, rather than a decisive, factor.

For example, FDR had wanted a woman in his cabinet in recognition of their relatively recent enfranchisement. He also needed a competent labor administrator, but did not want a union leader. In Frances Perkins, he found the combination of characteristics that he sought. From a different perspective, Oveta Culp Hobby (HEW, 1953–55) and Patricia Harris (HUD, 1977–79; HHS, 1979–81) were recruited for the political positions they represented rather than for the gender group they symbolized. Hobby had helped bring many Texas Democrats into Eisenhower's winning electoral coalition, while Harris was a respected civil rights activist, Black Democrat. President Reagan's midterm selection of Elizabeth Dole (Transportation, 1983–86) and Margaret Heckler (HHS, 1983–86) marked an attempt to bridge the "gender gap" as well as to enhance party unity and to cushion the impact of losses at the congressional elections in 1982.[10]

Finally, it must be noted that both the utility and influence of these women were limited by factors other than the political support capital which they represented. Virtually none had experience in electoral office and hence had little opportunity to acquire proficient political skills. Only Margaret Heckler had successfully run for elective office, while Patricia Harris has gained some experience in party politics. Although Perkins, Hobby, and Dole could claim some administrative capital via prior service as appointive public administrators, none had experience with the agency they were to head. Furthermore, none of the female cabinet members could make a strong claim to substantive expertise in their areas of responsibility. Thus, these individuals possessed few administrative, expertise, or political assets that might have enhanced their utility to or influence with the president. The relatively weak political influence of women secretaries is evident in the fact that they have rarely been positioned to become part of a president's inner circle, either by personal friendship or by departmental stature. Only Frances Perkins (FDR) could be considered a presidential confidant or the head of department central to the president's early policy agenda. The others were not only relative strangers to their presidents, but were appointed to head departments that were low-to-antagonistic to the president's priorities or else were newly established and beset by the problems of bureaucratic birth. In other words, female cabinet appointees have seldom added substantially to a president's political capital and have rarely exercised significant influence within an administration.

Even fewer Blacks and only one Hispanic have been appointed to the modern cabinet. Lyndon Johnson was the first president to make such an appointment, naming Robert Weaver to head the then-new Department of

Housing and Urban Development. With the exception of Nixon, subsequent presidents have each named one Black to their cabinets: William Coleman Jr. (1975–77), Patricia Harris (1977–81) and Samuel Pierce (1981–88). Each of these has been appointed to head an issue-area department responsible for programs of particular importance to minorities.... Reagan was the first President to name an Hispanic as a cabinet member when in 1988 he selected Lauro Cavazos as the Secretary of Education.

As interest group representatives, Harris and, especially, Coleman brought considerable political capital to their appointing presidents. Harris, in addition to being a symbolic representative of women, had been active in Democratic Party circles on civil rights issues. Whereas both Weaver and Harris might be considered well-educated, successful and prominent members of the Black community, neither had the constituency stature of William Coleman. Educated at Harvard Law, then a law clerk to Supreme Court Justice Felix Frankfurter, Coleman had co-authored the brief for the hallmark desegregation case of *Brown v. Board of Education* in 1954. In 1971, he was elected president of the NAACP Legal Defense and Education Fund. In recruiting Coleman (who was also a life-long Republican), President Ford gained considerable political support capital from an interest group that seldom identified with the modern Republican Party. Reaching out to Blacks (and women) through executive appointments was but one of the many efforts made by President Ford to help restore legitimacy and public support for the discredited government he had inherited in the wake of the Watergate scandal and President Nixon's resignation.

In contrast, the Reagan Administration gained little political capital from the appointment of Samuel Pierce in 1981. A New York labor lawyer who had served in the prior Republican administrations of Eisenhower and Nixon, Pierce was no minority leader and did little to improve relations between the Reagan presidency and Black Americans.

The Declining Political Character of Cabinet Recruitment

Despite its discontinuous character, the president's cabinet has persistently functioned as a mechanism and resource of presidential governance. Cabinet personnel have been treated herein as bearers of political capital that may add to a president's capacity to govern. Although the discussion has focused on capital of the political skills and political support variants, even this limited focus is suggestive of broad aspects of the evolution and problems of the modern presidency.

The scarcity of experienced politicians as well as of interest group leaders illustrates one way in which the quest for managerial control by the Chief Executive has hindered the presidency as a political institution. Indeed, the evidence suggests that the cabinet has atrophied as a political institution whose members are skilled political operants and/or potent political allies. Rather, the political qualities of cabinet personnel have become virtually residual: constituency representatives are merely symbolic (not actual) group leaders, while politicians who have lost or are losing their political base are more frequently recruited than those who can command independent power bases. While this tendency deprives presidents of certain political assets, it nonetheless has the virtue of producing cabinet secretaries who are likely to be dependent, and, therefore, relatively controlled, by presidents. Since this is in contrast to the historic independence of self-sufficient politicians who have served in earlier cabinets, the trend toward technocrats might be viewed as a move toward more manageable bureaucracy.

Since the 1937 Brownlow Committee's declaration of the president as the managerial head of the executive branch, presidents have sought to realize and exercise control over the so-called "fourth branch of government"—the bureaucracy. Theoretically, cabinet officers were to be a president's chief field officers in exercising this control. As administrative control became an increasingly important presidential goal, presidents have sought greater managerial resources to employ towards its achievement. Hence cabinet recruitment in the post-war period has come to emphasize the accumulation of administrative capital. Concomitantly, it has de-emphasized those political assets which might incur bargaining costs if a president were to secure political alliances with other elective, factional, or interest group leaders.

A second modern development has cast the president as the chief policy designer—a role that requires expertise in such a variety of fields that it is beyond the capacity of a single individual. In many ways, the growth of the Executive Office of the President can be explained as the cumulative effect of repeated efforts to provide presidents with the expert resources needed to function as chief policy designer. The Council of Economic Advisers, the National Security Council staff, and the Office of Science and Technology Policy are each prominent examples of new institutional assets available to presidents requiring diverse expertise capital. Similarly, the search for expertise capital has carried into cabinet recruitment as presidents have sought technocrats rather than political allies. Indeed, the search for technocrats such as labor, industrial, and agricultural economists, may have been pursued at the cost of seeking political allies, particularly with major political interest groups.

In a related development, the apparent substitution of expertise capital for political skills capital may have indirectly had an additional erosive effect on the political capabilities of an administration. Particularly during the last 20 years, policy expertise has tended to be recruited from the ranks of professional policy analysts, particularly those in think tanks and research institutions. The change from an "establishment" based set of policy experts to alternative sets of professional policy analysts has been most commented upon in the realm of foreign and national security affairs, where the shift was seen as symptomatic (if not catalytic) of the breakdown that occurred in the 1970s in the positive, bipartisan consensus of foreign policy.[11] Yet domestic issue networks have also become evident, each with its sets of competing policy professionals.

With so many intellectual and professional analysts now involved, policy making acquired something of the atmosphere and norms of academic politics.

Whereas the old "establishment" prided itself on anonymity (or at least avoided notoriety), the new professionals sought public recognition and reputation. Whereas the "old" expertise had performed what it regarded as informed service in the public interest, the "new" expertise prided itself on espousing analytical, partisan and ideological distinctions to advance its own careers and causes. In other words, the prime strategy of academic politics—drawing distinctions and emphasizing differences while simultaneously intellectualizing and personalizing disagreement—was transferred into the political arena with the recruitment of professional policy experts into administrative and decisionmaking counsels. As a consequence, the norm of the new policy experts—to develop and emphasize differences—was largely incompatible with the old political skills of compromise, accommodation and consensus-building. Thus the shift in the kinds of resources recruited into the presidential cabinets would seem to be reflective not only of waning political capabilities and capacities but the more fundamental displacement of operating norms supportive of productive politics and effective governance.

In sum, these two related trends are illustrative of and contributory to one of the central paradoxes of the modern American presidency. Against enormous structural and customary impediments, presidents have enhanced their managerial control of the executive branch and with it, significant influence over the direction of public policy. This managerial gain has apparently been realized at the cost of the capability to govern effectively. As one recent commentator noted, presidents form "administrations" rather than "governments."[12] But in a political system of separate institutions sharing power, it is only "governments" that have both the capacity and legitimacy to govern.

Notes

1. Samuel Lindsay observed over 50 years ago that "No single act of the President transcends in importance the appointment of his cabinet. The country forms its judgment of his underlying purposes and theories of government, it takes his measure and draws more conclusions from this single act than it does from his platform, his campaign pledges, his inaugural address or his first message to Congress. It represents in a vivid way the President's concept of the essential, vital and controlling organization of the executive government." See "The New Cabinet and Its Problems," *Review of Reviews*, April 1921, p. 382.
2. Roger Porter has used the term "adhocracy" to refer to an informal and changing policy organization that tends to neglect the need for overall policy coordination. See *Presidential Decision-Making: The Economic Policy Board*, (New York: Cambridge University Press, 1980). Graham Allison also uses the term in a discussion of the cabinet in "An Executive Cabinet," *Society*, (July/August, 1980), pp. 41–47, especially p. 44.
3. For a discussion of presidential personnel recruitment processes from Truman through Carter, see G. Calvin MacKenzie, *The Politics of Presidential Appointments* (New York: The Free Press Company, 1981), especially pp. 11–78.
4. This bears a resemblance to Richard Neustadt's perspective that presidential power is essentially persuasive in nature and that the ability to persuade requires "bargaining advantages." In that sense, "political capital" accrued through personnel

recruitment can be regarded as one source of "bargaining advantage." However, this approach differs in emphasis from Neustadt in the sense that he regards the Department heads primarily as officers the president must bargain with (thus expending some of his political capital negotiating with them.) In contrast, I emphasize the utility of cabinet members in providing the president with assets that can enhance (or diminish) his ability to "bargain" with others. On Neustadt's approach see *Presidential Power* (New York: John Wiley and Sons, Inc., 1980), especially pp. 26–33. . . .

5. The idea of "preventive assistance" is Richard R. Fenno's, see *The President's Cabinet*, (Cambridge: Harvard University Press, 1959), pp. 208 and 220.

6. For example, see Lloyd N. Cutler, "To Form a Government," *Foreign Affairs*, (Fall 1980): 126–143.

7. See for example, James L. Sundquist, "The Crisis of Competence in Our National Government" *Political Science Quarterly*, vol. 95, no. 2 (Summer 1980): 183–208.

8. Colin Campbell, *Managing the Presidency*, (Pittsburgh: University of Pittsburgh Press, 1986), pp. 55–6.

9. Edward Pendleton Herring, *Presidential Leadership*, (New York: Farrar and Rinehart, 1940), p. 92.

10. Elizabeth Dole is married to Senator Robert Dole, a moderate Republican who chairs the important Finance Committee and is an often-mentioned presidential hopeful. Margaret Heckler, a moderate Republican from Massachusetts, was defeated for reelection to the House in 1982, when redistricting pitted her against a Democratic congressional colleague who turned the election into a referendum on President Reagan's economic and military policies. As a Congresswoman Heckler has advocated women's rights and worked for the passage of legislation that addressed women's issues. While these actions brought her the endorsements of many women's groups, Heckler was never a leader of politically organized women. Furthermore, as an opponent of abortion, she forfeited the support of the National Women's Political Caucus.

11. The shift from an "establishment" to a "professional elite" in foreign policy has been persuasively recounted by I. M. Distler, Leslie H. Gelb, and Anthony Lake in *Our Own Worst Enemy, The Unmasking of American Foreign Policy*, (New York: Simon and Schuster, 1984), pp. 91–126.

12. Cutler, "To Form a Government."

CHAPTER SEVENTEEN

Judiciary

As a reading of Article III of the Constitution will quickly reveal, few things about the federal judiciary were stipulated by the delegates to the constitutional convention. The judiciary was one of the sources of potential conflict that the framers chose to skirt for the time being, and so they left many important details, pertaining even to power and structure, to be filled in later by Congress and by the judiciary itself. To put it another way, from the standpoint of the Constitution, there are few things about the judicial branch that are not changeable.

To view the judiciary as a *changing* institution, however, may at first seem to run contrary to the commonly held view that the courts, and especially the United States Supreme Court, were designed to be, and presumably are, rocks of stability within the political system. The judiciary was, after all, placed by the framers on an "island," set off from the changing issues of politics. The "judicial independence" of the courts was seemingly assured by making judicial positions appointive for life, rather than elective for set terms. Congress is even forbidden from reducing the salaries of the federal judges while they are in office.

The apparently unchanging independence of the courts can be deceiving. If the judges do not need to consult other public officials or consider public opinion in reaching decisions, then those decisions could presumably be made in a political "vacuum," the same today as yesterday, and the same tomorrow as today: the content of judicial decisions would not change to reflect even the most fundamental changes in society. But one important point that this view ignores is that judges, even on a court as revered as the United States Supreme Court, are human beings. Not only can human beings change their minds, but they are also mortal, and as the personnel on the benches change, so may the pervasive political orientation of "the Court," and so may its "opinions."

In fact, the United States Supreme Court has not been immune to altering its course or "changing its mind," sometimes in so fundamental and far-reaching a manner that it is said that an "era" of the Court has ended. Even when changes of mind have not been involved, the Court has seemed at times to be straining to find (or develop) constitutional principles to support a new "policy making" role for the judiciary as the basic issues of politics have changed. Within the power to interpret, there has been ample room for emphasizing some principles and deemphasizing others, and also apparently for inferring new ones and discarding old ones. Whether judges *should* feel bound by "original intent" or, alternatively, feel free to interpret differently for different times has been and continues to be intensely debated, as represented here by the readings from Robert Bork and Laurence Tribe. But regardless of whether a policy-making role for the judiciary is desirable, there is much factual support for the view that the Supreme Court has been and is, both attitudinally and behaviorally, a changing, political, policy-making institution.

First, there is the well-documented and now widely accepted view that the Court has, during at least three distinct periods of its history, played a role as "champion" of one particular cause or another, each time finding or inferring new principles to support its positions.* From founding until the Civil War era, the Court championed a strong national government, apparently seeing itself as the glue that could hold the union together. After the Civil War and until the Depression era, the Court applied new and expanded principles to protect the laissez-faire economic system from government regulation, but this position was eventually dropped as the weight of public opinion came down on the Court and made its position untenable. From the 1940s until at least recently, the Court has been seen primarily as protector of civil rights and civil liberties, as evidenced in the chapter with that title.

Second, there is firm evidence that the Court has not avoided "changing its mind" to the point of actually overturning its own, earlier decisions. Although this is by no means a "regular" occurrence, one justice has recently estimated that it has happened more than 150 times in the Court's history.** The case of *Gideon v. Wainwright* (see Chapter Five) is but one example.

Myths to the contrary notwithstanding, the Court is a changing, political, policy-making institution. The Court has already experienced three distinct periods in which an activist role has become quite clear, and experts have suggested that the recent appointment of several "conservatives" to the Court could have the effect of changing its emphasis again. In one of the readings of this chapter, David O'Brien examines indicators from the first full term of what he labels the Reagan/Rehnquist Court, and concludes that they do indeed point to a "sea change" in legal currents.

That Court appointments are viewed by presidents as a very important means for shaping the Court's political orientation is well documented in the selection by Chief Justice William Rehnquist himself, who defends the practice as "both normal and desirable." In the final reading of this chapter, John Moore documents the same tendency in appointments to lower levels of federal courts, finding that President Carter and then Presidents Reagan and Bush have effected their own "revolutions" on the lower courts.

No review of change in the federal judiciary could ignore the most important change that has occurred in the history of the court system, even though that change occurred just fourteen years after ratification of the Constitution. In 1803, in the case of *Marbury v. Madison*, the Supreme Court fundamentally changed its role in the separation of powers system by assuming a power not mentioned anywhere in the Constitution, the power of judicial review. More than any structural or behavioral change, this expansion of the judiciary's *power* has shaped the role of the Court in American government and politics. Chief Justice John Marshall's classic opinion in that case is the first reading of this chapter.

---

*Probably the most thorough treatment is Robert G. McCloskey, *The American Supreme Court* (Chicago: The University of Chicago Press, 1960)—*Editor's Note.*

**Justice Byron R. White, as quoted in David Edwards, *The American Political Experience* (Englewood Cliffs, N.J.: Prentice-Hall, Inc., 1985, p. 364).—*Editor's Note.*

61 / *Marbury v. Madison*
5 U.S. (1 Cranch) 137 (1803)

Judicial review, the power of the Court to declare laws null and void if they violate the Constitution, is recognized today as one of the Court's most important powers. Yet, no mention of this power is made in the Constitution itself. In the case of *Marbury v. Madison* (1803), the Court simply asserted this power, and it has had it ever since. It is little wonder that *Marbury v. Madison* is still recognized today as one of the most important decisions in the history of the United States Supreme Court.

As with many of the Court's "landmark" cases, *Marbury v. Madison* had humble beginnings. In the last days of President John Adams's administration, he made "midnight appointments" to a number of newly created judicial positions. The written appointments were properly signed and sealed before Adams's presidency ended, but through an oversight, they were not delivered. In fact, they were still in the desk of the secretary of state—the official charged with delivering them— when Adams's political foe, Thomas Jefferson, became president. James Madison, Jefferson's new secretary of state, chose not to deliver Adams's appointments, thereby leaving the positions open for the new president's own appointees.

William Marbury's appointment as Justice of the Peace for the District of Columbia was one of those that had not been delivered. Marbury petitioned the Supreme Court to issue a writ of mandamus ordering Madison to deliver the appointment. Although the Constitution did not provide for the Court to receive requests for writs of mandamus under its original jurisdiction, the Judiciary Act of 1789 did authorize the Supreme Court to consider such requests.

In the Court's written opinion, Chief Justice John Marshall expressed sympathy for Marbury's situation, but then asserted that the Court could not issue writs of mandamus despite the Judiciary Act's authorization.* That part of the Act was unconstitutional, Marshall argued, and hence it must be disregarded. This was the first assertion by the Court of its power of judicial review, a power that itself was not specifically mentioned in the Constitution.

. . .The following opinion of the Court was delivered by the *Chief Justice*.
Opinion of the Court

At the last term on the affidavits then read and filed with the clerk, a rule was granted in this case, requiring the secretary of state to show cause why a mandamus should not issue, directing him to deliver to William Marbury his commission as a justice of the peace for the county of Washington, in the District of Columbia.

No cause has been shown, and the present motion is for a mandamus. . . .

In the order in which the court has viewed this subject, the following questions have been considered and decided.

---

*Interestingly, John Marshall had been the secretary of state who failed to deliver William Marbury's appointment in the first place.—*Editor's Note.*

1st. Has the applicant a right to the commission he demands?

2d. If he has a right, and that right has been violated, do the laws of his country afford him a remedy?

3d. If they do afford him a remedy, is it a mandamus issuing from this court?

The first object of inquiry is,

1st. Has the applicant a right to the commission he demands?

His right originates in an act of congress passed in February, 1801, concerning the District of Columbia.

After dividing the district into two counties, the 11th section of this law enacts, "that there shall be appointed in and for each of the said counties, such number of discreet persons to be justices of the peace as the president of the United States shall, from time to time, think expedient, to continue in office for five years. .

It appears, from the affidavits, that in compliance with this law, a commission for William Marbury, as a justice of the peace for the county of Washington, was signed by John Adams, then President of the United States; after which the seal of the United States was affixed to it; but the commission has never reached the person for whom it was made out. . . .

It is, therefore, decidedly the opinion of the court, that when a commission has been signed by the President, the appointment is made; and that the commission is complete when the seal of the United States has been affixed to it by the Secretary of State. . . .

The discretion of the executive is to be exercised until the appointment has been made. But having once made the appointment, his power over the office is terminated in all cases where by law the officer is not removable by him. The right to the office is then in the person appointed, and he has the absolute, unconditional power of accepting or rejecting it.

Mr. Marbury, then, since his commission was signed by the President, and sealed by the Secretary of State, was appointed; and as the law creating the office, gave the officer a right to hold for five years, independent of the executive, the appointment was not revocable, but vested in the officer legal rights, which are protected by the laws of his country.

To withhold his commission, therefore, is an act deemed by the court not warranted by law, but violative of a vested legal right.

This brings us to the second inquiry; which is,

2d. If he has a right, and that right has been violated, do the laws of this country afford him a remedy?

The very essence of civil liberty certainly consists in the right of every individual to claim the protection of the laws, whenever he receives an injury. One of the first duties of government is to afford that protection. . . .

The government of the United States has been emphatically termed a government of laws, and not of men. It will certainly cease to deserve this high appellation, if the laws furnish no remedy for the violation of a vested legal right.

If this obloquy is to be cast on the jurisprudence of our country, it must arise from the peculiar character of the case.

It behooves us, then, to inquire whether there be in its composition any ingredient which shall exempt it from legal investigations, or exclude the injured party from legal redress. In pursuing this inquiry the first question which presents itself is, whether this can be arranged with that class of cases which come under the description of *damnum absque injuria;* a loss without an injury.

This description of cases never has been considered, and it is believed never can be considered, as comprehending offices of trust, of honor, or of profit. The office of justice of peace in the District of Columbia is such an office; it is therefore worthy of the attention and guardianship of the laws. It has received that attention and guardianship. It has been created by special act of congress, and has been secured, so far as the laws can give security, to the person appointed to fill it, for five years. It is not, then, on account of the worthlessness of the thing pursued, that the injured party can be alleged to be without remedy.

Is it in the nature of the transaction? Is the act of delivering or withholding a commission to be considered as a mere political act, belonging to the executive department alone, for the performance of which entire confidence is placed by our constitution in the supreme executive; and for any misconduct respecting which, the injured individual has no remedy?

That there may be such cases is not to be questioned; but that every act of duty, to be performed in any of the great departments of government, constitutes such a case, is not to be admitted. . . .

It follows, then, that the question, whether the legality of an act of the head of a department be examinable in a court of justice or not, must always depend on the nature of that act.

If some acts be examinable, and others not, there must be some rule of law to guide the court in the exercise of its jurisdiction.

In some instances there may be difficulty in applying the rule to particular cases; but there cannot, it is believed, be much difficulty in laying down the rule.

By the constitution of the United States, the President is invested with certain important political powers, in the exercise of which he is to use his own discretion, and is accountable only to his country in his political character and to his own conscience. To aid him in the performance of these duties, he is authorized to appoint certain officers, who act by his authority, and in conformity with his orders.

In such cases, their acts are his acts; and whatever opinion may be entertained of the manner in which executive discretion may be used, still there exists, and can exist, no power to control that discretion. The subjects are political. They respect the nation, not individual rights, and being intrusted to the executive, the decision of the executive is conclusive. The application of this remark will be perceived by adverting to the act of congress for establishing the department of foreign affairs. This officer, as his duties were prescribed by that act, is to conform precisely to the will of the President. He is the mere organ by whom that will is communicated. The acts of such an officer, as an officer, can never be examinable by the courts.

But when the legislature proceeds to impose on that officer other duties; when he is directed peremptorily to perform certain acts; when the rights of individuals are dependent on the performance of those acts; he is so far the officer of the law; is amenable to the laws for his conduct; and cannot at his discretion sport away the vested rights of others.

The conclusion from this reasoning is, that where the heads of departments are the political or confidential agents of the executive, merely to execute the will of the President, or rather to act in cases in which the executive possesses a constitutional or legal discretion, nothing can be more perfectly clear than that their acts are only politically examinable. But where a specific duty is assigned by law, and individual rights depend upon the performance of that duty, it seems equally clear that the individual who considers himself injured, has a right to resort to the laws of his country for a remedy.

If this be the rule, let us inquire how it applies to the case under the consideration of the court.

The power of nominating to the senate, and the power of appointing the person nominated, are political powers, to be exercised by the President according to his own discretion. When he has made an appointment, he has exercised his whole power, and his discretion has been completely applied to the case. If, by law, the officer be removable at the will of the President, then a new appointment may be immediately made, and the rights of the officer are terminated. But as a fact which has existed cannot be made never to have existed, the appointment cannot be annihilated; and consequently, if the officer is by law not removable at the will of the President, the rights he has acquired are protected by the law, and are not resumable by the President. They can not be extinguished by executive authority, and he has the privilege of asserting them in like manner as if they had been derived from any other source.

The question whether a right has vested or not, is, in its nature, judicial, and must be tried by the judicial authority. If, for example, Mr. Marbury had taken the oaths of a magistrate, and proceeded to act as one; in consequence of which a suit had been instituted against him, in which his defence had depended on his being a magistrate, the validity of his appointment must have been determined by judicial authority.

So, if he conceives that, by virtue of his appointment, he has a legal right either to the commission which has been made out for him, or to a copy of that commission, it is equally a question examinable in a court, and the decision of the court upon it must depend on the opinion entertained of his appointment.

That question has been discussed, and the opinion is, that the latest point of time which can be taken as that at which the appointment was complete, and evidenced, was when, after the signature of the President, the seal of the United States was affixed to the commission.

It is, then, the opinion of the Court,

1st. That by signing the commission of Mr. Marbury, the President of the United States appointed him a justice of peace for the county of Washington, in the District of Columbia; and that the seal of the United States, affixed thereto by the Secretary of State, is conclusive testimony of the verity of the signature, and of the completion of the appointment, and that the appointment conferred on him a legal right to the office for the space of five years.

2d. That, having this legal title to the office, he has a consequent right to the commission; a refusal to deliver which is a plain violation of that right, for which the laws of his country afford him a remedy.

It remains to be inquired whether,

3d. He is entitled to the remedy for which he applies. This depends on,

1st. The nature of the writ applied for; and,

2d. The power of this court.

1st. The nature of the writ. . . .

This writ, if awarded, would be directed to an officer of government, and its mandate to him would be, to use the words of Blackstone, "to do a particular thing therein specified, which appertains to his office and duty, and which the court has previously determined, or at least supposes, to be consonant to right and justice." Or, in the words of Lord Mansfield, the applicant, in this case, has a right to execute an office of public concern, and is kept out of possession of that right.

These circumstances certainly concur in this case.

Still, to render the mandamus a proper remedy, the officer to whom it is to be directed, must be one to whom, on legal principles, such writ may be directed; and the person applying for it must be without any other specific and legal remedy.

1st. With respect to the officer to whom it would be directed. The intimate political relation subsisting between the President of the United States and the heads of departments, necessarily renders any legal investigation of the acts of one of those high officers peculiarly irksome, as well as delicate; and excites some hesitation with respect to the propriety of entering into such investigation. Impressions are often received without much reflection or examination, and it is not wonderful that in such a case as this the assertion, by an individual, of his legal claims in a court of justice, to which claims it is the duty of that court to attend, should at first view be considered by some, as an attempt to intrude into the cabinet, and to intermeddle with the prerogatives of the executive.

It is scarcely necessary for the court to disclaim all pretensions to such jurisdiction. An extravagance, so absurd and excessive, could not have been entertained for a moment. The province of the court is, solely, to decide on the rights of individuals, not to inquire how the executive, or executive officers, perform duties in which they have a discretion. Questions in their nature political, or which are, by the constitution and laws, submitted to the executive, can never be made in this court.

But, if this be not such a question; if, so far from being an intrusion into the secrets of the cabinet, it respects a paper which, according to law, is upon record, and to a copy of which the law gives a right, on the payment of ten cents; if it be no intermeddling with a subject over which the executive can be considered as having exercised any control; what is there in the exalted station of the officer, which shall bar a citizen from asserting, in a court of justice, his legal rights, or shall forbid a court to listen to the claim, or to issue a mandamus directing the performance of a duty, not depending on executive discretion, but on particular acts of congress, and the general principles of law? . . .

. . . [W]here he is directed by law to do a certain act affecting the absolute rights of individuals, in the performance of which he is not placed under the particular direction of the President, and the performance of which the President cannot lawfully forbid, and therefore is never presumed to have forbidden; as for example, to record a commission, or a patent for land, which has received all the legal solemnities; or to give a copy of such record; in such cases, it is not perceived on what ground the courts of the country are further excused from the duty of giving judgment that right be done to an injured individual, than if the same services were to be performed by a person not the head of a department. . . .

This, then, is a plain case for a mandamus, either to deliver the commission, or a copy of it from the record; and it only remains to be inquired,

Whether it can issue from this court.

The act to establish the judicial courts of the United States authorizes the Supreme Court "to issue writs of mandamus in cases warranted by the principles and usages of law, to any courts appointed, or persons holding office, under the authority of the United States."

The Secretary of State, being a person holding an office under the authority of the United States, is precisely within the letter of the description, and if this court is not authorized to issue a writ of mandamus to such an officer, it must be because the law is unconstitutional, and therefore absolutely incapable of conferring the authority, and assigning the duties which its words purport to confer and assign.

The constitution vests the whole judicial power of the United States in one Supreme Court, and such inferior courts as congress shall, from time to time, ordain and establish. This power is expressly extended to all cases arising under the laws of the United States; and, consequently, in some form, may be exercised over the present case; because the right claimed is given by a law of the United States.

In the distribution of this power it is declared that "the Supreme Court shall have original jurisdiction in all cases affecting ambassadors, other public ministers and consuls, and those in which a state shall be a party. In all other cases, the Supreme Court shall have appellate jurisdiction."

It has been insisted, at the bar, that as the original grant of jurisdiction, to the Supreme and inferior courts, is general, and the clause, assigning original jurisdiction to the Supreme Court, contains no negative or restrictive

words, the power remains to the legislature, to assign original jurisdiction
to that court in other cases than those specified in the article which has been
recited; provided those cases belong to the judicial power of the United States.

If it had been intended to leave it in the discretion of the legislature to
apportion the judicial power between the supreme and inferior courts according to the will of that body, it would certainly have been useless to have proceeded further than to have defined the judicial power, and the tribunals in
which it should be vested. The subsequent part of the section is mere sur-
plusage, is entirely without meaning, if such is to be the construction. If congress remains at liberty to give this court appellate jurisdiction, where the
constitution has declared their jurisdiction shall be original; and original jurisdiction where the constitution has declared it shall be appellate; the distribution of jurisdiction, made in the constitution, is form without substance.

Affirmative words are often, in their operation, negative of other objects than those affirmed; and in this case, a negative or exclusive sense must
be given to them, or they have no operation at all.

It cannot be presumed that any clause in the constitution is intended
to be without effect; and, therefore, such a construction is inadmissible, unless
the words require it.

If the solicitude of the convention, respecting our peace with foreign
powers, induced a provision that the Supreme Court should take original
jurisdiction in cases which might be supposed to affect them; yet the clause
would have proceeded no further than to provide for such cases, if no further
restriction on the powers of congress had been intended. That they should
have appellate jurisdiction in all other cases, with such exceptions as congress might make, is no restriction; unless the words be deemed exclusive of
original jurisdiction. . . .

To enable this court, then, to issue a mandamus, it must be shown to
be an exercise of appellate jurisdiction, or to be necessary to enable them
to exercise appellate jurisdiction.

It has been stated at the bar that the appellate jurisdiction may be exercised in a variety of forms, and that if it be the will of the legislature that
a mandamus should be used for that purpose, that will must be obeyed. This
is true, yet the jurisdiction must be appellate, not original.

It is the essential criterion of appellate jurisdiction, that it revises and
corrects the proceedings in a cause already instituted, and does not create
that cause. Although, therefore, a mandamus may be directed to courts, yet
to issue such a writ to an officer for the delivery of a paper, is in effect the
same as to sustain an original action for that paper, and, therefore, seems
not to belong to appellate but to original jurisdiction. Neither is it necessary
in such a case as this, to enable the court to exercise its appellate jurisdiction.

The authority, therefore, given to the Supreme Court, by the act establishing the judicial courts of the United States, to issue writs of mandamus
to public officers, appears not to be warranted by the constitution; and it
becomes necessary to inquire whether a jurisdiction so conferred can be
exercised.

The question, whether an act, repugnant to the constitution, can become the law of the land, is a question deeply interesting to the United States; but, happily, not of an intricacy proportioned to its interest. It seems only necessary to recognize certain principles, supposed to have been long and well established, to decide it.

That the people have an original right to establish, for their future government, such principles, as, in their opinion, shall most conduce to their own happiness is the basis on which the whole American fabric has been erected. The exercise of this original right is a very great exertion; nor can it, nor ought it, to be frequently repeated. The principles, therefore, so established, are deemed fundamental. And as the authority from which they proceed is supreme, and can seldom act, they are designed to be permanent.

This original and supreme will organizes the government, and assigns to different departments their respective powers. It may either stop here, or establish certain limits not to be transcended by those departments.

The government of the United States is of the latter description. The powers of the legislature are defined and limited; and that those limits may not be mistaken, or forgotten, the constitution is written. To what purpose are powers limited, and to what purpose is that limitation committed to writing, if these limits may, at any time, be passed by those intended to be restrained? The distinction between a government with limited and unlimited powers is abolished, if those limits do not confine the persons on whom they are imposed, and if acts prohibited and acts allowed, are of equal obligation. It is a proposition too plain to be contested, that the constitution controls any legislative act repugnant to it; or, that the legislature may alter the constitution by an ordinary act.

Between these alternatives there is no middle ground. The constitution is either a superior paramount law, unchangeable by ordinary means, or it is on a level with ordinary legislative acts, and, like other acts, is alterable when the legislature shall please to alter it.

If the former part of the alternative be true, then a legislative act contrary to the constitution is not law: if the latter part be true, then written constitutions are absurd attempts, on the part of the people, to limit a power in its own nature illimitable.

Certainly all those who have framed written constitutions contemplate them as forming the fundamental and paramount law of the nation, and, consequently, the theory of every such government must be, that an act of the legislature, repugnant to the constitution, is void.

This theory is essentially attached to a written constitution, and, is consequently, to be considered, by this court, as one of the fundamental principles of our society. It is not therefore to be lost sight of in the further consideration of this subject.

If an act of the legislature, repugnant to the constitution, is void, does it, notwithstanding its invalidity, bind the courts, and oblige them to give it effect? Or, in other words, though it be not law, does it constitute a rule as operative as if it was a law? This would be to overthrow in fact what was established in theory; and would seem, at first view, an absurdity too gross to be insisted on. It shall, however, receive a more attentive consideration.

It is emphatically the province and duty of the judicial department to say what the law is. Those who apply the rule to particular cases, must of necessity expound and interpret that rule. If two laws conflict with each other, the courts must decide on the operation of each.

So if a law be in opposition to the constitution; if both the law and the constitution apply to a particular case, so that the court must either decide that case conformably to the law, disregarding the constitution; or conformably to the constitution, disregarding the law; the court must determine which of these conflicting rules governs the case. This is of the very essence of judicial duty.

If, then, the courts are to regard the constitution, and the constitution is superior to any ordinary act of the legislature, the constitution, and not such ordinary act, must govern the case to which they both apply.

Those, then, who controvert the principle that the constitution is to be considered, in court, as a paramount law, are reduced to the necessity of maintaining that courts must close their eyes on the constitution, and see only the law.

This doctrine would subvert the very foundation of all written constitutions. It would declare that an act which, according to the principles and theory of our government, is entirely void, is yet, in practice, completely obligatory. It would declare that if the legislature shall do what is expressly forbidden, such act, notwithstanding the express prohibition, is in reality effectual. It would be given to the legislature a practical and real omnipotence, with the same breath which professes to restrict their powers within narrow limits. It is prescribing limits, and declaring that those limits may be passed at pleasure.

That it thus reduces to nothing what we have deemed the greatest improvement on political institutions, a written constitution, would of itself be sufficient, in America, where written constitutions have been viewed with so much reverence, for rejecting the construction. But the peculiar expressions of the constitution of the United States furnish additional arguments in favour of its rejection.

The judicial power of the United States is extended to all cases arising under the constitution.

Could it be the intention of those who gave this power, to say that in using it the constitution should not be looked into? That a case arising under the constitution should be decided without examining the instrument under which it arises?

This is too extravagant to be maintained.

In some cases, then, the constitution must be looked into by the judges. And if they can open it at all, what part of it are they forbidden to read or to obey?

There are many other parts of the constitution which serve to illustrate this subject.

It is declared that "no tax or duty shall be laid on articles exported from any state." Suppose a duty on the export of cotton, of tobacco, or of flour; and a suit instituted to recover it. Ought judgment to be rendered in such a case? ought the judges to close their eyes on the constitution, and only see the law?

The constitution declares "that no bill of attainder or ex post facto law shall be passed."

If, however, such a bill should be passed, and a person should be prosecuted under it; must the court condemn to death those victims whom the constitution endeavors to preserve?

"No person," says the constitution, "shall be convicted of treason unless on the testimony of two witnesses to the same overt act, or on confession in open court."

Here the language of the constitution is addressed especially to the courts. It prescribes, directly for them, a rule of evidence not to be departed from. If the legislature should change that rule, and declare one witness, or a confession out of court, sufficient for conviction, must the constitutional principle yield to the legislative act?

From these, and many other selections which might be made, it is apparent, that the framers of the constitution contemplated that instrument as a rule for the government of courts, as well as of the legislature.

Why otherwise does it direct the judges to take an oath to support it? This oath certainly applies in an especial manner, to their conduct in their official character. How immoral to impose it on them, if they were to be used as the instruments, and the knowing instruments, for violating what they swear to support!

The oath of office, too, imposed by the legislature, is completely demonstrative of the legislative opinion on this subject. It is in these words: "I do solemnly swear that I will administer justice without respect to persons, and do equal right to the poor and to the rich; and that I will faithfully and impartially discharge all the duties incumbent on me as   , according to the best of my abilities and understanding agreeably to the constitution and laws of the United States."

Why does a judge swear to discharge his duties agreeably to the constitution of the United States, if that constitution forms no rule for his government? if it is closed upon him, and cannot be inspected by him?

If such be the real state of things, this is worse than solemn mockery. To prescribe, or to take this oath, becomes equally a crime.

It is also not entirely unworthy of observation, that in declaring what shall be the supreme law of the land, the constitution itself is first mentioned; and not the laws of the United States generally, but those only which shall be made in pursuance of the constitution, have that rank.

Thus, the particular phraseology of the constitution of the United States confirms and strengthens the principle, supposed to be essential to all written constitutions, that a law repugnant to the constitution is void; and that courts, as well as other departments, are bound by that instrument.

The rule must be discharged.

The decision in *Marbury v. Madison* would have important consequences not on-ly for the Court's own role in the system, but for the role of Congress (and by im-plication, the executive branch) as well. By asserting the power of judicial review, the Court established that Congress's power to legislate change was limited to what the Constitution allowed, and that the Court could exercise a "check" in cases of alleged discrepancies. By denying that it could exercise one power, the Court was *assuming* another power not mentioned in the Constitution.

62 / Judge Bork in Defense of Strict Construction

Robert H. Bork
Patrick B. McGuigan

When applying the Constitution, should judges feel free to interpret it as a chang-ing document, one whose broad principles may be applied differently today than they might have been in the very different circumstances that surrounded the framers? Or are judges bound to determine, to the best of their abilities, exactly what the framers had in mind, and then to apply their words with precisely that meaning today? A longstanding debate has raged over this important issue of jurisprudence, a debate that was vigorously and publicly joined in the 1980s by such notables as Attorney General Edwin Meese, Judge (and Reagan Supreme Court nominee) Robert H. Bork, and Harvard Law School Professor Laurence Tribe. The next two readings represent the opposing views of the "strict constructionists" and "loose constructionists." In the first of these readings, Judge Bork argues that judges are bound by the intent of the framers, and to act otherwise is to create a legislative judiciary.

(On September 5, 1985, Pat McGuigan conducted a lengthy interview with Judge Robert H. Bork in his chambers at the U.S. Court House in the District of Columbia. . . .)

Q: . . . First question: What is the proper role of judges in a democratic society?

A: The quick answer is: To try to discern the intent of the people who wrote the law they are applying, whether it is constitutional law or statutory law or precedential law.

Q: **In a speech three years ago to the Free Congress Foundation's Conference on Judicial Reform, you spoke of the difference between the "interpretivist" (or strict constructionist) school of constitutional and legal analysis and the "noninterpretivist" (or activist) school. Will you review that difference for our readers?**

A: There has recently grown up, in the law schools in particular, a school of constitutional philosophy which holds that judges are not properly bound by the intent of the framers of the Constitution, but may, indeed should, make new constitutional law, create new rights. And it is suggested that they may do so either because moral philosophy suggests inhibitions on legislative powers not found in the Constitution, or because judges think the legislative process is malfunctioning in some way that they themselves define.

    Interpretivists believe the contrary. They think the job of a judge is to understand the principle that the framers were trying to protect, and apply that principle in today's circumstances, which the framers could not have foreseen. But the idea is always to protect the value or the freedom that the framers were trying to protect—and not some new freedom.

Q: **In that 1982 speech, you maintained that if the notion that judges can draw their constitutional rulings from outside the Constitution "achieves entire intellectual hegemony in law schools, as it is on the brink of doing, the results will be disastrous for the constitutional law of this nation." Why would that be disastrous?**

A: Because you would have a small group of unelected, unrepresentative judges making the basic law of the nation, quite irrespective of the desires of the electorate, and quite irrespective of the meaning of the Constitution. That would bring minority tyranny in spades.

Q: **In your Bicentennial speech to the American Philosophical Society back in 1976 you said something that struck me as especially profound. I want to quote just one sentence. Your words were these: 'The case has been made, perhaps most effectively by Joseph Schumpeter, that the intellectual classes, given their typical desire to politicize all of society's processes, pose the greatest danger to the future of democratic government.' You said something along the same line in your 1982 speech at the Free Congress conference, expressing concern about what you called the "gentrification" of the Constitution.**

A: I was talking about the fact that if judges begin to create new personal freedoms on the theory that the times demand them or that it is the best moral view, or something of that sort, they will in fact enact as constitutional law the moral judgments of a particular socio-economic class to which they belong and to which they respond.

    Judges are not representative of the population at large—either socially or economically or religiously or any other way. They tend to respond to law school faculties, to clerks coming out of those law schools, to journalists, to members of the writing intellectual class. Those are groups with a point of view which does not run the full spectrum of American opinion. If judges simply enforced their own morality, you would get as constitutional law those moral views of a particular class, and a morality that is not by any means generally shared in this country. That's what I meant by the gentrification of the Constitution.

As to the first quotation, I was talking about the fact that the intellectual classes—until very recently, when a significant counter-intellectual movement arose—really seemed to want to politicize, and hence regulate, a great many aspects of life, including markets. What I was talking about was that democratic government is endangered when you politicize everything because it is not possible for representative institutions like Congress to make all of the millions of regulations that are then essential.

So that power necessarily shifts from elected representatives to vast bureaucracies. When you have a democratic government, in the sense that elected representatives are making the decisions, you necessarily have a more or less limited government, because they can't handle everything at once.

Q: In your speech on December 6, 1984, to the session at the American Enterprise Institute in which you were presented the Francis Boyer Award, you crafted what I thought was a powerful and succinct defense of the historically unique American political structure. Let me read that back to you. You said:

> Our constitutional liberties arose out of historical experience, and out of political, moral, and religious sentiment. They do not rest upon any general theory. Attempts to frame a theory that removes from democratic control areas of life the framers intended to leave there can only succeed if abstractions are regarded as overriding the constitutional text and structure, judicial precedent and the history that gives our rights life, rootedness and meaning. It is no small matter to discredit the foundations upon which our constitutional freedoms have always been sustained, and substitute as a bulwark only abstractions of moral philosophy.

These are powerful words and it is a sentiment not necessarily shared in legal circles. Could you elaborate a little bit about what you were driving at there?

A: Yes. The effort to create individual rights out of a general, abstract, moral philosophy, I think, is doomed to failure from the beginning because I don't think there is any version of moral philosophy that can claim to be absolutely superior to all others. What I was saying in the passage you quote is that the rights we enjoy, which were handed down to us, arose out of particular circumstances and particular sentiments and religious beliefs. They are not connected by a general philosophy. And—

Q: In essence, were they a blending? A compromise, if you will?

A: Well, they are a compromise, but also, they were quite specific. The framers had known certain kinds of abuses by government, and they wanted to make sure those abuses did not recur in our national government.

They didn't sit down and work out a utilitarian philosophy or a contractarian philosophy or something of that sort. If the framers intended to leave large areas of life to the democratic process, and we say, "No the framers' intention doesn't count because we have a moral philosophy that says they shouldn't have," then that casts doubt upon the freedoms the framers did give us because they are not supported by that abstract moral philosophy.

I think that approach undercuts the legitimacy and the prestige of our historically rooted freedoms.

Q: Many of your comments on the present state of constitutional and legal interpretation seem to me to reflect implicit criticism of the prevailing mentality in our law schools. What ideology...

A: May I just stop and say it is not implicit. It is explicit.

Q: Quite all right. What ideology then, if any, animates the law schools?

A: I doubt that there is a single ideology that animates law schools today. Instead, there are a lot of competing ideologies ranging from the law and economics group to the Critical Legal Studies people.

Among many constitutional law professors, there is a continual search for general philosophic principles about the nature of a just society which the professors would like judges to convert into constitutional law. This is a relatively new development and I can't say I understand all the reasons for it. Perhaps they just love playing with philosophy and find law too mundane and pedestrian. Or perhaps, in some cases, the professors have realized they are never going to get the electorate and their representatives to agree with them on sound social policy. A quick way, the only way, to the society they want is to get judges to make this society over.

The sin of wanting judges to do good things simply because the electorate won't do them is not confined to liberalism. Conservatives have been known to be infected with that desire, too. There are still a number of them around who want that.

Q: ...Turning for a moment to a specific area of the law flowing from what we have been talking about, how would the contending schools of interpretation—the interpretivists and the noninterpretivists—approach the constitutional legitimacy of, say, the death penalty? I am not necessarily asking for what the correct outcome is on the constitutionality (or lack

thereof) of the death penalty, but how would an interpretivist approach the matter and noninterpretivist approach it?

A: Well, I think for an interpretivist, the issue is almost concluded by the fact that the death penalty is specifically referred to, and assumed to be an available penalty, in the Constitution itself. In the Fifth Amendment and in the Fourteenth Amendment. It is a little hard to understand how a penalty that the framers explicitly assumed to be available, can somehow become unavailable because of the very Constitution the framers wrote.

I suppose the noninterpretivists would proceed, as some of them have, by saying, "Well, the standard, for example, of what is a cruel and unusual punishment under the Eighth Amendment is an evolving standard. It moves with the society's new consensus about what is consistent with human dignity, what is too cruel, etc., etc."

And then they say that evolving standard has now reached the death penalty, and eliminates it. But it is not made clear why the standard should evolve.

Q: In the absence of a constitutional amendment?

A: That's right. . . .

63 / The Myth of the Strict Constructionist: Our Incomplete Constitution

Laurence H. Tribe

According to Laurence Tribe, the strict constructionist's view that judges are limited to what "the writers intended" ignores the fact that constitutions and laws are the products of collective bodies, such that even if it could be resolved which writers' intentions should be considered, it is likely that more than one intention existed even among those original writers. Furthermore, given that imprecise language in the Constitution and the laws *requires* interpretation, the idea that judges can avoid *making* law is based on myth. Rather than perpetuating the myth, Tribe argues, judges should take responsibility for making the choices that interpreting the Constitution requires of them.

Some would argue that one justice or two would not make that much difference—and that even the many 5–4 splits would gradually disappear—if the Supreme Court were staffed, as they believe it should be, with men and women who understand that constitutional adjudication is simply the job of correctly reading the Constitution. If the Justices interpret our great charter in a straightforward manner—if they pay close attention to its words and avoid twisting or stretching their meanings—there will be few occasions for controversies that can be manipulated by well-chosen appointments. All that the President and the Senate need do is stop appointing "activist" judges who impose their own philosophies upon the document they are sworn to uphold, and appoint instead properly "restrained" jurists who know, and will not exceed, a judge's proper place. So the argument goes. It is simple, appealing, and plainly wrong.

Strict Constructionism Explained
In 1717 Bishop Benjamin Hoadly told the King of England that, in his opinion, "whoever hath an absolute authority to interpret any written laws is truly the Lawgiver to all intents and purposes, and not the person who first wrote them." Thus began a controversy that has continued unabated for the last two hundred and fifty years. Not everyone has agreed that the power of judicial review gives the Supreme Court wide discretion in reading the law. Justice Joseph Story argued in 1833 that the Court must give to the constitutional text only its ordinary and natural meaning: "Constitutions are instruments of a practical nature, founded on the common business of human life, adapted to common wants, designed for common use and fitted for common understanding." A century later Justice Owen Roberts described the Supreme Court's task in an even more limited and mechanical way: "to lay the article of the Constitution which is involved beside the statute which is challenged and to decide whether the latter squares with the former."

This approach to judicial review is usually known as strict constructionism, and its guiding principle is exclusive attention to the constitutional text. The Supreme Court's Justices must take the Constitution as they find it, and not make things up as they go along. Even if the Justices are appalled by the results this method produces, or believe that the Constitution's literal commands are severely out of step with the times, it is not their job to rewrite it. That prerogative belongs to the Congress and the President—and ultimately to the people, who retain the power to *amend* the Constitution. The watchword of strict constructionism is "restraint." The continuing popularity of this approach to constitutional interpretation is revealed by the fact that President Nixon announced a policy of appointing only strict constructionists to the Supreme Court; the same "judicial philosophy" [was purportedly a requirement] for nomination under President Reagan as well.

Why It Doesn't Work
The central flaw of strict constructionism is that words are inherently indeterminate—they can often be given more than one plausible meaning. If simply *reading* the Constitution the "right" way were all the Justices of the Supreme Court had to do, the only qualification for the job would be literacy, and the only tool a dictionary. But the meanings of the Constitution's

words are especially difficult to pin down. Many of its most precise commands are relatively trivial—such as the requirement that the President be thirty-five years old—while nearly all of its most important phrases are deliberate models of ambiguity. Just what does the Fourth Amendment prohibit as an "unreasonable search"? What exactly is the "speech" whose freedom the government may not "abridge"? What is it that we gain by being guaranteed the "equal protection of the laws"? And what, in heaven's name, is "due process"? Such vague phrases not only invite but *compel* the Supreme Court to put meaning *into* the Constitution, not just to take it out. Judicial construction inevitably entails a major element of judicial creation.

This is not to say that the Court is free to take the position of Humpty Dumpty, that "a word means just what I choose it to mean—neither more nor less." The Justices may not follow a policy of "anything goes" so long as it helps put an end to what they personally consider to be injustice. But the constitutional text is not enough—we need to search for, and explain our selection of, the *principles behind* the words.

Consider the First Amendment to the Constitution. Beyond dispute, it prohibits the Congress from dictating official religious beliefs, censoring newspapers, or punishing criticism of the government. The words of the First Amendment—which command that "Congress shall make no law respecting an establishment of religion, or prohibiting the free exercise thereof; or abridging the freedom of speech, or of the press"—could be read no other way. Yet not one word in the entire Constitution says that the *President* cannot do those things, even though such a notion seems unthinkable. What are we to make of this omission? A resort to the Constitution's text and *only* its text for an answer is a shortcut to a dead end. We must ask *why* the Congress is prohibited from violating our rights but the President is not. Is the President to be considered less of a threat to our liberty? Even if such a thought might have been plausible in 1791, when the First Amendment was ratified, it is certainly not plausible today: the modern American President is the repository of perhaps the world's greatest concentration of power; and that power is growing. We must look deeper than the surface of the Constitution's words.

The principle that animates the Bill of Rights, including the First Amendment, is that there are certain freedoms that are fundamental in determining the kind of society we wish to be. These freedoms must be protected from political compromise, and even democratically elected governments must fully respect them. In light of this principle, it is perfectly sensible to see the shield of the First Amendment as a bulwark of freedom against presidential as well as congressional acts. Indeed, it would be indefensible *not* to.

One of the most important problems of constitutional interpretation has been the question of the "incorporation" of the Bill of Rights into the Fourteenth Amendment, which declares that the states may not "deprive any person of life, liberty, or property, without due process of law." After the ratification of that amendment in 1868, the Supreme Court gradually recognized a glaring inconsistency in the constitutional scheme. The Bill of Rights, with its litany of fundamental liberties, had originally been understood and long been held to provide a shield only against intrusion by the *federal* govern-ment. Yet it seemed intolerable to declare that although the President and the Congress had no power to take our private property without compensa-tion, to break into our homes and spy on us at will, or to condemn us to prison or the gallows in trials before kangaroo courts, the states remained perfectly free to do so. That position was particularly intolerable after we fought the Civil War and added the Thirteenth, Fourteenth and Fifteenth Amendments to the Constitution, in part to protect some among us from the governments of the states in which we live. Therefore, over the course of a hundred years, the Supreme Court has gradually read into the Fourteenth Amendment's Due Process Clause most of the liberties guaranteed by the Bill of Rights. Even Justice Hugo Black, who is often considered the strictest constructionist who ever served on the Court, vigorously advocated this very practice.

Another problem emerged with the passage of the Fourteenth Amend-ment. That amendment, in addition to guaranteeing *due process* of law, pro-hibits the states from denying to anyone the *equal protection* of the laws. This latter provision was the basis of the Court's decision to strike down racial-ly segregated public schools in *Brown v. Board of Education.* On the same day in 1954 that it upheld Brown's challenge to Topeka's segregated schools, and another student's attack on segregation in Prince Edward County, Virginia, the Court was presented with an identical challenge to the segregated schools of the District of Columbia. The problem was that the Fourteenth Amendment requires only the *states,* and not the federal govern-ment, to provide equal protection of the laws; there is no parallel provision in the Bill of Rights.

A unanimous Supreme Court recognized the absurdity of denouncing racism in Virginia while condoning it across the Potomac River in Washington, D.C., and did not hesitate to read into the Fifth Amendment's Due Process Clause—which *does* apply to the federal government—a guarantee of equal protection of the laws. The literal result of this judicial innovation was to make the Equal Protection Clause of the Fourteenth Amendment wholly redundant, for if the Fifth Amendment's Due Process Clause includes pro-tection of equality, so must the identically worded Due Process Clause of the Fourteenth Amendment. This reading of the Constitution may seem odd in-deed if one looks only at the language of the document. But the reading is perfectly logical and laudable if one examines the principles embodied in that language, for there is no defensible reason to allow the national government to run roughshod over fundamental liberties that the fifty states and their cities are required to respect.

Chief Justice Marshall once wrote that we must remember that "it is a *Constitution* we are expounding." It is the grand charter of a democratic republic, the philosophical creed of a free people, and it was written in broad, even majestic language because it was written to evolve. The statesmen who wrote the Constitution meant the American experiment to endure without having to be reinvented with an endless series of explicit amendments to its basic blueprint. There is a message in the common adage "Ours is a

Constitution of limited powers." The Tenth Amendment makes that maxim a reminder that the federal government in particular may exercise only the powers ceded to it by the people in the Constitution. Perhaps even more important, the Ninth Amendment expressly states that even the Bill of Rights itself is not to be understood as an exhaustive list of individual liberties. The Ninth Amendment thereby invites us, and our judges, to expand on the panoply of freedoms that are uniquely our heritage. Thus the Constitution tells us, both implicitly and explicitly, that what it does *not* say must also be interpreted, understood, and applied.

A Related Fallacy: The Intent of the Framers
Another school of constitutional interpretation takes as its lodestar the intent of the authors of the Constitution. The task of the Supreme Court, when confronted by ambiguous or open-ended language, is simply to divine what the Framers and the authors of the amendments had in mind. This method employs historical research in addition to textual analysis. One obvious problem with asking "what they meant" is that we must first determine who "they" are. In the case of the Bill of Rights, do we defer to the intentions of the men— yes, it was men only—who drafted it and saw it as an essential safeguard against encroachment on fundamental freedoms, or to the intentions of those among them who saw the Bill of Rights as unnecessary and unwise, but acceded to its passage because otherwise some states might never have ratified the Constitution? And how should we understand the purpose of the Slave Trade Clause of Article I of the Constitution, which prohibits Congress from restricting the importation of slaves until 1808? Did the Framers mean by this provision that when they said, in the Declaration of Independence, "all men are created equal," they really meant "all *white* men"? Was this, too, merely a bargaining chip, a concession to the slaveholding states to entice them into the Union? Or did the Founding Fathers mean to give the South a two-decade grace period in which to phase out slavery before Congress did it for them? And how was this clause understood by the Southern legislators who ratified the Constitution?

The nagging doubt prompted by inquiries like these is that no collective body—be it the Congress or the Constitutional Convention or the aggregate of state legislatures—can really be said to have a *single*, ascertainable "purpose" or "intent." And even if such a mythical beast could be captured and examined, how relevant would it be to us today? Should the peculiar opinions held, and the particular applications envisioned, by men who have been dead for two centuries *always* trump contemporary insights into what the living Constitution means and ought to mean? Should we permit others to rule us from the grave not only through solemn enactments democratically ratified, but through hidden beliefs and premises perhaps deliberately left unstated?

Consider the Equal Protection Clause as an example. It was clearly intended to restrict racial discrimination against the recently emancipated slaves, but just what did the authors of the Fourteenth Amendment "count" as discrimination? Does a state deny equal protection by forcing blacks to attend segregated schools, use separate bathrooms, and sit only at the back of the bus? In *Plessy v. Ferguson* in 1898 a Supreme Court much closer to the source than we are today answered "no": separate but equal facilities are permissible. Half a century later a different group of Justices unanimously disagreed, because they recognized that, in a society dominated by white men, separate facilities for blacks were not likely ever to be "equal," and that, even if they were, enforced apartheid itself declared white supremacy and automatically denied equality to blacks. That decision may be hard to square with the specific, if for various reasons never expressed, agenda of those who gave us the Fourteenth Amendment. Historical evidence as to what "they" collectively had in mind is inconclusive, but it is quite possible that they had no objection to segregated schools as such. Schools even in some Northern states had been segregated for years. But public education in 1868 was not the crucial institution that it has since become. The right to own property was considered central to individual liberty, as was the right to make contracts, and we can safely say that the authors of the Equal Protection Clause "meant" to extend these rights to blacks as well as whites. In *Brown v. Board of Education* and the cases that followed it the Supreme Court was—and rightly so—less interested in the ways in which the *phrase* "equal protection" was implemented in the nineteenth century than in the sorts of inequalities which that *principle* should tolerate in the twentieth century.

Abdicating Responsibility for Tough Choices

The most serious flaw in both slavish adherence to the constitutional text and the inevitably inconclusive inquiry into the intent of those who wrote it is not just that these methods of judicial reasoning ask the wrong questions, but that they abdicate responsibility for the choices that constitutional courts *necessarily* make. The Supreme Court just cannot avoid the painful duty of exercising judgment so as to give concrete meaning to the fluid Constitution, because the constitutional rules and precepts that it is charged with administering lack that certainty which permits anything resembling automatic application. Strict constructionism in all of its variants is thus built on a conceit—which through the years has become a full-blown myth—that the Supreme Court does not *make* law, but *finds* law ready-made by others. In this mythology, the Justices do not really render their own opinions in deciding cases, for they are the mere mouthpieces of oracles beyond themselves; just as God spake by the prophets, so the Constitution speaketh by Supreme Court Justices. Even those who say they know it's not so—who claim, when wishing to sound sophisticated, that they realize some measure of choice is unavoidable—fall back on the myth when they criticize "activist" judicial decisions without specifying just *why* a particular "activist" interpretation strikes them as wrong.

Thus the members of the Court themselves occasionally duck responsibility for their substantive decisions about what the Constitution should be taken to mean by shoving the blame—or the credit—onto the document's supposedly plain words or onto the supposedly evident intentions of the

people who penned those words two hundred years ago. When Chief Justice
Taney declared that blacks were an "inferior class of beings" that could "justly
and lawfully be reduced to slavery for the white man's benefit," he claimed
that this was not *his* opinion but a conclusion dictated by the language of
the Constitution and the obvious intent of the men who wrote it.

But disclaimers that "the Constitution made me do it" are rarely more
persuasive than those that blame the devil. When Justice Black refused in
1967 to agree with the majority of the Court in *Katz v. United States* that
the Fourth Amendment restricts the government's power to put a tap on your
telephone line, it was not because *he* thought that electronic eavesdropping
was acceptable, but because the plain language of the Fourth Amendment
prohibits only "unreasonable *searches*," not unreasonable *wiretaps*. Naturally, such electronic invasions of privacy were not anticipated by men who
knew neither telephones nor tape recorders. Such are the unwholesome fruits
of what is sometimes called strict constructionism. Indeed, as the wiretap
example suggests, a Constitution frozen in eighteenth-century ice would soon
become obsolete; as the centuries pass, and technology changes basic patterns of life, that kind of Constitution would melt into meaningless words
signifying nothing.

Not all advocates of primary devotion to the Constitution's literal text
or to its authors' historical purpose adhere resolutely to the description of
those methods given here. Some searchers after the "original understanding"
of the Constitution allow a radical change in circumstances over the last two
hundred years to enter into the analysis; and some who seek answers to questions about the Constitution's meaning only among its clauses occasionally
give weight to the way that words were used by the Framers, or to the special
significance that the law has invested in certain terms. But such exceptions
and variations are to no avail because, in the end, the quest for a strict constructionist remains as futile as Diogenes' search for an honest man. The judge
capable of fulfilling the duty to make the Constitution meaningful to our
lives, and who can accomplish this task by simply "discovering" the meanings that someone else has put there, exists only in myth. Nor does it matter
whether we label the preferred method of passive discovery with such law
professors' terms as "strict constructionism," "originalism," "literalism," or
"mild interpretivism"; a delusion by any other name would sound as hollow.
Regardless of how one labels the technique or tries to fine-tune the mechanism,
there is simply no getting around the fact that whenever the Supreme Court
turns to the Constitution, it must inject a lot of substantive meaning into the
words and the structure, and thus the overall message, of that majestic but
incomplete document. That there is much a judge could *not* properly do in
the document's name is true enough. But that fact should not obscure the
wide range of choices that always remain in giving the Constitution contemporary meaning.

It may be that the most subtle danger of nearsighted examination of the
Constitution's text or of its authors' intentions is that, by making extremely
difficult choices seem easy, such examination stops the judicial inquiry just

when it becomes clear that more questions should be asked. Those crucial questions ask both *how* particular legal issues should be resolved and *who* should be trusted to resolve them. The allure of strict constructionism and of those who claim to practice it—their ability to make complicated issues sound simple and tough decisions easy—is precisely what should make us suspicious of it. For it threatens to put us to sleep at the very moments when we must be most alert to the choices that are in fact being made about the Constitution and its impact on our daily lives—choices whose shape is necessarily prefigured by the sorts of men and women we permit our Presidents to place on our nation's highest court.

64 / The Supreme Court: From Warren to Burger to Rehnquist

David M. O'Brien

In different periods of the Supreme Court's history, it has been known as a "champion" of one cause or another. In this view, the "Warren Court," named for Chief Justice Earl Warren (1953–1969), was known as a strong and active supporter of civil rights and civil liberties. More generally, Warren's Court became known as a "liberal" Court, choosing and deciding cases in a way that promoted individual rights, and especially the rights of minorities and of those accused of crimes.

The "Burger Court," named for Chief Justice Warren Burger (1969–1986), moved in a more "rightward" direction, though disappointing some conservatives who hoped that a number of Nixon and Reagan appointees would forge a new revolution to equal (and undo) the achievements of the Warren Court. David O'Brien suggests that Burger himself was a major factor in his Court's less-than-revolutionary behavior. Writing just after the first full term of what he labels the "Reagan/Rehnquist Court" (by then, including Reagan appointees O'Connor (appointed in 1981), Scalia (1986), and Kennedy (1987)), O'Brien argues that not only is Rehnquist's personality better suited to leading the Court in a fundamentally different direction, but also a conservative majority was now clearly in place.

The Supreme Court, of course, in a sense is always in transition. Within the marble temple, the justices are a close-knit group whose personal relations evolve and change. The docket each year brings new cases, affording fresh perspectives on old problems and opportunities for further reflection and negotiations. And the law clerks come and go, even if the justices remain the same.

From a broader political perspective, the Court swings back and forth with the country—much like a pendulum on a clock. For most of our history, the Court has been in step with major political movements, except during transitional periods or critical elections. The swing of electoral politics—through the power of presidential appointment—controls the composition of the bench and may temper the speed, if not shift the direction, of the Court. Public opinion also touches the justices' lives and may serve to curb them when they threaten to go too far or too fast in their rulings. But changes in the direction of the Court are ultimately moderated by its functioning as a collegial body, in which all nine justices share power and compete for influence.

The Court thus generally shifts direction gradually—on a piecemeal basis, incorporating and accommodating the views of new appointees. There are times, to be sure, when the Court makes rather sharp breaks with the past and charts a new course in constitutional law. This occurred in 1937 during the battle over FDR's "Courtpacking plan," and then again during the latter years of the Warren Court. The future of the Rehnquist Court, I will argue, holds the potential for as great a change, and perhaps for greater change than at any other time in the recent past. This is clear from the history of the Warren and Burger Courts and how the Rehnquist Court could differ.

The House That the Warren Court Built

The Warren Court (1953–1969) revolutionized constitutional law and American society. First, the unanimous and watershed school desegregation ruling, *Brown v. Board of Education,* in 1954 at the end of Warren's first year on the bench. Then, in 1962 *Baker v. Carr* announced the "reapportionment revolution" guaranteeing equal voting rights. And throughout the 1960s, the Court handed down a series of rulings on criminal procedure that extended the rights of the accused and sought to ensure equal access to justice for the poor. *Mapp v. Ohio* (1961), extending the exclusionary rule to the states, and *Miranda v. Arizona* (1966), sharply limiting police interrogations of criminal suspects, continue to symbolize the Warren Court's revolution in criminal justice.

These rulings became identified with an "egalitarian jurisprudence" that indelibly marks an era in the Court's history and elevated Warren above the ranks of most justices and to the status of one of our "great chief justices." The record of Warren and his Court remains, of course, riddled with irony and controversy. But, Warren did ultimately take command of his Court. Whether they agreed with him or not, as Justice Potter Stewart put it, "We all loved him." A big bear of a man with great personal charm, a real politician, he had the interest and capacity to lead the Court. Though by no means a legal scholar, he grew intellectually with the chief justiceship and won the Court over to his concern with basic principles of equality and fairness.

Still, like other chief justices, Warren could not lead until the others were willing to follow. Change comes slowly to the Court and we tend to forget that a chief justice is only first among equals. Even the force of a powerful intellect or personality may not overcome this basic fact of life in the marble temple.

The unanimity of *Brown v. Board of Education* tends to overshadow the fact that the "Warren Court" did not emerge for almost another decade. During that time in case after case involving criminal procedure, for example,

Warren frequently found himself in dissent along with liberal Justices Hugo Black, William O. Douglas and, after 1956 his close friend and advisor, Justice William J. Brennan, Jr. Justices Felix Frankfurter and John Harlan, apostles of judicial self-restraint, tended to hold sway over, if only to moderate at times, the brethren.

Not until the appointment of Justice Arthur Goldberg in 1962, and later those of Abe Fortas and Thurgood Marshall, was there a critical mass to support a liberal-egalitarian philosophy that placed individual rights above states' rights and boldly challenged the political process. The Warren Court then rather quickly forged new law with a rather broad brush, seeking "bright lines" when limiting the coercive powers of government, ensuring principles of equality, and opening up the electoral process.

The directions in which the Warren Court pushed the country remain controversial. Republican President Dwight Eisenhower himself later regretted his appointment of Warren as "the biggest damn-fooled mistake" he ever made. From public opposition and campaigns to "Impeach Earl Warren," Vice President Richard Nixon eventually forged a successful 1968 presidential campaign based on the theme of returning "law and order" to the country. He promised to appoint "strict constructionists" and advocates of judicial self-restraint who would resurrect a Frankfurterian view of the role of the Court.

Interior Redecorating and Minor Remodeling: The Burger Court Years
With his four appointments, Nixon achieved remarkable success in remolding the Court; if not in his own image, then in the ghost of Justice Frankfurter. Burger came to the Court with the agenda of reversing the "liberal-egalitarian jurisprudence" of the Warren Court. The era of the Warren Court came to an end. But, it left behind a series of landmark rulings that profoundly changed our constitutional landscape and a legacy that the Burger Court would not undo or overshadow.

As chief justice, Burger proved a considerable disappointment for conservatives. For one thing, though a devoted Republican, he came from the liberal wing of the party, in the mold of fellow-Minnesotan Harold Stassen. Quite simply, he proved too moderate for California Republicans like Nixon and Reagan.

Even more troubling was that Burger could not lead the Court intellectually. More of a lawyer than Warren, he was by no means a legal scholar and lacked a well-developed judicial philosophy. As one of his colleagues on the Court observed, Burger does not have a "legal mind" or a "taste for the law" outside of the area of criminal procedure. Rather than a coherent judicial philosophy, Burger tended to take positions on various issues on a case-by-case basis.

Moreover, he lacked the charisma of Warren and the demeanor and sharpness of mind of Chief Justice Charles Evans Hughes. With personal charm and a sense of humor, but also a temper, Burger did about all he could to promote collegial relations within the Court. Yet, his lack of precision in directing conference discussions occasionally led to confusion and frequently failed to flush out differences among the justices that needed to be hammered out. While this enhanced Burger's power in assigning opinions, and permitted him to later switch his votes, it troubled the brethren. Ironically, in spite of his interest in court management and basically managerial approach, Burger's personality and style was such that he had a hard time delegating responsibility and compromising with others. In the end, he was more interested (and his great accomplishments lie) in improving the administration of federal and state courts. Burger presided over the Court's functions, but did not lead the Court.

For the most part, centrists on the Court held sway. Eisenhower-appointee Potter Stewart, Kennedy-appointee Byron White, and Nixon-appointee Lewis F. Powell, Jr., in one way or another had all been touched by Frankfurter's philosophy of judicial self-restraint. And they provided the swing votes and moderating influence on the Burger Court.

More independent and less team players than some of the others are Justices Harry Blackmun and John Paul Stevens. Blackmun came to the Court as "the most conservative judge from the most conservative court of appeals in the country," at the urging of his high school buddy, Chief Justice Burger. He remains perhaps the hardest working, most self-consciously brooding justice, and perhaps Nixon's biggest disappointment. In his first years he voted almost 90 percent of the time with Burger but, after writing the abortion opinion in *Roe v. Wade* (1973), he has come to vote over 70 percent of the time with the liberal wing of the Court: Justices Brennan and Marshall. Likewise, Stevens, an appointee of President Gerald Ford in 1975, has demonstrated strong independent judgment. He considers himself a judicial conservative but without the political agenda of Nixon and Reagan appointees.

So it fell to Rehnquist to stake out the Court's conservative philosophy. He came to the Court in 1971 from the Department of Justice in the Nixon administration, though he had established his own conservative credentials years earlier. On the Court, he did not just stand his ground. Rehnquist articulated a consistent and well-developed judicial philosophy that turned out to be more compatible with the Reagan administration than that of Reagan's first appointee, Justice O'Connor (who was also considered for the post of chief justice, but had angered conservatives with her opinions on school prayer, libel, and affirmative action).

During Burger's tenure, the Court thus pretty much went its own way, pulled in different directions on different issues by either its most liberal or most conservative justices. There was no "constitutional counter-revolution" during the Burger Court, as some had predicted. Instead of a transformation, there were only modest "adjustments," as Burger noted when announcing his resignation. From the perspective of the Reagan administration, the Court headed by Burger accomplished little; it eschewed "bright lines" but lacked clear direction and appeared to drift from case to case.

In the final analysis, the Burger Court was one of transition, moderation, and self-restraint: a troubled and fragmented Court in the image of Felix Frankfurter. The legacy of the Burger Court (from 1969 to 1986) is likely to amount to little more than that of "a transitional Court": A Court divided between what the Warren Court accomplished and what the Rehnquist Court achieves and leaves behind. While the Court headed by Chief Justice Burger broke some new ground (as in tackling the problems of affirmative action and reverse discrimination), by and large it confined itself to minor remodeling— with a few new additions (as with the ruling on abortion)—in the house built by the Warren Court.

From Minor to Major Remodeling: The Rehnquist Court

. . . By all accounts, Rehnquist is a splendid chief justice. He has the intellectual and temperamental wherewithal to be a leader. No less important is the simple fact that there are now four justices who are more inclined than not to agree with him. Rehnquist has not moderated his views, which as an associate justice earned him the reputation of being the "Lone Ranger" for standing alone in 54 solo dissenting opinions. In his fifteen years as an associate justice, Rehnquist staked out his own conservative philosophy, for which Reagan elevated him to chief justice. Rehnquist has not turned his back on his record. Rather, with the addition of other Reagan justices [O'Connor, Scalia, Kennedy],* the Court has moved in Rehnquist's direction.

While Rehnquist is much less interested in the administrative side of the chief justiceship and the matters of judicial reform which preoccupied his predecessor, he wins praise for his crisp business-like conduct of the justices' private conferences. His wit and humor enliven oral arguments. That has made for more relaxed collegial relations among the justices off the bench as well. . . .

Whereas the Court in the mid-1980s often appeared unsure of itself and deeply fragmented, the Court under Chief Justice Rehnquist appears more self-confident. That may be because its more liberal members are in their eighties, while Rehnquist is 65 and Reagan's other justices are in their early fifties. But that is not all. Rehnquist's camp can dictate the Court's agenda, since it only takes four justices to grant cases review. Thus, when handing down *Webster*, Rehnquist announced that the Court would hear three more abortion cases in its 1989-1990 term.

[New Direction of the Court]

Rehnquist's majority also signaled that it does not want to waste time with "frivolous" appeals from indigents. Over the bitter dissent of Justices Brennan, Marshall and Stevens, the majority issued an extraordinary order barring a prison inmate, who since 1971 had filed over 73 petitions, from filing any more *in forma pauperis* petitions. That order, *In re MacDonald* (1988), symbolically represented the other recent rulings cutting back on the assistance of counsel and other protective benefits accorded the poor.

If there were any doubt that the Court would not abruptly change course, it ended with the one-two punch dealt affirmative-action programs. After

*Justice Clarence Thomas was added by President Bush in 1991—*Editor's Note.*

City of Richmond v. J. R. Croson Company, 57 U.S.L.W. 4132 (1989), state and local affirmative action programs are virtually impossible to defend, unless states and localities show concrete evidence of their past discrimination. Other rulings by the Rehnquist Court made it easier for white males to challenge court-approved affirmative action plans, even years after they have been put into place. Businesses will also find it easier to avoid liability for past discrimination in refusing to promote women....

Style and Modes of Analysis

There were few surprises in the Rehnquist Court's first full term [1988–89]. The major surprise came with the five-to-four ruling upholding an appellate court which overturned the conviction of a protester who burned an American flag when protesting the Reagan administration's foreign policies at a rally outside the 1984 Republican national convention. Reagan's last two appointees, Scalia and Kennedy, joined the three most liberal justices (Brennan, Blackmun and Thurgood Marshall) in upholding the First Amendment. It was one of a handful of cases in which they broke stride with Chief Justice Rehnquist and Justices O'Connor and White....

Rehnquist's majority displays an eagerness to overturn prior rulings with which it disagrees. At the same time, it appears to shrewdly and prudently calculate the importance of not appearing to break too radically with the past. Rehnquist's camp is thus often content to simply continue chipping away at landmark rulings.

This has been the practice when dealing with issues related to controversial rulings like *Miranda v. Arizona*, 384 U. S. 436, 16 L. Ed. 2d. 694 (1966), which held that police must inform suspects of their rights to remain silent, to have the presence of an attorney during police questioning, and to have one appointed for them if they are too poor to hire their own. Over the years, so many exceptions have been made that *Miranda* survives only as a hollow symbol of the Warren Court. Last term, the Rehnquist Court held that police do not have to honor *Miranda* when making routine traffic stops that result in the driver's arrest. Nor, held a bare majority in *Duckworth v. Eagan*, 57 U.S.L.W. 4942 (1989), must police use the exact language of *Miranda* when informing suspects of their rights.

Making exceptions to landmark rulings is not the only way Rehnquist's bloc is working its will. Four rulings in the 1988–1989 term expressly overturned prior decisions, and two others did that the year before. But the strategy of Rehnquist's bloc is often to reinterpret precedents in such a way as to reverse them without explicitly saying so. For instance, in a major ruling making it more difficult for women and minorities to prove on-the-job bias, a bare majority of the Court held in *Wards Cove Packing Co., Inc. v. Atonio*, 57 U.S.L.W. 4583 (1989), that they may no longer use statistics to prove discrimination and that *Griggs v. Duke Power Co.*, 401 U. S. 424 (1971), in Justice White's words, "should have been understood to mean" that!

More typically, the Rehnquist Court either refuses to extend or decides to carve out exceptions to prior rulings. In this respect, the Rehnquist Court is maintaining the practice that emerged when approving "good faith" and "inevitable discovery" exceptions to the Fourth Amendment's exclusionary rule, which bars the use at trial of evidence illegally obtained by police. In a series of cases, the Court held that evidence which the police illegally seized in good faith—in the mistaken belief that they were acting legally—may be admitted and used against the defendant. So too, the Rehnquist Court is inclined to uphold convictions based on the "harmless error" doctrine, which holds that not all procedural errors and failures to respect the rights of the accused merit the reversal of convictions and require the retrial of defendants.

On other matters of criminal procedure, the Rehnquist Court demonstrates a continuing aversion to "bright-line" rules which infringe on law-enforcement interests. The Rehnquist Court, for instance, is prone to look at the "totality of the circumstances" when addressing claims of coerced confessions and the denial of an accused's rights under the Fifth and Sixth Amendments....

In *DeShaney v. Winnebago County Department of Social Services*, 57 U.S.L.W. 4218 (1988), a bare majority of the Rehnquist Court also signaled the end of substantive due process analysis with respect to claims that the government in some circumstances has an affirmative obligation to protect or extend benefits to individuals. In this case, Rehnquist's majority declined to hold social workers accountable for violating a five-year-old boy's constitutional rights. They had failed to protect him from repeated beatings by his father which left him brain damaged, even though on occasion they had taken the child into custody as a precaution against abuse by his father.

DeShaney indicates as well that the Rehnquist Court is capable of painting just as broadly is the Warren Court, but in a different direction and away from bright-line rulings that burden governmental authorities.

Political Sensitivity

In the 1988–1989 term, however, the Rehnquist Court also seemed to gauge political wind when declining to bring down other landmark...rulings. [A good example of the Court's concern with the political fallout of its rulings is the abortion case of *Webster v. Reproductive Health Services*, 57, U.S.L.W. 5023 (1989).] To be sure, in *Webster* it was only O'Connor's resistance to "reconsidering" *Roe* that stopped the Rehnquist camp from moving further. But the political repercussions of reversing *Roe* must have weighed on the minds of others in Rehnquist's wing of the Court. The significance of expressly reaffirming or discarding *Roe* was certainly underscored for the Court by the unprecedented number of *amicus curiae* ("friend of the court") briefs—78 briefs in all, which were joined by hundreds of organizations on both sides of the abortion controversy....

Finally, there is one area which the Rehnquist Court appears as yet unwilling to tinker with: the First Amendment. Besides the flag desecration ruling, the Court affirmed First Amendment protection for newspapers publishing the names of rape victims and overturned a major portion of Congress's "dial-a-porn" law. However, several of the justices' opinions indicate that the Rehnquist Court might well alter its methods of First Amendment analysis with respect to government regulation of commercial speech and protection for privacy interests against claims of freedom of the press. Also, in *Ward v. Rock Against Racism*, 57 U.S.L.W. 4879 (1989), the Court indicated that it will no longer require governments to use the "least drastic means" available when imposing "time, place and manner" restrictions on the use of public forums such as city parks, streets and the like. In short, through a change in its methods of analysis the Rehnquist Court may well slightly devalue the First Amendment in deference to governmental regulation and protection for some interests in personal privacy and public decency.

The Rehnquist Court and Constitutional Politics

Changing times have brought the age of the Rehnquist Court. As reconstituted by Reagan, the Rehnquist Court could well prove to be one of the most lasting legacies of the Reagan era. Certainly, the mood, modes of analysis and directions of the Court have changed and will continue to change. In many ways, the Rehnquist Court now registers the prevailing national political consensus identified with the election and re-election of Reagan. The political process worked in imposing a measure of democratic accountability on the Court through Reagan's appointments. Whether the Rehnquist Court stays in tune with the times in the post-Reagan era remains to be seen.

Conclusion

The emergence of a solid conservative majority is unmistakable.... The Rehnquist Court has come of age and may well prove to be President Ronald Reagan's most lasting legacy.... He managed to turn the Court around and point it in new directions.

As an institution, the Court usually shifts course gradually. Moderate changes in legal currents come with the addition of new justices. But the first full term (1988–1989) of the Reagan/Rehnquist Court brought about the kind of sea-change that rarely occurs. And the forces within the Rehnquist Court are likely to gather momentum in future terms.

65 / Presidential Appointments: The Mixed Record of Court Packing

William H. Rehnquist

One of the fundamental principles embodied in the American constitution is judicial independence—independence of the federal judiciary from political pressures, and especially from the other branches of government. And yet it is going too far to say that the framers truly placed the courts on an "island separated from politics." One of the very important bridges that still links the judiciary to public opinion is the process by which judges are appointed to the courts, a process involving presidential appointment and Senate concurrence.

A much debated issue is whether presidents, in making appointments to the courts, should consider "political factors." In Senate hearings on Supreme Court appointments, it would be odd indeed if no one raised the issue. And certainly, some presidents have seen the appointment power as a license to politicize the Court. Chief among those was Franklin Roosevelt who, growing impatient with the majority of the "nine old men" who declared key New Deal legislation unconstitutional, proposed to Congress a scheme (which was never adopted) that would have allowed him to "pack" the Court with more sympathetic justices. While stopping short of such drastic measures, other presidents have also attempted to affect judicial decision-making through carefully chosen appointments. In the following reading, Chief Justice William Rehnquist defends this practice but also argues that institutional constraints have intervened to make it only partially successful.

Had Franklin Roosevelt only been more patient—had he but recognized the great wisdom in Henry Ashurst's advice to him—"Time is on your side; *anno domini* is your invincible ally"—he could have avoided the defeat for himself personally and for the Democratic party when the Senate rejected his Court-packing plan, and still have accomplished his goal. Before elaborating on this point, it may be well to define the use of the word *pack*, which seems to me the best verb available for the activity involved despite its highly pejorative connotation. It need not have such a connotation when used in this context; the second edition of Webster's unabridged dictionary defines the verb *pack* as "to choose or arrange (a jury, committee, etc.) in such a way as to secure some advantage, or to favor some particular side or interest." Thus a president who sets out to pack the Court does nothing more than seek to appoint people to the Court who are sympathetic to his political or philosophical principles.

There is no reason in the world why a president should not do this. One of the many marks of genius that our Constitution bears is the fine balance struck in the establishment of the judicial branch, avoiding subservience to the supposedly more vigorous legislative and executive branches on the one hand, and avoiding total institutional isolation from public opinion on the other. The performance of the judicial branch of the United States government for a period of nearly two hundred years has shown it to be remarkably independent of the other coordinate branches of that government. Yet the institution has been constructed in such a way that due to the mortality tables, if nothing else, the public will in the person of the president of the United States—the one official who is elected by the entire nation—have something to say about the membership of the Court, and thereby indirectly about its decisions.

Surely we would not want it any other way. We want our federal courts, and particularly the Supreme Court, to be independent of popular opinion when deciding the particular cases or controversies that come before them. The provision for tenure during good behavior and the prohibition against diminution of compensation have proved more than adequate to secure that sort of independence. The result is that judges are responsible to no electorate or constituency. But the manifold provisions of the Constitution with which judges must deal are by no means crystal clear in their import, and reasonable minds may differ as to which interpretation is proper. When a vacancy occurs on the Court, it is entirely appropriate that that vacancy be filled by the president, responsible to a national constituency, as advised by the Senate, whose members are responsible to regional constituencies. Thus, public opinion has some say in who shall become judges of the Supreme Court.

Whether or not it is, as I contend, both normal and desirable for presidents to attempt to pack the Court, the fact is that presidents who have been sensible of the broad powers they have possessed, and have been willing to exercise those powers, have all but invariably tried to have some influence on the philosophy of the Court as a result of their appointments to that body. Whether or not they have been successful in their attempts to pack the Court is a more difficult question. I think history teaches us that those who have tried have been at least partially successful, but that a number of factors militate against a president's having anything more than partial success. What these factors are can best be illustrated with examples from the history of presidential appointments to the Court.

Very early in the history of the Court, Justice William Cushing, "a sturdy Federalist and follower of Marshall" [Schachner, Vol. II, p. 901] died in September 1810. His death reduced the seven-member Court to six, evenly divided between Federalist appointees and Republican appointees. Shortly after Cushing's death, Thomas Jefferson, two years out of office as president, wrote to his former secretary of the treasury, Albert Gallatin, in these unseemingly gleeful words:

> I observe old Cushing is dead. At length, then, we have a chance of getting a Republican majority in the Supreme Judiciary. For ten years has that branch braved the spirit and will of the Nation. . . . The event is a fortunate one, and so timed as to be a godsend to me.

Jefferson, of course, had been succeeded by James Madison, who, though perhaps less ardently than Jefferson, also championed Republican ideals. Jefferson wrote Madison, "It will be difficult to find a character of firmness enough to preserve his independence on the same Bench with Marshall." [Dunne, p. 77] When he heard that Madison was considering Joseph Story and Ezekiel Bacon, then chairman of the Ways and Means Committee of the House of Representatives, he admonished Madison that "Story and Bacon are exactly the men who deserted us [on the Embargo Act]. The former unquestionably a Tory, and both are too young." [Dunne, pp. 78–79]

President Madison seems to have been "snakebit" in his effort to fill the Cushing vacancy. He first nominated his attorney general, Levi Lincoln, who insisted that he did not want the job and after the Senate confirmed him still refused to serve. Madison then nominated a complete dark horse, one Alexander Wolcott, the federal revenue collector of Connecticut, whom the Senate rejected by the mortifying vote of 24 to 9. Finally, in the midst of a Cabinet crisis that occupied a good deal of his time, Madison nominated Joseph Story for the Cushing vacancy, and the Senate confirmed him as a matter of routine three days later. Story, of course, fulfilled Jefferson's worst expectations about him. He became Chief Justice John Marshall's principal ally on the great legal issues of the day in the Supreme Court, repeatedly casting his vote in favor of national power and against the restrictive interpretation of the Constitution urged by Jefferson and his states' rights school. And Joseph Story served on the Supreme Court for thirty-four years, one of the longest tenures on record.

Presidents who wish to pack the Supreme Court, like murder suspects in a detective novel, must have both motive and opportunity. Here Madison had both, and yet he failed. He was probably a considerably less partisan chief executive than was Jefferson, and so his motivation was perhaps not strong enough. After having botched several opportunities, he finally preferred to nominate someone who would not precipitate another crisis in his relations with the Senate, rather than insisting on a nominee who had the right philosophical credentials. The lesson, I suppose, that can be drawn from this incident is that while for Court-watchers the president's use of his appointment power to nominate people for vacancies on the Supreme Court is the most important use he makes of the executive authority, for the president himself, the filling of Supreme Court vacancies is just one of many acts going on under the "big top" of his administration.

John Marshall was not the only member of the Court to have been appointed in the more than usually partisan atmosphere of a lame-duck presidential administration. In 1840, after the "hard cider and log cabin" campaign, William Henry Harrison, the Whig candidate for president, was elected over Martin Van Buren, the Democratic incumbent. Little more than a week before Harrison would take his oath on March 4, 1841, Justice Phillip Pendleton Barbour of Virginia died suddenly. Two days after Barbour's death Van Buren appointed Peter V. Daniel to be associate justice of the Supreme Court of the United States. A few days later, Martin Van Buren described in a letter to

Andrew Jackson, his mentor and predecessor, the appointment of Daniel: "I had an opportunity to put a man on the bench of the Supreme Court at the moment of leaving the government who will I am sure stick to the true principles of the Constitution, and being a Democrat *ab ovo* is not in so much danger of a falling off in the true spirit."

After frantic last-minute maneuvering between the Whig and Democrat factions in the Senate, Daniel was confirmed, and remained an ardent—nay, obdurate—champion of states' rights until his death in 1860.

Abraham Lincoln had inveighed against the Supreme Court's 1857 decision in the *Dred Scott* case during his famous debates with Stephen A. Douglas in 1858 when both sought to be elected United States senator from Illinois. Lincoln lost that election, but his successful presidential campaign two years later was likewise marked by a restrained [but] nonetheless forceful attack on this decision and by implication on the Court's apparent institutional bias in favor of slaveholders. Within two months of his inauguration, by reason of the death of one justice and the resignation of two others, Lincoln was given three vacancies on the Supreme Court. To fill them he chose Noah Swayne of Ohio, David Davis of Illinois, and Samuel F. Miller of Iowa. All were Republicans who had rendered some help in getting Lincoln elected President in 1860; indeed, Davis had been one of Lincoln's principal managers at the Chicago Convention of the Republican party.

In 1863, by reason of expansion in the membership of the Court, Lincoln was enabled to name still another justice, and he chose Stephen J. Field of California, a War Democrat who had been the chief justice of that state's supreme court. In 1864, Chief Justice Roger B. Taney finally died at the age of eighty-eight, and Lincoln had an opportunity to choose a new chief justice.

At this time, in the fall of 1864, the constitutionality of the so-called "greenback legislation," which the government had used to finance the war effort, was headed for a Court test, and Lincoln was very much aware of this fact. He decided to appoint his secretary of the treasury, Salmon P. Chase, who was in many respects the architect of the greenback legislation, saying to a confidant, "We wish for a Chief Justice who will sustain what has been done in regard to emancipation and the legal tenders. We cannot ask a man what he will do, and if we should, and he should answer us, we should despise him for it. Therefore, we must take a man whose opinions are known" (2 Warren 401).

In all, then, Lincoln had five appointments. How successful was Lincoln at packing the Court with these appointments? The answer has to be, I believe, that he was very successful at first. In the all-important *Prize Cases*, 2 Black 635 (1863), decided in 1863, the three Lincoln appointees already on the Court—Swayne, Miller, and Davis, joined with Justices Wayne and Grier of the Old Court to make up the majority, while Chief Justice Taney and Justices Nelson, Catron, and Clifford dissented. It seems obvious that this case would have been decided the other way had the same justices been on the Court who had decided the *Dred Scott* case six years earlier. Charles Warren, in his *The Supreme Court in United States History*, describes these cases as being not only "the first cases arriving out of the Civil War to be decided by [the Court], but they were far more momentous in the issue involved than any other case; and their final determination favorable to the government's contention was almost a necessary factor in the suppression of the war." [Warren, Vol. II, pp. 380–381].

But immediately after the war, a host of new issues arose which could not really have been foreseen at the time Lincoln made his first appointments to the Supreme Court. The extent to which military tribunals might displace civil courts during time of war or insurrection was decided by the Supreme Court in 1866 in the famous case of *Ex Parte Milligan*, 4 Wall. 2. While the Court was unanimous as to one aspect of this case, it divided 5 to 4 on the equally important question of whether Congress might provide for trial by military commissions during time of insurrection even though the president alone could not. On the latter question, the Lincoln appointees divided two to three.

During the postwar Reconstruction Era, three new amendments to the United States Constitution were promulgated, and the construction of those amendments was also necessarily on the agenda of the Supreme Court. The first important case involving the Fourteenth Amendment to come before the Court was that of the Slaughterhouse Cases, in which the applicability of the provisions of that amendment to claims not based on racial discrimination was taken up by the Court. Of the Lincoln appointees, Justice Miller wrote the majority opinion and was joined in it by Justice Davis, while Chief Justice Chase and Justices Field and Swayne were in dissent.

The ultimate irony in Lincoln's effort to pack the court was the Court's first decision in the so-called Legal Tender Cases, *Hepburn v. Griswold*, 8 Wall. 603. In 1870 the Court held, in an opinion by Chief Justice Chase, who had been named Chief Justice by Lincoln primarily for the purposes of upholding the greenback legislation, that this legislation was unconstitutional. Justice Field joined the opinion of the Chief Justice, while the other three Lincoln appointees—Miller, Swayne, and Davis—dissented. Chief Justice Chase's vote in the Legal Tender Cases is a textbook example of the proposition that one may look at a legal question differently as a judge from the way one did as a member of the executive branch. There is no reason to believe that Chase thought he was acting unconstitutionally when he helped draft and shepherd through Congress the greenback legislation, and it may well be that if Lincoln had actually posed the question to him before nominating him as Chief Justice, he would have agreed that the measures were constitutional. But administrators in charge of a program, even if they are lawyers, simply do not ponder these questions in the depth that judges do, and Chase's vote in the Legal Tender Case is proof of this fact.

In assessing Lincoln's success in his effort to pack the Court, it seems that with regard to the problems he foresaw at the time of his first appointments—the difficulties that the Supreme Court might put in the way of successfully fighting the Civil War—Lincoln was preeminently successful in his efforts. But with respect to issues that arose after the war—the use of military courts, the constitutionality of the greenback legislation, and the construction of the Fourteenth Amendment—his appointees divided from one another regularly. Perhaps the lesson to be drawn from these examples is that judges may think very much alike with respect to one issue, but quite differently from one another with respect to other issues. And while both presidents and judicial nominees may know the current constitutional issues of importance, neither of them is usually vouchsafed the foresight to see what the great issues of ten or fifteen years hence are to be.

By the time Theodore Roosevelt had succeeded to the presidency immediately after the turn of the century, issues arising out of the territorial expansion of the United States following the Spanish-American War and the governmental regulation of trusts and monopolies were issues high on the nation's agenda, issues that had been scarcely spots on the horizon at the time Lincoln appointed Salmon Chase Chief Justice. When President Roosevelt learned of the illness of Associate Justice Horace Gray of Massachusetts in 1902, his attention naturally turned to Chief Justice Oliver Wendell Holmes, Jr., of the Judicial Court of Massachusetts. But he was not going to buy a pig in a poke.

He wrote to his great and good friend Senator Henry Cabot Lodge of Massachusetts, as follows:

Dear Cabot,
. . . Now as to Holmes: if it becomes necessary you can show him this letter. First of all, I wish to go over the reasons why I am in his favor. He possesses the high character and the high reputation both of which should if possible attach to any man who is to go upon the highest court of the entire civilized world. His father's name entitles the son to honor; and if the father had been an utterly unknown man the son would nevertheless now have won the highest honor. The position of Chief Justice of Massachusetts is in itself a guarantee of the highest professional standing. Moreover, Judge Holmes has behind him the kind of career and possesses the kind of personality which make a good American proud of him as a representative of our country. . . .

Finally, Judge Holmes' whole mental attitude, as shown for instance by his great Phi Beta Kappa speech at Harvard is such that I should naturally expect him to be in favor of those principles in which I so earnestly believe. . . .

The majority of the present Court who have, although without satisfactory unanimity, upheld the policies of President McKinley and the Republican party in Congress, have rendered a great service to mankind and to this nation. The minority—a minority so large as to lack but one vote of being a majority—have stood for such reactionary folly as would have hampered well-nigh hopelessly this people in doing efficient and honorable work for the national welfare, and for the welfare of the islands themselves, in Porto Rico and the Philippines. No doubt they have possessed excellent motives and without doubt they are men of excellent personal character; but this no more excuses them than the same conditions excused the various upright and honorable men who took part in the wicked folly of secession in 1860 and 1861.

Now I should like to know that Judge Holmes was in entire sympathy with our views, that is with your views and mine and Judge Gray's, for instance, just as we know that ex-Attorney General Knowlton is, before I would feel justified in appointing him. Judge Gray has been one of the most valuable members of the Court. I should hold myself as guilty of an irreparable wrong to the nation if I should put in his place any man who was not absolutely sane and sound on the great policies for which we stand in public life.

> Faithfully yours,
> Theodore Roosevelt

P.S.—Judge Gray's letter of resignation to take effect upon the appointment of his successor, or as I may otherwise desire, has just come, so that I should know about Judge Holmes as soon as possible. How would it do, if he seems to be all right, to have him come down here and spend a night with me, and then I could make the announcement on the day that he left after we have talked together? [Roosevelt]

Holmes was duly appointed an associate justice, and largely fulfilled Theodore Roosevelt's expectations of him with respect to the so-called Insular Cases, which were a great issue at that time, although they are scarcely a footnote in a text on constitutional law today. But he disappointed Roosevelt with his dissenting opinion in the *Northern Securities* case, a disappointment Roosevelt is said to have expressed with the phrase: "Out of banana I could have carved a Justice with more backbone than that."

Although Franklin D. Roosevelt was understandably disappointed that he had had no opportunities to fill a vacancy on the Supreme Court during his first term in office, the vacancy occasioned by the retirement of Justice Van Devanter to which he appointed Justice Black was the first of eight vacancies that Roosevelt would have the opportunity to fill during his twelve years as President. There is no doubt that Roosevelt was keenly aware of the importance of judicial philosophy in a justice of the Supreme Court; if he were not, he never would have taken on the institutional might of the third branch with his Court-packing plan. Indeed, when it appeared during the battle in the Senate over the Court-packing bill that a compromise might be achieved in which Roosevelt would be allowed to appoint only two new justices instead of six, he pondered with several of his intimates whom he might choose in a way that he had not felt it necessary to do when he might have had the opportunity to choose six.

Majority Leader Joe Robinson of Arkansas was moved by considerations other than pure party loyalty to lead the fight for the President's Court-packing plan in the Senate. He had long wished to top off his long career of public service with a seat on the high bench, and many knowledgeable Washingtonians assumed that he would certainly be Franklin Roosevelt's first appointment to the Court. Leonard Baker, in his work *Back to Back: The Duel Between FDR and the Supreme Court*, describes the situation in the Senate this way:

> The day Willis Van Devanter sent his resignation to the White House, Joe Robinson's colleagues considered his appointment as a replacement a sure thing. So did Robinson. He came into the Senate chamber that afternoon with a wide grin on his face and feeling almost jubilant. His fellow senators of both parties, who were also his old and warm friends, swarmed toward him to congratulate him, shake his hand, slap him on the back. Some even called him "Mr. Justice." This situation, the high probability that Joe Robinson would be named to the Court, was one of the reasons Robinson had been able to secure pledges to support the Court bill compromise. His colleagues assumed that the appointment to the Court would be forthcoming as soon as Joe Robinson delivered passage of the Court bill. Some senators, wavering on judicial reform, had decided to go along as a favor to Robinson. They had much affection for him and wanted him to achieve his ambitions. [p. 248]

But Roosevelt's more liberal advisers were already cautioning him about nominating Robinson; he would be sixty-five years old that summer, and it was thought that his outlook as a justice might be more closely akin to the majority of the nine old men than Roosevelt would wish....

About a week after Van Devanter's resignation, Roosevelt was cruising on the Potomac with some of his friends, all of whom except Henry Morgenthau, Jr., secretary of the treasury, had retired belowdecks. Baker describes their conversation in these words:

> "If Brandeis resigns," speculated the President, "whom do you think I should appoint to succeed him—Landis or Frankfurter?" The first reference was to James M. Landis, a brilliant young New Dealer, and the second was to Felix Frankfurter of the Harvard Law School who had been a philosophical mentor to the New Deal.
>
> Morgenthau replied that he considered Landis the better choice.
>
> "Frankfurter would rate a more popular opinion."
>
> Morgenthau agreed, saying: "Yes, I suppose he would, but I believe that the public would have more confidence in Landis."
>
> "Well," said the President, "I think I would have a terrible time getting Frankfurter confirmed."

Morgenthau agreed, commenting that "one of the troubles with Frankfurter is that he is over-brilliant."

A few moments later Morgenthau brought the conversation from the realm of speculation to the immediate problem, the retirement of Willis Van Devanter and the expectation that Joe Robinson would succeed him. "What," he asked the President, "are you going to do about Joe Robinson?"

"I cannot appoint him," announced the President.

"Why not?"

"Because he is not sufficiently liberal."

"I am certainly glad to hear you talk that way," said Morgenthau. "The things that you have done and talked to me about the last ten days have encouraged me tremendously because after all I am a reformer."

Several months later the President returned to the question of appointing Joe Robinson. "If I had three vacancies, I might be able to sandwich in Joe Robinson." But he continued that he had no idea of who was going to resign after Van Devanter, or if anyone would. [Pp. 249–250]

This view is confirmed by observations of then Secretary of the Interior Harold L. Ickes in his diary:

Mr. Justice Van Devanter, on the nineteenth, sent his resignation to the President, to take effect at the end of this Term of Court. He tipped this off to a favorite newspaper correspondent before his letter could possibly reach the White House.

Not only the enemies of the President's Court plan but many of his friends at once rushed to get behind Senator Joe Robinson, to fill this vacancy. In fact, it seemed to me that the enemies were more interested in booming Robinson than anyone else, and the reason is not far to seek. . . .

I had an appointment with the President just before noon after he had taken cognizance of what was going on on behalf of Robinson. He said to me that if he had three or four appointments to make, it might be alright to appoint Robinson "just to even things up." I told him that I didn't think he could afford to appoint Robinson if his was to be the only appointment, and the President seemed to be emphatically of that opinion. [Ickes, Vol. II]

In rapid succession, as the so-called nine old men retired or died, Franklin Roosevelt appointed first Senator Hugo Black of Alabama, then Solicitor General Stanley Reed of Kentucky, then Professor Felix Frankfurter of Massachusetts, then SEC Chairman William O. Douglas of Connecticut and Washington, then Attorney General Frank Murphy of Michigan. During his third term Roosevelt appointed Attorney General Robert H. Jackson of New

York, Senator James F. Byrnes of South Carolina, and law school dean Wiley B. Rutledge of Iowa to the Court.... [F]ive of these Justices—Black, Reed, Frankfurter, Douglas, and Jackson—remained on the Court at the time of the Steel Seizure Case in 1952.

In the short run the effect of the change in membership on the Court's decisions was immediate, dramatic, and predictable. Social and regulatory legislation, whether enacted by the states or by Congress, was sustained across the board against constitutional challenges that might have prevailed before the Old Court. When Franklin Roosevelt in 1941 elevated Harlan F. Stone from associate justice to Chief Justice in place of Charles Evans Hughes, the periodical *United States News* commented, "The new head of the Court also will find no sharp divergence of opinion among his colleagues." *The Washington Post* echoed the same sentiment when it foresaw "for years to come" a "virtual unanimity on the tribunal." [Mason, p. 576]

These forecasts proved to be entirely accurate in the area of economic and social legislation. But other issues began to percolate up through the judicial coffee pot, as they have a habit of doing. The Second World War, which occupied the United States from 1941 until 1945, produced numerous lawsuits about civil liberties. During the war, the Court maintained a fair degree of cohesion in deciding most of these cases, but quite suddenly after the war, the predicted "virtual unanimity" was rent asunder in rancorous squabbling the like of which the Court had never seen before.

A part, but only a part, of the difference was of judicial philosophy. Understandably, seven justices who agreed as to the appropriate constitutional analysis to apply to economic and social legislation might not agree with one another in cases involving civil liberties. These differences manifested themselves infrequently during the war years, but came into full bloom shortly afterward. In a case called *Saia v. New York*, 334 U.S. 558 (1948), the Court held by a vote of 5 to 4 that a local ordinance of the city of Lockport, New York, regulating the use of sound trucks in city parks, was unconstitutional. Four of the five justices in the majority were appointees of Franklin Roosevelt, but so were three of the four justices in the minority. Seven months later the Court all but overruled the *Saia* case in *Kovacs v. Cooper*, 336 U.S. 53 (1949), with one of the *Saia* majority defecting to join the four dissenters for the *Kovacs* majority. These two cases provide but one of abundant examples of similar episodes in the Court's adjudication during the period from 1945 to 1949.

Thus history teaches us, I think, that even a "strong" president determined to leave his mark on the Court—a president such as Lincoln or Franklin Roosevelt—is apt to be only partially successful. Neither the president nor his appointees can foresee what issues will come before the Court during the tenure of the appointees, and it may be that none has thought very much about these issues. Even though they agree as to the proper resolution of current cases, they may well disagree as to future cases involving other questions when, as judges, they study briefs and hear arguments. Longevity of the appointees, or untimely deaths such as those of Justice Murphy and Justice

Rutledge, may also frustrate a president's expectations; so also may the personal antagonisms developed between strong-willed appointees of the same president.

All of these factors are subsumed to a greater or lesser extent by observing that the Supreme Court is an institution far more dominated by centrifugal forces, pushing toward individuality and independence, than it is by centripetal forces pulling for hierarchical ordering and institutional unity. The well-known checks and balances provided by the framers of the Constitution have supplied the necessary centrifugal force to make the Supreme Court independent of Congress and the president. The degree to which a new justice should change his way of looking at things when he "puts on the robe" is emphasized by the fact that Supreme Court appointments almost invariably come one at a time, and each new appointee goes alone to take his place with eight colleagues who are already there. Unlike his freshman counterpart in the House of Representatives, where if there has been a strong political tide running at the time of a particular election there may be as many as seventy or eighty new members who form a bloc and cooperate with one another, the new judicial appointee brings no cohorts with him.

A second series of centrifugal forces is at work within the Court itself, pushing each member to be thoroughly independent of his colleagues. The chief justice has some authority that the associate justices do not have, but this is relatively insignificant compared to the extraordinary independence that each justice has from every other justice. Tenure is assured no matter how one votes in any given case; one is independent not only of public opinion, of the president, and of Congress, but of one's eight colleagues as well. When one puts on the robe, one enters a world of public scrutiny and professional criticism which sets great store by individual performance, and much less store upon the virtue of being a "team player."

...The Supreme Court is to be independent of the legislative and executive branch of the government; yet by reason of vacancies occurring on that Court, it is to be subjected to indirect infusions of the popular will in terms of the president's use of his appointment power. But the institution is so structured that a brand-new presidential appointee, perhaps feeling himself strongly loyal to the president who appointed him, and looking for colleagues of a similar mind on the Court, is immediately beset with the institutional pressures I have described. He identifies more and more strongly with the new institution of which he has become a member, and he learns how much store is set by his behaving independently of his colleagues. I think it is these institutional effects, as much as anything, that have prevented even strong presidents from being any more than partially successful when they sought to pack the Supreme Court.

Bibliography

Baker, Leonard. *Back to Back: The Duel Between F.D.R. and the Supreme Court.* New York: The Macmillan Company, 1967.

Dunne, Gerald T. *Justice Joseph Story*. New York: Simon & Schuster, 1970.

Ickes, Harold L. *The Secret Diary of Harold L. Ickes*. 3 vol. New York: Simon & Schuster, 1954.

Mason, Alpheus Thomas. *Harlan Fiske Stone: Pillar of the Law*. New York: Viking Press, 1956.

Roosevelt, Theodore. *The Letters of Theodore Roosevelt*, ed. Elting E. Morison. Cambridge, Mass.: Harvard University Press, 1951.

Schachner, Nathan. *Thomas Jefferson*. New York: Appleton-Century-Crofts, 1951.

Warren, Charles. *The Supreme Court in United States History*. (3 Vols.) Boston: Little, Brown & Company, 1923.

66 / Righting the Other Federal Courts

W. John Moore

Though appointments to the Supreme Court generally gain more attention than presidents' appointments to the lower levels of federal courts, the latter are also important positions, and presidents have more than sufficient reason to try to "pack" these courts with co-ideologues. President Jimmy Carter made enough liberal appointments to the lower courts to affect his own mini-revolution, according to John Moore, but the conservative appointments during the Reagan and Bush presidencies have more than offset Carter's accomplishment. Not only have the conservative judges halted the liberal activism of Carter's appointees, some experts have concluded, but they have replaced the latter with their own conservative activism.

In the annals of American jurisprudence, *King v. Palmer* hardly qualifies as a landmark decision. The holding [in December of 1991] by the U.S. Court of Appeals for the District of Columbia Circuit ruled on the definitely Byzantine but hardly thrilling issue of attorneys' fees.

But *King v. Palmer* has considerable symbolic importance for what it says about the direction of the federal courts. In deciding that environmental lawyers could not get the higher fees they sought, the appeals court split on partisan grounds. All seven of the judges appointed by Presidents Reagan and Bush voted together, refusing to award the higher fees. All four of the judges appointed by President Carter dissented.

Such rulings, with factions of Reagan-Bush appointees opposed to all Carter-appointed jurists remain unusual, even on the ideologically polarized D.C. Circuit, perhaps the nation's most important appeals court because of its oversight of government rule making. But increasingly, like the D.C. Circuit, the 12 other appeals courts have become judicial battlegrounds, with ideological warfare waged between conservative Reagan-Bush appointees and their more liberal Carter colleagues.

As *King v. Palmer* also showed, Reagan-Bush judges now have the majority on most appeals courts to determine the outcomes of most cases, especially the most controversial and ideological ones. Simple numbers are the main reason.... More than half of the nation's 828 federal appeals and district court judges were appointed by Reagan or Bush.

Much has been made of the transformation of the Supreme Court from a liberal to a conservative court over the past dozen years, a revolution that is possibly Reagan's most important legacy. Less attention has been paid to the unprecedented takeover of the rest of the federal judiciary....

"We are moving towards the greatest imbalance in terms of partisanship that we have had since President Truman left office" in 1953, said Sheldon Goldman, a political science professor at the University of Massachusetts (Amherst) and an expert on federal judicial appointments.

Most of these judicial appointees are true-blue conservatives. During the Reagan Administration, according to its critics, likely nominees, especially at the appellate court level, were forced to pass ideological litmus tests that ensured appointments of conservatives with a clear agenda. Judicial restraint, fidelity to the Constitution and a halt to the liberal appointments made by Carter were the real objectives, Republicans said.

Perhaps more than in any other policy area, Bush has preserved Reagan's legacy in judicial nominations. Bush's nominees have been slightly younger, often with Ivy League backgrounds and better pedigrees than Reagan's nominees. More of them are women, fewer are academics, many are graduates of duty in U.S. Attorneys' offices.

Though Bush's nominees remain just as conservative, they haven't attracted the negative publicity of some Reagan choices.... "Bush's effort to place ideologues on the court is being pressed with as much intensity as it was by Ronald Reagan," Nan Aron, executive director of the liberal Alliance for Justice, said.

Conservatives, often unhappy with Bush's track record in other areas, wax euphoric over the President's judicial nominations. "A tour de force," cheered Clint Bolick, vice president and director of litigation at Washington's conservative Institute for Justice.... "He has been even better than Reagan," Bolick added. "Bush has made the judiciary more solidly conservative without spending a lot of political capital on the issue."...

The impact of the Reagan-Bush appointments is a topic of heated debate. "The judiciary is beginning to know its place in our governmental system," said Thomas L. Jipping, director of the Free Congress Research and Education Foundation's Center for Law and Democracy, a Washington-based conservative advocacy group. In this sense, the Republican appointees have practiced the conservative principle of judicial restraint, Jipping added.

Just as important, according to other conservatives, the Reagan-Bush judges have stymied the liberal activism that characterized the judicial philosophy of Carter appointees.... "People like that represent the worst judicial activism has to offer," Jipping said.

But Elliot Mincberg, legal director at Washington's People for the American Way, a liberal public-interest group, said many of the Reagan-Bush appointees practice a conservative brand of judicial activism. "These judges are more conservative on free-expression and privacy cases," he said. "They tend to give more weight to the government interest in cases and less interest to the public interest."

Legal scholarship conducted on the outcomes of cases Reagan-Bush judges have decided supports the thesis that Reagan's and Bush's appointments have generally produced the desired results. At the same time, the studies show a schism between Carter and Reagan-Bush judges on a wide range of issues. Unlike Carter's judges, the newest Republican judges are more likely to approve corporate mergers, rule against criminal defendants, reject claims of racial and sexual discrimination, deny citizen groups access to the courts and, as in *King v. Palmer,* oppose higher fees for lawyers.

On abortion decisions, the results are not surprising, with Reagan-Bush appointees far more hostile to abortion rights than either Carter appointees or even those appointed by President Nixon. "Presidents Carter and Reagan have indirectly influenced abortion jurisprudence by appointing judges who shared their platform-based policy predilections," concluded a study by University of Kansas professor C.K. Rowland and graduate student Steve Alumbaugh in the October 1990 issue of *Judicature.*

Still Supreme

On any important constitutional issue, such as abortion rights, the nation's 179 appellate judges and 649 district court judges are not empowered to make decisions that clash with existing Supreme Court precedent.... [I]t is the appointments of conservatives to the nation's highest court that has the overwhelming impact on jurisprudence. With Reagan-Bush appointees having a comfortable ... majority, the message sent to the lower court judges on some issues, such as criminal rights for defendants and death penalty cases, is clearly conservative.

The federal judiciary is hierarchical and authoritarian, said Herman Schwartz, a professor at the American University's Washington College of Law. Judges don't like to be reversed, and so they almost always follow precedent, no matter what their own ideological predilections might be, he added.

On the other hand, conservatives also have to wait for the Supreme Court to rule, with abortion just one key example. Reagan-Bush judges on the 6th Circuit, for example, in 1988 overturned Ohio statutes imposing restrictions on abortion. "The law does not change as rapidly as the judges," Schwartz noted.

But law bubbles up to the Court as well. A significant reason is the simple difference in volume of cases. In a typical term, the Court hears approximately 130 cases. The 13 appellate courts, on the other hand, consider 30,000 cases annually. Moreover, it is on the appeals courts that some of the intellectual heroes of the conservative movement have landed: exponents of the "Chicago school" law and economics doctrines such as Frank H. Easterbrook and Richard A. Posner on the 7th Circuit; libertarians such as Alex Kozinski on the 9th Circuit and the less well known Pasco M. Bowman II on the 8th Circuit; a strong conservative such as Edith Hollan Jones, recently a contender for a seat on the Supreme Court, on the 5th Circuit. Among the Reagan-Bush appointees, conservatives criticize as too liberal only Carol Los Mansmann of the 3rd Circuit, but former Reagan Administration officials described her record as exceptional.

"The genius of the Reagan-era appointment process is that they [aides selecting judges] looked for these people," said William E. Kovacik, a professor at George Mason University School of Law.

Critics charge that these judges represent the worst elements of conservative, result-oriented judging.

Given the number of cases and aggressively conservative judges, the appellate courts clearly have an effect on public policy. For example, . . . conservative star J. Harvie Wilkinson III, who was subjected to intense Senate scrutiny before joining the 4th Circuit in 1984, has written opinions striking down an affirmative action plan in Richmond, Va., permitting the government to seize an alleged criminal's assets used to pay attorneys' fees and holding that a fired worker can't sue his employer for age bias if he previously agreed to binding arbitration. All three decisions were upheld by the Supreme Court.

In the 6th Circuit, two Reagan-appointed judges took a tough stance in a sexual harassment case, holding that the plaintiff can't win unless she can show that the alleged harassment had an impact on work performance and personal well-being. It is a much tougher standard than anything adopted by the Supreme Court, Melanne Verveer, vice president of People for the American Way, said.

At the district court level, the selection process becomes a bit murkier, because of the role Senate Republicans play in the process. Many of the trial court judges have strong local Republican Party connections. The district court judges are a diverse lot. One is a sister of Donald Trump. Another is a former reporter who was nominated for a Pulitzer prize in 1971. . . .

Conservatives are generally pleased with the Reagan-Bush district court judges. "We only find about 10 per cent that we are less than enthusiastic about," Free Congress's Jipping said. "And the explanation of that is pork barrel politics."

District court judges—fact finders and initial trial judges—are not lacking in clout. Nor are the lower court judges prohibited from issuing important decisions. A former Reagan-appointed judge, in a decision later reversed on appeal, allowed children to be kept out of school because the parents objected to "secular humanism" being taught in the classroom.

Meanwhile, conservatives point to the rulings by the still-substantial number of Carter-appointed judges as proof positive that liberal activists remain at large—and influential.

"It doesn't matter if most of the judges were appointed by Reagan and Bush if you draw a Carter judge," said Washington lawyer Richard K. Willard, an assistant attorney general during the Reagan Administration; the Carter judges continue as liberal activists.. . .

Sparring Partners

The Carter Administration, given only four years in office, nevertheless effected its own mini-revolution on the courts. First, Carter appointed 264 federal judges, more than any of his three predecessors and more than Reagan did in his first term or Bush could before January 1993. Second, the Carter Administration accomplished its main goal of increasing the number of blacks, women and minorities on the federal bench.

The number of black judges named during Carter's term jumped to an unprecedented 14.3 per cent. Approximately 15.5 per cent of Carter-appointed judges were women. Republican Presidents Ford and Nixon combined named only two women to the federal bench.

Like Reagan, Bush has not evinced much interest in putting minorities on the bench. Liberal critics have dubbed Bush's judges white, male and wealthy; almost 25 per cent of them millionaires, according to the Alliance for Justice. Although his record is better than Reagan's and close to Carter's on naming women to the bench, only 4.8 per cent of Bush's judges are black. He has also appointed two physically disabled federal judges.

Some key Republicans remain nonplussed about the numbers of women and minorities as criteria to gauge judicial nominations. "The general feeling was that in the Carter Administration, the first criteria were these arbitrary characteristics of race and gender and not competence or fidelity to the Constitution," former Attorney General Edwin Meese III, Reagan's key adviser on judicial nominations, said in an interview. Other Republican legal experts argued that all the focus on the race, gender and ethnic backgrounds of Carter appointees simply ignored the fact that many of those nominated to the bench were liberal activists with an agenda.

But it's the Reagan-Bush judges who are more typically described as survivors of rigid ideological screening. Certainly, there is an ideological chasm separating judges appointed by a Republican or Democrat during the past 15 years. "Since I have been on this court, I have judges who came at cases more from a liberal angle, and now there are judges, more of them, who come at it from a conservative angle," Judge Carolyn D. King of the U.S. Circuit Court of Appeals for the 5th Circuit, a self-described Republican and a Carter appointee, said.. . .

Research has shown that the Reagan-Bush appointees may have formed a voting bloc, but that judges appointed by Nixon or Ford usually join them. On the other hand, the federal judiciary has not yet become so predictable that the result of every case is known once the names of the judges on the panel are known. Federal judges are notoriously unhappy about being described as mere stand-ins for the President who appointed them or as ideologues with an agenda that makes their every decision all but predictable.

Looking at the Results

Many recent studies show that the Reagan-Bush appointees differed from Carter judges in their decisions in a number of areas, including the following:

Abortion   According to the study by Rowland and Alumbaugh, opposition to abortion rights "could hardly have been more dramatic." Reagan appointees opposed abortion rights in 77 per cent of the cases, while Carter-appointed judges did so in only 13 per cent of the cases, they concluded.

Access to the courts   Carter judges are four times likelier than Reagan appointees to grant standing to public-interest groups, according to a February 1991 study in the *Journal of Politics* by Rowland and Eastern Michigan University professor Bridget Jeffery Todd. For Reagan judges, "where you stand depends in large measure on who you are," the study said. Reagan appointees slammed the courtroom door on civil rights groups, environmentalists and labor unions far more often than they did on corporations or the federal government. "President Reagan's injection of vigilant gatekeepers into the lower federal judiciary may vitiate participation in the federal political system for disadvantaged citizens," the study said. Carter judges permitted standing in fewer than half of the cases for both groups, but were more willing to grant courtroom access to groups seeking new kinds of "social regulation."

Antitrust   Carter judges retained more of the old-time religion than did Reagan-Bush appointees to appellate courts, voting more than twice as often to reject the corporate acquisitions, according to study by George Mason's Kovacic in the *Fordham Law Review.*

But in what is perhaps conservatives' most resounding intellectual victory, the differences between the judges over antitrust law have become muted. For example, judges on the same panel voted the same way in more than 90 per cent of the cases. Moreover, conservative antitrust theory has become so accepted and uncontroversial that some Carter-appointed judges such as Stephen G. Breyer on the 1st Circuit have "accumulated antitrust voting records that match or exceed the conservatism of prominent [Reagan] appointees like Richard Posner," Kovacic wrote.

Civil rights   Here there remains a major gulf between Carter and Reagan-Bush appointees. According to a 1989 study by Rowland and University of Houston professor Robert Carp, Reagan-Bush appointees agreed with plaintiffs that filed racial discrimination suits 13 per cent of the time; Carter appointees upheld the discrimination claims in 59 per cent of the cases.

Criminal law   "The degree of polarization between Reagan and Carter [judges]," according to one study, "is unprecedented." Carter judges are more than twice as likely as Reagan judges to support criminal defendants, the *Law and Society Review* said, noting that the Reagan appointees' record was not surprising but that the Carter judges' positions were not expected to be quite so liberal. "The differences in support [for criminal defendants] resemble differences one would expect if Presidents Carter and Reagan were Judges Carter and Reagan."

Environment   Reagan-Bush judges are likelier to issue rulings "that would reduce the burden of compliance" in meeting Clean Air Act and Clean Water Act standards than are judges put on the federal bench by Carter, Kovacik wrote in the *Boston College Environmental Affairs Law Review* last year. Moreover, Reagan judges take a dim view of citizen efforts to enforce the environmental laws on their own. *(See NJ, 2/13/88, p. 388.)*

Guessing the Future
...According to some judicial experts, the conservative choke hold on the federal judiciary, especially the Supreme Court, could restrict any new Democratic President's liberal innovations. The obvious solution for a Democratic President would be to transform the judiciary as quickly as possible.

That may not be an easy task. University of Massachusetts scholar Goldman cautioned that..., unless there is an increase in the size of the federal judiciary, ... Democrats will need [many] years in power to undo the damage.

Other legal experts disputed that assessment, noting that the Democrats, through their control of Congress and the Presidency, could expand the size of the judiciary and quicken the pace of the nominations process....

Changes in the lower courts might be joined by a speedy remake of the high court. Among the Associate Justices who could leave the Supreme Court within the next President's first term are the 83-year-old Blackmun, 71-year-old John Paul Stevens and 74-year-old Byron R. White.* Even Chief Justice William H. Rehnquist and Associate Justice Sandra Day O'Connor are considered possible candidates for retiring at an earlier age than some recent Justices, according to legal scholars.

Such a makeover at the Supreme Court would more than compensate for continued Republican holdovers on the lower courts. Only a transformation such as this would influence the conservative control of the judiciary. Even if Democratic federal judges were in the majority, they would still be hampered by a conservative Court, the American University's Schwartz said.

Conservative analyst Bruce E. Fein agreed, asserting that the conservatives have triumphed. "The judicial revolution created under Reagan and that has continued to some extent under Bush is there for the next 30 or 40 years," he said. "The entire intellectual climate has been so acutely altered over the last decade that the victory in the appointments process is assured."

---

* Ages are as of January, 1992—*Editor's Note.*

CHAPTER EIGHTEEN

Policy-making Institutions and Process

As the cumulative evidence of the previous chapters attests, dramatic changes in the institutions and behavior of American government and politics, as well as in the environment within which governing and politics take place, have resulted in a policy-making process that is far more complex today than the framers of the Constitution could possibly have envisioned. Principles such as federalism and separation of powers, which may seem simple in theory, have proven to be extraordinarily complicated in practice, and increasingly so as demands on government have come to outweigh resources. Creative expansion in the means by which interests may be expressed to government in a modern, pluralist society has made the forging of majority support for policies a much more difficult job for presidents and legislators alike.

The first two readings of this chapter are case studies in policy making in the *new* American context. Former President Jimmy Carter recalls the difficulties he faced when trying to develop a coherent energy policy in the age of hyperpluralism and ad hoc coalition-building, where success often requires going directly to the people (via television, of course) for support. Philip Brenner and William LeoGrande describe Congress's role in developing its own policy toward Nicaragua in the 1980s, and argue that it exemplifies just how much things have changed from the days when Congress was but a bit player on the foreign policy stage.

In the final selection, Benjamin Ginsberg and Martin Shefter argue that years of divided government have resulted in what they call "institutional combat" between the executive and legislative branches, with the consequence of increased difficulty in adopting and implementing policies to solve the nation's problems.

67 / A Case in Limits on Presidential Problem-Solving

Jimmy Carter

In the following excerpt from his presidential memoirs, former president Jimmy Carter tells of the difficulties of developing and promoting a policy to deal with the energy shortage of the 1970s. It is a story of using television to help set the nation's (and thereby, Congress's) agenda, and of the difficulty inherent in developing a coherent policy when passage would require the support of some ad hoc coalition of disparate special interests. Foremost, though, it is the story of how difficult it can be for presidents to forge policy changes quickly within the separation of powers system, even with the increased powers of the presidency.

From my earliest days in office, there were serious problems with distribution of fuel even when it was produced within our own country. We had plenty of American natural gas, but it was not going to the right places. That first winter, as we began work with congressional leaders and others on an energy program, the northeastern parts of the country were suffering from a severe shortage of gas. Many schools and factories had to be shut down—another stark reminder of the need for quick and vigorous action.

I went to the areas most damaged by the lack of fuel, both to marshal emergency aid and to arouse Congress. On February 1, less than two weeks after Inauguration Day, the law I sought was passed, giving me extraordinary powers to deal with the natural-gas shortage. Unfortunately, the almost unbelievable speed of Congress in enacting this legislation was not a harbinger of things to come.

Moving with exceeding haste myself, I announced that within ninety days a national energy plan would be made public and sent to Congress for immediate action. This was a major decision—and a controversial one. Because of the short time allowed for completing the project, creating a plan would require maximum coordination among the many agencies involved and would not permit the extensive consultation with congressional leaders that might insure swifter action once our legislation was sent to Capitol Hill. Nevertheless, I felt that the urgency of the issue required such quick action on my part. The plan needed to be completed without delay if Congress was to decide the matter during the first year.

I was more concerned about the difficulty of arousing public support for so complicated a program. First, awareness of the problem had been low; the energy question had rarely come up during the 1976 campaign. Then, on my visit to the areas of gas shortage people had asked me, "Mr. President, is there really a shortage? Aren't the gas companies just holding back supplies to squeeze more money out of us?" The skepticism about oil and gas companies was pervasive, leading many people to doubt the need for any sacrifice or new legislation. This doubt would continue to plague our efforts during the months ahead.

In order to emphasize the importance of the energy problem and to bring it home to the average American family, I devoted my first "fireside chat" to the subject. Wearing a cardigan sweater, I sat by an open fire in the White House library on the night of February 2, 1977, and outlined as clearly as possible what we needed to do together.

> Our program will emphasize conservation. The amount of energy being wasted which could be saved is greater than the total energy that we are importing from foreign countries. We will also stress development of our rich coal reserves in an environmentally sound way, we will emphasize research on solar energy and other renewable energy sources, and we will maintain strict safeguards on necessary atomic energy production.
>
> The responsibility for setting energy policy is now split among more than 50 different agencies, departments, and bureaus in the federal government. Later this month, I will ask the Congress for its help in combining many of these agencies in a new energy department to bring order out of chaos. . . . Utility companies must promote conservation and not just consumption. Oil and natural gas companies must be honest with all of us about their reserves and profits. We will find out the difference between real shortages and artificial ones. We will ask private companies to sacrifice, just as private citizens must do. . . . Simply by keeping our thermostats . . . at 65 degrees in the daytime and 55 degrees at night we could save half the current shortage of natural gas. . . . We can meet this energy challenge if the burden is borne fairly among all our people—and if we realize that in order to solve our energy problems we need not sacrifice the quality of our lives.

In order to give individual members of Congress maximum encouragement from the folks back home and help them resist the onslaught of lobbyists, I needed to arouse and sustain public interest in the energy issue. Following the fireside chat, I began a series of public forums within the White House and around the country to emphasize the importance of the legislation. It was like pulling teeth to convince the people of America that we had a serious problem in the face of apparently plentiful supplies, or that they should be willing to make some sacrifices or change their habits to meet a challenge which, for the moment, was not evident.

On April 18, 1977, I addressed the nation on the energy crisis. Two days later, I presented my energy plan to a joint session of Congress. It was my first visit to the House chamber. At the beginning of my speech, I stated that because of the nature of the subject, I did not expect applause. This was one time Congress lived up to my expectations.

We continued to meet with the key members of both Houses of Congress, trying to gain support for our proposals. Predictably, those from oil-producing states were intensely interested in the legislation; I knew that Senator Long would be a key figure in determining whether it would pass or fail.

> *I talked to Senator Long again . . . and asked him to come up and meet me later on in the day, which he did. Senator Long is one of the shrewdest legislative tacticians who has ever lived. He always takes the attitude that he's innocent, doesn't quite know what is going on, and the other senators put things over on him, but that he'll do the best he can. He's a shrewd negotiator, and I like him.*
>
> Diary, April 21, 1977

I did like him, but I soon learned that he and the other senators from oil-producing states were busy plotting strategy to short-circuit our plans and substitute legislation of their own, some of which was being drafted by the law firms representing the nation's oil companies.

As is often the case, the opposition forces were not very much in evidence at first, and the House finished its work on the omnibus bill expeditiously, with a final vote on our entire proposal on August 5. This was a remarkable exhibition of leadership by the Speaker, Chairman Ashley, and others who worked with them. Congress had not seen anything like it in many years. Both Houses of Congress also acted responsibly in approving our plan for a new Department of Energy, and accepted my nomination of Jim Schlesinger as the first secretary.

However, on our proposals for a comprehensive energy policy, we encountered far more serious difficulties in the Senate, where the energy industry lobbies chose to concentrate their attention. They launched a media campaign to convince the public that there really was no problem that could not be overcome if only the oil producers, public utility companies, and nuclear power industry were relieved of government interference and left to run their own business.

In the meantime, their spokesmen in the Senate were forming a quiet coalition with some of the liberals, who were characteristically uncompromising on any of their own demands. They did not want any deregulation of oil or gas prices; the producers wanted instant and complete decontrol. The liberals wanted all increased revenues from higher prices to go to social programs; the producers wanted all the resulting funds retained by the energy companies, to be used for increasing production. The liberals favored solar-power projects as a panacea for the world's energy woes; the oil producers wanted minimum competition from any energy sources they could not control. Some consumer groups saw expensive gasoline and restrictive legislation as essential for the elimination of the large gas-guzzling vehicles; the automobile companies wanted low fuel prices and no restraints on the size or style of cars. One group wanted to do away with all nuclear power plants;

another wanted to remove the existing safety regulations, which, it claimed, were hamstringing the industry. The environmentalists wanted ever stricter air pollution standards; the coal producers, utility companies, and automobile manufacturers wanted to eliminate those we already had.

For a variety of conflicting reasons, all these powerful groups rejected the balanced legislation we introduced. Their combined strength constituted an ample majority in the Senate. The division of the United States into energy producing and consuming regions also insured an equivalent division in Congress.

Our only hope was to take our case to the public and work to produce acceptable legislative compromises that could attract a bare majority of votes and still preserve the benefits of our original proposals.

> *The influence of the special interest lobbies is almost unbelievable, particularly from the automobile and oil industries.*
> Diary, June 9, 1977

The weeks dragged on. By the middle of October, the scheduled end of the congressional year had passed with the Senate work still unfinished. It looked as if the senators would produce five separate energy bills—but not in the forms I wanted. Key provisions concerning gas decontrol and taxation were altered to make them much more to the liking of the oil companies. All this new language bore little resemblance to our proposals, which had been passed virtually intact by the House. Any conference committees that might be formed would still face a formidable task in trying to get both Houses to agree on exactly the same bill. Nevertheless, the congressional leaders concurred with me that the work must be completed before final adjournment, and the legislative calendars were cleared of other important business to permit uninterrupted work on energy.

Tempers in the Senate were running high on both substantive and jurisdictional questions. Whose committee would play the lead role—Jackson's or Long's? They were unable to resolve their dispute within the Senate chambers. At the suggestion of the Democratic congressional leaders, I decided to bring the two contending committee chairmen together in the White House, hoping this maneuver would ease the strain.

It didn't work.

> *Met with the congressional leaders for breakfast, and we discussed almost exclusively the energy legislation. I particularly wanted Scoop Jackson and Russell Long there, so that we could have it out among a group of Democrats concerning their differences, which are very deep and personal. I thought Russell acted very moderately and like a gentleman, but Scoop . . . was at his worst. . . . At the same time, he is supporting my positions much more closely than Russell is. . . . Long said he would recommit the bill to committee if the Jackson amendments pass, and Jackson said he would call for*

> *recommitment if his amendments fail. And of course, recommit-*
> *ting the bill to the Finance Committee would kill it.*
>
> Diary, October 25, 1977

The primary argument was about a natural-gas law. Both committees had produced their own separate bills on the subject. In addition to wanting his legislation approved by the Senate, Long also wanted to keep his "negotiating points"—provisions highly favorable to the energy companies—some of which he claimed to be willing to trade away in conference with the House in order to protect other parts of the Senate bills. Of course, this process would also leave him the undisputed conference spokesman on the most vital questions. Jackson wanted either his own bill or major amendments in the Finance Committee bill. After heated debate, Long finally prevailed and the Senate passed the last bill on October 31.

Now we had one good House bill and five separate Senate bills—one each to phase out natural-gas price controls, favor increased use of coal instead of oil and gas, provide tax breaks for those who would use energy more efficiently, reform electric utility rates, and encourage other means of conserving energy. The most divisive issue was decontrol of natural-gas prices, with the Senate narrowly in favor of removing the limits on the price of gas.

The conferees were ready to begin their most concentrated work. Unfortunately, in trying to be fair to both consumers and the oil companies, the leaders in both Houses formed conference committees whose members were *exactly* divided on the most controversial issues. For instance, all 18 members of the Senate Energy Committee, divided 9 to 9 on decontrol, were appointed as the conferees!

We kept plugging away without much success. By December 15, agreement had been reached on only the three bills that had come from Jackson's Energy and Natural Resources Committee—conservation, coal conversion, and electricity rates. The final versions were close enough to our original proposals to be acceptable. The Senate refused to consider the tax measures until after a decision was made on natural-gas decontrol. Because we did not want to split up the entire package and permit a crippling postponement of the more difficult and important parts, we had given our encouragement to the House when it refused to vote on just three-fifths of the total package. We felt certain that if we accepted the three relatively attractive and popular bills, we would never get the other two. No basis for further compromise could be found, so Congress adjourned without passing any of the bills. The deadlock would have to be resolved in 1978.

It was one of my few major disappointments of the year, but it was serious, because everyone realized the bills were our most important legislation. *Congressional Quarterly* wrote, "The first session of the 95th Congress could be said to have had two agendas: energy and everything else." On all other domestic issues, I had done extremely well, but on energy I still had a long way to go. At least I had confronted an issue which had been postponed too long—I could now understand why—and the energy issues had become clearly defined.

68 / Congress and Nicaragua: The Limits of Alternative Policy Making

Philip Brenner
William M. LeoGrande

Until the 1970s, it was commonplace to view Congress's role in foreign policy-making as that of a bit player to the president's star. Though Congress might not give the president everything he asked for, neither did it actively challenge his exclusive leadership in this area. But for reasons enumerated by Philip Brenner and William LeoGrande, the situation changed dramatically in the 1970s, and since then Congress has been much more assertive. Though an exceptional case even today, Congress's development of its own alternative to the administration's Nicaragua policy demonstrates how far Congress can go in affecting foreign policy.

On March 24, 1989, President George Bush announced an historic accord that marked the end of a war between two semisovereign powers. The announcement culminated four weeks of negotiations by Secretary of State James A. Baker and marked the administration's first foreign policy success. In these meetings, however, Baker was not representing the United States. He was the emissary of the executive branch, and the agreement was with the U.S. Congress over policy toward Nicaragua.

Few analysts of U.S. policy toward Nicaragua have ignored Congress, and several even have focused on congressional actions.[1] Indeed, it would have been difficult to overlook the role Congress played in policy making toward Nicaragua in the 1980s. The Iran-contra affair emanated directly from the congressional cutoff of aid to the Nicaraguan armed opposition, or contras: the ban forced members of the executive branch to use unconstitutional means when they chose to continue their contra funding.

The prevailing scholarly view, however, has been that Congress had a minor part in shaping U.S. policy. The framework into which most scholars have placed Congress relegates it to the category of elements that must be considered in explaining the twists and turns of U.S. policy. Though many might disagree with his judgment about the Iran-contra affair, Rep. Henry Hyde, R-Ill., in effect captured the conventional executive-oriented wisdom about Congress when he wrote:

> [T]he Founding Fathers intended to vest the general control of foreign affairs in the President.... [T]here are Members of the House and Senate who do not believe that communism in Central America is a grave threat to peace and freedom...; there are

Members who concede the threat in the abstract, but wish to do little about it beyond talking; and there are Members who acknowledge the threat and wish to challenge it.... The strange alliance between the unbelieving and the believing-but-unwilling has made a mockery of our foreign policy: we have had one policy one year and another policy the next.... Too little have we acknowledged that our own convolutions have made the task of the Executive even more difficult.[2]

In contrast, Secretary of State Baker's negotiations on Capitol Hill seemed to evidence an appreciation for how much the role of Congress had evolved.[3] Rather than treating Congress as merely a source of influence, Baker implicitly acknowledged the legislative branch as an equal, with a distinctive policy. Indeed, for much of the 1980s the administration and Congress each had its own policy toward Nicaragua. Neither one quite prevailed, though each branch undertook extraordinary efforts to achieve its policy ends. Each influenced the other and thus contributed to the inconsistency that characterized both the legislature's and the executive's Nicaragua policies.

The notion that Congress might have its own foreign policy is consistent with, though different from, the now common observation that in the 1970s the legislature began to involve itself extensively in foreign policy making and to defer less to executive initiatives.[4]

Analysts have attributed the reorientation to several factors. Among them are a breakdown in the post-World War II consensus about the role of the United States in the world, precipitated by the Vietnam War; a series of relatively weak presidents; new members who came to Congress with an activist agenda; and the development in the legislative branch of mechanisms— such as improved information resources, increased staff, and subcommittees that could hold hearings and do independent investigations—that enhanced Congress's ability to initiate and shape policy.

These changes, along with major congressional initiatives on war powers, intelligence activities, covert action, human rights, and arms sales, led two observers in 1979 to describe Congress's new foreign policy-making role as a "revolution."[5] Yet the revolution seemed short-lived. The arrival of a strong president in 1981, and the subsequent congressional deferral to him on military spending, arms sales, human rights, and covert action, suggested that the pendulum had swung partially back, placing Congress in a decidedly secondary role.

Still, members of Congress were active on foreign policy issues in the 1980s, especially on policies toward Nicaragua, El Salvador, and southern Africa. But the view of Congress as secondary engendered the characterization that congressional activism was no more than interference in executive branch policy making. In its positive aspect, the caricature portrayed an image in which the legislature intruded to correct executive branch excesses or to help the executive branch avoid pitfalls.[6] As a criticism, it painted Congress as irresponsibly preventing the successful implementation of U.S. foreign policy, either through "micromanagement" or personal diplomacy.[7] In either case, U.S. policy was cast as the policy of the administration.

This framework would be adequate to explain congressional behavior with respect to Nicaragua until 1983. From then on, however, subgroups in the legislature developed alternative U.S. policies toward Nicaragua. As is the case with any plans that might be appropriately termed a policy, these policies included clear sets of goals, strategies for achieving the goals, and instruments to implement the strategies.

Congressional policy—that is, the policy of the institution as a whole articulated in its votes—was sometimes an expression of one or another of the subgroups' policies. At other times, when compromises were struck among the groups advocating alternative policies, it was an amalgam. And for about one and a half years in mid-decade, congressional policy was coincident with the administration's, because Senate and House Republicans advocated positions that were essentially the same as the executive's, and they prevailed. Indeed, during the time that the Senate was controlled by the Republican party, it was the House that offered an alternative policy, and congressional policy was often a compromise between the administration and the House that did not always reflect a consistent relationship between goals, strategies, and methods.

The fact that a distinctive congressional policy toward Nicaragua was evident in voting does not indicate that there was a consensus in the legislature about the policy. Congress was polarized on the issue, and throughout the 1980s large blocs of members were absolutely consistent in their opposing positions.

Notably, Nicaragua policy generated divisions within the administration as well, though not with the extremes found in Congress. The conflicts between agencies over Nicaragua policy frequently meant that one agency's actions contradicted the efforts of another.[8] Even official pronouncements by President Ronald Reagan were not clear guides to U.S. policy. At times they were intended to mislead U.S. allies, the public, Congress, and the Nicaraguan government, and at other times they may have reflected the president's ignorance of what some administration officials were doing.[9] In effect, congressional policy may have appeared more fragmentary than the administration's only because members of Congress were so much more accessible and willing to speak openly to journalists and scholars than were administration officials.

Congress rarely sets out to develop its own foreign policy. Most members are content to let an administration lead and to reach a bipartisan compromise cooperatively. The Nicaraguan case was unusual in this regard, though it was not unique. Congress appears to have developed and pursued distinctive policies toward El Salvador and southern Africa as well, and an analysis of congressional policy toward Nicaragua may suggest why the legislature deviated from its normal pattern in those cases. . . .

Congress and Contra Aid

During the 1980s the development of the congressional-executive conflict over Nicaragua proceeded in stages. In the first period, from January 1981 until the spring of 1983, the president set the policy agenda, and Congress acquiesced. The second period lasted approximately two years, during which time an increasing number of members opposed the administration's policy and began to develop alternatives. In the third period, from the spring of 1985 to the spring of 1986, one group among the Democrats came to ascendance, and their choice carried Congress. The fourth period lasted less than a year, ending with the close of the 99th Congress in January 1987. During this time Congress adopted a position that was essentially the same as the administration's. From January 1987 until March 1989, however, House Democrats defined a distinctive congressional policy, and this formed the basis of the settlement achieved with the Bush administration in March 1989. . . .

January 1987 to March 1989   In the wake of the Republicans' losses in the 1986 elections and the exposure of the Iran-contra scandal, the House majority that supported Reagan's Nicaragua policy evaporated. The House voted in March 1987 to deny release of the last $40 million from the $100 million package [of contra aid] approved the previous year; the vote was 230–196. Since only a joint resolution (which requires presidential concurrence) could block release of the funds, opponents of contra aid had no hope of overriding a presidential veto. But even though the vote was largely symbolic and aid continued to flow, the emergence of a firmer congressional resolve against aid was evident.

During 1987 the administration delayed any further requests for military support of the contras to avoid voting in the midst of the congressional investigation of the Iran-contra affair. The White House and the House Democratic leadership did agree to provide $20.7 million in food and medicine during the first half of fiscal 1988.

Meanwhile, efforts emerged in the region to secure a negotiated solution to the Nicaraguan war. These began in December 1986 with a new proposal by Costa Rican president Oscar Arias. . . . Arias's plan . . . would not have required the United States to remove its forces or military aid from the region. But it called for the termination of aid to all guerrilla forces in Central America, including the contras. This plan was endorsed in principle by El Salvador, Guatemala, and Honduras on February 16. One month later the Senate lauded it by a 97–1 vote (S. Con. Res. 24). Then in August the United States proposed a new diplomatic initiative endorsed by House Speaker Jim Wright and President Reagan. Their plan was quickly superseded by the Central Americans themselves. On August 7, 1987, all five Central American presidents—including Nicaragua's Daniel Ortega—signed the Esquipulas accord, which was in essence the same as the February Arias plan. . . . Under the Esquipulas agreement the five countries were pledged to establish pluralist democracies, hold free elections, halt support for regional insurgents, and seek national reconciliation with their own armed opponents.[10]

Progress on the diplomatic front reduced Reagan's chances of winning new military aid. Members of Congress wanted to underscore their support for regional peace efforts by acting in accord with the call for a contra aid ban. But many also felt that the contras had been encouraged to fight by the United States and should not be summarily abandoned. The matter of funding them faced Congress squarely in 1988, when the administration reported that the guerrilla forces had run out of money. On February 3 the House narrowly defeated (211–219) President Reagan's request for $36.25 million in military and nonmilitary assistance. The president's request also included a number of hidden costs that brought the total value of the package to some $60 million.

The administration still hoped it might prevail in April, when the Democratic leadership brought its own aid package to the floor. Sponsored by Rep. David Bonior, D-Mich., it included $16 million in food and medicine for the contras and $14.6 million for aid to Nicaraguan children victimized by the war. The Bonior proposal was approved initially, 215–210, but was finally defeated, 208–216, by staunch supporters of the contras, who felt that the Bonior plan provided too little, and by a few staunch opponents of contra aid, who felt that the plan provided too much. A few weeks later, however, the Republicans acquiesced and accepted the Democrats' proposal, preferring it to no aid at all.

The House, in its final vote on contra aid during the Reagan administration, handily rejected an amendment to the fiscal 1989 intelligence authorization bill that would have enabled the administration to resume military aid by drawing on the CIA's contingency fund. At that point, on May 26, 1988, a clear majority wanted to support the peace process that was moving rapidly within Nicaragua.

On March 23 the Nicaraguan government had signed a sixty-day cease-fire agreement with the contra political leadership. The so-called Sapoa accord—named for the Nicaraguan border town where it was signed—included plans for negotiations aimed at a permanent cease-fire, amnesty for contra soldiers, and government guarantees of free expression.... The agreement specified that the contras could receive humanitarian aid through neutral international organizations such as the Red Cross.

The Sapoa agreement, particularly the section on humanitarian aid, significantly undercut the rationale and legitimacy of the Reagan administration's contra aid program. Though the cease-fire broke down several times in the next year and the contra military leaders seemed opposed to it, the peace process continued to move forward with an announcement of elections in Nicaragua, the creation of a powerful and legitimate electoral council, and the willingness of the Nicaraguan government to allow international observers to monitor the electoral process. It became more difficult for the administration to portray the Nicaraguan government as intransigent, belligerent, and totalitarian and to justify support for the contra war. In effect, Sapoa led to the March 1989 agreement between Congress and the Bush administration that brought the policies of the two branches into synchronization.

The Legislative Struggle for an Alternative

The congressional effort to fashion an alternative policy toward Nicaragua was extraordinary. It absorbed the energies of an unusually large number of members and staff, particularly when assessed in relation to the size of the region involved and the level of proposed expenditure. It also attracted considerable effort by the administration and interest groups. This attention suggests the importance that was attached to the issue, but it only begins to indicate how a distinctive congressional policy developed. Four factors contributed to the emergence of an alternative policy in Congress: internal congressional activities; executive branch activities; domestic, nongovernmental activities and events; and regional activities and events.

Internal Congressional Activities   House Democrats prepared themselves to engage the president over Nicaragua and El Salvador policies even before Ronald Reagan took office. They selected Michael Barnes to chair the Inter-American Affairs (subsequently renamed Western Hemisphere) Subcommittee over the sitting chair, Gus Yatron, D-Pa., because Barnes had Latin American expertise and a more liberal voting record. With the loss of several liberal senators in the 1980 election and the switch in party control in the other chamber, House Democrats reasoned that they would need to have strength in this important subcommittee in order to challenge aggressive administration policies in Central America.

As the executive's policy emerged through covert action and directives that had no need for legislative corroboration, the Western Hemisphere Affairs Subcommittee had to develop a role for itself. It did this by regularly focusing public and media attention on Nicaragua, through trips to the region, and through an increasing number of hearings, especially after 1982.

The intelligence oversight committees themselves were deeply involved in overseeing Nicaragua policy, though this proved frustrating for many members because of the necessary secrecy attached to the deliberations of these panels. . . .

Senators and representatives outside the intelligence committees also wanted to be involved in shaping the policy, and their desires generated additional congressional activity. The total number of hearings about Central America in the House and Senate increased nearly 50 percent from 1982 to 1983 and more than doubled from 1983 to 1984. The number of hearings stayed at the 1984 level for the next three years.

From 1983 until 1988, more than one hundred senators and representatives traveled to Nicaragua to meet with government officials, to observe elections, and even to consult with the contras. The trips added to the level of knowledge about Nicaragua inside Congress, reinforced the members' interest in the war, and contributed to the sentiment that Congress was capable of developing its own Nicaragua policy.

Both Democrats and Republicans worked to develop alternatives through several informal panels. . . .

It was Speaker Wright, though, who played the most remarkable role in developing a congressional policy toward Nicaragua. Distrusted by liberals while he was House majority leader, he emerged in 1987 as a central figure when he spearheaded a diplomatic initiative that forced the administration to endorse the Esquipulas plan. As he involved himself in discussions with foreign leaders and forged a consensus among Democrats, he took on an unprecedented role for a Speaker as Congress's foreign policy spokesperson on Nicaragua.[11]

Executive Branch Activities   As Congress struggled to define a coherent policy toward Nicaragua, the most powerful external influence on its behavior was naturally the executive branch. The president made support of the contras the centerpiece of his entire foreign policy. He focused on them in several State of the Union addresses, in a speech before a joint session of Congress, and in numerous radio and television appeals. And he used his personal charm effectively to persuade some members of Congress—especially Republicans—to back contra aid.[12] . . .

Above all, the administration had the ability to seize the initiative in ways that forced Congress to respond. In 1984 it opened a seeming diplomatic offensive by sending a special envoy to negotiate with the Nicaraguan government, and in 1985 it unilaterally imposed economic sanctions. Its control of classified information enabled it to use selective leaks for maximum effect. And because it was responsible for the contra operation, it had considerable leverage over the actions taken by the guerrillas.

Yet the administration's actions were not well coordinated and contributed to a sense in Congress that the executive was in disarray over its Nicaragua policy. This sense provided an opening for Congress to assert itself. Members saw that while one administration official asserted that the United States was pursuing diplomatic avenues, another would disavow diplomatic efforts and threaten military intervention. Claims that the contras were only supposed to interdict arms were contradicted by officials who leaked information about a wider war.[13] Ultimately, the administration's credibility with Congress was eroded by years of obfuscation—from the 1984 harbor mining to the Iran-contra scandal—that in part resulted from various officials charting their own policies. Thus in 1988, when officials claimed that the administration sought a peaceful solution by sustaining the contras, few believed them. As House Majority Whip Tony Coelho, D-Calif., remarked, "Yesterday's vote [to deny funding] was the White House not understanding the power of peace."[14]

The Iran-contra scandal not only opened the most gaping hole in the administration's credibility, but it also indicated to Congress that the obsession with overthrowing the Nicaraguan government was tearing at the very fabric of the Constitution and was distorting U.S. objectives in other foreign policy areas. . . .

Domestic, Nongovernmental Activities and Events   In analyzing the major votes for contra aid from 1983 to 1988, we conclude that shifts in the congressional majority were produced by a combination of member replacement and conversion. Both sides had large blocs of members who voted consistently, and the narrow, winning coalitions thus hung on the votes of swing members and those brought in by elections. This situation encouraged extensive lobbying efforts by both opponents and supporters of contra aid and made the 1984 and 1986 elections major determinants in congressional policy toward Nicaragua....

Whether the lobbying campaigns had any effect on the media is uncertain. But the media themselves contributed to the development of congressional policy by helping to define a common wisdom about Nicaragua policy and aid to the contras. Editorials on contra aid in the *New York Times* and the *Washington Post* before major votes from 1983 to 1988 tended to be critical of the Nicaraguan government. Calling them "Nicaragua's leftist tyrants," the *Times* charged in 1986 that "the Sandinistas have ... installed a totalitarian security system.... The Sandinista junta has also meddled in its neighbors' affairs...." The *Post* asserted in 1986 that unquestionably "the Sandinistas are communists of the Soviet or Cuban school." Editorials also were hostile toward the administration's policy. In 1985, for example, the *Times* declared that "there is nothing unpatriotic about this resistance to the contra war." The contras, it asserted a year later, were organized by the CIA and "offer little hope of a democratic redemption." Still, both papers favored some form of aid to the contras. For example, the *Post* called on Congress in April 1985 to stop military aid to the contras, but "if it is not going to support that cause with either indirect or direct military means ... it ought to support it with other means: diplomatic, political and economic."[15]...

There was also consistent public opposition to contra funding and to U.S. military intervention against Nicaragua.[16] When pollsters first began asking about aid to the contras in early 1983, they found that about 60 percent of the public opposed aid and only about 25 percent favored it. These proportions remained unchanged over the succeeding years. In March and April of 1986, 62 percent of respondents opposed aiding the contras, and less than 30 percent were in favor, though a majority favored some effort to "prevent the spread of communism in Central America." Still, over time there was decreasing approval for the use of force, and polls taken in mid-1988 still showed 57 percent opposed and only 27 percent in favor of contra aid.[17]

Overall, the 1986 election had an even greater effect on congressional policy than the 1984 landslide did, and in the opposite direction. When the Democrats regained majority control of the Senate, the White House could no longer count on victories there. This dominance reinvigorated House Democrats, who envisioned that with majorities in both chambers they might be able to legislate the elusive congressional alternative to the executive's policy.

Regional Activities and Events   What continued to animate the congressional search for an alternative was, as many saw it, the inappropriateness of the administration's policy for the evolving situation in Nicaragua. Indeed, after 1983 the House in particular was sensitive to regional diplomatic initiatives to end the contra war. Many members repeatedly signaled their desire to avoid direct U.S. military involvement and to support negotiated solutions to the problems they perceived. When negotiations seemed to make headway, House majorities did pull back on contra aid. When they bogged down, House Democrats found it more difficult to muster a majority against contra military assistance....

It was the Esquipulas plan that set in motion the final movement toward a congressional policy. That Speaker Wright had joined President Reagan in proposing a bipartisan alternative the day before the Central American presidents met and had quickly acceded to the Esquipulas plan added an incentive for members to support a diplomatic approach to the achievement of their objectives for Nicaragua: their own leader now was heavily involved in the peace process. Although the initial plan was implemented only in part, members of Congress became extraordinarily sensitive to President Arias's interpretations of how well proposed contra aid plans would correspond to the August 1987 Esquipulas accords....

An Evolving Congressional Policy

...By 1985 there was a widely shared belief that the administration wanted to use the contras and the CIA to overthrow the Nicaraguan government.[18] A majority of representatives sought, in contrast, to demilitarize, to find ways to pressure the Nicaraguans to increase the participation of non-Sandinistas, and to end alleged support for insurgencies in other countries. Even most liberals by this point expressed disapproval of the Sandinista-led Nicaraguan government, though they hoped to pressure the Nicaraguans through nonmilitary means.[19]

Slowly, over the next two years, as the factors outlined in the preceding section affected them, members experimented with policy formulations that might achieve the objectives a majority had begun to articulate. The twists and turns of congressional policy were not merely passive reactions to differing pressures and events. They were proactive efforts to forge a workable policy that could consistently command majority support. At the same time, a large minority bloc in the House consistently supported aid to the contras, which in most years included military assistance.

The outlines of the congressional policy are evident from public statements and interviews by a cross section of Congress and ultimately from the March 1989 bipartisan agreement. In effect, the policy supported by a majority of Congress stipulated four points:

1. The two primary goals of U.S. policy should be, first, to achieve a pluralist, democratic political system in Nicaragua but without overthrowing the Nicaraguan government by force of arms; and second, to prevent the Nicaraguan government from committing aggression against neighboring countries.
2. The United States should achieve its objectives by using diplomatic means. In this regard, the United States should encourage and support the countries in Central America in their efforts to develop regional mechanisms for the promotion and maintenance of peace.[20]
3. The United States, however, should maintain pressure on the Nicaraguan government to engage in an internal dialogue with

the armed and unarmed opposition, to open up its political system to non-Sandinista groups, to implement regional agreements, to reduce the size of its military, and to reduce its links to the Soviet Union and countries in the Warsaw Pact and Council of Mutual Economic Assistance.[21]

4. In addition, because the poor economies of Central America contribute to instability and discourage regional cooperation, the United States should provide regional economic assistance and support regional development plans.

It was these basic points that were embodied in the 1989 bipartisan agreement.... The 1989 bipartisan agreement took Nicaragua off the congressional agenda until after the February 1990 Nicaraguan elections. The surprise victory of opposition candidate Violeta Chamorro and the demobilization of the contras after her inauguration in April marked the end of the covert war....

The Limits of Alternative Foreign Policy Making

...An assessment of the limits of alternative congressional policy making ... depends on one's vantage point. If the focus is on means, the congressional policy was significant. Congress eventually determined that the contras would not be the instrument of policy and that diplomacy would take precedence over military means. It also reduced the likelihood that there would be direct U.S. military intervention in Nicaragua. With respect to policy aims, congressional policy departed less dramatically from the executive's. But Congress nonetheless helped to make U.S. policy aims accord with those of countries in the region. Notably, the Arias plan required internal as well as external changes in Nicaragua's politics. Finally, if an assessment were to focus on the effect of the policy on Nicaragua, it could well be argued that the administration's ability to act unilaterally overwhelmed Congress's will to restrain the executive. Congressional pressure may have influenced Nicaragua's decision to institute internal reforms, but the executive's low-intensity war had a greater direct effect on conditions in Nicaragua.

Whatever its limitations, however, the emergence of an alternative congressional policy toward Nicaragua was significant because the circumstances that led Congress to develop its own policy toward Nicaragua were not unique. In this case, Congress began to develop its own policy when the Reagan administration refused to accede to early congressional attempts to moderate the policy. Administration intransigence and persistence escalated the conflict between the branches, which was exacerbated by elements of deceit and obfuscation.

The Democrats might have simply used the congressional power of the purse to veto the executive's policy, but many moderate to conservative Democrats were concerned about Nicaragua's behavior and wanted the United States to remain involved in Central America. Others may have wanted merely to avoid appearing irresponsible and believed that by proposing an alternative they could escape the inevitable charge that they had abandoned Nicaragua to communists. Moreover, liberal and moderate Democrats feared that the administration's policy was leading toward a widening of the war and the direct involvement of U.S. troops. As the conflict with the administration persisted and Nicaragua policy remained a seemingly visible issue, Democrats felt ever more compelled to conceptualize a full-blown alternative to the administration's policy.

[Administrations today do] not have the salve of the post-World War II consensus that was repeatedly able to smooth over differences between the branches in the 1950s and 1960s. Today, there is no consensus about the U.S. role in the world, about the way in which the United States should respond to developments in the Third World, or about which U.S. interests are vital and deserve military and paramilitary intervention. Differences over these fundamental issues are bound to arise again, as they did in the case of Nicaragua, and they are likely to prompt congressional efforts to modify administration behavior. This is the legacy of the 1970s foreign policy "revolution" in Congress: now members of Congress believe they should appropriately struggle with these issues. Until a new foreign policy consensus emerges between the executive and legislature, then, we are likely to witness efforts by legislators to develop distinctive congressional policies that contribute significantly to U.S. foreign policy.

Notes

We would like to thank Elizabeth Cohn and Kimberly Heimert for their research assistance on this [selection].

1. The most thorough examination of congressional activity on Nicaragua is Cynthia J. Arnson, *Crossroads: Congress, the Reagan Administration, and Central America* (New York: Pantheon, 1989). See also Morris J. Blachman and Kenneth E. Sharpe, "Central American Traps: Challenging the Reagan Agenda," *World Policy Journal* 5 (Winter 1987–1988): 1–28; Roy Gutman, *Banana Diplomacy: The Making of American Policy in Nicaragua, 1981–1987* (New York: Simon & Schuster, 1988); Victor Johnson, "Congress and Contra Aid," in *Latin America and Caribbean Contemporary Record, 1987–1988*, ed. Abraham F. Lowenthal (New York: Holmes & Meier, 1989); Peter Kornbluh, *Nicaragua: The Price of Intervention* (Washington, D.C.: Institute for Policy Studies, 1987); William M. LeoGrande, "The Contras and Congress," in *Reagan Versus the Sandinistas*, ed. Thomas W. Walker (Boulder, Colo.: Westview Press, 1987), 202–227; and Robert A. Pastor, *Condemned to Repetition: The United States and Nicaragua* (Princeton, N.J.: Princeton University Press, 1987).
2. House Select Committee to Investigate Covert Arms Transactions with Iran and Senate Select Committee on Secret Military Assistance to Iran and the Nicaraguan Opposition, *Report of the Congressional Committees Investigating the Iran-Contra Affair*, H. Rept. 100–433, S. Rept. 100–216, November 1987, 100th Cong., 1st sess. (Washington, D.C.: U.S. Government Printing Office, 1987), 668, 669. (Hereafter cited as *Iran-Contra Report.*)
3. Notably, Baker's meetings with congressional leaders occurred in Congress, and Baker engaged in the negotiations personally.
4. For example, see Philip Brenner, *The Limits and Possibilities of Congress* (New York: St. Martin's Press, 1983); Cecil V. Crabb, Jr., and Pat M. Holt, *Invitation*

to Struggle: Congress, the President and Foreign Policy, 3d ed. (Washington, D.C.: CQ Press, 1989); I.M. Destler, "Executive-Congressional Conflict in Foreign Policy: Explaining It, Coping with It," in *Congress Reconsidered,* 3d ed., ed. Lawrence C. Dodd and Bruce I. Oppenheimer (Washington, D.C.: CQ Press, 1985); Thomas M. Franck and Edward Weisband, *Foreign Policy by Congress* (New York: Oxford University Press, 1979); Susan Webb Hammond, "Congress and Foreign Policy," in *The Congress, the President and Foreign Policy,* ed. Edmund S. Muskie et al. (Lanham, Md.: University Press of America, 1986); and Charles W. Whalen, *The House and Foreign Policy* (Chapel Hill: University of North Carolina Press, 1982).

5. Franck and Weisband, *Foreign Policy by Congress,* 3–9.
6. For example, Pastor, *Condemned to Repetition,* 275, writes that "Congress plays the role of balancer of U.S. national interests."
7. Dick Cheney, "Congressional Overreaching in Foreign Policy," in *Foreign Policy and the Constitution,* ed. Robert A. Goldwin and Robert A. Licht (Washington, D.C.: American Enterprise Institute, 1990), 106–108.
8. See Gutman, *Banana Diplomacy.*
9. Gutman, *Banana Diplomacy,* chap. 14; Kornbluh, *Nicaragua,* chap. 4; Bob Woodward, *Veil: The Secret Wars of the CIA* (New York: Simon & Schuster, 1987), 296–297, 389–390.
10. John Felton, "The Peace Option to Get a Fresh Airing in Upcoming Talks on Regional Plan," *Congressional Quarterly Weekly Report,* March 14, 1987, 462–463; John Felton, "Arias' Plan Has Yet to Bring Real Peace to the Political Factions on Capitol Hill," *Congressional Quarterly Weekly Report,* August 15, 1987, 1892–1893.
11. John Felton, "Nicaragua Peace Process Moves to Capitol Hill," *Congressional Quarterly Weekly Report,* November 14, 1987, 2789–2791.
12. Arnson, *Crossroads,* 197–198.
13. Gutman, *Banana Diplomacy,* chap. 7; Woodward, *Veil,* chap. 13.
14. John Felton, "Contra-Aid Denial Shifts Burden to Democrats," *Congressional Quarterly Weekly Report,* February 6, 1988, 237.
15. "The Nicaraguan Horror Show," *New York Times,* March 18, 1986, A26; "The President's Nicaragua Appeal," *Washington Post,* March 18, 1986, A10; "Contadora or Contra?" *New York Times,* April 23, 1985, A26; "Congress on Nicaragua," *Washington Post,* April 23, 1985, A14.
16. William M. LeoGrande, *Central America and the Polls* (Washington, D.C.: Washington Office on Latin America, 1987), 25–29.
17. Ibid. See also Richard Sobel, "Public Opinion About United States Intervention in El Salvador and Nicaragua," *Public Opinion Quarterly* 53 (Spring 1989): 115; Gallup Organization, "U.S. Assistance to Nicaragua," *Gallup Report* (July 1988): 11.
18. John Felton, "House, in Dramatic Shift, Backs 'Contra' Aid," *Congressional Quarterly Weekly Report,* June 15, 1985, 1139–1140; Pastor, *Condemned to Repetition,* 250–251.
19. Gutman, *Banana Diplomacy,* 289.
20. Though there was broad support for this general objective, conservative Democrats and Republicans diverged from the full implications of this goal. The Contadora treaties, for example, would have required the demilitarization of Central America, including a reduction in U.S. military aid and an end of the U.S. military presence there. Many Democrats, but not a majority of Congress, embraced this requirement as an objective of U.S. policy.

21. A broad underlying theme evident in congressional deliberations was that the United States should thwart the development of communism in Central America. Members rarely were clear about what this objective meant, however. For some, communism was a code word for the Soviet Union and countries allied with it in military and economic pacts. For others, communism signified a system of state ownership or single party rule. To a small number of members, a state was communist merely if it exhibited anti-U.S. sentiments.

69 / Institutional Combat and the Erosion of Governmental Power

Benjamin Ginsberg
Martin Shefter

Though separation of powers has always implied some competition between the legislative and executive branches, Benjamin Ginsberg and Martin Shefter argue that many years of divided government resulted in a system of "dual sovereignty." Each party attempted to strengthen the branch it controlled at the expense of the other, with negative consequences for the policy-making process.

...The collapse of political party organizations and the decline of voter turnout have combined to produce a deadlock in the electoral arena that gives the Democrats a stranglehold on Congress and the Republicans a decided edge in contests for the presidency. As each side entrenches itself within its own governmental bastions, American politics is coming to center on the efforts of competing forces to strengthen the institutions they control while undermining those dominated by their opponents. In this way, institutional combat is supplanting electoral competition as the decisive form of political struggle in the United States.

This political pattern undermines the governing capacities of the nation's institutions, diminishing the ability of America's government to manage domestic and foreign affairs, and contributing to the erosion of the nation's international political and economic standing....

Institutional Combat and the Erosion of Governmental Power
...There are three major ways in which contemporary Political patterns exacerbate the historic fragmentation of the American state. First, as the Democrats seek to weaken the presidency and to strengthen the administrative and coercive capabilities of Congress while the Republicans attempt to undermine Congress and increase the autonomy of the White House, a system

approaching dual sovereignty has emerged in the United States. Second, contemporary electoral processes do not provide for political closure. The question of who will govern is not resolved in elections. As a result, the "winners" have difficulty forming a government, and public officials are compelled to pay as much heed to the impact of policies on domestic struggles as to their implications for collective national purposes. Finally, as bureaucratic agencies have become battlegrounds in, and weapons of, political combat, their ability to effectively implement public policies has been seriously eroded.

Dual Sovereignty   Conflict between the political forces controlling Congress and those controlling the presidency is built into the American system of government. Today, however, the separation of powers mandated by the constitution is becoming what amounts to a system of dual sovereignty. In a separation of powers system, the power to govern is shared by disparate institutions. If government is to function, each branch must secure a measure of cooperation from the others. For example, the framers of the constitution provided roles for both the president and Congress in the enactment of legislation. However, the growing prominence of institutional combat in America means that such cooperation often cannot be secured.

A noteworthy example of the extent to which institutional combat has disrupted the system of shared powers is the difficulty President Bush encountered in forming an administration during his first year in office. During the Reagan years, congressional Democrats had effectively used the weaponry of RIP to attack the administration. In its early weeks, the Bush administration found itself similarly threatened by the flood of allegations and revelations that emerged in the course of the Senate's confirmation hearings on the nomination of John Tower to the position of secretary of defense. Ultimately, Democrats were able to defeat Tower, marking the first time in American history that the Senate refused to confirm a cabinet appointment made by a newly elected president.

The Bush administration subsequently adhered to extraordinarily complex procedures to check the backgrounds of appointees, in an effort to protect itself from further attack either in the confirmation process or in the course of later policy conflicts. As a result, during much of Bush's first year in office, hundreds of top-level, policy-making positions remained unfilled, greatly impeding the president's ability to govern.[1]

The increasing prevalence of institutional combat, by disrupting the traditional system of shared powers, has encouraged the major branches of government to develop various formal and informal means of governing autonomously. Thus, the Republicans have undertaken to strengthen the presidency and to enhance its ability to pursue both foreign and domestic objectives independently of Congress. . . . [T]he Reagan administration sought to place control of major foreign and defense policies in the hands of the president's National Security Council. Moreover, it sought to circumvent Congress and rely on the Treasury Department and the Federal Reserve to manage the nation's economy. In a similar vein, through Executive Order 12291, which centralized control over federal regulations in the OMB, President Reagan sought to disrupt ties between Congress and administrative agencies, a disruption that would greatly enhance the legislative powers of the presidency.

The Democrats, for their part, have sought to strengthen Congress and to provide it with the capacity to develop and implement policies independently of the White House. Congress has greatly increased its autonomous control over policy formulation by establishing or bolstering such congressional agencies as the Congressional Budget Office (CBO) and the General Accounting Office (GAO), as well as by expanding the staffs of its committees and subcommittees.... Congress has also enhanced its ability to act autonomously by drafting detailed statutes that reduce the discretion of executive agencies, and by deploying its augmented staff to monitor agency compliance with the priorities of Congress, its committees, and its subcommittees.

Congress and the White House are thus able to pursue independent and even contradictory policies. The example that has most frequently been commented on involves policy toward Central America. At the same time that the administration was seeking to mobilize support in the Central American region for the contra forces in Nicaragua, House Speaker Jim Wright and other members of Congress were conducting their own negotiations with Central American heads of state premised upon American abandonment of the contras. But this is not the only time Congress and the president embarked upon contradictory courses of action. While the Reagan administration was pursuing policies of "constructive engagement" in southern Africa, Congress enacted trade sanctions against the Afrikaner regime. Similarly, while the Reagan administration, concerned with the fate of American military bases, sought to buttress the power of Philippines dictator Ferdinand Marcos, Chairman Stephen Solarz of the House Subcommittee on Asian Affairs was conducting hearings on Marcos's business dealings with the intention of discrediting him....

Despite their various efforts, neither presidents nor Congress have acquired sufficient formal authority to govern autonomously. As a result, they have frequently sought to work through other institutions, including nongovernmental entities. The problems confronting presidents and the Congress are akin to those faced by rulers in early modern Europe. Seeking glory abroad and grandeur at home, but not commanding the apparatus of a modern state, those rulers were compelled to draw on the resources of nongovernmental institutions. Contemporary America possesses such a state apparatus, but neither the White House nor Congress acting on its own is able to control it fully. The institutional expedients executive and legislative officials have adopted to cope with this problem bear striking resemblances to those devised by Renaissance princes.

Lacking adequate revenue systems, monarchs in the sixteenth and seventeenth centuries made use of tax farmers and bankers for funds.[2] This, in effect, is what the Reagan and Bush administrations have done over the past decade. The United States, of course, created an enormously productive revenue system in the 1940s based upon the progressive income tax. This system permitted politicians to win the support of a host of disparate interests by regularly enacting new spending programs. The Reagan administration managed, through the rate reductions and indexing provisions of the 1981 tax act, to disrupt this regime of interest-group liberalism by reducing the flow of tax receipts upon which it depended. Unable to secure commensurate reductions in domestic spending, however, and committed to an enormously costly military buildup, the administration was compelled to tap new revenue sources. It did so by devising twentieth-century equivalents to the fiscal techniques of Renaissance monarchs, techniques that have endured during the Bush years.

To make up the difference between tax receipts and governmental expenditures, the Reagan and Bush administrations were compelled to borrow $2 trillion through banks and other financial institutions. Approximately one-third of this sum has been supplied by foreign creditors, principally the Japanese.... [T]he Reagan and Bush administrations have fought to keep American markets open to Japanese products. Japanese financial institutions, in turn, have used profits earned in the American market (by such firms as Toyota and Sony) to purchase U.S. Treasury securities. The financial relationship between America and Japan was codified in the May 1984 report of the Japan–United States Yen-Dollar Committee.[3] Through this extraordinary relationship, the Japanese supply the U.S. Treasury with monies they collect from American consumers, while of course retaining a healthy share for themselves. This is a system of tax farming in all but name.

The White House has also resorted to fifteen-thand sixteenth-century practices in the realm of foreign and military policy. To bolster their military strength, Renaissance princes depended upon *condottieri*, mercenaries, and privateers.[4] Although the United States possesses an enormous military and intelligence apparatus, since the Vietnam War presidents have had to contend with congressional restrictions on its use. To circumvent limits on its freedom of action in such areas as Central America and Iran, the Reagan administration raised funds from foreign potentates and worked through private firms and free-lance operators like Richard Secord and Albert Hakim to hire mercenaries, organize military operations, and conduct diplomatic negotiations. As in early modern Europe, the conduct of public affairs was placed in private hands.

In modern Europe's formative period, rulers employed private parties not only to make war abroad but also to enforce the law at home. Lacking an extensive administrative apparatus, they relied upon such practices as bounty hunting and rewarding complainants and witnesses in order to assist the identification, apprehension, and prosecution of lawbreakers. For similar reasons, bounty hunting was common on the American frontier through the nineteenth century. Lately, the Congress, lacking full control over an administrative apparatus, has revived these techniques. Regarding environmental regulation, Congress has sought to involve private parties in law enforcement by authorizing citizens to bring suit against alleged polluters.[5] An incentive for such "private attorneys general" has been provided by requirements that convicted polluters pay attorneys' fees that generally far exceed costs to those who brought the suit.

This reversion to tax farming, privateering, and bounty hunting carries with it serious administrative costs. Modern states abandoned these practices precisely because they were inefficient, prone to abuse, and ultimately incompatible with popular sovereignty. Tax farming imposed heavy burdens on citizens while yielding inadequate revenues to the state. Over the past decade, the profits collected from American consumers by foreign manufacturers have greatly exceeded the funds provided by foreign financial institutions to the U.S. Treasury—to say nothing of the interest that the Treasury has obligated itself to pay to foreigners in order to secure these funds. Moreover, this method of raising revenue gives creditors inordinate leverage over the state. As John Brewer says of tax farming in seventeenth-century England, "in surrendering the task of tax gathering to some of its major creditors, the government ran the risk of financial subordination to ... [a] consortium controlling the two major sources of state income, namely loans and taxes."[6] The United States faces precisely this problem with regard to Japan, which is why the Reagan and Bush administrations have not been in a position to insist that it open its markets to American firms or purchase military aircraft directly from U.S. manufacturers.

States abandoned the use of mercenaries and privateers because, lacking loyalty to the nation they ostensibly served, they typically placed their own interests first. America relearned this lesson in its dealings with arms merchants and private military contractors in the Iran-contra affair. And just as bounty hunters were indifferent to larger public concerns such as the rights of the accused, private litigants cannot be expected to consider the ramifications for other public goals and policies of the suits they choose to bring— for example, the economic burden of alternative methods of pollution control. Thus administrative expedients that were already inadequate in the early modern era are even less well suited to the governance of a twentieth-century state.

No Winners, No Losers ... Under present circumstances, electoral competition does not create winners with the power to make and implement policies, nor does it substantially reduce the losers' opportunities to exercise influence. This absence of political closure exacerbates the historical fragmentation of the American state and leads to a policy-making process that is not well suited to the achievement of collective national purposes. Increasingly, four characteristics have come to dominate the formulation and implementation of public policy in the United States: support-shopping, burden-shifting, weapon-forging, and political paralysis. These features are by no means new to the American policy-making process, but they have become intensified at the very time that the United States faces competitive pressures from states whose policy-making processes are more coherent.

In the case of support-shopping, the persistence of divided control of government and the intensification of institutional conflict means that presidential proposals are as likely to be greeted with suspicion as enthusiasm on Capitol Hill. Presidents are able to strike deals with the leadership of

Congress on some issues, but they often must shop for support on an issue-by-issue, member-by-member basis. As a result, all programs tend to acquire a distributive component: Support is purchased by providing members of Congress with specific benefits for the interests or constituencies they represent, raising the costs of government programs and diffusing their impact.. . .

The necessity of building majorities on a piecemeal basis also enables members of Congress to demand that, in exchange for their support, the interests for which they speak be relieved of the costs and burdens associated with new programs. This allows powerful interests to shift these burdens to others—often to the public treasury.. . .

The absence of political closure has a third implication for the formation of public policy. Because conflicts are not resolved in the electoral arena and continue unabated within the governmental process, public officials must focus on the implications of programs and policies for institutional struggles as a condition for exercising power. Under these circumstances, contending forces undertake to forge weapons of institutional combat as much as to serve collective national purposes when fashioning public policies.

This tendency is exacerbated by the diminution of accountability in contemporary American politics. When there are no clearcut winners and losers, responsibility for the success or failure of policies to address national problems is diffused, and public officials are better able to avoid being held accountable for the consequences of their decisions.[7] This lessened accountability diminishes what might otherwise be a major constraint upon politicians' willingness to give priority to the pursuit of institutional and political advantage when fashioning policies.

The Reagan and Bush administrations' tolerance of enormous budget deficits and their program of deregulation provide examples of this phenomenon. As was noted previously, a major reason why Republican administrations have been prepared to accept the economic risks of unprecedented deficits is the constraint these deficits impose on congressional power. Similarly, the Republicans have pressed for deregulation in part because the congeries of interests that surround many regulatory policies are important Democratic bastions. In this effort, the administration often overlooked potential costs and risks. For instance, relaxation of regulatory restraints on financial institutions permitted many S&Ls to shift from their traditional role as home mortgage lenders into potentially more lucrative but dangerously speculative areas. Even as many S&Ls began to suffer heavy losses, the administration's commitment to deregulation did not wane.

A concern for institutional and political advantage can also color the way officials respond to the initiatives of their opponents. For example, congressional Democrats regularly vote for lower levels of military spending than the White House proposes, not because they are less committed to the nation's defense, but because they have come to identify the defense establishment as an important institutional bastion of the Republicans.

Finally, contemporary electoral processes can lead to political paralysis because they reinforce governmental fragmentation and division. In a number of important areas, institutional divisions have impeded the federal government from responding to situations that both Democrats and Republicans regard as important national problems. Bipartisan commissions, whose members are composed of both presidential and congressional appointees, are one device to which policy makers have resorted on a number of recent occasions to deal with problems that the regular institutions of government found themselves unable to handle. Such commissions were created to resolve conflicts over the impending collapse of the Social Security system, the closing of military bases, the basing of MX missiles, the crisis in Central America, and the budget deficit.[8] The first two of these commissions were successful, but the remaining three were unable to overcome the deep divisions between Congress and the White House.

. . .The dangers facing the United States in the 1990s are not as immediate as those that the nation confronted on the eve of the Civil War or in the aftermath of the 1929 stock market crash. Nevertheless, America's political processes impede governmental responses adequate to the challenges that the nation faces. . . .

Notes

1. "With 115 Nominations Awaiting Votes, Fingers Point Fast and Furious," *New York Times*, 28 Aug. 1989, sec. B, p. 6.
2. Margaret Levi, *Of Rule and Revenue* (Berkeley and Los Angeles: University of California Press, 1988), chap. 5.
3. Robert Gilpin, *The Political Economy of International Relations* (Princeton: Princeton University Press, 1987), 328–36.
4. William McNeill, *The Pursuit of Power* (Chicago: University of Chicago Press, 1982), chap. 3.
5. Barry Boyer and Errol Meidinger, "Privatizing Regulatory Enforcement," *Buffalo Law Review* 34 (1985): 833–956.
6. John Brewer, *The Sinews of Power: War, Money, and the English State, 1688–1783* (New York: Knopf, 1989), 93.
7. Lloyd Cutler, "Now Is the Time for All Good Men . . .," *William and Mary Law Review* 30 (Winter 1989): 387–402.
8. On the Social Security Commission see R. Kent Weaver, *Automatic Government* (Washington, D.C.: Brookings Institution, 1988), chap. 2; Paul Light, *Artful Work: The Politics of Social Security Reform* (New York, Random House, 1985).

PART FOUR

The Outputs

One political scientist has defined politics in terms of "who gets what, when, and how,"* and another as the "authoritative allocation of values."** Both definitions emphasize the making of decisions concerning how things of value are allocated within society. We have, in earlier chapters of this book, read about several sources of "inputs" into the policy-making process, and about governmental institutions charged with making, applying, and interpreting various types of decisions. In this part of the book, we will consider the policy process from the standpoint of its end products; that is, the "outputs." In particular, we will focus upon two related questions:

1. Who "controls" the outputs of the system; in other words, who rules?
2. Who receives the (most) benefits from the system; in other words, who wins?

*Lasswell, Harold D., *Politics: Who Gets What, When, How?* (New York: Meridian Books, 1958).—*Editor's Note.*
**Easton, David, *A Systems Analysis of Political Life* (New York: Wiley, 1965)—*Editor's Note.*

CHAPTER NINETEEN

Who Rules?

Although the answers that have been offered to the question of "who rules" in American politics are many and varied, most are related to one or the other of two competing theories of the distribution of power in American society: the "elitist" theory and the "pluralist" theory. The basic tenet of elitism holds that it is the few at the top who wield real power in American politics. According to C. Wright Mills, recognized as one of the chief architects of the elitist theory, America has been ruled throughout its history by a "power elite," formed from corporate, political, and military "cliques" with overlapping interests. Pluralism, on the other hand, holds that American society is characterized by many groups with competing interests, all of whom win some of the time and lose some of the time. Robert Dahl, with whom pluralism is most often associated, argues that the fragmentation of power among governmental institutions has made decentralization of power one of the continuities in American politics, and that this helps to ensure continuation of the pluralistic alternative to elitism.

Which view is correct? Is rule dominated by a few at the top, or is it shared among the many competing groups in American society? Recent evidence, collected by political scientists such as Thomas Dye, fails to support either view in totality. Instead, Dye concludes that "our research on institutional elites produces evidence of both hierarchy and polyarchy in the nation's elite structure."

70 / The Power Elite

C. Wright Mills

In this excerpt from C. Wright Mills' classic book, Mills argues that American society
has, throughout its history, been ruled by a "power elite" made up of corporate,
political, and military "cliques" with overlapping interests. Although changes have
occurred over time in the relative positions of these three cliques within the collective elite, it has always been the case that some version of this power elite has
ruled. (Note that Mills was writing in 1957, during what he called the fifth epoch
of the power elite. What do you think he would say today? Are we still in the fifth
epoch that he described?)

Except for the unsuccessful Civil War, changes in the power system of the
United States have not involved important challenges to its basic legitimations. Even when they have been decisive enough to be called 'revolutions,'
they have not involved the resort to the guns of a cruiser, the dispersal of an
elected assembly by bayonets, or the mechanisms of a police state.[1] Nor have
they involved, in any decisive way, any ideological struggle to control masses.
Changes in the American structure of power have generally come about by
institutional shifts in the relative positions of the political, the economic, and
the military orders. From this point of view, and broadly speaking, the
American power elite has gone through four epochs, and is now well into
a fifth.

1

I. During the first—roughly from the Revolution through the administration
of John Adams—the social and economic, the political and the military institutions were more or less unified in a simple and direct way: the individual
men of these several elites moved easily from one role to another at the top
of each of the major institutional orders. Many of them were many-sided men
who could take the part of legislator and merchant, frontiersman and soldier,
scholar and surveyor.

Until the downfall of the Congressional caucus of 1824, political institutions seemed quite central; political decisions, of great importance; many
politicians, considered national statesmen of note. 'Society, as I first remember
it,' Henry Cabot Lodge once said, speaking of the Boston of his early boyhood,
'was based on the old families; Doctor Holmes defines them in the "Autocrat"
as the families which had held high position in the colony, the province and
during the Revolution and the early decades of the United States. They
represented several generations of education and standing in the community
... They had ancestors who had filled the pulpits, sat upon the bench, and
taken part in the government under the crown; who had fought in the Revolution, helped to make the State and National constitutions and served in the

army or navy; who had been members of the House or Senate in the early days of the Republic, and who had won success as merchants, manufacturers, lawyers, or men of letters.'[2]

Such men of affairs, who—as I have noted—were the backbone of Mrs. John Jay's social list of 1787, definitely included political figures of note. The important fact about these early days is that social life, economic institutions, military establishment, and political order coincided, and men who were high politicians also played key roles in the economy and, with their families, were among those of the reputable who made up local society. In fact, this first period is marked by the leadership of men whose status does not rest exclusively upon their political position, although their political activities are important and the prestige of politicians high. And this prestige seems attached to the men who occupy Congressional position as well as the cabinet. The elite are political men of education and of administrative experience, and, as Lord Bryce noted, possess a certain 'largeness of view and dignity of character.'[3]

II. During the early nineteenth century—which followed Jefferson's political philosophy, but, in due course, Hamilton's economic principles—the economic and political and military orders fitted loosely into the great scatter of the American social structure. The broadening of the economic order which came to be seated in the individual property owner was dramatized by Jefferson's purchase of the Louisiana Territory and by the formation of the Democratic-Republican party as successor to the Federalists.

In this society, the 'elite' became a plurality of top groups, each in turn quite loosely made up. They overlapped to be sure, but again quite loosely so. One definite key to the period, and certainly to our images of it, is the fact that the Jacksonian Revolution was much more a status revolution than either an economic or a political one. The metropolitan 400 could not truly flourish in the face of the status tides of Jacksonian democracy; alongside it was a political elite in charge of the new party system. No set of men controlled centralized means of power; no small clique dominated economic, much less political, affairs. The economic order was ascendant over both social status and political power; within the economic order, a quite sizable proportion of all the economic men were among those who decided. For this was the period—roughly from Jefferson to Lincoln—when the elite was at most a loose coalition. The period ended, of course, with the decisive split of southern and northern types.

Official commentators are likely to contrast the ascendancy in totalitarian countries of a tightly organized clique with the American system of power. Such comments, however, are easier to sustain if one compares mid-twentieth-century Russia with mid-nineteenth-century America, which is what is often done by Tocqueville-quoting Americans making the contrast. But that was an America of a century ago, and in the century that has passed, the American elite have not remained as patrioteer essayists have described them to us. The "loose cliques" now head institutions of a scale and power not then existing and, especially since World War I, the loose cliques have tightened up. We are well beyond the era of romantic pluralism.

III. The supremacy of corporate economic power began, in a formal way, with the Congressional elections of 1866, and was consolidated by the Supreme Court decision of 1886 which declared that the Fourteenth Amendment protected the corporation. That period witnessed the transfer of the center of initiative from government to corporation. Until the First World War (which gave us an advanced showing of certain features of our own period) this was an age of raids on the government by the economic elite, an age of simple corruption, when Senators and judges were simply bought up. Here, once upon a time, in the era of McKinley and Morgan, far removed from the undocumented complexities of our own time, many now believe, was the golden era of the American ruling class.

The military order of this period, as in the second, was subordinate to the political, which in turn was subordinate to the economic. The military was thus off to the side of the main driving forces of United States history. Political institutions in the United States have never formed a centralized and autonomous domain of power; they have been enlarged and centralized only reluctantly in slow response to the public consequence of the corporate economy.

In the post–Civil-War era, that economy was the dynamic; the 'trusts'—as policies and events make amply clear—could readily use the relatively weak governmental apparatus for their own ends. That both state and federal governments were decisively limited in their power to regulate, in fact meant that they were themselves regulatable by the larger moneyed interests. Their powers were scattered and unorganized; the powers of the industrial and financial corporations concentrated and interlocked. The Morgan interests alone held 341 directorships in 112 corporations with an aggregate capitalization of over $22 billion—over three times the assessed value of all real and personal property in New England. With revenues greater and employees more numerous than those of many states, corporations controlled parties, bought laws, and kept Congressmen of the 'neutral' state. And as private economic power overshadowed public political power, so the economic elite overshadowed the political.

Yet even between 1896 and 1919, events of importance tended to assume a political form, foreshadowing the shape of power which after the partial boom of the 'twenties was to prevail in the New Deal. Perhaps there has never been any period in American history so politically transparent as the Progressive era of President-makers and Muckrakers.

IV. The New Deal did *not* reverse the political and economic relations of the third era, but it did create within the political arena, as well as in the corporate world itself, competing centers of power that challenged those of the corporate directors. As the New Deal directorate gained power, the economic elite, which in the third period had fought against the growth of 'government' while raiding it for crafty privileges, belatedly attempted to join it on higher levels. When they did so they found themselves confronting other interests and men, for the places of decision were crowded. In due course, they did come to control and to use for their own purposes the New Deal institutions whose creation they had so bitterly denounced.

But during the 'thirties, the political order was still an instrument of small propertied farmers and businessmen, although they were weakened, having lost their last chance for real ascendancy in the Progressive era. The struggle between big and small property flared up again, however, in the political realm of the New Deal era, and to this struggle there was added, as we have seen, the new struggle of organized labor and the unorganized employed. This new force flourished under political tutelage, but nevertheless, for the first time in United States history, social legislation and lower-class issues became important features of the reform movement.

In the decade of the 'thirties, a set of shifting balances involving newly instituted farm measures and newly organized labor unions—along with big business—made up the political and administrative drama of power. These farm, labor, and business groups, moreover, were more or less contained within the framework of an enlarging governmental structure, whose political directorship made decisions in a definitely political manner. These groups pressured, and in pressuring against one another and against the governmental and party system, they helped to shape it. But it could not be said that any of them for any considerable length of time used that government unilaterally as their instrument. That is why the 'thirties was a *political* decade: the power of business was not replaced, but it was contested and supplemented: it became one major power within a structure of power that was chiefly run by political men, and not by economic or military men turned political.

The earlier and middle Roosevelt administrations can best be understood as a desperate search for ways and means, within the existing capitalist system, of reducing the staggering and ominous army of the unemployed. In these years, the New Deal as a system of power was essentially a balance of pressure groups and interest blocs. The political top adjusted many conflicts, gave way to this demand, sidetracked that one, was the unilateral servant of none, and so evened it all out into such going policy line as prevailed from one minor crisis to another. Policies were the result of a political act of balance at the top. Of course, the balancing act that Roosevelt performed did not affect the fundamental institutions of capitalism as a type of economy. By his policies, he subsidized the defaults of the capitalist economy, which had simply broken down; and by his rhetoric, he balanced its political disgrace, putting 'economic royalists' in the political doghouse.

The 'welfare state,' created to sustain the balance and to carry out the subsidy, differed from the 'laissez-faire' state: 'If the state was believed neutral in the days of T.R. because its leaders claimed to sanction favors for no one,' Richard Hofstadter has remarked, 'the state under F.D.R. could be called neutral only in the sense that it offered favors to everyone.' The new state of the corporate commissars differs from the old welfare state. In fact, the later Roosevelt years—beginning with the entrance of the United States into overt acts of war and preparations for World War II—cannot be understood entirely in terms of an adroit equipoise of political power.

2

We study history, it has been said, to rid ourselves of it, and the history of the power elite is a clear case for which this maxim is correct. Like the tempo of American life in general, the long-term trends of the power structure have been greatly speeded up since World War II, and certain newer trends within and between the dominant institutions have also set the shape of the power elite and given historically specific meaning to its fifth epoch:

I. In so far as the structural clue to the power elite today lies in the political order, that clue is the decline of politics as genuine and public debate of alternative decisions—with nationally responsible and policy-coherent parties and with autonomous organizations connecting the lower and middle levels of power with the top levels of decision. America is now in considerable part more a formal political democracy than a democratic social structure, and even the formal political mechanics are weak.

The long-time tendency of business and government to become more intricately and deeply involved with each other has, in the fifth epoch, reached a new point of explicitness. The two cannot now be seen clearly as two distinct worlds. It is in terms of the executive agencies of the state that the rapprochement has proceeded most decisively. The growth of the executive branch of the government, with its agencies that patrol the complex economy, does not mean merely the 'enlargement of government' as some sort of autonomous bureaucracy: it has meant the ascendancy of the corporation's man as a political eminence.

During the New Deal the corporate chieftains joined the political directorate; as of World War II they have come to dominate it. Long interlocked with government, now they have moved into quite full direction of the economy of the war effort and of the postwar era. This shift of the corporation executives into the political directorate has accelerated the long-term relegation of the professional politicians in the Congress to the middle levels of power.

II. In so far as the structural clue to the power elite today lies in the enlarged and military state, that clue becomes evident in the military ascendancy. The warlords have gained decisive political relevance, and the military structure of America is now in considerable part a political structure. The seemingly permanent military threat places a premium on the military and upon their control of men, materiel, money, and power; virtually all political and economic actions are now judged in terms of military definitions of reality: the higher warlords have ascended to a firm position within the power elite of the fifth epoch.

In part at least this has resulted from one simple historical fact, pivotal for the years since 1939: the focus of elite attention has been shifted from domestic problems, centered in the 'thirties around slump, to international problems, centered in the 'forties and 'fifties around war. Since the governing apparatus of the United States has by long historic usage been adapted to and shaped by domestic clash and balance, it has not, from any angle, had suitable agencies and traditions for the handling of international problems.

Such formal democratic mechanisms as had arisen in the century and a half of national development prior to 1941, had not been extended to the American handling of international affairs. It is, in considerable part, in this vacuum that the power elite has grown.

III. In so far as the structural clues to the power elite today lies in the economic order, that clue is the fact that the economy is at once a permanent-war economy and a private-corporation economy. American capitalism is now in considerable part a military capitalism, and the most important relation of the big corporation to the state rests on the coincidence of interests between military and corporate needs, as defined by warlords and corporate rich. Within the elite as a whole, this coincidence of interest between the high military and the corporate chieftains strengthens both of them and further subordinates the role of the merely political men. Not politicians, but corporate executives, sit with the military and plan the organization of war effort.

The shape and meaning of the power elite today can be understood only when these three sets of structural trends are seen at their point of coincidence: the military capitalism of private corporations exists in a weakened and formal democratic system containing a military order already quite political in outlook and demeanor. Accordingly, at the top of this structure, the power elite has been shaped by the coincidence of interest between those who control the major means of production and those who control the newly enlarged means of violence; from the decline of the professional politician and the rise to explicit political command of the corporate chieftains and the professional warlords; from the absence of any genuine civil service of skill and integrity, independent of vested interests.

The power elite is composed of political, economic, and military men, but this instituted elite is frequently in some tension: it comes together only on certain coinciding points and only on certain occasions of 'crisis.' In the long peace of the nineteenth century, the military were not in the high councils of state, not of the political directorate, and neither were the economic men—they made raids upon the state but they did not join its directorate. During the 'thirties, the political man was ascendant. Now the military and the corporate men are in top positions.

Of the three types of circle that compose the power elite today, it is the military that has benefitted the most in its enhanced power, although the corporate circles have also become more explicitly intrenched in the more public decision-making circles. It is the professional politician that has lost the most, so much that in examining the events and decisions, one is tempted to speak of a political vacuum in which the corporate rich and the high warlord, in their coinciding interests, rule.

It should not be said that the three 'take turns' in carrying the initiative, for the mechanics of the power elite are not often as deliberate as that would imply. At times, of course, it is—as when political men, thinking they can borrow the prestige of generals, find that they must pay for it, or, as when during big slumps, economic men feel the need of a politician at once safe and possessing vote appeal. Today all three are involved in virtually all widely ramifying decisions. Which of the three types seems to lead depends upon 'the tasks of the period' as they, the elite, define them. Just now, these tasks center upon 'defense' and international affairs. Accordingly, as we have seen, the military are ascendant in two senses: as personnel and as justifying ideology. That is why, just now, we can most easily specify the unity and the shape of the power elite in terms of the military ascendancy....

...The power elite does, in fact, take its current shape from the decisive entrance into it of the military. Their presence and their ideology are its major legitimations, whenever the power elite feels the need to provide any. But what is called the 'Washington military clique' is not composed merely of military men, and it does not prevail merely in Washington. Its members exist all over the country, and it is a coalition of generals in the roles of corporation executives, of politicians masquerading as admirals, of corporation executives acting like politicians, of civil servants who become majors, of vice-admirals who are also the assistants to a cabinet officer, who is himself, by the way, really a member of the managerial elite.

Neither the idea of a 'ruling class' nor of a simple monolithic rise of 'bureaucratic politicians' nor of a 'military clique' is adequate. The power elite today involves the often uneasy coincidence of economic, military, and political power....

Notes

1. Cf. Elmer Davis, *But We Were Born Free* (Indianapolis: Bobbs-Merrill, 1953), p. 187.
2. Henry Cabot Lodge, *Early Memoirs*, cited by Dixon Wecter, *The Sage of American Society* (New York: Scribner's, 1937), p. 206.
3. Lord James Bryce, *The American Commonwealth* (New York: Macmillan, 1918), vol. I, pp. 84–5. In pre-revolutionary America, regional differences were of course important; but see: William E. Dodd, *The Cotton Kingdom* (Volume 27 of the Chronicles of America Series, edited by Allen Johnson) (New Haven: Yale University Press, 1919), p. 41; Louis B. Wright, *The First Gentlemen of Virginia* (Huntington Library, 1940), Chapter 12; Samuel Morison and Henry S. Commager, *The Growth of the American Republic* (New York: Oxford University Press, 1950), pp. 177–8; James T. Adams, *Provincial Society, 1690–1763* (New York: Macmillan, 1927), p. 83.

71 / Pluralist Democracy in the United States

Robert A. Dahl

Robert Dahl begins this selection by considering elements of the "elitist" and "popular" answers to the question "Who ought to govern?" He then suggests that America's answer to the question has been that the people should rule, but not by giving absolute sovereignty to "the majority." The "pluralist solution" provides for multiple centers of power, with opportunities available for all interested groups to influence the negotiations leading to the making of policy. No single group, including "the majority," can dictate all policy in such a system.

Who Ought to Govern?

It is impossible to say when men first became conscious of their political institutions. We know that for at least two thousand years before the first settlers came to America there had been in the Western world a distinct consciousness of political systems and an awareness of differences among them. During these twenty centuries men asked questions about politics, particularly during eras of great change and crisis when old systems confronted new ones. It is not a great step from becoming keenly aware that communities do have and probably must have governments—institutions for settling conflicts, enforcing rules, and perhaps even making rules—to the question, "Who ought to govern?" Because this question—like many other questions about politics— is likely to come to the fore in times of political disturbance and change, it was one of the most important questions that confronted the Founders gathered in Philadelphia in 1787 to discuss constitutional problems. As we shall see in the next chapter, they were by no means agreed on an answer. For they reflected, among other influences, the history of ancient controversies, controversies that still persist in our own day and will not die, I imagine, as long as men continue to ask questions.

Although the question, Who ought to govern? had been answered in many different ways, two sets of replies were particularly significant in 1787 and remain so down to the present day. One, which we may call the aristocratic point of view, holds that government should be in the hands of those who are best qualified to govern because of their special virtues and knowledge and that the number of these properly qualified rulers is, in any community, almost certain to be a minority. The other, the democratic point of view, holds that everyone should govern since, ideally, no adult should be governed without his consent; that political virtue and wisdom are not lodged exclusively in any identifiable group of persons; and that if consent is to mean anything, every adult must be quite free to participate in all political decisions without fear or favor.

The debate between those who espouse these conflicting doctrines would not have endured so long if each viewpoint did not have a good deal to be said for it—and each runs into some rather serious problems.

The aristocratic solution (which has nothing intrinsically to do with birth) is frequently used, even in democracies, for governing organizations where superior skills are crucial to the success of the organization and where, it is supposed, these superior skills can be more or less definitely defined and identified. In the early years of the Civil War many units elected their commanding officers; but the results were generally thought to be disastrous, and today even the most ardent exponents of democratic doctrine do not defend this method of governing military units. The perennial appeal of the aristocratic answer, then, is that it focuses directly on the problems of *fitness* to rule and stresses the importance of having good leadership, of giving authority to *skillful, wise,* and *virtuous* men (or women). Leadership is a persistent problem in all political systems—not least in democracies.

Yet it is one thing to govern a family, a ship, an army, a business firm, or a government bureau—and quite another to govern a community or a nation. As a matter of fact even in those institutions where 'aristocratic' solutions are supposed to work best, they have often produced notoriously incompetent leaders. Whatever may be the justification for the aristocratic solution for providing leadership in certain situations, there are four major objections to applying the aristocratic doctrine to the political system of an entire community.

First, the standards of skill, wisdom, and virtue required are unclear. Men of great learning are not always virtuous, and men of virtue are not always learned. After nearly twenty-five centuries, almost the only people who seem to be convinced of the advantages of being ruled by philosopher-kings are . . . a few philosophers. Though indispensable as advisers and occasionally skillful in politics, scholars as a group have not greatly impressed others with their competence as rulers. The skills of the businessman or military leader are highly specialized, and very different from those required in government: Ulysses S. Grant, a great general, and Herbert Hoover, a great businessman, were not great Presidents. In sum, it is easy to propose in the groves of academe that the skillful, wise, and virtuous should rule; but it is difficult to establish practical criteria for identifying persons with superior skill, wisdom, and virtue in politics. There seems to be a very strong and very human tendency to solve the problem by defining skill, wisdom, and virtue in the image of one's own self, group, or class. Was it by chance that Plato, a philosopher, concluded that the best rulers would be philosophers?

In the second place, even if the criteria were much clearer than they are, how are these criteria to be applied? How are the rulers to be selected? In a mad scramble for power, the wise and virtuous are likely to be trampled to death. Popular election would turn the whole process upside down. Hereditary aristocracies have always been subject to the great gamble of genetics and early environment; there is no guarantee that the first born son of a wise and virtuous father may not be a dullard, or a scoundrel, or both. One might propose that the rulers should be chosen by the wise and virtuous. But of course this only pushes the problem one stage farther back: Who is wise and virtuous enough to choose the wise and virtuous men who will choose the rulers?

Third, can a process designed to select only the wise and virtuous also insure that the leaders so chosen have widespread consent for their government? If it is said that surely the wise and virtuous would have general consent for their rule, then why not adopt the democratic solution and allow the people to choose their leaders? If, on the other hand, one objects that the people might not choose wise and virtuous leaders, then, since they are not the choice *of* and *by* people must they be imposed *on* the people? If so, would not the attempt to impose leaders on the people degenerate into a trial by battle in which the strongest, not the wisest and most virtuous, would win?

Finally, even if the skillful, wise, and virtuous could somehow be chosen as rulers, how can we be sure that they will not be corrupted by power? Lord Acton's famous proposition about power is, surely, an overstatement:* wags have sometimes proposed that it be amended to read: 'Power corrupts, and the absence of power corrupts absolutely.' Nonetheless, the dangers created by the mysterious alchemy of power are too familiar to be laughed aside.

To suppose, as many people do, that the argument for government by superior beings is as obsolete as the thick walls of a medieval fortress is to overlook the fact that many of the arguments for rule by an elite of unusual virtues and talents have been employed by some powerful twentieth century opponents of democracy, namely, Facists, Nazis, and Communists. Plato might be horrified to hear a defense of aristocracy from such sources; still, the idea obviously continues to have great appeal.

For anyone convinced by these objections to aristocratic government, the main alternative in the United States ever since Colonial times has always been popular government. In the eyes of the democrat, no one group can be found with such clearly superior talent and virtue to entitle it to rule. In the proper condition—and it is the job of a democracy to foster and maintain these conditions—practically everyone has sufficient knowledge and virtue to share, directly or indirectly, in the task of governing. In any case, even though I may lack technical knowledge as to the best or most efficient means, is anyone else likely to know better than I what ends are best for me?

However, every species of government has its special problems. These are some questions that an advocate of popular government must face up to honestly:

- How is it possible to provide and maintain a real equality of influence and power over government? Underneath all the trappings and rituals of democracy, won't power be concentrated in the hands of a minority—men of great wealth, or political skill, or determination, or simply with better opportunities?

See the analysis of Arnold Rogow and Harold D. Lasswell, *Power, Corruption and Rectitude,* Englewood Cliffs, N.J.: Prentice Hall, 1963.—*Author's Note.*

- If everyone is to have an equal say, how can the decisions of the government be made with sufficient knowledge and expertness? Aren't the problems of modern governments too complex for ordinary citizens to understand—particularly if they devote only a small part of their time to the effort of understanding the issues?
- How can a popular government act vigorously, speedily, and decisively, particularly in crises? Can a popular government have a strong, energetic executive? If not, how can it survive? If so, will he not be a source of great danger?
- How can a system of popular government ever cope with the twin problems of faction: On the one hand, how can larger groups with the greatest number of votes be prevented from exploiting and tyrannizing smaller groups with fewer votes? On the other hand, will there not be constant dissension, unrest and even subversion by discontented minorities who find their aims thwarted by more populous groups?
- Can a system really operate with the consent of *all*? Isn't this necessarily only a cloak for the interests of those who rule, whether these are a majority or some oligarchy that manages to dominate by accumulating the resources with which to rule?

These are not abstract questions but live issues. They were very much alive to the Founders in 1787; they had less experience to build on than we, and much of their experience suggested pessimistic answers. In one way or another every popular government must surmount these problems, else it ceases to exist as a popular government. To cast an eye toward the travail of new nations is to see how difficult the problems are. But we need not look so far afield: these problems were not solved, once and for all, when the thirty-nine men at Philadelphia signed The Constitution of the United States.

The Sovereign Majority

[Government by] "the People" is an ambiguous phrase. Do these famous words mean that whenever a majority is discontented with the government it should be free to change it? if they are not permitted to do so, then can we say that they have given their approval, in any realistic sense, to the processes of government? Yet if every majority must be free to alter the rules of government, what is the significance of a "Constitution"? How can a constitution be more binding than ordinary law? Is there no legitimate way by which groups smaller than a majority can receive guarantees that the rules they agree to abide by will be more or less permanent and will not change at the whim of the next legislature?

These are difficult questions to answer, and no answers seem to command universal agreement. To gain "the consent of all" consistently applying the principle that the majority should be sovereign gives rise to serious problems, both logical and practical. Perhaps under certain unusual conditions, such as a very high degree of homogeneity, among a very small body of citizens, these problems could be solved.

In practise, however, popular governments have moved toward a rather different solution.

A Pluralistic Solution

The practical solutions that democratic countries have evolved are a good deal less clear than a straightforward application of the principle of majority rule. These solutions seem less 'logical,' less coherent, more untidy, and a good deal more attainable. Patterns of democratic government do not reflect a logically conceived philosophical plan so much as a series of responses to problems of diversity and conflict, by leaders who have sought to build and maintain a nation, to gain the loyalty and obedience of citizens, to win general and continuing approval of political institutions, and at the same time to conform to aspirations for democracy. However, some common elements can be discovered.

For one thing, in practise, countries with democratic regimes use force, just as other regimes do, to repel threats to the integrity of the national territory....

Second, many matters of policy—religious beliefs and practises, for example—are effectively outside the legal authority of any government....

Third, a great many questions of policy are placed in the hands of private, semi-public, and local governmental organizations such as churches, families, business firms, trade unions, towns, cities, provinces, and the like. These questions of policy, like those left to individuals, are also effectively beyond the reach of national majorities, the national legislature, or indeed any national policy-makers acting in their legal and official capacities....

Fourth, whenever a group of people believe that they are adversely affected by national policies or are about to be, they generally have extensive opportunities for presenting their case and for negotiations that may produce a more acceptable alternative. In some cases, they may have enough power to delay, to obstruct, and even to veto the attempt to impose policies on them.

Now in addition to all these characteristics, the United States has limited the sovereignty of the majority in still other ways. In fact, the United States has gone so far in this direction that it is sometimes called a pluralistic system, a term I propose to use here.

The fundamental axiom in the theory and practise of American pluralism is, I believe, this: Instead of a single center of sovereign power there must be multiple centers of power, none of which is or can be wholly sovereign. Although the only legitimate sovereign is the people, in the perspective of American pluralism even the people ought never to be an absolute sovereign; consequently no part of the people, such as a majority, ought to be absolutely sovereign.

Why this axiom? The theory and practise of American pluralism tend to assume, as I see it, that the existence of multiple centers of power, none of which is wholly sovereign, will help (may indeed be necessary) to tame power, to secure the consent of all, and to settle conflicts peacefully:

- Because one center of power is set against another, power itself would be tamed, civilized, controlled, and limited to decent human purposes, while coercion, the most evil form of power, will be reduced to a minimum.
- Because even minorities are provided with opportunities to veto solutions they strongly object to, the consent of all will be won in the long run.
- Because constant negotiations among different centers of power are necessary in order to make decisions, citizens and leaders will perfect the precious art of dealing peacefully with their conflicts, and not merely to the benefit of one partisan but to the mutual benefit of all the parties to a conflict.

These are, I think the basic postulates and even the unconscious ways of thought that are central to the American attempt to cope with the inescapable problems of power, conflict, and consent....

Periods of Moderate Conflict

If you were to pick at random any year in American history since the Constitutional Convention to illustrate the workings of the political system, you would stand a rather good chance of being able to describe American politics during that year as follows:

- Important government policies would be arrived at through negotiation, bargaining, persuasion, and pressure at a considerable number of different sites in the political system—the White House, the bureaucracies, the labyrinth of committees in Congress, the federal and state courts, the state legislatures and executives, the local governments. No single organized political interest, party, class, region, or ethnic group would control all of these sites.
- Different individuals and groups would not all exert an equal influence on decisions about government policies. The extent of influence individuals or groups exerted would depend on a complex set of factors: their political skills, how aroused and active they were, their numbers, and their access to such political resources as organization, money, connections, propaganda, etc. People who lacked even suffrage and had no other resources— slaves, for example—would of course be virtually powerless. But because *almost* every group has some political resources—at a minimum, the vote—most people who felt that their interests were significantly affected by a proposed change in policy would have some influence in negotiations.
- All the important political forces—particularly all the candidates and elected officials of the two major parties—would accept (or at any rate would not challenge) the legitimacy of the basic social, economic, and political structures of the United States. Organized opposition to these basic structures would be confined to minority

movements too feeble to win representation in Congress or a single electoral vote for their presidential candidate.

- Political conflict would be moderate.
- Changes in policies would be marginal.

. . .These characteristics do not always fit American politics. But most of the time the American political system does display these characteristics.

Why should this be so? Our paradigm of conflict . . . suggests four reasons:

The political institutions reward moderation and marginal change, and discourage deviant policies and comprehensive changes.

In the United States there is a massive convergence of attitudes on a number of key issues that divide citizens in other countries.

As one result, ways of life are not seriously threatened by the policies of opponents.

On issues over which Americans disagree, overlapping cleavages stimulate conciliation and compromise.

72 / Who's Running America Today?

Thomas R. Dye

Which view of power in America is correct: elitism or pluralism? Thomas Dye reviews the evidence and concludes that today there are elements "of both hierarchy and polyarchy in the nation's elite structure."

Institutional Power in America

Power in America is organized into large institutions, private as well as public—corporations, banks, investment firms, governmental bureaucracies, media empires, law firms, universities, foundations, cultural and civic organizations. The nation's resources are concentrated in a relatively few large institutions, and control over these institutional resources is the major source of power in society. The people at the top of these institutions—those who are in a position to direct, manage, and guide institutional programs, policies, and activities—compose the nation's elite. . . .

The first task confronting social science is to develop an operational definition of national elite. Such a definition must be consistent with the notion that great power resides in the institutional structure of society; it must also enable us to identify by name and position those individuals who possess great power in America. Our own definition of a national institutional elite produced 7,314 elite positions. Taken collectively, individuals in these positions controlled more than one half of the nation's industrial assets; more than one half of all the assets in communications and utilities; two thirds of all banking assets; more than three quarters of all insurance assets; and they directed the nation's largest investment firms. They commanded nearly half of all assets of private foundations and universities, and they controlled the television networks, the national press, and major newspaper chains. They dominated the nation's top law firms and the most prestigious civic and cultural associations and occupied key federal government posts in the executive, legislative, and judicial branches and the top military commands.

Our selection of positions of institutional power involved many subjective judgments, but it provided a starting place for a systematic inquiry into the character of America's elite structure. It allowed us to begin investigation into a number of important questions: Who are the people at the top of the institutional structure of America? How did they get there? What are their backgrounds, attitudes, and values? How concentrated or dispersed is their power? Do they agree or disagree on the fundamental goals of society? How much cohesion or competition characterizes their interrelationships? How do they go about making important policy decisions or undertaking new policy directions?

Hierarchy and Polyarchy among Institutional Elites

Before summarizing our data on institutional elites, it might be helpful to gain some theoretical perspectives on our findings by suggesting *why* we might expect to find evidence of either hierarchy or polyarchy in our results.

European social theorists—notably Weber and Durkheim—provide theoretical explanations of why social structures become specialized in advanced societies, and why coordination mechanisms are required. These theorists suggest that increasing functional *differentiation* of elites occurs with increasing socioeconomic development. In a primitive society, it is difficult to speak of separate economic, political, military, or administrative power roles; in primitive life, these power roles are merged together with other roles, including kinship, religion, and magical roles. But as separate economic, political, bureaucratic, and military institutions develop, and specialized power roles are created within these institutions, separate elite groups emerge at the top of separate institutional structures. The increased division of labor, the scale and complexity of modern social organizations, and specialization in knowledge, all combine to create functional differentiation among institutional elites. This suggests polyarchy among elites in an advanced society such as the United States.

Yet even though specialized elite groups are required to direct relatively autonomous institutional sectors, there must also be some social mechanisms to coordinate the exercise of power by various elites in society. This requirement of *coordination* limits the autonomy of various institutional elites. Thus, specialization acts to bring elites together, as well as to force them apart. Social theory does not necessarily specify *how* coordination of power is to be achieved in modern society. Nor does it specify *how much* unity is required to maintain a relatively stable social system or, conversely, how much competition can be permitted. Certainly there must be *some* coordination if society is to function as a whole. The amount of coordination can vary a great deal, however, and the mechanisms for coordination among elites differ from one society to another.

One means of coordination is to keep the relative size of elite groups small. This smallness itself facilitates communication. If there are relatively few people who actually direct institutional activity, then these people can have extraordinary influence on national policy. What's more, the small size of these groups means that institutional leaders are known and accessible to each other. Of course, policy-planning groups, governmental commissions, and advisory councils, or informal meetings and conferences, are instrumental in bringing "specialists" together. But how small *is* America's elite? C. Wright Mills, wisely perhaps, avoids any estimate of the size of "the power elite"; he says only that it is "a handful of men."[1] Floyd Hunter estimates the size of "top leadership" to be "between one hundred and two hundred men."[2] We have already indicated that our definition of the elite produces an estimated size of 7,314 positions occupied by 5,778 individuals—considerably more than implied in the power elite literature, but still few enough to permit a great deal of personal interaction.

Another coordinating mechanism is to be found in the methods by which elites are recruited. The fact that elites who are recruited to different institutional roles share the same social class and educational backgrounds should provide a basis for understanding and communication. Social homogeneity, kinship links, similarity of educational experience, common membership in clubs, common religious and ethnic affiliations, all help to promote unity of outlook. Yet at the same time we know that a certain amount of "circulation of elites" (upward mobility) is essential for the stability of a social system. This means that some heterogeneity in social background must be tolerated. But again social theory fails to quantify the amount of heterogeneity that can be expected.

A related mechanism for coordination is common career experiences. If elite members were drawn disproportionately from one career field—let us say industry or finance—there would be greater potential for unity. But again, social theory does not tell us how much, if any, commonality in career lines is functionally requisite for coordination of specialized elites.

Still another form of coordination is a general consensus among elites on the rules to resolve conflicts and to preserve the stability of the social system itself. Common values serve to unify the elites of various institutional systems. Moreover, agreement among elites to abide by the rule of law and to minimize violence has a strong utilitarian motive, namely to preserve stable working arrangements among elite groups. Finally, unifying values also legitimize the exercise of power by elites over masses, so the preservation of the value system performs the dual function of providing the basis of elite unity, while at the same time rationalizing and justifying for the masses the exercise of elite power. Unfortunately, social theory does not tell us *how much* consensus is required among elites to facilitate coordination and preserve a stable social system. Social theory tells us that elites must agree on more matters than they disagree, but it fails to specify how broad or narrow the range of issues can be.

Because social theory suggests *both* convergence and differentiation among institutional elites, it is possible to develop competing theoretical models of the social system—models which emphasize either hierarchy or polyarchy. For example, the notion of the "power elite" developed by C. Wright Mills implies *hierarchy* among economic, political, and military power-holders. The idea suggests unity and coordination among leaders of functionally differentiated social institutions. Mills speculates that a large-scale, centralized, complex, industrial society *necessitates* coordination. . . .[3] Thus, the hierarchical or elitist model rests upon the theoretical proposition that increasing complexity requires a high degree of coordination, and consequently a great concentration of power.

In contrast, the polyarchical or pluralist model emphasizes differentiation in institutional structures and leadership positions—with different sets of leaders and different institutional sectors of society and with little or no overlap, except perhaps by elected officials responsible to the general public. According to this view, elites are largely specialists, and leadership roles are confined to a narrow range of institutional decisions. These specialists are recruited through separate institutional channels—they are not drawn exclusively from business or finance. Further, the functional specialization of institutional elites results in competition for power, a struggle in which competing elites represent and draw their strength from functionally separate systems of society. How do pluralists assume coordination is achieved among elites? The argument is that functionally differentiated power structures produce an equilibrium of competing elites. Resulting checks and balances of competition are considered desirable to prevent the concentration of power and assure the responsibility of elites.

In short, social theory postulates both hierarchy *and* polyarchy among elites in the social system. It is the task of systematic social science research to determine just *how much* convergence or differentiation exists among elites in the national system.

Who's Running America? Summary of Findings
Our findings do not all fit neatly into either an hierarchical, elitist model of power, or a polyarchical, pluralist model of power. We find evidence of both hierarchy and polyarchy in the nation's institutional elite structure. Let us try to summarize our [principal] findings. . . .

1. Concentration of Institutional Resources   The nation's resources are concentrated in a relatively small number of large institutions. More than one half of the nation's industrial assets are concentrated in 100 industrial corporations; two thirds of U.S. banking assets are concentrated in the fifty largest banks; and one half of our assets in communications and utilities are concentrated in fifty corporations. More than three quarters of the nation's insurance assets are concentrated in just fifty companies; fifty foundations control 40 percent of all foundation assets; twenty-five universities control two-thirds of all private endowment funds in higher education; three network broadcasting companies control 70 percent of the television news and entertainment; and fifteen newspaper empires account for more than one half of the nation's daily newspaper circulation. It is highly probable that thirty Wall Street and Washington law firms exercise comparable dominance in the legal field; that fifteen Wall Street investment firms dominate decision-making in securities; and that a dozen cultural and civic organizations dominate music, drama, the arts, and civic affairs. Federal government alone now accounts for 22 percent of the gross national product and two thirds of all government spending. More importantly, concentration of resources in the nation's largest institutions is increasing over time.

2. Individual versus Institutional Resources   The resources available to individuals in America are infinitesimal in comparison with the resources available to the nation's largest institutions. Personal wealth in itself provides little power; it is only when wealth is associated with top institutional position that it provides the wealth-holder with any significant degree of power.

Managerial elites are gradually replacing owners and stockholders as the dominant influence in American corporations. Most capital investment comes from retained earnings of corporations and bank loans, rather than from individual investors.

Nonetheless, personal wealth in America is unequally distributed: The top fifth of income recipients receives over 40 percent of all income, while the bottom fifth receives less than 5 percent. This inequality is lessening very slowly over time, if at all.

3. The Size of the Nation's Elite   Approximately 6,000 individuals in 7,000 positions exercise formal authority over institutions that control roughly half of the nation's resources in industry, finance, utilities, insurance, mass media, foundations, education, law, and civic and cultural affairs. This definition of the elite is fairly large numerically, yet these individuals constitute an extremely small percentage of the nation's total population—less than three-thousandths of 1 percent. However, this figure is considerably larger than that implied in the "power elite" literature.

Perhaps the question of hierarchy or polyarchy depends on whether one wants to emphasize numbers or percentages. To emphasize hierarchy, one can comment on the tiny *percentage* of the population that possesses such great authority. To emphasize polyarchy, one can comment on the fairly large *number* of individuals at the top of the nation's institutional structure; certainly there is room for competition within so large a group.

4. Interlocking Versus Specialization   Despite concentration of institutional resources, there is clear evidence of specialization among institutional leaders. Eighty-five percent of the institutional elites identified in our study were specialists, holding only one post of the 7,314 "top" posts. Of course, many of these individuals held other institutional positions in a wide variety of corporate, civic, and cultural organizations, but these were not "top" positions as we defined them. Only 15 percent of our institutional elites were interlockers holding more than one top post at the same time.

However, the multiple interlockers—individuals with six or more top posts—not surprisingly turned out to be giants in the industrial and financial world. Another finding is that there was a good deal of vertical overlap—top position-holders who have had previous experience in other top corporate, governmental, and legal positions—more so than there is horizontal (concurrent) interlocking. Only one quarter of governmental elites have held high corporate positions, and nearly 40 percent of the corporate elites have held governmental jobs. Yet even this vertical overlapping must be qualified, for most of the leadership experience of corporate elites was derived from *corporate* positions, and most of the leadership experience of governmental elites was derived from *government and law*.

There are, however, important concentrations of combined corporate, governmental, and social power in America. Large corporations such as AT&T have many interlocking director relationships with industrial corporations, banks, utilities, and insurance companies. There are identifiable groupings of corporations by interlocking directorships; these groupings tend to center around major banks and regions of the country. In addition, there is concentration of power among the great, wealthy, entrepreneurial families—the Rockefellers, Mellons, duPonts, Fords. One of the most important of these concentrations over the years has been the Rockefeller family group, which has had an extensive network in industrial, financial, political, civic, educational, and cultural institutions.

5. Inheritors versus Climbers   There is a great deal of upward mobility in American society, as well as "circulation of elites." We estimate that less than 10 percent of the top corporate elites studied inherited their position and power; the vast majority climbed the rungs of the corporate ladder. Most governmental elites—whether in the executive bureaucracy, Congress, or the courts—also rose from fairly obscure positions. Elected political leaders frequently come from parochial backgrounds and continue to maintain ties with local clubs and groups. Military leaders tend to have the largest percentage of rural, southern, and lower-social-origin members of any leadership group.

6. Separate Channels of Recruitment   There are multiple paths to the top. Our top elites were recruited through a variety of channels. Governmental leaders were recruited mainly from law and government; fewer than one in six was recruited from the corporate world. Military leaders were recruited exclusively through the military ranks. Most top lawyers rose through the ranks of the large, well-known law firms, and mass media executives were recruited primarily from newspaper and television. Only in the foundations, universities, and cultural and civic associations was the formal leadership drawn from other sectors of society.

7. *Social Class and Elite Recruitment*   Individuals at the top are overwhelmingly upper- and upper-middle-class in social origin. Even those who climbed the institutional ladder to high position generally started with the advantages of a middle-class upbringing. Nearly all top institutional elites are college-educated, and half hold advanced degrees. Elites are notably "Ivy League": 54 percent of top corporate leaders and 42 percent of top governmental leaders are alumni of just twelve well-known private universities. Moreover, a substantial proportion of corporate and government leaders attended one of just thirty-three private "name" prep schools.

Very few top corporate or governmental elites are women, although more women are now being appointed to top corporate boards. A greater number of women serve in top positions in the cultural world, but many of these women do so because of their family affiliation.

It is clear that very few blacks occupy any positions of authority in the institutional structure of American society. We estimated that in 1980 only about ten blacks served as directors of the nation's corporations, banks, or utilities.

Corporate elites are somewhat more "upper-class" in origin than are governmental elites. Governmental elites had slightly lower proportions of private prep school types and Ivy Leaguers than corporate elites, and governmental elites were less eastern and urban in their origins than corporate elites. Governmental leaders in our study had more advanced professional degrees (generally law degrees) than did corporate elites.

8. *Conflict and Consensus among Elites*   Elites in all sectors of American society share a consensus about the fundamental values of private enterprise, limited government, and due process of law. Moreover, since the Roosevelt era, elites have generally supported liberal, public-regarding, social welfare programs—including social security, fair labor standards, unemployment compensation, a federally aided welfare system, government regulation of public utilities, and countercyclical fiscal and monetary policies. Elite consensus also includes a desire to end minority discrimination—and to bring minority Americans into the mainstream of the political and economic system. Today's liberal elite believes that it can change people's lives through the exercise of governmental power—eliminate racism, abolish poverty, uplift the poor, overcome sickness and disease, educate the masses, and generally *do good*.

While American politics continue in this liberal tradition, there has been a growing disillusionment among elites with government interventions in society, and a reaffirmation of the role of the home, the community, and the free market in shaping society. The neoconservatives are still liberal and public-regarding in their values, but inflation, Watergate, civil unrest, and Vietnam combined to dampen their enthusiasm for large, costly government programs. Even among neoliberals there is a realization that many old liberal programs and policies are inadequate to society's needs today, and they are committed to a search for "new ideas" to foster economic growth and cure society's ills.

Elites from all sectors of society (even leaders of blacks, women, and youth) believe in equality of opportunity rather than absolute equality. Elites throughout American history have defended the principle of merit. Absolute equality, or "leveling," has never been part of the nation's elite consensus.

Elite disagreement does occur *within* this consensus over fundamental values. However, the range of disagreement is relatively narrow and tends to be confined to means rather than ends. Specific policy disagreements among various elite groups occur over questions such as the oil depletion allowance, federal versus state and local control of social programs, tax reform, specific energy and environmental protection proposals, and specific measures for dealing with inflation and recession.

9. Factionalism among Elites   Traditional pluralist theory emphasizes competition between Democrats and Republicans, liberals and conservatives, labor and management, and other conventional struggles among interest groups. Elitist theory, on the other hand, emphasizes underlying cohesion among elite groups, but still admits of some factionalism. A recognized source of factionalism is the emergence of new sources of wealth and new "self-made" individuals who do not fully share the prevailing values of established elites. Since the eve of World War II, new bases of wealth and power have developed in independent oil-drilling operations, the aerospace industry, computer technology, real estate development in the Sunbelt (from southern California to Florida), discount drugs and merchandising, fast foods, and low-cost insurance. We have labeled these new elites "the Sunbelt *cowboys*."

The *cowboys* are not liberal or public-regarding, or as social welfare–oriented as are the *yankees*, our label for the established institutional elites. The *cowboys* tend to think of solutions to social problems in much more individualistic terms, and they are generally moderate to conservative on most national policy issues.

Despite the self-importance of many new persons of wealth, established eastern institutional wealth and power continue to dominate national life. New wealth is frequently unstable and highly sensitive to economic fluctuations.

10. An Oligarchic Model of National Policy-Making   Traditional pluralist theory focuses attention on the activities of the proximate policy-makers in the policy-making process, and the interaction of parties, interest groups, President and Congress, and other public actors in the determination of national policy. In contrast, our oligarchic model of national policy-making views the role of the proximate policy-makers as one of deciding specific means of implementing major policy goals and directions which have *already been determined* by elite interaction.

Our oligarchic model assumes that the initial resources for research, study, planning, organization, and implementation of national policies are derived from corporate and personal wealth. This wealth is channeled into foundations, universities, and policy-planning institutions, where corporate representatives and top wealth-holders exercise ultimate power on the governing boards. Thus, the foundations provide the initial seed money to analyze social problems, to determine national priorities, and to investigate new policy directions. Universities and intellectuals respond to the research emphases *determined by the foundations* and produce studies that conform to these predetermined emphases. Influential policy-planning groups—notably the Council on Foreign Relations, the Business Roundtable, the American Enterprise Institute, and the Brookings Institution—may also employ university research teams to analyze national problems. But their more important function is consensus-building among elites—bringing together individuals at the top of corporate and financial institutions, the universities, the foundations, and the top law firms, as well as the leading intellectuals, the mass media, and influential figures in government. Their goal is to develop action recommendations—explicit policy recommendations having general elite support. These are then communicated to the proximate policy-makers directly and through the mass media. At this point federal executive agencies begin their research into the policy alternatives suggested by the foundations and policy-planning groups. The role of the various public agencies is thus primarily to fill in the details of the policy directions determined earlier. Eventually, the federal executive agencies, in conjunction with the intellectuals, foundation executives, and policy-planning-group representatives, prepare specific legislative proposals, which then begin to circulate among "the proximate policymakers," notably White House and congressional committee staffs.

The federal law-making process involves bargaining, competition, persuasion, and compromise, as generally set forth in pluralist political theory. But this interaction occurs *after* the agenda for policy-making has been established and the major directions of policy changes have already been determined. The decisions of proximate policy-makers are not unimportant, but they tend to center about the *means* rather than the *ends* of national policy. . . .

Who's Running America? Theory and Research

Systematic research on national leadership is no easy task. Most of the serious social science research on elites in America has concentrated on local communities. Frequently, analysts have extrapolated the knowledge derived from *community* power studies to *national* power structures. As a result, much of our theorizing about power in America rests on inferences derived from the study of community life. Yet to assume that national elites are comparable to community elites not only violates the laws of statistical sampling but also runs contrary to common-sensical understanding of the size and complexity of institutions at the national level.

We do not yet have sufficient evidence to confirm or deny the major tenets of elitist or pluralist models of national power. Our research on institutional elites produces evidence of both hierarchy and polyarchy in the nation's elite structure. If we were forced to summarize our views of the elitist-pluralist debate in the light of our findings, we could do no better than to draw upon a brief statement that appears near the end of G. William Domhoff's book, *The Higher Circles:*

> If it is true, as I believe, that the power elite consist of many thousands of people rather than several dozen; that they do not meet as a committee of the whole; that there are differences of opinion between them; that their motives are not well known to us beyond such obvious inferences as stability and power; and that they are not nearly so clever or powerful as the ultraconservatives think—it is nonetheless also true, I believe, that the power elite are more unified, more conscious, and more manipulative than the pluralists would have us believe, and certainly more so than any social group with the potential to contradict them. If pluralists ask just how unified, how conscious, and how manipulative, I reply that they have asked a tough empirical question to which they have contributed virtually no data.[4]

But we shall avoid elaborate theorizing about pluralism, polyarchy, elitism, and hierarchy in American society. Unfortunately, theory and conceptualization about power and elites have traditionally been so infected with ideological disputation that it is presently impossible to speculate about the theoretical relevance of our data on institutional leadership without generating endless, unproductive debate. . . .

Notes

1. C. Wright Mills, *The Power Elite* (New York: Oxford University Press, 1956), p. 7.
2. Floyd Hunter, *Top Leadership, U.S.A.* (Chapel Hill: University of North Carolina Press, 1959), p. 176.
3. Mills, *The Power Elite*, pp. 8–9.
4. William Domhoff, *The Higher Circles* (New York: Random House, 1970), p. 299.

CHAPTER TWENTY

Who Wins?

Many governmental programs have been developed precisely to alter the answer to the question "who wins?," economically speaking. While some have unquestionably been designed to maintain the status quo or to make it easier for the already well-off to "win more," other programs—especially many that were designed from the 1930s through the 1960s—were intended to place lids on accumulation and/or to redistribute wealth from richer to poorer through various social programs. It is the latter programs that are evaluated in the first two selections of this chapter, both of which were written prior to the "Reagan revolution" of the 1980s.

While neither selection disputes a finding of tremendous growth in programs designed to regulate the economy and to redistribute wealth, and while neither expresses much pleasure with the net consequences of these programs, different values lead the authors to quite different conclusions about who ultimately "wins." In fact, these two readings exemplify the tension that exists between two of the most basic values in American society: equality and individual freedom (or in Susan Love Brown et al.'s terms, *humanitarianism/altruism* and *individualism*).

Edward S. Greenberg, writing in 1979, is troubled by the unequal distribution of economic rewards that continued to be the case in America; Susan Love Brown et al. are troubled more by the growing lack of individual freedom. In the abstract, Greenberg would favor development of redistributive programs to achieve greater equality; however, even in the abstract Brown et al. would see them as contrary to the values of voluntarism and individualism. Greenberg is saddened to find that massive redistributive programs have resulted in little actual redistribution of wealth, and in fact, in some cases aided the well-off more than the poor. Brown et al. are saddened that the growth in such programs has led to reduction of freedom and its enjoyment in the United States.

So—what would these authors say about who wins from the United States' social policies? It is clear that the answer, to some extent, depends on one's values. Greenberg concludes that, contrary to the stated purpose for many governmental programs, they actually helped the better-off more than the poor. Brown et al. conclude that whenever individual freedom suffers, everyone in society loses.

In the final reading, Kevin Phillips—writing just after the presidency of Ronald Reagan—suggests that who wins (or at least, who is intended to win) is actually cyclical. The Reagan presidency came on the heels of a period when redistribution to the lower classes was emphasized in federal programs. Then came the Reagan years, a period Phillips describes as "the triumph of upper America"; and now, American politics could be poised for another swing to the left.

73 / Government Growth and Inequality

Edward S. Greenberg

Edward Greenberg documents tremendous growth in size, cost, and functions of government from the 1930s through the time of his writing in the late '70s. Despite the general growth and development during those decades of programs designed for redistribution of the wealth, Greenberg finds merit in the argument that the United States government continued to serve the interests of the rich at the expense of the poor.

On Government Size and Growth

Government in the United States has grown so enormously and transformed its activities to such an extent over the past several decades that it is barely recognizable to many Americans. It has become for many citizens the object of concern and even alarm, for the process of growth and transformation seems to them destined to continue unabated into the foreseeable future....

The Size of the Federal Government   In fact, the popular mood is a response to a very real development—namely, the enormous, nay explosive growth of governmental activities over the past handful of decades. Adam Smith, John Locke, Thomas Jefferson, Herbert Spencer and other antistatists of the past three centuries would no doubt be horrified by developments if they could visit the contemporary American republic. Instead of the passive agency they had envisioned, they would see a government that has become an active, potent engine of society that touches on almost every facet of the lives of Americans. The would see a modern "positive state"[1] that regulates business and the economy in general; that provides welfare payments to the poor and disabled; that regulates labor-management relations; that distributes monthly payments to the elderly; that owns vast quantities of land, equipment, and plants; that helps educate the nation's children; that regulates communications and commerce; that undertakes vast explorations in outerspace and under the seas; and that takes for public use a healthy portion of every working American's paycheck. What they would see in all of these diverse governmental activities, mostly products of this century, is nothing less than a revolution in the tasks, goals, and functions of the American state....

On Government Bias

Complaints about the operations of modern government in the United States are not confined to those which focus on its impressive growth in size and reach, however, though these complaints remain the most popular and widely articulated. A secondary though increasingly evident theme heard in recent years speaks to the existence of a persistent structural bias in governmental programs towards the needs and interests of the well-to-do and the privileged in American life. Behind the universalistic, nationalistic, and egalitarian rhetoric that accompanies almost every program, one finds a more sobering reality in which the vast financial, legal, and personnel resources of government are fairly consistently used to bolster the position of those persons and institutions already predominant in the private economy.

We know, for instance, that the primary dollar flow from the enormously swollen national defense budgets are directed primarily to the coffers of a relative handful of giant corporations and defense contractors, while federal subsidies flow to a wide range of industries, ranging from ship building to the aerospace industry. Federal regulatory commissions, instituted to protect the public interest against abuses from powerful and concentrated business enterprises (Interstate Commerce Commission, Federal Trade Commission, . . . Federal Communications Commission, etc.) today almost universally serve to protect and advance the interests of the very groups they are charged to regulate. Despite a handful of housing programs directed toward the needs of the poor, the overwhelming effect of federal policy (mortgage and interest deductions on federal income taxes, as well as FHA lending practices) has been to subsidize the housing of middle- and upper-income groups. As to the progressive income tax, most people are now generally aware that its progressive character is seriously undermined by the barrage of tax breaks favorable to those wealthy in property—capital gains, income-splitting, tax-free bonds, interest payment deductions, accelerated depreciation allowances, and a host of others.

Unfortunately, these listings could be almost infinitely expanded. We are beginning to become aware of the fact, for instance, that the Social Security System, the pride of the New Deal and of reform liberalism, is in its overall effect one of the most regressive programs in the entire federal arsenal. Most importantly, its financing is built upon a taxing system that taxes a low wage earner at higher effective rates (taxation as a percentage of income) than that for the high wage earner. Agricultural subsidy programs of the federal government flow disproportionately to the largest farmers in the United States and help speed the process by which smaller farmers are driven off the land. Enormous increases in federal health care spending over the past decade, mainly through medicare and medicaid, while not doing much in the way of improving the health of the American people, has done admirably well in improving the financial health of doctors, hospitals, drug companies, and medical equipment manufacturers. The list could go on, ad infinitum, ad nauseam, but the point remains, we believe, unarguable. Its programs make the federal government one of the principal instrumentalities for the maintenance and stabilization of the entire system of inequality derived from the normal operations of the market economy.[2]

While this enumeration certainly does not exhaust the list of popular complaints, it should serve to establish the existence of a growing popular concern that government is increasingly unable to accomplish decent and humane outcomes with its swollen budgets and employment roles. The federal government seems neither efficient nor just. It cannot seem to satisfy the very expectations which called forth its heightened activity in the first place. Paradoxically, with enhanced size, penetration, and impact, government has experienced a simultaneous loss of respect and a decline in its legitimate authority. Corporate and financial leaders decry its inability to control inflation or establish an environment conducive to adequate capital accumulation. Labor leaders decry its inability to foster an economy that is capable of providing employment for all Americans. The poor and dissident scoff at its presentations to justice, and point to its class biases. And almost all elements of American society protest at the high costs of this decreasingly effective machinery....

The Modern Positive State: Myth and Reality

By most indications, it would seem that the United States has transcended the problems that have historically plagued capitalism. Giant corporations are blessed with the productive, financial, and technical capacity to produce goods and services in quantities hithertofore never even imagined. Significant and strategically located elements of the work force are directly represented by labor unions in regularized and stable collective bargaining arrangements, transposing the classic labor-management confrontation from the factory floor and the streets to the negotiating table and regulatory agency office. America's position as the preeminent power in the world capitalist system gives it access to cheap raw materials in the Third World and favorable access to markets for its finished goods and agricultural products all over the nonsocialist world, in developed and less developed nations alike.

Such a confluence of favorable structural developments, it is safe to say, has never before occurred. It is not surprising, therefore, to find many social thinkers making the claim that the endemic problems of capitalism, which both the friends and foes of capitalism have always acknowledged, have been decisively and irrevocably erased, opening up a new era of growth and promise. The "American century," in this view, is no mere flight of the imagination or a publicist's construction, but a budding reality, soon to reach full flower.[3]

The reality of mature capitalism in the United States, however, is another matter entirely. In fact, there is a cruel paradox at work in the very processes of growth and concentration that its major economic actors pursue so assiduously. Capitalism's economic success leads to a number of disturbing and potentially disruptive contradictions. Success at one level of the system creates a new set of severe problems at another level that the major corporations are unable to solve by their own devices, and in consequence of that dilemma, they generally turn to the government for assistance. Some of these new difficulties involve, among a host of others, excess productive capacity, technological unemployment, excessive research and development costs, insufficient investment outlets, and poverty and social instability among competitive sector workers. However, state intervention introduces an additional dilemma into the equation. While it helps to lessen the impact of some of the problems, the act of intervention itself creates new problems; namely, bloated governmental budgets, bureaucratization, inefficiency, and the inevitable outcomes of permanent inflation and fiscal crisis. . . .

Such a massive pool of unemployed, underemployed, and exploited labor represents a potentially disruptive and explosive mixture. The problem of social control and management that is inherent in any social organization is heightened by the laws of motion of the capitalist mode of production since it constantly adds to that pool, while it at the same time raises the expectations for mass consumption so necessary for further economic advance. Control and management of this troublesome problem can take many forms ranging from the benign to the repressive. Modern capitalism is most likely to utilize options toward the benign end of the scale, though one should not for a moment ignore the frequent use of repressive methods: police, courts, and prisons. In fact, these repressive means represent one of the fastest growing areas of the budgets of all levels of government in the United States. The principal instrument for the treatment of this explosive mixture under modern capitalism, however, is the system of welfare.

The welfare commitment of the federal government began in a serious way with the Social Security Act of 1935. Under one provision of the act, the federal government agreed to contribute to state and locally administered programs of aid to the aged, the blind, the disabled, and dependent children. It was thought, at the time, that these welfare measures were a response to a specific and temporary emergency, and that especially with the old-age insurance provisions of that same Social Security Act coming into effect, the welfare program would gradually wither away.

Since that time two things have happened that have led to the widespread contemporary concern with the "welfare problem." First, the average welfare recipient is no longer an elderly, white person, but a young, black mother and her children. Fully 25 percent of the nation's black population receive some form of welfare, whereas only 4 percent of the white population do so.[4] The deep-seated racism of American society alone, given no other changes in the welfare system, would have helped to generate hostility to welfare spending. In addition, however, a second change has occurred over the past two decades—a rapid and significant increase in the relief rolls, a phenomenon most often called the "welfare explosion." In cities such as Baltimore, New York, St. Louis, and San Francisco, one in seven residents is on welfare. In Boston, one in six is on welfare, while in Detroit, Los Angeles, and Philadelphia, the proportion is one in eight.[5] The expansion since 1965 has been especially significant, with aid to families of dependent children (AFDC) the most prominent component. In the decade of the 1960s, AFDC expanded 107 percent with most of that increase taking place in the later half (71 percent) of the decade.[6]

While there has been an enormous increase in the number of people receiving welfare benefits, such programs in no way threaten the structure of inequality. Most pointedly, neither the total amount of money involved nor the average payment per recipient is anywhere near a level that would have *significant* redistributive effects. Since 1950, for instance, total welfare expenditures by all levels of government have not exceeded 4 percent of total personal income. Moreover, total welfare expenditures as a percentage of total personal income has actually *declined* since the Great Depression. Finally, despite the increase in the number of recipients, an expansion in the number of people served and an increase in the size of payments, the average payment to each recipient has actually declined over the past two decades when compared to the median income of employed males. In 1950, the average welfare payment was almost 20 percent of the median income, whereas in 1974 it had fallen to under 16 percent.

Any redistributive impact of welfare spending is also diminished by the fact that recipients pay some taxes and thereby help finance their own benefits. While the poor largely escape federal taxes, they are subject to highly regressive state and local taxes that finance over one-half of welfare expenditures. While there is no way to calculate accurately how much they contributed to the $32.6 billion welfare bill in 1976, it certainly amounts to several billions. . . .

While attitudes about the role of the state have changed dramatically since the 1930s, the general attitudes about the poor still persist. Opinion survey after opinion survey shows that most Americans tend to blame the poor rather than more general economic and social forces for their poverty. One becomes poor, it is generally assumed, because one is too lazy to work, too stupid to take advantage of opportunities, or too sinful to cease procreation. The attitudes toward the poor, not unnaturally, are reflected in the administration of welfare programs.

By far the most important respect in which welfare programs reflect the general societal hostility toward the poor is in the meagerness of their benefits. Without exception, benefits are so minimal that a recipient family totally dependent on them cannot hope to escape even the government's own definition of poverty. In 1973, for instance, the average national monthly welfare payment to a family of four was only $195.00 per person. A year's payments thus equaled $2,348 or less than one-half of the official poverty line for a family of four. The state is itself, therefore, a prime contributor to the perpetuation of poverty. There is no way, despite widespread thinking to the contrary, that people can live in any fashion approaching decency while on public welfare.[7]

For those who are forced by their situation to accept welfare benefits, further attacks on their esteem and dignity are forthcoming in the administration of welfare.[8] Some of the methods are subtle; some are blatant. Application procedures are often accompanied by harsh and disrespectful treatment by officials, demands for extensive documentary proof of poverty, long waits in crowded offices, demands for repeated filing of application forms, long delays in application investigations, and arbitrary rejections of applicants who meet all formal requirements of eligibility. The welfare system has also been rampant with arbitrary terminations from welfare rolls, even though technical requirements of eligibility are met.

> *Mr. G, a single man on Home Relief, received a letter telling him to report to Welfare the following morning to discuss his housing accommodation. When he arrived an hour late, he was severely chastised by his worker. Mr. G answered back and was then disqualified from further benefits for "obnoxious behavior". . . .*[9]

. . . However, one might respond that despite low benefits and harsh treatment, the welfare system is better than no system at all, and that the rise of governmental welfare activities in the 1930s and their continued expansion for four decades demonstrates the emergence of a mature positive state, concerned with accepting the responsibility for the well-being of all of its citizens, and the progressive humanization of the social and economic environment.

There is strong reason to suspect this description of the welfare state as inexorably more humane and generous, because it fails to make sense of the fact that welfare programs experience alternating periods of expansion and contraction, not perpetual growth. The best effort to explain this accordion-like pattern of welfare expenditures is the groundbreaking study of social welfare in the United States by Francis Fox Piven and Richard A. Cloward, *Regulating the Poor.* They claim that welfare spending is not so much a reflection of concern about the quality of the lives of the poor as an effort to maintain civil order, low wage labor, and inequality.

In their study they demonstrate that welfare rolls have always expanded in response to massive disruptions of civil order, and not to the widespread economic distress of the poor. They show, for instance, that from 1928 to 1933, despite serious unemployment (15 million by 1933), precipitous diminution of wages, spiraling farm failure, and drops in farm income (the latter fell 80 percent between 1929 and 1932), and resultant widespread poverty and economic distress, government did not respond to the crisis until serious threats to public order were evident. In the early 1930s there were increasing cases of the seizure of relief offices by the poor, organized resistance in both rural and urban areas to evictions, and rent riots. In 1931 there were two national hunger marches on Washington, including encampment by the "Bonus Army" of veterans. In Detroit there were massive marches by auto workers under the red banner of communism. In 1932, of course, there was also the revolutionary alteration in the electorate and the emergence of the national Democrats as the dominant party. It was in response to all of these cumulative events that the state moved in 1933 to expand welfare (through emergency relief, public works, and the Civilian Conservation Corps) and head off civil turmoil. In 1934 and 1935 additional turmoil and threats of civil disorder in the form of labor union unrest, and the combined onslaught of Huey Long, Francis Townsend, and Father Coughlin on the New Deal led to both expansions in direct relief, public works, and the passage of the Social Security Act. Most interesting, however, when the threat of turmoil was past in 1936, there was a massive trimming of the welfare rolls. After the 1936 election came the termination of emergency relief and massive cuts in public works. With the end of the threat to civil order (but not, it should be pointed out, an end to widespread economic distress) came a massive contraction of relief rolls.

The same phenomenon was at work in the explosion of the welfare rolls in the 1960s. Piven and Cloward demonstrate persuasively that the expansion of rolls was not a response to the economic distress and poverty, but to turmoil in the black ghettoes. Poverty was a severe problem in the 1950s and the early 1960s, but welfare rolls did *not* expand in response. With the technological modernization of southern agriculture came widespread rural unemployment in the 1950s, running as high as 37 percent among farm workers. With unemployment came poverty and hunger, but there is no evidence whatever that either state or federal government acted as a result. In fact, the 1950s witnessed quite the reverse in the South—the imposition of rigid restrictions and requirements and the paring of rolls.

The principal response to rural poverty has usually been urban migration, and the pattern was repeated in this case. The migration of southern blacks to urban areas, particularly outside of the South, was overwhelming. Literally millions left the farms during this period and became urban dwellers. Most of them found urban life every bit as severe as life in the rural South. In the late 1950s and early 1960s the national nonwhite unemployment rate fluctuated between 10 and 13 percent (about twice the white unemployment rate), and the subemployment rate (those only sporadically employed) in urban ghettoes reached 33 percent in the mid-1960s. And yet, even in the face of massive economic distress, severe restrictions remained on welfare eligibility. If welfare spending is, in fact, a response to distress, rolls should have rapidly expanded between 1950 and 1964, but that was generally not the case. From 1950 to 1965, total welfare recipients in all categories increased by only 1.8 million from 6.0 million to 7.8 million. From 1965 to 1971, however, the number of recipients shot up by almost 6 million to 13.5 million.

How are we to explain such an explosive expansion? To Piven and Cloward the answer is quite simple. The expansion was a political response to the widespread urban violence of the middle sixties and the growing power of black political, civil rights, and welfare groups and the perceived threat to both civil order and entrenched political power. The state commitment to the welfare of the poor which failed to be mobilized by need, was mobilized by trouble. With the decline of troubles, with the threat of civil disorder receding, we once again hear widespread demands that the welfare rolls be pared and that welfare recipients take jobs. From state to state we are beginning to see a significant contraction in the number of welfare recipients now that turmoil no longer threatens, although economic distress is every bit as severe for millions of families. We can expect such a state of affairs to continue if Piven and Cloward are correct, until the outbreak of the next round of civil conflict and political disruption.

Public welfare serves another important function, according to Piven and Cloward: it helps to maintain a pool of low wage labor to meet the personnel requirements of the private industrial and economic system. In nondisruptive times, the welfare system operates to persuade, even to force many people to take low-paying, demeaning, and even dangerous jobs. The system uses several devices to accomplish this goal. First, relief in non-threatening times is restricted to persons who are of little immediate use to the economy—the elderly, the disabled, children, and mothers of young children.[10] Welfare payments have generally been denied to able-bodied males no matter what their state of poverty. As long as the potential existed for some present or future employment, benefits were not forthcoming. Fully 25 percent of the poor in the United States live in families headed by employed males, yet welfare benefits are usually denied to them. Welfare agencies have also traditionally attempted to deny benefits to mothers in any way involved with a man. If we see one of the functions of welfare as keeping people in the low wage labor pool, then these behaviors are no longer perplexing. The goal is to prevent benefits from reaching employable men. The commitment of the welfare system to the alleviation of poverty is, consequently, highly suspect relative to its other objectives.

Another method to accomplish the same goal is to tie relief payments to local economies. By turning over most of the administration of welfare to state and local governments, the state ensures that relief payments will in no area exceed the lowest wages paid in the local economy. If relief payments were to exceed the lowest rungs of the wage scale, there would be no incentive for people to take such low-paying jobs. In the South, it has been traditional to deny welfare to blacks in order to force them to take work as menials. It was and still is common practice to cut welfare during periods of "full employment" (e.g., cotton picking time) to ensure the availability of low wage labor.

Finally, Piven and Cloward claim that the demeaning and contemptuous treatment of welfare recipients also serves a personnel function by making welfare so unattractive and oppressive that most people would take *any* work rather than face the indignities of the welfare recipient. The system creates an outcast class that no rational person, given a choice, would join. The constant ritual-like degradation of the welfare recipient, whether at the hands of the welfare workers, elected officials, or newspaper editorials, is aimed not at the recipient alone, but at any able-bodied, potentially employable worker.

Public welfare, therefore, which looks at first glance to be proof of the commitment of the modern American state to social justice, to the alleviation of widespread economic distress, and to the attenuation of severe inequalities, looks quite different upon careful examination. While no one can deny that the state is more involved in these areas than it was prior to the New Deal, or that it is slightly redistributive, it still remains true that public welfare hardly dents inequality, does little to alleviate poverty, and does much to assault the self-esteem of its beneficiaries. There is strong reason to believe, if we accept Piven and Cloward's intriguing analysis, that the welfare system mainly serves the dual functions of maintaining both civil order and a pool of cheap labor for the private sector. . . .

Notes

1. "Positive state" is the general term we shall use to indicate the tendency of all modern capitalist governments to be active and interventionist to one degree or another, rather than inactive and passive. We use it in preference to the term "welfare state" which has too many emotional implications and is theoretically vague and undeveloped.
2. For a complete discussion of these issues as well as extensive source references see Edward S. Greenberg, *Serving the Few: Corporate Capitalism and the Bias of Government Policy* (New York: John Wiley, 1974). Also see Edward S. Greenberg, *The American Political System: A Radical Analysis* (Cambridge: Winthrop, 1977).
3. For leading statements in this vein, see the work of Daniel Bell, *The Coming Of Post-Industrial Society* (New York: Basic Books, 1973) and *The End of Ideology* (New York: Free Press, 1960).
4. Thomas Dye, *Understanding Public Policy* (Englewood Cliffs, N.J.: Prentice-Hall, 1972), p. 90. As of 1975, moreover, over 44% of all AFDC expenditures were going to black people. Table #550, *Statistical Abstracts of the United States* (Washington D.C.: U.S. Department of Commerce, 1977), p. 350.
5. Ibid., p. 88.
6. Francis Fox Piven and Richard A. Cloward, *Regulating the Poor: The Functions Of Public Welfare* (New York: Pantheon, 1971), p. 186.
7. It does no good, moreover, to reply that people should get off of welfare and take jobs. All available research suggests that for the most part recipients are either aged, young children, the mothers of young children, or incapacitated males. The best estimate is that only one percent of the males in the universe of welfare recipients are employable. (See *Office of the President, 1967 Budget Report*). Given their lack of skills and an economy that thinks of a 6–7 percent unemployment rate as normal, finding work is highly problematic for most welfare recipients.
8. Most of the remainder of the discussion of welfare is based on the brilliant analysis of the subject by Piven and Cloward, *Regulating the Poor*.
9. Ibid., p. 159.
10. In this respect it is similar to Social Security (in its support of persons of no immediate use to the economic system).

74 / Individualism: The Staff of Life

Susan Love Brown, Karl Keating, David Mellinger, Patrea Post, Stuart Smith, Catriona Tudor

The authors of this essay consider the merits of humanitarianism and individualism as competing values, and argue that individualism is not only the superior value but also the basic founding principle of the United States. Since social programs that obligate citizens to share benefits with others conflict with individualism, the freedom of everyone in society ultimately suffers from adoption of such programs.

It is late on the evening before your final exam in microbiology. It's been a very tough semester, but by burning the proverbial midnight oil you might be able to get on with your life.

Just as one scientific smudge is beginning to distinguish itself from another, there comes a knock on your door. Tearing yourself away from the fascination of cells and germs, you open the door only to be deluged by the tears of your neighbor. You sigh because you remember this scene from before.

Your neighbor has played an interesting role this semester. Although studying the same subjects as you, it is not with the same vigor. Instead, there is much more emphasis on "extra-curricular activities." There is perhaps one of these interruptions each week with much the same outcome after each. And since your neighbor looks upon you as "so understanding and such a good listener," you usually get the call to man the tissue box.

What may have started as genuine sympathy at the beginning now borders on genuine contempt. This person has kept you from doing some important things during the course of the semester, and now the timing is really crucial.

The dilemma is what to do. You've probably made the decision already, but reconsider it from two points of view—the humanitarian (altruist) and the individualist.

The humanitarian/altruist has a deep, unselfish concern for the welfare of his fellow man. His actions do not consider himself, and in fact, some of them are detrimental to his own well being. But he is convinced he must not be selfish, and so he sits quietly listening to his neighbor because of his neighbor's need and his own unselfish determination. He will not think about the fact that he will surely fail the test in the morning.

On the other side of the issue, the individualist has little difficulty in making his decision. His prime concern is himself, so the neighbor is quickly shooed out of the room bringing the quiet necessary for study.

Many people, beguiled by what they feel is a doctrine of humanitarian benevolence, think of themselves (or would like to think of themselves) as altruists. But the person who consistently practices altruism would regard it as a moral obligation to sacrifice at every opportunity, his happiness for others, his welfare for others, and ultimately his own life for others. People can preach altruism but they cannot live it. Nor should they, for the genuine altruist voluntarily enslaves himself to the need and desires of every other person. The genuine altruist—if there could really be such a thing—is not a man but a doormat.

The philosophical doctrine which recognizes the moral correctness of self-interest is individualism. It maintains that the individual is justified in pursuing his own self-interest and that, accordingly, he is not morally obligated to place the welfare of the group above his own. That such actions demonstrably result in a more productive and prosperous free society is merely a desirable consequence, not a principle.

Does this mean that the individualist rejects any sense of concern for others? Of course not. But it does mean that he recognizes as concerns only those relationships which he has voluntarily entered. Because he values human life he may assist those who are in genuine need, but the "obligation" is to his own values, not to the other person. The individualist does not regard it as an obligation to subordinate his own self-interest to the desires of others. And he would certainly resist any attempt to impose that alleged obligation upon him by force—nor would he attempt to impose it on others. What is important about this person is that he is not stringent, but flexible, and that he does not operate according to obligation or conceit, but by logical thought and reason and by self consideration.

It is quite true, of course, that individuals benefit from association with other individuals. One who lives the life of a hermit, removed from human association, must provide for himself and do without the company of others. One who lives in a voluntary association with others receives the benefits of the knowledge of others, the benefits of the production of others, and the benefit of the company of others.

But again, the real issue concerns the terms on which this association takes place. Is it voluntary or is it compulsory? Is it based on a mutual recognition of individual rights or the abrogation of them?

If all associations are voluntary, then the result is a free society in which each individual can make the most of his or her life. The only condition then is that no individual or group of individuals violate the rights of any other individual or group of individuals.

However, if men are compelled by law to serve the interests of others, it is not cooperation—it is slavery.

The Bill of Rights of the United States Constitution did not establish the sovereignty of "society," but the sovereignty of the individual. Neither did it require that the individual serve the State, the king, the nobility, the society, the rich, the poor, the public interest, the fatherland, or humanity. As long as the individual did not initiate force against others, he was to be free to live his own life without fear in accordance with his own convictions. It was individualism that was the basis of the most free and progressive nation on earth.

The philosophy of individualism grows out of a concept of rights, and this concept grows out of observing the basic nature of man as a human being.

For instance, if you were a hermit living in a clearing surrounded by impenetrable forests and never encountered any other human beings, the concept of individual rights would have no meaning. You would be responsible only to yourself. But when human beings live together it becomes evident that certain rules must be established to protect their lives, or to define how they may act in relation to other individuals.

However, on a purely social basis, it makes no difference if one believes that he has the right to his own life and is not obliged to blindly serve another or if one believes that sacrifice for others is a virtue. It is when one enters the political arena that the question of who is obliged to serve whom is no longer merely a matter for debate—it then becomes a question settled by legalized force.

By means of the coercive arm of the State, those opposed to individualism seek to impress upon the individual his obligation to others. The humanitarian seeks medical care for all—by force. He would encourage brotherhood—by force. *He would make men good—by force.* It is important to note that in a political system based on individual freedom a human being may practice any form of morality he wishes (including self-sacrifice) provided that he does not initiate force against others. But in a political system based on self-sacrifice the freedom to act upon one's beliefs is obliterated, because the humanitarian seeks to force his sense of "duty" upon everyone else—he employs force to make one human being sacrifice for another.

"To be a socialist," declared Nazi socialist Joseph Goebbels, "is to submit the I to the thou; socialism is sacrificing the individual to the whole."[1]

"We are going to take all of the money that we think is unnecessarily being spent and take it from the 'haves' and give it to the 'have-nots' that need it so much."[2] President Johnson.

Stalin: "True Bolshevik courage does not consist in placing one's individual will above the will of the Comintern. True courage consists in being strong enough to master and overcome one's self and subordinate one's will to the will of the collective, the will of the higher party body."[3]

"Ask not what your country can do for you—ask what you can do for your country."[4] President Kennedy.

Hitler: "It is thus necessary that the individual should finally come to realize that his own ego is of no importance in comparison with the existence of his nation . . . that the higher interests involved in the life of the whole must here set the limits and lay down the duties of the interests of the individual."[5]

But observe the contradiction in this argument. Humanitarians say that human beings must forget themselves in order that the "common good" can be served. But what is the "common good" but the sum of what is good for each individual that makes up a society? Therefore, how can the good of society be separated from the good of the individuals who compose it?

When each individual is allowed to live his life to its fullest extent without subjection to compulsion, then he is achieving the greatest good for himself. Since the initiation of force is not permitted in a free society, each individual is free to pursue his goals to the limit of his own capabilities. However, if the right of the individual to live in accordance with his own principles is prevented by State force, the individual's "good" is incalculably reduced. If the "good" for each individual is substantially reduced, then it follows that the "common good" is substantially reduced.

Americans have traditionally accepted both charity and self-interest as desirable components of human character, and have admired the person who demonstrates a balance of these two values in his actions.

However, a false notion has crept into our thinking that sacrifice of self is the "good" and individualism is the "bad." Therefore (so the thinking goes), since charity is desirable, it should be the philosophy of the land, and the government should see that it is expanded. In view of this, it is not hard to understand how most people are misled into "buying" governmental humanitarianism. But advocating forced charity is like wanting cold steam or hot ice. Charity by definition must be a voluntary action. To force it is to pervert the character trait (voluntary good will) that prompts it. The results of forced charity will never be what people expect. Because humanitarianism is food for tyranny, this nation is moving steadily toward totalitarianism instead of a free society.

When Hitler shouted that it was the duty of the good German citizen to sacrifice for the fatherland, he would have shouted in vain were it not that too many "good" German citizens had been brought up to believe precisely that. As long as people choose to believe that virtue lies in service first to "society" or to the "common good" or to the "fatherland" or to the "public interest," there will continue to be dictators to see that virtue prevails.

It is by taking humanitarianism to its logical political consequence that dictatorships are established and the rights of individual people ravaged.

Controlled housing. Controlled prices. Controlled wages. Controlled business. Controlled unions. Controlled money. Controlled banking. Controlled television. Controlled news. *Controlled people.*

Notes

1. Arthur M. Schlesinger, *The Vital Center* (New York: Houghton-Mifflin, 1962), p. 54.
2. *Lost Angeles Times,* March 3, 1965.
3. Arthur M. Schlesinger, op. cit., p. 56.
4. Milton Friedman, *Capitalism and Freedom* (Chicago: The University of Chicago Press, 1962), p. 2.
5. Cited by Ayn Rand, *The Fascist New Frontier* (New York: Nathaniel Branden Institute, 1963), p. 4.

75 / The Cyclical Politics of Rich and Poor

Kevin Phillips

Just as governmental leadership and policies change over time, which economic groups "win" from government's policies may change as well. Kevin Phillips, longtime Republican activist and commentator, suggests in the following reading that such a change occurred during the Reagan years, and another, reactive change may be in the offing. After decades of redistribution of wealth to the lower income groups, conditions were right for a shift in the other direction when Ronald Reagan became president. Promising to end growth in welfarism and to restore incentives for wealth, President Reagan led the way to a decade of rich becoming richer and poor becoming poorer. Now, Phillips argues, the pendulum is poised to swing back again in favor of more liberal reforms. Such shifts in "who wins" from governmental policy are themselves not new in American politics, but the stakes may be higher this time around.

The 1980s were the triumph of upper America—an ostentatious celebration of wealth, the political ascendancy of the richest third of the population and a glorification of capitalism, free markets and finance. But while money, greed and luxury had become the stuff of popular culture, hardly anyone asked why such great wealth had concentrated at the top, and whether this was a result of public policy. Despite the armies of homeless sleeping on grates, political leaders—even those who professed to care about the homeless—had little to say about the Republican party's historical role, which has been not simply to revitalize U.S. capitalism but to tilt power, policy, wealth and income toward the richest portions of the population. The public understood this bias, if we can trust 1988 opinion polls; nevertheless, the Democrats shunned the issue in the election of 1988, a reluctance their predecessors had also displayed during previous Republican booms.

That discussion is now unfolding. From Congress to the executive branch, "money politics"—be it the avarice of financiers or outright corruption of politicians—is shaping up as a prime political theme for the 1990s. Class structures may be weak in the United States, but populist sensitivities run high. Wealth in this country has always been fluid, volatile and migratory. Unlike Europe, we have needed no revolutions for its redistribution. In America the reallocation of income and assets has usually followed consumer fads, population shifts and technological innovations. But politics and political ideologies have also been important keys to the cashbox. Changing popular and governmental attitudes toward wealth have always influenced who gets what. Decade after decade illustrates the point; the Reagan era was not unique.

The 1980s were a second Gilded Age, in which many Americans made and spent money abundantly. Yet as the decade ended, too many stretch limousines, too many enormous incomes and too much high fashion foreshadowed a significant shift of mood. A new plutocracy—some critics were even using the word "oligarchy"—had created a new target for populist reaction. A small but significant minority of American liberals had begun to agitate the economy's losers—minorities, young men, female heads of households, farmers, steelworkers and others. Television audiences were losing their early-eighties fascination with the rich. And many conservatives, including President George Bush himself, were becoming defensive about great wealth, wanton moneymaking and greed.

No fixed caste, class, ideology or geographic section has long governed America's lively pursuit of money and success. Sectional competition has been pursued always and everywhere, and has yielded every kind of regional advantage. Relative affluence in the United States has moved West (almost from the first days of settlement), gone North (after the Civil War) or South (with the rise of the Sunbelt). The 1980s boom in the Boston-Washington megalopolis, coupled with hard times on the farm and in the Oil Patch, produced a familiar conservative economic geography—a comparative shift of wealth toward the two coasts. *And* toward income groups already well off.

This preference was nothing new. Twice before in the last hundred years, wealth also further accumulated in the hands of those *already rich*—during the late nineteenth century, then again during the 1920s. To some extent, these buildups have also served the larger purpose of stimulating capitalist growth, entrepreneurialism and technological innovation. Avarice was only one ingredient. At other times, and also for at least partly valid public policy reasons, Washington has gone in the opposite direction and redeployed upper-income assets to fatten thinner wallets, expand low-income purchasing power and rebuild the social fabric of poorer Americans. So debtors have occasionally gained as have creditors. Farmers have outmaneuvered bankers, although rarely, but regardless of the direction it's hard to overstate the importance of American politics to American wealth—and vice versa.

Candor in these matters is rare. But in the words of an iconoclastic journalist of the Reagan era, William Greider, "Concentration of wealth was the fulcrum on which the most basic political questions pivoted, a dividing line deeper than region or religion, race or sex. In the nature of things, government might choose to enhance the economic prospects for the many or to safeguard the accumulated wealth held by the few, but frequently the two purposes were in irreconcilable conflict. The continuing political struggle across this line, though unseen and rarely mentioned, was the central narrative of American political history, especially in the politics of money." Greider's thesis is generally supported by history. Since the American Revolution the distribution of American wealth has depended significantly on *who controlled the federal government, for what policies, and in behalf of which constituencies.*

From this perspective, the Reagan era reversed what late-twentieth-century Americans had become used to. The liberal style that prevailed from 1932 to 1968 had left a legacy of angry conservatives indignant over two generations of downward income redistribution. A reorientation in the opposite direction was all but inevitable in the 1980s—and there were precedents aplenty.

In the years after 1790, when Alexander Hamilton persuaded Congress to assume debts incurred by the states during the Revolution, the result was a redistribution of wealth to bondholders, many of whom had bought the low-valued debt instruments as speculation. Then in the 1870s, restoration of the gold standard squeezed out the last vestiges of Civil War inflation, providing a similar preference to creditors over debtors. And the Harding-Coolidge tax cuts of the 1920s, in which the top individual federal income tax rate fell from 73 percent to 25 percent, furnish yet another example of realignment upward. This periodic upward bias is as much a fact of U.S. history as the liberal bias with which it alternates.

Even in this most optimistic of countries, economic individualism yields to community-minded reform on a cyclical basis as the public grows indignant over the political distribution of wealth. By the mid-1920s, and especially during the New Deal, muckraking interpretations of the economic motives of conservative governance were a dime a dozen. Historian Charles Beard became famous for his *Economic Interpretation of the U.S. Constitution* and other books arguing the premise that the Founding Fathers and their descendants had served their own class interests as well as American patriotism. Populist or progressive periods have often nurtured such materialistic views, and the 1990s are likely to regard the Reagan era as a seamless web of preoccupation with wealth and moneymaking. By 1989, after all, the statistics *were* in: once again, just as in the 1790s, the 1880s and the 1920s, conservative and upper-bracket groups had been the major gainers. As a percentage of overall national income, the shift wasn't big, of course. Yet increases of two, three and four points in the share of income held by the top 1 percent of Americans—accompanied, meanwhile, by some decline in the bottom two fifths of the population—have been the stuff of major economic and political movements....

...Only for so long will strung-out $35,000-a-year families enjoy magazines articles about the hundred most successful businessmen in Dallas or television programs about the life-styles of the rich and famous. And the discontents that arise go well beyond lower-class envy or the anticommercial bias of academe.

A century ago established lawyers, diplomats, doctors and bank presidents—and, in particular, patrician landowners and other old-money families—seethed over the erosion of their relative wealth and importance as muddy-booted nouveau riche railroad barons and stockjobbers flourished, a frustration that foreshadowed similar public distaste in the late 1980s for corporate raiders, Wall Street inside traders and thirty-one-year-old investment bankers earning a million dollars a year. The historian Richard Hofstadter, looking at the Progressive movement as it culminated in Theodore Roosevelt's third-party bid for the presidency on the 1912 Bull Moose ticket, has argued that Progressivism drew heavily on the resentment of old money for new. How much the 1990s will follow this familiar pattern remains to be seen, but George Bush, a scion of the Eastern Establishment, for all his loyalty to Ronald Reagan, chose to echo "TR" in the 1988 campaign by deploring "this fast-buck stuff...I don't have great respect for just going out and stacking up money." Bush refreshed this theme in his inaugural address, for just as Ronald Reagan had replaced Richard Nixon's bias toward "Middle America" with nouveau riche ostentation, Bush represented a shift from the aggressiveness of the new rich to the defensiveness, even social conciliation, of established wealth.

Some amplifications are in order. Political terminology can be confusing, even contradictory, during these periods. The late Harvard economist Joseph Schumpeter has described how capitalism, at its zenith, is profoundly creative, profoundly destructive—and profoundly *unconservative* by any standard except its respect for market forces and moneymaking. Populists and progressives are not alone in opposing the "malefactors of great wealth." Upholders of traditional or aristocratic values, such as they are in the United States, have also been periodic critics— not just Theodore Roosevelt but also Henry Cabot Lodge and Charles Francis Adams, to say nothing of his cousins Henry and Brooks. A minor but vaguely similar dissent on the part of Southern traditionalists was also apparent during the last crescendos of the Roaring Twenties.

To be sure, historical parallels are dangerous, but history can teach certain general lessons well enough to suggest certain tentative precedents for not only what *happened* during the Reagan years but what *may occur in reaction* during the 1990s. While neither Democrats nor Republicans like to acknowledge their role in the concentration and dispersal of wealth, these roles have always been present, lurking beneath the rhetoric of individualism, market forces and free enterprise, on one side, or fairness and social justice, on the other. Excesses in one direction have always bred a countermovement in the other direction, and the Reagan era certainly had its excesses.

The shift to the right in late-twentieth-century U.S. politics—the odd mix of conservatism and populism that I described two decades ago in my book *The Emerging Republican Majority*, and that provided elements of the strategy for the 1968 GOP presidential campaign—was fading by the 1988 election. One sign that the Republican presidential cycle had reached late middle age in the 1980s was an intensified ideological focus on free markets and capitalist values. *Money and business had become fashionable—again.* History suggests that GOP cycles tend to stage capitalist blow-offs as they mature, which is what happened in the 1920s. The Reagan administration, from the beginning, was openly committed to copying the economic style and incentives of the Calvin Coolidge years, though Reagan's revival of the Roaring Twenties was more precarious and debt-dependent than the original era.

By the time of the Democratic and Republican conventions in 1988, the boosterish style of the Reagan era—from entrepreneur worship to roller-coaster stock markets—was already yielding to a more restrained, centrist tone. That was clear in *both* parties. As summer turned to autumn each groped toward a different successor politics. George Bush presented himself as a low-key activist and reformer, casting an occasional well-bred aspersion toward those who did nothing but pursue money. Both candidates eschewed the values of the glitterati. Michael Dukakis, who originally styled himself as the architect of Massachusetts' economic "miracle," assumed a more populist stance by October, but by that time it was too late for him to benefit from Democratic themes of economic discontent.

. . . [T]he portrait of what the 1988 debate largely ignored [includes]: the new political economics, intensifying inequality and pain for the poor, the unprecedented growth of upper-bracket wealth, the surprisingly related growth of federal debt, global economic realignment, foreigners gobbling up large chunks of America, the meaninglessness of being a millionaire in an era with nearly a hundred thousand "decamillionaires." Part of the portrait is international—Britain and Japan displayed a similar concentration of wealth—but mostly it is about which *American* individuals, groups, economic sectors and regions profited, and which lost.

We are talking about a major transformation. Not only did the concentration of wealth quietly intensify, but the sums involved took a mega-leap. The definition of who's rich—and who's no longer rich—changed as radically during the Reagan era as it did during the prior great nouveau riche periods of the late nineteenth century and the 1920s, periods whose excesses preceded the great populist upheaval of the Bryan era and the New Deal.... [T]he political pendulum has swung back in the past, and may be ready to swing again. The 1990s could easily be another watershed decade. But this time the stakes are unusually high, in light of America's new status as a debtor nation, a situation not seen since World War I. Some relative decline in our circumstances seems inevitable—indeed, has *already* taken place. Powerful currents of global change are operating quite beyond our power to offset them.

Yet perhaps a part of America's challenge and opportunity is more traditional: as they have in the past, liberals once more favor bringing extremes of wealth, debt and inequality under control through taxation and regulation.... [T]he 1980s political and economic debate ended amid hints that America's other political-economic traditions were on the rise, with their distaste for survival-of-the-fittest economics, new talk of a "kinder, gentler nation," belief in a more activist role for government and demand for more attention to the weaker portions of society. U.S. history records significant achievements for *those* cycles, too.

The Articles of Confederation

The Constitution of the United States of America

The Articles of Confederation

To all to whom these presents shall come, we the undersigned delegates of the states affixed to our names send greeting. Whereas the delegates of the United States of America in Congress assembled did on the fifteenth day of November in the year of our Lord One Thousand Seven Hundred and Seventy-seven, and in the second year of the independence of America, agree to certain articles of confederation and perpetual union between the states of New-hampshire, Massachusetts-bay, Rhodeisland and Providence Plantations, Connecticut, New York, New Jersey, Pennsylvania, Delaware, Maryland, Virginia, North Carolina, South Carolina, and Georgia in the words following, viz.

"Articles of confederation and perpetual union between the states of New-hampshire, Massachusetts-bay, Rhodeisland and Providence Plantations, Connecticut, New York, New Jersey, Pennsylvania, Delaware, Maryland, Virginia, North Carolina, South Carolina and Georgia.

Article I
The stile of this confederacy shall be "The United States of America."

Article II
Each state retains its sovereignty, freedom, and independence, and every power, jurisdiction, and right, which is not by this confederation expressly delegated to the United States, in Congress assembled.

Article III
The said states hereby severally enter into a firm league of friendship with each other for their common defense, the security of their liberties, and their mutual and general welfare, binding themselves to assist each other against all force offered to, or attacks made upon them, or any of them, on account of religion, sovereignty, trade, or any other pretense whatever.

Article IV
The better to secure and perpetuate mutual friendship and intercourse among the people of the different states in this union, the free inhabitants of each of these states—paupers, vagabonds, and fugitives from justice excepted—shall be entitled to all privileges and immunities of free citizens in the several states; and the people of each state shall have free ingress and regress to and from any other state, and shall enjoy therein all the privileges of trade and commerce, subject to the same duties, impositions, and restrictions as the inhabitants thereof respectively, provided that such restrictions shall not extend so far as to prevent the removal of property imported into any state, to any other state of which the owner is an inhabitant; provided also that no imposition, duties, or restriction shall be laid by any state on the property of the United States, or either of them.

If any person guilty of, or charged with treason, felony, or other high misdemeanor in any state shall flee from justice, and be found in any of the United States, he shall upon demand of the governor or executive power of the state from which he fled be delivered up and removed to the state having jurisdiction of his offense.

Full faith and credit shall be given in each of these states to the records, acts, and judicial proceedings of the courts and magistrates of every other state.

Article V

For the more convenient management of the general interests of the United States, delegates shall be annually appointed in such manner as the legislature of each state shall direct, to meet in Congress on the first Monday in November, in every year, with a power reserved to each state to recall its delegates, or any of them, at any time within the year, and to send others in their stead for the remainder of the year.

No state shall be represented in Congress by less than two, nor by more than seven members; and no person shall be capable of being a delegate for more than three years in any term of six years; nor shall any person being a delegate, be capable of holding any office under the United States for which he, or another for his benefit, receives any salary, fees, or emolument of any kind.

Each state shall maintain its own delegates in a meeting of the states, and while they act as members of the committee of the states.

In determining questions in the United States in Congress assembled, each state shall have one vote.

Freedom of speech and debate in Congress shall not be impeached or questioned in any court, or place out of Congress, and the members of Congress shall be protected in their persons from arrests and imprisonments during the time of their going to and from, and attendance on Congress, except for treason, felony, or breach of the peace.

Article VI

No state without the consent of the United States in Congress assembled shall send any embassy to, or receive any embassy from, or enter into any conference, agreement, or alliance or treaty with any king, prince, or state; nor shall any person holding any office of profit or trust under the United States, or any of them, accept any present, emolument, office, or title of any kind whatever from any king, prince, or foreign state; nor shall the United States in Congress assembled, or any of them, grant any title of nobility.

No two or more states shall enter into any treaty, confederation, or alliance whatever between them without the consent of the United States in Congress assembled, specifying accurately the purposes for which the same is to be entered into, and how long it shall continue.

No state shall lay any imposts or duties which may interfere with any stipulations in treaties entered into by the United States in Congress assembled, with any king, prince, or state, in pursuance of any treaties already proposed by Congress to the courts of France and Spain.

No vessels of war shall be kept up in time of peace by any state, except such number only as shall be deemed necessary by the United States in Congress assembled, for the defense of such state, or its trade; nor shall any body of forces be kept up by any state in time of peace, except such number only as in the judgment of the United States, in Congress assembled, shall be deemed requisite to garrison the forts necessary for the defense of such state; but every state shall always keep up a well-regulated and disciplined militia, sufficiently armed and accoutered, and shall provide and constantly have ready for use, in public stores, a due number of field pieces and tents, and a proper quantity of arms, ammunition, and camp equipage.

No state shall engage in any war without the consent of the United States in Congress assembled, unless such state be actually invaded by enemies, or shall have received certain advice of a resolution being formed by some nation of Indians to invade such state, and the danger is so imminent as not to admit of a delay till the United States in Congress assembled can be consulted: nor shall any state grant commissions to any ships or vessels of war, nor letters of marque or reprisal, except it be after a declaration of war by the United States in Congress assembled, and then only against the kingdom or state and the subjects thereof, against which war has been so declared, and under such regulations as shall be established by the United States in Congress assembled, unless such state be infested by pirates, in which case vessels of war may be fitted out for that occasion and kept so long as the danger shall continue, or until the United States in Congress assembled shall determine otherwise.

Article VII

When land-forces are raised by any state for the common defense, all officers of or under the rank of colonel shall be appointed by the legislature of each state respectively by whom such forces shall be raised, or in such manner as such state shall direct, and all vacancies shall be filled up by the state which first made the appointment.

Article VIII

All charges of war, and all other expenses that shall be incurred for the common defense or general welfare, and allowed by the United States in Congress assembled, shall be defrayed out of a common treasury, which shall be supplied by the several states in proportion to the value of all land within each state, granted to or surveyed for any person, as such land and the buildings and improvements thereon shall be estimated according to such mode as the United States in Congress assembled shall from time to time direct and appoint. The taxes for paying that proportion shall be laid and levied by the authority and direction of the legislatures of the several states within the time agreed upon by the United States in Congress assembled.

Article IX

The United States in Congress assembled shall have the sole and exclusive right and power of determining on peace and war, except in the cases mentioned in the sixth article—of sending and receiving ambassadors—[of] entering into treaties and alliances, provided that no treaty of commerce shall be made whereby the legislative power of the respective states shall be restrained from imposing such imposts and duties on foreigners, as their own people are subjected to, or from prohibiting the exportation or importation of any species of goods or commodities whatsoever—of establishing rules for deciding in all cases, what captures on land or water shall be legal, and in what manner prizes taken by land or naval forces in the service of the United States shall be divided or appropriated—of granting letters of marque and reprisal in times of peace—[of] appointing courts for the trial of piracies and felonies committed on the high seas and establishing courts for receiving and determining finally appeals in all cases of captures, provided that no member of Congress shall be appointed a judge of any of the said courts.

The United States in Congress assembled shall also be the last resort on appeal in all disputes and differences now subsisting or that hereafter may arise between two or more states concerning boundary, jurisdiction, or any other cause whatever; which authority shall always be exercised in the manner following:

Whenever the legislative or executive authority or lawful agent of any state in controversy with another shall present a petition to Congress, stating the matter in question and praying for a hearing, notice thereof shall be given by order of Congress to the legislative or executive authority of the other state in controversy, and a day assigned for the appearance of the parties by their lawful agents, who shall then be directed to appoint by joint consent, commissioners or judges to constitute a court for hearing and determining the matter in question: but if they cannot agree, Congress shall name three persons out of each of the United States, and from the list of such persons each party shall alternately strike out one, the petitioners beginning, until the number shall be reduced to thirteen; and from that number not less than seven nor more than nine names, as Congress shall direct, shall in the presence of Congress be drawn out by lot, and the persons whose names shall be so drawn, or any five of them, shall be commissioners or judges to hear and finally determine the controversy; so always as a major part of the judges who shall hear the cause shall agree in the determination: and if either party shall neglect to attend at the day appointed, without showing reasons, which Congress shall judge sufficient, or being present shall refuse to strike, the Congress shall proceed to nominate three persons out of each state, and the secretary of Congress shall strike in behalf of such party absent or refusing; and the judgment and sentence of the court to be appointed, in the manner before prescribed, shall be final and conclusive; and if any of the parties shall refuse to submit to the authority of such court, or to appear to defend their claim or cause, the court shall nevertheless proceed to pronounce sentence, or judgment, which shall in like manner be final and decisive, the judgment or sentence and other proceedings being in either case transmitted to Congress and lodged among the acts of Congress for the security of the parties concerned: provided that every commissioner, before he sits in judgment, shall take an oath to be administered by one of the judges of the supreme or superior court of the state where the cause shall be tried, "well and truly to hear and determine the matter in question, according to the best of his judgment, without favor, affection, or hope of reward": provided also that no state shall be deprived of territory for the benefit of the United States.

All controversies concerning the private right of soil claimed under different grants of two or more states, whose jurisdiction as they may respect such lands, and the states which passed such grants are adjusted, the said grants or either of them being at the same time claimed to have originated antecedent to such settlement of jurisdiction, shall on the petition of either party on the Congress of the United States, be finally determined as near as may be in the same manner as before prescribed for deciding disputes respecting territorial jurisdiction between different states.

The United States in Congress assembled shall also have the sole and exclusive right and power of regulating the alloy and value of coin struck by their own authority, or by that of the respective tests—fixing the standard of weights and measures throughout the United States—regulating the trade and managing all affairs with the Indians, not members of any of the states, provided that the legislative right of any state within its own limits be not infringed or violated—establishing and regulating post offices from one state to another throughout all the United States, and exacting such postage on the papers passing through the same as may be requisite to defray the expenses of the said office—appointing all officers of the land forces in the service of the United States, excepting regimental officers— appointing all the officers of the naval forces, and commissioning all officers whatever in the service of the United States—making rules for the government and regulation of the said land and naval forces, and directing their operations.

The United States in Congress assembled shall have authority to appoint a committee to sit in the recess of Congress, to be denominated a "Committee of the States," and to consist of one delegate from each state; and to appoint such other committees and civil officers as may be necessary for managing the general affairs of the United States under their direction—to appoint one of their number to preside, provided that no person be allowed to serve in the office of president more than one year in any term of three years: to ascertain the necessary sums of money to be raised for the service of the United States, and to appropriate and apply the same for defraying the public expenses—to borrow money or emit bills on the credit of the United States, transmitting every half-year to the respective states an account of the sums of money so borrowed or emitted—to build and equip a navy—to agree upon the number of land forces, and to make requisitions from each state for its quota in proportion to the number of white inhabitants in each state; which requisition shall be binding, and thereupon the legislature of each state shall appoint the regimental officers, raise the men, and clothe, arm and equip them in a soldier-like manner at the expense of the United States, and the officers and men so clothed, armed, and equipped shall march to the place appointed, and within the time agreed on by the United States in Congress assembled: but if the United States in Congress assembled shall, on consideration of circumstances, judge proper that any state should not raise men, or should raise a smaller number of men than the quota thereof, and that any other state should raise a greater number of men than the quota thereof, such extra number shall be raised, officered, clothed, armed, and equipped in the same manner as the quota of such state unless the legislature of such state shall judge that such extra number cannot be safely spared out of the same, in which case they shall raise, officer, clothe, arm, and equip as many of such extra number as they judge can be safely spared. And the officers and men so clothed, armed, and equipped shall march to the place appointed, and within the time agreed on by the United States in Congress assembled.

The United States in Congress assembled shall never engage in a war, nor grant letters of marque and reprisal in time of peace, nor enter into any treaties or alliances, nor coin money, nor regulate the value thereof, nor ascertain the sums and expenses necessary for the defense and welfare of the United States, or any of them, nor emit bills, nor borrow money on the credit of the United States, nor appropriate money, nor agree upon the number of vessels of war to be built or purchased, nor the number of land or sea forces to be raised, nor appoint a commander-in-chief of the army or navy, unless nine states assent to the same: nor shall a question on any other point, except for adjourning from day to day, be determined unless by the votes of a majority of the United States in Congress assembled.

The Congress of the United States shall have power to adjourn to any time within the year, and to any place within the United States, so that no period of adjournment be for a longer duration than the space of six months, and shall publish the journal of their proceedings monthly, except such parts thereof relating to treaties, alliances, or military operations, as in their judgment require secrecy; and the yeas and nays of the delegates of each state on any question shall be entered on the journal when it is desired by any delegate; and the delegates of a state, or any of them, at his or their request shall be furnished with a transcript of the said journal, except such parts as are above excepted, to lay before the legislatures of the several states.

Article X

The committee of the states, or any nine of them, shall be authorized to execute, in the recess of Congress, such of the powers of Congress as the United States in Congress assembled, by the consent of nine states, shall from time to time think expedient to vest them with; provided that no power be delegated to the said committee for the exercise of which, by the Articles of Confederation, the voice of nine states in the Congress of the United States assembled is requisite.

Article XI

Canada acceding to this confederation, and joining in the measures of the United States, shall be admitted into, and entitled to all the advantages of this union: but no other colony shall be admitted into the same unless such admission be agreed to by nine states.

Article XII

All bills of credit emitted, monies borrowed, and debts contracted by, or under the authority of Congress, before the assembling of the United States, in pursuance of the present confederation, shall be deemed and considered as a charge against the United States, for payment and satisfaction whereof the said United States and the public faith are hereby solemnly pledged.

Article XIII

Every state shall abide by the determinations of the United States in Congress assembled on all questions which, by this confederation, are submitted to them. And the articles of this confederation shall be inviolably observed by every state, and the union shall be perpetual; nor shall any alteration at any time hereafter be made in any of them, unless such alteration be agreed to in a Congress of the United States, and be afterward confirmed by the legislatures of every state.

And whereas, it hath pleased the Great Governor of the World to incline the hearts of the legislatures we respectively represent in Congress to approve of, and to authorize us to ratify, the said Articles of Confederation and perpetual union: Know ye, That we the undersigned delegates, by virtue of the power and authority to us given for that purpose, do by these presents, in the name and in behalf of our respective constituents, fully and entirely ratify and confirm each and every of the said Articles of Confederation and perpetual union, and all and singular the matters and things therein contained: and we do further solemnly plight and engage the faith of our respective constituents, that they shall abide by the determinations of the United States in Congress assembled, on all questions which, by the said confederation, are submitted to them. And that the articles thereof shall be inviolably observed by the states we respectively represent, and that the union shall be perpetual. In witness whereof we have hereunto set our hands in Congress.

Done at Philadelphia in the State of Pennsylvania the ninth day of July in the year of our Lord One Thousand Seven Hundred and Seventy-eight, and in the third year of the independence of America.

The Constitution of the United States of America

We the People of the United States, in Order to form a more perfect Union, establish Justice, insure domestic Tranquility, provide for the common defence, promote the general Welfare, and secure the Blessings of Liberty to ourselves and our Posterity, do ordain and establish this Constitution for the United States of America.

Article I

Section. 1. All legislative Powers herein granted shall be vested in a Congress of the United States, which shall consist of a Senate and House of Representatives.

Section. 2. The House of Representatives shall be composed of Members chosen every second Year by the People of the several States, and the Electors in each State shall have the Qualifications requisite for Electors of the most numerous Branch of the State Legislature.

No Person shall be a Representative who shall not have attained to the age of twenty-five Years, and been seven Years a Citizen of the United States, and who shall not, when elected, be an Inhabitant of that State in which he shall be chosen.

Representatives and direct Taxes shall be apportioned among the several States which may be included within this Union, according to their respective Numbers, *which shall be determined by adding to the whole Number of free Persons, including those bound to Service for a Term of Years, and excluding Indians not taxed, three fifths of all other persons.*[1] The actual Enumeration shall be made within three Years after the first Meeting of the Congress of the United States, and within every subsequent Term of ten Years, in such manner as they shall by Law direct. The Number of Representatives shall not exceed one for every thirty Thousand, but each State shall have at Least one Representative; and until such enumeration shall be made, the State of New Hampshire shall be entitled to chuse three, Massachusetts eight, Rhode-Island and Providence Plantations one, Connecticut five, New-York six, New Jersey four, Pennsylvania eight, Delaware one, Maryland six, Virginia ten, North Carolina five, South Carolina five, and Georgia three.

When vacancies happen in the Representation from any State, the Executive Authority thereof shall issue Writs of Election to fill such Vacancies.

The House of Representatives shall chuse their Speaker and other Officers; and shall have the sole Power of Impeachment.

Section. 3. The Senate of the United States shall be composed of two Senators from each State, *chosen by the Legislature thereof,*[2] for six Years; and each Senator shall have one Vote.

Immediately after they shall be assembled in Consequence of the first Election, they shall be divided as equally as may be into three Classes. The Seats of the Senators of the first Class shall be vacated at the Expiration of the second Year, of the second Class at the Expiration of the fourth Year, and of the third Class at the Expiration of the sixth Year, so that one third may be chosen every second

Year; *and if Vacancies happen by Resignation, or otherwise, during the Recess of the Legislature of any State, the Executive thereof may make temporary Appointments until the next Meeting of the Legislature, which shall then fill such Vacancies.*[3]

No Person shall be a Senator who shall not have attained the Age of thirty Years, and been nine Years a Citizen of the United States, and who shall not, when elected, be an Inhabitant of that State for which he shall be chosen.

The Vice President of the United States shall be President of the Senate, but shall have no Vote, unless they be equally divided.

The Senate shall choose their other Officers, and also a President pro tempore, in the Absence of the Vice President, or when he shall exercise the Office of President of the United States.

The Senate shall have the sole Power to try all Impeachments. When sitting for that Purpose, they shall be an Oath or Affirmation. When the President of the United States is tried, the Chief Justice shall preside: And no Person shall be convicted without the Concurrence of two thirds of the Members present.

Judgment in Cases of Impeachment shall not extend further than to removal from Office, and disqualification to hold and enjoy any Office of Honor, Trust or Profit under the United States: but the Party convicted shall nevertheless be liable and subject to Indictment, Trial, Judgment and Punishment, according to Law.

Section. 4. The Times, Places and Manner of holding Elections for Senators and Representatives, shall be prescribed in each State by the Legislature thereof; but the Congress may at any time by Law make or alter such Regulations, except as to the Places of chusing Senators.

The Congress shall assemble at least once in a Year, and such Meeting shall be on the first Monday in December, unless they shall by Law appoint a different Day.[4]

Section. 5. Each House shall be the Judge of the Elections, Returns and Qualifications of its own Members, and a Majority of each shall constitute a Quorum to do Business; but a smaller Number may adjourn from day to day, and may be authorized to compel the Attendance of absent Members, in such Manner, and under such Penalties as each House may provide.

Each House may determine the Rules of its Proceedings, punish it Members for disorderly Behavior, and, with the Concurrence of two thirds, expel a Member.

Each House shall keep a journal of its Proceedings, and from time to time publish the same, excepting such Parts as may in their judgment require Secrecy; and the Yeas and Nays of the Members of either House on any question shall, at the Desire of one fifth of those Present, be entered on the journal.

Neither House, during the Session of Congress, shall, without the Consent of the other, adjourn for more than three days, nor to any other Place than that in which the two Houses shall be sitting.

Section. 6. The Senators and Representatives shall receive a Compensation for their Services, to be ascertained by Law, and paid out of the Treasury of the United States. They shall in all Cases, except Treason, Felony and Breach of the Peace, be privileged from Arrest during their Attendence at the Session of their respective Houses, and in going to and returning from the same; and for any Speech or Debate in either House, they shall not be questioned in any other Place.

No Senator or Representative shall, during the Time for which he was elected, be appointed to any civil Office under the Authority of the United States, which shall have been created, or the Emoluments, whereof shall have been encreased during such time; and no Person holding any Office under the United States, shall be a Member of either House during his continuance in Office.

Section. 7. All Bills for raising Revenue shall originate in the House of Representatives; but the Senate may propose or concur with Amendments as on other Bills.

Every Bill which shall have passed the House of Representatives and the Senate, shall, before it become a Law, be presented to the President of the United States; if he approve he shall sign it, but if not he shall return it, with his Objections to that House in which it shall have originated, who shall enter the Objections at large on their Journal, and proceed to reconsider it. If after such Reconsideration two thirds of that House shall agree to pass the Bill, it shall be sent, together with the Objections, to the other House, by which it shall likewise be reconsidered, and if approved by two thirds of that House, it shall become a Law. But in all such Cases the Votes of both Houses shall be determined by Yeas and Nays, and the Names of the Persons voting for and against the Bill shall be entered on the Journal of each House respectively. If any Bill shall not be returned by the President within ten Days (Sundays excepted) after it shall have been presented to him, the Same shall be a Law, in like Manner as if he had signed it, unless Congress by their Adjournment prevent its Return, in which Case it shall not be a Law.

Every Order, Resolution, or Vote to which the Concurrence of the Senate and House of Representatives may be necessary (except on a question of Adjournment) shall be presented to the President of the United States; and before the Same shall take Effect, shall be approved by him, or being disapproved by him, shall be re-passed by two thirds of the Senate and House of Representatives, according to the Rules and Limitations prescribed in the Case of a Bill.

Section. 8. The Congress shall have Power to lay and collect Taxes, Duties, Imposts and Excises, to pay the Debts and provide for the common Defence and general Welfare of the United States; but all Duties, Imposts and Excises shall be uniform throughout the United States;

To borrow Money on the credit of the United States;

To regulate Commerce with foreign Nations, and among the several States, and with the Indian Tribes;

To establish an uniform Rule of Naturalization, and uniform Laws on the subject of Bankruptcies throughout the United States;

To coin Money, regulate the Value thereof, and of foreign Coin, and fix the Standard of Weights and Measures;

To provide for the Punishment of counterfeiting the Securities and Current Coin of the United States;

To establish Post Offices and post Roads;

To promote the Progress of Science and useful Arts, by securing for limited Times to Authors and Inventors the exclusive Right to their respective Writings and Discoveries;

To constitute Tribunals inferior to the Supreme Court;

To define and punish Piracies and Felonies committed on the high Seas and Offences against the Law of Nations;

To declare War, grant Letters of Marque and Reprisal, and make Rules concerning Captures on Land and Water;

To raise and support Armies, but no Appropriation of Money to that Use shall be for a longer Term than two Years;

To provide and maintain a Navy;

To make Rules for the Government and Regulation of the land and naval Forces;

To provide for calling forth the Militia to execute the Laws of the Union, suppress Insurrections and repel Invasions;

To provide for organizing, arming, and disciplining, the Militia, and for governing such Part of them as may be employed in the Service of the United States, reserving to the states respectively, the Appointment of the Officers, and the Authority of training the Militia according to the discipline prescribed by Congress;

To exercise exclusive Legislation in all Cases whatsoever, over such District (not exceeding ten Miles square) as may, by Cession of particular States, and the Acceptance of Congress, become the Seat of the Government of the United States, and to exercise like Authority over all Places purchased by the Consent of the Legislature of the State in which the Same shall be, for the Erection of Forts, Magazines, Arsenals, dock-Yards, and other needful Buildings;—And

To make all Laws which shall be necessary and proper for carrying into Execution the foregoing Powers, and all other Powers vested by this Constitution in the Government of the United States, or in any Department or Officer thereof.

Section. 9. The Migration or Importation of such Persons as any of the States now existing shall think proper to admit, shall not be prohibited by the Congress prior to the Year one thousand eight hundred and eight, but a Tax or duty may be imposed on such Importation, not exceeding ten dollars for each Person.

The Privilege of the Writ of Habeas Corpus shall not be suspended, unless when in Cases of Rebellion or Invasion the public Safety may require it.

No Bill of Attainder or ex post facto Law shall be passed.

No Capitation, or other direct, Tax shall be laid, unless in Proportion to the Census or Enumeration herein before directed to be taken.

No Tax or Duty shall be laid on Articles exported from any State.

No Preference shall be given by any Regulation of Commerce or Revenue to the Ports of one State over those of another: nor shall Vessels bound to, or from, one State, be obliged to enter, clear, or pay Duties in another.

No Money shall be drawn from the Treasury, but in Consequence of Appropriations made by Law; and a regular Statement and Account of the Receipts and Expenditures of all public Money shall be published from time to time.

No title of Nobility shall be granted by the United States: And no Person holding any Office of Profit or Trust under them, shall, without the Consent of the Congress, accept of any present, Emolument, Office, or Title, of any kind whatever, from any King, Prince, or foreign State.

Section. 10. No State shall enter into any Treaty, Alliance, or Confederation; grant Letters of Marque and Reprisal; coin Money; emit Bills of Credit; make any Thing but gold and silver Coin a Tender in Payment of Debts; pass any Bill of Attainder, ex post facto Law, or Law impairing the Obligation of Contracts, or Grant any Title of Nobility.

No State shall, without the Consent of the Congress, lay any Imposts or Duties on Imports or Exports, except what may be absolutely necessary for executing its inspection Laws: and the net Produce of all Duties and Imposts, laid by any State on Imports or Exports, shall be for the Use of the Treasury of the United States; and all such Laws be subject to the Revision and Control of the Congress.

No State shall, without the Consent of Congress, lay any Duty of Tonnage, keep Troops, or Ships of War in time of Peace, enter into any Agreement or Compact with another State, or with a foreign Power, or engage in War, unless actually invaded, or in such imminent Danger as will not admit of delay.

Article II

Section. 1. The executive Power shall be vested in a President of the United States of America. He shall hold his office during the Terms of four Years, and, together with the Vice President, chosen for the same Term be elected as follows:

Each State shall appoint, in such Manner as the Legislature thereof may direct, a Number of Electors, equal to the whole Number of Senators and Representatives to which the Senate may be entitled in the Congress: but no Senator or Representative, or Person holding an Office of Trust or Profit under the United States, shall be appointed an Elector.

The Electors shall meet in their respective States, and vote by Ballot for two Persons, of whom one at least shall not be an inhabitant of the same State with themselves. And they shall make a List of all the Persons voted for, and of the Number of Votes for each; which List they shall sign and certify, and transmit sealed to the Seat of the Government of the United States, directed to the President of the Senate. The President of the Senate shall, in the Presence of the Senate and House of Representatives, open all the Certificates, and the Votes shall then be counted. The Person having the greatest Number of Votes shall be the President, if such Number be a majority of the whole Number of Electors appointed; and if there be more than one who have such Majority, and have an equal Number of Votes, then the House of Representatives shall immediately chuse by Ballot one of them for President; and if no Person have a majority, then from the five highest on the List the said House shall in like Manner chuse the President. But in chusing the President, the votes shall be taken by States, the Representation from each State having one Vote; A quorum for the purpose shall consist of a Member or Members from two thirds of the States, and a majority of all the States shall be necessary to a Choice. In every Case, after the Choice of the President, the Person having the Greatest Number of Votes of the Electors shall be the Vice President. But if there should remain two or more who have equal Votes, the Senate shall chuse from them by Ballot the Vice President.[5]

The Congress may determine the Time of chusing the Electors, and the Day on which they shall give their Votes; which Day shall be the same throughout the United States.

No Person except a natural born Citizen, or a Citizen of the United States, at the time of the Adoption of this Constitution, shall be eligible to the Office of President; neither shall any Person be eligible to that Office who shall not have attained to the Age of thirty-five Years, and been fourteen Years a Resident within the United States.

The Case of the Removal of the President from Office, or of his Death, Resignation, or Inability to discharge the Powers and Duties of the said Office, the Same shall devolve on the Vice President, and the Congress may by Law provide for the Case of Removal, Death, Resignation or Inability, both of the President and Vice President, declaring what Officer shall then act as President, and such Officer shall act accordingly, until the Disability be removed, or a President shall be elected.

The President shall, at stated Times, receive for his Services, a Compensation which shall neither be encreased nor diminished during the Period for which he shall have been elected, and he shall not receive within that Period any other Emolument from the United States, or any of them.

Before he enter on the Execution of his Office, he shall take the following Oath or Affirmation:—"I do solemnly swear (or affirm) that I will faithfully execute the Office of President of the United States, and will to the best of my Ability, preserve, protect, and defend the Constitution of the United States."

Section. 2. The President shall be Commander in Chief of the Army and Navy of the United States, and of the Militia of the several States, when called into the actual service of the United States; he may require the Opinion, in writing, of the principal Officer in each of the executive Departments, upon any Subject relating to the Duties of their respective Offices, and he shall have Power to grant Reprives and Pardons for Offences against the United States, except in Case of Impeachment.

He shall have Power, by and with the Advice and Consent of the Senate, to make Treaties, provided two thirds of the Senators present concur; and he shall nominate, and by and with the Advice and Consent of the Senate, shall appoint Ambassadors, and other public Ministers and Consuls, Judges of the supreme Court, and all other Officers of the United States, whose Appointments are not herein otherwise provided for, and which shall be established by Law; but the Congress may by Law vest the Appointment of such inferior Officers, as they think proper, in the President alone, in the Courts of Law, or in the Heads of Departments.

The President shall have Power to fill up all Vacancies that may happen during the Recess of the Senate, by granting Commissions which shall expire at the End of their next Session.

Section. 3. He shall from time to time give to the Congress information of the State of the Union, and recommend to their Consideration such Measures as he shall judge necessary and expedient; he may, on extraordinary Occasions, convene both Houses, or either of them, and in Case of Disagreement between them, with Respect to the Time of Adjournment, he may adjourn them to such Time as he shall think proper; he shall receive Ambassadors and other public Ministers, he shall take Care that the Laws be faithfully executed, and shall Commission all the Officers of the United States.

Section. 4. The President, Vice President, and all civil Officers of the United States, shall be removed from Office on Impeachment for, and Conviction of, Treason, Bribery, or other Crimes and Misdemeanors.

Article III

Section. 1. The judicial Power of the United States, shall be vested in one Supreme Court and in such inferior Courts as the Congress may from time to time ordain and establish. The Judges, both of the supreme and inferior Courts, shall hold their Offices during good Behavior, and shall, at stated Times, receive for their Services, a Compensation, which shall not be diminished during their Continuance in Office.

Section. 2. The Judicial Power shall extend to all Cases, in Law and Equity, arising under this Constitution, the Laws of the United States, and Treaties made, or which shall be made, under their Authority;—to all Cases affecting Ambassadors, other public Ministers and Consuls;—to all Cases of admiralty and maritime Jurisdiction;—to Controversies to which the United States shall be a Party;—to

Controversies between two or more States;—*between a State and Citizens of another State*;[6]—between Citizens of different States;—between Citizens of the same State claiming Lands under Grants of different states, *and between a State, or the Citizens thereof, and foreign States, Citizens, or Subjects.*[7]

In all cases affecting Ambassadors, other public Ministers and Consuls, and those in which a State shall be Party, the supreme Court shall have original Jurisdiction. In all other Cases before mentioned, the supreme Court shall have appellate Jurisdiction, both as to Law and Fact, with such Exceptions, and under such Regulations as the Congress shall make.

The Trial of all Crimes, except in Cases of Impeachment, shall be by Jury; and such Trial shall be held in the State where the said Crimes shall have been committed; but when not committed within any State, the Trial shall be at such Place or Places as the Congress may by Law have directed.

Section. 3. Treason against the United States, shall consist only in levying War against them, or in adhering to their Enemies, giving them Aid and Comfort. No person shall be convicted of Treason unless on the Testimony of two Witnesses to the same overt Act, or on Confession in open Court.

The Congress shall have Power to declare the Punishment of Treason, but no Attainder of Treason shall work Corruption of Blood, or Forfeiture except during the Life of the Person attainted.

Article IV

Section. 1. Full Faith and Credit shall be given in each State to the public Acts, Records, and judicial Proceedings of every other State. And the Congress may by general Laws prescribe the Manner in which such Acts, Records, and Proceedings shall be proved, and the Effect thereof.

Section. 2. The Citizens of each State shall be entitled to all Privileges and Immunities of Citizens in the several States.

A Person charged in any State with Treason, Felony, or other Crime, who shall flee from Justice, and be found in another State, shall on Demand of the executive Authority of the State from which he fled, be delivered up, to be removed to the State having Jurisdiction of the Crime.

No Person held to Service or Labour in one State, under the Laws thereof, escaping into another, shall, in Consequence of any Law or Regulation therein, be discharged from such Service or Labour, but shall be delivered up on Claim of the Party to whom such Service or Labour may be due.[8]

Section. 3. New States may be admitted by the Congress into this Union; but no new State shall be formed or erected within the jurisdiction of any other State; nor any State be formed by the Junction of two or more States, or Parts of States, without the Consent of the Legislatures of the States concerned as well as of the Congress.

The Congress shall have Power to dispose of and make all needful Rules and Regulations respecting the Territory or other Property belonging to the United States; and nothing in this Constitution shall be so construed as to Prejudice any claims of the United States, or of any particular State.

Section. 4. The United States shall guarantee to every State in this Union a Republican Form of Government, and shall protect each of them against Invasion; and on Application of the Legislature, or of the Executive (when the Legislature cannot be convened) against domestic Violence.

Article V

The Congress, whenever two thirds of both Houses shall deem it necessary, shall propose Amendments to this Constitution, or, on the Application of the Legislatures of two thirds of the several States, shall call a Convention for proposing Amendments, which, in either Case, shall be valid to all Intents and Purposes, as Part of this Constitution, when ratified by the Legislatures of three fourths of the several States, or by Conventions in three fourths thereof, as the one or the other Mode of ratification may be proposed by the Congress; Provided that no Amendment which may be made prior to the Year One thousand eight hundred and eight shall in any Manner affect the first and fourth Clauses in the Ninth Section of the first Article; and that no State, without its Consent, shall be deprived of its equal Suffrage in the Senate.

Article VI

All Debts contracted and Engagements entered into, before the Adoption of this Constitution, shall be as valid against the United States under this Constitution, as under the Confederation.

This Constitution, and the Laws of the United States which shall be made in Pursuance thereof; and all Treaties made, or which shall be made, under the Authority of the United States, shall be the supreme Law of the Land; and the Judges in every State shall be bound thereby, any Thing in the Constitution or Laws of any State to the Contrary notwithstanding.

The Senators and Representatives before mentioned, and the Members of the several State Legislatures, and all executive and judicial Officers, both of the United States and of the several States, shall be bound by Oath or Affirmation, to support this Constitution; but no religious Test shall ever be required as a Qualification to any Office or public Trust under the United States.

Article VII

The Ratification of the Convention of nine States, shall be sufficient for the Establishment of this Constitution between the States so ratifying the Same.

Done in Convention by the Unanimous Consent of the States present the Seventeenth Day of September in the Year of our Lord one thousand seven hundred and eighty seven and of the Independence of the United States of America the twelfth. In witness whereof We have hereunto subscribed our Names.

* * *

Articles in addition to, and amendment of, the Constitution of the United States of America, proposed by Congress, and ratified by the several States, pursuant to the Fifth Article of the original Constitution.

Amendment I

[Ratification of the first ten amendments was completed December 15, 1791]

Congress shall make no law respecting an establishment of religion, or prohibiting the free exercise thereof; or abridging the freedom of speech, or of the press; or the right of the people peaceably to assemble, and to petition the Government for a redress of grievances.

Amendment II

A well regulated Militia, being necessary to the security of a free State, the right of the people to keep and bear Arms, shall not be infringed.

Amendment III

No Soldier shall, in time of peace be quartered in any house, without the consent of the Owner, nor in time of war, but in a manner to be prescribed by law.

Amendment IV

The right of the people to be secure in their persons, houses, papers, and effects, against unreasonable searches and seizures, shall not be violated, and no Warrants shall issue, but upon probable cause, supported by Oath or affirmation, and particularly describing the place to be searched, and the persons or things to be seized.

Amendment V

No person shall be held to answer for a capital, or otherwise infamous crime, unless on a presentment or indictment of a Grand Jury, except in cases arising in the land or naval forces, or in the Militia, when an actual service in time of War or public danger; nor shall any person be subject for the same offence to be twice put in jeopardy of life or limb; nor shall be compelled in any criminal case to be a witness against himself, nor be deprived of life, liberty, or property, without due process of law; nor shall private property be taken for public use, without just compensation.

Amendment VI

In all criminal prosecutions, the accused shall enjoy the right to a speedy and public trial, by an impartial jury of the State and district wherein the crime shall have been committed, which district shall have been previously ascertained by law, and to be informed of the nature and cause of the accusation; to be confronted with the witness against him; to have compulsory process for obtaining witness in his favor, and to have the Assistance of Counsel for his defence.

Amendment VII

In Suits at common law, where the value in controversy shall exceed twenty dollars, the right of trial by jury shall be preserved, and no fact tried by a jury, shall be otherwise re-examined in any Court of the United States, than according to the rules of the common law.

Amendment VIII

Excessive bail shall not be required, nor excessive fines imposed, nor cruel and unusual punishments inflicted.

Amendment IX

The enumeration in the Constitution, of certain rights, shall not be construed to deny or disparage others retained by the people.

Amendment X

The powers not delegated to the United States by the Constitution, nor prohibited by it to the States, are reserved to the States respectively, or to the people.

Amendment XI

[January 8, 1798]

The Judicial power of the United States shall not be construed to extend to any suit in law or equity, commenced or prosecuted against one of the United States by Citizens of another State, or by Citizens or Subjects of any Foreign State.

Amendment XII

[September 25, 1804]

The Electors shall meet in their respective states and vote by ballot for President and Vice President, one of whom, at least, shall not be an inhabitant of the same state with themselves; they shall name in their ballots the person voted for as President, and in distinct ballots the person voted for as Vice President, and they shall make distinct lists of all persons voted for as President, and of all persons voted for as Vice President, and of the number of votes for each, which lists they shall sign and certify, and transmit sealed to the seat of the government of the United States, directed to the President of the Senate:—The President of the Senate shall, in the presence of the Senate and House of Representatives, open all the certificates and the votes shall then be counted;—The person having the greatest number of votes for President, shall be the President, if such number be a majority of the whole number of Electors appointed; and if no person have such majority, then from the persons having the highest numbers not exceeding three on the list of those voted for as President, the House of Representatives shall choose immediately, by ballot, the President. But in choosing the President, the votes shall be taken by states, the representation from each state having one vote; a quorum for this purpose shall consist of a member or members from two thirds of the states, and a majority of all the states shall be necessary to a choice. And if the House of Representatives shall not choose a President whenever the right of choice shall devolve upon them, *before the fourth day of March next following,*[9] then the Vice President shall act as President as in the case of the death or other constitutional disability of the President.—The person having the greatest number of votes as Vice President, shall be the Vice President, if such number be a majority of the whole number of Electors appointed, and if no person having a majority, then from the two highest numbers on the list, the Senate shall choose the Vice President; a quorum for the purpose shall consist of two-thirds of the whole number of Senators, and a majority of the whole number shall be necessary to a choice. But no person constitutionally ineligible to the office of President shall be eligible to that of Vice President of the United States.

Amendment XIII

[December 18, 1865]

Section 1. Neither slavery nor involuntary servitude, except as a punishment for crime whereof the party shall have been duly convicted, shall exist within the United States, or any place subject to their jurisdiction.

Section 2. Congress shall have power to enforce this article by appropriate legislation.

Amendment XIV

[July 28, 1868]

Section 1. All persons born or naturalized in the United States, and subject to the jurisdiction thereof, are citizens of the United States and of the State wherein they reside. No State shall make or enforce any law which shall abridge the privileges or immunities of citizens of the United States; nor shall any state deprive any person of life, liberty, or property, without due process of law; nor deny to any person within its jurisdiction the equal protection of the laws.

Section 2. Representatives shall be apportioned among the several States according to their respective numbers, counting the whole number of persons in each State, excluding Indians not taxed. But when the right to vote at any election for the choice of electors for President and Vice President of the United States, Representatives in Congress, the Executive and Judicial officers of a State, or the members of the Legislature thereof, is denied to any of the male inhabitants of such State, being twenty one years of age, and citizens of the United States, or in any way abridged, except for participation in rebellion, or other crime, the basis of representation therein shall be reduced in the proportion which the number of such male citizens shall bear to the whole number of male citizens twenty one years of age in such State.

Section 3. No person shall be a Senator or Representative in Congress, or elector of President and Vice President, or hold any office, civil or military, under the United States, or under any State who having previously taken an oath, as a member of Congress, or as an officer of the United States, or as a member of any State legislature, or as an executive or judicial officer of any State, to support the Constitution of the United States, shall have engaged in insurrection or rebellion against the same, or given aid or comfort to the enemies thereof. But Congress may by a vote of two thirds of each House remove such disability.

Section 4. The validity of the public debt of the United States authorized by law, including debts incurred for payment of pensions and bounties for services in suppressing insurrection or rebellion shall not be questioned. But neither the United States nor any State shall assume or pay any debt or obligation incurred in aid of insurrection or rebellion against the United States, or any claim for the loss or emancipation of any slave; but all such debts, obligations, and claims shall be held illegal and void.

Section 5. The Congress shall have power to enforce, by appropriate legislation, the provisions of this article.

Amendment XV

[March 30, 1870]

Section 1. The right of citizens of the United States to vote shall not be denied or abridged by the United States or by any State on account of race, color, or previous condition or servitude.

Section 2. The Congress shall have power to enforce this article by appropriate legislation.

Amendment XVI

[February 25, 1913]

The Congress shall have power to lay and collect taxes on incomes, from whatever source derived, without apportionment among the several States, and without regard to any census or enumeration.

Amendment XVII

[May 31, 1913]

The Senate of the United States shall be composed of two Senators from each State, elected by the people thereof, for six years; and each Senator shall have one vote. The electors in each State shall have the qualifications requisite for electors of the most numerous branch of the State legislatures.

When vacancies happen in the representation of any State in the Senate, the executive authority of such State shall issue writs of election to fill such vacancies: *Provided,* That the legislature of any State may empower the executive thereof to make temporary appointments until the people fill the vacancies by election as the legislature may direct.

This amendment shall not be so construed as to affect the election or term of any Senator chosen before it becomes valid as part of the Constitution.

Amendment XVIII

[January 29, 1919]

Section 1. *After one year from the ratification of this article the manufacture, sale, or transportation of intoxicating liquors within, the importation thereof into, or the exportation thereof from the United States and all territory subject to the jurisdiction thereof for beverage purposes is hereby prohibited.*

Section 2. *The Congress and the several States shall have concurrent power to enforce this article by appropriate legislation.*

Section 3. *This article shall be inoperative unless it shall have been ratified as an amendment to the Constitution by the legislatures of the several States, as provided in the Constitution, within seven years from the date of submission hereof to the States by the Congress.*[10]

Amendment XIX

[August 26, 1920]

The right of citizens of the United States to vote shall not be denied or abridged by the United States or by any State on account of sex.

Congress shall have power to enforce this article by appropriate legislation.

Amendment XX

[February 6, 1933]

Section 1. The terms of the President and Vice President shall end at noon on the 20th day of January, and the terms of Senators and Representatives at noon on the 3rd day of January, of the years in which such terms would have ended if this article had not been ratified; and the terms of their successors shall then begin.

Section 2. The Congress shall assemble at least once in every year, and such meeting shall begin at noon on the 3rd day of January unless they shall by law appoint a different day.

Section 3. If, at the time fixed for the beginning of the term of the President, the President elect shall have died, the Vice President elect shall become President. If a President shall not have been chosen before the time fixed for the beginning of his term, or if the President elect shall have failed to qualify, then the Vice President elect shall act as President until a President shall have qualified; and the Congress may by law provide for the case wherein neither a President elect nor a Vice President elect shall have qualified, declaring who shall then act as

President, or the manner in which one who is to act shall be selected, and such person shall act accordingly until a President or Vice President shall have qualified.

Section 4. The Congress may by law provide for the case of the death of any of the persons from whom the House of Representatives may choose a President whenever the right of choice shall have devolved upon them, and for the case of the death of any of the persons from whom the Senate may choose a Vice President whenever the right of choice shall have devolved upon them.

Section 5. Sections 1 and 2 shall take effect on the 15th day of October following the ratification of this article.

Section 6. This article shall be inoperative unless it shall have been ratified as an amendment to the Constitution by the legislatures of three fourths of the several States within seven years from the date of its submission.

Amendment XXI

[December 5, 1933]

Section 1. The eighteenth article of amendment to the Constitution of the United States is hereby repealed.

Section 2. The transportation or importation into any State, Territory, or possession of the United States for delivery or use therein of intoxicating liquors, in violation of the laws thereof, is hereby prohibited.

Section 3. This article shall be inoperative unless it shall have been ratified as an amendment to the Constitution by conventions in the several States, as provided in the Constitution, within seven years from the date of the submission hereof to the States by the Congress.

Amendment XXII

[February 26, 1951]

Section 1. No person shall be elected to the office of the President more than twice, and no person who has held the office of President, or acted as President, for more than two years of a term to which some other person was elected President shall be elected to the office of President more than once. But this Article shall not apply to any person holding the office of President when this Article was proposed by the Congress, and shall not prevent any person who may be holding the office of President, or acting as President, during the term within which this Article becomes operative from holding the office of President or acting as President during the remainder of such term.

Section 2. This article shall be inoperative unless it shall have been ratified as an amendment to the Constitution by the legislatures of three fourths of the several States within seven years from the date of its submission to the States by the Congress.

Amendment XXIII

[March 29, 1961]

Section 1. The District constituting the seat of Government of the United States shall appoint in such manner as the Congress may direct:

A number of electors of President and Vice President equal to the whole number of Senators and Representatives in Congress to which the District would be entitled if it were a State, but in no event more than the least populous State; they shall be in addition to those appointed by the States, but they shall be considered, for the purposes of the election of President and Vice President, to be electors appointed by a State; and they shall meet in the District and perform such duties as provided by the twelfth article of amendment.

Section 2. The Congress shall have power to enforce this article by appropriate legislation.

Amendment XXIV

[January 23, 1964]

Section 1. The right of citizens of the United States to vote in any primary or other election for President or Vice President, for electors for President or Vice President, or for Senator or Representative in Congress, shall not be denied or abridged by the United States or any state by reason of failure to pay any poll tax or other tax.

Section 2. The Congress shall have power to enforce this article by appropriate legislation.

Amendment XXV

[February 10, 1967]

Section 1. In case of the removal of the President from office or of his death or resignation, the Vice President shall become President.

Section 2. Whenever there is a vacancy in the office of the Vice President, the President shall nominate a Vice President who shall take office upon confirmation by a majority vote of both Houses of Congress.

Section 3. Whenever the President transmits to the President pro tempore of the Senate and the Speaker of the House of Representatives his written declaration that he is unable to discharge the powers and duties of his office, and until he transmits to them a written declaration to the contrary, such powers and duties shall be discharged by the Vice President as Acting President.

Section 4. Whenever the Vice President and a majority of either the principal officers of the executive departments or of such other body as Congress may by law provide, transmit to the President pro tempore of the Senate and the Speaker of the House of Representatives their written declaration that the President is unable to discharge the powers and duties of his office, the Vice President shall immediately assume the powers and duties of the office as Acting President.

Thereafter, when the President transmits to the President pro tempore of the Senate and the Speaker of the House of Representatives his written declaration that no inability exists, he shall resume the powers and duties of his office unless the Vice President and a majority of either the principal officers of the executive department[s] or of such other body as Congress may by law provide, transmit within four days to the President pro tempore of the Senate and the Speaker of the House of Representatives their written declaration that the President is unable to discharge the powers and duties of his office. Thereupon Congress shall decide the issue, assembling within forty-eight hours for that purpose if not in session. If the Congress, within twenty-one days after receipt of the latter written declaration, or, if Congress is not in session, within twenty-one days after Congress is required to assemble, determines by two-thirds vote of both Houses that the President is unable to discharge the powers and duties of his office, the Vice President shall continue to discharge the same as Acting President; otherwise, the President shall resume the powers and duties of his office.

Amendment XXVI

[June 30, 1971]

Section 1. The right of citizens of the United States, who are 18 years of age or older, to vote shall not be denied or abridged by the United States or by any state on account of age.

Section 2. The Congress shall have power to enforce this article by appropriate legislation.

Amendment XXVII

[May 7, 1992]

No law varying the compensation for the services of the Senators and Representatives shall take effect until an election of Representatives shall have intervened.

Editor's Notes

1. Italics are used throughout to indicate passages that have been altered by subsequent amendments. In this case see Amendment XIV.
2. See Amendment XVII.
3. Ibid.
4. See Amendment XX.
5. See Amendment XII.
6. See Amendment XI.
7. Ibid.
8. See Amendment XIII.
9. See Amendment XX.
10. Repealed by Amendment XXI.

ACKNOWLEDGMENTS (Continued)

"Presidential Power: Restoring the Balance," by Theordore J. Lowi. From *Political Science Quarterly*, Volume 100, Number 2, Summer 1985. Copyright © 1985 by The Academy of Political Science. Reprinted by permission.

"The Bill of Rights, Incorporation, and the Erosion of Constitutional Federalism," by Charles Rice. From "The Bill of Rights and the Doctrine of Incorporation," by Charles Rice from *The Bill of Rights: Original Meaning and Current Understanding*, edited by Eugene W. Hickok (Charlottesville, Virginia: 1991). Reprinted by permission of the University Press of Virginia.

"Competitive Federalism—Three Driving Forces," by John Shannon. From *Intergovernmental Perspective*, Fall 1989.

"State and Local Governments Go International," by John Kincaid. From *Intergovernmental Perspective*, Spring 1990.

"The Law of Appropriateness in Intergovernmental Relations," by David J. Kennedy. Reprinted with permission from *Public Administration Review*. Copyright © by the American Society for Public Adminsitration (ASPA), 1120 G Street NW, Suite 700, Washington, DC 20005. All rights reserved.

"Does Affirmative Action Mean Reverse Discrimintion?" by Glenn A. Phelps. Reprinted with the permission of Lexington Books, an imprint of Macmillan, Inc. From *Contemporary Debates on Civil Liberties: Enduring Constitutional Questions*, edited by Glenn A. Phelps and Robert A. Poirier. Copyright © 1985 by Lexington Books.

"Seventeen Words: The Quite Revolution of the Fourteenth Amendment," by Fred W. Friendly and Martha J.H. Elliot. From *The Constitution: That Delicate Balance*, by Fred W. Friendly and Martha J.H. Elliott. Copyright by McGraw-Hill Book Company. Reprinted by permission of the publisher.

"Equal Justice under Law: The Supreme Court and Rights of the Accused, 1932–1991," by David J. Bodenhamer. Reprinted with the permission of The Free Press, a division of Macmillan, Inc. From *Crucible of Liberty: 200 Years of the Bill of Rights*, edited by Raymond Arsenault. Copyright © 1991 by Raymond Arsenault.

"Development of the Right of Privacy," by John Brigham. Reprinted with the author's permission from *Civil Liberties and American Democracy*, by John Brigham (Washington, D.C.: CQ Press, 1984).

"Race, Rights, Taxes, and the Conservative Ascendance," by Thomas Byrne Edsall and Mary D. Edsall. From "The Conservative Ascendance" in *Chain Reaction: The Impact of Race, Rights, and Taxes on American Politics*, by Thomas Byrne Edsall and Mary D. Edsall. Reprinted by permission of W.W. Norton & Company, Inc.

"How the ERA Was Lost," by Jane J. Mansbridge. From *Why We Lost the ERA*, by Jane J. Mansbridge. Reprinted by permission of the publisher, The University of Chicago.

"New Values in the Pursuit of Office," by Alan Ehrenhalt. From *The United States of Ambition*, by Alan Ehrenhalt. Copyright © 1991 by Alan Ehrenhalt. Reprinted by permission of Times Books, a division of Random House, Inc.

"Change in American Electoral Behavior: 1952–1988," by Norman R. Luttbeg. From *American Electoral Behavior 1952–1988*, by Michael M. Gant and Norman R. Luttbeg. Copyright 1991, pp. 179–188. Reproduced by permission of the publisher, F.E. Peacock Publishers, Inc., Itasca, Illinois.

"The Mass Media, Political Trust, and Participation," by M. Margaret Conway. From *Political Participation in the U.S.*, second edition, by M. Margaret Conway (Washington, D.C.: CQ Press, 1991), pp. 81–92. Reprinted with permission of the publisher.

"The Postmodern Election," by W. Lance Bennett. From *The Governing Crisis: Media, Money and Marketing in American Elections*, by W. Lance Bennett. Copyright © 1992. Reprinted with permission of St. Martin's Press, Incorporated.

"The Selling of the President 1988," by Nicholas J. O'Shaughnessy. From *The Phenomenon of Political Marketing*, by Nicholas J. O'Shaughnessy. Copyright © 1990 by Nicholas J. O'Shaughnessy. Reprinted with permission of St. Martin's Press, Incorporated and The Macmillan Press, Ltd. U.K.

"The 1980s: Realignment at Last?" by Nelson W. Polsby and Aaron Wildavsky. From *Presidential Elections*, Eighth Edition, by Nelson W. Polsby and Aaron Wildavsky. Copyright © 1988, 1991 by Nelson W. Polsby and Aaron Wildavsky. Abridged with the permission of The Free Press, a division of Macmillan, Inc.

"Black Politics and Presidential Elections," by Lenneal J. Henderson, Jr. From *The New Black Politics*, Second Edition, edited by Michael B. Preston, Lenneal J. Henderson, Jr., and Paul L. Puryear. Copyright by Lenneal J. Henderson, Jr. Reprinted by permission of the author.

"Proposals for Reforming the Electoral College," by Stephen J. Wayne. From *The Road to the White House 1992: The Politics of Presidential Elections*, by Stephen J. Wayne. Copyright © 1992. Reprinted with permission of St. Martin's Press, Incorporated.

"Structure as Strategy: Presidential Nominating Politics in the Post-Reform Era," by Elaine Ciulla Kamarck. Reprinted from *The Parties Respond: Changes in the American Party System*, edited by L. Sandy Maisel, 1990, by permission of Westview Press, Boulder, Colorado.

"Evaluating the New Nominating System: Thoughts after 1988 from a Governance Perspective," by W. Wayne Shannon. From *Nominating the President*, edited by Emmett H. Buell, Jr., and Lee Sigelman. Copyright © 1991 by The University of Tennessee Press. Reprinted by permission of The University of Tennessee Press.

"The Decline and Possible Resurrection of Parties," by Stephen A. Salmore and Barbara G. Salmore. From *Candidates, Parties, and Campaigns: Electoral Politics in America*, Second Edition, by Stephen A. Salmore and Barbara G. Salmore (Washington, D.C.: CQ Press, 1989), pp. 19–38. Reprinted with permission of the publisher.

"The Impact of Direct Marketing on the Parties," by R. Kenneth Godwin. From *One Billion Dollars of Influence*, by R. Kenneth Godwin, pp. 3, 101–110, 116. Copyright © 1988 by Chatham House Publishers, Inc.

"The Changing Styles of American Party Politics," by Gary R. Orren. From *The Future of American Political Parties: The Challenge of Governance*, edited by Joel L. Fleishman, pp. 6, 8–27, 30, 40–41. New York: The American Assembly.

"The Changing Nature of Interest Group Politics," by Allan J. Cigler and Burdett A. Loomis. From *Interest Group Politics*, Third Edition, by Allan J. Cigler and Burdett A. Loomis (Washington, D.C.: CQ Press, 1991), pp. 1–28. Reprinted with permission of the publisher.

"PACs and Campaign Finance," by Herbert E. Alexander. From *Financing Politics: Money, Elections, & Political Reform*, Fourth Edition, by Herbert E. Alexander (Washington, D.C.: CQ Press, 1992), pp. 56–61. Reprinted with permission of the publisher.

"Proposals for Change in the Federal Election Campaign Law," by Michael J. Malbin. From "Looking Back at the Future of Campaign Finance Reform: Interest Groups and American Elections," by Michael J. Malbin, from *Money and Politics in the United States: Financing Elections in the 1980s*, pp. 232, 266–270. Copyright © 1984 by the American Enterprise Institute.

"The Paradox of Interest Groups in Washington—More Groups, Less Clout," by Robert H. Salisbury. From *The New American Political System*, Second Edition, edited by Anthony King. Reprinted with the permission of The American Enterprise Institute for Public Policy Research, Washington, D.C.

"Journalism: Power by Default," by James David Barber. Originally titled "The Presidential Beat." From *The Pulse of Politics*, by James David Barber, pp. 8–12. Reprinted by permission of the author.

"From Whistle Stop to Sound Bite," by Sig Mickelson. From *From Whistle Stop to Sound Bite: Four Decades of Politics and Television*, by Sig Mickelson, pp. 151–157, 160–165, 167, and 170–176. Copyright © 1989 by Praeger Publishers, an imprint of Greenwood Publishing Group, Inc., Westport, Conn. Reprinted with permission.

"Diplomacy in a Television Age: The Dangers of Teledemocracy," by David R. Gergen. From *The Media and Foreign Policy*, edited by Simon Serfaty. Copyright by The Macmillan Press Ltd., U.K. Reprinted with the permission of the publisher.

"Challenge and Change in the Two Congresses," by Roger H. Davidson and Walter J. Oleszek. From *Congress and Its Members*, Second Edition, by Roger H. Davidson and Walter J. Oleszek (Washington, D.C.: CQ Press, 1985), pp. 433–444. Reprinted with permission of the publisher.

"Congress: The First 200 Years," by Thomas P. O'Neill, Jr. From *National Forum: The Phi Kappa Phi Journal*, Volume LXIV, Number 4, Fall 1984. Copyright © by Thomas P. O'Neill, Jr. By permission of the publishers and the author.

"The Class of '74 and the New Way of Doing Business," by Burdett Loomis. Reprinted from *The New American Politician*, by Burdett Loomis. Copyright © 1988 by Basic Books, Inc. Reprinted by permission of Basic Books, a division of HarperCollins Publishers.

"Power in the Reform and Post-reform House" by Lawrence C. Dodd and Bruce I. Oppenheimer. From *Congress Reconsidered*, Fourth Edition, by Lawrence C. Dodd and Bruce I. Oppenheimer (Washington, D.C.: CQ Press, 1989), pp. 39–64. Reprinted with permission of the publisher.

"The Stewardship Doctine," by Theodore Roosevelt. From *The Autobiography of Theodore Roosevelt*, by Theodore Roosevelt. Copyright 1913 Charles Scribner's Sons: copyright renewed 1941 Edith K. Carow Roosevelt. Reprinted with permission of Charles Scribner's; Sons, an imprint of Macmillan Publishing Company.

"The Proper Scope of Presidential Powers," by William Howard Taft. From *The President and His Powers*, by William Howard Taft (1916). Reprinted with permission of the publisher, Columbia University Press.

"The Leadership Problem in America," by Bert A. Rockman. From *The Leadership Question*, by Bert A. Rockman, pp. 4–15. Copyright © 1984 by Praeger Publishers, an imprint of Greenwood Publishing Group, Inc., Westport, Conn. Reprinted with permission.

"The Actor President in the Age of Fiction," by James David Barber. From *The Presidential Character: Predicting Performance in the White House*, Third Edition, by James David Barber. Reprinted with permission of the author.

"Democracy and the Growing Bureaucracy," by David Nachmias and David H. Rosenbloom. From *Bureaucratic Government USA*, by David Nachmias and David H. Rosenbloom. Copyright © 1980. Reprinted with permission of St. Martin's Press, Incorporated.

"The Waning Political Capital of Cabinet Appointments," by Margaret Jane Wyszomirski. From *The Presidency in Transition*, Volume VI, Number I, 1989. Permission granted by the Center for the Study of the Presidency, publisher of *Presidential Studies Quarterly*.

"Judge Bork in Defense of Strict Construction," by Robert H. Bork and Patrick B. McGuigan. From *Ninth Justice: The Fight for Bork*, by Patrick B. McGuigan and Dawn M. Weyrich, pp. 285–290. Copyright © 1990 by The Free Congress Foundation. Used by permission of The Free Congress Foundation.

"The Myth of the Strict Constructionist: Our Incomplete Constitution," by Laurence H. Tribe. From *God Save This Honorable Court*, by Laurence H. Tribe. Copyright © 1985 by Laurence H. Tribe. Reprinted by permission of Random House, Inc.

"The Supreme Court from Warren to Burger to Rehnquist," by David O'Brien. From *Political Science*, Winter 1987, Volume 20, Number 1. David O'Brien is a Professor of Government at the University of Virginia and author, among other books and articles, of *Storm Center: The Supreme Court in American Politics*, Third Edition (Norton, 1993), and co-author of *The Politics of American Government* (St. Martin's, 1994). Reprinted with permission of the author.

"Presidential Appointments: The Mixed Record of Court Packing," by William H. Rehnquist. From *The Supreme Court*, by William Rehnquist. Copyright © 1987 by William Rehnquist. By permission of William Morrow & Company, Inc.

"Righting the Other Federal Courts," by W. John Moore. From *National Journal*, January 25, 1992, pp. 200–205. Reprinted by permission.

"A Case in Limits on Presidential Problem-Solving," by Jimmy Carter. From *Keeping Faith*, by President Jimmy Carter (Bantam Books). By permission of International Creative Management.

"Congress and Nicaragua: The Limits of Alternative Policy Making," by Philip Brenner and William M. LeoGrande. From *Divided Democracy: Cooperation and Conflict Between the President and Congress*, edited by James A. Thurber (Washington, D.C.: CQ Press, 1991), pp. 219–253. Reprinted with permission of the publisher.

"Institutional Combat and the Erosion of Governmental Power," by Benjamin Ginsberg and Martin Shefter. From *Politics by Other Means*, by Benjamin Ginsberg and Martin Shefter. Copyright © 1990 by Basic Books, Inc. Reprinted with permission of Basic Books, a division of HarperCollins Publishers.

"The Power Elite," by C. Wright Mills. From *The Power Elite*, by C. Wright Mills, pp. 269–278. Copyright © 1956 by Oxford University Press, Inc. Renewed © 1984 by Yaraslava Mills. Reprinted by permission.

"Pluralist Democracy in the United States," by Robert A. Dahl. From *Pluralist Democracy in the United States: Conflict and Consent*, by Robert A. Dahl, pp. 7–10, 22–24, 325–326. Reprinted by permission.

"Who's Running America Today?" by Thomas R. Dye. From *Who's Running America? The Bush Era*, Fifth Edition, by Thomas R. Dye, copyright © 1990, pp. 271–283. Reprinted by permission of Prentice-Hall, Englewood Cliffs, N.J.

"Government Growth and Inequality," by Edward S. Greenberg. From *Understanding Modern Government*, by Edward S. Greenberg. Copyright © 1979 by Macmillan Publishing Company. Reprinted with permission of Macmillan Publishing Company, Inc.

"Individualism: The Staff of Life," by Susan Love Brown et al. From *The Incredible Broad Machine*, by Susan Love Brown et al., pp. 130–138. Copyright © 1974 World Research, Inc., P. O. Box 9359, San Diego, CA 92109. Reprinted by permission of the publisher.

"The Cyclical Politics of Rich and Poor," by Kevin Phillips. From *The Politics of Rich and Poor*, by Kevin Phillips. Copyright © 1990 by Kevin Phillips. Reprinted by permission of Random House, Inc.

About the Author

Robert Harmel (Ph.D., Northwestern University) is a professor of political science at Texas A&M University. With special research interests in both American government and comparative politics, Professor Harmel has authored or coauthored published work on political parties, state legislatures, and the presidency. Among these publications are *Parties and Their Environments: Limits to Reform?* (with Kenneth Janda, 1982) and an edited volume, *Presidents and Their Parties* (1984). His most recent work includes a study of the development of party organizations in the Texas legislature, analysis of the development of new right-wing parties in social democracies, and a National Science Foundation-sponsored study of party change. He regularly teaches classes on American government, political parties, and comparative politics.